BELIZE

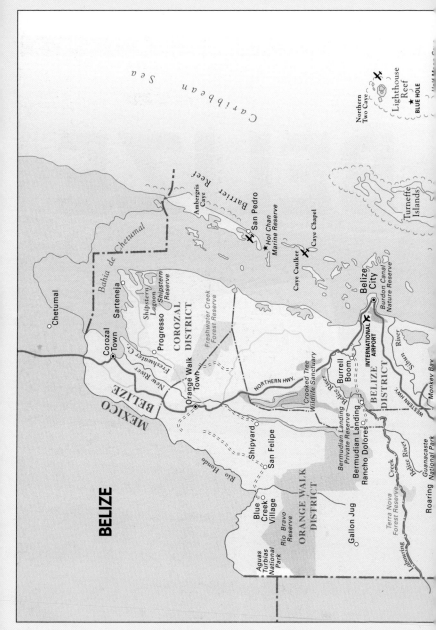

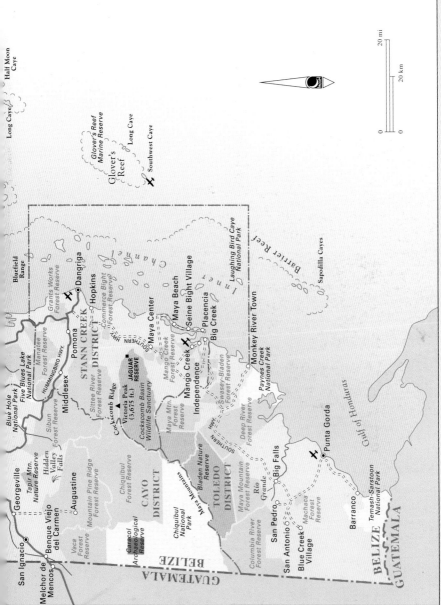

© AVALON TRAVEL PUBLISHING, INC.

MOON HANDBOOKS

BELIZE

FIFTH EDITION

CHICKI MALLAN & PATTI LANGE

PHOTOGRAPHS BY OZ MALLAN

AVALON
TRAVEL

MOON HANDBOOKS:
BELIZE
FIFTH EDITION

Chicki Mallan & Patti Lange

Published by
 Avalon Travel Publishing
 5855 Beaudry St.
 Emeryville, CA 94608, USA

Please send all comments,
corrections, additions,
amendments, and critiques to:

MOON HANDBOOKS: BELIZE
Avalon Travel Publishing
5855 Beaudry St.
Emeryville, CA 94608, USA
email: info@travelmatters.com
www.travelmatters.com

ISBN: 1-56691-343-8
ISSN: 1533-9130

Printing History
 1st edition—1991
 5th edition—September 2001
 5 4 3 2 1

Editor: Marisa Solís
Series Manager: Erin Van Rheenen
Copy Editor: Jean Blomquist
Graphics Coordinator: Erika Howsare
Production: Alvaro Villanueva, Marcie McKinley
Map Editor: Naomi Dancis, Robby Peckerar
Cartographers: Kat Kalamaras, Mike Morgenfeld, Ben Pease
Index: Monica Smersh

Front cover photo: © Joel Simon, 1999

Distributed in the United States and Canada by Publishers Group West

Printed in China through Colorcraft Ltd., Hong Kong

Dedicated to the family

CONTENTS

INTRODUCTION..**1–50**
The Land 3
   Waterways of Belize; Habitats of Inland Belize; Caves; The Weather
Flora..9
   Forests of Belize; Trees; Flowers
Fauna...16
   Birds of Belize; Cats; Monkeys; Rodents; Other Interesting Mammals; Lizards;
   Snakes; Other Reptiles; Insects and Arachnids
The Sea 28
   Estuaries; Mangroves; Sea-Grass Beds; The Reef
Sea Life 31
   Fish; Sea Mammals; Sea Turtles; Shellfish; Other Sea Animals
History 36
   The Ancients; Colonial History; Independence
Government and Economy 42
The People..47
   The Maya; Polyglot; Literacy

SPECIAL TOPICS

The Belize National Anthem *2*
Weather Information *8*
Exotic Fruits and Nuts of Belize *14–15*
The Quetzal—Worth a Trip *17*
Birds of Belize *18–19*
Jaguars 1, Hunters 0 . . . . *20*
Differences Between Moths
   and Butterflies *27*
Longest Reefs in the World *29*
Protect the Marine Heritage *30*
Manatee Breeding Program *33*
Belize History in a Nutshell *40*
What's in a Name? *42*
Ecotourism *43*
Marie Sharp Success Story *44*
Belize Association of Louisiana (BAL) . . . *50*

ON THE ROAD **51–92**
Highlights 51
   Sight-Seeing; Recreation
Water Sports 52
   Snorkeling and Scuba Diving; Fishing; Boating; Canoeing and Kayaking; Other
   Water Sports
Adventures on Land...57
   On the Trail; Sports
Entertainment and Events 60
   Festivals; Dances of the Maya; Music of Belize
Accommodations 63

Food **64**
Pre-Columbian Agriculture; Gastronomical Adventure
Health and Safety **66**
Traveler's Disease; Other Diseases; Sunburn; Healing; Be Sensible—Stay Safe
Getting There **77**
By Air; From Mexico; By Car; By Boat
Getting Around **80**
By Air; By Bus; By Rental Car; By Cruise Ship
Tours Organized in the United States **83**
Touring with Experts; Tour Operators
Information **85**
Tourist Information; Using the Telephone in Belize, Money; Nuts and Bolts Info to
Know Before You Go
What to Take **86**
Cameras and Picture Taking **87**

SPECIAL TOPICS

Live-Aboard Dive Boats 52
Emergency Numbers for
  Accident Evacuation 54
Journey into the Maya Underworld 58
National Holidays in Belize 60
Feast of San Luis 61–62
Save the Lobster 66

Hospital/Clinic Phone Numbers 68
Simple First-Aid Guide 73–76
Women Travelers 76
Airlines Serving Belize 79
Car Rentals 81
Road Distances from Belize City to: 82
Baby Safari 89–91

MUNDO MAYA **93–106**
Maya Archaeological Sites **94**
Sites in Northern Belize; Sites in Western Belize; Sites in Southern Belize;
Other Sites

BELIZE DISTRICT **107–140**
Belize City **107**
Orientation; Sights; Recreation; Accommodations; Food; Nightlife; Shopping;
Services; Information; Getting Around
Vicinity of Belize City **126**
Gales Point; The Belize Zoo and Tropical Education Center; The Bermudian
Landing Community Baboon Sanctuary; The Road to Altun Ha
Crooked Tree **135**
Crooked Tree Wildlife Sanctuary; The Village; Guides and Tours;
South of Crooked Tree

SPECIAL TOPICS

Baron Bliss .114
Drinking Water in Belize City 121
Beta No Litta 124

The Beginning of an Animal
  Adventure: The Belize Zoo 129–130
Crooked Tree Cashew Festival . . .137–138

THE CAYES 141–185
The Land and Sea 141
Fauna 143
  Birds
History 144
  The Maya; Spanish Speakers; Buccaneers; Tourists
Practicalities 145
  Accommodations and Food; Getting There
Ambergris Caye 145
  The Land; History; The Ocean; Scuba Diving; Boating, Snorkeling, and Fishing;
  Accommodations; Food; Entertainment; Shopping; Services and Information;
  Getting There; Getting Around
Caye Caulker 167
  The Land; Flora and Fauna; History; The People; Tourism; Officialdom; Orientation;
  Water Activities; Accommodations; Food; Nightlife and Entertainment; Island Art and
  Gift Shops; Services and Information; Transportation
Other Popular Cayes 180
  Caye Chapel; St. George's Caye; South Water Caye
Lesser Known Cayes 183
  Bluefield Range; English Caye; Goff's Caye; Laughing Bird Caye; Montego Caye;
  Spanish Lookout Caye; French Louis Caye; Long Caye; And Many More Cayes

SPECIAL TOPICS
The Mangroves and Turtle Grass 143
Reef Fish 149
Introductory Diving Courses 151
Turtle Pens Turned
  Swimming Pools 181
The Gray Lady 182

THE ATOLLS 186–199
Introduction 186
  Diving around the Atolls
Turneffe Islands Atoll 188
  Diving; Accommodations
Lighthouse Reef Atoll 192
  Orientation; Diving; Half Moon Caye; Northern Two Caye
Glover's Reef Atoll 197

SPECIAL TOPIC
Searching for Sunken Treasure 191

COROZAL DISTRICT 200–209
Corozal Town 200
  Orientation; Sights and Recreation; Accommodations; Food; Shopping and
  Services; Getting There

East of Corozal Town. 207
Shipstern Wildlife Nature Reserve; Sarteneja

ORANGE WALK DISTRICT 211–217
Introduction. 211
The Land
Lamanai Archaeological Zone. 212
Orange Walk Town 213
Sights and Recreation; Accommodations; Food; Getting There
West of Orange Walk Town. 215
Rio Bravo Research Station; Chan Chich

CAYO DISTRICT 218–258
Introduction. 218
History; Inland Adventure; Cayo Arts and Crafts
Along the Western Highway 222
Practicalities; Guanacaste National Park
Belmopan. 227
Orientation; Accommodations; Food; Getting There
South of Belmopan. 230
Along Hummingbird Highway; Adventure Trips and Jungle Accommodations
West of Belmopan 232
Accommodations and Food
Georgeville to Mountain Pine Ridge. 235
Sights; Accommodations
Georgeville to San Ignacio. 240
San Ignacio 241
Orientation; Sights; Activities; Accommodations and Food Downtown;
Accommodations Just Outside of Town; Entertainment and Services; Getting There
Vicinity of San Ignacio 249
North of Town; South of Town; West of Town
To the Guatemala Border. 255
San José Succotz; Benque Viejo del Carmen

SPECIAL TOPICS

A Damming Project . . . .*220*   *Pass Up the Plastic, Please* *224*

STANN CREEK DISTRICT. 259–290
Introduction. 259
The Land; On the Road
History and the People. 261
Maya; Garifuna; White Settlers

Dangriga 266
   Accommodations; Food; Getting There; Services
Along the Southern Highway 270
   Hopkins; Sittee
Cockscomb Basin 272
   Cockscomb Basin Wildlife Sanctuary
Placencia Peninsula 274
   Maya Beach; Seine Bight
Placencia Town 279
   Orientation; Sights; Water Sports; Other Recreation; Accommodations; Food;
   Practicalities; Getting There; Getting Around

SPECIAL TOPICS

   Garifuna History . . . .*262*   *Kulcha Shack Menu—A Few*
   Garifuna Settlement Day . . . .*264–265*   *Garifuna Dishes* *278*
                                 Monkey River Village *282–283*

TOLEDO DISTRICT **291–308**
Introduction 291
   The Land; Activities; History
Ecotourism 293
Punta Gorda 296
   Orientation; Sights; Recreation; Accommodations; Food; Entertainment; Shopping;
   Information and Services; Getting There; Into Guatemala from Punta Gorda
West of Punta Gorda 304
   Archaeological Sites; Maya Villages; San Antonio Village; Blue Creek Reserve;
   Additional Accommodations in Maya Country; Getting There

SPECIAL TOPICS

   Guest Villages of the Toledo District . . .*292*   *Conservation Organizations in Belize* . .*295*
   Coffee, Tea, or Iguana? . . . .*294–295*   *Butterflies* *305*

ACROSS BELIZE'S BORDERS **309–329**
Guatemala (Tikal) 309
   History; The Ruins; Tikal Accommodations and Food; Getting There
Mexico 319
   Chetumal; Bacalar
Maya Sites of Mexico 320
   Tulúm; Cobá; The Cobá Ruins; West of Chetumal; State of Campeche
Honduras 326
   San Pedro Sula; Tegucigalpa; Copán; Practicalities

SPECIAL TOPIC

Travel in Guatemala *318*

BOOK LIST **330**

ACCOMMODATIONS INDEX **333**

RESTAURANTS INDEX **335**

GENERAL INDEX **337**

MAPS

BELIZE . . . . ii–iii

INTRODUCTION
Global Rainforest Zone 10–11

MUNDO MAYA
Maya Archaeological Sites 95
The World of the Maya 96–97
Altun Ha 101
Cahal Pech 103
Xunantunich 104

BELIZE DISTRICT
Belize District 108
Belize City 110–111
Belize City Downtown 112
Belize Zoo 128
To Baboon Sanctuary
    from Belize City 131
Belize City to Altun Ha
    and Crooked Tree 134
Crooked Tree Wildlife Sanctuary . . . 136

THE CAYES
The Cayes 142
Ambergris Caye 146
San Pedro 148
San Pedro Downtown 154
Caye Caulker 169

THE ATOLLS
The Atolls 187
Turneffe Islands 189
Lighthouse Reef 193
Glover's Reef 198

COROZAL DISTRICT
Corozal District 201
Corozal Town 202

ORANGE WALK DISTRICT
Orange Walk District 211

CAYO DISTRICT
Cayo District 219
From Belize City West 223
Guanacaste National Park 226
Belmopan 228
West Belize and Mountain
    Pine Ridge Area 234
Cayo Cottage Country 237
San Ignacio 242

STANN CREEK DISTRICT
Stann Creek District 260
Dangriga 267
Cockscomb Basin
    Wildlife Sanctuary 273
Northern Placencia Area 276
Southern Placencia Area 277

TOLEDO DISTRICT
Toledo District 293
Punta Gorda Town 298

ACROSS BELIZE'S BORDERS
Across Belize's Borders 310
Tikal 313
The Road to Tikal 317

MAP SYMBOLS

═══	Primary Road	⊛	National Capital	▪	Other Location
══	Secondary Road	◉	District Capital	▲	Mountain
=========	Unpaved Road	○	City/Town	🦢	Waterfall
- - - - -	Trail/Footpath	★	Point of Interest	⩙	Archaeological Site
✈	International Airport	•	Accommodation	▯	Gas Station
✗	Airfield/Airstrip	▾	Restaurant/Bar	⟨⟩	Reef

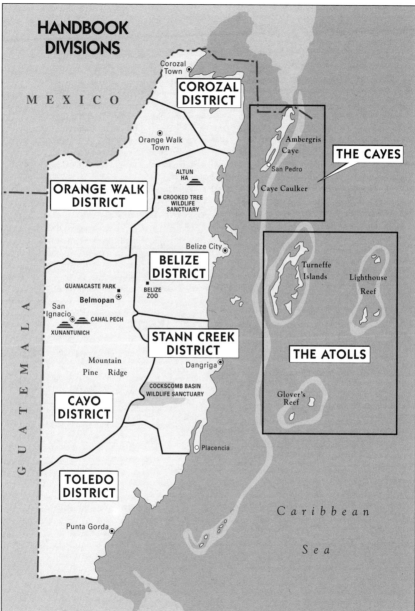

HANDBOOK DIVISIONS

MEXICO

Corozal Town

COROZAL DISTRICT

Orange Walk Town

ALTUN HA

THE CAYES

Ambergris Caye

San Pedro

Caye Caulker

ORANGE WALK DISTRICT

CROOKED TREE WILDLIFE SANCTUARY

Belize City

BELIZE DISTRICT

GUANACASTE PARK

Belmopan

BELIZE ZOO

Turneffe Islands

Lighthouse Reef

San Ignacio

CAHAL PECH

XUNANTUNICH

STANN CREEK DISTRICT

THE ATOLLS

Mountain Pine Ridge

Dangriga

COCKSCOMB BASIN WILDLIFE SANCTUARY

CAYO DISTRICT

Glover's Reef

G U A T E M A L A

Placencia

TOLEDO DISTRICT

Caribbean

Punta Gorda

Sea

© AVALON TRAVEL PUBLISHING, INC.

ABBREVIATIONS

a/c—air-conditioned, air
   conditioning
BETA—Belize Eco-Tourism
   Association
BZE$—Belize dollars
C—centigrade
d—double occupancy
F—Fahrenheit
FAP—full American plan
   (3 meals/day)
4WD—four-wheel drive

h/c—hot and cold
MAP—modified American plan
   (breakfast/dinner)
MC—MasterCard
MET—Mountain Equestrian Trails
NAUI—National Association of
   Underwater Instructors
PADI—Professional Association
   of Dive Instructors
pp—per person
PUP—People's United Party

q—quadruple occupancy
RV—recreational vehicle
s—single occupancy
s/d—single or double occupancy
t—triple occupancy
tel.—telephone number
UDP—United Democratic Party
US$—American dollars
YH—youth hostel

ACKNOWLEDGMENTS

The people of Belize are sensational. Everyone is willing to take a few minutes to answer questions and share personal knowledge; they actually welcome our intrusion into their lives. Thanks to the kind folks who just liked to chat about their country and finished with "Would you like to come to my house for dinner?" Thank you all for accepting our Riley and making him feel so welcome, even when he fussed. We're also fortunate to know a few of the same kind of folks in the States who share our excitement for Belize, such as Steve Cox and Sherry Boyd at International Expeditions, and Cully Erdman and Lucy Wallingford at Slickrock. Writing *Moon Handbooks: Belize* continues to be a labor of love, and lest we forget, thanks to all of our readers who keep us returning to Belize.

ABOUT THE PRICES IN THIS BOOK

As numbers go, relatively few people have shared the wonderful secret of Belize over the years. But as it happens, the secret is out—more and more adventurers, divers, sun-worshippers, and curiosity-seekers are discovering Belize. All of this attention is bringing about rapid changes to the country. Please use the prices given only as a guide; they change frequently. We've tried to furnish accurate addresses as well as email, fax, and telephone numbers where you can verify these facts. If you find the numbers have changed, we would appreciate knowing about that as well. All prices are in U.S. dollars, except where noted.

ACCOMMODATION RATINGS

Under US$25
US$25–50
US$50–100
US$100–150
US$150+

WE WELCOME YOUR COMMENTS

We strive to keep our books as up-to-date as possible and would appreciate your help. If you find that a resort is not as we described, or discover a new restaurant or other information that should be included in our book, please let us know. Our map-makers make extraordinary effort to be accurate, but if you find an error, let us know that as well.

We're especially interested in hearing from female travelers, RVers, outdoor enthusiasts, expatriates, and local residents. We are always interested in hearing from the tourist industry, which specializes in accommodating visitors to Belize. Happy traveling! Please address your letters to:

Moon Handbooks: Belize
Avalon Travel Publishing
5855 Beaudry St.
Emeryville, CA 94608 USA
email: info@travelmatters.com

KATHY ESCOVEDO SANDERS

INTRODUCTION

Belize is a lot of things to its visitors. Think of unbelievably clear blue water and diving along a protected reef rich with brilliant sea life. Amen! And there's so much more. Some call a visit to Belize—with its twisting jungle trails overhung with exotic vines, orchids, and bromeliads—a walk through the Garden of Eden. The air is alive with the calls of toucans and parrots, and there's always a chance to see myriad animals from the regal jaguar to the roaring howler monkey. All around the country magnificent waterfalls cut through stone mountains with multitudes of caves. Many visitors are eager to explore mysterious Maya ruins whose deserted temples and ball courts whisper the names of rulers long past. Belize is home to a polyglot people who have maintained a variety of traditions and cultures for hundreds of years. So far this isolated country has not paved over nature's wonders. Generally speaking, Belize is ecotourism in action.

Early recorded comments following Columbus's fourth voyage to the New World led the Spaniards to hastily conclude that the swampy shoreline was unfit for human habitation. How things have changed! Today this little-known destination is stepping quietly into the world of tourism. The government has recognized priorities and is establishing clear guidelines as the country welcomes more and more visitors. "Our tourism is based on our wildlife, the forests, the flora and fauna," proclaimed Victor Gonzalez, former Permanent-Secretary of Belize's Ministry of Tourism and the Environment. The country, on the cutting edge of the ecotourism phenomenon, actively protects its natural resources: wildlife, tracts of rainforest and unsullied swamplands, innumerable Maya archaeological sites, varied cultural heritages, and the largest barrier reef in the Western Hemisphere.

Unfortunately, big companies from a variety of countries want to get in on the development cusp. They wave U.S. dollars in front of this low-budget country, and there are frequently a few who are tempted to give it all away. But for the most part, Belize has managed to remain intact, even though a few areas have been logged more than they should, several outsiders have wreaked havoc on cayes for "development," and the rumor mill works

THE BELIZE NATIONAL ANTHEM

LAND OF THE FREE

O, Land of the Free by the Carib Sea,
Our manhood we pledge to thy liberty!
No tyrants here linger, despots must flee
This tranquil haven of democracy.
The blood of our sires which hallows the sod,
Brought freedom from slavery oppression's rod,
By the might of truth and the grace of God.
No longer shall we be hewers of wood.

Arise! ye sons of the Baymen's clan,
Put on your armours, clear the land!
Drive back the tyrants, let despots flee—
Land of the Free by the Carib Sea!

Nature has blessed thee with wealth untold,
O'er mountains and valleys where prairies roll;
Our fathers, the Baymen, valiant and bold
Drove back the invader; this heritage bold
From proud Rio Hondo to old Sarstoon,
Through coral isle, over blue lagoon;
Keep watch with the angels, the stars and moon;
For freedom comes to-morrow's noon.

they were selective and removed only a couple of species of trees.

Today Belize has one of the most peaceful, stable governments in all of Central America. Its growing population numbers about 240,000 (22.6 people per square mile), a quarter of whom live in Belize City. (This city has its share of crime; tourists should be aware of this and keep their eyes open.)

Edging the unspoiled Western Caribbean, Belize only recently realized its enormous potential for tourism. Divers, among the first tourists to visit this tropical country, have quietly enjoyed the Belize Reef for decades—thanks, Jacques Cousteau! Independent travelers and special-interest groups (bird-watchers, archaeologists, and nature buffs) have discovered the country's beautiful cayes (meaning "islands," pronounced KEES) lying off the Caribbean coast, as well as inland rainforests and a vast number of archaeological centers. More and more middle-aged and senior travelers from the United States are looking into Belize as a viable, warm-weather, budget location to spend their retirement years. And at the same time, foreign industries are finding the Belizean government cooperative and willing to make tax concessions to attract outside investments. This in turn provides jobs for the locals, which the emerging country desperately needs.

The people of Belize are very aware of the importance of the pristine natural treasures in their own backyard. They realize these natural resources must be protected, and they have opted for a long-term investment in a tourism that attracts people curious about natural history. Today thousands of rainforest acres have been declared reserves, hunting certain animals (which in other parts of the world are already extinct) is illegal, and the lavish coast with miles of reef is strictly regulated. The beautiful atolls and surrounding underwater marine world that is considered second to none in the world have their reserves as well. And ordinary farmers and landowners are banding together to form parts of their land into private reserves.

overtime spreading the word about still another large tract of land that might be torn up for a new resort.

Belize is tucked into the corner of Mexico's Yucatán Peninsula and is an important part of the region called **Mundo Maya** (Maya World), five countries that have been home to the Maya for 3,000 years. An English-speaking country, Belize was called British Honduras from 1862 until 1973, when it once again became Belize in anticipation of its independence from England.

Belize was the favored hideout for pirates until pirating went out of favor. Then those hard-drinking, high-seas robbers discovered an even more lucrative profession: stripping the forests of trees to fill the holds of their ships and later fetch high prices at home in England. Fortunately,

THE LAND

Belize lies on the east coast of Central America. Its 8,866 square miles of territory are bordered on the north by Mexico, on the west and south by Guatemala, and on the east by the Caribbean Sea. From the Rio Hondo border with Mexico to the southern border with Guatemala, Belize's mainland measures 180 miles long, and is 68 miles across at its widest point. It's roughly the same size as the state of Massachusetts. Offshore, Belize has more than 200 cayes. Both the coastal region and the northern half of the mainland are flat, but the land rises in the south and west (in the Maya Mountains) to over 3,000 feet above sea level. Mangrove swamps cover much of the humid coastal plain. The Maya Mountains and the Cockscombs form the country's backbone, rising 3,675 feet to **Victoria Peak,** Belize's highest point.

The uninhibited growth of the jungle takes over everything, including old Maya structures.

In the west, the Cayo District contains the **Mountain Pine Ridge Reserve.** At one time a magnificent pine forest, it was destroyed in the lower plains over the decades by fires and lumber removal, and only a few straggler pine trees remain in the arid foothills. However, the upper regions of Mountain Pine Ridge provide spectacular scenery, and thick forest encompasses the **Macal River** as it tumbles over huge granite boulders. **Hidden Valley Falls** plunges 1,000 feet to the valley below. The **Rio Frio** cave system offers massive stalactites and stalagmites to the avid spelunker. The diverse landscape includes limestone-fringed granite boulders.

Over thousands of years, what was once a sea in the northern half of Belize has become a combination of scrub vegetation and rich tropical hardwood forest. Near the Mexican border much of the land has been cleared, and it's here that the majority of sugar crops are raised, along with family plots of corn and beans. Most of the northern coast is swampy with a variety of grasses and mangroves that attract hundreds of species of waterfowl. Rainfall in the north averages 60 inches annually, though it's generally dry November–May.

Significant rainfall in the mountains washes silt and nutrients into the lower valleys to the south and west, forming rich agricultural areas. In southern Belize it rains most of the year, averaging 150 inches or more. The coastal belt attracts large farms that raise an ever-expanding variety of crops. A dense rainforest thrives in this wet, humid condition with thick ferns, lianas, tropical cedars, and palms.

WATERWAYS OF BELIZE

Heavy rains, deluging the mountains strung across the center of Belize, feed the rivers and waterways that flow from the mountains to the sea. For decades the rivers were the highways of the country. A few are deep enough to be navigable and are still used for hauling logs: Blue Creek, Rio Hondo, New River, Belize River,

*exploring the caves
along the Macal River*

Sibun River, Macal River, Rio Grande, Moho River, Tumex River, and Sarstoon River. Some of the most beautiful areas of the country surround these rivers.

HABITATS OF INLAND BELIZE

Belize has several productive habitats that support a startling variety of life. Each habitat is dependent on the soil and available water.

Marshy Havens
Belize is dotted with rivers, lagoons, and swamps. Low forests grow up around these wetlands and provide an environment for insects, birds, mammals, and reptiles. Bamboo, logwood, red mangrove, and white mangrove are among the species that find footholds in the soggy soil and grow into thickets. Numerous insects, agouti, basilisk lizards, iguanas, paca, and waterfowl are among the many creatures that inhabit these fringe forests. The wetlands themselves play host to many creatures: crocodiles, fish, turtles, and hundreds of bird species. A boat ride into one of the wetlands will give you an opportunity to see a great variety of waterfowl. The lakes of Belize (such as those at Crooked Tree) are wintering spots for many flocks of North American duck species. Among others, you might see the blue-winged teal, northern shoveler, and lesser scaup, along with a variety of wading birds feeding in the shallow waters, including numerous types of heron, snowy egret, and (in the summer) white ibis.

We once watched a peregrine falcon hunt at Crooked Tree. First the wary bird slowly circled high above the lake watching its prey and then plummeted to attack a flock of American coots. Seconds before the falcon reached the ducks, the flock spotted it and began squawking loudly—warning the whole family—and diving into the water (where the falcon will not follow). After watching the falcon dive for the ducks over and over again, we moved on in our canoe feeling more secure about the destiny of these American coots.

Broadleaf Jungle and Cohune Forests
By certain scientific definitions there is no true "rainforest" in Belize; the quantity of rainfall is insufficient and is not evenly spread throughout the year. Instead, the magnificent broadleaf jungle of Belize is considered "moist tropical forest." Depending on its maturity this forest may have a single, double, or even triple canopy, triple being the oldest and rarest. Definitions aside, the broadleaf jungles of the Maya Mountains and parts of northern and western Belize create beneath their crowns relatively cool, damp environments that yield an explosion of life. Towering mahogany, ceiba, figs, and guanacaste live here. Bromeliads, orchids, and other epiphytes cover the limbs of these jungle giants.

Lianas and vines drip from the branches to the ground. Mushrooms of many varieties and other fungi digest the remains of fallen trees. Leaf cutter ants, termites, butterflies, and spiders abound. Hummingbirds, parrots, toucans, and woodpeckers flit between trees. Anteaters, howler and spider monkeys, squirrels, and margays move among the branches. Jaguars and pumas are plentiful. Boa constrictors, fer-de-lance, and other snakes are common, as are many species of lizards.

Broadleaf forests thrive in clay soils enriched by alluvial runoff from streams and rivers. In places, cohune palms, which are typically scattered throughout the forest, grow in thick concentrations. This cohune forest forms a dense cover or canopy. Even so, many of the jungle giants will penetrate it as they reach upward into the sunlight. Many of the same epiphytes, vines, and animals frequent these areas.

Pine Forests and Savanna
Pine forests grow up around areas of low moisture and sandy soil. These conditions exist in certain lowland areas and the low mountains of western Belize. With its typically open canopy, the pine forest allows much more light to reach the ground. Plant and animal life is less diverse here. Palmetto palms, scrub oak, and various grasses grow in close association with pine forests. In fact, standing pines are frequently surrounded by savanna or grassland. Foxes and jaguarundis, deer, mice, squirrels and other rodents, armadillos, hawks and owls, rat snakes, and fer-de-lance frequent these areas.

CAVES

From small rock shelters to miles of underground passageways, cave systems riddle the subterranean corridors of Belize. The ancient Maya used caves in the prehistoric past, and it is believed they sat untouched for 2,000 years before modern man rediscovered them. Modern-day mapping and research only began in the 1960s. Since then more than three hundred caves have been explored and probably 150 miles of passages have been mapped, including the Cebada and Petroglyph caves, two of the largest underground chambers in the

world. Caves are found all over the country, but most are centered in the southern and western areas of Belize. As discovered, the caves reveal intriguing stories of the Maya. Modern-day cavers give them Maya names out of respect to the Maya.

Approximately 200 million years ago the beginning stages of limestone formation occurred, creating what in part gives today's Belize its extensive cave system. It was during this Cretaceous period that life under the ocean started to create what is now limestone. Millions of sea creatures left a legacy with their deaths: skeletons formed a thick layer (6,000 feet in some areas) of what is now limestone, the backbone of the cave systems. Sea levels fell and the mountains impelled themselves upward. After 120 million years and with the help of wind, rain, and faulting, the Maya Mountains were created, and flowing underground rivers carved out channels, rooms, and caverns.

Large populations of Maya were concentrated in these limestone foothills, where water supplies and clay deposits were plentiful. The Maya used caves for utilitarian as well as religious and ceremonial purposes. Caves were a source of fresh water, especially during dry periods. Clay pots of grain were safely stored for long periods of time in the cool air. Pure or virgin water that dripped from stalactites was used for ceremonial purposes. Some caves were used as burial chambers.

Looting of caves has been a problem for decades, and as a result all caves are considered archaeological sites. If caving solo, permission must be granted from the Department of Archaeology (and sometimes the Department of Forestry) in Belmopan, tel. 8/22106.

Belize's neighbor, Mexico, is renowned for its cave and cenote diving, but so far this is not an option for the visitor to Belize. Researchers have done very little study of cenote diving, in part due to the remote and difficult locations of the cave entrances (but that is slowly changing). Cenotes are created when the constant ebb and flow of underground rivers and lakes erodes the underside of limestone containers. In certain places, the surface crust eventually wears so thin that it caves in, exposing the water below, and at the same time creating steep-walled caverns—natural wells. Around these water sources, Maya villages grew. Some of the wells are shallow— seven meters below the jungle floor; some are treacherously deep at 90 meters underground. In times of drought, the Maya fetched water by carving stairs into slick limestone walls or by hanging long ladders into abysmal hollows that led to the underground lakes.

Notable Caves

The most spectacular cave system in Belize is the **Chiquibul,** west of the Maya Mountains and close to the Guatemalan border. Miles and miles of passageways riddle this system, including **Cebada,** the largest in Belize.

The Toledo District has two major cave systems, one near Blue Creek Village and the other north of Blue Creek, **Little Quartz Ridge.** Located in pristine surroundings, the **Blue Creek Cave System** includes a large walk-through cave with some passages that force you to crawl through on hands and knees.

In the Cayo District, north of the Maya Mountains, **Caves Branch** offers tourists easy access to incredible sights. Many hotels and tour operators run trips that include floating on inner tubes in and out of black passageways. Caves Branch is close to the highway, allowing easy access and logistical planning. **St. Herman's Cave, Petroglyph Cave,** and the (inland) **Blue Hole** are part of this system, all part of a nature reserve. Many lodges are situated literally on top of these caves and offer outings and various modes of transport through the caves.

Vaca Plateau is partly in the Mountain Pine Ridge area and includes the **Rio Frio Cave,** undoubtedly the most popular cave (due to its easy access) in the Cayo District. Ask at any hotel or at Eva's Cafe in San Ignacio to visit this small cave.

Underwater Caves

Many submerged sinkholes, most beautifully the Blue Hole, occur in the ocean. **Giant Cave,** off of Caye Caulker, is believed to be one of the longest underwater caves in the world. Other underwater caves are also found off of Caye Chapel, Ambergris Caye, and Columbus Caye. Diving these caves is highly unlikely for the average diver—local dive shops just are not equipped or trained for this type of undertaking, regardless of how much you are willing to spend to go under.

Animals/Critters

Skeletons aren't the only things living in caves. Bats, bugs, fish, and crabs are also found in many caves. The most prolific of these are the bats, hundreds of them in some caves. Some ceilings of caves are covered with what look like reverse sinkholes—holes that go up. Bats cling to the ceilings, often attracted to warm pockets of air. Their urine and other bodily secretions slowly eat away at the limestone, creating these holes. The bats' sense of smell attracts them back to these same holes or "homes." Bats are harmless to humans; most that live in the caves are insect-eating bats. Their eyesight is excellent, as is their use of echolocation; fly-bys occur only if they go after the bugs attracted to your headlamp. Some scientists give the warning about a pulmonary disease that can be carried in the dry dust of bat droppings. If you are concerned, ask your doctor and perhaps wear a breathing mask of some sort.

Mythology

The ancient Maya believed that upon entering a cave, one entered the underworld, or Xibalba, the place of beginnings and of fright. The Maya believed there were nine layers of the underworld, and as much as death and disease and rot was represented by the underworld, so was the beginning of life. Caves were a source of water for the Maya, a source of life. The underworld was also an area where souls had hopes of defeating death and becoming ancestors. As a result, rituals, ceremonies, and even sacrifices were performed in caves, evidenced today by many pots, shards, implements, and burial sites.

Caves were important burial chambers for the ancient Maya, and over 200 skeletons have been found in more than 20 caves. One chamber in Caves Branch was the final earthly resting spot for 25 individuals. Many of these burial chambers are found deep in the caves, leading to speculation that death came by sacrificing the living, as opposed to carrying in the dead. Some burial sites show possible evidence of commoners being sacrificed to accompany the journey with an elite who had died—but who really knows?

Cave Archaeology

The first written accounts related to archaeology began in the late 1800s. A British medical officer by the name of Thomas Gann wrote of his extensive exploration of caves throughout the country, stemming from his fascination with the ancient Maya. In the late 1920s he was also part of the first formal study of some ruins and caves in the Toledo District, and his papers give insight no one else can give to modern-day archaeologists.

Little else was done until 1955, when the Department of Archaeology was created by the government of Belize. Starting in 1957, excavations were organized throughout the years under various archaeologists. Excavations in the 1970s led to many important archaeological discoveries, including pots, vessels, and altars. In the 1980s a series of expeditions was undertaken to survey the Chiquibul cave system. Other finds during this time period include a burial chamber and one cave with over 60 complete vessels and other ceremonial implements.

Today projects are underway in many caves around the country. The Department of Archaeology does not have a museum—they've been talking about one for years. In the past, individuals wanting to see artifacts in the vaults have been able to make an appointment to visit, but not anymore. It is possible that groups might be able to make arrangements. As with many things in government, funding is a constant roadblock for further studies; excavations come in last on the government's to-do list. Fortunately many universities and private organizations have ongoing programs to push the work forward. Opportunities for the amateur archaeologist to participate in surveys and studies pop up once in a while. For more information, contact the Department of Archaeology in Belmopan at tel. 8/22106.

Safety

Go with a guide! Do not play Indiana Jones, regardless of how tempting it is. Once lured into the world of darkness, with each step it becomes more and more difficult to turn back. Flash floods occur. What might seem like a minor rain where you are can create instant high-rises in water levels that can easily sweep you away, resulting in injury and, more likely, drowning. These caves are dark! Once past the entrance all natural light disappears, making it necessary to wear headlamps and carry spare flashlights and batteries. With such limited vision, it is easy to hit stalactites and whack your head on sloping and shallow ceilings, so wear a hard hat. Twisting, turning corridors make it very easy to lose your sense of direction. Local guides know the mazelike caves like you know your way around your kitchen. Finally, respect life in the cave—don't use forming stalactites as handholds, because body oils destroy years of growth. Never disturb or remove anything. If you do and you're caught, your new "hotel" will be the jailhouse.

THE WEATHER

The climate in Belize is subtropical with a mean annual temperature of 79°F, so you can expect a variance between 50–95°F. Belize has definite wet and dry seasons. The dry season generally lasts November–May and the wet season June–November.

Note: In the tropics it's not unusual to have rain in the dry season; it just falls in shorter spurts. The amount of rainfall varies widely from north to south. Corozal in the north receives 40–60 inches while Punta Gorda in the south averages 160–190 inches with an average humidity of 85 percent. Occasionally during the winter "northers" sweep down from North America across the Gulf of Mexico, bringing rainfall, strong winds, and cooling temperatures. Usually lasting only a couple of days, they often interrupt fishing and influence the activity of lobster and other fish. Fishermen invariably report increases in their catches several days before a norther.

The "mauger" season, when the air is still and the sea is calm, generally comes in August; it can last for a week or more. All activity halts while locals stay indoors as much as possible to avoid the onslaught of ferocious mosquitoes and other insects.

Hurricanes

Belize lies in a hurricane belt. Though for many years this powerful phenomenon seldom occurred, Belize has had firsthand experience with five in recent history. Since 1787, 21 hurricanes

WEATHER INFORMATION

	JAN.	FEB.	MARCH	APRIL	MAY	JUNE
AVERAGE INCHES OF RAINFALL (BELIZE CITY)	2.98	1.45	1.68	0.04	5.41	14.01
	JULY	AUG.	SEPT.	OCT.	NOV.	DEC.
	4.59	8.18	10.41	8.40	4.58	7.0
	JAN.	FEB.	MARCH	APRIL	MAY	JUNE
AVERAGE INCHES OF RAINFALL (PUNTA GORDA)	10.32	2.51	0.09	0.28	3.74	13.13
	JULY	AUG.	SEPT.	OCT.	NOV.	DEC.
	28.67	25.38	27.32	14.50	2.60	9.10
	JAN.	FEB.	MARCH	APRIL	MAY	JUNE
MEAN HIGHS AND LOWS IN DEGREES FAHRENHEIT	82/66	83/66	85/68	87/71	87/72	85/72
	JULY	AUG.	SEPT.	OCT.	NOV.	DEC.
	85/72	87/73	85/72	84/70	82/68	81/66
	JAN.	FEB.	MARCH	APRIL	MAY	JUNE
HUMIDITY	73%	68%	67%	74%	75%	85%
	JULY	AUG.	SEPT.	OCT.	NOV.	DEC.
	82%	82%	82%	67%	75%	89%

have hit the small country in varying degrees of intensity. In 1931, 2,000 people were killed and almost all of Belize City was destroyed. The water rose nine feet in some areas, even onto Belize City's swing bridge. Though forewarned by Pan American Airlines that the hurricane was heading their way, most of the townsfolk were unconcerned, believing that their protective reef would keep massive waves away from their shores. They were wrong! The next devastation came with Hurricane Hattie in 1961. Winds reached a velocity of 150 mph, with gusts of 200 mph; 262 people drowned. It was after Hurricane Hattie that the capital of the country was moved from Belize City (just 18 inches above sea level) to Belmopan. Then in 1978, Hurricane Greta took a heavy toll in dollar damage, though no lives were lost. The two most recent hurricanes were Mitch in 1999 and Keith in 2000. The Belizeans are survivors, they pick up the pieces of their lives and homes, and bravely rebuild.

FLORA

Belize is a Garden of Eden. Four thousand species of native flowering plants include 250 species of orchids and approximately 700 species of trees. It is one of the few countries where thousands of acres of forest are still in a semipristine condition. The country is divided into several ecological life zones: subtropical moist, subtropical lower montane moist, subtropical lower montane wet, subtropical wet, tropical moist-transition to subtropical, and tropical wet-transition to subtropical. A botanist can recognize the life zones by the types of natural vegetation that occur. The determining factor of these zones is the amount of rain that falls. Even the common mangrove grows differently depending on which life zone it is in. The trees in the subtropical moist forest along the northern coast are shorter than those growing in the wetter zones in the south. The tallest mangroves occur in the tropical wet-transition to subtropical in the southern Toledo District.

FORESTS OF BELIZE

Most of the country's forests have been logged off and on for more than 300 years. The areas closest to the rivers and coast were the hardest hit because boats could be docked and logs loaded and taken farther out to sea to the large ships used to haul the precious timber. For years small patches were burned for use as *milpas* (cornfields) by the Maya. Today the government is trying to educate the people about the advantages of using other farming methods. However, it will take a long time to break a tradition that goes back millennia.

Flying over the countryside gives you a view of the patchwork landscape of cleared areas and secondary growth. Belize consists of four distinct forest communities: pine-oak, mixed broadleaf, cohune palm, and riverine forests. Pine ridge forests are found in sandy, dry soils. Also in these soils large numbers of mango, cashew, and coconut palm are grown near homes and villages. The mixed broadleaf forest is a transition area between the sandy pine

soils and the clay soils found along the river. Often the mixed broadleaf forest is broken up here and there and doesn't reach great height; it's species-rich but not as diverse as the cohune forest. The cohune forest area is characterized by the cohune palm, which is found in fertile clay soil where a moderate amount of rain falls throughout the year. The cohune nut was an important part of the Maya diet. Archaeologists have a saying that when they see a cohune forest, they know they'll find evidence of the Maya.

The cohune forest gives way to the riverine forest along river shorelines, where vast amounts of water are found year-round from excessive rain and from the flooding rivers. About 50–60 tree varieties and hundreds of species of vines, epiphytes, and shrubs grow here. Logwood, mahogany, cedar, and pine are difficult to find along the easily accessible rivers because of the extensive logging. The forest is in different stages of growth and age. To find virgin forest, it's necessary to go high into the mountains that divide Belize. Because of the rugged terrain, lack of roads, and distance from the rivers, these areas were left almost untouched. Even in the 2000s few roads exist. If left undisturbed for many, many years, the forest will eventually regenerate itself.

Among the plant life of Belize look for mangroves, bamboo, and swamp cypresses, as well as ferns, vines, and flowers creeping from tree to tree, creating a dense growth. On topmost limbs, orchids and air ferns reach for the sun. As you go farther south you'll find the classic tropical rainforest, including tall mahoganies, *campeche, sapote,* and ceiba, thick with vines.

TREES

Bull Horn Acacia
The bull horn acacia, or cockspur, is named after the large paired thorns that occur along its stems and branches. Depending on your point of view, these thorns may remind you of the armament of a bull or rooster. What is certain is that this tree has developed an amazing symbiotic (or cooperative) relationship with ants.

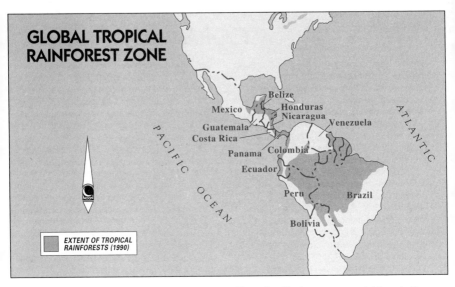

GLOBAL TROPICAL RAINFOREST ZONE

Belize
Mexico — Honduras
Nicaragua
Guatemala — Venezuela
Costa Rica
Panama — Colombia
Ecuador
Peru — Brazil
Bolivia

PACIFIC OCEAN

ATLANTIC

MOON

EXTENT OF TROPICAL
RAINFORESTS (1990)

The acacia provides food and shelter for the ants, and they in turn protect the tree. Tunneling into the thorns near the tips, the ants hollow out areas for their colonies. They find various forms of food along the branches of the acacia. In turn, foraging animals and insects, as well as passing humans who brush against the plant, are viciously attacked. The ants' painful stings are enough to drive away even large animals. Each acacia may be colonized by several groups of ants, but as the colonies grow larger, they attack each other, with one colony eventually prevailing.

Ceiba
The ceiba with its towering gray trunk is one of the tallest trees in the jungle. Specimens nearly 100 feet tall are not uncommon, and some grow to twice that. Found in tropical zones around the world, the ceiba has many names. It is called the cotton tree in Belize for the fluff surrounding its seeds. This same material, commercially referred to as "kapok," has been used to stuff furniture and pillows. Young ceiba have large, somewhat blunt thorns on their trunks. The number of these thorns seems to diminish as the tree matures. Ceiba are commonly found in mature broadleaf jungle.

The tall ceiba is a very special tree to the Maya religion. Considered the tree of life, even today it remains undisturbed whether it has sprouted in the middle of a fertile Maya *milpa* (cornfield) or anywhere else.

Guanacaste
The guanacaste, a member of the mimosa family, occurs from Mexico to Venezuela. Sacred to the Maya, it was called *pich*. A mature guanacaste, or tubroos, is an impressive sight with its huge gray trunk, spreading branches, and wide canopy. Total height can reach 130 feet with a six-foot-diameter trunk. The fruits, favorites of monkeys and other animals, have an earlike shape, giving rise to the name "monkey ear tree." The wood of the tubroos is durable and light, making it ideal for furniture and dugout canoes, or *pitpans*. Guanacaste trees inhabit mature broadleaf forests as well as secondary forests. You can see a giant specimen at Lamanai Ruins and an even larger one in Guanacaste Park just north of the Western Highway at the Belmopan turnoff.

Gumbo-Limbo
With its outer layer shedding in thin papery strands, the reddish inner bark of the gumbo-

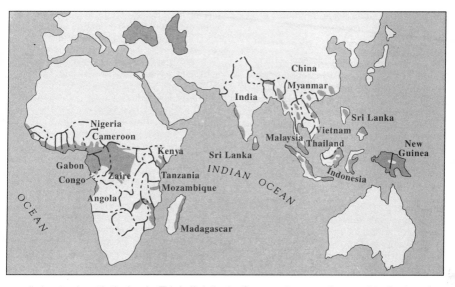

limbo stands out in the jungle. This half-clothed appearance has given rise to the name "naked Indian." The Maya have for centuries used gumbo-limbo bark in preparations to treat skin rashes, especially those caused by the poison-wood tree. Fortunately gumbo-limbos grow in close proximity to these troublemakers. Of little use for lumber, saplings are cut for use as fence posts. Amazingly they soon become living fences as they sprout leaves and begin life anew. Tolerant of shade, the gumbo-limbo is often found in mature broadleaf jungle.

Locust
Also called *pac* by the Maya, the locust tree emits an aromatic resin. For centuries the Maya have used this sap for incense. Called *copal,* traces of this burnt resin have been found in some of the many caverns that dot the Cayo District and Maya Mountains. Locust trees are usually found in broadleaf jungle.

Palms
A wide variety of palm trees and their relatives grow in Belize: some are short, others bear fruit, and still others produce oil. Though similar, various palms have distinct characteristics. Royal palms are tall with smooth trunks.

Queen palms are often used for landscaping and bear a sweet fruit. Thatch palms are called *chit* by the Maya; the frond of this tree is used extensively for roof thatch. Coconut palms serve the Belizeans well. One of the 10 most useful trees in the world, the coconut palm produces oil, food, drink, and shelter. The tree matures in six to seven years and then, for five to seven years, bears coconuts, a nutritious food also used for copra (dried coconut meat that yields coconut oil) and valued as a money crop by the locals.

Pines
Pine forests are less productive and diversified than broadleaf jungle but work well on the poor sandy soils of the Mountain Pine Ridge (Belizeans use "ridge" to mean forest) and lowland areas. Lowland areas support pines and savanna. The Caribbean and ocarpo are the two species most prevalent. The Caribbean has thick, rough bark and is more resistant to fire, an asset in the Mountain Pine Ridge where lightning strikes are common. It is one of the dominant trees in Belizean pine forests. With smoother bark and a less hardy constitution, the ocarpo does not fare as well in the face of fire. Pine lumber and sap have been

important products in Belize since the turn of the century.

Poisonwood

The poisonwood is named for its toxic sap, which causes extreme skin reactions similar to those from poison ivy. The skin blisters, itches, and swells. Some locals have a resistance to the sap's harmful effects. Called *chechem* by the Maya, poisonwood is often present in mixed hardwood forests. Avoid contact with leaves, stems, and bark. If you do run afoul of a poisonwood tree, your Belizean guide will know what to do. While he or she looks for a gumbo-limbo, an oral antihistamine or cortisone lotion may offer some relief.

Quamwood

The quamwood is known for its glowing yellow flowers, which festoon the tree and carpet the ground under it in spring. The tree takes its name from the local name for the curassow or quam, a large bird that favors its seeds. Quamwood trees are usually found in broadleaf jungle and dense forests.

Strangler Fig

Imagine a creepy, leafy parasite that starts its cycle as a seed deposited by a monkey or bird somewhere in the high jungle canopy. As the fig gets down to business, it sends a tendril to the ground to take root. Leaves and branches begin to grow from the budding plant. As they do, off-shoots of the original tendril begin a long process of surrounding the hapless victim's trunk. Over time the fig sends its branches above the crown of the host tree. Overshadowed above and enveloped below, the host dies. Victorious, the strangler fig is left to tower alone, a tree with a hollow heart where once the trunk of its victim stood.

Fruit Trees

Central America grows delicious sweet and sour oranges, limes, and grapefruit. Avocado is abundant, and the papaya tree is practically a weed. The *sapote* (mammee) tree grows tall (50–65 feet) and full, providing not only welcome shade but also an avocado-shaped fruit with brown fiber on the outside and a vivid salmon-pink flesh that makes a sweet snack (the flavor is similar to a sweet yam). It also produces chicle, the sap formerly used for chewing gum. Another unusual fruit tree is the *guaya* (part of the litchi nut family). This rangy evergreen thrives on sea air and is commonly seen along the coast and throughout Belize. Its small, green, leathery pods grow in clumps like grapes and contain a sweet, yellowish, jellylike flesh—tasty! The calabash tree, a friend to the indigenous people for many years, provides a gourd used for containers.

When visiting in the summer, you'll see *flamboyanes* (royal poinciana) everywhere. As its name implies, when in bloom it is the most flamboyant tree around, with wide-spreading

high forests of Belize

PHIL LANIER

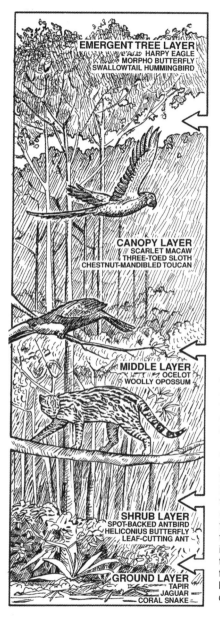

EMERGENT TREE LAYER
HARPY EAGLE
MORPHO BUTTERFLY
SWALLOWTAIL HUMMINGBIRD

CANOPY LAYER
SCARLET MACAW
THREE-TOED SLOTH
CHESTNUT-MANDIBLED TOUCAN

MIDDLE LAYER
OCELOT
WOOLLY OPOSSUM

SHRUB LAYER
SPOT-BACKED ANTBIRD
HELICONIUS BUTTERFLY
LEAF-CUTTING ANT

GROUND LAYER
TAPIR
JAGUAR
CORAL SNAKE

branches covered in clusters of brilliant orange-red flowers. These trees line sidewalks and plazas and when clustered together present a dazzling show.

FLOWERS

Orchids

In remote areas of Belize one of the more exotic blooms, the orchid, is often found on the highest limbs of tall trees. Of the 71 species reported in Belize, 20 percent are terrestrial (growing in the ground) and 80 percent are epiphytic (attached to a host plant—in this case trees—and deriving its moisture and nutrients from the air and rain). Both types grow in many sizes and shapes: tiny buttons, spanning the length of a long branch; large-petaled blossoms with ruffled edges; or intense, tiger-striped miniatures. The lovely flowers come in a wide variety of colors, some subtle, some brilliant. The black orchid is Belize's national flower. All orchids are protected by strict laws, so look but don't pick.

Nature's Hothouse

In spring, flowering trees are a beautiful sight—and sound—attracting hundreds of singing birds throughout the mating season. While wandering through the jungle landscapes you'll see, thriving in the wild, a gamut of plants we so carefully nurture and coax to survive in a pot on a windowsill at home. Here in its natural environment, the croton exhibits wild colors, the pothos grows one-foot-long leaves, and the philodendron splits every leaf in gargantuan glory.

White and red ginger are among the more exotic herbs that grow in Belize. Plumeria (called *frangipani* in the South Pacific) has a wonderful fragrance and many colors. Hibiscus and bougainvillea bloom in an array of bright hues. A walk through the jungle will introduce you to many delicate strangers in the world of tropical flowers. But you'll find old friends, too, such as the common morning glory, creeping and climbing for miles over bushes and trees. Viny coils thicken daily. Keeping jungle growth away from the roads, utility poles, and wires is a constant job because warm, humid air and ample rainfall encourage a lush green wonderland.

EXOTIC FRUITS AND NUTS OF BELIZE

Tamarind

An edible pod about an inch in width and three to eight inches in length, the tamarind is reminiscent of a dark-colored string bean. The pulp around and between the two to six seeds is brown and can be 11 percent acidic, though as much as 20 percent sugar—rather sweet and sour in taste. Used in cold drinks, preserves, and chutneys, it is 3.3 percent protein, high in minerals, and an excellent source of vitamin B. You see stacks of them in public markets, and children enjoy them straight from the tree, a healthy snack said to be as high in food value as maize or wheat.

BOB RACE

Cacao

Considered a stimulant plant along with coffee, the cacao bean is used to make chocolate products, including the world's favorite candy. The pods are yellow to greenish in color and look like a type of squash hanging from the tree. If you split the pod you'll find 10–20 seeds surrounded by a white creamy flesh that makes a tasty drink. Children enjoy the seeds fresh from the tree though the seeds must be dried and roasted before they acquire the familiar chocolate flavor that Americans know and love.

BOB RACE

Bananas

Bananas come in a variety of shapes and sizes, from the tiny lady finger variety that grows in hands of about 75 fruits to the giant Cavendish, a plantain used for cooking that produces hands with about 15 fruits. The lady finger grows four to six inches long and weighs about two ounces; it has a wonderful, refreshing flavor. Most of the production in Belize is of the large market-size variety. The time from blossom to ripe fruit stage may be as short as 75 days. When a stalk of bananas is harvested, the top of the tree is whacked off and the leaves are dispersed around the base, where a new shoot grows; within eight months it will bear another stem of bananas. The cycle repeats itself for seven years before the entire tree must be replaced.

BOB RACE

Pineapple

Tropical fruits have some peculiar family traits. The pineapple, for example, is one of the bromeliad family, which is usually an epiphyte (meaning that it lives on trees and gets its nutrients from what floats around in the breeze). However, a few distant relatives of the bromeliad grow on the ground; the pineapple is one of the most famous. Each stem flowers only once and dies after fruiting. But nature in its constant battle to keep going sends up another side shoot that takes over. The plant grows to about three feet tall, and the size of the fruit ranges from small (about six to seven inches tall) to the large hybrids (as tall as 12–15 inches). A sweet fruit that personifies the tropics, the pineapple is a favorite all over the world.

BOB RACE

The *Sapote*

Also known as the mammee fruit, it grows on a tall tree that for hundreds of years has been a sacred tree to the Maya. Historians say this was the fruit that kept Cortés and his army alive on their march from Mexico City to Honduras. The oval fruit is three to six inches long and covered with a brown fibrous skin. The flesh is a beautiful salmon pink and surrounds an avocado-like seed. The "taste" of the fruit must be "acquired" by most outsiders. The texture is somewhat like a sweet potato, and the flavor reminds me of a chestnut—but taste is in the tongue of the taster. It is used in a thick jam called *crema de mamey colorado,* while the seed's commercial value becomes greater when roasted and mixed with cacao in making chocolate.

The Cashew Nut

The amazing diversity among tropical botanical relatives continues to confuse many people. For instance, did you know that the mango is a relative of the cashew nut? Actually, the family comprises some 400 species in about 60 genera around the world, but mostly in the warm-weather countries. It is said that the cashew tree furnishes food and remedies to the poor, provides a refreshing beverage to the sick, a sweetmeat for tables of the affluent, and good timber and resin for industrial use. The cashew tree is a large, spreading evergreen that grows up to 40 feet in height, often with a crooked trunk and branches. The fruit is bizarre: The fleshy fruit part is called the cashew apple; the nut (the true fruit) is a kidney-shaped bean that hangs from the bottom of the "apple." It is about an inch long and covered with a thick shell. The shell contains acid substances that severely burn the skin at the touch. The cashew is roasted and then peeled to reveal a white kernel of delicate flavor. The cashew apple is a soft fleshy fruit that gives a zesty juice. It is made into jam and a wonderfully flavorful wine.

The Sapodilla Fruit

The sapodilla tree at one time was highly prized for its milky latex, which was used for many years in the production of chewing gum. It bears a fruit prized by the locals from southern Mexico, Central America, and northern South America. Fruits grow two to three inches in diameter, the skin is rough and brown, and the flesh is yellowish-brown, granular, and very sweet. Unless it is well ripened, granules stick to the teeth and feel like chewing gum. This is another "taste" that must "grow" on you.

The Passion Fruit

The name and the flower of the passion fruit may be more familiar to people than the actual fruit. Again, this beautiful purple-flowered fruit has several unlikely relatives: papaya, pumpkin, and melon. Actually there are both purple and yellow passion fruits. Both have high acidic content and are generally used for juice. Many people grow the tree strictly as an ornament because of its colorful, unusual flowers.

BOB RACE

FAUNA

Nature lovers will find a fantasyland in Belize. A walk through the jungle brings you close to myriad animal and bird species, many of which are almost extinct in other Central American countries—and the world. Tread softly—more than likely you won't see many of the beasties mentioned here since they're experts at hiding in trees, behind thick vines, in old logs, in hidden burrows, or just blending in with their background. But with concerted effort, a light step, and sharp eyes, you might get lucky.

BIRDS OF BELIZE

Since a major part of Belize is still undeveloped and covered with trees and brush, it isn't surprising to find exotic, rarely seen birds across the landscape. The Belizeans are beginning to realize the great value in this (almost) undiscovered treasure trove of nature, which attracts both scientists and laypeople, and are making rapid progress in protecting natural habitats. The birds in Belize have until recent years been free of pest sprays, smog, and encroaching human beings. If you're a serious bird-watcher, you know all about Belize. Change is coming as more people, exploring these still-undeveloped tracts in the wilderness areas of Belize, intrude into the habitat of the birds. Still, there are more birds to watch here than in almost any other location in Central America.

Belize, with its marsh-rimmed shores and lakes, nearby cornfields, and tall, humid forest, is worth a couple of days to the ornithologist. One of the more impressive birds to look for is the spectacularly hued keel-billed toucan. This is the national bird of Belize and is often seen perched high on a bare limb in the early morning. Others include chachalacas (held in reverence by the Maya), screeching parrots, and, occasionally, the ocellated turkey. A good book that zeros in on the birds and animals of Belize is *Jungle Walk, Birds and Beasts of Belize* by Katie Stephens. No color, but along with sketches of the creatures, she gives good down-

to-earth descriptions of their habits. The book is available through International Expeditions, US$4.95 plus tax, postage, and handling; to order call 800/633-4734. At the Audubon Society Office in Belize City at 12 Fort St., pick up a copy of the *Checklist of the Birds of Belize* by Wood, Leberman, and Weyer, published by the Carnegie Museum of Natural History, Pittsburgh, Pennsylvania. Another excellent bird book that deals with the entire Yucatán Peninsula is *100 Common Birds of the Yucatán Peninsula,* with full-color photos, written by Barbara MacKinnon. It's available through Amigos de Sian Ka'an, Apto. Postal 770, Cancún, Quintana Roo 77500, Mexico.

toucan at home in the shade at the Belize Zoo

THE QUETZAL—WORTH A TRIP

Though the ancient Maya made abundant use of the dazzling quetzal feathers for ceremonial costume and headdress, they hunted other fowl in much larger quantities for food; nonetheless, the quetzal is one of the few birds mentioned in the pre-Columbian era and it is almost extinct. Though the colorful bird is not found in Belize, we mention it because bird-watchers continuing into Guatemala or Costa Rica will want to visit its habitats. The Guatemalan government has established a quetzal sanctuary not too far from the city of Cobán. The beautifully designed reserve is open to hikers, with several miles of good trails leading up into the cloud forest. For the birder this could be a worthwhile detour to search out the gorgeous quetzal. The Cobán tourist office, INGUAT, hands out an informative leaflet with a map and description of the quetzal sanctuary. If in Costa Rica, take a trip into the Monteverde Cloud Forest Reserve for a possible glimpse of these shy, beautiful birds.

BOB RACE

Acorn Woodpecker

This creature best known for storing its supper in individual holes burrowed into tree trunks, allowing the nut to dry out without fermenting. As part of a "commune," the male birds share the breeding females, who then lay their eggs in a communal nest. The young hang around the nest for several years "helping out at home" before leaving to raise their own families. The woodpecker has black and white feathers with a red patch on the top of its head.

Jabiru Stork

The largest flying bird in the Americas is the jabiru stork, which grows four to five feet tall and has a wing span of 9–12 feet. Though the birds are scarce in the rest of the Western Hemisphere, Belize boasts a healthy community of breeding storks. Building the nest is a major construction job. The brooding nest is generally built in a high tree in an open area above the rainforest; a favorite spot is in the Crooked Tree Wildlife Sanctuary. The cumbersome birds weave a platform, measuring as much as 10 feet across, from large branches. The hatchlings (two to four) are an indiscriminate gray that eventually changes into the adult coloration of black beak, white body, and black head, with a bright red band below the

neck. Occasionally seen in a farmer's field, from a distance the stork looks like a bent old man wearing a red tie. The birds feed in and around swamps and ponds, preferring snails, frogs, small mammals, fish, and especially reptiles.

Keel-billed Toucan

The national bird of Belize, the keel-billed toucan is instantly recognizable by its large colorful bill, yellow front, black body, and splash of red beneath the tail. Inhabitants of the forest, toucans follow each other in small ragged flocks as they forage for fruit and small prey in the trees. Not known for their singing, toucans make short, hoarse squawks. Like that of the woodpeckers and hornbills to whom they are related, their flight has an undulating motion to it. These birds are especially numerous in sections of the Cayo, Orange Walk, and Toledo Districts.

King Vulture

Certainly the king vulture or King John crow is one of the more brilliantly colored large birds of Central America. The body is white with black flight feathers on the wings, but the visual fireworks start from the shoulders up. A bright orange neck and beak, purplish head, grayish folds at the cheeks, white eyes surrounded by red, and an orange-yellow warty growth above the beak make the King John crow a real show-stopper. But, like its lesser brethren the turkey and black vultures, the king must content itself with carrion, the leftovers of the animal world. The king vulture is the only vulture in Belize to prefer forested areas, locating its food by sight alone. Rare throughout its range, the king vulture is a remarkable sight as it soars over forested valleys, hills, and mountainsides. For most visitors, though, the surest opportunity to observe this royalty is at the Belize Zoo.

Magnificent Frigate Bird
Daring show-offs, frigate birds swoop and soar in breathtaking abandon, often along the shores in San Pedro and Belize City. Easily identified by their black overall color, scissor tails, and swept-back wing tips, female frigate birds have white heads and short bills while males have long black bills. The magnificent frigate bird got its name from the male's inflatable red pouch below the neck. Males inflate this twin-lobed sac only during mating displays. Frigate birds are pirates at heart, bullying other birds into releasing catches of fish in midair. Thus, these airborne buccaneers gain a dishonest meal without so much as getting their feet wet. The man-o'-war bird, as it is sometimes called, can be a tolerant neighbor at home though. At Half Moon Caye they peacefully share nesting areas with rare red-footed boobies and other birds. At mealtime, of course, they revert to their pirate ways. You can easily observe all this from a treetop platform erected by the Belize Audubon Society.

Ocellated Turkey
The "peacock" of Belize, the ocellated turkey is so named because of the eyelike rings on its tail. The blue warty head sports a reddish beak. The body and legs also have a red cast. Turkeys especially like open woodland and forest edge where they hunt and peck for seeds, grasses, and fruit. They congregate in flocks of about a dozen birds most of the year. Feeding in early

---

BIRDS OF BELIZE

Marsh Birds
roseate spoonbill
white ibis

Wading Birds
American flamingo

Water Birds
black-bellied tree-duck
fulvous tree-duck
white-fronted goose

Lowland Birds
barred antshrike
black-headed saltator
blue-crowned motmot
blue tanager
boat-billed flycatcher
clay-colored robin
crimson-collared tanager
golden-olive woodpecker
keel-billed toucan
kisadee flycatcher

masked tityra
olivaceous flycatcher
rufous-tailed hummingbird
singing blackbird
social flycatcher
spotted-breasted wren
violaceous trogon
white-tipped brown jay
yellow-throated euphonia

Birds in the Dense Forest
acorn woodpecker
black-faced grosbeak
brown woodpecker
collared trogon
flint-billed woodpecker
golden-crowned warbler
golden-olive woodpecker
gray-headed vireo
green jay
jabiru stork
keel-billed toucan
lineated woodpecker

little tinamou
lowland wood-wren
olivaceous creeper
red-crowned tanager
ruddy quail dove
short-billed pigeon
spotted-breasted wren
spotted wood-quail
sulphur-bellied flycatcher
violaceous trogon
white-bellied emerald
white-fronted dove
white-throated robin

Birds at Beaches, Bays, and Adjacent Ocean
black tern
black vulture
brown pelican
laughing gull
least tern
magnificent frigate bird
royal tern

morning and late afternoon, turkeys select nesting sites in low horizontal branches. Considerable droppings mark these sites in white. In spring to early summer they begin their mating ritual. Like their North American counterparts, ocellated males put on elaborate displays and come equipped with spurs for jousting with rivals. They and their northern cousins are the only wild turkeys in the world. Ocellated turkeys are readily observed in Orange Walk District at the Rio Bravo Conservation Area run by Programme for Belize.

Sooty Tern

The sooty tern is not the only seabird that lacks waterproof feathers, but it is the only one that will not land and rest on passing ships or drifting debris. The bird feeds on tiny fish and squid that swim close to the surface of the sea. While hovering close to the water they snatch their unsuspecting prey. The birds nest April–September, and if left undisturbed a colony can raise 150–200 chicks in a summer. Humans are the sooty tern's only predators. If frightened, the parent birds panic, leaving the eggs exposed to the hot tropical sun or knocking the young out of the nest where they cannot fend for themselves.

CATS

Jaguar

Seven species of cats are found in North America; five are distributed tropically. The jaguar is heavy-chested with sturdy, muscled forelegs, a relatively short tail, and small, rounded ears. Its tawny coat is uniformly spotted; the spots form rosettes: large circles with smaller spots in the center. The jaguar's belly is white with black spots. The male can weigh 145–255 pounds, females 125–165 pounds. Largest of the cats in Central America and third-largest cat in the world, the jaguar is about the same size as a leopard. It is nocturnal, spending most daylight hours snoozing in the sun. The male marks an area of about 65 square miles and spends its

---

sooty tern
spotted sandpiper

Birds Seen at Lagoons, Tidal Flats, Shallow Estuaries, and Mangrove Swamps
American coot
American widgeon
black vulture
common egret
great blue heron
great-tailed grackle
jacana
killdeer
laughing gull
little blue heron
Louisiana heron
magnificent frigate bird
mangrove swallow
mangrove warbler
olivaceous cormorant
reddish egret
royal tern
snowy egret
spotted sandpiper
yellow-crowned night heron

Birds Seen in Villages and Overgrown Fields
black vulture
clay-colored robin
common ground-dove
gray saltator
groove-billed ani
ruddy ground-dove
singing blackbird
tropical house wren
tropical mockingbird
Vaux's swift

Birds Seen at Partially Cleared Archaeological Sites, Woodland Edge, or Scrubby, Deciduous Woodland
altamira oriole
Aztec parakeet
black-headed saltator
blue-black grassquit
blue-gray gnatcatcher
boat-billed flycatcher
cave swallow
common ground-dove
ferruginous pygmy owl

golden-fronted woodpecker
gray saltator
groove-billed ani
hooded oriole
laughing creeper
lesser nighthawk
mangrove vireo
masked tityra
olivaceous flycatcher
pauraque
peppershrike
plain chachalaca
red-eyed cowbird
rose-throated coptinga
ruddy ground-dove
social flycatcher
spotted-breasted wren
tropical kingbird
white-bellied wren
white-browed wren
white-fronted dove
white-lored gnatcatcher
white-winged dove
yellow-billed elaenia
Yucatán jay

nights stalking deer, peccaries, agoutis, tapirs, monkeys, and birds. If hunting is poor and times are tough, the jaguar will go into rivers and scoop fish with its large paws. The river is also a favorite spot for the jaguar to hunt the large tapir when it comes to drink. Females begin breeding at about three years and generally produce twin cubs.

For years the rich came to Belize on safari to hunt the jaguar for its beautiful skin. Likewise, hunting margay, puma, ocelots, and jaguarundis was a popular destructive sport in the rainfor-est. All of that has changed. Hunting any en-dangered species in Belize is not allowed. To preserve the cats, as well as other unusual ani-mals including the tapir, paca, and dozens of bird species, Belize has designated approxi-mately 155 square miles as **Cockscomb Basin Wildlife Sanctuary** (see "Cockscomb Basin" in the Stann Creek District chapter).

While much of the wildlife in the preserve is nocturnal, traces of animals are found by those who trek along the old logging tracks or climb up into the Cockscomb Range, including the

JAGUARS 1, HUNTERS 0

Jaguars, the biggest predators in the New World, need lots of space to roam. So it's ironic that Belize, a country so small it would fit into the hip pocket of Texas, claims to have the greatest con-centration of jaguars on earth.

Apparently the cats are hanging in there and even growing in numbers. After international hunting groups brought the possibility of hunting the big cats once again before the Belize government, Alan Ra-binowitz, a leading authority on jaguars with Wildlife Conservation International (the foreign service arm of the New York Zoological Society), helped it to decide that the numbers of jaguars were not enough to justify hunting. Rabinowitz did a premier study more than a decade ago on the big cat and at that time encouraged the government to protect the an-imals. Since 1981, hunting jaguars has been banned, and 102,000 acres of forest in the Cockscomb Basin Wildlife Sanctuary have been set aside for the big cat. Jaguars, which once ranged from the Grand Canyon to Argentina, have virtually disappeared in the United States and are rare or endangered elsewhere.

Changes in the countryside, such as a decline in cattle ranching, have made the jaguar more popular. Pastures have been replaced by citrus orchards, and fruit is now the country's number two export, after sugar. For jaguars at least, citrus farmers make bet-ter neighbors than ranchers, who have a deep prej-udice against the prowling meat-eaters.

The new appreciation, pride, and concern ex-pressed by Belizeans about their wildlife and their environment is the most striking change that has occurred in Belize. The image of the jaguar has changed from that of a night-stalking, dangerous livestock killer to a source of pride and awe. Jaguars are now featured on Belizean currency, postage stamps, and nearly every tourist brochure.

The most vocal advocates of jaguar protection in Belize are people involved in the country's escalat-ing tourism business. Rabinowitz strongly advises the government to maintain its moratorium on jaguar hunting. His report is reassuring and sees the in-creasing public support for jaguars as an important ally in ensuring the majestic cat's survival.

PATTI LANGE

highest peak in Belize, Victoria Peak (3,675 feet). South Stann Creek and the Swasey branch of the Monkey River both flow through the preserve and are good stop-offs for a cooling swim while hiking the basin. When planning a visit, go to Maya Center (a small town) first and ask about a guide, who might also take you to a minor Maya ceremonial center within the preserve. You can reach the Cockscomb Basin Wildlife Sanctuary from the Southern Highway, which parallels the coast between Dangriga and Placencia. Sadly, the jaguar is still illegally hunted for its skin. The animal's greatest predator is the human. By establishing Cockscomb preserve and others like it, Belize hopes to keep the big cat around for many centuries to come.

Margay

The smallest of the Belizean cats is the margay, usually weighing in at about 11 pounds and marked by a velvety coat with exotic designs in colors of yellow and black large beautifully patterned eyes, and a tail that's half the length of its body. The bright eye shine indicates it has exceptional night vision. A shy animal, it is seldom seen in open country, preferring the protection of the dense forest. The "tiger cat," as it is called by locals, hunts mainly in the trees, satisfied with birds, monkeys, and insects as well as lizards and figs.

Jaguarundi

Larger and not nearly as catlike as the margay, this black or brown feline has a small flattened head, rounded ears, short legs, and a long tail. It hunts by day for birds and small mammals in the rainforests of Central America.

Ocelot

The ocelot is another of nature's great works of art, with a beautiful striped and spotted coat. Average weight is about 35 pounds. A good climber, the cat hunts in trees as well as on the ground. Its prey includes birds, monkeys, snakes, rabbits, young deer, and fish. Ocelots usually have litters of two but can have as many as four.

Puma

The puma is also known as the cougar or mountain lion. The adult male measures about six feet in length and weighs up to 198 pounds. It thrives in any environment that supports deer, porcupine, or rabbit. The puma hunts day or night.

MONKEYS

Black Howler Monkey

In Creole the howler monkey is referred to as "baboon" and in Spanish it's called *saraguate,* though it has no close connection to its African relatives. Because the howler prefers low-lying tropical rainforests under 1,000 feet of elevation, Belize is a perfect habitat, boasting a healthy family of 1,500 howlers. They are more commonly found near the riverine forests, especially on the Belize River and its major branches. The howler monkey, along with its small cousin the spider monkey, also enjoys the foothills of the Maya Mountains. To protect the howler monkey, the **Bermudian Landing Community Baboon Sanctuary** was organized to help conserve the lands where it lives. Thanks to an all-out effort involving local property owners, the Belize Ministry of Natural Resources, the U.S. World Wildlife Fund, the Belize Audubon Society, and the Peace Corps, the land that provides for the howler will be saved. The sanctuary is an ideal place for researchers to study its habits and perhaps discover the key to its survival among encroaching humans. Concentrations of the howler are reasonably accessible to visitors in Belize.

The adult howler monkey is entirely black and weighs 15–25 pounds. Its most distinct trait is a roar that can be heard up to a mile distant. A bone in the throat acts as an amplifier; the cry sounds much like that of a jaguar. The howler's unforgettable bark is said by some to be used to warn other troops away from its territory. Locals, on the other hand, say the howlers roar when it's about to rain, to greet the sun, to say good night, or when they're feeding.

The howlers live in troops that number four to eight and no more than 10, consisting of one adult male and the rest females and young. Infants nurse for about 18 months, making the space between pregnancies about 24 months. Initially, "mom" carries her young clutched to her chest; once they're a little older, they ride piggyback. The troop sleeps, eats, and travels together. The howlers primarily eat leaves, but include flowers and fruit in their diet (when available). Highly selective, they require particular segments of certain trees and blossoms: sapodilla, hog-plum, bay cedar, fig, and buket trees. The locals even put up with the monkey's occasional invasion of cashew trees. Although the baboon has a couple of natural predators—the jaguar and the harpy eagle—its worst foe is deforestation by humans. An unexpected boon to the area has been the reappearance of other small animals and bird species that are also taking advantage of the protected area.

Spider Monkey

Smaller than howlers, spider monkeys live in troops of a dozen or more, feeding on leaves, fruits, and flowers high in the jungle canopy. Slender limbs and elongated prehensile tails assist them as they climb and swing from tree to tree. With a border of white around their faces, adults look like little old people. Baby spider monkeys are winsome in appearance too, and often are captured for pets. So curious and mischievous are they, however, that frustrated owners frequently cage or even release them back into the wild. Without the skills to survive or the support of a troop, such freed orphans are doomed to perish. Unlike howler monkeys, which may allow human proximity during their midday siesta, spider monkeys rarely approve. They usually dissolve into the forest canopy. On occasion, they have been known to aim small sticks, urine, and worse at intruders. Though not as numerous in Belize as howler monkeys because of disease and habitat loss, they remain an important part of the country's natural legacy.

RODENTS

Agouti

A small rodent relative of the rabbit and paca, the agouti or "Indian rabbit" has coarse gray-brown fur and a hopping gait. It is most often encountered scampering along a forest trail or clearing. Not the brightest of creatures, it makes up for this lack of wit with typical rodent libido and fecundity. Inhabiting the same areas as the paca, these two seldom meet, as the agouti

minds its business during the day and the paca prefers nighttime pursuits. The agouti is less delectable than the paca. Nonetheless, it is taken by animal and human hunters and is a staple food of jaguars.

Paca

The paca or gibnut is a quick, brownish rodent about the size of a large rabbit with white spots along its back. Nocturnal by habit and highly prized as a food item by many Belizeans, the gibnut is more apt to be seen by the visitor on an occasional restaurant menu than in the wild. Similar in flavor to its rabbit cousin, in Belize the gibnut is frequently fried or stewed—and it's not bad. In fact, when it comes to cuisine, the paca has been dubbed by the British press "the royal rat" after the queen took a taste during a visit in 1994.

OTHER INTERESTING MAMMALS

Anteater

Without a tooth in its head the tamandua—or anteater—makes a fine living by tearing into termite and ant nests with sharp curved claws and slurping up the inhabitants. The anteater's tapered snout and long, sticky, saliva-coated tongue are perfectly adapted to this business. Ants and termites, of course, are a hard lot to stomach, but the anteater makes the most of it by employing equally tough innards. The tamandua wears a dark saddle over a lighter brown coat, and its wiry hair and thick skin offer some protection against the attacks of enraged ants. Living both on the forest floor and in the treetops, the anteater uses its prehensile tail for balance or as an extra hand upstairs. Solitary by nature, anteater mothers do allow youngsters to ride along on their backs.

Coati

A member of the raccoon family, the coati—or quash—has a long, ringed tail, masked face, and lengthy snout. Sharp claws aid the coati in climbing trees and digging up insects and other small prey. Omnivorous, the quash also relishes jungle fruits. A sensitive, agile nose helps it sniff out trees bearing these favored goodies. Usually seen in small troops of females and young, coatis have an amusing, jaunty appearance as they cross a jungle path, tails at attention. The occasional solitary male is referred to as a coatimundi or solitary coati.

Honduran White Bat
A sight that most people will never see is the two-inch Honduran white bat. It lives only in the jungles of Central America. Cuddly-looking little creatures, they have white fur with pink ears and nose. Like most bats, they feed at night on the local fruit trees found in the jungle or in a farmer's backyard. During the day, they sleep in groups of 2–15 in a "tent" they fashion by biting through the veins of a heliconia leaf (much like a large banana leaf) near the midrib until the sides droop. The result is a tent where they cluster under the midrib while hanging upside down by their feet. The drooping leaf protects them from the sun and rain as they sleep. The leaf also creates a perfect camouflage against predators. During the day the bright sunlight filters through the leaf, bathing the bats' fur in green hues. The green tone makes it hard for enemies, such as monkeys and snakes, to spot the bats.

Peccary
Next to deer, peccaries are the most widely hunted game in Central America. Other names for this piglike creature are musk hog and javelina. Some compare these nocturnal mammals to the wild pigs found in Europe, though in fact they are native to America.

Two species found in Belize are the collared and the white-lipped peccaries. The feisty collared peccary stands one foot at the shoulder and can be three feet long, weighing as much as 65 pounds. It is black and white with a narrow semicircular collar of white hair on the shoulders. In Spanish *jabalina* means "spear," descriptive of the two spearlike tusks that protrude from its mouth. This more familiar peccary lives in deserts, woodlands, and rainforests, and travels in groups of 5–15.

Also with tusks, the white-lipped peccary or warrie is reddish-brown to black and has an area of white around the mouth. This larger animal, which can grow to four feet long, dwells deep in tropical rainforests and at one time lived in herds of 100 or more. They are more dangerous

than their smaller cousins and should be given a wide berth.

Tapir
The national animal of Belize, the South American tapir is found from the southern part of Mexico to southern Brazil. It is stout-bodied (200–300 kgs or 91–136 lbs.), with short legs, a short tail, small eyes, and rounded ears. Its nose and upper lip extend into a short but very mobile proboscis. Totally herbivorous, tapirs usually live near streams or rivers in the forest. They bathe daily and also use the water as an escape when hunted either by humans or by their prime predator, the jaguar. Shy, unaggressive animals, they are nocturnal with a definite home range, wearing a path between the jungle and their feeding area. The tapir is said to have bad eyesight, and if attacked it lowers its head and blindly crashes off through the forest; it's been known to collide with a tree and knock itself out in its chaotic attempt to flee! "April the Tapir" is a star attraction at the Belize Zoo. A birthday celebration is held for her each year to the delight of hundreds of Belizean schoolchildren. April gets her vegetarian "cake," and the children get the real thing as well as a good visit with the national animal. Many people attend the party, which doubles as a popular fund-raiser to help support the zoo. (See the special topic "The Belize Zoo" in the Belize District chapter.)

LIZARDS

Belize is inhabited by a great variety of lizards, from a skinny two-inch miniature gecko to a chameleon-like black anole that changes colors to match the environment, either when danger is imminent or as subterfuge to fool the insects it preys upon. At mating time, the male anole puffs out its bright red throat fan to make sure all female lizards will see it. Some lizards are brightly striped in various shades of green and yellow; others are marked with earthy colors that blend with the gray and beige limestone dotting the landscape. Skinny as wisps of thread running on hind legs or chunky and waddling with armorlike skin, the variety is endless—and fascinating!

Basilisk Lizard

The basilisk lizard looks like a tiny Godzilla with its crested head and back. It's a basic brown with dark stripes on the sides. When disturbed, the basilisk proves to be equally entertaining as it tears around at breakneck speed. All you are likely to see is a flash of legs and elbows as it streaks off into the brush. In fact, its nickname, Jesus Christ lizard, comes from its ability to run across swampy areas and creeks with its webbed hind feet. Don't believe it? Just watch!

Iguana

Found all over Central America, lizards of the family *Iguanidae* include various large plant-eaters, in many sizes and typically dark in color with slight variations. The young iguana is bright emerald green. The common lizard grows to three feet long and has a blunt head and long flat tail. Bands of black and gray circle its body, and a serrated column reaches down the middle of its back, almost to its tail. During mating season, it's common to see brilliant orange males on a sunny branch hoping to attract girlfriends.

Very large and shy, the lizard uses its forelimbs to hold the front half of its body up off the ground while the two back limbs remain relaxed and splayed alongside its hindquarters. However, when the iguana is frightened, its hind legs do everything they're supposed to, and the iguana crashes quickly (though clumsily) into the brush searching for its burrow and safety. This reptile is not aggressive, but if cornered it will bite and use its tail in self-defense. The iguana mostly enjoys basking in the bright sunshine along the Caribbean. Though they are mainly herbivores, the young also eat insects and larvae. Certain varieties in some areas of southern Mexico and Central America are almost hunted out—for example, the spiny-tailed iguana in the central valley of Chiapas, Mexico. A moderate number are still found in the rocky foothill slopes and thorn-scrub woodlands. It is not unusual to see locals along dirt paths carrying sturdy specimens by the tail to put in the cook pot.

From centuries past, recorded references attest to the medicinal value of this lizard, partly explaining the active trade of live iguanas in the marketplaces of some parts of Belize. Iguana stew is believed to cure or relieve various human ailments, such as impotence. The unlaid eggs of iguanas caught before the nesting season are considered a delicacy. Another reason for their popularity at the market is their delicate white flesh, which tastes much like chicken. If people say they're having "bamboo chicken" for dinner, they are dining on iguana.

Several other species of iguana live in Belize, from the small to a gargantuan six feet long. Their habits are much the same, however. They all enjoy basking in the sun, sleeping in old hollow trees at night, and eating certain tender plants. The female can lay up to a hundred eggs, and when the pale green or tan hatchlings

Iguanas love the sun.

emerge from the rubbery egg skins, they scoot about quickly. One of the iguana's serious predators is the hawk. If an iguana sunbathing high in the trees senses a winged shadow it flings itself from the tree either into a river below or the brush, skittering quickly into hiding. However, the human still remains its most dangerous predator.

SNAKES

Snakes roam the Belize jungles and plains. The much-maligned animal is shunned by most humans, and in some cases that's a wise move. Belize has more than 20 kinds of poisonous snakes; nine are deadly. Most of these you will likely never see. Many others are harmless, and anyone who will be wandering in the bush should try to learn the difference. Pick up the Audubon Society's booklet, *Snakes of Belize*. It's full of good information from herpetologist Dora Weyer and detailed drawings by Ellen MacRae, who lives in Caye Caulker.

Boa Constrictor

The boa or wowla is one of the most handsome reptiles in the forest, and its dark and light brown leafy pattern serves as good camouflage. Boas hunt for birds, lizards, and small mammals in trees and on the ground. Holing up during the day, boas prefer to hunt at night. They are able to sense the presence of prey through very sensitive heat receptors and their senses of smell and sight. As the name implies, they kill their prey by constriction, primarily suffocating their victims. Only about six feet fully grown, wowlas pose little threat to humans but may bite if provoked. They freeze or retreat when approached. Some uninformed people kill boas as well as other snakes on sight. This is unfortunate, not only because people are rarely injured by snakes, but also because snakes help reduce the number of rodents, which keenly compete with many other creatures for food.

Coral Snake

Coral snakes are found only in the New World, mostly Central and South America, with a few in the southern United States. In all, there are about 50 species. The coral snakes in Belize av-

erage about 31 inches long. The true coral is highly poisonous and a bite is usually fatal unless treated. The harmless false coral is also found here. Its body is slender, with no pronounced distinction between head and neck. In Belize, the true coral snake is banded in a red-yellow-black-yellow-red sequence (this is not the case in other countries). If you don't know for sure, don't approach a banded snake with those colors. Remember, red means stop! One jingle says: "Red and yellow kill a fellow; red and black, a friendly Jack." Usually nocturnal, coral snakes spend the day in mossy clumps under rocks or logs.

Corals do not look for trouble and seldom strike, but will bite if stepped on; their short fangs, however, can be stopped by shoes or clothing. Even though the locals call this the "20-minute snake" (meaning if you are bitten and don't get antivenin within 20 minutes, you'll die), it's actually more like 24 hours.

The chances of the average tourist's being bitten by a coral (or any other snake) are slim. Reportedly, most snakebite victims are children. However, if you plan on extensive jungle exploration, check with your doctor before you leave home. Antivenin is available, doesn't require refrigeration, and keeps indefinitely. It's wise to be prepared for an allergic reaction to the antivenin—bring an antihistamine and Adrenalin (epinephrine). The most important thing to remember if bitten: *don't panic and don't run.* Physical exertion and panic cause the venom to travel through your body much faster. Lie down and stay calm; have someone carry you to a doctor. (See the special topic "Simple First-Aid Guide" in the On the Road chapter.)

Fer-de-lance

This fellow is bad news. Often aggressive, the fer-de-lance, or yellow-jawed tommygoff, is a nocturnal pit viper that comes from the same family as the cascabel (tropical rattler), water moccasin, and the jumping viper. The fer-de-lance can be found anyplace: in thick jungle, savanna grass, or out in the open chasing prey. This nasty specimen can grow over eight feet long. It comes from litters of up to 75, and until it reaches adolescence it sports a prehensile tail and can and will swing and jump from any tree. As it matures it comes to the ground and pretty well stays there. It attacks with two fangs from either a coiled or extended position and will attack more than once if given the opportunity. The adult has an arrow-shaped head, is thick-set, and its dorsal coloring ranges from dark brown to olive to gray to red. It has 30 paired triangles along its sides, lighter in color and edged in black, which form a row of dark diamonds the length of the snake's back. The underside is cream or yellow beneath the jaw to the throat. The mouth is large and contains two hollow, retractable fangs, larger in proportion to its size than any other snake's. Its venom is highly poisonous and should be treated immediately. Carrying a **Cutter's Snake Bite Kit** is a possible last-ditch effort when there's nothing else, but be advised that most doctors discourage cutting the wound. Do not use a tourniquet and do not ingest alcoholic beverages. If you ask advice from a rural local about where to go if bitten, he/she might suggest a snake doctor who is little more than a healer. However, some Belizeans say, "Do not *ever* go to a snake doctor!" In a desperate situation, you must make a choice.

For more information, *Poisonous Snakes of the World* is available from the Superintendent of Documents, U.S. Government Printing Office, Washington, DC.

OTHER REPTILES

Central American River Turtle

Woe the poor hicatee, too tasty for its own good! A well-armored herbivore, the hicatee or Central American river turtle has been overhunted by humans in the rivers and lagoons where it lives. Its diet consists of fruits, grasses, and other vegetarian fare found along the waterways. Hicatees sleep on the bottom during the day and feed at night. They mate in late spring and early summer and lay eggs in the fall to mid-December. Capable of growing to nearly 50 pounds, they rarely get the chance to do so today. As in neighboring countries, their numbers continue to decline and the Belize government has yet to declare any protection for these hard-pressed reptiles.

Crocodile

Though often referred to as alligators, Belize has only crocodiles, the American (up to 20 feet) and Morelet's (to eight feet). Crocodiles have a well-earned bad reputation in Africa, Australia, and New Guinea as man-eaters, especially the larger saltwater varieties. Their American cousins are fussier about their cuisine, preferring fish, dogs, and other small mammals to people. The territories of both species overlap in estuaries and brackish coastal waters. Able to filter excess salt from its system, only the American crocodile ventures to the more distant cayes. Endangered throughout their ranges, both crocs are protected by international law and should be left undisturbed. Often seen floating near the edge of lagoons or canals during midday, they are best observed at night with the help of a powerful flashlight. When caught in the beam, their eyes glow an eerie red. Crocodiles are most abundant in the rivers, swamps, and lagoons of the Belize City, Orange Walk, and Toledo Districts as well as areas around the Turneffe Islands.

INSECTS AND ARACHNIDS

Any tropical jungle has literally tens of thousands of what most people call bugs—insects and arachnids. Some are annoying (mosquitoes and gnats), some are dangerous (black widows, bird spiders, and scorpions), and others can cause discomfort (botflies) or painful bites (red ants). Many, however, are beautiful (butterflies and moths), and *all* are fascinating studies in evolved socialization and specialization.

Botfly

Ah, the lowly botfly! It looks like the common household variety, but this one has developed an unpleasant trick. By depositing eggs on mosquitoes, the botfly allows its young to be transported to an unsuspecting host. As the mosquito feeds, a botfly larva is roused by the body heat of the warm-blooded host and drops onto the unsuspecting human or animal. Burrowing quickly under the skin, the maggot sets up housekeeping. To breathe, it sticks a tiny tube through the skin (I'm not making this up), and there it stays until one of two things happen: you kill it, or it graduates and leaves home. Though uncomfortable and distasteful, it's not a serious health problem. To rid yourself of this pesky boarder, Sharon Matola of the Belize Zoo suggests dab-

DIFFERENCES BETWEEN MOTHS AND BUTTERFLIES

1. Butterflies fly during the day; moths fly at dusk and during the night as well.
2. Butterflies rest with their wings folded straight up over their bodies; most moths rest with their wings spread flat open.
3. All butterflies have bare knobs at the ends of both antennae (feelers); moths' antennae are either plumy or hairlike and end in a point.
4. Butterflies have slender bodies; moths are plump. Both insects are of the order *Lepidoptera*—lepidopterists, bring your nets!

bing a glob of Vaseline petroleum jelly over the air hole. This strategy draws out the varmint, intent on home repair but hopelessly mired. It is easy enough, then, to squash the squishy freeloader. Another suggested method, which she credits to Mr. Gregorio Sho, is especially effective for the head area: Take a tiny piece of tobacco (I'm not making this up either) and stick it in the air hole. Overnight, nicotine destroys the teenage maggot. The next day you can squeeze out the ungrateful boarder at your leisure.

Butterflies and Moths

Belize has an abundance of beautiful moths and butterflies. Of the 90,000 types of butterflies in the world, a large percentage are seen here. You can see, among others, the magnificent blue morpho, orange-barred sulphur, copperhead, cloudless sulphur, malachite, admiral, calico, ruddy dagger-wing, tropical buckeye, and emperor. The famous monarch is also a visitor during its annual migration from the Florida peninsula to the Central American mountains and Mexican highlands, where it spends the winter. Trying to photograph a (live) butterfly is a testy business. Just when you have it in your crosshairs, the comely critter flutters off to another spot!

Firefly

The poor firefly is really a misnomer. It's not a fly and it surely has no fire. Quite the contrary; it's a flying beetle that turns on a glow on the underside of its abdomen when nature's cycle brings

together certain chemicals. When you see a tree in the forest literally *aglow* with tiny flashing lights, you know that it's mating season. Both males and females locate each other by flashing an on/off pattern special to their genus. However, sometimes in a hunger frenzy a female will fool the male of another species by imitating his flashing pattern—when the poor love-struck male approaches, she eats him! Even in the larval stage, the young can glow, perhaps to scare away predators. Occasionally fireflies eat each other, but most other jungle predators, such as birds, toads, and others searching for supper, stay away from them because the chemicals in their bodies taste *so* bad.

Leaf Cutter Ant

A visitor's first glimpse of these industrious insects is likely to be a column of ants carrying green leaf cuttings across a jungle path. A quick look around may uncover an intersection where two ant "highways" cross, ants from both directions managing to get through with their leafy burdens. On first glance one would think the leaves themselves must be the object of all this effort and organization. The reality is more surprising; the ants are farmers! In a special section of their nest the insects use the cuttings as a growth medium for a preferred fungus. This cultivated fungus is what the ants harvest for food. The nest may be dozens of feet across and 10 or more feet deep, sheltering millions of ants. Like all ants, leaf cutters are highly organized, with different-sized members doing different tasks. Oddly the tiny worker ants are the laborers. Soldiers and breeding males are larger. The queen is largest and longest-lived, with a life span of more than a dozen years.

Termite

A rival to the ant's reputation for industry is that of the termite. These critters are big on building roundish nests resembling a hornet's in appearance and constructed of wood, mud, and saliva. Such termite towns are found in almost any convenient place: a hollow tree, a limb, under a porch, in a hole in the ground. The only stipulation seems to be that they must be near their favorite meal: wood is the appetizer, main course, and dessert. Unassuming, termites like to live their lives avoiding the limelight—or any light for that matter. Their nests provide them a safe dark place, ventilation, and protection from the elements. They also provide anteaters with a handy larder.

Scorpion

One of the arachnids (according to Mr. Webster: any of a class of arthropods comprising mostly air-breathing invertebrates, spiders and scorpions, mites and ticks), these pesky little creatures are believed by some scientists to be the first land animals. They can grow up to about five inches long and are equipped with robust claws. But it's the curled-up tail that you want to really avoid. When cornered, stepped on, or trapped, the scorpion uses its tail and deposits what can be a fatal sting to humans. Everyone has heard that when in a jungle, never put on your shoes without checking the insides—good advice—and always give your clothes a good visual going over and a vigorous shake before putting them on. For another precaution, carry a sleeping net if you're sleeping under a *palapa* (thatch roof, usually made of palm leaves). We have seen scorpions drop from *palapa* roof/ceilings many times.

Tarantula

This is an ugly, furry guy, but fortunately not fatal to humans. Its bite can cause a lot of pain but will not kill. It can grow to about six inches in diameter, and some species migrate in large groups. Once while driving on a highway in a California desert, about a hundred yards ahead I saw a lane-wide black spot moving across to the other side of the road; it was dozens and dozens of tarantulas. Yes, they live in desert *and* jungle. Some folks feed and train these arachnids as pets. Others in the jungle report stepping on them at night, so *do* wear shoes when you're out wandering, even on village sidewalks. The tarantula is able to live for long periods without food or water.

THE SEA

The Belize coast is blessed with a rich abundance of sea life, if not the sandy beaches one finds at many resorts in the Caribbean. The sandy bottom that many beachgoers worship is actually a desert supporting a limited amount of undersea life. Belize's underwater bounty, on the other hand, is due to many complex interactions among river estuaries, mangroves, sea-grass beds, and reefs.

ESTUARIES

The marshy areas and bays at the mouths of rivers where saltwater and fresh water mix are called estuaries. Here, nutrients from inland are carried out to sea by currents and tides to nourish reefs, sea-grass beds, and the open ocean. Many plants and animals feed, live, or mate in these waters. Conch, crabs, shrimp, and other shellfish thrive here. Several types of jellyfish and other invertebrates call this home. Seabirds, shorebirds, and waterfowl of all types frequent estuaries to feed, nest, and mate. Crocodiles, dolphins, and manatees are frequent visitors. Rays, sharks, and tarpon hunt and mate here. During the wet season the estuaries of Belize pump a tremendous amount of nutrients into the sea.

MANGROVES

Mangroves live on the edge between land and sea, forming dense thickets that act as a protective border against the forces of wind and waves. Four species grow along many low-lying coastal areas on the mainland and along island lagoons and fringes. Of these, the red mangrove and the black mangrove are most prolific. Red mangrove in excess of 30 feet is found in tidal areas, inland lagoons, and river mouths, but always close to the sea. Its signature is its arching prop roots. Black mangrove grows almost double that height. Its roots are slender, upright projectiles that grow to about 12 inches, protruding all around the mother tree. Both types of roots provide air to the tree. Another species, white mangrove, grows inland along riverbanks. The buttonwood mangrove thrives in drier areas of the cayes and mainland.

Mangrove thickets are nurseries without equal, harboring immature fish and a variety of shellfish. Barnacles, crabs, immature gray snappers, jellyfish, snails, and sponges hide among or cling to the latticework of roots. Bonefish nose about the shallows and tarpon lie in wait. Birds of many species use the mangrove branches for roosting and nesting sites, including blackbirds, herons, kingfishers, pelicans, and roseate spoonbills.

Less happily for humans, even mosquitoes and biting flies find homes among the tangle. The mud beneath mangrove thickets is often malodorous with decaying plant matter. For these reasons many developers would like nothing better than to eliminate mangroves. Fortunately the government is enforcing laws that make it difficult to disturb these natural wonders.

SEA-GRASS BEDS

Standing on Ambergris Caye and looking seaward, many tourists are surprised to see something dark in the shallow water just offshore. They expect a sandy bottom typical of many Caribbean islands. However, it is this "dark stuff" that eventually will make their day's snorkeling, fishing, or dining experience more enjoyable. What they are noticing is sea grass, another of the ocean's great nurseries.

Sea grasses are plants with elongated, ribbonlike leaves. Just like the land plants they evolved from, sea grasses flower and have extensive root systems. They live in sandy areas around estuaries, mangroves, reefs, and open coastal waters. Turtle grass has broader tapelike leaves and is common down to about 60 feet. Manatee grass, found to depths of around 40 feet, has thinner, more cylindrical, leaves. Both cover large areas of seafloor and intermix in some areas, harboring an amazing variety of marine plants and animals. Barnacles, conch, crabs, and many other shellfish proliferate in the fields of sea grass. Anemones, seahorses, sponges, and starfish live here. Grunts, filefish, flounder, jacks, rays, and wrasses feed here. Sea turtles and manatees often graze in these lush marine pastures.

THE REEF

Running parallel to the coast is the Belize Reef, the longest in the Western Hemisphere and fifth-longest in the world. Scattered offshore and protected by the reef are more than 200 cayes; just outside of it lie three of the Caribbean's four atolls: **Glover's Reef, Turneffe Islands,** and **Lighthouse Reef.** An atoll is a ring-shaped coral island surrounding a lagoon, always beautiful, and almost exclusively found in the South Pacific. The three types of cayes are **wet cayes,** which are submerged part of the time and can support only mangrove swamps; **bare coral outcroppings** that are equally uninhabitable; and **sandy islands** with palm trees, jungle shrubbery, and their own set of animals. The more inhabited cayes lie in the northern part of the reef and include Caye Caulker, Ambergris Caye, St. George's Caye, and Caye Chapel.

The sea is a magical world. Humanity is just beginning to learn of the wonders within its depths. Some dreamers predict that a time is coming when the world's oceans will provide humans with all needed nutrients, and that people will live comfortably side by side with the fish of the sea. For now, men and women are content just to look at what's there, often through a small, round window on a diving mask.

Coral

The Belize Reef has such extraordinarily clear water that looking through a diving mask brings you into a world of color. The myriad hues of coral are rainbowlike: pale pinks, flashy reds, deep purples, flamboyant greens, and a multitude of colors in between.

Coral is a unique limestone formation that grows in innumerable shapes, such as delicate lace, trees with reaching branches, pleated

---

LONGEST REEFS IN THE WORLD

Great Barrier Reef, Australia:	1,600 km
S.W. Barrier Reef, New Caledonia:	600 km
N.E. Barrier Reef, New Caledonia:	540 km
Great Sea Reef, Fiji Islands:	260 km
Belize Reef:	250 km
S. Louisade Archipelago Reef, Papua New Guinea:	200 km

mushrooms, stovepipes, petaled flowers, fans, domes, heads of cabbage, and stalks of broccoli. Corals are formed by millions of tiny carnivorous polyps that feed on minute organisms and live in large colonies of individual species. These small creatures can be less than half an inch long or as large as six inches in diameter. Related to the jellyfish and sea anemone, polyps need sunlight and clear saltwater not colder than 70°F to survive. Coral polyps have cylinder-shaped bodies. One end is attached to a hard surface (the bottom of the ocean, the rim of a submerged volcano, or the reef itself), and the mouth end is encircled with tiny tentacles that capture its minute prey with a deadly sting.

Coral reefs are formed when polyps attach themselves to each other. Stony coral polyps, for example, connect with a flat sheet of tissue between their middles. They develop their limestone skeletons by extracting calcium from the seawater and depositing calcium carbonate around the lower half of the body. They reproduce from buds or eggs. Occasionally small buds appear on the adult polyp; when the buds mature, they separate from the adult and add to the growth of existing colonies. Eggs, on the other hand, grow into tiny forms that swim away and settle on the ocean floor. When developed, these begin a new colony.

How a Reef Grows

As these small creatures continue to reproduce and die, their sturdy skeletons accumulate. Over eons, broken bits of coral, animal waste, and granules of soil contribute to the strong foundation for a reef that will slowly rise toward the surface. To grow, a reef must have a base no more than 82 feet below the water's surface. In a healthy environment it can grow one to two inches a year. One small piece of coral represents millions of polyps and many years of construction.

Reefs are divided into three types: atoll, fringing, and barrier. An **atoll** can be formed around the crater of a submerged volcano. The polyps begin building their colonies on the round edge of the crater, forming a circular coral island with a lagoon in the center. Thousands of atolls occupy the world's tropical waters. A **fringing reef** is coral living on a shallow shelf that extends outward from shore into the sea. A **barrier reef** runs parallel to the coast, with water separating it from the land. Sometimes it's actually a series of reefs with channels of water in between. This is the case with some of the larger barrier reefs in the Pacific and Indian oceans.

The Belize Reef is a barrier reef that extends from the tip of Mexico's Isla Mujeres to Sapodilla Caye in the Bay of Honduras. This 180-mile-long reef is known by various names (Belize Reef is the most common). The beauty of the reef attracts divers and snorkelers from distant parts of the world to investigate the unspoiled marine life.

The Meaning of Color

Most people interested in reefs already know they're in for a brilliant display of colored fish. In the fish world, color isn't only for exterior decoration. Fish change hues for a number of reasons, including anger, protection, and sexual attraction. This is still a little-known science. For example, because of groupers' many colors, marine biologists are uncertain how many species of groupers exist—different species or different moods? A male damselfish clearly im-

---

PROTECT THE MARINE HERITAGE

To ensure that the waters of Belize, particularly the reefs, remain healthy for everyone's enjoyment, please respect the following protective regulations:

1. No person shall buy, sell, export, or attempt to export black coral in any form, except under a license obtained from the Fisheries Administrator.

2. No person shall have in his possession any turtle June 1–Aug. 31, take any turtle found on the shores of Belize, export any turtle or articles made from turtle other than under a license granted by the Minister.

3. No person shall take fish (mollusk, scale, crustacea) using scuba equipment, except under a special permit from the Fisheries Administrator.

4. No person shall take, buy, sell, or have in possession crawfish March 15–July 14, or conch July 1–September 30.

5. No person shall take, buy, or sell any coral at any time.

parts his aggression and his desire for love by turning vivid blue. Some fish can transform into as many as 12 recognizable color patterns within seconds. These color changes, along with other body signals, combine to make communication simple between members of a species. Scientists have discovered that a layer of color-bearing cells lies just beneath a fish's transparent scales. These cells contain orange, yellow, or red pigments; some contain black, others combine to make green or other hues. A crystalline tissue adds white, silver, or iridescence. Color changes when the pigmented cells are revealed, combined, or masked, creating the final result. Fish communicate in many other surprising ways, including electrical impulses and flashing bioluminescence (body light). If fish communication intrigues you, read Robert Burgess's book *Secret Languages of the Sea* (Dodd, Mead and Company).

Conservation

The Belizean government has strict laws governing the reef, with which most divers are more than willing to comply to preserve this natural phenomenon and its inhabitants. However, there are always a few who care only for their own desires. Recently an American bought Hatchett Caye; he has remodeled it and the local newspaper reported that he dynamited part of a nearby reef to better fit his idea of a tropical hideaway for tourists.

It takes hundreds of years to form large colonies of coral, so please *don't* break off pieces of coral for souvenirs. After a very short time out of water, the polyps lose their color and only a piece of chalky white coral remains—just like the pieces you can pick up while beachcombing. Strict fines await those who remove *anything* from the reef. (Spearfishing is also against the law.)

SEA LIFE

FISH

Angelfish

Few fish display more heavenly beauty than these disc-shaped denizens with their rounded heads, flat vertical bodies, and swept-back fins. The adult queen angelfish glistens with a burst of neon blues and yellows. It can be distinguished from the similar blue angelfish by the dark crown with light blue border on its forehead. The adult French angelfish is black overall with tasteful flecks of yellow on the sides. All live in and around the reef, pecking out a living of small shellfish and marine growth. Shy by nature, they may be approached if the diver does not pay them too much direct attention. They are found both inside and outside the barrier reef and often travel in mated pairs.

Barracuda

With its six-foot maximum length, jaws of ragged teeth, and habit of swimming directly up to divers, a large barracuda can be an unnerving sight to the novice. As with groupers, the 'cuda is territorial and investigates intruders. Yet a barracuda can make good company, following a diver around like a dog. Like their freshwater cousins (pickerel and muskellunge), however, barracuda may strike at bright objects that look like injured fish. For that reason it is best not to dive near them wearing shiny watches and jewelry. Move slowly and deliberately. As with many creatures, if you like their company, avoid staring. On the other hand, a direct look or swimming toward them usually will cause barracuda to maintain more distance.

Bluestriped Grunt

These common reef fish school in large numbers in shady areas during the day. Coloration includes thin irregular blue stripes edged in black that run from nose to tail over a yellow background. The tail fin is black with a trailing edge of yellow. The bluestriped grunt is often confused with the white grunt. The latter has stripes only on the head with the rest of the body a checkerboard of yellow and blue. At night these fish move out from the reef in search of shellfish in grassy or sandy areas. When grunts grind their strong molars they produce a croaking sound that is amplified by an air bladder. It is this distinct sound that gives rise to their name.

Grouper

Groupers are saltwater members of the bass family, exhibiting the heavy muscular body and large head, lips, and fins characteristic of their kind. Most members grow to about three to four feet in length. The jewfish, however, may reach eight feet and weigh hundreds of pounds. Solitary hunters, they lie in wait for smaller fish near caves, piers, reefs, and wrecks. When a likely candidate swims within range, they dart forward and open their cavernous jaws, sucking in their next meal. Rows of needle-sharp teeth ensure there is no escape. The Nassau grouper is easily identified by chocolate stripes that run more or less vertically along the length of its lighter body. It is curious and quick to approach divers. The black grouper has dark irregular horizontal patches against a pale background. Not as outgoing, it will linger near divers if ignored. Groupers of these and other species are especially numerous at Hol Chan Marine Reserve and the atolls.

Parrot Fish

The beaky mouth that gives the parrot fish its name is actually a set of fused upper and lower front teeth—the better to eat coral polyps. The result is a sandy cloud excreted by parrot fish at regular intervals as they flap about the reef with their pectoral fins. Parrot fish come spruced up in an amazing palette of bright colors. Since these colors and patterns change with age, identification is often tricky. But most divers can learn to spot several colorful characters. The largest of the group, the blue parrot fish is evenly colored a light to dark blue. Young and old midnight parrot fish appear alike in dark blue with bright blue markings on the face and head. The rainbow parrot fish is easily identified by a copper head and tail separated by a wide band of greenish blue. Adult stoplight parrot fish usually sport a calico brown and white body with a cranberry belly, tail, and dorsal fin. The queen parrot fish has a green to bluish cast but appears to have applied makeup of blue stripes bordered by yellow around the mouth and eyes.

Yellowtail Snapper

This handsome fish often swims singly or in schools. Easily identified, the yellowtail snapper has a streamlined shape with a bright yellow line running from the eye down the center of the body and covering both lobes of the deeply V-shaped tail. The background of the body is a light shimmering blue above and white beneath. Yellow spots punctuate the upper sides. Curious and fast, these fish haven't a shy bone in their bodies and will readily approach divers.

SEA MAMMALS

Bottle-nosed Dolphin

Bottle-nosed dolphins, called *pampas* locally, are marine mammals that breathe through a blowhole on top of their heads and are not to be confused with the dolphinfish or dorado. Bottle-nosed dolphins are frequently sighted near mainland beaches as well as offshore cayes and atolls. Intelligent and playful, they will catch a free ride at the bow of passing boats. During these displays their speed, strength, and intelligence are most evident. It is not unheard of for divers to encounter dolphins singly or in pods; females tend to interact more freely than males. Single dolphins may swim very close and even allow you to touch them. Remember that these are big, powerful animals. Do not hang onto the dorsal fin or impede the animal; dolphins have been known to play roughly with those who do the same. Mothers with young may make a couple or more close passes—a wonderful experience. Or one dolphin may gain your attention while the rest move off in another direction.

Manatee

The manatee is an elephantine creature of immense proportions with gentle manners and the curiosity of a kitten. Though scarce today, this enormous animal, often called the sea cow, at one time roamed the shallow inlets, bays, and estuaries of the Caribbean in large numbers. The manatee is said to be the basis of myths and old seamen's references to mermaids. In South America certain indigenous tribes revere this particular mammal. The Maya hunted the manatee for its flesh, and its image frequently appears in ancient Maya art. In modern times, the population has been reduced by the encroachment of large numbers of people in the manatees' habitats along the river ways and shorelines. Ever-growing numbers of motorboats inflict often-deadly gashes on the nosy creatures.

MANATEE BREEDING PROGRAM

There's great concern in the world of animals about the falling numbers of manatees. Belize is one of several locations in the world where they are still seen. Until recently one of the favorite tours for visitors was a trip to the mammals' favorite water holes, where tourists could jump in and swim with the manatees. Although these animals are gentle and curious, it upsets their natural instincts and habits to have humans swimming around. The government has established rules guarding the observation of the manatee. Guides can bring their boats in slowly and only within a certain distance, and once the mammal is spotted, the motors are to be turned off, and then poles are used to move around. Manatees are frequently injured while investigating a boat and tangling with a propellor.

The state of Florida, under the auspices of the Miami Seaquarium and Dr. Jesse White, has begun a captive-breeding program, hoping to learn more about the habits of the manatee and to try to increase the declining numbers. Several manatees have been born in captivity; they along with others that have recuperated from injury or illness will be or have been released into Florida's Crystal River, where boat traffic is restrict-

ed. They are tagged and closely observed. Florida maintains a 24-hour hotline for people to report manatees in need of help for any reason. Rescues have included removing an adult male from a cramped storm drain and rushing to newborns that somehow managed to get separated from their mothers and washed ashore. These newborns are readily accepted by surrogate-mother manatees and are offered nourishment (by way of a thumb-sized teat under the front flipper) and lots of TLC. Medical aid is given to mammals that have been slashed by boat propellers as a result of cruising boats. The manatee has a playful curiosity and investigates anything found in its underwater environment, many times sustaining grave damage.

Information gained in Florida is helping manatees everywhere.

At birth the manatee weighs 60–70 pounds; it can grow up to 13 feet long and weigh more than a ton. Gray with a pinkish cast and shaped like an Idaho potato, it has a spatulate tail, two forelimbs with toenails, pebbled coarse skin, tiny sunken eyes, numerous fine-bristled hairs scattered sparsely over its body, and a permanent Mona Lisa smile. The head of the mammal seems small for its gargantuan body, and its preproboscidean lineage includes dugongs (in Australia), hydrax, and elephants. The mana-tee's truncated snout and prehensile lips help to push food into its mouth. As the only aquatic mammal that exists solely on vegetation, the manatee grazes on bottom-growing grasses and other aquatic plant life. It ingests as much as 495 pounds per day, cleaning rivers of oxygen-choking growth. It is unique among mammals in that it constantly grows new teeth—worn teeth fall out and are replaced. Posing no threat to any other living thing, it has been hunted for its oil, skin, and flesh, which is said to be tasty.

The mammal thrives in shallow warm water and has been reported (infrequently, however) in shallow Belize bays. One spring evening in the bay at Consejo Shores in Belize, a curious manatee spent about an hour lazily swimming the cove, lifting its truncated snout, and often its entire head, out of the water about every four minutes. The few people (this author included) who were standing on a small dock in the bay were thrilled to see the shy animal. They are around; just keep looking. Belize reportedly has the largest population of manatees in the world, except perhaps for the Florida Sanctuary in the United States.

In neighboring Guatemala, the government is sponsoring a manatee reserve in Lago de Izabal. In the United States the mammal is found mostly at inshore and estuarine areas of Florida. It is protected under the Federal U.S. Marine Mammal Protection Act of 1972, the Endangered Species Act of 1973, and the Florida Manatee Sanctuary Act of 1978. It is estimated that their total population numbers about 2,000.

SEA TURTLES

In Belize sea turtles come in three varieties: green, hawksbill, and loggerhead. All have paddlelike flippers instead of feet and use the front set like wings and the rear ones to steer. Yet, as well adapted to the ocean as they are, they all have to surface to breathe. For that reason many die in the nets of fishermen throughout the world. The largest of the three, the green turtle, is so named for the green fat that encircles its body. In centuries past, mariners relied on these turtles and their eggs for sustenance. Smallest of the sea turtles, the hawksbill has been heavily hunted for its shell, which is marketed as tortoise shell. The plates of this attractive shell overlap like the shingles of a house. The loggerhead or larga is distinguished by its large head, heavy neck, and heart-shaped shell.

Sea turtles are still eaten in Belize and elsewhere. Green and loggerhead turtles are legally hunted November–April. Hawksbill turtles are now fully protected in Belizean waters. As the number of sea turtles continues to dwindle worldwide, responsible travelers avoid consuming any kind of sea turtle product.

People create other hazards for turtles too. Habitat destruction, nesting disruption, and floating plastic debris threaten all three species. When people dredge turtle-grass beds they destroy a primary food source for turtles. When they erect hotels, condominiums, and other buildings on turtle beaches or when they steal eggs, they disrupt key nesting sites and hatching. When they leave plastic bags and other debris floating about in the water, turtles mistake them for a favorite food, jellyfish, and suffocate upon swallowing them. On northern Ambergris Caye, Greg Smith and a group of enlightened landowners have created a sea turtle sanctuary along a six-mile stretch of beach. Their aim is to ensure nesting areas for turtles of all three species.

SHELLFISH

Conch

A large seagoing member of the snail family, the conch spends its time dragging itself around sea-grass beds, where it feeds. It uses a leathery foot for locomotion and even has eyes to detect motion. The top of the shell is a yellowish brown. Underside, the shell is bright pink and white around the shell opening. The horny brown foot blocks entrance. As tasty as they are numerous, conch are caught by free-diving fishermen who sell their catches in Belize City, San Pedro, and elsewhere. Conch meat is served raw in ceviche, fried, stewed, and added to soups. Conch season lasts October–June. After that, the conch are allowed to reproduce in peace.

Spiny Lobster

Spiny lobsters lack the large claws of their Maine relatives. Instead, they have hard spiky shells and antennae. These antennae are quite long and are useful in detecting and fencing with enemies. In fact, the protruding antennae usually are an alert diver's first indication that a lobster is at home. Bottom dwellers, spiny lobsters hide out in the reef by day, emerging by night to feed. When caught out in the open, the lobster uses its powerful tail to propel itself away from would-be gourmands, human or otherwise. Near the reef, it retreats into the first handy cranny. A favorite of seafood lovers everywhere, lobsters are legally taken in Belize by trap or free diving. Size limits are enforced; scuba divers are not allowed to take lobster. The season begins June 15 and ends February 15. It is illegal to have lobsters in one's possession out of season, and hefty fines result from infractions. Only close management will prevent these crustaceans from being overexploited. You can do your part by refusing lobster out of season.

Feather Duster Worm

Appearing like a small flower or feather duster, this worm lives in a tube buried in the reef or sand. Its head protrudes with a flowery spiral of fronds that serve as gills and a means of collecting food. This parasol may be solid yellow, gray, or white, or it may have bands of white and red. These fronds are extremely sensitive to disturbances in the water near the worm. Get too close or move too suddenly and the feather duster disappears in a flash into the tube.

OTHER SEA ANIMALS

Nurse Shark

Divers often see the sluggish nurse shark resting on sand bottoms or swimming lazily about the reef. The skin varies from a shimmering copper to a slate gray. The eyes are small and light, and two barbels appear under the snout. The shape of the head, somewhat like a vacuum cleaner, may aid the nurse shark as it feeds along the bottom on crustaceans. When it comes to behavior, there is not much to report. More interesting is the shark's effect on humans. People often back away or become pests, pulling at fin or tail. Such rudeness can earn a bite. It's best to show some decorum and restraint.

Green Moray Eel

The leathery skin of this moray is an even shade of green or olive from head to tail. The long undulating fins, top and bottom, assist it in swimming. The largest of several species of eel in Belizean waters, the green moray reaches lengths of up to six feet. It hides in reef crevices during the day, venturing out at night to feed. Like all moray eels, the green moray must open and close its mouth to breathe, revealing a flash of bristling sharp teeth. Morays are easygoing but will inflict nasty bites when molested or when groping hands are thrust into their dens.

Rays

Almost alien in appearance, rays fly through the water with the greatest of ease. The species in Belizean waters include stingrays, eagle rays, and manta rays. As defense they have camouflage, speed, and, in the case of stingrays and eagle rays, poisonous spines. Stingrays spend most of their time on the ocean bottom, often covered to the eyes with sand. The rest of the time they search for shellfish by shoveling the bottom with their pointed snouts. Stingrays are easy to get along with. When walking in shallows, a shuffling gait will give rays ample warning of your approach. They will simply flutter out of the way. Divers need only treat stingrays with a modicum of respect and the rays will return the favor. Never pull or poke at them. Freewheeling eagle rays are a graceful sight as they wing past the edge of a reef or pier. But don't even think about hitching a ride; they have several poisonous spines at the base of their tails. A bad scrape with one of these will spoil your whole day! Manta rays have no such spines, but just as you wouldn't appreciate some lout grabbing you by the shoulders, show the peaceful manta the same courtesy.

HISTORY

THE ANCIENTS

Earliest Humans

During the Pleistocene epoch (about 50,000 B.C.), when the level of the sea fell, people and animals from Asia crossed the Bering land bridge into the American continent. For nearly 50,000 years, humans continued the epic trek southward. It is believed that the first people reached Tierra del Fuego, at the tip of South America, in approximately 1000 B.C.

As early as 10,000 B.C., Ice Age man hunted woolly mammoth and other large animals roaming the cool, moist landscape of Central America. Between 7000 and 2000 B.C., society evolved from hunters and gatherers to farmers. Such crops as corn, squash, and beans were independently domesticated in widely separated areas of Mesoamerica after about 6000 B.C. The remains of clay figurines from the pre-Classic period, presumed to be fertility symbols, marked the rise of religion in Mesoamerica, beginning about 2000 B.C.

Around 1000 B.C. the Olmec culture, believed to be the earliest in the area and the predecessors to the Maya, began to spread throughout Mesoamerica. Large-scale ceremonial centers grew along Gulf Coast lands, and much of Mesoamerica was influenced by the Olmecs' religion of worshiping strange jaguarlike gods. They also developed the New World's first calendar and an early system of writing.

Classic Period

The Classic period, beginning about A.D. 300, is now hailed as the peak of cultural development among the Maya. Until A.D. 900, they made phenomenal progress in the development of artistic, architectural, and astronomical skills. They constructed impressive buildings during this period, and wrote codices (folded bark books) filled with hieroglyphic symbols that detailed complicated mathematical calculations of days, months, and years. Only the priests and the privileged held this knowledge and continued to learn and develop it until, for some unexplained reason, the growth suddenly halted. A new militaristic society was born, built around a blend of ceremonialism, civic and social organization, and conquest.

The Mystery of La Ruta Maya

For hundreds of years, modern scholars of the world have asked, "What happened to the Maya people?" Their world included today's countries called Belize, Honduras, Guatemala, El Salvador, and southern Mexico. We know that many Maya descendants survive today, but not the intelligentsia. However, their magnificent structures, built with such advanced skill, still stand. Many carvings, statues, and even a few colored frescoes remain. All of this art depicts a world of intelligent human beings living in a well-organized, complex society. It's apparent that their trade and agricultural methods supported the population for many centuries. They used intensive systems of farming by terracing foothill slopes and constructing raised beds in valley bottoms where soil fertility could be enriched by trapping alluvial deposits and adding organic supplements. Scholars agree the Maya were the most advanced of all ancient Mesoamerican cultures. Yet all signs point to an abrupt work stoppage. After about A.D. 900, no buildings were constructed and no stelae, which carefully detailed names and dates to inform future generations of their roots, were erected. So what happened?

Anthropologists and historians do know that perhaps as many as 500,000 Maya were killed by diseases such as smallpox after the arrival of the Spaniards into the New World. But no one really knows for sure what halted the progress of the Maya culture.

A Society Collapses

Priests and noblemen, the guardians of religion, science, and the arts, conducted their ritual ceremonies and studies in the large stone pyramids and platforms found today in ruins throughout the jungle. Consequently, more specific questions arise: What happened to the priests and noblemen? Why were the centers

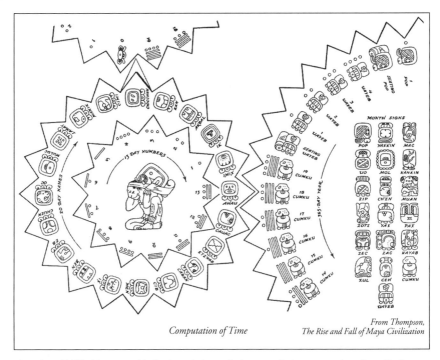

Computation of Time

From Thompson,
The Rise and Fall of Maya Civilization

abandoned? What happened to the knowledge of the intelligentsia? They studied the skies, wrote the books, and designed the pyramids. Theories abound. Some speculate about a revolution of the people or decentralization with the arrival of outside influences. Others suggest that the people were tired of subservience and were no longer willing to farm the land to provide food, clothing, and support for the priests and nobles. Another theory is that there just wasn't enough land to farm and provide food and necessities for the large population. Whatever happened, it's clear that the special knowledge concerning astronomy, hieroglyphics, and architecture was not passed on to Maya descendants. Sociologists who have lived with the indigenous people in isolated villages are convinced that this privileged information is not known by today's Maya. Why did the masses disperse, leaving once-sacred stone cities unused and ignored? It's possible that lengthy periods of drought, famine, and epidemic caused the people to leave their once-glorious sacred centers. No longer important in day-to-day life, these structures were ignored for a thousand years and faced the whimsy of nature and its corroding elements.

The Maya question may never be answered with authority. One nonconforming theory suggests that these stone cities were built by people from outer space. Another considers the possibility that today's Maya are no relation to the people who built the structures, made near-perfect astronomical observations, and discovered infinity a thousand years ago.

Secrets of the Ruins

With today's technology, astronauts have seen many wonders from outer space, spotting overgrown structures within the thick uninhabited jungle of La Ruta Maya. These large treasures of knowledge are just waiting to be reopened. But until the funds and plans are in hand, these mounds are left unsung and untouched in hopes that looters will not find them before archaeologists are able to open them up. Looters generally are not interested in the knowledge gained from an artifact; they're primarily interested in the dollars. Not only has much been lost in these criminal actions, but their heavy-handed methods have also destroyed countless artifacts. As new finds are made, the history of the Maya develops new depth and breadth. Archaeologists, ethnologists, art historians, and linguists continue to unravel the ongoing mystery with constant new discoveries of temples and artifacts, each with a story to tell.

COLONIAL HISTORY

The pre-Columbian history of Belize is closely associated with all of its nearby neighbors: Mexico, Guatemala, and Honduras. The Maya were the first people to inhabit the land referred to as La Ruta Maya. They planted *milpas* (cornfields), built ceremonial centers, and established villages with large numbers of people throughout the region. Hernán Cortés passed through the southern part of the country on his trek northward searching for treasure. In 1530 the conquistador Montejo attacked the Nachankan and Belize Maya, but his attempt to conquer them failed. This introduction of Spanish influence did not have the impact on Belize that it did in the northern part of the Caribbean coast until the Caste War.

Hernán Cortés and Other Explorers
After Columbus's arrival in the New World, other adventurers traveling the same seas soon found the Yucatán Peninsula. In 1519, 34-year-old Cortés sailed from Cuba against the will of the Spanish governor. With 11 ships, 120 sailors, and 550 soldiers, he set out to search for slaves, a lucrative business with or without the blessings of the government. His search began on the Yucatán coast and eventually encompassed most of Mexico. However, he hadn't counted on the ferocious resistance and cunning of the Maya. The fighting was destined to continue for many years—a time of bloodshed and death for many of his men. This "war" didn't *really* end on the peninsula until the Chan Santa Cruz people finally made peace with the Mexican federal government in 1935, more than 400 years later.

Cortés

Although the Maya in Mérida, in Yucatán, Mexico, were a long distance from Belize and not directly bothered by the intrusion of the Spanish, the actions of the Spanish Franciscan priests toward the Mérida Maya would have a great influence on Belize in the years that followed. The Catholic priests were wiping out ceremonies and all other traces of the Maya, further setting the stage for the bloodshed to come. The ripple effect that followed eventually exploded into the Caste War, which, in turn, brought both Maya and mestizos across the borders of Belize.

Diego de Landa was the Franciscan priest who, while trying to gather the Maya into the fold of Christianity, leaned on them and their beliefs with a heavy hand, destroying thousands of Maya idols, many of their temples, and all but four of their books. Because his methods were often cruel, in 1563 he was called back to Spain after colonial civil and religious leaders accused him of "despotic mismanagement." He spent a year in prison, and while his fate was being decided, he wrote a book, *Relaciones de las Cosas de Yucatán,* defending himself against the charges. This book gave extensive information about the

Maya, their beliefs, the growth and preparation of their food, the structure of their society, the priesthood, and the sciences—essentially a broad insight into the culture that otherwise would have been lost forever. Fortunately, he included in his book a one-line formula that, when used as a mathematical and chronological key, opened up the science of Maya calculations and their great knowledge of astronomy. De Landa returned to the Yucatán Peninsula and lived out his remaining years, continuing his previous methods of proselytizing until his death in 1579.

Catholicism

Over the years, the majority of Maya were indeed baptized into the Catholic faith. Most priests did their best to educate the people, teach them to read and write, and protect them from the growing number of Spanish settlers who used them as slaves. The Maya practiced Catholicism in their own manner, combining their ancient beliefs, handed down throughout the centuries, with Christian doctrine. These mystic yet Christian ceremonies are still performed in baptism, courtship, marriage, illness, farming, house building, and fiestas.

Pirates and Subjugation

While all of Mesoamerica dealt with the problems of economic colonialism, the Yucatán Peninsula had an additional problem: harassment by vicious pirates who made life in the coastal areas unstable. In other parts of the Yucatán Peninsula the passive people were ground down, their lands taken away, and their numbers greatly reduced by the European settlers' epidemics and mistreatment.

British buccaneers sailed the coast, attacking the Spanish fleet at every opportunity. These ships were known to carry unimaginable riches of gold and silver from the New World back to the king of Spain. The Belizean coast became a convenient place for pirates to hole up during bad weather or for a good drinking bout. And, though no one planned it as a permanent layover, by 1650 the coast had the beginnings of a British pirate lair/settlement. As pirating slacked off on the high seas, British buccaneers discovered they could use their ships to carry logwood back to a ready market in England. These early settlers were nicknamed the Baymen.

In the meantime, the Spanish desperately tried to maintain control of this vast New World they had grasped from across the ocean. But it was a difficult task, and brutal conflicts continually flared between the Spanish and either the British inhabitants or the Maya. The British Baymen were continually run out but always returned. Treaties were signed and then rescinded. However, the British relentlessly made inroads into the country, importing slaves from Africa beginning in the 1720s to laboriously thrash through the jungles and cut the timber—work that the fiercely independent Maya resisted with their lives.

In 1763 Spain "officially" agreed to let the British cut logwood. The decree allowed roads (along the then-designated frontiers) to be built in the future, though definite boundaries were to be agreed upon later. For nearly 150 years the only "roads" built were narrow tracks to the rivers; the rivers became Belize's major highways. Boats were common transport along the coast and somehow road building was postponed, leaving boundaries vaguely defined and countrymen on both sides of the border unsure. This was the important bit of history that later encouraged the Spanish-influenced Guatemalans to believe that Belize had failed to carry out the 1763 agreement by building roads, so it was their turf. Even after Spain vacated Guatemala, Guatemalans tried for generations to assume ownership across the existing Belize borders. Since 1988, however, the boundary disagreement *appears* to have blown over with the Guatemalan threat of a takeover stopping on their side of the frontier. But because no official agreements have been made, most believe this conflict is still unresolved.

Treaty of Paris

Politically, Belize (or, more to the point, its timber) was up for grabs, and a series of treaties did little to calm the ping-pong effect between the British and the Spanish over the years. One such agreement, the Treaty of Paris, did little to control the Baymen—or the Spanish. With license, British plantation owners continued to divest the forests of logs, leaving Belize with nothing more than a legacy of brutality and tyrannical control over the slaves (who worked under cruel conditions while making rich men of their masters). The Spanish continued to claim sovereignty over the land but never settled in Belize. They continued their efforts to take over by sporadically harassing and attacking the Baymen—only to fail each time when the British returned and held on to their settlement.

The Baymen held on with only limited rights to the area until the final skirmish in 1798 on St. George, a small caye just off Belize City. The Baymen, with the help of an armed sloop and three companies of a West Indian regiment, won the battle of St. George's Caye on September 10, ending the Spanish claim to Belize once and for all. After that battle Belize was ruled by the British Crown until gaining its independence in 1981.

During the first 400 years after Europeans arrived, nothing much was done to develop the country, not even (as mentioned) roads or railroads, and you can count on one hand how many historic buildings are standing (because few were ever built). Maya structures don't count—they were here before the British and will be here for many years to come.

Land Rights
In 1807, slavery was *officially* abolished in Belize by England. This was not agreeable to the powerful British landowners, and in many quarters it continued to flourish. Changes were then made to accommodate the will of the powerful. The local government no longer *gave* land to settlers as it had for years (the British law now permitted former slaves and other "coloureds" to hold title). The easiest way to keep them from possessing the land was to charge for it—essentially barring the majority in the country from landownership. So, in essence, slavery continued.

Caste War
It was inevitable that the Maya would eventually erupt in a furious attack. This bloody uprising in the Yucatán Peninsula in the 1840s was called the Caste War. Though the Maya were farmers and for the most part not soldiers, in this savage war they took revenge on every white man, woman, and child by rape and murder. When the winds of war reversed themselves and the Maya were on the losing side, vengeance on them was merciless. Some settlers would immediately kill any Maya, regardless of his beliefs. Some Maya were taken prisoner and sold to Cuba as slaves; others left their villages and hid in the jungles, in some cases for decades. Between 1846–50 the population of the Yucatán Peninsula was reduced from 500,000 to 300,000. Guerrilla warfare ensued, with the escaped Maya making repeated sneak attacks upon the white settlers. Quintana Roo, adjacent to Belize along the Caribbean coast, was considered a dangerous no-man's-land for more than a hundred years until, in 1974, with the promise of tourism, the territory was admitted to the Federation of States of Mexico.

Growing Maya Power
Many of the Maya who escaped slaughter during the Caste War fled to the isolated jungles of Quintana Roo and Belize. The Maya revived the religion of the "talking cross," a pre-Columbian oracle representing gods of the four cardinal directions. This was a religious/political marriage. Three determined survivors of the Caste War—a priest, a master spy, and a ventriloquist—all wise leaders, knew their people's desperate need for divine leadership. As a result of their leadership and advice from the talking cross, the shattered people came together in large numbers and began to organize. The community guarded the location of the cross, and its advice made the Maya strong once again.

BELIZE HISTORY IN A NUTSHELL

The peaceful country of Belize is a sovereign democratic state of Central America located on the Caribbean. The government is patterned on the system of parliamentary democracy and experiences no more political turmoil than any other similar government, such as Great Britain or the United States.

Important Dates
1862: Became a British colony
1954: Attained universal adult suffrage
1964: Began self-government
1981: Attained full independence

They called themselves Chan Santa Cruz ("People of the Little Holy Cross"). As their confidence developed so did the growth and power of their communities. Living very close to the Belize (then British Honduras) border, they found they had something their neighbors wanted. The Chan Santa Cruz Maya began selling timber to the British and in return received arms, giving the Maya even more power. Between 1847 and 1850, in the years of strife during the Caste War in neighboring Yucatán, thousands of Maya, mestizo, and Mexican refugees who were fleeing the Spaniards entered Belize. The Yucatecans introduced the Latin culture, the Catholic religion, and agriculture. This was the beginning of the Mexican tradition in northern Belize, locally referred to as "Spanish tradition." The food is typically Mexican with tortillas, black beans, tamales, squash, and plantain (a type of banana that can be cooked). For many years these mestizos kept to themselves and were independent of Belize City. The colonial administration kept its distance, and a community-appointed headman made and kept the laws. Both Hispanic and non-Hispanic Belizeans who live in the northern area speak Spanish. Today all the towns and cities of Belize come under the jurisdiction of the central Belizean government.

The Sugar Industry

Though most of the refugees ultimately returned to their homes in Mexico, the ones who stayed and began farming the land were making the first real attempt at much-needed agriculture. Large tracts that had been cleared of trees were empty, and rich landowners were willing to rent acreage (cheaply) to the refugees for farming. Until then almost all foodstuffs had been imported from other countries (and to this day it's not unusual to see many tinned foods from Australia, England, and the United States on market shelves).

The mestizos settled mostly in the northern sections of the country, which is apparent by the Spanish names of the cities: Corozal, San Estevan, San Pedro, and Punta Consejo. By 1857, the immigrants were growing enough sugar to supply Belize, with enough left over to export the surplus (along with rum) to Britain. After their success proved to the tree barons that sugarcane could be lucrative, the big landowners became involved. Even in today's world of low-priced sugar, the industry is still important to Belize's economy.

Timber

For 300 years Belize was plundered and neglected—and not just by swashbuckling pirates and hard-living buccaneers. Its forests were denuded of valuable logwood (the heart of which provided rich dyes for Europe's growing textile industry until manmade dyes were developed). When the demand for logwood ceased, plantation owners found a viable substitute for their logging interests—removing mahogany trees from thick virgin forests. For three centuries the local economy depended on exported logs and imported food.

In a 1984 Audubon Society report, it was noted that despite the widespread use of slash-and-burn farming by the Maya a millennium ago, and the more recent selective logging of logwood and mahogany since the 16th century, Belize still has extensive forests. The large-scale abandonment of farms with the decline of the Maya civilization about A.D. 900 permitted forest regeneration that has attained what plant ecologists consider to be "climax" status. The removal of logwood had little effect on the forest structure. It's in today's economy that logging can cause serious damage to the forest with the indiscriminate removal of large tracts of trees, no matter the variety, because of modern methods and high-tech equipment.

INDEPENDENCE

In 1862 Belize officially became the colony of British Honduras, though it had been ruled by the British crown since 1798. The average Belizean had few rights and a very low living standard. Political unrest grew in a stifled atmosphere. Even when a contingent of Belizean soldiers traveled to Europe to fight for the British in World War I, the black men were scorned. But when these men returned from abroad, the pot of change began to boil. Over the next 50 years, the country struggled through power plays, another world war, and economic crises. But always the seed was there—a growing desire to be independent. The colonial system had been falling apart around the world, and when India gained its freedom in 1947 the pattern was set. Many small undeveloped countries soon began to gain independence and started to rely on their own ingenuity to build an economy that would benefit the people.

Even though Belize was self-governing by 1964, it was still dominated by outside influences until September 1981, when it gained its independence from the British Crown. But change comes slowly. This third-world country is learning through hard knocks how to be self-sustaining, self-motivated, self-governing—noncolonial. In the process of finding methods to become financially independent and raise the standard of living, Belizean leaders are discovering that the country's natural assets may indeed hold the key to bringing in dollars in the form of tourism, an industry they never before dreamed of. The government is proceeding slowly to design the proper tourist growth to fit into its scheme to preserve the ethnic cultures, the animals, the reef, and the forests. Belize is becoming a role model for other developing countries that need tourism dollars but are not willing to sacrifice their cultures and natural resources. In September 1981 the Belizean flag was raised—the birth of a new era! Belize joined the United Nations, the Commonwealth, and the Non-Aligned Movement. Its work is cut out for it.

GOVERNMENT AND ECONOMY

GOVERNMENT

The infant country's first parliamentary elections were held in 1984. The government is directed by a prime minister; a bicameral legislature, the National Assembly, comprises an appointed Senate and an elected House of Representatives. Belize has two active political parties, PUP (People's United Party) and UDP (United Democratic Party). George Price and Manuel Esquivel have been elected prime minister back and forth. As in most democracies, the rhetoric can get very animated, but Belize is a peaceful, law-abiding country, and its citizens are proud to rule themselves.

Though the country has grown on all fronts, including economically, it is still a poor country and needs money. One of the newest "events" on the money-raising agenda is the sale of citizenship for hard currency. It isn't easy to obtain, and applicants must go through rigorous scrutiny. Even that doesn't please everyone; many citizens in the country object to selling their patrimony. The cost to obtain citizenship is between US$75,000 and US$85,000 per family. The number of families accepted is limited to 500 per year. Anyone interested should contact the nearest Belize Consulate or Embassy; in the United States, write or call: 2535 Massachusetts Dr. NW, Washington, DC 20008; 202/332-9636, fax 202/332-6741.

WHAT'S IN A NAME?

No one knows for sure where the name of Belize originated or what it means. The country was called Belize long before the British took the country over and renamed it British Honduras. In 1973, the locals changed it back to the original Belize as a first step on the road to independence. There are several well-known theories for its meaning. Some say it's a corruption of the name Wallis (pronounced wahl-EEZ), from the pirate (Peter Wallace) who roamed the high seas centuries ago and visited Belize. Others suggest that it's a distortion of the Maya word *belix*, which means muddy river. Still others say it could be a further distortion of the Maya word *belikin* (which is also the name of the local beer). And of course it could be another of those mysterious Maya secrets we may never learn.

ECONOMY

One of the exciting aspects of a developing country is watching how the people's creative genius can turn them into entrepreneurs. The United States is a great example of this and a good role model for countries just putting their toes into the sea of world commerce. Belize has been independent since 1981, and after a few false moves is beginning to see the start of a glowing future. The *Belize Investment Code* states, "Foreign investment is welcome as long as it creates jobs and expands Belizean talent and skills; infuses foreign financial resources and good managerial skills into Belize; produces for export markets; utilizes indigenous raw materials; and engages in environmentally sound projects which make technological advances and increase the capital stock of the nation." Developing and improving the country's infrastructure promises big changes. For example, the government has brought electricity to 98 percent of outlying villages.

However, some critics in the country say Belize should take a hard look at what's happening. These locals are questioning how much of the country they are willing to give away to enter mainstream economics. An editorial in the local paper, *Amandala,* put it succinctly:

What we poor Belizeans have to consider is just exactly what all are we prepared to sell in order to achieve so-called "development." We've been poor for centuries in this country, and while none of us are prepared to sell our mother, we have been selling our motherland. We may not be prepared to sell our children, but we have no problem selling our children's future. We may not think we are selling our souls, but some of us are certainly selling our bodies.

We argue, when we sell our assets, that we have to get into this development race now, but when a nation sells resources which are nonrenewable, then it is giving up some of its sovereignty for money—speculative money.

ECOTOURISM

The many natural wonders of Belize include: the only barrier reef in the Western Hemisphere, a jaguar sanctuary, Maya ruins, a great variety of birds, hundreds of cayes, and cultures virtually unchanged in the past few hundred years. Thanks to many eco-oriented organizations and individuals, these natural wonders are fiercely protected and monitored for their future existence.

Ecotourism is environmentally sound and culturally friendly tourism. It is the "business" of preventing tourism from spoiling the environment. This is done through education and protection of flora and fauna while keeping alive the natural, sustainable, and renewable resources. Its purpose is all encompassing: for the past to remain alive, the present to continue to grow, and for the future to exist for many generations to come.

Many organizations in Belize promote ecotourism in their creed and environmental objectives, including Belize Eco-Tourism Association and Belize Audubon Society; hotels and individuals do the same on a smaller scale.

It doesn't take much effort to keep in line with these ideals. Here are some things you can do:

When you're in the water, don't touch, collect, or move coral and other defenseless species; leave the animals alone. If you must fish and or hunt, take only the legal size and the legal limit, and only if it is in season. Make conscious choices on what you eat, and where you eat and visit. Ask questions, read books—educate yourself so you know that hawksbill turtles are always protected and which fish and turtles are illegal to take and when. Be involved—join an active organization that promotes such ideals and is pro-environment. Ask before you take tours—most, if not all, are spouting the ecotourism slogan because it's catchy and people want to hear it.

The government is involved, largely through the efforts of the great conservation groups in the country. Those in the know maintain and protect flora and fauna in addition to educating both nationals and foreigners about what is endangered, how not to disrupt wildlife habitats, and how to advance resource sustainability. "We seek to keep the government informed of the problems faced in natural resource management and encourage action to be taken in haste," says the Belize Audubon Society.

Certainly these are words to ponder for any developing country.

Tourism and Ecotourism

Tourism is gradually heading to the top of the list of moneymakers in the country, especially a version of it called "ecotourism." What exactly is ecotourism? Well, it depends on whom you ask. It can be anything from a walk around the Belize Zoo, to tenting in the jungle, to participation in hard-core scientific fieldwork. The general concept is easy enough to understand. Fundamentally, ecotourism means to visit a place making as little environmental impact as possible and meanwhile helping sustain the indigenous populace, thereby encouraging the preservation of scarce wildlife and habitat.

One promising step in that direction has been the rise of ecology-minded organizations such as the Belize Eco-Tourism Association and its code of ethics and the Toledo Eco-Tourism Association with its Village Guesthouse Program. Others involved with educating as well as preserving include: the Belize Zoo and Tropical Education Center, Community Baboon Sanctuary at Bermudian Landing, Programme for Belize with its Rio Bravo Conservation and Management Area, the Sea Turtle Sanctuary on Ambergris Caye, and Slate Creek Preserve in the Cayo District. Along with the government, these organizations are among those spearheading responsible tourism development and environmental protection.

Can it work? As Belize is seeing, it probably can (if the government and members of the tourist industry properly appeal to and serve those adventurous travelers who prefer real jungle to the sanitized versions of movies and amusement parks). Both local and outside investors are catching on, and the Belizean government is helping further by giving tax concessions to legitimate business, not just gold-plated Wall Street names. A few Americans who have taken the plunge into the bureaucracy describe a moderate amount of paperwork involved, such as establishing residency and obtaining work permits. Although it can take time, it isn't so difficult that it discourages potential investors.

Belize Industries

The economy of Belize was traditionally based on logwood, mahogany, and chicle export. Today

MARIE SHARP SUCCESS STORY

Belize is a country where the little guy with a big idea can still make that dream come true. Marie Sharp, a native of Stann Creek District, came up with a sizzling idea one day in her kitchen—why not make and bottle a local hot sauce? **Melinda's** hot sauce, one of Belize's most successful products, was the result. It has since found its way into almost every restaurant and home in Belize, and into more than a dozen states in the United States, including Hawaii. This is a gourmet chile pepper sauce made from the notorious habañero pepper grown only on the Yucatán Peninsula, where Belize is located. Pepper lovers the world over agree that the *habanero Capsicum chinense* is the hottest pepper known to humans. Marie and Jerry Sharp grow their own on their 400-acre plantation in the Maya Mountain foothills just outside Dangriga in southern Belize.

In 1983, Marie planted five acres of peppers. After bringing along a healthy crop, she was offered a ridiculous US50 cents a gallon for the peppers. She refused to give her peppers away and began experimenting with recipes to make a hot sauce. After some time she came up with the perfect recipe, which includes onions and carrots, pureed raw habañero, lime juice, vinegar, garlic, and salt. With ingredients like that, how could it miss? To get the bright red color she wanted, it was necessary to use only specially cultivated all-red peppers.

After a lot of hard work, including several packaging and marketing classes in the United States, Marie selected the label "Melinda's. Proud Product of Belize."

Marie, meanwhile, is now buying peppers from local farmers to meet demand and has branched out to market other delicious products. Her fruit jams and spreads, all made of pure, natural ingredients, including fruits raised in the sweet earth of Belize, are already becoming equally famous. And, yes, she moved out of the family kitchen some time ago.

tourism, agriculture, fisheries, and small manufactured goods give the country an important economic boost. The main exports are sugar, citrus, bananas, lobster, and timber. Thanks to tax concessions given to foreign investors, Belize has experienced a diversification of manufacturing industries, such as plywood, veneer manufacturing, matches, beer, rum, soft drinks, furniture, boat-building, and battery assembly.

The Belize Bank offers U.S. dollar accounts for its international business corporations. This has been a big factor in attracting foreign investors.

Fishing

Belize has maintained a viable fishing industry. For years Belize fishing co-ops have been exporting rock and spiny lobster to the United States. At first it was almost a giveaway, but as the fishermen began working together through co-ops, prices have risen and fishermen manage to make a good living. In recent years fishing has been controlled to prevent the "fish-out" of the lobster by closing the season Feb. 15–June 15 and limiting the size of the lobsters removed. The main export markets for scale fish are the United States, Mexico, and Jamaica. With the help of Canadian government agencies, Belizean fishermen are trained in many fields of the fishing industry. They are learning modern processing techniques, navigation, and marine engineering.

Mariculture and Aquaculture

Mariculture is a fairly new activity in Belize. Shrimp are being harvested near the Monkey River with two species of shrimp introduced from Ecuador. Another shrimp farm is being developed near Quashie Trap Lagoon in southern Belize District. Another farm in its beginning stages will introduce the American lobster on Turneffe Islands to Caribbean waters in an attempt to stimulate faster growth. At Turneffe Islands' Northern Bogue, the spiny lobster is being raised in enclosed submerged pens. Many new "fish-growing" industries are also in the planning stages for Belize. The newest is a shrimp hatchery to be located at Mile 5 on the Western Highway. Taiwan will be providing facilities to rear post-larvae (baby shrimps) so that Belize will not be so dependent on imported larvae, a system that has kept the

bananas

growth of the shrimp industry in slow motion. The Taiwanese will assist in developing the process while training Belizean Fishing Department personnel.

Sugarcane

Sugar has continued throughout the years to be the primary moneymaker for the country, despite low sugar prices in recent years. England was for years the major export/import partner for Belize. Although Belize exports to other countries, England is still an active importer for Belize, along with the United States.

Bananas

One of the attractive investments is establishing banana plantations in Belize's southern coastal region; so far the land costs are reasonable. Limestone soil (washed down from the nearby mountains), a warm climate, and an annual rainfall of 130 inches make the area perfect for growing bananas.

This cow dines on tasty water plants during the dry season.

Citrus Fruit

Stann Creek offers excellent conditions for raising citrus fruit, first introduced into the country in the early 1920s. Nine hundred grafted trees were imported from Florida, and with a great deal of TLC tending them, they won blue ribbons at agricultural shows in England 1928–31. But as much as the Europeans were impressed with Belizean oranges, freight costs made shipping the whole fruit impossible and they had to be content with the juice.

Over the years, despite hurricanes that have flattened the trees and fluctuating prices, a combination of external events has given the Belizean citrus industry a big boost. In 1983 President Reagan removed taxes from Caribbean-grown citrus. Soon after, severe frosts damaged and limited fruit production in Florida and Texas, followed by a canker disease on Florida citrus that dealt another blow for the U.S. citrus industry. This enabled Belize to get a toehold in trading, and it has been climbing ever since.

Cattle

Not too many years ago, beef was either not available, tough and stringy (and therefore "cooked to tenderness"), or "cooked to death" for health reasons. The average Belizean family just didn't put beef on the table much. Beef growing was a depressed business. Most Belizeans grew up eating canned meat, fried chicken, and seafood, and that was just fine. However, a new breed of cattlemen came along (mostly from the United States) and showed the locals how cattle should be "wrangled." After a lot of hard work, the quality improved and the word was out—hamburgers are good! Government support of the industry has helped. And ranchers are learning the secrets of ranching in Belize. They are establishing pastures of higher-protein grasses that can support and fatten one animal per acre for one year. Next time you're in a restaurant in Belize, compliment the chef, or rather the rancher—order a tender, high-quality beefsteak raised in Belize.

THE PEOPLE

THE MAYA

The indigenous people, the Maya, inhabited the area that is now Guatemala, El Salvador, southern Mexico, Honduras, and Belize. Scientists believe that at one time the Maya, the first settlers in what is now called Belize, numbered about a million. The earliest known community in the Maya world was at Cuello, in Belize's Orange Walk District, dating to 2000 B.C. Here they were pottery makers and farmers. A few of the most powerful Maya ceremonial centers have been uncovered at Altun Ha, Lubaantun, Caracol, and Xunantunich (zoo-nahn-too-NEECH).

Physical Characteristics

Maya men average just over five feet tall, women just under five feet. Muscular-bodied, they have straight black hair, round heads, broad faces with pronounced cheekbones, aquiline noses, almond-shaped dark eyes, and eyelids with the epicanthic or Mongolian fold (a prolongation of a fold of the upper eyelid over the inner angle or both angles of the eye).

Stylized Beauty

Bishop Diego de Landa wrote in his *Relaciones* that when the Spanish arrived, the Maya still practiced the ancient method of flattening a newborn's head with a press made of boards. By pressing the infant's forehead, the fronto-nasal portion of the face was pushed forward, as can be seen in carvings and other human depictions from the pre-Columbian period; this was considered a very important sign of beauty. Further, they dangled a bead in front of a baby's eyes to encourage crossed eyes, another Maya beauty mark. They practiced dental mutilation by filing the teeth to give them different shapes or by making slight perforations and inlaying pyrite, jade, or turquoise. Tattooing and scarification were accomplished by lightly cutting a design into the skin and purposely infecting it, creating a scar of beauty. Adult noblemen often wore nosepieces to give the illusion of an even longer nose sweeping back into the long flat forehead.

Modern Maya

Although the Spanish were never successful in annihilating the Maya in Latin America, they destroyed many communities. The Maya wisely left the coastal areas (where most of the outsiders were) and lived deep in the jungle interior of Belize. That, together with the influx of Maya during the Caste War, created a fairly good-sized population of Maya in the country. More recent comers are Guatemala Maya escaping brutal treatment from the upper class. These people make up a large part of the hill areas of the Cayo, Toledo, and Stann Creek Districts.

The Maya Bloodline

Isolation of the indigenous people kept the Maya bloodline pure. The resemblance of today's Maya to the people of a thousand years ago is thus understandable, but still amazing. Three distinct Maya groups are found in Belize. Though the languages of these groups are related, they are different enough from each other that, even if you know one dialect, it's still difficult to understand another dialect. The locals call the Mopan and Yucatecs by the term Maya, and separate the Kekchi as a non-Maya group, although they, too, are Maya. Together the three groups make up about 12 percent of the entire population of the country. The Maya settlements are found in southwest Toledo, the upper Belize River Valley, and northwest Corozal/northern Orange Walk Districts. These villages have a south-to-north pattern of Kekchi-Mopan-Yucatec. The Kekchi migrated from Guatemala to work on sugar plantations. The Yucatec, who have had the most contact with mestizos, have experienced the biggest changes in their culture. A good example is Yo Creek in the Orange Walk District. Once an all-Maya agricultural village, its first language is Spanish and more Yucatecs than ever now work for wages outside the village.

POLYGLOT

Although the first settlers, outlawed pirates, did most of their own logging, it was the second wave of settlers—the British—that changed the face of the landscape now known as Belize. Cheap labor was needed to do the grueling timber work in thick, tall jungles. The British failed to force it on the maverick Maya, so they brought slaves from Africa, indentured laborers from India, and Caribs from distant Caribbean islands, as was common in the early 16th and 17th centuries. The Caribs, much like the Maya, were a detached group and never really gave in to slaving in the sugar fields. Much later, from 1958 to 1962, a group of Mennonites came looking for religious freedom and began a fine dairy and agricultural tradition. This assortment of nationalities eventually created a handsome group of people of multicolored skin and hair. Although English is the official language, a mixture of Spanish, African dialects, Carib, and English has become a patois called Creole that's pleasant to the ear, though it takes heavy-duty listening to understand. Most of the people of Belize are black-skinned Afro-Creole.

Creoles

The people who call themselves "Creoles" make up 60 percent of the population of Belize today. All Creoles share two distinctive traits: a degree of African ancestry and the use of the local English-Creole dialect. Skin color runs from very dark to very light, but European ancestry is usually apparent. Most Creoles believe themselves to be "true Belizeans" because their ancestors are thought to have been among the first settlers. This may not have been the case, however. Aside from the claims by resident Amerindians and European Baymen to first occupancy, many Creoles are descended from the immigrants who entered the country years after the Garifuna, Maya, East Indians, and Ladinos.

The center of Creole territory is Belize City, and half of the ethnic Creoles make up more than three-fourths of the city's population. Rural Creoles live along the highway between Belmopan and San Ignacio, in isolated clusters in northern Belize District, and in a few coastal spots to the south—Gales Point, Mullins River, Mango Creek, Placencia, and Monkey River Town.

Ladinos

Spanish-speaking Belizeans, descended from Amerindians and Europeans, normally are labeled "mestizos." While the term is appropriate in a racial connotation, Ladino better describes the cultural attributes of Mexican and Central American immigrants who have given up the distinct culture of their ancient ancestors. Once the predominant population (after immigration from the Yucatecan Caste War), Ladinos are now the second-most populous ethnic group of Belize. They occupy the old "Mexican-Mestizo corridor" that runs along New River between Corozal and Orange Walk. In west-central Belize—Benque Viejo and San Ignacio—indigenous people from Guatemala have recently joined the earlier Spanish-speaking immigrants from Yucatán.

Caribs and Garifuna

The Caribs came to the Caribbean islands around 1300 from South America. These warlike tribes lived mainly in the Amazon River Valley and Guiana lowlands, and it's said the fierce warriors ate their victims. They were experts in building and navigating large plank dugouts, as well as prolific trappers, farmers, and fishermen (they fished with poison darts). Being wanderers they moved from island to island every couple of years. In the 17th century, Africans who had escaped from slavery intermarried within the Carib groups who lived on the Windward Islands in the east Caribbean. The resulting group of people is called the Garinagu or Garifuna. No pure-blooded Caribs are left in Belize.

The Garifuna (also called Garinagu) inherited the independent bloodlines of their ancestors and strongly resisted control by the Europeans. However, their arrows were no match for colonial guns, and they were ultimately defeated by the Spanish. In 1796 about 5,000 Garifuna were forced to the Bay Islands off the coast of Honduras. Over the years they migrated to the coastal areas of Honduras, Nicaragua, Guatemala, and southern Belize. A small Garifuna settlement grew in Stann Creek, where they fished and farmed. They began bringing fresh produce to Belize City, but were not welcome to stay for more than 48 hours without getting a special permit—the Baymen wanted the produce but didn't want these independent thinkers around the city, fearing they'd help slaves escape or perhaps cause a loss of the Baymen's tight control. The Baymen tried to keep the Garifuna separated from the people of Belize City by any means possible. Rumors were spread about their religious beliefs—that they were devil worshipers and baby eaters. They did have their exotic and often ritualistic ceremonies—some still do—but the dancing and singing weren't always as evil as the manipulating politicians would have one believe. (A certain amount of prejudice and fear still exists.) The Garifuna tried many times to become part of the Public Meeting (the British governing system) but were effectively refused until November 19, 1832, when they were allowed to join the community. That event, **Garifuna Settlement Day,** continues to be a major national celebration and holiday each year.

Immigrants from India

From 1844 to 1917, under British colonialism, 41,600 East Indians were brought to British colonies in the Caribbean as indentured workers. They agreed to work for a given length of time for one "master." Then they could either return to India or stay on and work freely. Unfortunately, the time spent in Belize was not as lucrative as they were led to believe it would be. In some cases they owed so much money to the company store (where they received half their wages in trade and not nearly enough to live on) that they were forced to "reenlist" for a longer period. Most of them worked on sugar plantations in the Toledo and Corozal Districts, and many of

the East Indian men were assigned to work as local police in Belize City. In a town aptly named Calcutta, many of the population today are descendants of the original indentured East Indians. Forest Home near Punta Gorda also has a large settlement. About 47 percent of the ethnic group live in these two locations. The East Indians usually have large families and live on small farms with orchards adjacent to their homes. A few trade in pigs and dry goods in ma-and-pa businesses. East Indians normally speak Creole and Spanish. Apparently descendants from the original immigrants do not speak Hindi today. A small number of Hindi-speaking East Indian merchants live in Belize City and Orange Walk Town, but they are fairly new to the country and have no cultural ties with the descendants of earlier immigrants.

Mennonites

German-speaking Mennonites are the most recent group to enter Belize on a large scale. This group of Protestant settlers from the Swiss Alps wandered over the years to northern Germany, southern Russia, Pennsylvania, and Canada in the early 1800s, and to northern Mexico after World War I. For some reason the quiet, staid Mennonites disturbed local governments in these other countries, and restrictions on their isolated agrarian lifestyle have caused a nomadic past. Most of Belize's Mennonites first migrated from Mexico between 1958–62. A few came from

Garifuna drummers are an important part of any Garifuna celebration.

BELIZE ASSOCIATION OF LOUISIANA (BAL)

BAL is a great group of people living in Louisiana who were born in Belize or whose parents are from Belize. It is a social club; everyone gets together at parties, dances, fashion shows, and other special events. But the best part is that the profits all go to Belize. The group doesn't want cash. Instead, members donate toys for Christmas, books for Belizean libraries, summer clothes for adults and children, and sports equipment of all kinds; TACA airlines graciously hauls the goods to Belize. Medical supplies are always needed, even if it's just aspirin. And BAL tries to help one very special charity in Belize, HelpAge, a home for older folks in need. For this the group is always happy to get used bedding, sheets, blankets, pillows, etc.—hotels that turn over their bedding periodically are contacted in the hopes that they will donate the linens to BAL.

This is one of the most sincere charities I've come across. If anyone out there wants to donate, please contact Toucan Travel and ask for Dulce, who is from Belize. The address is 32 Traminer Dr., Kenner, LA 70065; tel. 504/465-0769. Remember, BAL isn't asking for cash, just goods in decent or new condition.

Peace River in Canada. They bought large blocks of land (about 148,000 acres) and began to farm. Shipyard (in Orange Walk District) was settled by a conservative wing; Spanish Lookout (in Cayo District) and Blue Creek (in Orange Walk District) were settled by more progressive members. In hopes of averting future problems with the government, Mennonites and Belize officials made agreements that guarantee the Mennonites freedom to practice their religion, use their language in locally controlled schools, organize their own financial institutions, and to be exempt from military service. Over the 30-plus years that Mennonites have been in Belize, they have slowly merged into Belizean activities. Although they practice complete separation of church and state (and do not vote), their innovations in agricultural production and marketing have advanced the entire country. Mennonite farmers are probably the most productive in Belize; they commonly pool their resources to make large purchases such as equipment, machinery (those that use machinery), and supplies. Their fine dairy industry is the best in the country, and they supply the domestic market with eggs, poultry, fresh milk, cheese, and vegetables.

Rastafarians

Primarily the Rastafarians live in Belize City, but a few have made homes in Caye Caulker and other parts of the country. Rastafarians are part of a religion that believes in the eventual redemption of blacks and their return to Africa. They are easily recognizable by their dreadlocks—uncombed and uncut long mats of hair (although not all dreadlock wearers are true Rastas). Their beliefs, according to the biblical laws of the Nazarites, forbid the cutting of their hair. Rastafarians use ganja (marijuana) in their rituals (which gets them in trouble in the wrong neighborhoods) and venerate Haile Selassie I, late emperor of Ethiopia, as their god. Selassie's precoronation name was Ras Tafari Makonnen, hence the name (Ras is simply an honorific title). He allegedly descended from King Solomon and the Queen of Sheba.

LITERACY

At one time only the children of the elite were able to attend school. The Belizeans have put a top priority on education; schools are available throughout the country, and today 90 percent of Belizeans are literate. (There is concern that the figure may change with the heavy influx of El Salvadoran refugees.) School is mandatory for Belizean children up to age 14. High school is neither mandatory nor free—most are run by religious groups with aid from the government. As a result, not all families can afford to educate their children beyond grammar school.

KATHY ESCOVEDO SANDERS

ON THE ROAD
HIGHLIGHTS

SIGHT-SEEING

Belize is peppered with ruins of known Maya settlements and cities. More are being discovered all the time. **Altun Ha, Cahal Pech, Lamanai, Lubaantun,** and **Xunantunich** are among the most interesting developed sites. Others, such as **Caracol, Chan Chich, El Pilar,** and **La Milpa,** are not fully excavated but captivating nonetheless. (See the Mundo Maya chapter.)

Day trips from Ambergris Caye, Belize City, Corozal, or San Ignacio to the ruins of Altun Ha, Lamanai, Xunantunich, and others can be arranged before or after arrival in Belize, either on your own in a rental car or with a group. For those who would like to stay at or within sight of Maya ruins, **Chan Chich Lodge, Lamanai Outpost Lodge,** and **Nabitunich** (see the Accommodations Index in the back of the book) all offer that experience.

RECREATION

For years the most well-known and publicized activities for visitors to Belize were diving and snorkeling. Without a doubt the Belize Reef (fifth longest in the world and longest in the Western Hemisphere) offers the diver a fulfilling experience observing the colors and variety of tropical fish and coral. Now, however, many inland attractions and activities are getting equal time. Belize is a country with a host of adventure travel and learning opportunities for all ages and abilities. The hard part is deciding which ones to choose on your next vacation. To make the most of your decision making, it's helpful to keep in mind the style of traveling you like, physical abilities, and whether you will be bringing children. A little thought given early on will help ensure your time in Belize is well spent and enjoyable.

A Matter of Style

Some folks enjoy getting dirty and being tested to the limits of their physical abilities. Others like to stay reasonably clean and experience the outdoors in a softer fashion. Some travelers like to trek through miles of muddy jungle in hopes of seeing a tapir. Others prefer to sight one in comfortable surroundings at the Belize Zoo. And while some travelers thrill to participate in a jungle research project, others are fascinated by a short visit to some excavated ruins and a guided tour. All of the above are available in Belize and can be arranged through travel agents, guides, hotels, or lodges. When making arrangements, ask lots of questions to ensure that a given activity is neither too tame nor too wild for your personal style of adventure.

A Matter of Age

Today senior travelers and parents traveling with children have many options. Active seniors enjoy Belize. Some like the tranquility of the palm-studded cayes. Many come to learn about the jungle and its creatures or about the ancient Maya ruins. ElderHostel offers fascinating tours for those who love the adventure of learning. Some resorts are designed to better accommodate the needs of active senior travelers.

Though lodges and hotels may offer discounts on accommodations for small children, Belize is best suited for families with kids old enough to enjoy outdoor activities and learning about nature. Many small children may do well at resorts, however, that offer safe beaches, games, and of course a visit to the zoo. Any of the tranquil beaches are a great place to give them their first look through the dive mask at the unique underwater world.

Photography

For the photographer, a world of beauty awaits: the sea, the people, and the natural landscape of the jungle, waterfalls, rivers, and archaeological sites. For those who want to film *everything*, small planes are available for charter in Belize City. Ask around the airports for a private pilot.

WATER SPORTS

SNORKELING AND SCUBA DIVING

Snorkeling Around

Not everyone who travels to Belize is a diver or even a snorkeler—at first. But one peek through the "looking glass"—a diving mask—will change that. The Caribbean is one of the most notoriously seductive bodies of water in the world. Turquoise blue and crystal clear with perfect tepid temperature, the protected Belizean coast (thanks to offshore reefs) is ideal for a languid float during hot humid days.

Even if you've never considered underwater sports in the past, you'll be willing—no, eager!—to learn. It's easy for the neophyte to learn how to snorkel. Once you master breathing through a tube, it's simply a matter of relaxing and floating. Time disappears once you are introduced, through a four-inch glass window, to a world of fish in rainbow colors of garish yellow, electric blue, crimson, and probably a hundred shades of purple. The longer you look, the more you'll discover: underwater caverns, tall coral pillars, giant tubular sponges, shy fish hiding on the sandy bottom, and delicate wisps of fine grass.

Diving Wonderland

For the diver, there's even more adventure. Reefs, caves, and rugged coastline harbor the

---

LIVE-ABOARD DIVE BOATS

Belize Aggressor III (120')
Aggressor Fleet, Ltd., P.O. Drawer K, Morgan City, LA 70381; 800/348-2628 or 504/385-2628, fax 504/384-0817

Offshore Express (50')
Coral Beach Dive Shop, San Pedro, Ambergris Caye; tel. 26/2817, email forman@btl.net

Belize Wave Dancer (120')
Peter Hughes Diving; 800/932-6237 or 305/669-9391, email dancer@peterhughes.com

unknown. Ships wrecked hundreds of years ago hide secrets as yet undiscovered. Swimming among the curious and brazen fish puts you literally into another world. This is raw excitement.

Expect to see an astounding variety of fish, crustaceans, and corals. Even close to shore, these amazing little animals create exotic displays of shape and form, dense or delicate depending on species, depth, light, and current. Most need light to survive; in deeper, low-light areas, some species of coral take the form of a large plate, thereby performing the duties of a solar collector. Sponge is another curious underwater creature; it comes in all sizes, shapes, and colors, from common brown to vivid red.

Be Selective

Diving lessons are offered at nearly all the dive shops in the country. Before you make a commitment, ask about the instructor and check his/her accident record; then talk to the locals or, if you're in a small village, ask at the local bar. Most of these divers are conscientious, but a few are not, and the locals know whom to trust.

Bringing your own equipment to Belize might save you a little money, depending on the length of your trip and means of transportation. But if plan to stay just a couple of weeks and want to join a group aboard a dive boat by the day, it's generally not much more for tank rental, which will save you the hassle of carrying your own.

Choose your boat carefully. Look it over first. Some aren't much more than fishing boats with little to make the diver comfortable. Ask questions! Does it have a platform to get in and out of the water? How many tanks of air may be used per trip? How many dives? Exactly where are you going? How fast does the boat go and how long will it take to get there? Remember, some of the best dive spots might be farther out at sea. A more modern boat (though it'll cost a little more) might get you extra diving time.

Detailed information is available for divers and snorkelers who wish to know about the dive sites they plan to visit. *Skin Diver* magazine puts out a very informative issue on Belize at least once a year, usually in June. Many pamphlets and books are available, especially for U.S.-based dive tours. Some have been in business for many years; check them out. Wherever diving is good, you'll almost always find a dive shop. On both

BOB RACE

Ambergris Caye and Caye Caulker, and in Belize City, dive shops offer day trips.

A few high-adventure dives require an experienced guide—not only recommended but also a necessity.

Underwater Hazards

A word here about some of the less-inviting aspects of marine society. Anemones and sea urchins live in Belize waters. Some can be dangerous if touched or stepped on. The long-spined black sea urchin can inflict great pain, and its poison can cause an uncomfortable infection. Don't think that you're safe in a wetsuit, booties, and gloves. The spines easily slip through the rubber and the urchin is encountered at all depths. They are more abundant in some areas than in others; keep your eyes open. If you should run into one of the spines, remove it quickly and carefully, disinfect the wound, and apply antibiotic cream. If you have difficulty removing the spine, or if it breaks, see a doctor—pronto! **Note:** Environmentalists discourage divers from wearing gloves to deter their touching the fragile coral. For some varieties, even with gloves, just one touch is the touch of death.

First Aid

Cuts from coral, even if just a scratch, will often become infected. Antibiotic cream or powder will usually take care of it. If you should get a deep cut, or if minute bits of coral are left in the wound, a serious and long-lived infection can ensue. See a doctor.

If you should get scraped on red or fire coral you may feel a burning sensation for just a few minutes or up to five days. In some, it causes an allergic reaction and will raise large red welts. Cortisone cream will reduce inflammation and discomfort. While it wouldn't be fair to condemn all red things, you'll notice in the next few paragraphs that many of the creatures to avoid are red!

Fire worms (also known as bristle worms) if touched will deposit tiny cactus-like bristles in your skin. They can cause the same reaction as fire coral. *Carefully* scraping the skin with the edge of a sharp knife (as you would to remove a bee stinger) *might* remove the bristles. Any leftover bristles will ultimately work their way out, but you might be very uncomfortable in the meantime. Cortisone cream helps to relieve this inflammation too.

Several species of sponges have fine sharp spicules (hard, minute, pointed calcareous or siliceous bodies that support the tissue) that should not be touched with the bare hand. The attractive red fire sponge can cause great pain; a mild solution of vinegar or ammonia (or urine if there's nothing else) will help. The burning lasts a couple of days, and cortisone cream soothes. Don't be fooled by dull-colored sponges. Many have the same sharp spicules.

Hands Off!

Some divers feel the need to touch the fish or coral they swim with. Touching coral injures it. Touching the wrong fish might injure you. Coral takes scores of years to grow a single inch. Grabbing onto a coral head damages it for years to come. Leave the reef in the same condition you found it so that others may enjoy it after you. Thoughtful divers *don't touch.*

Barracuda, moray eels, and sharks do not appreciate groping hands, and all have ample means to protect themselves. Enough said. Even

---

EMERGENCY NUMBERS FOR ACCIDENT EVACUATION

Always check with your dive master about emergency procedures *before* your boat heads out to sea. A safety decompression chamber is located on Ambergris Caye, tel. 26/2851.

Divers Alert Network (DAN): 800/446-2671 or 919/684-2948; dial this number for info about decompression chambers

Life Flight (air ambulance): Houston, TX, 713/704-4357 or 800/231-4357.

To get the proper help to you much sooner, it's important to have as much of the following information as possible ready to give the emergency service:
- name and age of the patient
- the problem
- when it happened
- name and telephone number of the doctor and medical facility treating the patient

Laughing Bird Caye

PATTI LANGE

sea turtles occasionally try to bite when tampered with by those wishing to prove how macho they are. Look, don't touch. In addition, sharks are attracted to blood, certain low frequency sounds (like those caused by an injured fish), electromagnetic disturbances, and certain shapes and color patterns. Avoid swimming with bleeding wounds. And while barracudas, like other predatory fish, can be excited by fish blood and jerky vibrations, they seem to be more visual hunters. They are likely to snap at something flashy, such as watches and bracelets, so leave your flashy jewelry at home.

A few seagoing critters resent being stepped on and can retaliate with a dangerous wound. The scorpion fish, hardly recognizable with its natural camouflage, lies hidden most of the time on a reef shelf or on the bottom of the sea. If you should step on or touch it you can expect a painful, dangerous sting. If this happens, see a doctor immediately.

The ray is another sinister fellow. Several varieties live in the Caribbean, including the yellow and southern stingrays. If you leave them alone they're generally peaceful, but if stepped on they will zap you with a tail that carries a poisonous sting capable of causing anaphylactic shock. Symptoms include respiratory difficulties, fainting, and severe itching. Go quickly to the doctor and describe what caused the sting. One diver suggests a shuffling, dragging-of-the-feet gait when walking on the bottom of the ocean. If bumped, the ray will quickly escape, but if stepped on it feels trapped and uses its tail for protection.

Jellyfish can also inflict a miserable sting. Avoid particularly the long streamers of the Portuguese man-of-war, though some of the smaller jellyfish are just as hazardous.

Don't let these what-ifs discourage you from an underwater adventure though. Thousands of people dive in Belize's Caribbean every day of the year and only a small percentage have accidents.

Safety References

Check with your dive master about emergency procedures before your boat heads out to sea. Ask about the decompression chamber in San Pedro. We tried calling the number we had, and were told it no longer existed which made us wonder about the chamber. However, after calling one of our dive shop friends on the caye, he explained that the chamber is still there and operational, but that it is run by volunteers who come running when there is a need. Ask your dive master until you are satisfied. Divers should also know that there's a decompression chamber in Houston, Texas, and another on Isla Cozumel, Mexico, tel. 987/2-2387.

FISHING

Wetting a hook in Belize will probably net you a fine dinner and a bag-full of pleasant memories. Inside the reef, anglers have a choice of several game and food fish. The flats are good hunting grounds for tarpon, bonefish, permit, and occasionally barracuda. In the mangroves, anglers are likely to snag a snook, tarpon, mangrove snapper, or mutton snapper. Outside the reef it's deep-sea fishing for red snapper and the big trophies such as marlin, sailfish, giant groupers, and tuna.

Fishing the flats of Belize has always been a challenge to fly fishermen; however, it's becoming one of the biggest fishing attractions in the Caribbean. Apparently, stalking the fish in the wadable surf is not as easy as it sounds. Belize offers many areas perfect for this type of fishing.

Increasingly Belize boat operators and resorts are turning to "catch-and-release" policies for many fish. The fisher is photographed or videotaped with the catch, and then the fish is released. Often a few food fish are kept to provide a meal while the rest are turned loose. A wise choice, these policies will help ensure that Belize remains an angler's dream for generations to come.

Boats and guides are plentiful in Belize City, Ambergris Caye, Caye Caulker, Corozal, Dangriga, Placencia, and Punta Gorda. Resorts that offer fishing packages include Belize River Lodge, El Pescador, Journey's End Caribbean Club, and Victoria House on Ambergris Caye; Manta Resort on Southwest Caye in Glover's Reef; Lighthouse Reef Resort on Northern Caye; and Turneffe Flats and Turneffe Island Lodge in the Turneffe Islands. It's easy to make arrangements through your hotel or tour opera-

tors in Belize and in the United States (see "Tour Operatators," below).

BOATING

Charters

Visitors have several options for chartering a boat with a captain and crew in Belize. Ambergris Caye, Belize City, Caye Caulker, and Moho Caye (just offshore Belize City) have boats available. Motor boats and sailboats are available. Bare boats (without captain and crew) are almost impossible to find, and the companies that once specialized in them are out of business. The reason is said to be damage done to the boats by encounters with submerged coral heads, shoals, and the like.

Private Cruising

If you plan to cruise to Belize in your own boat, you must contact the Belize Consulate about a permit for your vessel. Sailors will find numerous anchorages among the cayes and coastal villages of Belize. Motor boaters have limited opportunities to refuel, but marinas or dock facilities with gasoline do exist at Ambergris Caye, Belize City, Caye Caulker, Caye Chapel, Moho Caye, Placencia, and Punta Gorda.

The barrier reef provides calm inshore waters with none of the crashing surf or large swells of the open ocean. It is also pretty to observe

getting ready to paddle
the cayes

PATTI LANGE

as you approach. However, stay well clear of the reef as there are numerous coral heads that dot the water on the inland side of the reef. Good charts are a must in this area.

Bottom conditions that affect anchoring include mud around Belize City and river mouths, sand around the many cayes farther offshore, and grass beds near the inshore cayes. Avoid anchoring in coral or, if at all possible, grass beds. If there is no choice but to drop anchor in sea grass, make very certain the anchor has dug in properly and that you've allowed sufficient rope for tide, wind, and wave conditions before leaving the vessel.

Those interested in cruising these waters, especially the atolls, should talk to the locals to ascertain any local undersea hazards and the best approaches.

CANOEING AND KAYAKING

Canoeing
A paddle along one of Belize's rivers, lagoons, marshes, or reefs is a great way to get some exercise and enjoy the outdoors. One of the best ways to observe wildlife in Belize is by canoe. Dawn and dusk find many creatures at the water's edge for a drink. Nights are also productive as agoutis, crocodiles, and other wildlife can be spotted within the beam of a flashlight. Rent canoes at resorts and from independent operators. Bermudian Landing Baboon Sanctuary, Chan Chich, Gales Point, and San Ignacio are prime locations.

Kayaking
Kayaking is one of those off-the-wall activities that's growing all over the world and often in unlikely places. It is fast becoming a favorite in Belize. Kayakers have a choice of river trips, sea kayaking, or a combination. The rivers are gentle enough for even beginning kayakers. An ideal way to explore the coast is to paddle the calm water within the reef and touch on isolated cayes. Ambergris Caye, Dangriga, Glover's Reef, Placencia, and Punta Gorda all offer opportunities. For more information about kayaking and camping in Belize contact **Monkey River Expeditions,** 206/660-7777, fax 206/938-0978, or **Slickrock Adventures,** tel. 800/390-5715 (see "Tour Operators," below).

OTHER WATER SPORTS

Depending on where you are, additional water sports may be available. Because so many of these beaches are protected by the reef that runs parallel to Belize's eastern coast, calm **swimming beaches,** though shallow, are easy to find; finding a *sandy* beach is limited to certain areas. Many hotels have pools. You can also enjoy swimming inland in various rivers and lagoons. **Glass-bottom boats** are well worth the time for the nonswimmer or nonsnorkeler and are available at Ambergris Caye and Caye Caulker. While staying high and dry, it's possible to enjoy the beauties of the underwater gardens. Personal watercrafts are available at the Princess Hoteland Casino in Belize City, several resorts on Ambergris Caye, and at Tony's Inn and Beach Resort in Corozal. **Tubing** is becoming a popular Cayo activity in the dry season on the Macal and Mopan rivers; tubing through a few caves is also an alternative activity.

ADVENTURES ON LAND

ON THE TRAIL

Backpacking and Hiking
The whole country is a backpacker's delight. Catch a bus to Corozal, Dangriga, Placencia, Punta Gorda, or San Ignacio and use any of these as a base for venturing out into the countryside. All have numerous options for budget accommodations or camping. Hang out with the locals. Pick up some Spanish, Creole, or Mayan words and phrases. Eat the local food. It's fun and you can do it on a shoestring. And if you really want to get close to nature on a tight budget, try a visit to the Cockscomb Basin Wildlife Sanctuary, Crooked Tree Lagoon, or the

Programme for Belize research station in Rio Bravo Conservation Area.

Bird-watching

Birding is spectacular throughout Belize and serious bird-watchers come from all over the world. From north to south the variety of birds is broad and changes with the geography and the weather (see "Fauna" in the Introduction). Some of the more productive areas for water-fowl and shorebirds are the lagoons of Amber-gris Caye and inland around Crooked Tree Lagoon, Gales Point, New River Lagoon, North-ern Lagoon (below Belize City), and Shipstern Lagoon. Half Moon Caye has a bird sanctuary that contains the nesting sites of boobies, frigate birds, and more. The Maya Mountains and low-land jungles of southern Belize harbor Aztec parakeets, hummingbirds, scarlet macaws, and king vultures, among many others. The es-carpment of the Mountain Pine Ridge shelters

parrots, orange-breasted hawks, and a variety of songbirds. Northwestern Belize is rich in ocellated turkeys, toucans, and curassow, to name a few. There's a lot more to see in plant and animal life while birding (see "Nature Walks," below).

Bring binoculars and wear boots, lightweight long-sleeved shirts, and trousers if you plan to go birdwatching in jungle areas. Don't forget the bug repellent and be prepared for an occasion-al rain shower, even in the dry season.

The **Belize Audubon Society** is very active; write if you have questions, 12 Fort St., Belize City, Belize, C.A., tel. 2/35004 or 2/34985.

Nature Walks

Wherever you go in Belize you're never far from a chance to see unusual plants and wild-life. Minutes out of the heart of Belize City you may encounter anything from a boa or fox crossing the road to manatees in the Belize

JOURNEY INTO THE MAYA UNDERWORLD

Our guides, Pete and Ted, led us about three miles through dense rainforest on a narrow footpath, swinging large machetes. We stopped to swim once in a freshwater pond, and again for lunch at the base camp of an archaeology team that was here at the cave—which we later found out is named Actun Tunichil Muknal—earlier in the year. We donned hard hats with lights attached and swam into the cave entrance. Pete told us we were not just entering a cave, but entering the Maya under-world. He could not have been more correct. Leaving the warmth and brilliance of the sunlight behind, we entered the cave and felt the cool air as we were introduced to vast blackness. With headlamps on and carrying spare flashlights, we started our de-scent into Xibalba, the Maya underworld. Wading through underground streams we were sometimes ankle deep, sometimes waist deep in the cool water. The only illumination came from our headlamps, our field of vision narrow. Stumbling over hidden rocks and bumping into rock walls and unseen stalactites, we slowly journeyed over two miles into the cave.

Stalactites and stalagmites are found throughout the cave, and the Maya believed that these were the roots of the ceiba tree, connecting the under-world with the terrestrial. Our guide rapped his knuck-les on the dead stalactites and introduced us to the beautiful sound, with the pitch and tone of an organ chord.

Deities also inhabited the underworld. While on a rest break, Pete convinced us to turn out our lights. After a few moments, our ears were sensitized, and we heard the voices. Over the din of the river, we heard shrieks and laughter of both young and old, chatter of the ancients living on over the ages. Know-ing that sacrifices and other ceremonies took place inside this cave, it was easy to imagine the piercing screams of the victims, the chants of the leaders, and the songs to accompany the victim to the next world, and to smell the incense burning.

Continuing into the cave, we found physical evi-dence of the ancient Maya, first in the form of pottery shards, and then complete pots and large bowls. A little farther we entered the burial chamber and saw a skull embedded in the ground. Once again we turned off our lights, and with the flick of a lighter we observed millions of stars in the black world around us—the reflection of quartz in the earthen walls. What better place to bury a body for the jour-ney into the next dimension.

River. And you're not even in the jungle yet! Many hotels and resorts throughout the country have their own nature trails, some with signs identifying trees, termite nests, and other interesting flora and fauna.

Nature Study

When it comes to enjoying wildlife and the outdoors, some people want more than just fun. They want serious fun, the fun of learning about nature in more depth. This is becoming increasingly popular in Belize and is taking several forms. On Caye Caulker **Seeing Is Belizing** offers slide shows and talks on nature subjects. Maya Mountain Lodge in the Cayo District offers talks covering similar subjects as well as Maya ceramics. Chaa Creek Cottages has a Nature Study Center that houses exhibits, a library, and presentation room. On Blackbird Caye guests can participate in a dolphin research project. Lamanai Outpost Lodge offers guests the opportunity to involve themselves in a study of howler monkeys. And the list is growing all the time.

Cycling

Though at one time you seldom saw cyclists in Belize, you will find a growing number of comrades in Belize who are avid practitioners. However, consider a few things before you pack your bike and head for the nearest airport. If you haven't cycled in hot tropical humidity, you may first want to rent a bike in Belize for a short trial run before you plan a long trip. The humidity can be debilitating for some; for others it might take a day or two of easy riding before the body will acclimate. Another consideration is the roads of Belize. Only three roads are paved, and those are getting busier all the time. Traffic is getting heavy on the Western Highway, which is probably the best road in the country. Most of the other roads in Belize are narrow, filled with potholes, or are dirt, which can get pretty mushy in the rain. Rule of thumb: Always relinquish the roadway to motor vehicles approaching from the rear. Anyone trying to cycle around Belize City's narrow, crowded streets is looking for an accident to happen. Also, watch your bike like a hawk—take it to bed with you at night, or at least into your room. After all that, if you still want to bike the roads of Belize, have at it!

horseback riding in the mountains

For bicycling or mountain biking you have three practical options; rent on Ambergris Caye, in Belize City, or the Cayo District. Serious cyclists can ride as far as Belmopan, Corozal, Orange Walk, or San Ignacio in a day. Or once in the San Ignacio area, you can arrange bike rentals at several of the lodges or ask Bob Jones at **Eva's.** Mountain bikes are preferable and a patch kit is a wise precaution.

Horseback Riding

The horsey set will find no end of enjoyment in Belize. The Cayo alone offers numerous ranches, lodges, and independent operators who provide adventures on horseback. You can ride around a ranch and help herd cattle or explore jungle trails or archaeological sites. You can also find horses for hire near Altun Ha in Belize City District and Gallon Jug in Orange Walk District. Even Ambergris Caye has horses.

SPORTS

Golf
Golfers so far have one choice, Caye Chapel. Under new ownership, the course is being developed for a very high-end resort, or so we have heard.

Tennis
Tennis courts are scarce, but the tennis buff will be happy to know that a few resorts do have them: on Caye Chapel, **Villa Holiday Inn** in Belize City, and **Journey's End** on Ambergris Caye.

ENTERTAINMENT AND EVENTS

FESTIVALS

Come to the party! Certain holidays in Belize are signals to have fun. And the variety of activity on each holiday is vast. This is the time to sample the culture and cuisine of Belize traditions. When a public holiday falls on Sunday, it is celebrated on the following Monday. If you plan to visit during holiday time, make advance hotel reservations—especially if you plan to spend time in Dangriga during Settlement Day on November 19 (the area has limited accommodations).

Note: On a few holidays (Easter and Christmas), most businesses close for the day, and some close the day after Christmas, which is Boxing Day; on Good Friday most of the buses do not run. Check ahead of time.

NATIONAL HOLIDAYS IN BELIZE

January 1	New Year's Day
March 9	Baron Bliss Day
March or April	Good Friday
March or April	Holy Saturday
March or April	Easter Sunday
March or April	Easter Monday
May 1	Labour Day
May 25	Commonwealth Day
September 10	National Day
September 21	Independence Day
October 12	Columbus Day
November 19	Garifuna Day
December 25	Christmas Day
December 26	Boxing Day

Baron Bliss Day
On March 9 this holiday is celebrated with various activities, mostly water sports. In memory of English sportsman Baron Henry Edward Ernest Victor Bliss, who remembered Belize with a generous legacy when he died, a day of sailing and fishing was designated in his will. A formal ceremony is held at his tomb below the lighthouse in the Belize Harbor where he died on his boat. Fishing and sailing regattas begin after the ceremony.

Ambergris Caye Celebration
If you're wandering around Belize near June 26–29, hop a boat or plane to San Pedro and join the locals in a festival they have celebrated for decades, **El Dia de San Pedro,** in honor of the town's namesake, St. Peter. This is good fun; reservations are suggested. **Carnaval,** one week before Lent, is another popular holiday on the island. The locals walk in a procession through the streets to the church, celebrating the last hurrah (for devout Catholics) before Easter. Lots of good dancing competitions.

St. George's Caye Day
On September 10, 1798, at St. George's Caye off the coast of Belize, the British buccaneers fought and defeated the Spaniards over the territory of Belize. The tradition of celebrating this victory is still carried on each year, followed by a weeklong calendar of events from religious services to carnivals. During this week Belize City (especially) feels like a carnival with parties everywhere. On the morning of September 10, the whole city parades through the streets and enjoys local cooking, spirits, and music with an upbeat atmosphere that continues well into the beginning of Independence Day on September 21.

KATHY ESCOVEDO SANDERS

FEAST OF SAN LUIS

There is no question that the Feast of San Luis celebration is symbolic, but of what? It's doubtful that anyone really knows. So much of the ancient traditional culture has been mixed with the Christian religion that even the Maya aren't sure. We do know an all-night vigil begins the festival, during which traditional masks and costumes are blessed with smoke from burning incense and food offerings. According to Maya belief, a great power resides in the masks and it can be directed toward good or evil.

Drums announce the procession to the home of the prioste (holy man) each of the next nine days. Leading the marchers is a man dressed as the "holy deer," followed by the other characters of the dance, including *el tigre* ("the jaguar"), women portrayed by men, dogs, and finally, the hunters dressed in black. Four men carry an instrument called the marimba, which is played all the way into the prioste's house and intermittently during respites in the ceremonial dances. Some of the men shake rattles and an ongoing chant adds an exotic tone to the music of the dance.

The Tiger Dance
The ancient legend of the tiger is performed in a square. The four corners and the center of the space represent the Maya's five cardinal directions—north, south, east, west, and the center. Slowly and with grace the story of *el tigre* unfolds. With active movements the tiger chases and is chased by the men in red from each of the four corners and around the center. Were they the *bacabs,* the Maya guardians of directions? As a clown, the tiger impishly teases the hunters throughout the dance, stealing their hats or their rattles. At the finale the tiger is captured and killed; the hunters pantomime the killing and skinning of the tiger while the dancer steps out of his costume and runs away. Though performed with exaggerated elements of sincerity, it's a comedic performance, a warm-up of more serious things to come.

The Holy Deer Dance
The story of the holy deer, on the other hand, is performed with reverence instead of comedy, and continues for several days. The festivities include a lively procession to the San Antonio village church. The deer dances proudly, head high, acknowledges each of the other dancers, and then disappears into the forest. Enter the dogs sent by the hunters to seek out the deer. After a while the frightened deer/dancer is chased back by the dogs and with great drama the hunters kill the noble animal.

The Greased Pole
Preparations for the finale start two days ahead of time with an all-night vigil for the men who will cut down a tall tree to be used in the pole-climbing festivities. The pillar is about 60 feet long and made from a special tree, called *sayuc* in Maya. The tree is trimmed and the dancing continues, drawing larger and larger audiences. A great procession follows as the huge pole and a statue of San Antonio (which has been in the prioste's home) are carried to San Antonio's church on the top of the hill. Occasionally the long line of people stops and lays the pole on the ground. In silence and great solemnity the pole is "blessed" by the statue of San Antonio while women manipulate censers of burning incense, sending wisps of aromatic smoke wafting around the pole. Once at the church, saints are traded. The statue of San Antonio is returned to its place, more prayers are said, and the statue of San Luis, under a protective colorful canopy and flanked by a dozen flags, is carried out on a wooden platform to "bless" the pole. The procession of people, including the statue, then makes its way to the prioste's house for another night of social dancing.

The Finale
It's September 25, the climax day—

(continued on next page)

FEAST OF SAN LUIS
(continued)

and the end of the celebration. Preparations for raising the pole begin early in the morning to the steady, low beat of a drum. Under the watchful eyes of many anxious children, bars of soap are flattened with rocks, broken into small pieces, and dissolved in buckets of water. Next, melted lard is added and thoroughly mixed. The oily compound is then generously spread on the pole. How anyone could accomplish an upward movement on this mess is a mystery, although the first has the most slips. Prizes that have been stored at the prioste's house—a generous hand of bananas, a bottle of rum, and a small sum of money—are placed at the top of the pole for the climber who makes it all the way. He will earn it!

After a slow procession, eating, dancing, and more blessings, the grand finale (under the watchful eye of the saint) is about to begin.

The pole-raising brings a still moment; the only sound is the low beat of the drums. The aroma of incense permeates the air. Fifty men hold ropes while others hold forked sticks and the pole slowly begins to rise, but not without a few slippery sways that bring gasps from the anticipating crowd. Finally the long pole slips neatly into the hole.

Now the fun begins—at least for the onlookers. The tiger and the hunter characters are the first to attempt to climb the pole, followed by a dozen other men; to make it more difficult each has his feet tied together. Everyone has a good laugh watching the slipping and sliding. Finally a successful challenger with great determination inches his way to the top and reaches for his prize; the crowd cheers and the church bells ring out.

The men in the village take turns as the religious caretaker for special statues of the church. This is a privilege that includes bearing the expense for most of the ceremonies for the year—a costly honor.

National Independence Day

On September 21, 1981, Belize gained independence from Great Britain. Each year to celebrate, Belizeans enjoy carnivals on the main streets of downtown Belize City and district towns. Like giant county fairs, they include displays of local arts, crafts, and cultural activities, while happy Belizeans dance to a variety of exotic rhythms from *punta* rock to *soka* to reggae. Again, don't miss the chance to sample local dishes from every ethnic group in the country. With this holiday back to back with the celebration of the Battle of St. George's Caye, Belize enjoys two weeks of riotous, cacophonous partying.

Garifuna Settlement Day

On November 19, Belize recognizes the 1823 arrival and settlement of the first Garifuna (Black Caribs, also called Garinagu) to the southern districts of Belize. Belizeans from all over the country gather in Dangriga and Toledo to celebrate with the Garifuna. The day begins with the reenactment of the arrival of the settlers and continues with dancing to the local Garifuna drums and *punta* rock. Traditional food is available at street stands and local cafés. The language is called Garifuna and both words, Garifuna and Garinagu, are interchangeable.

DANCES OF THE MAYA

If you happen to be one of the lucky travelers in Belize on September 25, you should make an effort to visit **San Antonio Village** in the Toledo District. You have a good chance of seeing the **deer dance** performed by the Mopan and Kekchi Maya villagers. Dancing and celebrating begins around the middle of August, but the biggest celebration begins with a *novena* nine days before the feast day of San Luis.

Actually this festival was only recently revived. The costumes were burned in an accidental fire some years back at a time when (coincidentally) the locals had begun to lose interest in the ancient traditions. Thanks to the formation of the **Toledo**

Maya Cultural Council, the Maya once again are realizing the importance of recapturing their past. A grant from **Video Incorporated** broadcast company enabled the people to make new masks and costumes. In return the broadcasting company was granted permission to tape the festivities—a big concession for the secretive Maya. Before you decide to attend this days-long event, remember just that—it gets long. Ask the headman before you take any pictures.

MUSIC OF BELIZE

Like that of many Central American countries, the music of Belize has been heavily influenced by the rhythmic, exotic syncopations of Africa. This is toe-tapping, hip-swinging, hand-clapping music, and anyone who can just sit still and listen must be in a coma. If you manage to get to Belize in September during the festivals of the Battle of St. George's Caye and National Independence Day, you'll have an introduction to the raucous, happy music of a **jump up** (a street dance), **punta rock** (a spin-off from the original *punta,* a traditional rhythm of the Garifuna settlers in the Stann Creek District), **reggae** (everyone knows the beat of the steel drums adapted from the Trinidad cousins), **soka** (a livelier interpretation of reggae), and **brukdown** (a cadence begun in the timber camps of the 1800s, when the workers, isolated from civilization for months at a time, would let off steam with a full bottle of rum and begin the beat on the bottle—or the jawbone of an ass, a coconut shell, a wooden block—anything that made a sound. Add to that a harmonica, guitar, and banjo, and you've got *brukdown*). **Creole** folk songs tell the story like it is, sad or happy, with lyrics in the Creole patois of the people.

In the southern part of Belize in Toledo District, you'll likely hear the strains of ancient Maya melodies played on homemade wooden instruments designed before memory: Kekchi harps, violins, and guitars. In the west in Cayo District listen for the resonant sounds of marimbas and wooden xylophones—from the Spanish influence across the Guatemala border. In Corozal and Orange Walk Districts in the north, the infatuations of old Mexico are popularized with romantic lyrics and the strum of a guitar.

Tapes and Recordings

The music recording business is developing in Belize in its own original way—watch out Hollywood! If you want to hear Belizean music but can't get away, send for a catalog of cassette tapes available for overseas sales from **Sunrise Productions,** P.O. Box 137, Belmopan, Cayo District, Belize, C.A. Look for marimba music, Kekchi harp music, and the ever-loving **Waribagabaga and Children of the Most High,** combining their music of drums, turtle shells, and vocals sung in Garifuna. Also offered are typical jump up music and *punta* rock rhythms.

ACCOMMODATIONS

Picking the proper accommodations is as crucial to a good vacation as your choice of activities. That's why some folks would rather wait until they get to a destination to choose. That's not always a good idea in Belize, especially February–April, high season. Educating yourself about the kinds of accommodations available and then matching those with your budget and preferences will reap large rewards later.

In Belize basic budget rooms are still fairly easy to find; small modern lodgings are adding more rooms to alleviate the growing shortages, and upscale hotels have been built on Ambergris Caye and in Belize City in the last few years, with more going up in Stann Creek. Scattered about the rest of the countryside and coastal regions, small hotels and delightful intimate guest houses range from spartan cottages with kerosene lanterns on the riverbank to luxury cabañas built of rich tropical hardwoods and surrounded by the rainforest, glorious gardens, and well-manicured grass. The rooms offer access to thousands of acres of rainforest, nature reserves, rivers, waterfalls, beautiful flowers, wild animals, colorful birds, and modern Maya villages along with ancient ceremonial sites of their ancestors. On tiny cayes just offshore, simple cabins sit in perfect locations for easy-access scuba diving and snorkeling as well as world-class permit and bonefishing. Or for other serious divers and anglers, live-aboard boats offer accommodations and the opportunity to comfortably cruise to offshore cayes. Most of the hostelries in the country are small and intimate, which, in keeping with the small country, is what the tourist majority prefers. Note: In the more isolated areas, rooms may not have hot water, electricity, or telephones. Those staying in the Maya Guest Houses will also have to use an outhouse. Will adventurers let that stop them? It seems not.

As you look through the listings for hotels in this book, remember that in most cases you must add 7 percent tax, and in some cases an extra few percent for the use of credit cards. If you decide to stay in one of the low-key budget hotels, bring cash; most don't accept credit cards.

FOOD

PRE-COLUMBIAN AGRICULTURE

Enriching the Soil
Scientists believe Maya priests studied celestial movements. A prime function performed in the elaborate temples (built to strict astronomical guidelines) may have been charting the changing seasons and deciding when to begin the planting cycle. Farmers used the slash-and-burn method of agriculture (and the Maya still do today). When the time was propitious (before the rains began in the spring), Maya farmers cut the trees on a section of land, leaving stumps about a foot above ground. They spread downed trees evenly across the landscape to burn uniformly; residual ash was left to nourish the soil. At the proper time, they made holes with a pointed stick and dropped precious maize kernels into the earth, one by one. At each corner (the cardinal points) of the cornfield, they left offerings of pozole (maize stew) to encourage the gods to give forth great rains. With abundant moisture, crops were bountiful and rich enough to provide food even into the following year.

The Maya knew the value of allowing the land to lie fallow after two seasons of growth, and each family's milpa (cornfield) was moved from place to place around the villages scattered through the jungle. Often, squash and tomatoes were planted in the shade of towering cornstalks to make double use of the land. The coming of electricity to outlying areas brought pumps to transport water from rivers and lakes to irrigate crops. Outside of irrigation methods, today's Maya follow the same ancient pattern of farming as their ancestors. The government is suggesting more efficient management of the land with less destruction to the rainforest; this "alternate" farming method reuses a plot of ground, with the help of fertilizers, after it's been left fallow for a short time. Education, intended to teach the indigenous people alternatives to slash-and-burn, is beginning to take hold.

Maize
Corn was the heart of Maya nutrition, eaten at each meal. From it they made tortillas, stew, and both alcoholic and nonalcoholic beverages. Because growing corn was such a vital part of Maya life, it is represented in drawings and carvings along with other social and religious symbols. Corn tortillas are still a main staple of the Maya people. Grinding the corn into tortilla dough has been done by hand for centuries (and still is in isolated places). Others pay a few more cents and buy their tortillas by the kilo hot off the tomal (griddle). The Maya's combination of corn and beans provided a complete protein; they did not raise cattle, sheep, or pigs before Spanish times. They did include in their diets turtle, manatee, iguana, fresh seafood, and many small animals that roamed the jungle.

GASTRONOMICAL ADVENTURE

Taste as many different dishes as possible! You'll be introduced to spices that add a new dimension to your diet. Naturally you won't be wild about everything—it takes a while to become accustomed to squid served in its own black ink, for instance. A hamburger might not taste like one from your favorite "fast foodery" back home. Be prepared to come into contact with many new and different tastes—you're in

Belize, after all, a land of myriad cultures and cuisines. You will easily find Chinese, Mexican, Creole, and European dishes. Look for such delicacies as conch, conch soup, fried lobster, iguana, armadillo, shark, black beans and rice, great fried chicken, fried plantain, and papaya, and don't turn your nose up if someone invites you to a "boil up" (seafood stew). Though turtle is an endangered species, the law allows fishermen to take them at certain times of the year, so you may also see turtle offered on a menu—but perhaps if no one buys them the fishermen will quit catching them in their nets!

Seafood

You won't travel far before realizing that one of the favorite Belize specialties is fresh fish. All along the Caribbean and Gulf coasts are opportunities to indulge in piscine delicacies: lobster, shrimp, red snapper, sea bass, halibut,

cleaning conch, still an important staple along the Caribbbean coast

barracuda, conch, and lots more prepared in a variety of ways. Even the tiniest café will prepare sweet, fresh fish.

Try the unusual conch *(say kawnk),* which has been a staple in the diet of the Mayan and Central American along the Caribbean coast for centuries. It's often used in ceviche. Some consider this raw fish; actually, it's marinated in lime juice with onions, peppers, and a host of spices—no longer raw, and very tasty! In another favorite conch is pounded, dipped in egg and then cracker crumbs, and sautéed quickly (like abalone steak in California) with a squirt of fresh lime. Caution: If it's cooked too long it becomes tough and rubbery. Conch fritters are minced pieces of conch mixed into a flour batter and fried—delicious.

If you happen to be on a boat trip the crew will probably catch a fish and prepare it for lunch, maybe cooked over an open fire, or in a "boil up," seasoned with onions, peppers, and *achiote,* a fragrant red spice grown locally since the time of the early Maya.

Garifuna Style

A very ethnic way to prepare fish is to cook it in coconut milk and local spices; it's called *sere.* In many dishes plantain or green bananas are grated into various recipes, and seaweed is used now and then. All contribute to new and unique flavors.

Wild Game

Many ethnic groups in Belize are hunters, and if you explore the jungle paths very much, you'll see men and boys on foot or on bicycles with rifles slung over their shoulders and full game bags tied behind them. Jungle game varies. Wild duck is served during certain times of the year and is prepared in several ways that *must* be tried. Iguana is common, gibnut (a rabbitlike rodent) is said to be very tasty (I haven't tried it yet, but Queen Elizabeth has!), and the Maya eat a wide variety of wild game cooked in a spicy red sauce. If you're invited for dinner by a local Maya, don't be surprised to find the likes of crested guan, tinamou, brocket deer, peccary, armadillo, agouti, paca, turtle, iguana, and iguana eggs. This is the norm for people who live in and around the forest, although I didn't say it was all legal.

Hot Stuff!

All that grand Belizean fare wouldn't be authentic without a dash or two of Marie Sharp's hot sauce. You won't have to search far; it's at nearly every restaurant in the entire country. It comes in three levels of heat: mild, hot, and fiery hot (believe them). But be careful, the taste grows on people. Some take it back by the case.

Brewed in Belize

When it comes to "cases," many travelers wouldn't mind taking home a case or two of the local beer, Belikin. The familiar brown bottles with the white and green label are sold all over the country. Belikin also makes a very good premium beer and a marvelous stout. All three are every bit as good as most American beers and often are favorably compared to beers from the new microbreweries in the States. The official drinking age in Belize is 18.

Restaurants

Most small cafés that cater to Belizeans are open all day until about 10 P.M. Hotels with foreign tourists offer dinner early in the evening to cater to British, Canadian, and American tastes. Most hotels and restaurants add tax and a 20 percent service charge to the bill. It's still gracious to leave a few coins for the waiter. If the tip isn't added to the bill, leaving 10–15 percent is customary.

Stewed chicken is found on almost every menu in Belize, along with beans and rice, which is considered a "typical" dinner. Some of the more local restaurants offer gibnut, a rabbitlike rodent that was served to Queen Elizabeth when she visited some years back, causing British newspapers to print half-page headlines stating the queen was served rat in Belize. Oh, well; newspapers go to any lengths to be noticed.

A ploy many seasoned adventurers use when

SAVE THE LOBSTER

Since the influx of tourists into the small country of Belize, a very big concern has been the safety of the lobster beds off the coast, which have provided food and support for the locals for many years. Because the price of a lobster dinner in Caye Caulker, for instance, is so much cheaper than in the United States, the demand has increased rapidly. To keep tourists happy, a few fishermen supply the restaurants open season or closed, legal size or not! The population of lobster cannot continue to flourish with these illegal activities, and the collapse of the Belizean fishing industry will follow.

As a responsible traveler, you are urged not to order lobster during the closed season, which is Feb. 15–June 15. Also, if (during the open season) a restaurant is offering a lobster dinner for BZE$7–8, it is most likely a "short," which means it is under legal size. Minimum size for a lobster tail is four ounces. Ask around town for restaurants that sell legal-size tails, and then patronize them with a positive comment about saving the lobster.

All of the above advice goes for the conch as well. Closed season for conch is July–September, and the minimum size is three ounces of meat.

---

they're tired of eating cold food from their backpacks: in a village where no cafés exist go to the local pub, grocery store, church, or city hall and ask if there's a housewife in town who, for a fee, would be willing to include you at her dinner table. Almost always you'll find someone, usually at a fair price (determine price when you make your deal). With any luck you'll find a woman renowned for her cooking. You'll gain a lot more than food in this arrangement; the cultural swap is priceless.

HEALTH AND SAFETY

If you have any safety concerns about the country, call the Centers for Disease Control and Prevention in Atlanta, GA, 404/639-2888, before leaving the United States. Prescription drugs are unavailable in the tiny villages, so bring any necessary medicines in your backpack; in Belize City you should have no problem. Bring a bug repellent; some areas at some times of the day are really a nuisance. "No see-ums" and occasional sand flies can be a big problem as well—DEET works, Avon's Skin-So-Soft works great for *some* people (if you can stand the strong smell!).

TRAVELER'S DISEASE

Some travelers to foreign countries worry about getting sick the moment they leave their own country. But with a few simple precautions, it's not a foregone conclusion that you'll come down with something. The most common illness to strike visitors is traveler's disease, known by many names but, in plain Latin, it's diarrhea. No fun, it can cause uncomfortable cramping, fever, dehydration, and the need to stay close to a toilet for a few days. It's caused by, among other things, various strains of bacteria managing to find your innards, so it's important to be very careful about what goes into your mouth.

Studies show that the majority of tourists who get sick do so on the third day of their visit, and that traveler's illness is common in every country. They say that in addition to bacteria, a change in diet is equally to blame and suggest that the visitor slip slowly into the eating habits of the country, especially if the food tends to be spicier than you're use to. In other words, don't blast your tummy with the habañero or jalapeño pepper right off the bat. Work into the fried food, alcoholic drinks, local specialties, and new spices gradually; take your time changing over to foods you may never eat while at home, including the large quantities of wonderful tropical fruits that you'll want to eat in the tropics. Also beware mixing alcohol with longer-than-usual periods of time in the tropical sun. Alcohol changes the body chemistry and it becomes very difficult to handle excessive heat.

It's the Water

While the above theories are often valid, water is probably the worst culprit. According to locals, the water from the faucet in Belize City is safe, but smaller villages and more isolated areas are still "iffy"—you'd be wise to take special precautions. A good rule of thumb: if you're not sure about the water, ask the locals or the desk clerk at your hotel; they'll let you know the status. Hotels prefer healthy guests—they'll return. If you are in an area where water is a problem, you have two options. Drink bottled water if available, or drink carbonated beverages without ice. The carbonation lowers the pH enough to make it inhospitable for microorganisms to grow and live.

In the backcountry, hikers should carry their own water. If you drink from other sources, out of the tap or a crystal-clear pond, boil it or purify it with chemicals. That goes for brushing your teeth as well. If you have nothing else, a bottle of beer will make a safe (though maybe not sane) mouth rinse. If using ice, ask where it was made and if it's pure.

Giardia is a parasite that can be present in streams and ponds almost anyplace in the world. You can destroy it by boiling the water for 20–30 minutes. Or you can treat the water with iodine. An inexpensive water treatment kit that uses crystalline iodine is available from Recreational Equipment Incorporated. For more information, write P.O. Box 88125, Seattle, WA 98138-0125, 800/426-4840. The company also offers the more expensive Swiss-made Katadyn PF Pocket Water Filter for those who cannot tolerate iodine for either taste or thyroid reasons. Outdoor supply shops are a good place to check for the latest in portable water purifiers.

Hidroclonozone and **Halazone** are two types of water-purification tablets, but many brands are available at drugstores in all countries. You might also carry a small plastic bottle of liquid bleach (use 8–10 drops per quart of water) or iodine (use 5–7 drops per quart) to purify the water. Whichever you use, let the water stand for 20 minutes to improve the flavor. Even though it requires time and energy to purify water—and may make that backpack even heavier—don't get lazy in this department. You can get very sick drinking contaminated water, which you can't identify by its appearance—unless you travel with a microscope!

When camping on the beach where fresh water is scarce, use seawater to wash dishes and even yourself. Before leaving home, check at a sporting goods or marine shop for **Sea Saver Soap.** (A rub of bar soap on the bottom of pots and pans before setting them over an open fire makes for easy cleaning after cooking.)

Ciguatera

This is a toxin occasionally found in large reef fish. It is not a common circumstance, but it is possible for grouper, snapper, and barracuda to carry this toxin. If after eating these fish you experience diarrhea, nausea, numbness, or heart arrhythmia, see a doctor immediately. The toxin is found in certain algae on reefs in all the tropical areas of the world. Fish do nibble on the coral, and if they happen to find this algae, over a period of time it accumulates in their systems. The longer they live and the larger they get, the more probable it is they will carry toxin; it is not destroyed when cooked.

Other Sources of Infection

Money can be a source of germs. Wash your hands frequently, don't put your fingers in your mouth, and carry individual foil packets of disinfectant cleaners, such as Wash Up, or small bottles of Purell, which are handy and refreshing in the tropic heat. Hepatitis is another bug that you can contract easily if you're around it.

When in backcountry cafés, remember that fruits and vegetables, especially those with a thin edible skin (such as tomatoes), are a possible source of bacteria. If you like to eat street vendors' food (and some shouldn't be missed), use common sense. If you see the food being cooked (killing all the grubby little bacteria) before your eyes, have at it. If it's hanging there already cooked and being nibbled on by small flying creatures, pass it by. It may have been there all day, and what was once a nice sterile morsel could easily have gone bad in the heat, or been contaminated by flies. Be cautious of hotel buffets; raw shellfish, potato salad, and other cream-based salads may have been sitting out for hours—a potential bacteria source unless they are well iced.

Treatment

Remember, it's not just the visitor who gets sick from bacteria. Each year locals die from the same germs, and the government is working hard to remedy the sanitation problems. Tremendous improvements ultimately will be accomplished all over Belize, but it's a slow process. In the meantime, many careful visitors come and go each year with nary a touch of illness. If after all your precautions you still come down with traveler's illness, many medications are available for relief. You can buy most over-the-counter, but in the United States you may need a prescription from your doctor. **Lomotil** and **Imodium** antidiarrheal medications are common and certainly turn off the faucet after a few hours of dosing; however, they have the side effect of

HOSPITAL/CLINIC PHONE NUMBERS

Ambergris Caye
Lions Clinic, San Pedro Town, tel. 2/62073
San Pedro Health Center, San Pedro Town, tel. 2/63668

Belize District
Belize City Hospital, Belize City, tel. 2/31548
Belize Medical Associates, Belize City, tel. 2/30303

Caye Caulker
Health Center, tel. 2/22166

Cayo District
Public Hospital, Belmopan, tel. 8/22263
Good Shepherd Clinic, Benque Viejo, tel. 9/32243
San Ignacio Hospital, San Ignacio Town, tel. 9/22066
Spanish Lookout Clinic, Spanish Lookout, tel. 8/30149

Corozal District
Corozal Hospital, Santa Rita Hill, tel. 4/22076

Orange Walk District
Estrella Medical Center, Orange Walk Town, tel. 3/23927
Orange Walk Hospital, Orange Walk Town, tel. 3/22072

Stann Creek District
Dangriga Hospital, Dangriga Town, tel. 5/22078
Doctors Headquarters, Dangriga Town, tel. 5/22084
Stann Creek Medical Center, Dangriga Town, tel. 5/22138
Independence Health Centre, Independence Village, tel. 6/22019

Toledo District
Punta Gorda Hospital, Punta Gorda Town, tel. 7/22026

becoming a plug. These medications do not cure the problem, only the symptoms; if you quit taking it too soon your symptoms reappear and you're back to square one. In their favor, Lomotil and Imodium work faster than **Pepto Bismol** or **Kaopectate** antidiarrheals, and if you're about to embark on a seven-hour bus ride to Placencia you might consider either one of those "quick-stop" drugs a lifesaver. **Note:** Imodium no longer requires a prescription; Lomotil, however, does.

If you're concerned, check with your doctor before leaving home. Also ask the doctor about antibiotics to treat bacterial causes of diarrhea such as **Septra** and **Bactrim** (trimethoprim-sulfamethoxazole) or **Cipro** (ciprofloxacin), which may prove to be better against organisms with resistance to Bactrim or Septra. You should take antibiotics only if you develop diarrhea, not as prophylaxis. Something else to be aware of: Pepto Bismol can turn the tongue a dark brownish color—nothing to be alarmed about.

For those who prefer natural remedies, lime juice and garlic are both considered good when taken as preventatives. They need to be taken in large quantities. Douse everything with the readily available lime juice (it's delicious on salads, fresh fruit, and in drinks). You'll have to figure your own ways of using garlic (some believers carry garlic capsules, available in most health-food stores in the United States). Fresh coconut juice is said to help (don't eat the oily flesh; it makes your problem worse!). Plain, boiled white rice soothes the tummy. While letting the ailment run its course, stay away from spicy and oily foods and fresh fruits. Drink plenty of pure water. Don't be surprised if you have chills, nausea, vomiting, stomach cramps, or a fever. This could go on for about three days. But if the problem persists, or worsens—if the diarrhea becomes bloody, fever exceeds 102°F, vomiting persists—or you still have symptoms of dehydration, *please* see a doctor.

OTHER DISEASES

Many animals—cats, dogs, iguanas, and birds—can carry more than your average tick. A good rule of thumb: Don't handle the animals.

You can acquire parasites through contact with contaminated soil, sand, water, food, or insects. Generally they enter through the skin or by being inadvertently eaten. Simple steps will help keep your exposure to them at a minimum. Wear shoes/sandals even at the beach. If you love to sunbathe on the sand, have a beach towel under you. Use insect repellent to avoid other insects such as mosquitoes, "kissing" bugs, and biting flies (see below). Symptoms of a parasite infection include but are not limited to the following: fever, rashes, swollen lymph nodes, digestive problems, eye problems, or anemia. These will not all necessarily appear while you are traveling, but may take several weeks or months to develop.

Malaria

Avoid mosquito bites: prevention is key. This is important not only for malaria, but for dengue fever and especially for yellow fever, which has no specific therapy. No yellow fever immunization is required for travelers entering Belize except for those from countries where it is endemic, such as South America and parts of Africa. Yellow fever in Central America fortunately is rare. Dengue fever, however, occurs naturally in the region and is usually transmitted by mosquitoes that bite in the day, just the opposite of those that transmit malaria. Travelers are usually at low risk except during epidemics.

Use insect repellent that contains DEET (N,N-Diethyl metatoluamide). For adults, 30–35 percent DEET formulas are appropriate, for children, 6–10 percent DEET. Apply it to any exposed skin surfaces, including the back of the hands, feet, ankles, ears, and neck.

For those of you trekking into forest or jungle, one can also buy bed nets and clothing soaked or sprayed with permethrin, another insect repellent that lasts on the order of weeks to a few months. You can buy these items at military surplus, hardware, or backpacking supply stores.

As for medical prevention, consult your doctor. In Central America, prophylaxis is usually adequate with Aralen (chloroquine). The regimen is to take it once a week beginning one week before the trip, through the trip, and then for four more weeks after returning. Side effects are rare and usually do not require discontinuing the drug. They include upset stomach, headache, dizziness, blurred vision, and itching.

Other Parasites

The "kissing bug," also known as the assassin bug, spreads Chagas' disease, or American trypanosomiasis. The insect spreads the disease when it contaminates the bite wound with its own infected feces. The one-inch bug prefers to bite its victims while they sleep; the bugs drop from their hiding places in thatch or other rural houses. The bite is followed by fever and swollen glands. Early treatment with drugs can rid the victim of the parasite, so see a doctor immediately. Untreated, it can damage the heart and other organs years later.

Although it poses almost no risk to most travelers, watch out for the flesh-eating screwworm if you have open wounds. Primarily an affliction of livestock, the female screwworm fly lays up to 300 eggs on open wounds so its larva can feed on the flesh. Without treatment, it can be fatal. Scientists have rid the United States and Mexico of the pest by releasing sterile male flies; they are trying to push the screwworm out of Central America as far as Panama.

The annoying botfly is much more likely to plague the traveler. It is unsightly, painful, but not dangerous and easy to treat. It burrows under the skin; you either have to draw it out or squeeze it out. (See "Insects and Arachnids" under "Fauna" in the Introduction.)

Hepatitis A

Hepatitis A is a virus transmitted by the fecal-oral route and so occurs in areas of poor sanitation. It can be transmitted by person-to-person contact, contaminated water, raw shellfish, or uncooked fruits or vegetables. Symptoms include fatigue, fever, poor appetite, nausea, vomiting, dark urine, light-colored stools, aches, pains. As with yellow fever, there is no specific therapy. Prevention generally is the same as for preventing traveler's disease and includes washing your hands before you eat. The Centers for Disease Control and Prevention recommend a shot of gamma globulin to protect yourself before your trip.

Wash Your Hands

The best protection for so many of these transmitted diseases is to frequently wash your hands, disinfecting them. If you're not near soap and water use one of the new bottled disinfectants that you can slip into your backpack. Continue rubbing until it dries. Also, the small individual packets of disinfectants work well.

SUNBURN

Sunburn can spoil a vacation quicker than anything else, so approach the sun cautiously. Expose yourself for short periods the first few days; wear a hat and sunglasses. Apply a good sunscreen to all exposed areas of the body (don't forget your feet, hands, nose, ears, back of knees, and top of forehead—especially if you have a receding hairline). Remember that after every time you go into the water, sunscreen lotion must be reapplied. Even after a few days of desensitizing the skin, wear a T-shirt in the water to protect your exposed back, especially if you spend the day snorkeling, and thoroughly douse the back of your neck with sunscreen lotion. PABA—para-aminobenzoic acid—solutions offer good protection and condition the skin. PABA is found in many brand names and strengths, and is much cheaper in the United States than in Belize. **Note:** Some people are allergic to PABA and it is said to cause cancer in isolated cases; check with your doctor before using. The higher the number on sunscreen bottles, the more protection.

If, despite precautions, you still get a painful sunburn, do not return to the sun. Cover up with clothes if it's impossible to find protective deep shade (like that in the depths of a dark, thick forest). Keep in mind that even in partial shade (such as under a beach umbrella), the reflection of the sun off the sand or water will burn your skin. Reburning the skin can result in painful blisters that easily become infected. Soothing suntan lotions, coconut oil, vinegar, cool tea, and preparations such as Solarcaine or other sunburn relief products will help relieve the pain. Usually a couple of days out of the sun will cure it. Drink plenty of liquids (especially water) and take tepid showers (see the special topic "Simple First-Aid Guide").

HEALING

Most cities in Belize have a medical clinic. More than likely someone there speaks English. In the bigger cities you can usually find a doctor who will make a house call. When staying in a hotel, get a doctor quickly by asking the hotel manager; in the larger resorts, an English-speaking doctor is on call 24 hours a day. A taxi driver can be your quickest way to get to a clinic when you're a stranger in town. In small rural villages, if you have a serious problem and no doctor is around, you can usually find a *curandero.* These healers deal with the old natural methods (and maybe just a few chants thrown in for good measure). This person could be helpful in a desperate situation away from modern technology. Locals who live in the dense, jungle areas inhabited by poisonous snakes go to the local "snake doctor." Again, this might be a possibility in a remote emergency situation where you need help quickly, and yet, medical people say every time, *no matter what,* don't go to a snake doctor. A **Cutter's Snake Bite Kit** can be helpful if used immediately after a bite, though its use is controversial in medical circles because of the risk of infection. Making the cut and sucking the poison out could pass germs into the open wound.

Ancient Healing

A delightful lady from Chicago, **Rosita Arvigo,** and her husband, Greg Shropshire, have been practicing the ancient Maya art of healing for some years. Both are graduates of Chicago National College of Naprapathy; Rosita is a professor of botanical studies and has been a practicing herbalist for more than 20 years. She continues to be intrigued with the study and exploration of nature's healing herbs and has her own company, which specializes in these herbs. For some years in Belize's Cayo District, Rosita was a student of the late **Don Eligio Panti,** who lived to be over 100 years old. The Maya bush doctor spent most of his life healing people using only the ancient Maya method plus added techniques learned from a Carib Indian during the chicle days of the 1930s. Rosita was his assistant for a number of years. She and Don Eligio tried very hard to keep the ancient ways alive, especially valuable because only a few Maya really remembered the old ways. In most cases only one or two people in each village knew these ancient secrets and they were handed down within the family. This part of the culture has dimmed over the years with the intrusion of modern medicine, which often isn't available to most of the Maya, either by choice or by circumstances.

Rosito Arvigo with the late Don Eligio Panti, a revered Belizean bush doctor who perpetuated Maya healing methods

Rosita recorded Don Eligio's therapies, treatments, and remedies so that future generations of his people (and the world) will always have access to their effectiveness. Rosita offers her services to anyone who is willing to travel to her research headquarters, **Ix Chel Tropical Research Center,** located in the Cayo District. Early on she established the **Panti Trail,** a nature trail through her forest property where she introduced many of the plants used in Maya treatment.

While walking the Panti Trail, a lovely path through the woods, visitors learn about the medicinal or healing value of various roots, vines, plants, and trees; each has a sign with its name and an explanation. A booklet explains the use of each one. Here visitors will see the **grapevine,** which provides pure water to cleanse the navel of a newborn infant; the bark of the negrito tree, also called **dysentery bark,** which treats severe dysentery (and which was sold for high prices by druggists in Europe when pirates discovered it many years past). Tea made from the **China root** is used for blood building after an attack from parasites. Another tea made from **ki bix** acts as birth control by coating the lining of the uterus.

With a guide personally trained by Rosita or with just the small booklet, you will discover fruit and food sources that made it possible for the Maya of old to glean a good part of daily subsistence from the jungle. The breadnut (also known as the Ramon Tree), tasting something like a cross between a potato and a chestnut, served the Maya well for centuries when the corn crop was minimal. It can be stored up to a year, roasted over coals and eaten plain, or ground up and used to make tortillas.

This is just a tiny sampling of the information shared with visitors.

Self-Help

The smart traveler carries a first-aid kit of some kind. If backpacking, at least carry a minimal first-aid kit:

- adhesive tape
- insect repellent
- alcohol
- Lomotil or Imodium
- antibiotic ointment
- aspirin
- painkiller
- baking soda
- sterile, adhesive strips
- sunscreen
- cornstarch
- tweezers
- gauze
- water-purification tablets
- hydrogen peroxide
- iodine needle

Many first-aid products are widely available, but certain items, such as aspirin and plastic bandages, are sold individually in small shops and are much cheaper if bought in your hometown. Even if not out in the wilderness you should carry at least a few sterile strips, aspirin, and an antibiotic ointment or powder or both. Travelers should be aware that in the tropics, with its heavy humidity, a simple scrape can become infected more easily than in a dry climate. So keep cuts

and scratches as clean and as dry as possible.

Another great addition to your first-aid kit is David Werner's book, *Where There Is No Doctor.* You can order it from the Hesperian Foundation, P.O. Box 1692, Palo Alto, CA 94302. David Werner drew on his experiences living in Mexico's backcountry to create this practical, informative book. Also useful is Dirk Schroeder's *Staying Healthy in Asia, Africa, and Latin America,* from Moon Travel Handbooks.

Centers for Disease Control and Prevention

Check on your last tetanus shot before you leave home. If you anticipate backpacking in jungle regions, call the **International Traveler's Hotline** at the **Centers for Disease Control and Prevention,** 404/332-4559. This hotline advises callers of the conditions abroad, what areas are experiencing an outbreak of disease, and will make suggestions for immunizations. It is updated as conditions warrant. You can receive information by fax, or go online at www.cdc.gov. A booklet also is available for sale, *Health Information for International Travelers,* from the U.S. Government Printing Office. To obtain a copy, send US$5 to the Superintendent of Documents, U.S. Government Printing Office, Washington, DC 20402.

BE SENSIBLE—STAY SAFE

Leave expensive jewelry at home. Don't flaunt cameras and video equipment or leave them in sight in cars when sight-seeing, especially in some parts of Belize City. Remember, this is a poor country and petty theft is its number-one crime—don't tempt fate. (As in London, the police don't carry guns.) It is also wise not to wander around alone on foot late at night in Belize City— for the same reasons. Go out, with others if possible, and take a taxi. Most Belizeans are friendly, decent people, but, as in every community, a small percentage will steal anything—given the opportunity. Expect to be hustled, whether in the market, a café, or a bar. To the Belizeans, Americans and Canadians come off as "rich" whether they are or not. The local hustlers are quite creative when it comes to thinking of ways to con you out of some cash. Keep your wits about you, pull out of conversations that appear headed in that

SIMPLE FIRST-AID GUIDE

Acute Allergic Reaction

This, the most serious complication of insect bites, can be fatal. Common symptoms are hives, rash, pallor, nausea, tightness in the chest or throat, and trouble speaking or breathing. Be alert for symptoms. If they appear, get prompt medical help. Start CPR if needed and continue until medical help is available.

Animal Bites

Bites, especially on the face and neck, need immediate medical attention. If possible, catch and hold the animal for observation, taking care not to be bitten again. Wash the wound with soap and water (hold under running water for 2–3 minutes unless bleeding heavily). Do not use iodine or other antiseptic. Bandage. This also applies to bites by human beings. In case of human bites, the danger of infection is high. (See also "Rabies" and "Snakebites.")

Bee Stings

Apply cold compresses quickly. If possible, remove the stinger by gently scraping with a clean fingernail and continue cold applications till pain is gone. Be alert for symptoms of acute allergic reaction or infection requiring medical aid.

Bleeding

For severe bleeding, apply direct pressure to the wound with a bandage or the heel of the hand. Do not remove cloths when blood-soaked; just add others on top and continue pressure until bleeding stops. Elevate bleeding part above heart level. If bleeding continues, apply a pressure bandage to arterial points. Do not put on tourniquet unless advised by a physician. Do not use iodine or other disinfectant. Get medical aid.

Blister on Heel

It is better not to open a blister if you can rest the foot. If you can't, wash the foot with soap and water, make a small hole at the base of the blister with a needle (sterilized in 70 percent alcohol or by holding the needle in the flame of a match), drain fluid, and cover with strip bandage or moleskin. If a blister breaks on its own, wash with soap and water, bandage, and be alert for signs of infection (redness, festering) that call for medical attention.

Burns

Minor burns (redness, swelling, pain): apply cold water or immerse burned part in cold water immediately. Use burn medication if necessary. Deeper burns (blisters develop): immerse in cold water (not ice water) or apply cold compresses for 1–2 hours. Blot dry and protect with a sterile bandage. Do not use antiseptic, ointment, or home remedies. Consult a doctor. For deep burns (skin layers destroyed, skin may be charred): cover with sterile cloth; be alert for breathing difficulties and treat for shock if necessary. Do not remove clothing stuck to burn. Do not apply ice. Do not use burn remedies. Get medical help quickly.

Cuts

Wash small cuts with clean water and soap. Hold wound under running water. Bandage. Use hydrogen peroxide or other antiseptic. For large wounds, see "Bleeding." If a finger or toe has been cut off, treat severed end to control bleeding. Put severed part in a clean cloth for the doctor (it may be possible to reattach it by surgery). Treat for shock if necessary. Get medical help at once.

Diving Accident

There may be injury to the cervical spine (such as a broken neck). Call for medical help. (See also "Drowning.")

Drowning

Clear airway and start CPR even before trying to get water out of lungs. Continue CPR till medical help arrives. In case of vomiting, turn victim's head to one side to prevent inhaling vomitus.

Food Poisoning

Symptoms appear a varying number of hours after eating and are generally like those of the flu—headache, diarrhea, vomiting, abdominal cramps, fever, and a general sick feeling. See a doctor. A rare form, botulism, has a high fatality rate. Symptoms are double vision, inability to swallow, difficulty in speaking, and respiratory paralysis. Get to a hospital at once.

(continued on next page)

SIMPLE FIRST-AID GUIDE
(continued)

Fractures
Until medical help arrives, do not move the victim unless absolutely necessary. Suspected victims of back, neck, or hip injuries should not be moved. Suspected breaks of arms or legs should be splinted to avoid further damage before victim is moved, if moving is necessary.

Heat Exhaustion
Symptoms are cool, moist skin, profuse sweating, headache, fatigue, and drowsiness with essentially normal body temperature. Remove the victim to cool surroundings, raise the feet and legs, loosen clothing, and apply cool cloths. Give sips of saltwater—one teaspoon of salt to a glass of water—for rehydration. If the victim vomits, stop fluids and take the victim to a hospital as soon as possible.

Heat Stroke
Rush the victim to a hospital. Heat stroke can be fatal. The victim may be unconscious or severely confused. The skin feels hot and is red and dry with no perspiration. Body temperature is high. Pulse is rapid. Remove the victim to cool area and sponge with cool water or rubbing alcohol: use fans or air conditioning and wrap in wet sheets, but do not overchill. Massage arms and legs to increase circulation. Do not give large amounts of liquids. Do not give liquids if victim is unconscious.

Insect Bites
Be alert for an acute allergic reaction that requires quick medical aid. Otherwise, apply cold compresses and soothing lotions. If bites are scratched and infection starts (fever, swelling, redness), see a doctor. (See also "Spider Bites," "Bee Stings," and "Ticks.")

Jellyfish Stings
The symptom is acute pain and may include a feeling of paralysis. Immerse in ice water for 5–10 minutes or apply aromatic spirits of ammonia to remove venom from skin. Be alert for symptoms of acute allergic reaction and/or shock. If this happens, get the victim to a hospital as soon as possible.

Mosquito Bites
See "Insect Bites."

Motion Sickness
Get a prescription from your doctor if you anticipate boat travel and this illness is a problem. Many over-the-counter remedies are sold in the United States: Bonine and Dramamine are examples. If you prefer not to take chemicals or if these make you drowsy, then something new, the Sea Band, might work for you. It's a cloth band that you place around the pressure point of the wrists. For more information, write to Sea Band, 1645 Palm Beach Lake Blvd., Suite 220, W. Palm Beach, FL 33401.

Medication that's administered by adhesive patches behind the ear is also available by prescription from your doctor.

Muscle Cramps
Usually a result of unaccustomed exertion, the cramp can be relieved by "working" the muscle or kneading it with the hand. If in water, head for shore (you can swim even with a muscle cramp), or knead the muscle with your hand. Call for help if needed. Do not panic.

Mushroom Poisoning
Even a small ingestion may be serious. Induce vomiting immediately if there is any question of mushroom poisoning. Symptoms—vomiting, diarrhea, difficulty breathing—may begin in 1–2 hours or up to 24 hours. Convulsions and delirium may develop. Go to a doctor or hospital at once.

Nosebleed
Press bleeding nostril closed, pinch nostrils together, or pack with sterile cotton or gauze. Apply cold cloth or ice to nose and face. The victim should sit up, leaning forward, or lie down with head and shoulders raised. If bleeding does not stop in 10 minutes, get medical help.

Obstructed Airway
Ask if the victim can talk. If so, encourage the victim to try to cough up the obstruction. If the victim cannot speak, a trained person must apply the Heimlich maneuver. If you are alone and choking, try to forcefully cough object out. Or press your fist into your upper abdomen with a quick upward thrust, or lean forward and quickly press your upper abdomen over any firm object with a rounded edge (the back of a

chair, the edge of a sink, or a porch railing). Keep trying until the object comes out.

Plant Poisoning

Many plants are poisonous if eaten or chewed. Induce vomiting immediately. Take the victim to a hospital for treatment. If the leaves of the diffenbachia (common in the Yucatán jungle) are chewed, one of the first symptoms is swelling of the throat. (See also "Mushroom Poisoning.")

Poison Ivy, Poison Oak, or Poison Sumac

After contact, wash affected area with alkali-base laundry soap, lathering well. Have a poison-ivy remedy available in case itching and blisters develop.

Puncture Wounds

Usually caused by stepping on a tack or a nail, puncture wounds often do not bleed, so try to squeeze out some blood. Wash thoroughly with soap and water and apply a sterile bandage. Check with a doctor about tetanus. If pain, heat, throbbing, or redness develops, get medical attention at once.

Rabies

Bites from bats, raccoons, rats, or other wild animals are the most common threat of rabies today. Try to capture the animal, avoiding being bitten, so it can be observed; do not kill the animal unless necessary and try not to injure the head so the brain can be examined. If the animal can't be found, see a doctor, who may decide to use antirabies immunization. In any case, flush bite with water and apply a dry dressing; keep victim quiet and see a doctor as soon as possible. See also "Animal Bites."

Scrapes

Sponge scrapes with soap and water; dry. Apply antibiotic ointment or powder and cover with a nonstick dressing (or tape on a piece of cellophane). When healing starts, stop ointment and use antiseptic powder to help scab form. Ask a doctor about tetanus.

Shock

Shock can result from any kind of injury. Get immediate medical help. Symptoms may be pallor, a clammy feeling to the skin, shallow breathing, a fast pulse, weakness, or thirst. Loosen clothing, cover the victim with a blanket but do not apply other heat, and lay the person on the back with feet raised. If necessary, start CPR. Do not give water or other fluids.

Snakebites

If the snake is not poisonous, tooth marks usually appear in an even row. (The bite of a poisonous lizard, the Gila monster, shows even tooth marks.) Wash the bite with soap and water and apply a sterile bandage. See a doctor. If the snake is poisonous, puncture marks (1–6) can usually be seen. Kill the snake for identification if possible, taking care not to be bitten. Keep the victim quiet, and immobilize the bitten arm or leg, keeping it on a lower level than the heart. If possible, phone ahead to be sure antivenin is available and get medical treatment as soon as possible. Do not give alcohol in any form. If treatment must be delayed and a snakebite kit is available, use as directed.

Spider Bites

The black widow bite may produce only a light reaction at the place of the bite, but severe pain, a general sick feeling, sweating, abdominal cramps, and breathing and speaking difficulty may develop. The more dangerous brown recluse spider's venom produces a severe reaction at the bite, generally in 2–8 hours, plus chills, fever, joint pain, nausea, and vomiting. Apply a cold compress to the bite in either case. Get medical aid quickly.

Sprain

Treat a sprain as a fracture until the injured part has been X-rayed. Raise the sprained ankle or other joint and apply cold compresses or immerse in cold water. If swelling is pronounced, try not to use the injured part till it has been X-rayed. Get prompt medical help.

Sunburn

For skin that is moderately red and slightly swollen, apply wet dressings of gauze dipped in a solution of one tablespoon baking soda and one tablespoon cornstarch to two quarts of cool water. Or take a cool bath with a cup of baking soda to a tub of water. Sunburn remedies are helpful in relieving pain. See a doctor if the burn is severe.

Sunstroke

This is a severe emergency. See "Heat Stroke." Skin is hot and dry; body temperature is high. The victim may be delirious or unconscious. Get medical help immediately.

(continued on next page)

SIMPLE FIRST-AID GUIDE
(continued)

Ticks

Remove ticks attached to your skin immediately with tweezers by grasping the tick's head parts as close to your skin as possible and applying slow steady traction. Do not attempt to get ticks out of your skin by burning them or coating them with anything like nail polish remover or petroleum jelly. To avoid infection, take care to remove the whole tick. Wash area with soap and water. Check with a doctor or the health department to see if deadly ticks are in the area. If you remove a tick before it has been attached for more than 24 hours, you greatly reduce your risk of infection.

Wasp Stings

See "Bee Stings."

---

direction, and remember—you're in their country. Don't give out your hotel or room number freely or where they can be overheard by strangers.

Drugs on the Street

Don't be surprised if someone tries to sell you an illegal substance on the street; if you buy, don't be surprised if the same guy turns you in to the local authorities and earns a payoff. The police come down heavily on substance users in Belize. Despite the efforts of the local government, as well as U.S. and British governments, drug activity hasn't stopped. There are certain areas where it's worse than ever: Belize City and Orange Walk Town among the worst. This little country has lots of isolated countryside to grow marijuana, and there are those who do and sell it locally, or ship it to the States. On top of that, there is cocaine traffic through the country. Everyone should be aware of what's going on,

WOMEN TRAVELERS

For the independent woman, Belize is a great place for group or solo travel. Its size makes it easy to get around, English is spoken everywhere, and if you so desire, you won't be lacking for a temporary travel partner in any part of the country. You'll meet many fellow travelers at the small inexpensive inns and guest houses. Belizeans are used to seeing all combinations of travelers; solo women are no exception. It is not unusual for men (mostly Belizeans) to come up and ask what you are doing and if you're traveling alone. Never indicate the name of your hotel or your room number. Any woman who feels threatened at this point can lie—after all, you really could be meeting a partner or even a mother on the next corner, or next town. Admitting to being alone often brings invitations—legal and not so legal—and of course discretion is needed. (Remember, there is little loyalty among thieves or ganja salesmen.) Speaking of thieves, use common sense and a money belt for valuables. Always be aware of the people around you.

Cat calls from the locals are common, and as both-ersome as it may seem, the best way to handle this is to smile a brief hello and keep on walking. Ignoring them seems to increase the volume and intensity.

When away from the beach towns and cayes, notice what the local women are wearing and dress accordingly. Pants, skirts, or even long shorts will lessen the gawking that short shorts and small tank tops attract. Most of the small towns and villages are safe even at night, with the exception of Belize City—don't walk anywhere there at night even with friends; even during the day there are some neighborhoods you want to avoid.

Feminine supplies are found everywhere with the exception of the smallest outlying villages and some of the remote lodges. For extended stays, consider bringing vitamin supplements since menu-fare doesn't include many fresh fruits and vegetables once out of the main tourist areas. If you worry about your safety on the road, a small can of mace is a good tool for protection; however, the best tool to bring is common sense and an open mind. Most of the people you meet will be just great. Enjoy!

and don't take any unnecessary risks. All of this advice is valid in Paris, downtown Los Angeles, Jakarta, and many other large cities throughout the world.

Traveler Safety Tips

The Belize Tourist Board has issued the following list of common-sense safety tips to help visitors.

It's always prudent to get the lay of the land upon arrival. Once you strike out, be reasonably sure of your destination and have a clear idea of how to get there before departing.

Always be aware of your surroundings and keep to the main streets if you have to walk. Avoid walking alone in unknown neighborhoods.

It's best not to wear expensive jewelry when traveling. And, don't carry large amounts of money, your passport, or your plane tickets if not necessary; if you must carry these things, wear a moneybelt under your clothes. Most hotels have safety deposit boxes.

At night, take a taxi between locations. Throughout Belize, taxis can be identified by their green license plates.

In Belize City, taxi prices are set. Ask your bellman, receptionist, bus driver, or other service personnel for directions and taxi prices before proceeding to your next destination.

When driving alone at night in isolated areas (which isn't too smart), use good sense, lock your doors, and keep windows up. Always keep your valuables locked in the trunk or glove compartment. And picking up strangers isn't guaranteed anywhere; only you can decide that one. (We pick up plenty of hitchhikers in Latin America, but we are selective when we make that instant decision—usually backpackers with heavy packs get our sympathy). We try to stay off the road at night.

Crime

Most of the crime besides drugs in Belize is petty theft and burglary. In the rare event that a stranger approaches you and demands your valuable items, remember that "things" can be replaced!

On any public transport, keep your belongings close by.

In emergencies, yes, you can dial 911 for police assistance; fire 90; ambulance 90.

Keep your eyes open and be aware of people close by.

Do *not* bring firearms into the country.

Penalties for crimes against you will bring high fines and mandatory jail sentences in most cases.

GETTING THERE

You *must* have a current passport that will be good for six months beyond your planned departure date from Belize. You may be asked at the border to show a return ticket or ample money. You do not need a visa if you are a British Commonwealth subject or a citizen of Belgium, Denmark, Finland, Greece, Iceland, Italy, Liechtenstein, Luxembourg, Mexico, Spain, Switzerland, Tunisia, Turkey, the United States, or Uruguay, provided you have valid documents. Remember to save US$15 for **departure tax** when going home. Note: If flying with your cell phone, **please, please** make sure the phone is turned off when taking off (as requested by attendants), whether it is in your purse or your carry-on luggage, or your checked cases. It really *does* cause problems, like telling the pilot there's a fire on the plane, precipitating a forced landing wherever possible!

BY AIR

Belize is a small country that, without a national airline, is dependent on foreign airlines to bring visitors from the United States, Mexico, and the rest of Central America. However, this may change given the history of the commuter airlines within the country and how they have grown. To Belizeans, flying in and out of Belize was a far-fetched idea when American hero **Charles Lindbergh** paid a dramatic visit to the small Caribbean nation. At the time, 1927, Lindbergh was the world's most famous pilot, having completed his flight across the Atlantic nonstop from New York to Paris. It was shortly after his famous "Lindy Hop" that he paid a visit to Latin America in his ongoing effort to promote and develop commercial aviation. On his visit to Belize, the **Barracks Green** in Belize City served as his runway, and the sound of his well-known little craft, *The Spirit of St. Louis,* overhead attracted hundreds of curious spectators. This was an exciting event for Belizeans, the beginning of an idea that would develop into the important aviation industry that has since linked the isolated parts of Belize.

Philip Goldson International Airport

Most travelers planning a visit to Belize arrive at Philip Goldson International Airport nine miles from Belize City in Ladyville. In the airport several vendors sell Belizean and Central American arts and crafts; there's also a currency exchange. Check the observation deck upstairs and the bar/restaurant that serves decent versions of local food. Taxi fare to and from the international airport is about US$15 and rising. Transport to Belize is getting easier every year.

Board direct flights from **Louisiana, Texas, Florida, Cancún,** and several points in **Latin America** daily. Airlines serving Belize include **American, Continental,** and **TACA International.** Only charter flights serve visitors from Canada, and there are no nonstop flights from Europe.

After clearing customs you'll be besieged by taxi drivers offering rides into town. If you are not being picked up by a resort or tour company and you choose to rent a car, cross the parking lot where you'll find several rental car firms.

Belize City Municipal Airport

If you are connecting to a domestic flight or a flight to Tikal in Guatemala, check at the information desk. Some domestic flights to other parts of the country leave from the Belize City Municipal Airport, a 15-minute cab ride away, and are generally cheaper (see "Getting Around," below).

FROM MEXICO

Traveling to Belize via Mexico's state of Quintana Roo on the Yucatán Peninsula can be a cheaper way to get there. Or combining a vacation in both countries is also economical and a way to see a little more than usual. Shop around for budget flights from the United States into Cancún or even Isla de Cozumel (just a short ferry ride to Playa del Carmen and its efficient bus depot, then continue by bus). From Cancún it's immensely cheap and easy to travel the 218 miles by bus to Chetumal and then across the Rio Hondo.

Also from Cancún there is a direct flight to Belize City on Aerocaribe Airlines on Tuesday, Thursday, Saturday, and Sunday; cost is about US$415 round-trip, call Mexicana Airline, 800/237-6639. (This schedule often changes; I've also heard that if there are not enough passengers the flight is canceled.) Check with your travel agent. From Belize City it's easy to rent a car or catch that bus or boat.

The Rio Hondo forms a natural border between Quintana Roo and Belize. Chetumal is the only land link between the two countries and a departure point for Batty and Venus bus lines traveling to many points in Belize.

Henry Menzies Travel and Tours, P.O. Box 210, Corozal Town, Corozal District, Belize, C.A., tel. 4/22725 or 4/23414, runs a taxi service and has the run between Chetumal and Corozal down to a science. Henry guides first-timers across the border with great ease. Call a day or two in advance (if in

PATTI LANGE

AIRLINES SERVING BELIZE

INTERNATIONAL AIRLINES

American Airlines: U.S. 800/624-6262, Canada 800/433-7300; from Dallas, Ft. Worth, Miami

Continental Airlines: U.S. 800/231-0856, Canada 800/525-0280; nonstop from Houston

TACA Airlines: U.S. 800/535-8780, Canada 800/263-4039; from Houston, New Orleans, Miami, Los Angeles, New York Kennedy, and Washington Dulles

NATIONAL AIRLINES

Cari-Bee Air Service: tel. 2/44253; charters, domestic, international, ambulance

Maya Island Air: U.S. 888/755-3819 or 713/440-1867, Belize tel. 2/44234, fax 2/30031; municipal, international, San Pedro, Corozal, Caye Caulker, Dangriga, Big Creek, Punta Gorda, charters, ambulance

Tropic Air: U.S. 800/422-3435, Belize tel. 26/2012 or 2/45671, fax 26/2338; municipal, international, San Pedro, charters, daily flights to Tikal

---

Mexico). If possible don't wait to call from Chetumal; for some reason telephoning from there can be very difficult at times. And the problem is not the phone service in Belize, which is modern. The trip between Chetumal and Corozal takes about 20 minutes, including the border crossing. (No matter what your travel mode, don't go at peak times such as 8 A.M. or 5 P.M.—opening and closing hours—without expecting a long wait.) Menzies will take you any place you'd like to go in Belize. Make fare arrangements before you climb in the cab. Henry is a good, helpful driver and an excellent guide with a comfortable air-conditioned van.

BY CAR

If your own vehicle is a low-slung sports car, leave it home. Off the three main highways, roads are rough and potholed. When it rains, you'll heave through thick mud where tires cut deep ridges. The hot tropical sun appears and dries it into "cement" mounds. The higher the car the better; 4WD is best. If traveling by car you'll need Belizean insurance bought on the Belize side of the border with Belizean dollars (a couple of insurance offices are close to the border and in Corozal).

Note for the RV buff or hardy driver: The route between Brownsville, Texas, and the border of Belize is just under 1,400 miles. If you don't stop to smell the flowers along the way, you can make the drive in a few days. The all-weather roads are paved, and the shortest route is through Mexico by way of Tampico, Veracruz, Villahermosa, Escarcega, and Chetumal.

However, the Mexican government has recently changed its rules for travelers who are passing through Mexico to another country. Call a Mexico Government Tourism Office near you for more precise information; these rules change regularly.

BY BOAT

Daily boats from Punta Gorda (P.G.) make it easy to get to Puerto Barrios, Guatemala. Both leave P.G. around 8:30 A.M. The return fom Puerto Barrios leaves around 2 P.M. Call Paco's boat service, tel. 7/22246, or Requenas charter service, tel. 7/22070. Ask around at the Punta Gorda dock.

GETTING AROUND

BY AIR

By far the fastest and easiest way to move around Belize is by plane. The two "major" airlines are **Tropic Air** and **Maya Island Air.** Both are based at San Pedro on Ambergris Caye. Flying on either of these is always a great adventure. If you are leaving from the municipal airport, the runway looks about as long as two or three football fields. With the steady sea breeze, however, getting airborne is a cinch. Other airstrips look more like strips of mown grass or a short abandoned roadway, but they work just fine. Because these are such small planes, you not only watch the pilot handle the craft, you may also get to sit next to him. Coming in for a landing, you have an excellent vantage point from which to observe the runway looming large on approach. Best of all, flying low and slow in these aircraft allows you to get a panoramic view of the barrier reef, cayes, coast, and jungle.

Recently the FAA disclosed that the safety oversight by the Belize government and several other countries do not meet agency standards for airlines flying into the United States. The United States was describing freight planes. This has caused some understandable confusion and concern among travelers to Belize. For one thing, there are no Belizean passenger airlines flying to the States. Belizean commuter airlines all have an outstanding record of safety.

A parade of regular scheduled flights leave the municipal and international airports for airstrips offshore at Ambergris Caye, Caye Caulker, and Caye Chapel. If the scheduled flight happens to be full, another will taxi up shortly and off you go. Flight times to the cayes are 15 minutes or less. Other less-frequent flights fly the coast to Big Creek, Corozal, Dangriga, Placencia, and Punta Gorda. Corozal takes about 45 minutes with a stop at Ambergris Caye. Punta Gorda will take about an hour with a stop or two along the way. Chartered flights can be arranged at any time and to less frequented stops: Lighthouse Reef Resort on Northern Caye, Belmopan and Central Farms near San Ignacio, Blancaneaux Lodge airport in the Mountain Pine Ridge, and Gallon Jug airport near Chan Chich. Ask your travel agent for schedules or request them directly: **Tropic Air,** from the States, 800/422-3435, fax 713/521-9674, calling from Belize, 26/2012, email tropicair @btl.net. For **Maya Island Air,** call 2/44234.

BY BUS

Probably the cheapest way to get around the country is by bus, which, in most cases, is surprisingly good. Most buses offer regular schedules and run frequently; for longer trips it's best to reserve your seat the day before you wish to travel. Expect lively music in fairly modern vehicles where all the passengers have seats— some even show movies on longer trips. In most cases, standing is not allowed and the driver will pack passengers three to a seat if necessary. The exceptions are the afternoon buses to Punta Gorda.

Travel time from Belize City to Corozal or San Ignacio is about two hours, to Dangriga about four hours, and to Punta Gorda eight to 10 hours (this can be a bumpy ride). Fares average about US$2–4 to most destinations, about US$7–12 for the longer routes. Remember that these are not luxury buses; however, they are the cheapest way to travel. And for anyone who wants to meet the Belizean people, this is the way to go. Most of these buses make frequent stops and will pick up anyone on the side of the road anywhere—as long as space permits. The drivers will also drop you off wherever you wish if you holler when you want off.

To Mexico and Guatemala
Note: Batty bus lines was recently sold to **Novelo's Bus Co.;** at this moment we do not know if the names have been changed or not. However, if you have a problem and need to talk to someone in charge, call Novelo's at 2/71160. **Novelo's** and **Venus** lines serve Belize and go into Mexico and Guatemala. Get information

from tel. 2/71160. Get Venus bus line information on Magazine Road in Belize City, tel. 2/73354 or 77390, or on 7th Ave. in Corozal, tel. 4/22132. Both companies offer upscale charter tours as well.

To Crooked Tree
Dawson Buses leave Cinderella Plaza for Crooked Tree. **Jex Buses** pick up passengers in Belize City and go to Crooked Tree.

To Dangriga and Punta Gorda
Urbina buses travel from Belize City to Orange Walk, departing from Cinderella Plaza. Catch the **Z-Line** to go south to Dangriga and Punta Gorda, departing from the terminal on Magazine Road, tel. 2/73937.

James' Bus service travels to the southern part of the country, leaving Belize City from the Pound Yard Bridge.

To Cayo
Novelo buses travel to Belmopan, the Cayo District, and on to the Guatemalan border from the depot on W. Collet Canal, tel. 2/77372. **Carmen** buses also travel to the Cayo District, leaving from the Pound Yard Bridge.

BY RENTAL CAR

A rental car offers the independent traveler more freedom to experience Belize on a very personal level and at the driver's own pace, the itinerary changing with the urge or necessity. It also presents some challenges, not the least of which is to the pocketbook. Car rentals are expensive in Belize, but the pool of available cars is growing.

Rental companies offer small, midsize, and large 4WD vehicles. Vans and passenger cars are also available, some with air conditioning—they cost more, though prices have come down somewhat from a few years ago. Insurance is mandatory. Driving rules are U.S.-style, and it's wise to obtain an international driver's license before you leave home (about US$10 at most auto clubs). Gasoline also is quite costly, about US$3 a gallon. Tour guides, package trips, and drivers are available—pricey (though maybe not compared with the cost of a car and

gas)—but they offer some of the best ways to see the country.

Renting a car in Belize is usually a simple matter but is always subject to Murphy's Law. High deposits can be put on credit cards. If you know exactly when you want the car and where, it's helpful to make reservations.

Getting the Car
Check out the car *carefully* before you take it far. Drive it around the block and go over the following:

- Make sure there's a spare tire and working jack.
- Make sure all doors lock.
- Make sure the seats move forward, have no sprung backs, etc.
- All windows should lock, unlock, roll up and down properly.
- Trunk should lock and unlock.
- Check for proper legal papers for the car, with addresses and phone numbers of associate car rental agencies in towns you plan to visit in case of an unexpected car problem.
- Make sure horn, emergency brake, and foot brakes work properly.
- Make sure clutch, gearshift, and all gears work properly (don't forget reverse).
- Get directions to the nearest gas station; the gas tank may be empty. If it's full, it's wise to return it full, as you'll be charged top dollar per gallon of gas.
- Ask to have any damage, even a small dent, missing door knob, etc., noted on your contract, if it hasn't been already.
- Note the hour you pick up the car and try to return it before that time: a few minutes over could get you another full-day's rental fee.

CAR RENTALS

Avis: Radisson Fort George Hotel, tel. 2/31987, fax 2/30225
Crystal: Belize City, tel. 2/31600, fax 2/31900
National: Belize City, tel. 2/31586 or 2/52294
Budget: 771 Bella Vista, P.O. Box 863, Belize City, Belize, C.A. (ask for Alan Auil), tel. 2/32435 or 33986, fax 2/30237, email jmagroup@btl.net

ROAD DISTANCES FROM BELIZE CITY TO:

Belmopan:. . . . . 55 miles
Benque Viejo:. . . . . 81 miles
Corozal Town: . . . . 96 miles
Dangriga: . . . . 105 miles
Orange Walk Town:. . . . . 58 miles
Punta Gorda: . . . . 210 miles
San Ignacio: . . . . 72 miles

Vehicle Condition

If you plan to motor along the Northern Highway to Crooked Tree, Orange Walk, or Corozal, you can drive the older, cheaper cars some rental companies specialize in. However, if you want to drive the rougher stretches of the Hummingbird Highway, Manatee Road, or Southern Highway you'll need a 4WD vehicle in good shape. In less-traveled areas at night or on narrow, rutted jungle trails, the condition of the vehicle becomes critical. Once you've driven the teeth-rattling roads to Chiquibil Forest, Cockscomb Basin Wildlife Sanctuary, Chan Chich, or Lamanai Outpost Lodge, you'll understand. The local Suzuki dealership in Belize City runs the Budget Rent a Car franchise. Several recent rental experiences have indicated the cars are fairly new and well maintained.

Insurance

Mandatory car insurance from rental car agencies runs US$10–15 per day and covers only 80 percent of damages. In most cases in Belize, when an accident occurs the police take action first and ask questions later. With an insurance policy, most of the problems are eased over. Rental agencies also offer medical insurance for US$4–6 per day. Your private medical insurance should cover this, but check.

Payoff Time

When you pick up your rental car, the company makes an imprint of your credit card on a blank bill, one copy of which is attached to the papers you give the agent when you return the car. Keep in mind that the car agency limits how much you can charge on one credit card at one time (ask the maximum when you pick up the car). If you go over the limit be prepared to pay the balance in cash or with another credit card. Most travelers don't stay that long in the country, but it happened to us after staying several months in a foreign country.

BY CRUISE SHIP

For those who like traveling aboard ship, several cruise lines offer an opportunity to experience the romance of the sea along with stops at interesting cayes, ports of call, and even inland tours. Note that these ships can accommodate both active and relaxed lifestyles. And remember, airfare and port taxes are usually extra.

Niagara Prince offers a choice of two 12-day cruises from Belize City. Stops include Ambergris Caye, numerous smaller cayes, and Punta Gorda. Both cruises call on Livingston, Guatemala, and journey up the Rio Dulce to beautiful Lake Izabal. The ship boasts a stern swim-and-snorkel deck as well as a retractable boarding ramp built into the bow. A 21-foot glass-bottom boat is available for viewing reef life. Active senior travelers will find lots of company and camaraderie here. It accommodates 78 passengers. Rates are about US$1,490-2,525 per person double occupancy. Contact American Canadian Caribbean Line, Inc., 800/556-7450.

Other ships that make stops at Belize are *Norwegian Wind, Windstar, Enchanted Isle, Big Red Boat 2, Seabourn Legend, Bremen, Carnival Spirit,* and *Carnival Pride.* If you want more details about dates ships travel to and stop in Belize, contact Stanley Longsworth, Caribbean Shipping Agencies, Ltd, Box 352, Belize City, Belize, C.A., tel. 2/77396, email stanlong @btl.net.

TOURS ORGANIZED IN THE UNITED STATES

TOURING WITH EXPERTS

Have you finally decided to do it? Is this the first time you've ever left the border of your own country? Are you having heart palpitations because you don't know where to start to plan this once-in-a-lifetime trip? You can stop worrying now. The first time out is a good time to read this book thoroughly, and then if you still have doubts, book a tour with an experienced group. I know, I know—you don't want to be a bus-window looky-loo! You won't be. Today's tour travelers have a world of possibilities. You can get as involved as you want in any way you wish—all with the help and encouragement of an experienced escort. The tours will include real involvement, which can be snorkeling, diving, or climbing the tall Maya ruins (there's really no way possible to see the Belizean Maya sites from a bus window). OK, on the other hand you don't want to commit to a lot of hiking—just leave it to the expert escort. Plenty of magical places are just right for *you.* The escort can be a scuba diver, an archaeologist, a naturalist, or a zoologist. Plan your own trip with the help of one of these experienced operators.

Tours

One reason people choose a tour over independent travel is the luxury of having someone else handle all the details, especially the first time out—someone who knows about passports, visas, reservations, airline schedules, time changes, the best food, the safest water, and the most comfortable beds, plus the experience to be able to show you the best of what you wish to see.

Trip Choice

If you've chosen to visit Belize, you must be someone who's interested in jungles, diving, the Caribbean, nature, wild animals, flowers, trees, history of the West Indies, the Maya, archaeology, exotic cultures, or—just Belize. Following are descriptions of some of the adventures available and a few itineraries. If any of them sound good, remember, this is just the tip of the you-know-what. In most cases telephone numbers are toll free; call them and you'll have a live human to answer all the questions you've *ever* had about Belize—and a few of its neighboring countries. The following operators have been chosen on the basis of their knowledge; all of them have a sincere feeling for the country, maybe even a love affair. All have been dealing with Belize for some time, and as in the case of **Sea & Explore,** they are transplanted Belizeans who maintain close ties. If you need more tour operators to choose from, call **Belize Tourist Board** at 800/624-0686 and ask for the *Belize Sales Planner.*

TOUR OPERATORS

International Expeditions, Inc.

One of the finest tour companies in the United States with an intimate knowledge of Belize, International Expeditions, Inc. offers planned itineraries to suit all tastes. If you are one or a dozen people interested in something out of the ordinary, call and the staff will work with you in every way possible.

Naturalist guides have been trained in their fields, and most of them are either native Belizeans or have lived in Belize for some time and know their way around the country. Expeditions run 7–14 days with two- and three-day add-ons available. Among the itineraries offered is **Naturalist Quest,** an 10-day overview of the natural wonders of Belize, including an in-depth look at the unique fauna, the rainforest, or a concentrated study of the island and reef ecology. This program is available in many combinations that include snorkeling and scuba diving. The **Maya Heartland** expedition, escorted by an informed archaeologist, focuses on the ruins of the once-great ceremonial centers built by the sophisticated ancient Maya.

One of the newest programs, **Pharmacy from the Rainforest,** has been held in the Amazon as well, and is a very popular trip. However, you don't have to be a doctor or medical person to appreciate this; people with an interest in the treasure trove of medicines that continue to come from the jungles and rainforests of the tropics are entranced. Also during the trip, field expeditions will include the Maya Medicine Trail and a reception to meet Rosita Arvigo, noted traditional healer trained by bush doctor Eligio Panti. Travelers will have an opportunity to take part in an *ethnobotanical field collection,* part of ongoing research into plant-based cancer drugs. Those interested will have a look at **Succotz Village Centre for Mayan Culture, Preservation & Women's Development, The Midwifery Centre, Smithsonian Marine Biology Institute** on Carrie Bow Caye, and lots more. Workshop leaders are prominent working scientists in their fields. Side trips include Tikal, Xunantunich, Belize Zoo, and a visit to the Barrier Reef, a Garifuna village, and Cockscomb Basin.

Special expeditions are planned with a variety of themes, one taking in the **Garifuna Settlement Day** celebration (see the special topic "Garifuna Settlement Day" in the Stann Creek District chapter). Shorter excursions (three and four days) are planned for **Tikal** (see the Across Belize's Borders chapter), **Mountain Pine Ridge** (see the Cayo District chapter), the fabulous archaeological site of **Caracol** (see the Mundo Maya chapter), and the **Cockscomb Basin Wildlife Sanctuary** (see the Stann Creek District chapter). Hotels and restaurants are well chosen for comfort and adaptation to the area. For more information and prices contact International Expeditions, One Environs Park, Helena, AL 35080, 800/633-4734 or 205/428-1700, fax 205/428-1714.

Toucan Travel
This company is run by Dulce, a transplanted Belizean living in Louisiana. She relays her intimate knowledge of the country to tourists and specializes in Placencia. For more information, contact 32 Traminer Dr., Kenner, LA 70065, 800/747-1381, fax 504/464-0325.

Great Trips
Specializing in **Great Trips to Belize,** this company provides customized travel packages to ex-perienced travelers, sportspeople, and adventurers. For more information, contact Edgar at 119 4th St. SE, Montgomery, MN 56069, 800/552-3419 or 507/364-7713, fax 507/364-7569.

Sea & Explore
Owners Sue and Tony Castillo, native Belizeans, take pleasure and pride in sharing their country with visitors. They know every out-of-the-way destination, and go out of their way to match clients with the right areas of the country to suit their interests. Susan worked with the Belize Ministry of Tourism before coming to the United States. Whether you wish to see the cayes or the Maya sites, contact Sea & Explore, 1809 Carol Sue Ave., Suite E, Gretna, LA 70056, 800/345-9786 or 504/366-9985, fax 504/366-9986, email seaexplore-belize@worldnet.att.net.

Slickrock Adventures, Inc.
Slickrock Adventures, Inc., offers a nine-day kayak adventure based on a private island at Glover's Reef. This includes charter flights from Belize City, sailboat transfers to the reef, all guides (one American, one Belizean), hotel accommodations upon arrival and departure, all meals (daily fresh seafood), all kayak and camping equipment (bring your own sleeping gear), rustic cabins on Glover's Reef, and overnight trips to neighboring cayes by kayak. Experience is recommended but not required; weather can sometimes make for strenuous days. Although the trips are made during the dry season, tropical squalls can come along at any time, delaying the ongoing passage. Conditioning before the excursion is encouraged; kayakers can expect to paddle no more than nine miles per day, usually only three or four. Call or write for prices and more information: P.O. Box 1400, Moab, UT 84532, tel. 800/390-5715, slickrock@slickrock.com.

Far Horizons Cultural Discovery Trips
Mary Dell Lucas is known throughout the Maya world for her excellent archaeological knowledge and insight. Her company provides trips into the most fascinating Maya sites, regardless of location. Although Mary Dell Lucas is an archaeologist herself, she often brings specialists along with her groups. You can be assured that the trips with Far Horizons all have

an archaeological or cultural emphasis. For more information, call 800/552-4575, fax 505- 343-8076, or email journey@farhorizon.com, website: www.farhorizon.com.

INFORMATION

TOURIST INFORMATION

At the **Belize Tourist Board,** Central Bank Bldg, level 2, Gabourel Lane, Belize City, Belize, C.A., tel. 2/31913, fax 2/31943, email btbb@btl.net, you'll find brochures on a number of reserves and national parks and information on various sections of the country. You'll usually find someone who's willing to talk to you and answer your questions. Or in the United States, call Belize Tourist Office, 800/624-0686.

Belize Tourism Industry Associates, P.O. Box 62, Belize City, Belize, C.A., tel. 2/75717, fax 2/78710. These folks are also a source of good information about the country.

The **Embassy of Belize,** 2535 Massachusetts Dr. NW, Washington, DC 20008, 202/332-9636, fax 202/332-6741, and the **Caribbean Tourism Association,** 20 E. 46th St., New York, NY 10017, 800/624-0686 or 212/563-6011 are both good sources of information.

USING THE TELEPHONE IN BELIZE

All but two cities have one digit area codes, or city codes as they are sometimes known, Ambergris Caye (26) and Caye Caulker (22). If you dial from within the country to any city, please add a zero before the area code, (e.g. Ambergris Caye: 026). If calling from the United States or other country, you do not need to dial the zero before the area code (but you *will* need to dial the international access code—011—plus the country code for Belize—501—and finally, the area code and phone number). Some cities have just four digits in the body of the number, such as Ambergris Caye, where a phone number might be 26/0000; others have five digits, such as Belize City, which might be 2/00000. The lack of uniformity is due to a growing system, and as more telephones are added to the country, the numbering systems seem to change. Perhaps in the future things will be uniform; until then, here are a few area codes:

Belize District	2
Ambergris Caye	26
Caye Caulker	22
Corozal	4
Orange Walk	3
Cayo	8
San Ignacio	9
Dangriga	5
Placencia	6
Punta Gorda	7

Belize Online

Belize is dynamite online. Travelers cruising the Internet before a visit to Belize will discover a great variety of information on websites where you can get a good look at the country in vivid color and great design. Check out the website called **Belize Online, Tourist and Investment Guide,** which is endorsed by the Belize Tourism Industry Association and the Belize Tourist Board. For more information, contact the site at www.belize.com.

MONEY

The currency unit is the Belize dollar (BZE$), which has been steady at BZE$2 to US$1 for some years. While prices are given in US$ in this book, travelers should be prepared to pay in Belizean currency on the street, aboard boats, in cafés, and at other smaller establishments; however, carry both just in case. Of course, the larger hotels accept U.S. dollars. When you buy or sell currency at a bank, be sure to retain proof of sale. The following places are authorized to buy or sell foreign currency: Atlantic Bank Ltd., Bank of Nova Scotia, Barclays Bank, Belize Bank of Commerce and Industry, and Belize Global Travel Services Ltd. All are closed together near the plaza in Belize City and in other cities. Hours are Mon.–Fri. till 1 P.M., Saturday till 11 A.M.

At the Mexico-Belize border you'll be approached by money changers (and you can bet they don't represent the banks). Many travelers buy just enough Belize dollars to get them into the city and to the banks. Depending on your mode of transport and destination, these money changers can be helpful. Strictly speaking, though, this is illegal—so suit yourself. The exchange rate is the same, but you'll have no receipt of sale. If selling a large quantity of Belize dollars back to the bank, you might be asked for that proof.

Airport departure tax is US$15 (including security tax) when leaving the country, except for in-transit passengers spending fewer than 24 hours in the country. When entering the country and flying to any other in-country destination, a US$.75 charge is required to clear security.

Credit Cards and Traveler's Checks

Credit cards are taken only at the larger business establishments, so bring traveler's checks and cash as well. You will find representatives of Visa, MasterCard, and American Express at the four commercial banks in Belize City; there you can make cash advances against your card. Only account holders at the bank are authorized to use the ATM machines in Belize.

Tipping

Most restaurants and hotels include the tip on the check; if the tip isn't added to the bill, then 10–15 percent is the norm. It is not customary to tip taxi drivers unless they help you with your luggage.

NUTS AND BOLTS INFO TO KNOW BEFORE YOU GO

The electricity is 110/220 volt, 60 cycles. Removal of archaeological artifacts will get you thrown in jail. Religious services available are Protestant, Roman Catholic, and Anglican; ask for church locations at your hotel. While the water is said to be good from the tap in Belize City, experienced travelers still drink only bottled water. If you're looking for a water substitute, Coke signs are everywhere, and rum and Belikin beer are plentiful (both are made in Belize). Some travelers take advantage of the privilege and bring in one bottle of their own favorite liquor. The local time is Greenwich mean time minus six, the same as U.S. central time, year-round (no daylight savings time). Shops are generally open daily 8 A.M.–noon and 1–4 P.M., closed Sunday and public holidays. You can obtain visas for ongoing travel to Guatemala at the Guatemalan Embassy. When writing letters to Belize, abbreviate Central America as C.A. Be sure to include the periods; otherwise the U.S. Post Office will send your letters to California.

WHAT TO TAKE

Whatever time of year you travel to Belize, you can expect warm to hot weather. Most airlines allow you to check two suitcases, and you can bring another carry-on bag that fits either under your seat or in the overhead rack; this is fine if you're planning a one-destination trip to a self-contained resort and want a couple of changes of clothes each day. But if you plan on moving around a lot, you'll be happy if you keep it light— one bag and one carry-on.

Experienced women travelers pack small foldable purses into their carry-ons, leaving them with only one thing to carry while en route. And be sure to include a few overnight necessities in your carry-on in case your luggage doesn't arrive when you do. Valuables are safest in your carry-on stowed under the seat in front of you rather than in the overhead rack, whether you're on a plane, boat, or bus.

Safeguards

It's smart to keep passports, traveler's checks, money, and important papers in a hotel safe or on your person at all times. (It's always a good idea to keep one separate list of document numbers in your luggage and leave another copy with a friend back home. This expedites replacement in case of loss.) The do-it-yourselfer can sew inside pockets into clothes; buy extra-long pants, turn up the hem, and sew three-fourths of the way around, closing the last section with a piece of Velcro. Separate shoulder-holster pockets, money belts, and pockets around the neck inside clothing—all made of cotton—are available commercially. If you're going to be backpacking and sloshing in jungle streams, etc., put everything in zipper-lock plastic bags before placing them in pockets. Waterproof plastic tubes are available that will hold a limited number of items around your neck while swimming.

Clothing

A swimsuit is a must, and if you're not staying at one of the larger hotels, bring a beach towel. In today's Belize, you'll see a wide variety of clothing. Unless you want to attract a lot of attention, do not wear bikinis, short shorts, or revealing tight clothes while strolling the streets of Belize City. Save that for the beach areas or the pool at your hotel. If traveling November–January, bring along a light wrap since it can cool off in the evening. The rest of the year you'll probably carry the wrap in your suitcase. For women, a wraparound skirt is a useful item that can quickly cover up shorts when traveling through the villages and some cities (many small-village residents really gawk at women wearing shorts; whatever you do, don't enter a church wearing them). The wraparound skirt also makes a good shawl when it cools off. Cotton underwear is the coolest in the tropics, but nylon is less bulky and dries overnight, cutting down on the number needed. Be sure that you bring broken-in, comfortable walking shoes; blisters can wreck a vacation almost as much as a sunburn. For those planning long treks through the jungle, lightweight hiking boots give protection from scratching brush, flying biting insects that hover near the ground, and, yes, snakes.

Necessities

If you wear glasses and are planning an extended trip, it's a good idea to bring an extra pair or carry the lens prescription; the same goes for medication (make sure the prescription is written in generic terms). Bring your favorite toiletries and cosmetics as the selection here is small. American cigarettes are available but are pricey. If you smoke a pipe, bring plenty of tobacco since it's almost impossible to find.

Reading Material

Avid readers from the United States and Canada are in luck in Belize. Because the official language is English, you'll seldom have a hard time finding English-language books; however, don't expect a huge selection of best-sellers. Both small and large hotels have book-trading shelves. If they aren't obvious, ask at the desk. Most travelers are delighted to trade books. Many travelers come prepared with an "itty bitty" Book Light for rooms where there's either no electricity or dim bulbs. For books on Belize, see the Book List at the back of the book.

Backpacking

If you plan to hitchhike or use public transportation, don't use a large external-frame pack; crowded buses have very little room and it won't fit in most small cars or public lockers. Smaller packs with zippered compartments that will accommodate minipadlocks are most practical. A strong bike cable and lock secures the pack to a YH (Youth Hostel) bed or a bus/train rack. None of the above will deter the real criminal but might make it difficult enough to discourage everyone else.

Experienced backpackers travel light with a pack, an additional canvas bag, a small water- and mosquito-proof tent, a hammock, and mosquito netting.

CAMERAS AND PICTURE TAKING

Bring a camera to Belize! Nature and people combine to provide unforgettable panoramas, well worth taking home with you on film to savor again at your leisure. Many people bring simple cameras such as instants that are easy to carry and uncomplicated. Others prefer 35mm cameras that offer higher-quality pictures, are easier than ever to use, and are available in a variety of price ranges. They can come equipped with built-in light meter, automatic exposure, self-focus, and self-advance—with little more to do than aim and click. Traveling for a week or 10 days makes it practical to bring your digital camera. But unless you have many many media chips, any longer than that (if you're a *frequent snapper*), it's best to carry the old-fashioned camera and film. Of course the pro who also carries the newest high-tech computer equipment to download digital cameras will already know what to do.

Film

Two reasons to bring film with you: it's cheaper and more readily available in the United States. Two reasons *not* to bring quantities of film: space may be a problem and heat can affect film quality, both before and after exposure. If you're traveling for more than two weeks in a car or bus a good part of the time, carry film in an insulated case. You can buy a soft-sided insulated bag in most camera shops or order one out of a professional photography magazine. For the average vacation, if your film is kept in your room there should be no problem. Many varieties of Kodak film are found in camera shops and hotel gift shops in Belize. In the smaller towns, you may not be able to find slide film.

X-Ray Protection

If you carry film with you when traveling by plane, remember to take precautions. Each time film is passed through the security X-ray machine, a little damage is done. It's cumulative, and perhaps one time won't make much difference, but most photographers won't take the chance. Request hand inspection. With today's tight security at airports, some guards insist on passing your film and camera through the X-ray machine. If packed in your checked luggage, it's wise to keep film in protective lead-lined bags, available at camera shops in two sizes: the larger size holds up to 22 rolls of 35mm film; the smaller holds eight rolls. If you use fast film, ASA 400 or higher, buy the double lead-lined bag designed to protect more sensitive film. Carry an extra lead-lined bag for your film-loaded camera if you want to drop it into a piece of carry-on luggage. (These bags also protect medications from X-ray damage.)

If you decide to request hand examination (rarely, if ever, refused at the Belize airport), make it simple for the security guards. Have the film out of boxes and in clear canisters placed together in one clear plastic bag that you can hand the guard for quick examination both coming and going. The guard will also want to look at the camera; load it with film *after* crossing the border if possible.

Film Processing

For processing film the traveler has several options. Most people take their film home and have it processed at a familiar lab. Again, if the trip is lengthy and you are shooting many photos, it's impractical to carry used rolls around for more than a couple of weeks. Larger cities have one-hour photo labs. Kodak film mailers are another option, but most photographers won't let their film out of sight until they reach their favorite lab.

Camera Protection

Take a few precautions with your camera while traveling. At the beach, remember that a combination of wind and sand can really gum up the works and scratch the lens. On 35mm cameras keep a clear skylight filter on the lens instead of a lens cap so the camera can hang around your neck or in a fanny pack, always at the ready for the spectacular shot that comes when least expected. If something is going to get scratched, better a $15 filter than a $300 lens. It also helps to carry as little equipment as possible. If you want more than candids and you carry a 35mm camera, basic equipment can be simple. Of course there is the real camera bug who carries all the lenses. Get in shape! Padded camera cases are good and come in all sizes. A canvas bag is lighter and less conspicuous than a heavy photo bag but doesn't have the extra protection the padding provides.

Safety Tips

Keep your camera dry; carrying a couple of big zipper-lock bags affords instant protection. Don't *store* cameras in plastic bags for any length of time because the moisture that builds up in the bag can damage a camera as much as leaving it in the rain.

It's always wise to keep cameras out of sight in a car or when camping out. Put your name and address on the camera. Chances are if it gets left behind or stolen it won't matter whether your name is there or not, and don't expect to see it again; however, miracles do happen. (You

BABY SAFARI

It was time to update this book and a trip to Belize was on the calendar. There was no way I was going to leave my six-month-old with someone back home for weeks and weeks. But I had my doubts. Would he be safe, healthy, comfortable? Would we?

I knew after an hour on the plane with my husband, Eric, and our beautiful blond-headed baby boy, Riley (our first child), that this was going to be a good trip. He ate, slept, and cooed at all of the right times to the delight of our fellow travelers—and us! As it turned out, traveling with Riley in Belize was one of the most enjoyable experiences of our lives.

Reading about others who had traveled with babies intimidated me. The problems I read about ranged from painful earaches on the plane (I nursed him while taking off and landing and he was fine) to *vacuum socks*. Yes, vacuum. The article predicted the pressure on a plane would tighten the socks on the baby's feet and would cause extreme pain! While I suspected that was nonsense, I still took off his socks, just in case. Of course there were the usual fears of food contamination and bad water. So the plan was to keep him from eating or drinking anything other than from the cache we brought with us from home.

The other fear concerned finding competent health care outside the United States. What if something happened? We found out that there are lots of doctors in Belize—thankfully we didn't have to use one. We did, however, buy medivac insurance (that is, insurance for medical evacuation, which usually is by plane) just in case something really serious occurred that would require medical care back in the States. (Ask your insurance agent for more details).

What to Bring
The diaper issue. We opted to play it safe and bring diapers with us—all 210 of them, and we didn't have enough!. We hadn't investigated the availability of disposable diapers in local stores ahead of time. We should have known that no matter how far out of the way we might travel, we'd find parents, even in remote parts of the world, who have also discovered and love disposable diapers. (Pity the poor landfills.) In addition to the diapers, here's what else we brought: antibiotics from the pediatrician, bottled water, car seat, portable crib, stroller, and our very large backpack carrier. Whew! We, the champion light travelers in our previous lives, looked as though we were moving into the country permanently!

What We Learned
I had traveled all over the world with my seven older siblings and my parents since I was six weeks old, so I was no novice traveler. In fact, I was considered by my big traveling family to be the "gypsy travel queen." And yet I went berserk with my own little darling on his first big trip.

Best Traveling Time Is While Breast-feeding
Before we left, I had only introduced cereal and fruits to Riley. He ate so little prepared food that it was a waste of energy packing and carrying jarred food. And this was a learning time for him—he learned to love all the fresh fruit—mangos, pineapples, bananas, and melons—that I ate everyday. How easy it was to just feed him off my plate (even though the books say to wait a year before introducing solid food).

(continued on next page)

Patti, Riley, and Eric

BABY SAFARI
(continued)

Breast-feeding was ideal. I was discreet (never got any curious stares), it was easy, and no mixing or buying formula, or water worries. But if you do bring formula, bottled water is readily available.

It's a lot easier to travel with an infant that hasn't begun walking yet, because he can't run away as easily. (I know, because now Riley walks and gets into everything!)

More about Food

Jarred baby food was available, but after reading labels we discovered it was full of sugar and other additives that we preferred not to use. Now that he's a year old, we make sure that whatever he eats (potatoes, carrots, apples, etc.) has been cooked in boiling water when traveling out of the country. Cooked eggs and fruits that can be peeled are also safe choices. We mash them and mix combinations to form soupy pulps.

"Lets go to the top, dad!"

PATTI LANGE

Sleeping

All over the country we muscled a portable crib. We learned immediately that the biggest problem was getting him to sleep in the unfamiliar bed. He didn't like that at all, and had the lungs to tell everyone. For our sake and that of neighboring guests in thin-walled bedrooms, we mostly kept the crib folded and he bunked in with us. He liked to hear the howler monkeys, but we're not sure they liked hearing him.

Clothe or Not to Clothe

I was determined to keep Riley's tender skin out of the sun. I expected him to wear clothes with long sleeves, long pants, a floppy safari hat, and shoes while we trekked in the jungle and under the hot sun—while I wore shorts. That was OK for part of the time, but mostly he preferred to be free of anything. I worried the heat would bother him; it didn't. We made an effort to stay in the shade except where it was unavoidable, like when swimming; those times we depended on sunblock. Ask your doctor to recommend a brand for your baby. Be sure to double-check labels of bug repellant for DEET (a pesticide) and PABA (an acid) in sunblock; these additives can be too strong for your baby's skin. And if your baby sweats, make sure he wears some kind of a hat or headband around his forehead to keep the sunblock/bug repellent chemicals from dripping into his eyes (that is if he will keep it on).

Clothing also protected against flying, crawling, and biting critters that got past our overwhelming scrutiny during long treks in the rainforest.

Common Sense

Traveling in the tropics and staying in the jungle opens the door for scorpions, spiders, and mosquitoes that are either dangerous or which just plain make life miserable. Always zip suitcases when not using them. Always store baby shoes in closed cases, and before putting them on, be sure to look inside and give them a good hard shake to dislodge any foreign squatters—good advice for big shoes as well. Wherever possible, hang things to keep them off the floor.

Our backpack baby-carrier was the star of the trip. We used it all the time. Since Daddy is really tall, Riley had a bird's eye view of Belize. He would take his nap as we trekked the jungle, or point and gurgle at the monkeys. He stood on top of Maya temples and surveyed the jungle below, slept with Mom or Dad in hammocks, which even alone he couldn't crawl out of—smart, those Maya.

Make sure that your pack includes a stirrup for his feet; this adds support and a provides a chance for him to exercise his leg muscles when he wants to. Check that the pack is well padded around the leg holes for long trips, or it could cut off circulation in his legs.

Aren't Babies Grand?
Ultimately I learned to relax and let Riley be Riley. He was the opening for some truly great encounters, conversations, and interactions with people that I would probably never have had a chance to meet otherwise. It made me realize that despite the many previous trips to Belize (yes, even our honeymoon), I learned more about the people this time than ever before—through Riley's eyes.

Although I thought I knew it already, I learned just how much we have in common with people everywhere. We found kindness if Riley was fussing; both locals and fellow backpackers are quite understanding. Though most restaurants in southern Belize didn't have high chairs, 90 percent of the time a waitress or restaurant owner was anxious to take the baby, croon to him, admire his blue eyes and blonde-white hair, and hold him and play with him while we ate.

At first I had reservations. I didn't know these people and was worried about letting strangers hold him. But Riley loved all of them. One time he came back with cake crumbs on his face—he really loved that new taste. Once he was out of view for a few seconds when our waitress walked outdoors to show him the household turkey, and we nearly ran after him. I'm not advising anyone to let a total stranger disappear with a precious infant, but strangers can be involved in a child's life in ways that create a happy experience for all.

Riley opened doors. It was very easy to approach people, and people found it very easy to approach us. My little towhead amazed them just as much as they amazed him. At first he was curious. He stared into their dark eyes, reached out his tiny white fingers, and touched the black skin of many of his newfound friends and always followed it by a big smile. He learned early that these people were fun! If he could talk, he would say, "Belize rules, Mom!

can put a rider on most homeowner's insurance policies for a nominal sum that will cover the cost if a camera is lost or stolen.) It's a nuisance to carry cameras every second when traveling—especially for a long period. During an evening out, we always leave our cameras and equipment (out of sight) in the hotel room; so far everything has been intact when we return. However, if this makes you crazy with worry, some hotel safes are large enough to accommodate your equipment.

Cameras can be a help or a hindrance when trying to get to know the people. When traveling in the backcountry you'll run into folks who don't want their pictures taken. Keep your camera put away until the right moment. The main thing to remember is to ask permission first and then if someone doesn't want his/her picture taken, accept the refusal with a gracious smile and move on.

Underwater Photography
One of the delights for the amateur photographer is shooting the creatures of the Belizean reef in living color. If you're fortunate enough to have one of the upscale 35mm cameras put out by Nikonos or Hanimex, you've got it made. Even the simple cameras, such as Weathermatic put out by Minolta, will give you a lot of pleasure and good souvenirs to take home. The simpler, inexpensive cameras are generally usable only to a depth of 15 feet. The Nikonos and Hanimex are waterproof up to 150 feet. And last but not least, check out the *disposable* cardboard underwater cameras available at most photo shops and large discount stores in the United States. Obviously the resulting pix will not be publishable, but they're good enough to take home and put in your album to remember Belize and its underwater denizens.

Some hotels, resorts, and shops in Belize rent underwater cameras. Don't expect a large selection. Remember, when buying film the best for underwater is natural-, red-, or yellow-tint film; film such as Ektachrome with a bluish cast does not give the best results. A strobe or flash is a big help if shooting in deep water or into caves. Natural-light pictures are great if you're shooting in fairly shallow water. It's best to shoot on an eye-to-eye level when photographing fish. Be careful of stirring up silt from the bottom with your fins. Try to hold very still when depressing the shutter, and if you must stabilize yourself, *don't* grab onto any bright-colored coral—you will kill it. If it's colored, it's alive, so grab only the drab grayish-tannish coral; grabbing live coral can cut your hands and often cause infection. Enjoy the reef and make sure the reef enjoys you—this is a natural haven for fragile life that must be preserved and cared for.

Other Photo Information
Belize has some mighty fine local photographers. If you're not a camera carrier and decide you'd like to take home some great pictures, including underwater shots, check out the photo gallery and gift shop of **James Beveridge** on Caye Caulker—look for the sign that says Seaing Is Belizing.

BOB RACE

KATHY ESCOVEDO SANDERS

MUNDO MAYA

For several years five Latin American nations (Mexico, Belize, Guatemala, Honduras, and El Salvador) have discussed the need to preserve the remaining culture of the Maya, one of the greatest civilizations of all time. The Maya were dynamic engineers who created architecturally flamboyant buildings, massive reservoirs, more cities than were in ancient Egypt, and innovative farmlands. They developed a written language, tracked and recorded movements of the universe, and at its zenith the society numbered more than five million people. Present-day descendants of the Maya, along with thousands of structures hidden in thick tropical jungles, continue to tell the story of the past.

An ambitious project, tagged **Mundo Maya** ("World of the Maya"), has been designed to both exhibit and preserve, to see that the rapid growth of population—and tourism—will not destroy what has been quietly enduring nature and her elements for hundreds and in some cases as long as three thousand years. Many factors are involved in project decisions that will affect millions of people; not only the Maya who have lived in isolated pockets and out-of-the-way villages for centuries, but also the people of each country involved, plus thousands of visitors who are discovering this culture for the first time. La Ruta Maya ("The Maya Route") will encompass the entire area that was once inhabited by the Maya, who have left their footprints in the form of amazing stone structures all over the landscape.

The project requires the cooperation of five countries, concentrating on the preservation of natural resources and rainforests, including the birds and animals that live within their boundaries (already extinct in other parts of the world). Perhaps the most important challenge the countries face is to come up with a way to encourage the development that tourism dollars can bring without infringing upon the cultural, historical, and environmental heritage of the Maya people.

A way must be found to induce the population to stop cutting the rainforest to create pastureland for raising crops and grazing cattle. Several plans are being studied. Those who have been supporting themselves in traditional ways for centuries must be taught ways to make a living without destroying the surrounding rainforest.

Options include harvesting and selling such rain-forest products as coffee, cacao, medicines, and fruits, and raising water buffalo (which survive nicely in the wet rainforest) rather than cattle—the meat is a viable substitute for beef. And maybe the biggest moneymaker for the people of the future is tourism—rather, ecotourism.

The five governments involved took the first step when they met in October 1988 in Guatemala City, an event hosted by then-President Vinicio Cerezo Arevalo. One of the most innovative suggestions was to build monorail-type transportation that would travel the 1,500-mile route throughout the environmentally precarious landscape to avoid bringing roads into these areas. Road development invariably brings uncontrolled settlement and destruction. There was talk of a regional Mundo Maya tourist visa and a Eurail-type pass that would allow visitors to move freely across the borders of the five countries.

No doubt it will take years of planning and agreements before these ideas come to pass, but Mexico and Guatemala have made one of the first moves by creating two adjoining biosphere reserves totaling 4.7 million acres of wildlands.

MAYA ARCHAEOLOGICAL SITES

A thousand years before modern seafarers came along, the Maya inhabited Belize. They are believed to be the first *Homo sapiens* to populate the country. Archaeologists estimate that at one time, at least one million Maya lived in the area that is now called Belize. More Maya sites are discovered each year, and it's quite common for Belizean families to have ruins in their backyards without official archaeological knowledge. These are often small oratorio-style buildings or caves with artifacts that date back hundreds of years. As money becomes available, whether from the government or outside universities, more discoveries are made and it becomes apparent that Belize is a veritable treasure chest of Maya culture.

Hints for Touring the Archaeological Sites
Seven of the archaeological sites described below are open to the public. Four are visited widely and soon will be official reserves with supporting facilities. Right now visitors will find no bathrooms, snack bars, or even water in any of them. In some areas it's necessary to trek through tall grasses and jungle terrain, so dress accordingly. Wearing long pants and sturdy walking shoes with socks pulled over the cuffs (which have been previously sprayed with the type of insect repellent that can be applied to the skin) is one efficient way to approach these areas. Flying and crawling insects thrive in the jungle terrain. Of course the other usual mom-given tips apply: sunblock, a loose floppy hat, and a bottle of water all help to protect the body inside and out against the hot sun and its effects.

Know the locations and distances of the sites you wish to visit. Some are lengthy treks from the closest town. Other sites are on private property and can only be visited if prior permission is obtained. For more information visit the **Department of Archaeology** (tel. 8/22106) in Belmopan or the **Association for Belizean Archaeology** at the **Center of Environmental Studies** on Eve Street in Belize City.

SITES IN NORTHERN BELIZE

Santa Rita
Santa Rita was still a populated community of Maya when the Spanish arrived. One mile northeast of Corozal, the largest Santa Rita structure was explored at the turn of the century by Thomas Gann. Sculptured friezes and stucco murals were found along with a burial site that indicates flourishing occupation in the early Classic period (about A.D. 300), as well as during the late post-Classic period (A.D. 1350–1530). Two significant burials were found from distant periods in the history of Santa Rita: one from A.D. 300 was a female and the other was a king from a period 200 hundred years later. In 1985 archaeologists Diane and Arlen Chase discovered a tomb with a skeleton covered in jade and mica ornaments. Some believe that Santa Rita was part of a series of coastal lookouts. It has been excavated and

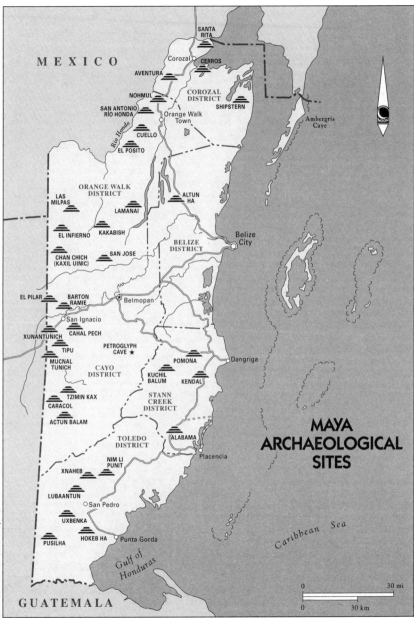

MEXICO

SANTA RITA

Corozal

CERROS

AVENTURA

NOHMUL

COROZAL DISTRICT

SHIPSTERN

SAN ANTONIO RÍO HONDA

Orange Walk Town

Río Hondo

CUELLO

EL POSITO

Ambergris Caye

LAS MILPAS

ORANGE WALK DISTRICT

ALTUN HA

LAMANAI

EL INFIERNO

KAKABISH

SAN JOSE

CHAN CHICH (KAXIL UINIC)

BELIZE DISTRICT

Belize City

EL PILAR

BARTON RAMIE

San Ignacio

Belmopan

XUNANTUNICH

CAHAL PECH

TIPU

PETROGLYPH CAVE ★

MUCNAL TUNICH

CAYO DISTRICT

POMONA

Dangriga

KUCHIL BALUM

KENDAL

TZIMIN KAX

CARACOL

STANN CREEK DISTRICT

ACTUN BALAM

ALABAMA

TOLEDO DISTRICT

Placencia

NIM LI PUNIT

XNAHEB

MAYA ARCHAEOLOGICAL SITES

LUBAANTUN

San Pedro

UXBENKA

PUSILHA

HOKEB HA

Punta Gorda

Caribbean Sea

Gulf of Honduras

GUATEMALA

0   30 mi

0   30 km

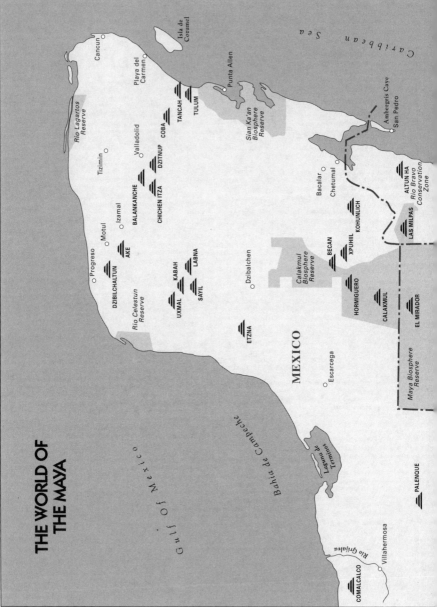

THE WORLD OF
THE MAYA

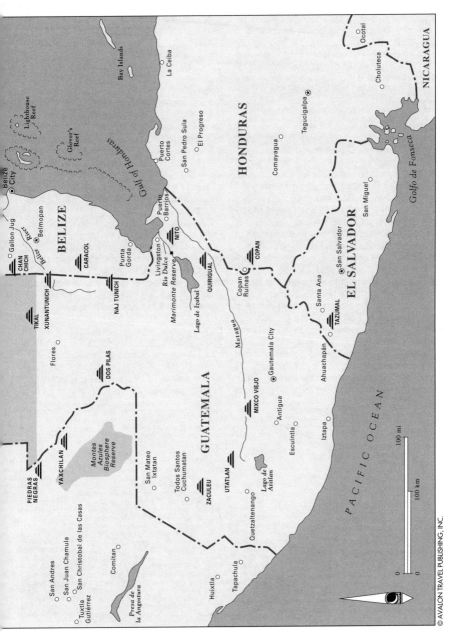

© AVALON TRAVEL PUBLISHING, INC.

somewhat reconstructed under the Chases' jurisdiction; only one structure is accessible to the public. Post-Classic murals, mostly destroyed over the years, combined Maya and Mexican styles that depict the ecumenical flavor of the period. Santa Rita is probably more appealing to an archaeologist than to the average tourist.

Cerros

Cerros was an important coastal trading center during the late pre-Classic period (350 B.C.–A.D. 250). It's situated on a peninsula in the Bay of Chetumal, across from the town of Corozal. Magnificent frescoes and stone heads were uncovered by archaeologist David Friedel; these signify that elite rule was firmly fixed by the end of the pre-Classic period. The tallest of its temples rises to 70 feet, and because of the rise in the sea level the one-time stone residences of the elite Maya are partially flooded. It would appear that Cerros not only provisioned the oceangoing canoes, but was in an ideal location to control ancient trade routes that traced the Rio Hondo and New River from the Yucatán to Petén and the Usumacinta basin. A plaster-lined canal for the sturdy, oversized ocean canoes was constructed around Cerros. Archaeologists have determined that extensive fishing and farming on raised fields took place, probably to outfit the traders. But always the question remains: Why did progress suddenly stop? You can reach Cerros by boat. (Hire it in Corozal at **Tony's Inn** or check with a travel agent in Corozal.) If you travel during the dry season (Jan.–April), you can get to Cerros by car.

Nohmul

Nohmul was a major ceremonial site. It is the tallest structure in the Orange Walk/Corozal Districts. Twin ceremonial groups are connected by a *sacbe* (raised causeway). The center shows it once catered to a thriving population in the late pre-Classic and late Classic periods (350 B.C.–A.D. 250 and A.D. 600–900) and controlled an area of about 12 square miles. Nohmul ("Big Hill") was named by the people living in the vicinity of the site.

The entrance to the site, in the sugarcane fields behind the village of San Pablo, is one mile down the road going west from the center of the village. Public transportation from Belize City, Orange Walk Town, and Corozal passes through the village of San Pablo several times daily. You can find simple accommodations in Orange Walk Town eight miles away.

Cuello

The ruins of Cuello were studied in the 1970s by a Cambridge University archaeology team led by Dr. Norman Hammond. A small ceremonial center, a proto-Classic temple, has been excavated. Lying directly in front is a

At Cuello, archaeologists have renovated the Maya ruins in the ancient manner by covering them with a white stucco coating.

large excavation trench, partially backfilled, where the archaeologists gathered the historical information that revolutionized previous concepts of the antiquity of the ancient Maya. Artifacts indicate the Maya traded with people hundreds of miles away. Among the archaeologists' out-of-the-ordinary findings were bits of wood that proved, after carbon testing, that Cuello had been occupied as early as 2600 B.C., much earlier than ever believed; however, archaeologists now find that these tests may have been incorrect, and the age is now in dispute. Also found was an unusual style of pottery—apparently in some burials clay urns were placed over the heads of the deceased. It's also speculated that it was here over a long period that the primitive strain of corn seen in early years was refined and developed into the higher-producing plant of the Classic period. Continuous occupation for approximately 4,000 years was surmised with repeated layers of structures all the way into the Classic period. However, archaeologists are still debating the accuracy of this backdating.

These structures (as in Cahal Pech) have a different look than most Maya sites. They are covered with a layer of white stucco, as they were in the days of the Maya.

The ruins of Cuello are on the same property as the rum distillery of the same name. It's about four miles west of Orange Walk Town on Yo Creek; taxis are available. This site isn't developed, cleared, restored, or ready for the average tourist, but if you're interested in more information, contact the Department of Archaeology in Belmopan, tel. 8/22106; if you're in the area ask at the distillery for permission to enter.

Lamanai

Set on the edge of a forested broad lagoon are the temples of Lamanai. One of the largest ceremonial centers in Belize, it was described as an imperial port city encompassing ball courts, pyramids, and the more exotic Maya features. Hundreds of buildings have been identified in the two-square-mile area. A few sites to look for:

The Mask Temple N9-56: Here two significant tombs were found, as well as two early Classic stone masks.

The High Temple N10-43: At 33 meters (10 feet) tall, this is the tallest securely dated pre-

Classic structure in the Maya area. Among many findings was a dish containing the skeleton of a bird and pre-Classic vessels dating to 100 B.C.

Temple N10-9: Dated to the 6th century A.D., this temple had structural modifications in the 8th and 13th centuries. Jade jewelry and a jade mask were discovered here as was an animal-motif dish.

The Ball Court: The game played in this area held great ritual significance for the Maya. In 1980, archaeologists raised the huge ball court marker stone disc and found lidded vessels containing miniature vessels with small jade and shell objects on top of a mercury puddle.

Archaeologist David Pendergast headed a team from the Royal Ontario Museum that, after finding a number of children's bones buried under a stela, presumed that human sacrifice was a part of the religion of these people. Large masks that depict a ruler wearing a crocodile headdress were found in several locations, hence the name Lamanai ("Submerged Crocodile"). Another unique find under a plain stone marker was a pottery container with a pool of mercury. Excavations reveal continuous occupation and a high standard of living into the post-Classic period, unlike other colonies in the region.

Lamanai is believed to have been occupied from 1500 B.C. to the 19th century, as evidenced by the remains of two Christian churches and a sugar mill. This site has not been cleared or reconstructed; the landscape is overgrown, and trees and thick vines grow from the tops of buildings—the only sounds are birdcalls echoing off the stone temple. To see above the thick jungle canopy you can climb to the top of the temple on ancient steps that are still pretty much in place, and don't be surprised if you find Indiana Jones's hat at the top—it's that kind of a place.

The trip to the site is great; it's located in Orange Walk District on the high banks of New River Lagoon about 50 miles northwest of Belize City. Most people travel by boat through tropical flora and fauna, and on the way you might see such exotics as black orchids, old tree trunks covered with sprays of tiny golden orchids, and a multitude of bird life, possibly even the jabiru stork (the largest flying bird in the New World with a wing span of 10–12 feet).

This area is a reserve so look for some wildlife you may not see in other, more inhabited areas. On the paths you'll see numbered trees that correspond to a pamphlet of information available from the caretakers at the entrance of Lamanai Reserve:

1. santa maria
2. cohune palm
3. trumpet tree
4. tubroos
5. cotton tree
6. allspice
7. red gumbo-limbo
8. pimenta palm
9. bucut
10. cedar
11. rubber tree
12. breadnut tree
13. copal tree
14. cordoncia

Bird-watchers, look around the Mask and High temples for the **black oropendola.** The **black vulture** is often spotted slowly gliding over the entire area. A woodpecker with a distinct double-tap rhythm and a red cap is the male **Guatemalan ivorybill.** Near the High Temple, the **collared** *aracari* sits on the highest trees and chirps like an insect; this is a variety of toucan. The **citreoline trogon** is covered with color: a yellow chest, black-and-white tail, and a back of blue and green. Though

it looks as if the **northern jacana** is walking on water, it's the delicate floating vegetation that holds the long-toed bird above the water as it searches along the water's edge for edible delicacies.

Other fauna spotted by those who live there are jaguarundi, agouti, armadillo, hicatee turtle, and the roaring howler monkey.

Chan Chich
In the northwestern corner of Belize in Orange Walk District, near the Guatemala border, an old overgrown logging road blazed originally by the Belize Estate and Produce Company (logging operators) was reopened. Here the Maya site of Chan Chich (Kaxil Uinich) was rediscovered. As recently as 1986 the only way in (for rare adventurers, pot farmers, or grave robbers) was with machete in hand and a canoe to cross the swiftly flowing river. After sweating and cutting into dense jungle to the end of the barely visible track, the adventurer's sudden reward was a 100-foot-tall rock-strewn hill—an introduction to another Maya ceremonial site! This complex has two levels of plazas, each with its own temples, all surrounded by unexcavated mounds.

When found, three of the temples showed obvious signs of looting with vertical slit trenches—open—just as the looters had left them. No one will ever know what valuable artifacts were removed and easily sold to private collectors all over the world. The large main temple on the

Altun Ha

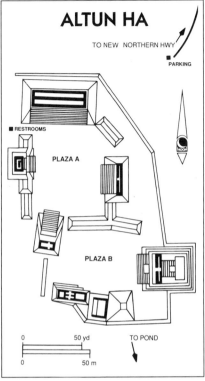

upper plaza had been violated to the heart of what appears to be one or more burial chambers. A painted frieze runs around the low ceiling. Today the only temple inhabitants greeting outsiders are small bats.

Chan Chich has a new guard: Belizean-born Barry Bowen, owner of the property, who has built a group of simple thatch cabañas in one of the plazas of the Maya site. Though deplored by some archaeology buffs, these cabañas are very popular with bird-watchers and Mayaphiles who agree with Bowen that they will serve as a deterrent to temple looters who think nothing of defiling the ancient stone cities, and marijuana growers who find these isolated spots perfect hiding places for their illegal crops. For more information about Chan Chich Lodge, see "West of Orange Walk Town" in the Orange Walk District chapter.

Altun Ha

Travel north 28 miles on the New Northern Highway from Belize City until it intersects with the Old Northern Highway. Take Old Northern Highway about 12 miles; a sign marks the Altun Ha access road. It's about one and a half miles to the archaeological site from here. It wasn't until the archaeologists came in 1964 that the name Rockstone Pond was translated into the Maya words Altun Ha. The site covers an area of about 25 square miles, most of which is covered by trees, vines, and jungle. Altun Ha, a trading center as well as a religious ceremonial center, is believed to have accommodated about 10,000 people. Archaeologists, working in the midst of a community of Maya families that have been living here for several centuries, have dated construction to about 1,500–2,000 years ago.

A team led by Dr. David Pendergast from the Royal Ontario Museum began work in 1965 on the central part of the ancient city, where upward of 250 structures have been found in an area of about 1,000 square yards. So far, this is the most extensively excavated of all the Maya sites in Belize. For a trading center, Altun Ha was strategically located—a few miles from **Little Rocky Point** on the Caribbean and a few miles from **Moho Caye** at the mouth of the Belize River, both believed to have been major centers for the large trading canoes that worked up and down the coasts of Guatemala, Honduras, Belize, the Yucatán, and all the way to Panama.

Near Plaza B, the **Reservoir,** also known as **Rockstone Pond,** is fed by springs and rain runoff. It demonstrates the advanced knowledge of the Maya in just one of their many fields: engineering. Archaeologists say that for centuries an insignificant little stream ran through the jungle. No doubt it had been a source of fresh water for the Maya—but maybe not enough. The Maya diverted the creek and then began a major engineering project, digging and enlarging a deep, round hole that was then plastered with limestone cement. Once the cement dried and hardened, the stream was rerouted to its original course and the newly built reservoir filled and overflowed at the east end, allowing the stream to continue on its age-old track. This made the area livable. Was all of this done before or after the temple structures were built? Is the completion of this reservoir what made the Maya elite choose to locate in this area? We may never know for sure. Today Rockstone Pond is surrounded by thick brush and the pond is alive with jungle creatures, including tarpon, small fish, and turtles and other reptiles.

The concentration of structures includes palaces and temples surrounding two main plazas. The tallest building (the Sun God Temple) is 59 feet above the plaza floor. At Altun Ha the structure bases are oval and terraced. The small temples on top have typical small rooms built with the Maya trademark—the corbel arch.

Pendergast's team uncovered many valuable finds, such as unusual green obsidian blades, pearls, and more than 300 jade pieces—beads, earrings, and rings. Seven funeral chambers were discovered, including the **Temple of the Green Tomb**, rich with human remains and traditional funerary treasures. Maya scholars believe the first man buried was someone of great importance. He was draped with jade beads, pearls, and shells. And it was next to his right hand that the most exciting find was located—a solid jade head now referred to as **Kinich Ahau** ("The Sun God"). Kinich Ahau is, to date, the largest jade carving found in any Maya country. The head weighs nine pounds and measures nearly six inches from base to crown. It is cared for by the Department of Archaeology in Belmopan.

Altun Ha was rebuilt several times during the pre-Classic, Classic, and post-Classic periods. Scientists believe that the site was abandoned due to violence and the desecration of the structures. This Maya ceremonial site is open to the public 9 A.M.–5 P.M.; small entrance fee.

SITES IN WESTERN BELIZE

Cahal Pech

Cahal Pech ("Place of the Ticks") is in San Ignacio in the Cayo District near **Tipu**. This medium-sized Maya site was discovered in the early 1950s, but scientific research did not begin until 1988, when a team from the University of San Diego began excavation. Thirty-four structures were compacted into a 2–3-acre area. Excavation is ongoing and visitors are welcome. Watching the archaeological team in action gives visitors an opportunity to see how ruins look before restoration and how painstaking the work can be. You'll pay a small fee at Cahal Pech, and you can visit a new, small museum where you will see artifacts found at the site. This site is within walking distance of San Ignacio.

Xunantunich

The word Xunantunich (zoo-nahn-too-NEECH, "Stone Lady") is derived from local legend. A thousand years ago, Xunantunich was already a ruin. It's believed to have been built some-

Cahal Pech

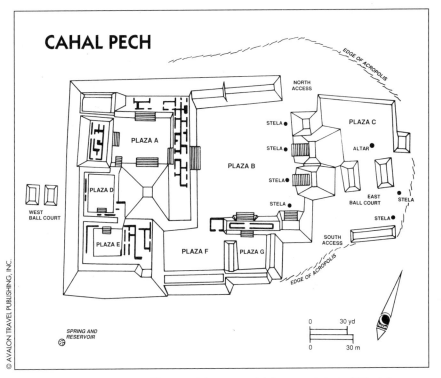

CAHAL PECH

EDGE OF ACROPOLIS

NORTH ACCESS

PLAZA C

STELA ●

STELA ●   ALTAR ●

PLAZA A

PLAZA B

STELA ●

STELA ●

PLAZA D

EAST BALL COURT

WEST BALL COURT

STELA ●

STELA ●

PLAZA E

PLAZA F   PLAZA G

SOUTH ACCESS

EDGE OF ACROPOLIS

0   30 yd

0   30 m

SPRING AND RESERVOIR

© AVALON TRAVEL PUBLISHING, INC.

time during A.D. 150–900, the golden age of the Maya. Though certainly not the biggest of Maya structures, at 135 feet high **El Castillo** is one of the taller structures (Maya or otherwise) in Belize. El Castillo has been partially excavated and explored. The eastern side of the structure displays an unusual stucco frieze (it looks new and fresh, as if it hasn't been too long since its reconstruction), and you can see three carved stelae in the plaza. Xunantunich contains three ceremonial plazas surrounded by house mounds. It was first opened by noted archaeologist Sir J. Eric Thompson in 1938 after centuries of neglect. As the first Maya ruin to be opened in the country, it has attracted the attention and exploration of many other archaeologists over the years.

In 1950, the University of Pennsylvania (noted for its years of outstanding work across the Guatemala border in Tikal) built a facility in Xu-

nantunich for more study. In 1954, visitors were invited to explore the site after a road was opened and a small ferry was built. In 1959, archaeologist Evan Mackie made news in the Maya world when he discovered evidence that part of Xunantunich had been destroyed by an earthquake in the late-Classic period. Some believe it was then that the people began to lose faith in their leaders—an unearthly sign from the gods. But for whatever reason, Xunantunich ceased to be a religious center long before the end of the Classic period.

This impressive Maya ceremonial site is well worth a visit and a climb—from the top the panorama encompasses the thick green Guatemalan Peten District, the Maya Mountains, and a grand view of the entire Cayo District and Belize jungle stretching for miles to the horizon. To get to the top, follow a path that meanders across the front and side of the structure. At the

XUNANTUNICH

PLAZA A-3

PLAZA A-2

GROUP B

TO SUCCOTZ'S FERRY

PLAZA A-1

PAVILION

RESTROOMS

EL CASTILLO

GROUP C

NOT TO SCALE

© AVALON TRAVEL PUBLISHING, INC.

top is a typical small Maya temple; watch out for the large step over a hole in the cement—it should be fixed by now! On one of our last visits, the site was empty except for one lone believer meditating on the very top of the roof of the temple in a perfect lotus position. He appeared to be in complete harmony with the blue sky and puffy white clouds above, the jungle below—and perhaps with the Maya gods of Xunantunich within.

To find Xunantunich, travel about eight miles south of San Ignacio on the Western Highway toward Benque Viejo and the Guatemala border. (Look for a small wooden sign on the side of the road that says Xunantunich.) At the river's edge, hop on the free, hand-cranked cable ferry. If driving, either park here or drive onto the ferry (it can handle two cars), and from the bank it's less than a mile farther up gentle hills to the site. The

short, leathery-faced, aged man who cranked the ferry for years and years has been replaced by a young, robust fellow said to be a relative of the stern-faced old Mayan. You pay a small fee to enter the grounds, and Elfego Panti, a very knowledgeable guide, will explain the site: the history, what's been restored, and what's in the future. This major center sits on a natural limestone ridge. The funky ferry operates daily 8 A.M.–5 P.M.

Caracol

Perhaps the largest site in Belize, Caracol ("Snail") is an enormous ceremonial center covering more than five square miles. On a low plateau deep in the **Chiquibul Forest Reserve,** evidence remains of primary rainforest. The tallest temple structure stands 136 feet above the plaza floor (just slightly higher than El Castillo at Xunantunich) with a base broad enough to rival any of the ruins at Tikal (in Guatemala). This Classic site is noted for the rare use of giant date glyphs on circular stone altars. Again the Maya exhibited their engineering skills, building extensive reservoirs and agricultural terraces. More of Caracol continues to be discovered by archaeologists Diane and Arlen Chase and their energetic assistants—student interns from Tulane University and University of Central Florida. According to John Morris, archaeological commissioner of Belize, a lifetime of exploration remains to be done within six to nine miles in every direction from today's discoveries. It's proving to have been a powerful site that controlled a very large area.

Many carvings are dated A.D. 300–600, indicating Caracol was settled about A.D. 300 and continued to flourish when other Maya sites were in decline. Carvings on the site also indicate that Caracol and Tikal engaged in ongoing conflicts, each defeating the other on various occasions. After a war in A.D. 562, however, Caracol dominated the area for more than a century. A former archaeological commissioner named the site Caracol because of the numerous snail shells found there.

You can reach Caracol by forestry road through Douglas DeSilva (formerly called Augustine) in the Mountain Pine Ridge. However, although the site is only 30 miles farther on, visitors are advised to travel with 4WD vehicles as the road is extremely rough. **Note:** The "new" road is an all-weather track, but is still bad during downpours. The closest accommodations are near the Douglas DeSilva Forestry Station and in and around the Cayo District. Gas is not available along this road, so it behooves visitors to make all arrangements necessary to carry ample fuel. Camping is not allowed in the area without permission from the Forestry Department in Belmopan. The **Department of Archaeology** and/or the **Forestry Department, Western Division** must be informed before any visits, for permission and advice on accessibility.

SITES IN SOUTHERN BELIZE

Lubaantun
Northwest of Punta Gorda, north of the Columbia River and one mile beyond San Pedro is the Maya ruin of Lubaantun ("Place of the Fallen Stones"). It was built and occupied during the late-Classic period (A.D. 730–890) and first noticed in 1875 by refugees from the southern United States who left the States during and after the Civil War. Its ridge location gives it a commanding view of the entire countryside. Eleven major structures are grouped around five main plazas, in addition to smaller plazas, for a total of 18 plazas and three ball courts. Most of the structures are terraced, and the tallest structure rises 50 feet above the plaza,

from which you can see the Caribbean Sea, 20 miles distant. Notice that some corners of structures are rounded. Lubaantun's distinct style of architecture sets it apart from Maya construction in some parts of Latin America. This large late-Classic site has been studied and surveyed several times by familiar names, such as Thomas Gann and, more recently, by Norman Hammond in 1970. Distinctive clay whistle figurines (similar to those found in Mexico's Isla Jaina) illustrate lifestyles and occupations of the era. Other artifacts include a unique, carved glasslike skull, obsidian blades, grinding stones (much like those still used today to grind corn), beads, shells, turquoise, and shards of pottery. From all of this archaeologists have determined that the city flourished until the 8th century A.D. It was a farming community that traded with the highland areas of today's Guatemala, and the people worked the sea and maybe the nearby cayes just offshore. To get to Lubaantun from Punta Gorda, go 1.5 miles west past the gas station to the Southern Highway, then take a right. Two miles farther you'll come to the village of San Pedro. From here go left around the church to the concrete bridge; cross and go almost a mile—the road is passable during the dry season. Park before you reach the aged wooden bridge. This site has not been made into a park, so it's largely overgrown with brush and jungle; wear your hiking boots and long pants.

Caracol

Nim Li Punit

Right off the Southern Highway before the San Antonio turnoff, 25 miles north of Punta Gorda town, you'll find Nim Li Punit (a 15-minute walk from the highway along a trail marked by a small sign). The site has enjoyed only preliminary excavations (1970) and is believed to have held a close relationship with nearby Lubaantun. One of the memorable finds was a 30-foot-tall carved stela, the tallest ever found in Belize—and in most of the rest of the Maya world. About 25 stelae have been found on the site dated A.D. 700–800. Rediscovered in 1974, the site was looted almost immediately. However, the looters missed a tomb later uncovered by archaeologist Richard Leventhal in 1986. If you're not driving a car, it's best to make arrangements to see these ruins and the villages with a guide before your arrival in Punta Gorda.

Uxbenka

Found only recently (1984), Uxbenka has revealed more than 20 stelae, seven of which are carved. One dates from the early Classic period, an otherwise nonexistent period in southern Belize and a rare date for stelae in the entire Maya area. The site is perched on a ridge overlooking the traditional Maya village of Santa Cruz and provides a grand view of the foothills and valleys of the Maya Mountains. Here you'll see hillsides lined with cut stones resembling massive structures. This method is unique to the Toledo District.

Uxbenka ("Old Place") was named by the people of nearby Santa Cruz. It's located just outside Santa Cruz, about three miles west of San Antonio Village. The most convenient way to see the site is with a rental car. However, if you're staying in San Antonio or Punta Gorda ask around town; a local may be willing to take you around and act as a guide. Arrange your price in advance.

OTHER SITES

A few other sites that have been documented are in various stages of excavation: **Actun Balam,** near Caracol in the Cayo District, **Tzimin Kax** ("Mountain Cow"), in the Cayo District, and **Pusilha,** on the Moho River near Lubaantun.

This is far from a complete list. As growth in the country continues and money becomes available, the mysterious Mundo Maya will continue to reveal itself.

Rio Azul

Beyond Blue Creek and across the border into Guatemala is one of the newest and most exciting archaeological sites, Rio Azul. Without roads, it is not yet accessible from the Belizean side, but it has produced new and exciting artifacts, such as a screw-on-lid pottery jar—a few more pieces to fit into the puzzle of the advanced Maya civilization.

KATHY ESCOVEDO SANDERS

BELIZE DISTRICT

Of all the districts, probably the Belize District most clearly defines the country. Here on the banks of Haulover Creek the country was founded, its hopes were kindled, its present success was forged, and many of its greatest problems have arisen. It is a district of much ethnic diversity. It is also a district that encompasses swamps, mangroves, thickets, marshes, broad leaf forest, and a couple of hundred cayes. It juxtaposes Maya ruins with the commercial capital of the country, Belize City, where the population is also the most heavily concentrated. Within the Belize District to the east are island playgrounds, the largest of them Ambergris Caye; to the west are the Baboon Sanctuary and the Belize Zoo; to the north rises the pyramid of Altun Ha; and to the south lie the lagoons of the Gales Point area.

BELIZE CITY

Belize City straddles the estuaries of Haulover Creek, part of the Belize River that empties into the Caribbean Sea. In this bustling harbor-city of about 80,000 (mostly Afro-Creoles), small businesses abound. With independence, Belize is implementing slow but sure changes. However, if you want to get a taste of what colonial life was like "back when," don't wait. Come before the town is spiffed up, painted, and high-rises line the coast. Visit before the old swing bridge is replaced—there is nothing quite like watching the traffic jams when the low-lying bridge across Haulover Creek closes to cars while it pivots to allow tall-masted boats to pass through. (If you happen to drive across the swing bridge after dark, be sure to turn your headlights down as there's a hump in the bridge—car headlights blind oncoming traffic.) Haulover Creek is a name left over from the time when cattle were attached to each other by a rope wrapped around their horns and "hauled" across the river.

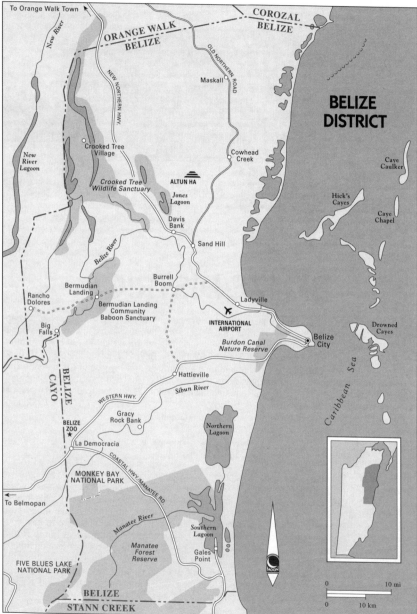

To Orange Walk Town

ORANGE WALK
BELIZE

COROZAL
BELIZE

New River

OLD NORTHERN ROAD

Maskall

NEW NORTHERN HWY.

BELIZE
DISTRICT

New
River
Lagoon

Crooked Tree
Village

Cowhead
Creek

Caye
Caulker

*Crooked Tree
Wildlife Sanctuary*

ALTUN HA

Jones
Lagoon

Hick's
Cayes

Caye
Chapel

Davis
Bank

Belize River

Sand Hill

Burrell
Boom

Bermudian
Landing

Ladyville

Drowned
Cayes

Rancho
Dolores

Bermudian Landing
Community
Baboon Sanctuary

INTERNATIONAL
AIRPORT

Belize
City

Big
Falls

*Burdon Canal
Nature Reserve*

BELIZE

Hattieville

CAYO

WESTERN HWY.

Sibun River

Caribbean Sea

Gracy
Rock Bank

Northern
Lagoon

BELIZE
ZOO

La Democracia

COASTAL HWY./MANATEE RD.

MONKEY BAY
NATIONAL PARK

To Belmopan

Manatee River

*Southern
Lagoon*

FIVE BLUES LAKE
NATIONAL PARK

Manatee
Forest
Reserve

Gales
Point

MOON

BELIZE

STANN CREEK

0   10 mi

0   10 km

© AVALON TRAVEL PUBLISHING, INC.

ORIENTATION

Most travelers planning a visit to Belize arrive at Belize's **Philip Goldson International Airport.** Commuter flights to the cayes and other towns come and go from the Belize City Municipal Airport. From the international airport, you'll approach the city from the northwest on the Northern Highway, passing the **Belize Biltmore Plaza** along the way. At the edge of the city the highway changes its name to **Freetown Road** at the intersection with Central American Boulevard, the first large street you cross. To reach the **Belize City Municipal Airport,** turn left at this intersection onto what is called from this point **Princess Margaret Drive,** and follow it to St. Matthew Street, where another left leads to the terminal. Otherwise, continuing straight on Freetown Road eventually puts you at Barracks Road. A left here heads to the edge of the sea and northward toward **The Princess Hotel and Casino;** turn right and you are aimed toward an intersection with **Queen Street** and access to the heart of the city.

The Flavor of the City

Visitors should know ahead of time that Belize City is no Caribbean "paradise" in terms of a Cancún or Cozumel. The city appears at first glance to be old and run-down, and, though it's perched on the edge of the gorgeous Caribbean, it is without beaches. Antiquated clapboard buildings on stilts—unpainted, weathered, tilted, and streaked with age—line the narrow streets but are slowly being replaced by concrete structures. The banks of the Belize River, meandering through the middle of the city, are often dirty and smelly—face it, the country is not only old, but it's also poor; that's the *downside.* The *upside* is that you'll find, tucked here and there, almost-white sedate public structures—and very few modern glitzy buildings. The people, for the most part, are friendly and their future is glowing. Schools are everywhere, trendy shops are popping up, and some of the simplest bars are gathering places for the most interesting people. It's Somerset Maugham country—at least for a while longer.

Culture Shock

After a few days in Belize City visitors get over the culture shock and no longer notice the "rundown" condition of the city. Instead, they'll begin to feel somewhat comfortable strolling the streets, while the sensation of living in an era past takes over. If pirate captain Lafitte came swaggering down the street today, he'd fit right into some of these neighborhoods. But there's more to this friendly city—it's an excitement in the air, an electricity that's buzzing with growth, dreams, plans—it's history in the making. Ten years from now Captain Lafitte probably won't recognize the city—however, he'd still have to watch his wallet. And we *know* he'd be shocked to find a traffic light or two in Belize City.

Crime and the City

Like many other countries, Belize has its share of problems with drugs and crime. In fact, over the last several years violent crime increased noticeably in the capital. The government and police are still criticized for not taking stronger action in the face of the rising mayhem, much of it gang- and drug-related. The government has taken steps to battle crime, including stiffer enforcement of the law and the use of the Tourist Police, who are here specifically for the protection of tourists. Only time will tell if these and future measures will have the desired effect.

In the meantime, use the common sense that would apply in any city. Before you venture out, have a clear idea of how to get where you're going and stick to main streets if you're walking. At night, don't walk. Take a taxi between destinations and keep the windows rolled up—or if you are driving—keep the windows up and the doors locked. Don't flash money, jewelry, and other temptations, but if you're threatened, hand them over. And in emergencies, call 911 for the police, 90 for fire or ambulance.

Hub of the Nation

While the country of Belize has become the "sweetheart" of the adventure-traveler, Belize City is not for everyone. However, there are many practical reasons travelers include Belize City in their explorations. At certain times of the year it becomes difficult to find comfortable accommodations within one's budget in the major caye resorts. In fact, during certain holidays it's

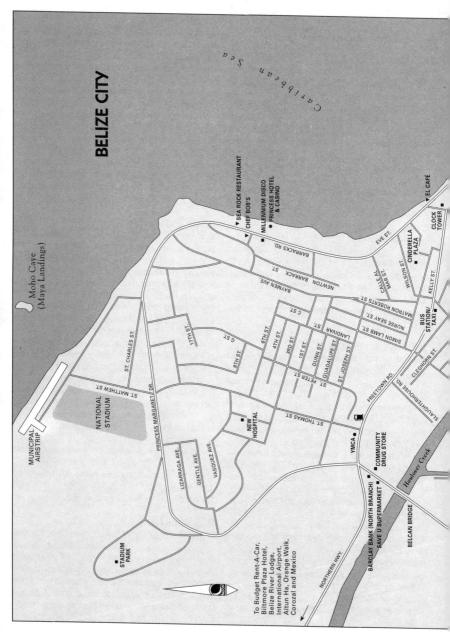

BELIZE CITY

Caribbean Sea

Moho Caye
(Maya Landings)

MUNICIPAL AIRSTRIP

NATIONAL STADIUM

ST. MATTHEW ST.

ST. CHARLES ST.

17TH ST.

G ST.

8TH ST.

6TH ST.

4TH ST.

3RD ST.

1ST ST.

DUNN ST.

ST. PETER ST.

GUADALUPE ST.

ST. JOSEPH ST.

LANDIVAR ST.

C ST.

SIMON LAMB ST.

NURSE SEAY ST.

MATRON ROBERTS ST.

NEWTON BARRACK ST.

BAYMEN AVE.

BARRACKS RD.

CALLE AL MAR ST.

WILSON ST.

EVE ST.

KELLY ST.

CINDERELLA PLAZA

CLOCK TOWER

EL CAFÉ

BUS STATION/ TAXI

CLEGHORN ST.

SLAUGHTERHOUSE RD.

FREETOWN RD.

ST. THOMAS ST.

NEW HOSPITAL

YMCA

COMMUNITY DRUG STORE

SAVE U SUPERMARKET

BARCLAY BANK (NORTH BRANCH)

BELCAN BRIDGE

Haulover Creek

NORTHERN HWY.

PRINCESS MARGARET DR.

LIZARRAGA AVE.

GENTLE AVE.

VASQUEZ AVE.

STADIUM PARK

To Budget Rent-A-Car,
Biltmore Plaza Hotel,
Belize River Lodge,
International Airport,
Altun Ha, Orange Walk,
Corozal and Mexico

SEA ROCK RESTAURANT

CHEF BOB'S

MILLENNIUM DISCO

PRINCESS HOTEL & CASINO

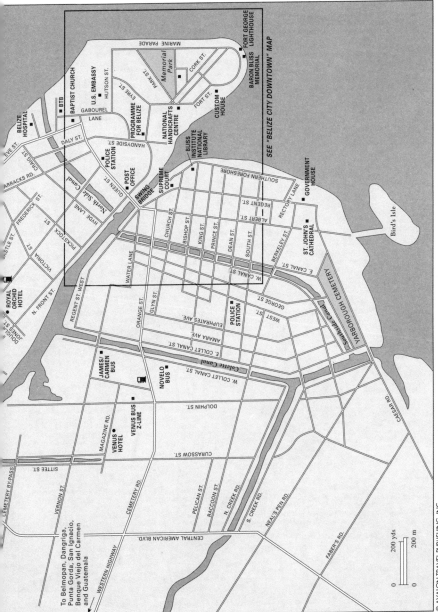

© AVALON TRAVEL PUBLISHING, INC.

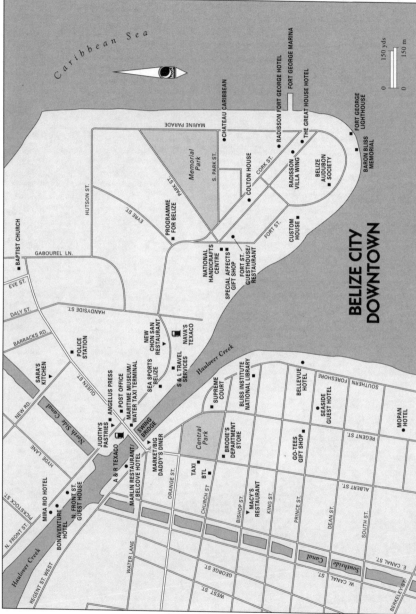

Caribbean Sea

MARINE PARADE

Memorial Park

S. PARK ST.

PARK ST.

HUTSON ST.

EYRE ST.

BAPTIST CHURCH

GABOUREL LN.

EVE ST.

DALY ST.

HANDYSIDE ST.

BARRACKS RD.

QUEEN ST.

SARA'S KITCHEN

POLICE STATION

NEW RD.

ANGELUS PRESS

POST OFFICE

MARITIME MUSEUM/ WATER TAXI TERMINAL

NEW CHON SAN RESTAURANT

SEA SPORTS BELIZE

S & L TRAVEL SERVICES

NAVA'S TEXACO

Haulover Creek

HYDE LANE

North Side Canal

JUDITH'S PASTRIES

SWING BRIDGE

A & R TEXACO

MARLIN RESTAURANT/ BELCOVE HOTEL

MIRA RIO HOTEL

N. FRONT ST. GUEST HOUSE

BONAVENTURE HOTEL

N. FRONT ST.

PICKSTOCK ST.

REGENT ST. WEST

Haulover Creek

MARKET/BIG DADDY'S DINER

TAXI

BTL

BRODIE'S DEPARTMENT STORE

Central Park

ORANGE ST.

WATER LANE

GEORGE ST.

CHURCH ST.

MACY'S RESTAURANT

BISHOP ST.

KING ST.

GO-TEES GIFT SHOP

PRINCE ST.

ALBERT ST.

DEAN ST.

REGENT ST.

SOUTH ST.

SUPREME COURT

BLISS INSTITUTE NATIONAL LIBRARY

BELLEVUE HOTEL

SEASIDE GUEST HOTEL

MOPAN HOTEL

SOUTHERN FORESHORE

WEST ST.

W. CANAL ST.

E. CANAL ST.

Southside Canal

BERKELEY ST.

CHATEAU CARIBBEAN

RADISSON FORT GEORGE HOTEL

FORT GEORGE MARINA

THE GREAT HOUSE HOTEL

FORT GEORGE LIGHTHOUSE

BARON BLISS MEMORIAL

COLTON HOUSE

CORK ST.

RADISSON VILLA WING

BELIZE AUDUBON SOCIETY

FORT ST.

CUSTOM HOUSE

PROGRAMME FOR BELIZE

NATIONAL HANDICRAFTS CENTRE

SPECIAL AFFECTS GIFT SHOP

FORT ST. GUESTHOUSE/ RESTAURANT

BELIZE CITY DOWNTOWN

0   150 yds
0   150 m

© AVALON TRAVEL PUBLISHING, INC.

almost impossible to find any accommodations without reservations. Because of the number and variety of accommodations in Belize City, it's a good base for forays into other parts of the country on day trips.

Belize City has access to rivers, ocean, and three of the five major roads in the country: the Northern Highway, Western Highway, and Manatee Highway. The city is ideally located for reaching any part of the country within a day's time. Because of this access, Belize City is also where you'll find the headquarters of the bus lines, rental car agencies, and airlines, as well as water taxis to get to the cayes.

The People
The people in Belize City, at least 95 percent of them, are really wonderful, friendly people. Strolling the city you have a chance to meet many of them, and to get acquainted with their lifestyle. Many still follow the old traditions, but the younger generation is rolling "full speed ahead" into the 21st century. If you stay in Belize City long enough, and are on foot, you may very well be hassled for money or to buy drugs. Be polite but firm and don't linger.

Stocking Up
Whether you're heading off by bus to Punta Gorda, driving to the Rio Bravo Research Center in Orange Walk District, cycling out to the Cayo District, or catching the boat to the Turneffe Islands, there is nowhere in the country better suited for stocking up on necessary provisions. Supermarkets, pharmacies, hardware stores, and bike shops have a greater selection than you will find elsewhere.

SIGHTS

North of the Swing Bridge
An early morning stroll through the weathered, old clapboard buildings of Belize City gives you a genuine feeling of the city. This is when people are rushing off to work, kids are all spiffed up on their way to school, and housewives are out and about doing their daily shopping.

For most travelers, Belize City revolves around the **swing bridge** at Haulover Creek. You reach it from either airport from the northwest side of

town. This is where you catch boats to the cayes, do your banking, post a letter, buy local handicrafts, and much more. The streets are crammed with small shops (many operated by East Indian and Chinese merchants), a stream of pedestrians on the sidewalks, and lots of traffic.

On this side of the creek, Queen and Front Streets are the crucial thoroughfares. As you face the swing bridge a look to the right will reveal the **Texaco Station;** a look to the left reveals the **Marine Terminal,** home to the **Caye Caulker Water Taxi Association fleet** and the boats that take you to the cayes and the new **Maritime Museum.** On the corner to the left, the post office is in the multistory wooden building.

Moving down Front Street on your right you'll find **Sea Sports Belize** dive shop, 83 N. Front St. and **The Image Factory,** 91 N. Front St., an art gallery featuring Belizean artists.

Keep walking, taking all the roads that go to the right, and you'll come to the **Fort George Lighthouse.** The sea breeze can be very pleasant here as you glimpse numerous cayes as well as ships at anchor offshore. Once you round the point, the road becomes Marine Parade and

BOB RACE

BARON BLISS

Henry Edward Ernest Victor Bliss, also known as the "Fourth Baron Bliss of the former Kingdom of Portugal," was born in the County of Buckingham, England. He first sailed into the harbor of Belize in 1926, though he was too ill to go ashore because of food poisoning he had contracted while visiting Trinidad. Bliss spent several months aboard his yacht, the *Sea King,* in the harbor, fishing in Belizean waters. Although he never got well enough to go ashore, Bliss learned to love the country from the sea and its habitués—the fishermen and officials in the harbor all treated him with great respect and friendliness. On the days that he was able only to languish on deck, he made every effort to learn about the small country. He was apparently so impressed with what he learned and the people he met that before his death he drew up a will that established a trust of nearly two million dollars for projects to benefit the people of Belize.

So far, more than a million dollars in interest from the trust has been used for the erection of the Bliss Institute, Bliss School of Nursing, Bliss Promenade, an In-transit Lounge at the Belize International Airport, plus contributions to the Belize City water supply, the Corozal Town Board and Health Clinic, and for land for the building of Belmopan.

An avid yachtsman, Bliss stipulated that money be set aside for a regatta to be held in Belize waters, a focal point of the gala Baron Bliss Day celebrations each year. The baron's white granite tomb is at the point of Fort George in Belize City, guarded by the Bliss Lighthouse.

---

runs past the modern Radisson Fort George Hotel and **Memorial Park,** a grassy salute to the 40 Belizeans who lost their lives in World War I, and ends at Hutson Street. The **U.S. Embassy** sits at the end of the block on the right. The old colonial house was built in New England, dismantled, and transported to Belize as ship's ballast. It was reconstructed 120 years ago and houses the entire U.S. Embassy, which has been in Belize since 1840.

From the **Radisson Fort George Dock** you'll get a good view of the harbor. Originally this was Fort George Island; until the 1850s it was the location of the army barracks. The strait separating the island from the mainland was filled in during the early 1920s and dedicated as a memorial park for the dead of World War I. Today it is the site of the **Baron Bliss Memorial** and the Radisson Fort George Hotel. After World War II, visiting dignitaries from England surveyed the country armed with plans for various agricultural projects to help the people, but they couldn't find a place to stay. So accommodations went to the top of their priority list and became one of the first postwar projects in the colony. An easygoing, low-key charmer with excellent service and tasty meals, Fort George was the best hotel in town. Today the hotel is part of the Radisson chain and has taken over the Villa hotel across the street, one block off the waterfront.

In general, the Fort George area is one of the most pleasant in Belize City. Meander the neighborhood and you'll pass some lovely homes and a few that have become charming old guest houses. The new **Mirab** department store is here. You'll notice it—square, stark, and rather ugly in this quaint neighborhood.

South of the Swing Bridge

As you cross the bridge, fishing boats at anchor bob in the current. You're in for quite a spectacle if you are lucky enough to be there as the bridge is opened to allow boat traffic upstream.

On the south side of the bridge, you'll encounter even more traffic and more local color. Vendors sell fruits, vegetables, clothes, incense, jewelry, and cold drinks along the southeast side of the bridge. Bliss Promenade skirts the waterfront and eventually brings you to the **Bliss Institute;** social functions and seminars are held here. It is also the location of a theater, museum, and library, as well as the **National Arts Council.**

In the main business section of Regent and Albert Streets (originally called Front and Back Streets—the only streets in 18th-century Belize City) you'll see old brick slave houses, with timber-and-shingle second floors. Slaves were kept in chains in the brick basements when they were not working in the fields.

The Market

Saturday-morning market in Belize City will never be the same. The seedy old colonial marketplace on the southern side of the swing bridge has been replaced by a three-story concrete structure. It's not quite as crowded as the old tin-roofed, open-sided building, but friendly people still sell vegetables, skinned iguanas, fish, meats, and exotic fruits, as well as Belizean handicrafts. When you're strolling through the market and a lovely black lady with a bright-colored kerchief wrapped around her head says, "Try a tamarind, darlin'," go ahead (peel it and enjoy the flesh around the seeds). A tamarind is tasty and looks like a dark-reddish-brown string bean; it has the texture of dried fruit. Man doesn't live by apples alone—the tropics have many exotic fruits to be tried.

Albert Street, just before you reach Belize City's **Central Park,** is the banking center of the city.

The market square offers frequent flea-market activity with a mishmash of gewgaws set out on small blankets, park benches, makeshift tables or the ground. This is a colorful scene with owners huddling close together under brilliant-hued umbrellas to screen out the hot sun. On close examination, it looks as though everyone is selling the same "attic treasures." This is the location of the original courthouse built in 1818. It has since been twice rebuilt (once after a demolition in 1878, and again after a fatal fire in 1918 that took the life of then-governor William Hart Bennett). Today there is no courthouse, just a bit of green in the middle of the city.

The **Supreme Court building** sits between Central Park and Haulover Creek. The antiquated town clock atop the white clapboard building shows a different time from all four sides—each wrong since the clock stopped running many years ago; however, the current rumor is it's going to be repaired and will show the same time on all four sides. Does that mean that everyone will be expected to arrive on time?

The structure is decorated with a graceful white-metal filigree stairway that leads to the long veranda overlooking the square.

Church and State

Belize has the oldest Protestant church in Central America, **St. John's Anglican Cathedral.** This lovely old building, the only typically British structure in the city, is surrounded by well-kept green lawns. The slaves in Belize in 1812 helped to erect this graceful piece of architecture using bricks brought as ballast on sailing ships from Europe. Several Mosquito Coast kings from the Waiki tribe were crowned in this cathedral with ultimate pomp and grandeur; the last was crowned in 1815.

Behind the cathedral, at the southern end of Regent Street and also on Southern Foreshore, is a newish museum in the old **Government House,** which, before Hurricane Hattie and the ensuing construction of Belmopan, was the home and office of the governor general, the official Belizean representative of the Queen of England. (Today the governor general can be found in Belmopan at Belize House.) For a long time it was used as a guest house for visiting VIPs and a place for social functions. Queen Elizabeth and Prince Philip were houseguests here on their visit in 1994. The old wooden buildings (built 1812–14) are said to have been designed by acclaimed British architect Christopher Wren, and until recently were described "as elegant as it gets." It's surrounded by sprawling lawns and wind-brushed palms facing the sea along Southern Foreshore.

Museums and Art Galleries

The museums and art galleries in Belize City offer the visitor a taste of Belize, past and present. The grand **Government House Museum** was built in the 1800s and played a significant role in the early development of Belize. Wander through the wood structure and into the private lives of rulers and politicians of days gone by. Antique lovers will enjoy the period furniture as well as the silverware and glassware collections. On the water's edge, stroll the grounds and enjoy the solitude of the city. Open Mon.–Fri. 8:30 A.M.–4:30 P.M., admission US$2.50.

The **Maritime Museum,** at the swing bridge, has displays of fish and local marine life downstairs; upstairs are models of various boats used past and present in Belize as well as photos and bios of local fishermen and boatbuilders. Open daily 8 A.M.–4 P.M., admission US$2.

The Image Factory, a few doors down from the Maritime Museum, has an eclectic mix of oils and watercolors. The goal of this museum is to encourage Belizean artists to create whatever they wish. Drop in and you might see an artist at work—someone is usually around to discuss the meanings behind the pieces.

The Image Factory also has museumlike displays of "things Belize." You might find a bug collection from someone's 30 years of bug hunting, or art by Belizean children from another time; a printmaking exhibit, or a collection of photographs capturing the history of fire in Belize, who knows, but it's a worthwhile browse. It's not a fancy place, but it's the closest thing to a true art gallery.

The **Bliss Institute** also has revolving displays of artwork.

RECREATION

Diving and Snorkeling
Minutes from Belize City are four cayes with excellent wall dives and idyllic snorkeling. **Hugh Parkey's Dive Connection,** P.O. Box 1818, Belize City, Belize, C.A., tel. 2/34526, 888/223-5403, fax 2/78808, email hugh@belizediving.com, offers a full-service PADI dive shop at the Radisson Marina. Snorkel and dive trips are offered on the newest and biggest day-trip boat fleet to the surrounding cayes, as well as day trips to the Blue Hole. Hugh Parkey also offers scuba instruction and years of local knowledge to divers, in addition to other adventures like manatee watching and inland trips.

Sea Sports Belize, at 83 N. Front St., tel. 2/35505, fax 2/75213, email seasprtsbz@btl.net, offers scuba trips to local reefs and the atolls, instruction, a once a year IDC, snorkeling, and fishing.

Live-Aboard Dive Boats
The *Belize Aggressor III,* 800/348-2628, docks at the Radisson Marina when not out at sea. It's 120 feet long with nine cabins, a wet bar on the sundeck, and a whirlpool. It makes seven-day trips to Lighthouse Reef and the Turneffe Islands with five dives per day. Call for rates.

Another, with all the needed amenities, is the *Wave Dancer.* **Peter Hughes Diving,** 800/932-6237 or 305/669-9391, has a fleet of top-end dive boats that go to Turneffe Islands, Lighthouse, and Glover's Reef. The boat accommo-

dates 20 guests on a dive adventure they will not soon forget. Guests have a choice of five dives per day on two separate sites.

Marinas
Boat owners note: Vessels traveling to the area must have permission before entering Belize. Contact the Belize Embassy in Washington, DC, 202/332-9636.

Rogue's Point, **Radisson Fort George Hotel,** 2 Marine Parade, tel. 2/33333, email rdfgh@btl.net, is a picturesque place to tie up, especially morning and evening. The pier is 550 feet long and, besides being home to dive boats, provides slips for visiting boaters. Fuel, security, a deli, fresh water, and garbage disposal are just some of the services offered.

Belize Resort and Marina, tel. 2/35350, email mohocaye@btl.net, VHF 16, on Moho Caye is just a few minutes from Belize City. The small, protected marina has slips for US$.50 a foot per day. They also offer fuel, oil, ice, laundry services, showers, and access to the mainland. A small bar and restaurant will keep you fed if you don't feel like going into the city. Day-trippers can come here for lunch. The water taxi runs every half hour or so and is free if you eat on the island. If not, cost is US$2.50.

The **Princess Hotel and Casino,** tel. 2/32670, has marina facilities; call for information.

ACCOMMODATIONS

Most hotels all over the country add about 20 percent to listed prices for taxes and service charge. And if the business accepts a credit card (many don't), be prepared to pay 3–5 percent more. One of the publications put out by the Belize Tourist Board says you can find rooms from US$12 and up. Well, the "and up" rooms are easy to find, but you'll have to look a little harder to find the cheapies—and then you should study them carefully. Expect community bathrooms and only cold water in some. But ample economy-types are around for those willing to search for them. Upscale hotels are growing in size—literally; many have added rooms in response to the keen interest in Belize.

Under $25

The small, simple **North Front Street Guest House,** 124 N. Front St., Belize City, Belize, C.A., tel. 2/77595, offers eight rooms with shared bath. Near the center of town, it is within walking distance of the water taxis. The neighborhood isn't the greatest—definitely take a taxi at night. Write or call for more information.

In the same neighborhood is the **Bonaventure Hotel,** tel. 2/44248 or 44134, fax 2/31134; it's very simple, smells old, and has shared bathrooms, but it is cheap. Rooms with private bath are more expensive.

The **Belcove Hotel,** 9 Regent St., West Belize City, Belize, C.A., tel. 2/73054, features 11 simple rooms with ceiling fans and either private or shared baths with h/c water. Rates are US$15 s/d with shared bath, US$20 with private bath and US$40 for a/c and TV. Take a taxi at night.

The best of the budget is the **Seaside Guest House,** 3 Prince St., Belize City, Belize, C.A., tel. 2/78339, email friends@btl.net, a little gem with clean rooms and a comfy environment, the tone set by the Society of Friends, which runs the inn. A dorm room is available with four beds for US$10 per person; private double rooms are US$24.It has hot water in the community bathroom, a sea view, a wonderful orchid display, and it's kept cool by the tradewinds. A bulletin board lists bus schedules, other budget hotels in the country, and other useful information. It's quiet and is only six blocks from the bus station and three blocks from the central square. A good breakfast is available (beans, eggs, toast, orange juice, and tea or coffee US$4). This is a great place to meet travelers from around the world. Please note that reservations are not confirmed until they have received a check. Write for more information.

A reader told us about the **Downtown Guesthouse,** 5 Eve St., tel. 2/33851. It is clean, cheap, and has hot water. With private bath US$20; with shared bath US$10. If you check it out, let us know.

$25–50

On Moho Caye, just a short water-taxi ride from the city, **Maya Landings,** P.O. Box 86, Belize City, Belize, C.A., tel. 2/35350, fax 2/35466, rates are about US$50. Offers four comfortable rooms, a restaurant, and a marina.The restaurant serves good versions of local cuisine and rooms come with h/c water, full private bath, ceiling fans, and windows looking out on the cayes. Credit cards OK. Extra marina slips are available for visitors. A courtesy water taxi takes guests and restaurant patrons to and from Moho Caye and the mainland. Call or write for more information and directions to the water-taxi landing.

$50–100

Trends Guesthouse, 91 Freetown Road, tel. 2/36066, email edsan@btl.net, has comfy rooms with a/c and cable TV within a short distance from everything.

The **Royal Orchid,** P.O. Box 279, Belize City, Belize, C.A., tel. 2/32783, fax 2/32789, is a four-story on the corner of Douglas Jones Street and New Road. Rooms are about US$55. All rooms have h/c water, private baths, a/c, and TV.

Fort Street Guest House is a delightful small guest house in a charming old Victorian building, P.O. Box 3, Belize City, Belize, C.A., tel. 2/30116, fax 2/78808, email fortst@btl.net. In the United States, contact Magnum Belize, 800/447-2931. US$75. The Parkeys (owners) and their staff enjoy making guests feel at home and sharing information about the city and sight-seeing on the cayes and in the countryside. (Hugh Parkey also operates a dive service—dive packages are available.) Conveniently located, the guest house is within easy walking distance of the entire Fort George area as well as the action around the swing bridge area. The cooking here remains outstanding and a favorite with local Belizeans for a special evening out. By night the simple, tropical Victorian decor takes on a crystal, linen, and candlelight sparkle. Lime garlic shrimp has its followers, as does the longtime signature dessert, Death by Chocolate Cake, with chocolate ice cream and topping.

The relaxing Casablanca-style decor of the rooms with wooden shutters, wicker furniture and slow-moving ceiling fans, is special! Some rooms share a bath, some have a private bath. Put your order in the night before and fresh coffee is delivered to your room at 7 A.M. Rates include breakfast.

An on-site tour company, **Jaguar Adventures Tours and Travel,** tel. 2/36025, offers experienced, friendly guides to just about anything you could possibly want to do while in the country.

Colton House, 9 Cork St. (just around the corner from the Radisson Hotel) Belize City, Belize, C.A., tel. 2/44666, another favorite, is just down the street. US$75. This old charmer is owned and operated by Alan and Ondina Colton. It's obvious from the sparkling hardwood floors that a lot of love (and labor) went into renovating the house, which is more than 60 years old. Some of its appeal lies in the white wooden hanging swings on the front porch, the green plants scattered about, and the sheer white curtains on the windows. Bedrooms are fan cooled. Both of the Coltons are usually on hand to give good information about Belize; they live downstairs. The Coltons offer five rooms, all with private bathrooms. The Garden Room has a fridge, microwave, TV, and toaster. Colton's does not offer food, but it's near quite a few restaurants. Close by is a Chinese café, and just around the corner is the Fort Street Restaurant.

The **Mopan Hotel,** US$60 or US$80 with a/c, 55 Regent St., Belize City, Belize, C.A., tel. 2/77351 or 73356, fax 2/75383, is another simple, friendly place. This old-timer has the bar that's been known far and wide as a meeting place for both locals and travelers for decades. The friendly old house has 12 rooms, private bathrooms, with a/c in some.

The **Villa Boscardi B&B,** P.O. Box 1501, Belize City, C.A., tel. 2/31691, email boscardi @btl.net, US$65, is a small, quaint, comfortable inn between the city and the airport, perfect for a weary traveler. A full breakfast is included in the room rate, plus free drop-offs or pickups from the airport, excluding Sundays.

Chateau Caribbean, 6 Marine Parade, Belize City, C.A., tel. 2/30800, email chateaucar@btl.net. Rates start at US$80—a bit pricey for the condition. It has been around for a long time and it shows. This old wooden building has great porches and catches wonderful breezes but is in need of some TLC. The rooms are worn but have private baths, cable TV, and a/c. The restaurant has a variety of tasty dishes and pleasant servers.

Biltmore Plaza, Mile 3, New Northern Highway, Belize City, C.A., U.S. tel. 800/528-1234, Belize tel. 2/32302, fax 2/32301, US$85. One of the more modern Belize City hotels is comfortable and attractive. Seven miles from the airport in the Bella Vista area near town and across the highway from Budget Rent a Car, the Bilt-

more is a convenient stop for those intending to stay overnight before renting a vehicle. You'll find nothing rustic about these 92 rooms; they're midsize, with good beds, TV, direct-dial phones, and tile bathrooms and showers, and the upper story opens onto cool verandas. All the rooms surround a green garden with a pool in the middle that has a swim-up bar. The **Victorian Room** is an upscale dining room open daily 7 A.M.–11 P.M. The **Squires Lounge** is adjacent to the restaurant and opens at 4:30 P.M. for predinner drinks or a handy game of darts. This really gives the feeling of an English pub; were they still around, you might find a group of British soldiers having an ale and tossing darts.

The **Bellevue Hotel,** 5 S. Foreshore, P.O. Box 428, Belize City, Belize, C.A., tel. 2/77051, fax 2/73253, email bellevue@btl.net or fins@btl.net, is a charming landmark hotel that was built as a private home in the early 1900s. US$65–85. The family that built this hotel has owned and operated it for the past 46 years. Most of the rooms are large with private bathrooms, a/c, and telephones. The hotel features a garden/pool, restaurant, bar, and a lively disco with live band on Friday nights plus happy hour and karaoke.

$100–150

The **Great House,** 13 Cork St., Belize City, Belize, C.A., tel. 2/33400, fax 2/33444, email greathouse@btl.net, US$105. This beautiful colonial structure, originally built in 1927, was renovated and restored a few years ago, and is now a charming hotel. The six spacious rooms each have a different color scheme and offer queen-size beds, a/c, in-room safe deposit boxes, and all the modern conveniences. Downstairs is a mini-mall. If you can catch him, ask owner Steve Maestre about the months they spent raising the building over five feet—while living in it! The on-site restaurant, **The Smokey Mermaid,** has a built-in smokehouse and specializes in smoked fish, meats, and assorted fresh breads. Beer lovers: Steve claims they have the coldest beer in town. The outdoor dining area has wooden multilevel decks made out of sapodilla wood—wood so hard they couldn't nail it but had to drill through it. Fruit trees, tropical plants, and flowers flourish, creating a comfortable garden atmosphere.

The **Princess Hotel and Casino,** Kings Park, Belize City, C.A., tel. 2/32670, email princessbz@btl.net, standard rooms are about US$125. Formerly the Fiesta Inn (in last edition), the hotel has brought big gaming to this little country. A modern casino similar to Vegas awaits you. Bring your wallet!

The 118 rooms all have a/c, cable TV, and a typical bland look. They are comfortable with views of the ocean but seem to be missing the charm of Belize. Everything you need is here: pool, gift shop, beauty salon, conference facilities, bars, restaurants, and a tour desk. There are also a variety of suites.

An on-site marina has docking facilities for visiting boats, is home to SeaSports Belize, and has WaveRunner rentals.

US$150+

One of the older upscale hotels in Belize City is the **Radisson Fort George Hotel,** 2 Marine Parade (on the waterfront), P.O. Box 321, Belize City, Belize, C.A., tel. 2/77400 or 77242, fax 2/73820. In the United States or Canada, call 800/333-3333 or fax 402/498-9166. Rates start at US$169. Rooms are nicely appointed, with private baths, a/c, TV, and minibars; some have ocean views. Across the street at the Villa, all rooms have a view of the ocean. The hotel has two swimming pools and its own marina. The dining room serves a daily full buffet breakfast and offers a different dinner special each day; on Thanksgiving count on a U.S.-style turkey dinner. You'll also find the Seventh Heaven Guest Deck, a bookstand, and a gift shop. And if you see a big bowl of bananas in the lobby, help yourself!

Inside the Fort George compound is **Rachel's Art Gallery,** which carries prints and original art by various artists, including those by Rachel herself. **Emory King Real Estate** also has a small office here. (The main office is at 9 Regent St., tel. 2/77453.)

Near the Airport

Don't be misled by the name **Embassy Suites,** tel. 2/52226. It's not an embassy-type and needs some TLC, but it's conveniently located across the street from the Philip Goldson Airport. You can actually see the terminal from the basic rooms; the one we looked at smelled smoky. The owners are nice people that are very helpful,

have passenger vans, and will arrange tours for their guests. They also rent cars at comparable prices. They cater to school and church groups, and give groups over eight good rates on meals and rooms. US$35 pp for room and three (set) meals. Dining room available for all guests. Rooms with private bathroom US$50, with king bed US$65, suites start at US$89.

By the New Northern Highway near the international airport, the **Belize River Lodge,** P.O. Box 459, Belize City, Belize, C.A., tel. 2/52002, email bzelodge@btl.net, is ready for the fishermen. It sits on a lush bank of the Belize *Olde River.* Up to 16 guests stay in the beautiful mahogany lodge, run by Marguerite Miles and Mike Heusner. They specialize in flats fishing, either from the lodge or a mothership cruise. Both options offer great fishing areas; flats, cayes, barrier reef, Belize River, Sibun River, and many other desirable locations. Go for tarpon, permit, bonefish, snook, jacks, barracuda, grouper and more. Write or call for more information. A six-night package costs about US$1,949 pp.

FOOD

For years it was the custom for international travelers to Belize to eat in their hotels, where simple food was prepared. Few restaurants were available, and even those were really nothing to speak of. However, more and more travelers are now opting to try the cuisine of the country. As a result, a few more restaurants open each year.

Local Cuisine

While in Belize take the opportunity to try the country favorites: Creole-style beans, rice, and stewed chicken. Favorite side dishes are coleslaw and fried plantain (large cooking bananas). Fried chicken and potato salad are Sunday-best dinners. And fresh fish is beginning to come in fancy wrappings. If staying at a guest house, ask if the cook makes fry jacks (bread dough that is flattened into thin, small round cakes and fried) for breakfast. One of the staples of the Caribbean for years has been conch: conch fritters, stewed conch, even conch ceviche. Will the conch still exist 30 years from now? Who knows, but efforts are being made to "farm" them.

Belize street

Fragile Foods from the Sea

Don't order seafood out of season. The ocean is being exploited, and even some fishermen somehow don't realize that if you keep eating the babies of any species, they don't grow up to produce. The once-prolific lobster is becoming scarce in Belizean waters. And conch (really the staple of the Caribbean people) is not nearly as easy to find as it once was. Most reputable restaurateurs go along with the "rules" and don't buy fragile seafood undersized or out of season; however, a few have no scruples. Closed season for lobster is Feb. 15–June 15, and conch season is closed July 1–September 30. Lobster season has been shifted to help the crawly red critters get ahead of the hunt.

Wild Game

For the adventurous, at least one restaurant in Belize City—**Macy's**—serves wild game. The old favorites, such as venison, are seldom seen on menus because of their position on the about-to-become-extinct list. Even "bamboo chicken" (iguana) is getting harder to find; however, an iguana program will soon make it a "farm" product. But you will see some dishes that you probably won't find anyplace else. For the most part, **armadillo** and **gibnut** are fixed in a stew. **Turtle,** another species getting scarce and on a don't-hunt list, was on the menu last visit—it's your choice: boycott or tell the owners your feelings.

Hotel Food

Belize City is not a "gourmet delight" *yet,* but things are looking up. Hotels are beginning to discover good chefs, and a few outstanding restaurants are becoming known outside the country. All of the more luxury-oriented hotels offer continental cuisine in lovely surroundings, though the food is apt to be a little pricey. And don't forget the small hotels. Some of the guest houses have some of the tastiest meals around.

The **Bellevue Hotel** is known for good food and a bar upstairs that overlooks the water. The **Radisson Fort George Hotel** serves a beautiful buffet with a multitude of delicious seafood delicacies. The **Princess Hotel** has a whole selection of dining experiences on the premises and **The Smokey Mermaid** at the Great House is the newest kid on the block that offers many great dishes.

International Food

Among the better small restaurants is the **Fort Street Restaurant,** 4 Fort St., tel. 2/30116. Fort Street is a popular spot with an excellent menu for a special candlelight dinner, but don't give short shrift to breakfast and lunch. (We had one of the great Thanksgiving dinners away from home at Fort Street.) **Chef Bob's,** 164 Newtown Barrack St., tel. 2/34201, a short walk from the Princess Hotel, is popular with upscale travelers. And if you like that sort of thing, you can rub shoulders with the hoity crowd while enjoying a glass of wine, and a good steak or tasty pasta.

Belizean Specialties
Macy's Restaurant, 18 Bishop St., is a good bet for excellent Creole food at reasonable prices. If you see conch fritters on the menu, give them a try. **Three Amigos,** 2 King Street, is another favorite for inexpensive, typical Belizean fare.

Simple and Good
Big Daddy's Diner, on the top floor of the public market, has good eggs and fry jacks for breakfast as well as a nice view of the water taxis. **Sara's Kitchen,** on New Road, has great "stew beans" and rice as well as other specials. (Don't miss out on the cow foot soup on Saturday.)

Chinese Cooking
You'll find a lot of Chinese food in Belize City. Some of the better places include the **Chateau Caribbean Hotel,** 6 Marine Parade, tel. 2/30800, **Timmy's Place** on St. Thomas St., and **New Chon San Palace,** 184 N. Front Street.

Other Cuisines
For Indian dishes, check out **Natraj, Gateway of India,** 5 Amara Ave., tel. 2/74723, where you'll find a menu that includes chicken tika, mutton

egg fry, and fish baryani. The **Sea Rock Restaurant,** 190 New Town, tel. 2/34105, features a large selection of Indian dishes.

Snacks and Sweets
Ice-cream lovers go to **Scoops,** Gaol Lane at Eve St., for ice-cream cones and sundaes. Or for a tropical fruit drink and more ice cream, stop in at **Bluebird Ice Cream Parlour,** Albert Street. You can always check out the deli case at **Brodie's Department Store,** with lusciouslooking cold cuts and sandwiches to go.

NIGHTLIFE

Travelers looking for nightlife in Belize City will find the best at hotels such as the **Bellevue,** where the views of the harbor are great at sunset and music goes on often until the wee hours of the morning. **Club Excess** is "a real disco" by local standards. **Linsberg** bar lounge offers disco with happy hour and karaoke. A pirated **Planet Hollywood,** on Queen Street, is a decent-sized disco for those wanting to shake their booty.

Look around, ask at your hotel, take a taxi; something's always going on at night in Belize. (As tempting as some activities might be, we recommend you keep things legal.)

SHOPPING

Gifts and Souvenirs
At 3 Fort Street, across from the Fort Street Guest House, sits an old warehouse. But don't be fooled: The **National Handicrafts Centre,** tel. 2/33636, is one of the best sources of Belizean arts and crafts in the country. Inside you'll find carved wooden plaques and bowls, jewelry, bags, ceramics, slate carvings, baskets, maps, music, and more. **Note:** Bringing black coral jewelry or any other form of the coral into the United States is illegal.

Nearby is **Special Affects,** #1 Fort Street, tel. 2/35973, a large shop that is tastefully decorated and full of special treasures. Most of the goods are made in Belize.

Rachel's Art Gallery, in the courtyard of the Radisson Fort George Hotel, 2 Marine Parade,

---

DRINKING WATER IN BELIZE CITY

Use your common sense as far as food and water are concerned. The water in Belize is said to be potable and is used by most everyone. The water is commonly runoff from rooftops that is then stored in cisterns or tanks. In some cases, it's perfectly safe; in others, it's iffy! If you're concerned, bottled water is for sale. In case it's not available, carry a small bottle of laundry bleach as a backup. Add a couple of drops per quart of water, shake, and let stand 30 minutes before drinking. Another option is to travel with a small, portable water purifier. (See "Health and Safety" in the On the Road chapter.)

artisan with Ziricote carving

is a small shop big on the quality of Belizean paintings and prints displayed. A talented artist herself, Rachel also has a few of her own pieces for sale.

Sings, near Brodies, has a great selection of reasonably priced T-shirts as well as a collection of junky knickknacks.

At **Brodie's Department Store,** Albert and Regent Streets, tel. 2/77070, and you'll find a modern boutique where you can collect lots of goodies to take home.

On days that cruise ships are in town, many shops and vendors set out tables in the Memorial Park near where passengers disembark. Wood and slate carvings, books, T-shirts, and Belizean specialty foods are just some of the goods you find.

Groceries and Sundries
Brodie's Department Store, Albert and Regent Streets, tel. 2/77070, is an institution in Belize. It's a modern emporium that sells a wide

variety of foodstuffs and personal hygiene products, shampoos, soaps, aspirin, toilet tissue, razors, shoe polish, and much, much more. Across the street is another modernish supermarket, **Ro-Macs.**

Stock up on your way into or out of the north edge of town at **Sav U Supermarket.** This modern, air-conditioned market sells everything any supermarket in the United States would carry, and it's reasonably priced.

Film and Photo Processing
Photo processing in Belize has come a long way in the last several years. Now you can get fast, professional processing of slides or prints at **Belize Photo Lab,** corner of Bishop and Canal Streets, tel. 2/74991; **Spooner's 1-Hour Minilab,** 89 Front St., tel. 2/31043. And both chrome and print film is available.

SERVICES

Money Matters
Go south over the bridge on Albert Street and you run into a string of banks, including **Atlantic Bank,** 6 Albert St., tel. 2/71255; **Bank of Nova Scotia,** Albert St., tel. 2/77027; **Barclay's Bank,** 21 Albert St., tel. 2/77211; **Belize Bank,** 60 Market Square, tel. 2/77132. All the banks keep the same hours and days: Mon.–Thurs. 8 A.M.–1 P.M., Fri. 8 A.M.–1 P.M. and 3–6 P.M. Keep in mind most banks don't accept ATM cards from the United States—you need to have an account with the bank. The exception is Barclay's Bank, which currently accepts foreign ATM cards.

Be prepared for some additions on your bills for taxes and service charges:
• Sales tax 8%
• Hotel room tax 7%
• Service charge (a tip placed on a bill) 10%
• Airport departure tax US$15
• Airport security fees: from international airport to domestic airport in Belize is US$.75; international airport to foreign international airport is US$1.25; and a **Protected Areas Conservation Trust** fee of US$7.50.

If you use your credit card, it will cost you a little more at most businesses. Ask how much, if that's a problem. You will be approached by street vendors selling Belize dollars for less than the official rate. You might be lucky and hook up with an honest peddler (and many are), but on the other hand you might find the guy who has already cheated a lot of tourists in the exchange business. The official rate of exchange is two Belize dollars for one U.S. dollar.

Post Office

To post a letter or pick up stamps, stop by the **Paslow Building,** at the corner of Queen and Front Streets. Lots of folks buy the beautiful Belize stamps for framing and for gifts. They really are lovely. If you just want to post a letter, expect a letter to the United States to travel for US$0.30, a postcard for US$0.15; to Europe a letter will cost BZE$0.75, and a postcard is BZE$0.40. If you visit in the outlying cities or cayes, bring your mail to Belize City to post. It's more apt to get to its destination quickly.

Emergency Numbers

For the **police,** call 911. For **fire** and **ambulance,** call 90.

Medical Services

If you should need a doctor, **Belize Medical Associates** is located at 5791 St. Thomas St., tel. 2/30303. **Karl Heusner Memorial Hospital** is on Princess Margaret Dr., tel. 2/31548 or 31564.

Downtown pharmacies are **Community Drug Store,** Albert St., tel. 2/73842; **Brodie's Department Store,** Albert and Regent Streets, tel. 2/77070; and **Central Drug Store,** 1 Market Square, downtown.

Internet Services

To email home, Angelus Press on Queen Street and BTL on Church Street both offer email services. Many of the larger hotels also offer email services.

INFORMATION

Tourist Information

For general information sources and a list of consulates, see "Information" in the On the Road chapter. While in Belize City, visit or call the **Belize Tourist Board,** at the New Central Bank building on Gabourel Lane, tel. 2/31913, email info@travelbelize.org, for information on re-

serves, national parks, and various sections of the country.

There is a desk at the water-taxi terminal that might prove helpful.

Travel Agents

Want to book transportation, tours, or accommodations? **S & L Travel Services,** 91 N. Front St., P.O. Box 700, Belize City, Belize, C.A., tel. 2/75145 or 77593, fax 2/77594, email sltravel @btl.net, is easy to find. Owners Sarita and Lascelle Tillet run a first-class and very personable operation. They've been in business for over 25 years; we have worked with them for more than 10 years. They can get as creative as you like, whether you want a custom vacation, a photo safari, a birding adventure, or anything else you can imagine. You also can get all the usual things—airline tickets, car rentals, hotel reservations.

To the east and on the left is another agency, **Belize Travel Adventures,** 168 N. Front St., Belize City, Belize, C.A., tel. 2/32618. Using local agencies to make arrangements is often better than trying to wing it completely on your own. These agencies can get you all the information you need, and when rooms are tight (a not too infrequent situation Feb.–April), they are more likely to be able to get you accommodated.

Jaguar Adventures Tours and Travel, 4 Fort St., Belize City, C.A., tel. 2/36025, email jaguaradv@btl.net, is located at the Fort Street Hotel and offers night walks at the Belize Zoo, cave tubing trips, visits to Maya ruins, snorkeling the reef, and diving the atolls, to name a few.

Universal Travel Services, 14 Handyside St., tel. 2/30963, fax 2/32120, is another reputable option.

Conservation Organizations

The **Belize Audubon Society** has offices and representatives all over the country. It is a splendid source of information for travelers who wish to investigate any of the wildlife reserves in Belize. In each case the society is involved in managing the reserves. It has the most up-to-date information about current seasonal conditions, and can tell you when and if you can use each reserve. Ask about the **Community Baboon Sanctuary** at Bermudian Landing, **Cockscomb Basin Wildlife Sanctuary, Crooked Tree**

BETA NO LITTA

Whether in Creole or plain English, the message comes through! Keep our country clean. The **Belize Eco-Tourism Association** (BETA), along with businesses, resorts, and individuals, is sponsoring an antilittering campaign to clean up the roadsides and to protect the environment. Where you see the green signs, someone has adopted that portion of the road and makes certain it is kept clean. Hurray BETA!

Sanctuary, and **Half Moon Caye Natural Sanctuary.** Roughing it at these locations (and that's pretty much the way it is at all of them) is not for everyone, but for those willing to stay in very basic accommodations or camp, each of these offers unique experiences. The office at 12 Fort St., tel. 2/34985 or 35004, can answer tourists' questions. Stop by to buy books on natural history or to pick up free pamphlets on parks. Bird-watchers, ask about the *Belize Bird Guide.* This office is also where you can arrange overnight accommodations in Cockscomb Basin Wildlife Sanctuary.

Near the Fort Street District is the **Programme for Belize,** 1 Eyre Street, P.O. Box 749, Belize City, Belize, C.A., U.S. tel. 617/259-9500, Belize tel. 2/75616, fax 2/75635, email pfbel@btl.net, is the group that manages the **Rio Bravo Conservation Area** with the support of the Belize Audubon Society, The Nature Conservancy, and the World Wildlife Fund. Stop in here to arrange for accommodations or tours at Rio Bravo in Orange Walk District.

Publications

In most of the large hotels, you'll find a shop with English-language novels and popular history and picture books put out by Belize's own **Cubola Productions.** It publishes a selection of history books, an atlas of the country, and several collections of short stories and poems written by locals. They aren't necessarily all Pulitzer quality, but they give a great insight into the country from the early days to today. Several bookstores in town are worth investigating.

Though the **Angelus Press,** 10 Queen St.,

tel. 2/35777, north of the swing bridge, is a large stationery shop, it offers a good selection of books about Belize, maps, paper supplies, pens, and stamps, plus all kinds of equipment for architects, etc. There is also a good selection at the **Book Centre,** tel. 2/77457.

For complete, accurate survey maps of the entire country, check out the **Survey Department,** above the post office on Queen St., tel. 2/73221. The **Belize Tourist Board** also has maps available; they're not of Survey Department caliber, but they'll get you around. And of course, Emory King's *Road Guide* for the country is charming, though not necessarily perfectly accurate.

If you're looking for **local newspapers,** you'll find several in the city; *Amandala* is our favorite.

For American news, check with the Radisson and Fort Street Guest House. Between the two you can generally find the *Miami Herald, Newsweek,* and/or *Time.* **Brodie's** also carries American magazines and some books.

GETTING AROUND

Getting around the city by foot is fairly easy since most of it is clustered close together. However, if you wish to see Belize City's outlying areas you can go by taxi, bus, boat, or plane.

By Rental Car

Belize City has various rental car agencies. They are all expensive. **Budget Rent a Car,** Mile 3, Northern Highway, tel. 2/32435 or 33986, fax 2/30237, offers new cars that are well maintained. When you're out in the wilderness, that's what counts. **Avis,** tel. 2/52385, another reputable agency, has cars at both the international (tel. 2/52385) and municipal (tel. 2/34619) airports. **Hertz** is in a convenient location half a block from the Radisson, tel. 2/35395.

Safari Car Rental, 73 Eve St., tel. 2/35395, fax 2/30268, U.S. tel. 800/447-2931, offers all four-door 4WD vehicles and a small pickup for driving around town. Other companies have offices in town; these just happen to be our favorites. Price them all—you never know when you can make a good deal. And of course, always check out your car thoroughly.

If you're driving the **Western Highway,** start your trip odometer at the cemetery; if you're driving the **Northern Highway,** start the odometer at the northern edge of town just north of the intersection of the Northern Highway with Central American Blvd./Princess Margaret Drive. Using your odometer from Belize City will help you track your location and mileage. The mileage signs are easy to see alongside the road.

Two **gas stations** that are easy to find downtown are **A & R Texaco** on North Front Street, just upriver from the swing bridge where the water taxis park, and **Nava's Texaco** on North Front Street, down the street from the post office about a block and on the right. You'll find **Shell** and **Esso** stations around town, as well as on the way out of town on the Northern and Western Highways.

By Taxi

Taxi fares are *supposed to be* controlled by the government. Even so, they should be determined before getting in the cab. From the international airport to Belize City, the fare is usually US$15; from the municipal airstrip expect to pay US$5. The fare for one passenger carried between any two points within Belize City (or any other district town) is US$2.50.If you plan to make several stops, tell the cabbie in advance and ask what the total will be; this eliminates lots of misunderstandings. Generally speaking, most of the city is accessible on foot, even the bus stations. Taxis can be hired by the hour (US$15) for long trips out of town.

By Bus

You'll find a choice of buses available going off in all directions. Since the schedules change regularly, contact the companies when you're ready to travel. Fares are reasonable. The bus lines are:

Novelo Bus Service, West Collet Canal, tel. 2/77372; **Venus Bus Lines,** Magazine Road, tel. 2/73354 or 77390; **Z-Line Bus Service,** Magazine Road, tel. 2/73937; in Dangriga, tel. 5/22211. Other small lines, which don't have phone numbers, are **Jex Buses,** which depart from 34 Regent Street and from the Pound Yard Bridge to Crooked Tree, and **Pooks** and **Russell's** which go the Bermudian Landing.

By Sea

You now have a choice of boats to get to the cayes or other coastal communities. One point of departure is the water terminal at the swing bridge. Daily scheduled trips go to and from Caye Caulker and Ambergris Caye throughout the day. Another terminal is at the Texaco Station, 73 N. Front St., tel. 2/30413, where the *Rainbow Runner* leaves for both destinations. Fares cost US$7.50 one-way to Caulker, US$12.50 to Ambergris.

Most of the water taxis will stop at Caye Chapel or Caye Caulker on their way to Ambergris Caye if you alert the captain as you board. On calm, sunny days it's a very pleasant trip. In windy or rainy weather, a light wrap comes in handy. Or take the *Andrea,* which is enclosed, from the dock at the Bellevue Hotel. Transit to Caye Caulker takes about 45 minutes; the trip between Belize City and Ambergris takes about 75 minutes. The trips cost about US$10 one-way, less than US$20 round-trip.

By Air

The Belizean commuter planes provide a great service in and out of Belize City to the outlying airports all over the country. In many cases taking the plane really beats the bumpy, rough (often muddy) roads for long distances (like to Punta Gorda). Call for current schedules and prices. Two airlines offer regularly scheduled flights to all districts in Belize: **Tropic Air,** tel. 2/62338 (international airport), tel. 2/45671 (municipal airport), U.S./Canadian tel. 800/422-3435, email tropicair@btl.net; and **Maya Island Air,** tel. 2/31140 or 35371, U.S. tel. 800/521-1247, email mayair@btl.net.

Other planes available for charter from the municipal airport include **Caribee Air,** tel. 2/44253; **Javier's Flying Service,** tel. 2/35360; and **Su-Bec Air,** tel. 2/34906 or 30388.

By Tour

Savvy travelers know Belize offers much for the visitor to see and many ways to do it: travel independently with a rental car or by bus, hire a taxi, or travel with a tour operator who provides transportation as well as guidance. For those interested in letting someone else do the driving, various tour operators are reliable. In Belize City, for example, Sarita and Lascelle Tillet of **S & L Travel**

Services, P.O. Box 700, 91 N. Front St., Belize City, Belize, C.A., tel. 2/75145 or 77593, fax 2/77594, email sltravel@btl.net, operate as a husband/wife team. They drive late-model air-conditioned sedans or vans and travel throughout the country with airport pickup available. The Tillets have designed several great **special-interest vacations** and will custom design to your interests, whether they be the Maya archaeological zones (including Guatemala's Tikal), the cayes, or the caves and the countryside. Lascelle is a great bird-watcher; he always seems to spot the unique before anyone else and knows the names and living habits of each winged creature—it was he who pointed out our first jabiru stork in Belize.

Formerly Belize Mesoamerica, **Adventure Expeditions Belize,** 4 S. Park St., P.O. Box 1217, Belize City, Belize, C.A., tel. 2/30748, fax 2/30750, is another reputable Belizean tour agency. Tell the agents what you want and they will make it easy for you. They have an office at the Belize International Airport and offer tours to all the attractions in the country, whether natural history, archaeology, or adventure.

Other reputable agencies include; **Jaguar Adventures Tours and Travel,** 4 Fort St., Belize City, C.A., tel. 2/36025, email jaguaradv@btl.net; **Belize Travel Adventures,** 168 N. Front St., tel. 2/33064, fax 2/33196, and **Belize Tours & Expeditions,** tel./fax 2/35721.

VICINITY OF BELIZE CITY

GALES POINT

To get to Gales Point by car choose either the Manatee Highway or the Hummingbird Highway; make sure it's not raining! Going by way of the Hummingbird is about 25 miles longer. It's a drive best done in daylight because it's safer and there's such a lot to see—beautiful jungle views, Maya villages, and the Maya Mountains in the distance.

A small village originally established by logwood cutters sits on a two-mile-long peninsula that juts into the Southern Lagoon; both are called Gales Point. Gales Point is about 15 miles north of Dangriga in Stann Creek District and 25 miles south of Belize City.

Southern Lagoon
The lagoon is part of an extensive estuary surrounded by thick mangroves. Their tangled roots provide the perfect breeding grounds for sport fish, crabs, shrimp, lobster, and a host of other marine life. Rich beds of sea grass line the bottom of the lagoon and support a population of manatees. These gentle mammals are often seen basking on the surface of the water or coming up for air (which they must do about every four minutes). This concentration of manatees is a popular spot for boaters to bring visitors to observe the manatees.

Access from Belize City by boat is a pleasant way to Gales Point. The boat winds through mangrove-lined canals and across the Sibun River before going through the Northern and Southern Lagoons.

Accommodations
Manatee Lodge, P.O. Box1242, Belize City, Belize, C.A., U.S. tel. 877/462-6283, Belize tel./fax 2/12040. On the northern end of Gales Point, visitors here have access to a completely different wildlife habitat that exists in the broad expanse of shallow brackish water and mangroves called the Southern Lagoon. The number of shorebirds and waterfowl is impressive, and to encourage guests to see local wildlife, the lodge provides each room with a canoe. Binoculars and bug repellent are a must. A motor boat and guide are US$125 per half-day for a group of up to four people. Expeditions to other area nature reserves can be arranged along with round-trip ground/water transport between Belize International Airport and Gales Point (ask for prices). The lodge caters to birders and independent travelers who enjoy the outdoors. You can fish for a little diversion (some rods are available at the lodge). The kids especially seem to enjoy baiting a hook and seeing what comes up on the other end of the line. Snook and snapper are likely and tasty catches. The lodge will prepare them for lunch or dinner. Fly-fishing for the small tarpon of the lagoon can be fun. The lodge also has a couple of Sunfish sailboats for the enjoyment of guests.

The eight rooms of the lodge are spacious, have private bathrooms, and are connected to the main buildings by elevated walkways. Children under six are free, 6–12 half price. Room rates are US$87.50 s, US$105 d; breakfast US$5.50–7.50, lunch US$7.50, dinner US$13.50.

The Shores, tel. 2/12023, email shores @btl.net, is another pleasant resort located at Gale's Point on the sea about halfway between Belize City and Dangriga near the Creole village of Gale's Point. Visitors find lots of beach to explore, and during nesting season they may see the hawksbill sea turtle laying her eggs. Diving lessons are available or river trips in canoes, dive trips to nearby cayes or at the nearby reef. The lodge is airy and the cabañas offer private baths, family-style buffets for breakfast, lunch, and dinner are included in the price, US$60 per person per night, double occupancy.

To the Belize Zoo

On Freetown Road headed out of Belize City, turn left onto Central American Boulevard and cross the Belcan Bridge. At the first big intersection you come to—it has a turnaround in the center of the intersection—take a right and you are now on Cemetery Road, which becomes the Western Highway. Set the trip odometer at 1. Follow the Western Highway to about Mile 28 and look for the turnoff on the right.

THE BELIZE ZOO AND TROPICAL EDUCATION CENTER

The Zoo

The Belize Zoo, established in 1983, has continued to grow from a backyard enterprise into a one-of-a-kind zoo where the happy animals practically smile at you. The zoo is located on 1,600 acres and uses 29 acres to house 20 varieties of mammals, 12 bird species, and six types of reptiles. Over 125 creatures live and thrive here; all are native to Belize. The zoo keeps animals that were either orphaned, injured and rehabilitated, those born in the zoo, or are gifts from other zoos. The environment is as natural as possible, and each animal lives in its own shady jungle compound; no steel bars here.

Sharon Matola, the founding director of the Belize Zoo, tells the story of the zoo with affection and love: "Some people call it funky; others say that it's the best zoo they have ever seen, and everyone tells us that the animals who live at the Belize Zoo seem . . . well, they seem so happy. Welcome to the Belize Zoo!" This zoo is probably the single-most important educational tool of the country. Ten thousand children visit the zoo each year.

Many zoo supporters in and out of the country obtained pledges, raised contributions, and held fund-raisers to build successful new housing for the animals. Since the zoo moved to its new headquarters in 1991, it has added a spacious waterbird compound (in 1993), and several valuable new boarders have moved in: two jabiru storks; Ellen the black jaguar; C. T. Katun, a male spotted jaguar; and a jaguarundi.

Everyone loves the old-timers, like April, the Baird tapir—also known as a mountain cow. (An old superstition says that the tapir can skin a person alive with its nose.) Sometimes when you go to visit this 500-pound tapir, she's happily submerged in her own pond. She's a hands-on favorite. When she trundles over to get a closer look at the curious visitor, it is evident that the personal touches of animal care and wildlife education have produced a unique zoo experience. She now has a roommate, which is part of the zoo's philosophy to keep the animals happy. April is a representative of Belize's national animal, and her birthday is celebrated every year with a big birthday party, all kids invited.

No one can ignore Rambo the colorful toucan, or Sugar, the pretty little purring ocelot. A favorite of the kids is Sweetboy, the otter, who tumbles and plays in the water to a great audience.

Wildlife Awareness

The zoo's hand-painted, homespun signs provide simple educational messages that help visitors to laugh as well as learn. A glance at the sign in front of the peccary enclosure tells visitors, "We are warries, and we like the way we smell." Warries are members of the piglike peccary family. Peccaries do smell funny, but a sign explains the purpose of this odd scent in a way that helps observers to appreciate this animal's unusual natural history.

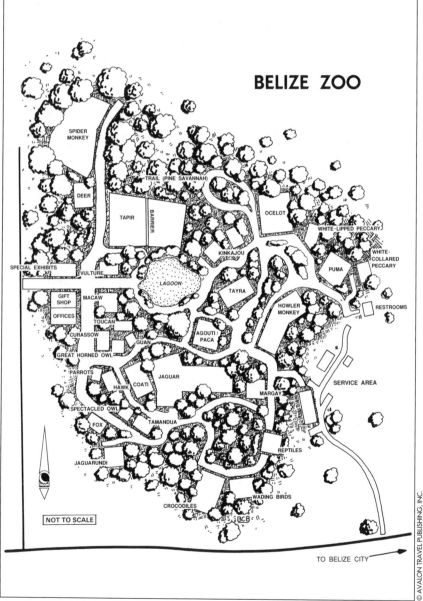

BELIZE ZOO

SPIDER MONKEY

TRAIL (PINE SAVANNAH)

DEER

TAPIR

BARRIER

OCELOT

WHITE-LIPPED PECCARY

KINKAJOU

WHITE-COLLARED PECCARY

SPECIAL EXHIBITS

VULTURE

LAGOON

TAYRA

PUMA

RESTROOMS

GIFT SHOP

MACAW

HOWLER MONKEY

OFFICES

TOUCAN

CURASSOW

GUAN

AGOUTI / PACA

GREAT HORNED OWL

PARROTS

JAGUAR

HAWK

COATI

MARGAY

SERVICE AREA

SPECTACLED OWL

FOX

TAMANDUA

JAGUARUNDI

REPTILES

WADING BIRDS

CROCODILES

BCB

NOT TO SCALE

TO BELIZE CITY

© AVALON TRAVEL PUBLISHING, INC.

THE BEGINNING OF AN ANIMAL ADVENTURE: THE BELIZE ZOO

Director Sharon Matola started the Belize Zoo in January 1983—the beginning of an accidental career. Coming to Belize to begin a zoo and build a wildlife-education program was not what she considered part of her destiny. She always loved animals and arrived in Belize to manage a small collection of local animals for a Nature film company. However, after she had worked only five months on the project, funds were severely reduced, and it became evident that the group of animal "film stars" would have to be disbanded.

Get Rid of the Animals?

Sharon says that besides the fact that these wild cats, birds, anteaters, and snakes had become her friends and companions, logic entered the picture. Once a wild animal has become semitamed and dependent on people for care, returning to a life in the wild is impossible.

As an alternative, she decided, "This country has never had a zoo. Perhaps if I offered the chance for Belizeans to see these unique animals, their existence here could be permanently established."

And so a zoo was born. From the very beginning, the amount of local interest shown in the zoo was incredible. The majority of the people in Belize live in urban areas, and their knowledge of the local fauna is minimal. The Belize Zoo offered many Belizeans the opportunity to see the animals that share their country. It was touching to see the looks on the faces of small children who were experiencing for the first time the animals of their homeland. The modest beginnings hinged on the simple idea that children deserved the chance to grow up knowing animals, especially those living in the thick forests and jungles not too many miles from their city homes.

School Programs

This initial interest was exciting and prompted Sharon to begin a countrywide education program. She took colorful slides of the animals to schools along with invitations for the teachers to bring their students—free of charge—to the new zoo. Those modest beginnings have evolved into a major wildlife awareness program that has touched the hearts of thousands of children and adults throughout Belize. The zoo now has a collection of Belizean fauna that numbers well over one hundred species. The zoo staff is a dedicated crew of Belizean zookeepers who not only provide excellent care for the animals but also travel around the nation with wildlife-education programs.

A Success Story

This type of progressive wildlife education has helped to bring about a growing pride among the

(continued on next page)

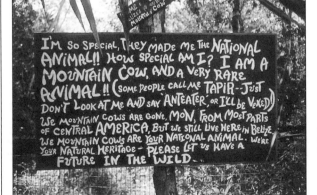

The "backyard" feeling is promoted by these clever signs at each exhibit.

THE BEGINNING OF AN ANIMAL ADVENTURE: THE BELIZE ZOO

(continued)

people of Belize for the animals of their country. This sense of pride will lead to a feeling of propriety that will ultimately help to ensure the animals' future in the Belizean wild. The zoo's success story will develop further, and the future is an exciting one. Using a master plan for development that was donated by zoo architects from Seattle, Washington, the goal is to display each Belizean animal in a natural, wild setting.

Of course, the usual problem prevailed: how to support this project. Raising money to implement this master plan has been a local as well as an international effort. It wasn't easy, but slow and steady progress continues. A visit to the Belize Zoo is fun, inspiring, and educational for the local as well as foreign visitors. The funky, "down-home" approach puts people from all walks of life in touch with the magic of the animals, which are the natural heritage of this unspoiled, tropical country, and more, natural treasures of the entire world. Thank you, Sharon Matola!

April, the national animal, loves the attention she gets at the Belize Zoo.

Special events at the zoo further enhance wildlife awareness efforts. Every child in the nation is invited to come to the zoo and join the celebration of their national animal's birthday. Besides singing "Happy Birthday" to a tapir, eating cake, and being entertained by Rose Tattoo (the famous clown of Belize), the children learn more about their special natural heritage and all the reasons for protecting it.

One of the zoo's important messages is to let visitors know where they can view the animals of Belize in the wild. When watching the howler monkeys playing in the trees at the zoo, a nearby sign informs zoo guests that they can see these monkeys at the Bermudian Landing Community Baboon Sanctuary. A walk by the jaguar exhibit not only provides an impressive look at these beautiful big cats but also encourages visitors to visit the Jaguar Preserve in the Cockscomb Basin Wildlife Sanctuary—"the only place in the world where the big cats can roam protected and forever free."

Protecting the country's animals is vital. Today, throughout Central America, much of the wildlife is standing on the brink of extinction. To lose forever the roaring call of the howler monkey, the scarlet macaw's dramatic flashes of red, or the discreet presence of the mighty jaguar would be a tragedy.

The Belize Zoo is becoming increasingly well

known throughout the world. The unique educational programs and the conservation efforts of the zoo have consistently made international environmental news. Funds are always needed to support "dream projects" for the future: a reptile exhibit, a butterfly flight room, and, with the promise of help from the Monterey Bay Aquarium, a new "water world" exhibit. If you wish to help, it's easy! When visiting the zoo, ask about becoming a member to show your support.

The zoo is at Mile 29 on the Western Highway, open daily 10 A.M.–5 P.M. The admission is US$6.50

Note: The local buses will drop you off only on the highway (you must ask the driver to stop at the zoo road). From there it's about a mile walk to the zoo. You can also take taxis from Belmopan for under US$10, depending on how many people are going. From Belize City, escorted tours make day trips to the zoo and back; ask at your hotel.

The Belize Tropical Education Center
Across the street from the zoo is the Education Center. Meetings are held here for zoological news, reports, and educational seminars attended and given by people involved with zoology from around the world. A dormitory can

accommodate 30 people; there are outdoor showers and flush toilets. Great nature trails weave through the 84-acre site, and bird-watchers can avail themselves of a bird-viewing deck. The Green Iguana Breeding Project is but one of a variety of programs at the zoo that you can observe. There is a small gift shop. For more information, contact Tropical Education Center, P.O. Box 1787, Belize City, Belize, C.A., tel./fax 8/13004, email belizezoo@pobox.com.

THE BERMUDIAN LANDING COMMUNITY BABOON SANCTUARY

Driving the Northern Highway
If you are driving to Bermudian Landing from downtown Belize City, leave town on Freetown Road. You'll pass through the intersection with Central American Boulevard (to the left) and Princess Margaret Drive (to the right). Continue straight out of town. As you cross this major intersection, the road becomes the Northern Highway; set your trip odometer just a couple of hundred yards farther, where the road begins a gentle bend to the right.

Expect a good deal of traffic in the mornings and afternoons on the stretch past the Bella

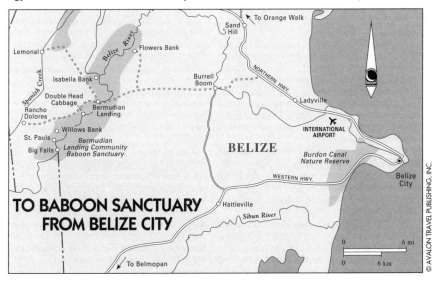

TO BABOON SANCTUARY FROM BELIZE CITY

© AVALON TRAVEL PUBLISHING, INC.

Vista suburb and the Belize Biltmore Hotel. You'll encounter lots of school buses, vehicles pulling over to pick up riders, and speed bumps. The **Belize River** is off to the left. At about Mile 5.5, you'll come to **Haulover Bridge** (one-way traffic at a time) and continue skirting the river northward on Northern Highway.

About seven miles past Burrell Boom, you'll be in Bermudian Landing. Check in with the sanctuary manager for up-to-date information on directions, room and board, and guide fees.

the monkey). Homeowners agreed to leave the monkey's food trees, hogplums and sapodillas, and small strips of forest between cleared fields as aerial pathways for the primates, as well as 60 feet of forest along both sides of waterways.

BOB RACE

The landowners signed voluntary pledges promising to follow the management plans set forth by Horwich and Lyon—and a sanctuary was born. At last count more than 70 landowners (in eight villages covering 18 square miles along a stretch of the Belize River that measures 20 miles) were taking part.

Home of the Black Howler Monkey

When zoologist Robert Horwich from the University of Wisconsin at Milwaukee began a population survey throughout the range of the howler monkey, it was the beginning of what would become the first viable animal sanctuary. One of the six species of howler monkeys in the world, the black howlers are the largest monkeys in the Americas. Horwich spent time in the howler's range, which covered southern Mexico, northeast Guatemala, and Belize. Until then, no one had formally studied the primate and its rainforest habitat.

The results were disturbing. In Mexico the monkeys were hunted by the locals for food, and their living habitat was fast being eliminated with the destruction of the rainforest. Conditions in Guatemala were only slightly better. Here, too, the monkeys were hunted by locals in the forests around Tikal, and as the forest habitat shrank in the country, so too did the numbers of howler monkeys.

It was the last survey that was surprising. In Belize, at Bermudian Landing, the communities of monkeys were strong and healthy, the forest was intact, and the locals seemed genuinely fond of the noisy creatures. This was definitely a place to start talking wildlife reserve.

Horwich, with the help of Jon Lyon, a botanist from the State University of New York, began a survey of the village. After many meetings with the town leaders, excitement grew about the idea of saving the "baboon" (the local name for

Excellent Results

According to sanctuary manager Fallett Young, the monkey population has grown to a whopping 2,000. By now sanctuary management may have acted on the plan to move some of the troops south into the Cockscomb Basin Wildlife Sanctuary.

One of the outgrowths of this innovative plan in Belize is the knowledge that educating the people about conservation and arousing in them a basic fondness for all of nature has been much more successful than enacting a stringent hunting law. The managers of the sanctuary are local villagers who understand their neighbors; much of their time is spent with children at schools and adults in interested villages. Part of their education includes basic farming techniques and sustained land use that eliminates the constant need to cut forest for new *milpas* (cornfields); this might be the most important feature of learning for the forest inhabitants.

Another result is the unhindered growth of 100 species of trees, vines, and epiphytes. The animal life is thriving as well—anteaters, armadillos, iguanas, hicatee turtles, deer, coati, amphibians, reptiles, and about 200 species of birds.

A museum at Bermudian Landing gives visitors an overview of rainforest ecology along with specific information and lore about the black howler monkey and other animals living within the sanctuary. From the museum, visitors can explore three miles of forest trails that surround Bermudian Landing. Be aware that the trails are on private land and visitors should not infringe on private property. A trail is maintained and it's required that all who visit have a guide for orientation. The trails are marked with numbered signs that correspond with information provided in a (good) book, *Community Baboon Sanctuary,* available in most gift shops, at the sanctuary, or through the sanctuary. It's always a thrill to watch the bright-eyed black monkey as it sits within five feet of you on a wild-lime tree branch, happily munching the leaves. They seem to know they're protected here. Group trips and/or guides from local hotels are available. Ask at Bermudian Landing about locals who provide home-cooked meals and informal accommodations; in Belize City, ask at the Audubon Society Office, 12 Fort St., tel. 2/34985 or 35004.

The tourist brings in a few extra dollars for the subsistence economy of the area. Plans include building guest cabañas, selling wood carvings created by locals, and offering visitors a trip down the river into monkey country.

If it all sounds perfect, it isn't! Some people from the more urban areas come to the sanctuary to kidnap baby monkeys to sell for pets. The only way anyone can kidnap a baby howler is by killing the mother, since she will never relinquish her young without a fight. A lively debate continues among traditional conservationists about allowing the people to live within a wildlife preserve. However, Belize's grassroots conservation is proving that it can succeed. Other countries such as Australia and Sierra Leone are watching carefully to see how this same concept can be adapted to the needs of their own endangered species without disturbing the people who have lived on the land for many generations.

Accommodations and Food
Situated on a lush hillside is the **Howler Monkey Lodge,** P.O. Box 694, Belize City, Belize, C.A., tel./fax 2/12158, email jungled@btl.net. Formerly the Jungle Drift Lodge, it has been remodeled and provides simple accommodations, some with porches that overlook the river and its lovely bank. The resort is 300 yards from the natural history museum sponsored by the World Wildlife Fund. On 20 acres the owners have fashioned their little piece of paradise with a selection of eight basic cabins with h/c water, private baths, electric lamps, and fans US$40–60. In addition they offer three more cabins, smaller, and with a garden view, US$20. Meals are served family style. Breakfast US$6, lunch US$5, dinner US$9, complimentary coffee 7–9 A.M. The lodge offers canoes and kayaks for rent. Ask about the crocodile night adventure and fully guided canoe trips through the sanctuary. All guides here are licensed. This is a good hub to investigate Crooked Tree, Altun Ha, river and village tours. Reservations are suggested.

Getting There
By Bus: Both **Pooks** and **Russell's** buses, travel Mon.–Sat. No service on Sunday. There's a bus around noon and 5 P.M., Mon.–Fri. and 2 P.M. on Sat. Contact the Belize Audubon Society for schedules.

By Car: It's an easy drive and well signed once you're on the Northern Highway.

By Taxi or Tour: This is close enough to the city or either airport that you can consider a taxi or an escorted tour for a day trip. Negotiate taxi prices ahead of time. Check with your hotel or travel agent for a tour.

THE ROAD TO ALTUN HA

Back on the Northern Highway, continue past the Burrell Boom turnoff (to the Baboon Sanctuary) and continue to about Mile 19, where the road forks; the right fork leads to Altun Ha and Maskall Village.

Ten and a half miles from the intersection, you reach the Altun Ha entrance. The ruins of Altun Ha have become one of the more popular day trips to Maya archaeological sites for groups and individuals venturing from Belize City, Ambergris Caye, and Caye Caulker. It was from a tomb at Altun Ha that archaeologists unearthed the largest Maya jade carving ever found (see the Mundo Maya chapter). There is a gift shop and toilet facilities at the entrance. Cost is US$5 per person.

Mayan Wells Restaurant, tel. 2/12039, is close to the ruins and offers typical Belizean fare, Tuesday through Saturday. Closes at 5 P.M.

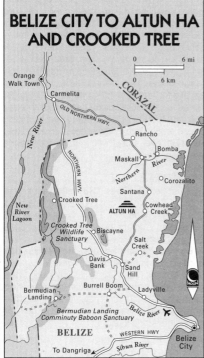

BELIZE CITY TO ALTUN HA AND CROOKED TREE

Orange Walk Town
Carmelita
CORAZAL
OLD NORTHERN HWY.
New River
NORTHERN HWY.
Rancho
Bomba
Maskall
Northern River
Corozalito
Santana
Crooked Tree
ALTUN HA
Cowhead Creek
New River Lagoon
Crooked Tree Wildlife Sanctuary
Biscayne
Salt Creek
Davis Bank
Sand Hill
Burrell Boom
Ladyville
Bermudian Landing
Bermudian Landing Comminuty Baboon Sanctuary
Belize River
BELIZE
WESTERN HWY
Belize City
To Dangriga
Sibun River

0   6 mi
0   6 km

© AVALON TRAVEL PUBLISHING, INC.

Accommodations

Maruba Lodge lies about a mile out of Maskall Village, P.O. Box 300703, Houston, TX 77230, 713/799-2031 or 800/552-3419; in Belize 3/22199, email maruba@flash.com, US$175–400. If you were to judge this resort by the neighborhood, you might think it a simple place. But once the car is parked and you walk up the palm-lined walkway, you enter a tropical, eclectic world where the guest is royalty. Ducking under the *palapa* (thatch roof), you enter the dark, cool lobby alongside the dining room. You are transported to a different level of existence. Stone couches with cushy pillows cov-

ered in African prints invite you to relax. Colorful tables in the dining room are set using palm fronds and flowers from the grounds as place mats and promise a meal as unusual as the decor.

The resort focuses on pampering the body and soul, as is evidenced by the focal points spread around the grounds. A tiny, glass-decorated chapel; a palapa-covered stone chess table; a pool that seems to spring from the jungle complete with small waterfalls.

The rooms are spread out on the grounds for privacy and are addressed by name—moon, fertility, bondage, to name a few. All continue the eclectic motif-carved masks, mosaic tile floors, standing candles, cement fountains, tiled tubs, screened shuttered windows and fresh flowers on the bed and in the bathroom. Each is different, all have private bath and electricity.

The restaurant often offers wild game, including gibnut. Conch soup, and sweet, spicy smoked chicken, and hibiscus are just a sampling of the creative menu.

At the bar, you will find viper rum with a warning label that reads for "real men only." Instructions on how to properly down a shot of this potent rum will be given by owner/bartender Nicky. Conservatives might not like it here.

Massages, mud wraps, manicures and pedicures are all available plus a gym. Packages are available with tours to the reefs, ruins, and inland destinations. Rooms start at US$175 and max out at US$400. Prices are for doubles and include breakfast. Many plans are available; call for specifics.

Getting to Altun Ha and Maruba

For those who want to bus it, ask at your hotel for current schedules and make sure there is a return bus the same day if you do not plan on staying in the area. Altun Ha is close enough to the city that a taxi is your best bet, or try a tour operator that specializes in these trips. Those going to Maruba should ask at the hotel about transfers when making reservations.

CROOKED TREE

Crooked Tree is 33 miles northwest of Belize City and three miles off the Northern Highway. After you take the turnoff to Crooked Tree, it's another two miles down the dirt road and over a mile-long narrow causeway. (Be prepared to give way to allow another vehicle coming from the opposite direction to pass.) Hunting and fishing are not permitted.

History
Crooked Tree is a network of inland lagoons, swamps, and waterways. **Crooked Tree Lagoon** is up to a mile wide and more than 20 miles long. Along its banks lies the town of **Crooked Tree.** It was settled during the early days of the logwood era, an island surrounded by fresh water, accessible only by boats traveling up the Belize River and Black Creek. The waterways were used to float the logs out to the sea.

CROOKED TREE WILDLIFE SANCTUARY

The wildlife sanctuary is divided into two sections. The largest is a series of six connected lagoons open to visitors and accessible by boat and road. A smaller water area, Mexico/Jones Lagoon, is not open to tourists.

Flora and Fauna
Crooked Tree Wildlife Sanctuary was established to protect its most famous habitant, the amazing **jabiru stork,** largest flying bird in the Western Hemisphere. Multitudes of birds find the sanctuary a safe resting spot during the dry season, with enormous food resources along the shorelines and in the trees. After a rain, thousands of minuscule frogs (no more than an inch long) seem to drop from the sky. They're fair game for the **agami heron, snowy egret,** and **great egret**—quick hunters with their long beaks. A fairly large bird, the **snail kite** picks up the **apple snail** all around the lake, then returns to its nesting tree and gorges—a dead giveaway with piles of empty snail shells underneath. Two varieties of ducks, the **black-bellied whistling duck** and the **Muscovy,** nest in trees along the swamp. All five species of **kingfishers** live in the sanctuary, and you can see **ospreys** and **black-collared hawks** diving for their morning catch. On one trip, we watched from our dory as a **peregrine falcon** repeatedly tried but failed to nab one of a flock of floating **American coots.** Black Creek, with its forests of large trees, provides homes to **black howler monkeys, Morelet's crocodiles, coatimundi, turtles,** and **iguana.**

Crooked Tree Audubon Society Visitor's Center

Audubon Society

Although several organizations had a hand in founding the park with financial aid, ongoing credit for supervision goes to the Belize Audubon Society. The society, with the continued help of devoted volunteers, maintains a small business center/museum in a small building on the right just after you cross the causeway. Do sign in; this validates the sanctuary and gives the society a reason to sponsor it. You will always find a knowledgeable curator willing to answer questions about the birds and flora encountered at the sanctuary.

THE VILLAGE

The village is divided into three neighborhoods: **Crooked Tree, Pine Ridge,** and **Stain,** with a total population of 800. Villagers operate farms, raise livestock, and have a small fishery. Visitors will find the village spread out on the island; it consists of a cricket field, four churches, and neat wooden houses (many on stilts) in the middle of large, well-kept plots of land, each with its own tank to catch rainwater—a tranquil community.

Crooked Tree mainly attracts nature lovers. But visitors will find barefoot boys going home for lunch with fishing poles over their shoulders and, maybe, a string of healthy-looking fish. Ladies with floppy hats gabbing over back fences always flash a friendly smile with a gracious hello. And if you indulge in conversation, you'll have a chance to hear the lovely soft Creole patois that is common throughout the country. While strolling through the village you might see local boys playing football, racing horses, or having a hard workout on the cricket field.

The Cashew Seed/Nut

The village is also known for its thick stand of cashew trees. In the past, the trees yielded a mild infusion into the budgets of the local women. Once a year they picked, processed, and sold about 400–500 quarts of bulk cashew nuts to a distributor in Belize City, who then packaged and sold them to the consumer. A new business is growing in Crooked Tree. The townspeople will be doing what they did before, only now they will go on to package the nuts for visitors and

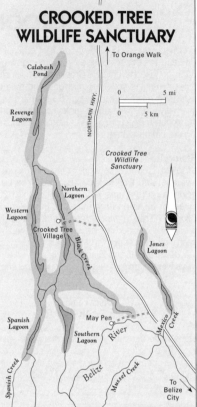

local consumers in shops and hotels around the country.

The cashew is very unusual—it's the only plant that grows its seed on the outside of the fruit (see the special topic "Exotic Fruits and Nuts of Belize" in the Introduction). One bean-shaped pod hangs from the bottom of each fruit—one fruit, one cashew nut. (No wonder they're expensive!) The shell contains a highly irritating poison that for most people causes blisters and inflammation. Those who handle the nuts wear gloves; however, processing removes all poison. The fruit is juicy and makes delicious jelly and wine. We had our first chilled sample of the wine at the back fence of our guide's cousin's house in Crooked Tree—tasty and very refreshing!

CROOKED TREE CASHEW FESTIVAL

The "crooked tree" is the cashew tree that grows prolifically in the small community of the same name, Crooked Tree Village. This small island, located in one of the many inland waterways of Belize, puts on a colorful festival that celebrates the cashews that the women have been picking for years.

The cashew festival is a time of fun like an old-fashioned backyard fair. Visitors will find good Caribbean food, including fry jacks (bread dough that is flattened into thin, small round cakes and fried) and johnny cakes, and great Punta music.

Most people will see for the first time the way the green cashew is processed. The fruit (the cashew "apple") can be either red or yellow, and both have the seed hanging from the bottom of the apple. The apple can be stewed, or made into jam and wine; tasty!

The seedpod hanging from the bottom of the fruitpod is roasted in an open fire on the ground. The fire stabilizes the highly acidic oil, at the same time making the pod brittle for cracking. The nut is partially cooked during this step in the processing. The seeds are raked to cool evenly and quickly.

(continued on next page)

CROOKED TREE CASHEW FESTIVAL
(continued)

The cashews are then cracked by hand, one at a time. From that point, they can be made into a luscious spread, or after further roasting they are bagged and sold under the name, Cashews With a Cause. The cause is a true example of an effective sustainable natural resource development. International Expeditions has been a guiding force in this project that began in 1992.

TOM GRASSE

The small village now attracts a few tourists with several small intimate bed-and-breakfast–type accommodations. A few days here is always fun: canoe along the lagoon, visit the Maya site Chau Hiix, watch the immense collection of birds that visit, but mostly, meet the people of this fine little village. A sure fire way to get to know Belize a little better.

The bagged nuts can be purchased at gift shops throughout the country. In the States, they can be ordered through International Expeditions, One Environs Park, Helena, Alabama 35080, 800/633-4734, fax 205/428-1714.

OZ MALLAN

Crooked Tree Cashew Festival

The first weekend in May, the village of Crooked Tree hosts its annual Cashew Festival. It's a lot of fun, a hometown fair with regional arts, music, folklore, dance, crafts, and of course a chance to sample cashew wine, cashew jellies, stewed cashews, and the locally raised and processed nuts—a new industry for Crooked Tree. If you're lucky enough to be here at this time, be sure to watch a demonstration showing how the cashew nut is processed—interesting stuff. International Expeditions, Inc., was instrumental in setting up the new Crooked Tree Cashew Producers Association, a great boon for the townsfolk.

Accommodations and Food

This is a low-key tourist area with just a few places to stay overnight, and a couple of places to have a cold drink and a simple meal.

Turn left at the junction and bear left at the next fork in the road. That dirt track will take you to the waterside and the **Crooked Tree Bird's Eye View Resort,** U.S. tel./fax 570/588-1184, email birdseye@btl, Belize tel. 2/32040, fax 2/24869. All rooms are spacious and have h/c water and private baths, US$60–80, 30 percent less expensive in the summer. A dorm-type room sleeps eight US$5 pp. Meals are available: US$7 for breakfast and lunch, dinner US$10. The resort has boat rentals, and many tours for bird-watching as well as to special sites; ask about airport pickups.

Sam Tillett's Hotel and Tours, Crooked Tree Village, Belize District, Belize, C.A., tel./fax 2/12026, email samhotel@btl.net, is a small hotel that's clean, has private baths, with fans US$30, plus one double with a/c US$40, and the Jabiru Suite US$50. Ask Sam about his budget rooms for US$10–15 with outside bathroom. Meals are available, breakfast and lunch US$4, dinner US$6. Camping US$5.They serve typical Belizean food: stew chicken, vegetable salads, local fish, fry jacks, and johnny cakes. All rooms have hot/cold water. These are charming people, and Sam is full of knowledge of wildlife in the area, and many stories about the "old days!"

Everyone is welcome to dine at **Triple J's,** and **Suzette's Burger Bar** is a fine little spot for burgers and hot dogs. A small gift shop across from Sam's Tillett's Hotel specializes in locally made herbal skin and beauty products.

Getting There

Independent travelers can catch the **Jex Bus** to Crooked Tree in Belize City at 34 Regent St. at 10:55 A.M., and from the Pound Yard Bridge at 4:30 P.M., 5:15 P.M., and 9:10 P.M. From Crooked Tree to Belize City buses leave at 5:15 A.M., 6:00 A.M., 6:30 A.M., and 7 A.M. This is fine for those who plan to spend the night. Check with the Audubon Society for further transportation information, rates, and an updated schedule. Other options are to go by taxi or with a local tour operator.

GUIDES AND TOURS

One recommended way to visit Crooked Tree is to hire a local guide who really knows his digs. Options include boat, horseback, and walking tours. The best way to really experience the lagoon is by boat. **Sam Tillett,** tel. 2/12026, email samhotel@btl.net, is an excellent local guide and owner of a small hotel. Ask him if he's available to paddle you around the lagoon in his dugout canoe (a dory); this silent transport (with a trawling motor) enables you to get very close to the shoreline without a motor that might tangle with thick plants, such as water lilies (called "tum

Crooked Tree cruise canoe

tum") that grow on the surface of the lagoon. A profusion of wild ocher pokes up from the water covered with millions of pale pink snail eggs. Grazing cows wade into the shallows of the lagoon to munch on the tum tum, a delicacy that keeps them fat and fit when the grasses turn brown in the dry season.

If you can't get in touch with Sam, check with the people at the Belize Audubon Society office in Belize City and they will be happy to have a guide and boat waiting for you when you arrive. Sam also offers Belize City airport pickup, and auto tours of the main sights of the country as well as horses with a guide.

SOUTH OF CROOKED TREE

Chau Hiix Ruins

Archaeological site Chau Hiix is being studied nearby. Archaeologists have made some startling discoveries, including a ball court and ball-court marker, along with small artifacts. Preliminary studies indicate the site was occupied from 1200 B.C. to A.D. 1500. **Sapodilla** **Lagoon** is south of Crooked Tree on Spanish Creek. A small guest house, aptly named Chau Hiix Lodge, is available near the site.

BOB RACE

KATHY ESCOVEDO SANDERS

THE CAYES

Along the coast of Belize, more than 200 cayes (pronounced KEES and derived from the Spanish word *cayo*) lie off the mainland. They range in size from no more than a half-block-long patch of mangrove forest to the largest, Ambergris Caye, which is 25 miles long and nearly 4.5 miles across at its widest point. Some of these islands are inhabited by people, others only by wildlife.

THE LAND AND SEA

Until recently, while boating off the coast of Placencia, you would pass what in the distance looked like a tiny house rising straight from the sea. The small wood structure sat on a caye that just barely provided enough ground around the building to keep it dry. A caye starts as a tiny dot of mangrove, which in turn attracts birds, guano, and bits of sand in the breeze; it continues to grow until it's a true little island. This is just one example of how tiny pieces of mangrove take hold, collect bits of earth and other plant materials on the breeze and from birds, and soon there's an island. Any place where an individual can build on an island while it continues to grow is truly unique. In Belize, the locals say it is "rising." Perhaps this funny little house was a form of "homesteading" the sea. But this story has a sad ending—a hurricane wiped out the house and most of the "little" caye.

Most of the cayes lie within the protection of the Belize Reef (almost 200 miles long), which parallels the mainland. Without the protection of the reef—in essence a breakwater—the islands would be washed away by the constantly pounding surf. Within the reef, the sea is calm, shallow, and inviting; in some areas with a white sandy bottom, the color of the water is a rich aqua—even more inviting. Mangroves provide wonderful breeding grounds for the magnificent sea life that attracts divers worldwide.

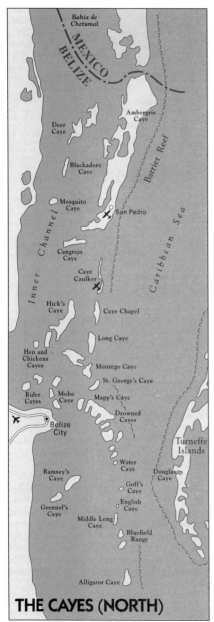

THE CAYES (NORTH)

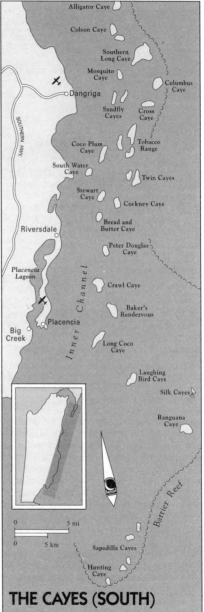

THE CAYES (SOUTH)

© AVALON TRAVEL PUBLISHING, INC.

FAUNA

The uninhabited islands are alive with all manner of exotic wildlife, though fewer animals and birds are seen on the larger cayes as more people visit them. However, you will see the common **iguana,** which can grow to more than six feet (a local food source), along with its smaller cousin, the **wishwilly** or **spiny-tailed iguana** (note the lethal-looking jagged spines that run down its back); both avowed vegetarians and usually harmless, they can devastate a garden in

---

THE MANGROVES AND TURTLE GRASS

Developers and certain segments of the tourism industry frown upon two Belizean ecosystems: mangroves and the accompanying grass flats.

Many people see mangroves as an eyesore, a breeding place of mosquitoes and sand flies. As beachfront property becomes more desirable, developers are tempted to remove mangroves and turtle grass to make way for white beaches, clear swimming areas, and hotels.

Fortunately biologists and naturalists are informing those interested in development that without the mangroves and the turtle grass, the cayes will erode and lose landmass.

A good example of erosion can be seen at the Split on Caye Caulker. Originally this was a shallow ditch dug across the island for easy dory transport, but in 1961 Hurricane Hattie blasted through the small ditch, making a much larger cut. It was made worse in the early 1980s when a small resort cut down the protecting mangroves to create a beach. Since then, the erosion has continued and the buttonwood mangrove trees along the edge have fallen one by one into the swiftly flowing waters of the channel. As the mangroves and grasses are uprooted, cayes lose their "anchors."

What makes turtle grass important? Lobster, conch, and stone crab proliferate in the protection of the wispy grass. And it's an important food source for Belize's manatees and sea turtles. These marine creatures, globally endangered, are just two that have managed to survive in Belize's waters. Turtle grass, along with a variety of mangroves, is a natural hatchery for many fish species, which in turn provide the fry to feed larger fish, pelicans, cormorants, and other seabirds.

Mangroves are salt-resistant, growing where most other plant life finds it impossible. In Belize, two species of the four known in the country—the red mangrove and the black mangrove—shield large areas of the Belizean coastline and hundreds of cayes. Red mangrove in excess of 30 feet grows in tidal areas, inland lagoons, and river mouths, but always close to the sea. Its signature is its arching prop roots. Black mangrove grows almost double that height. Its roots are slender, upright projectiles that grow to about 12 inches, protruding all around the mother tree. Both types of roots provide air to the tree. Another species, white mangrove, grows inland along riverbanks. The buttonwood mangrove thrives in drier areas of the cayes and mainland.

Mangroves are amazingly resilient, second only to the barrier reef in providing hurricane protection. When wiped out, they immediately begin to grow again. They propagate by their prop roots and by seeds that germinate on the tree. As soon as the seeds hit the mud, they begin their growth cycle. If the seeds fall into the water, they can survive for six months floating and bobbing until they happen upon the right conditions in which to set down roots.

Mangrove cayes nurture invertebrates and reptiles, including boa constrictors, iguanas, and saltwater crocodiles. Sea turtles, including loggerhead and hawksbill, thrive on encrusted sponges and crustaceans clustered at the roots. Wading birds, spoonbill, ibis, and heron feed around the roots; frigates, pelicans, and cormorants roost and nest in the rich, green foliage.

Mangroves and turtle grass are Belize's most important ecosystems. Again, Belizeans are becoming role models to other developing countries with their choice of priorities. And though the tourist dollar is very important to the economy, the people are making decisions that will protect their natural assets; they are choosing today the type of tourist who will visit the country in the future.

no time. Also lurking in the underbrush are **opossum, armadillo, raccoon, peccary, deer, paca (gibnut),** and maybe even **ocelot.** The **giant blue land crab** is an unusual critter, as is the **hermit crab,** which moves into the closest vacant shell and often leaves it behind—sometimes in the crook of a tall tree. Two snakes make their home on the islands: the **boa constrictor** and the **black-tailed indigo.** Both are good rat catchers and supposedly harmless to adults (at least those too big to be crushed). These snakes will bite if cornered; do guard small pets and children. The many frogs and lizards are fun to search out, especially the **Central American basilisk.** This small lizard often streaks past, upright on its hind legs—even along the surface of the water. It's often referred to by the locals as the Jesus Christ lizard. The black **anole** has a colorful habit of spreading a bright, salmon-pink throat pouch when claiming territory or looking for a female.

BIRDS

The most impressive members of this wild kingdom, however, are the birds that thrive on the multitude of cayes, whether they're tiny mangrove patches or busy tourist destinations. Colorful land birds number in the hundreds, including 27 varieties of migrant warblers. Birdwatchers will also find the **magnificent frigate bird, brown pelican, cormorant, royal tern, laughing gull,** and **brown-** and **red-footed boobies.** The best time to be a watcher on the cayes is during September and October, when thousands of birds are migrating south. Many go no farther and spend the winter right here. Wading birds have found the islands the perfect place to live year-round. Look for the **snowy egret, green heron, great egret, cattle egret, little blue heron,** and **great blue heron,** plus many, many others.

HISTORY

THE MAYA

The first "islanders" on the cayes were the Maya. Little is known about the culture of the cayes in that era except on Ambergris Caye, where shards of pottery still litter the ground at Marco Gonzalez, Chac Balam, and Santa Cruz. Remnants indicate that Ambergris Caye was an important hub for trading. It is possible to visit these sites, and it's best to go with a guide. Contact the Belize Tourist Board in Belize City, tel. 2/31913; or in San Pedro on Ambergris Caye, contact the San Pedro Town Board at 26/2198 or 2402, fax 26/2492. They will put you in touch with someone who knows the ins and outs of Maya territory on the island.

SPANISH SPEAKERS

In the mid-1800s, Spanish-speaking refugees from Mexico's Caste War came for relief from the killing and bloodletting between the Maya and the Mexicans. Many of these people stayed in Belize, starting dynasties that continue to grow several generations later.

BUCCANEERS

By the 17th century, pirates found the cayes around the Belizean mainland perfect for lying low, riding out a storm, resting, drinking rum, refurbishing their ships, and replenishing water and food supplies. Small treasures of gold coins and antiquated bottles dating from the era indicate the pirates used these islands regularly. In the past, locals "strenuously" discouraged outsiders from using metal detectors for fear they'd find one of the legendary "gold treasures" buried on the island by pirates.

TOURISTS

The cayes first opened the doors to tourism with a boat that made the trip from Belize City in the 1920s. But it really began in earnest when the cayes started to attract a large influx of fishermen and divers in the 1960s. One of these islands, Ambergris, is one of the most popular diving hubs in Belize.

PRACTICALITIES

ACCOMMODATIONS AND FOOD

At one time the only island with a hotel was Ambergris, and that came surprisingly early in its history. But it was many years before any of the other cayes had the same amenities. Caye Caulker was next with friendly folks who would rent out an extra room or hammock space with guests/tourists welcome to join the family for meals. That has all changed. About 25 cayes now offer simple to elaborate accommodations. Some cayes offer an entire island with one exclusive hotel. It doesn't always mean the hotel falls into the luxury category; in fact, many of these are "diving" islands with simple cabinlike accommodations. However, guests have a selection of prime vacation options if they want to dive or fish. These resorts are generally noted for excellent food.

Almost everything must be brought over by boat, including food, furniture, fuels, everyday living essentials, and building materials. Expect the prices to be a little higher than on the mainland for similar lodging and meals.

Note: Most hotels offer special rates during the summer and early fall. Also, a 7 percent government tax is added to your room rate, and in many hotels a 10–15 percent service charge is also tacked on. In some cases an extra 4–5 percent is charged for the use of a credit card. This raises the quoted rate considerably! Prices also change frequently; traveler's checks usually are accepted.

Make reservations as soon as you decide to travel to the cayes—especially if you are planning your trip December–March. In most cases accommodations are limited, and even on the largest island, Ambergris, reserve well in advance.

GETTING THERE

Each caye has its own method of transport. Caulker and Ambergris have regular daily public transport. For some, you must make arrangements with private boat owners. The resorts can give you details. Private yachts and seaplanes may land at a few of the cayes. Check with the Belize Embassy in Washington, DC, for rules concerning paperwork when bringing in a foreign-registered vessel. A few cayes have small airstrips for charter planes (available in Belize City). Remember that when you leave the protection of the barrier reef to get to the atolls, you will be in open sea and it can get quite choppy. Those who tend toward seasickness should come prepared with their favorite preventatives.

AMBERGRIS CAYE

Ambergris is the largest caye along the Belizean coast, and if it weren't for a very small canal separating the island from the Yucatán mainland, Ambergris could easily have been part of Mexico. In fact, Mexico has occasionally staked its claim over the years. As for its name, ambergris is a waxy substance occasionally found floating in or on the shores of tropical seas. Believed to originate in the intestines of the sperm whale, it is rare and valuable, used in the manufacture of perfume.

San Pedro is the only town on Ambergris and for years has been the main tourist attraction of Belize. This is changing with the development of hotels and guest houses all over the country. But despite its many new hotels and golf carts, this small island still offers the "feeling" of old Belize and I hope it will never change. Activities are pretty low-key, but if you're looking you will find a couple of discos and bars with a lively nightlife. For a special holiday celebration, visit San Pedro during El Dia de San Pedro, June 26–29.

Enjoy a Belikin beer at one of the waterfront hangouts and watch the sometimes-hectic but mostly quiet traffic in the harbor. At one time cars were really a rarity, but more are showing up on the sandy roads. However, since the government eliminated the duty on electric golf carts, hundreds of these quiet vehicles—instead of cars—are now on the island. The carts are brought over on barges.

Don't be surprised if a local Creole comes into the bar or café where you're having a Belikin and offers to sell you an old beer bottle filled with a potion made in his kitchen from seaweed; it is said to ease hangovers, cure ulcers, and soothe colicky babies. No hard sell here; he's just offering a needed service. The waitresses and potion-peddlers will be happy to talk to you, tell you about their families, their island, their lives. Many of these friendly, sociable people can trace their family roots to the beginnings of Ambergris, even before James Blake bought the island (see "History," below).

Enjoy Belize for what it is and don't expect something it isn't: a luxury resort—à la Cancún. It's becoming more and more upscale, Belizean style.

THE LAND

Twenty-five-mile-long Ambergris is three-quarters of a mile off the Belize Reef and 35 miles from Belize City. Its beach runs parallel to the reef except at Rocky Point, where they briefly come together. Four and a half miles north of Rocky Point, at Boca Bacalar Chico, a narrow channel separates Belize and Mexico. Legend says the ancient Maya dug the scant strait by hand so that they could bring their canoes through rather than go all the way around the peninsula. In dry years when the water receded, it was impossible to get a boat through, so in 1899 the Mexican government dug the channel deeper and wider to allow its warships easy access to the other side of the peninsula.

Ambergris Caye was formed by an accumulation of coral fragments. That, along with the silt emptied nearby from the Rio Hondo, has created a lovely bit of terra firma where people have been making a living as fishermen since pre-Hispanic times. The caye is made up of mangrove swamps, 12 lagoons, a plateau, and sand ridges. The largest lagoon, fed by 15 creeks, is 2.5-mile-long **Laguna de San Pedro** on the western side of the village. San Pedro sits on a sand ridge at the southern end of the is-

land. Over the years the constant wind, rain, and tide have reduced the shoreline and beachfront of the village by 30 feet. The water surrounding the caye offers rich fishing grounds and has supported the people for more than 300 years. At the southern end of Ambergris, navigable channels (often only big enough for a skiff) meander in and out of mangrove swamps and small and large lagoons. The backside is a haven for myriad varieties of birds, including the rare spoonbill.

HISTORY

The Maya

As with the rest of Belize, the first people on the caye were the Maya. They managed to rout the invading Spaniards as early as 1508. Very little is known about these Maya. However, a small post-Classic site in the Basil Jones area and a few jade and carved ornaments have been found along with obsidian flakes and fragments of pottery. At the southern end of the caye, the ruins of Marco Gonzalez are also considered of strategic importance. It is presumed that because of the location of Ambergris Caye (in the center of the sea-lane) it was a stopover for Maya traders traveling up and down the coast. And because of its close proximity to Mexico, no doubt it had great military value as well.

The Blakes

Between 1848–49, during the Caste War on the Yucatán Peninsula, Yucatecan mestizos migrated to Belize, and four families were the first permanent residents of what has developed into present-day San Pedro on Ambergris Caye. Before long there was a population of 50 self-sufficient fishermen, who were also growing corn and vegetables. Life was idyllic for these people—until 1874 and the coming of the Blake family.

James Blake paid the Belize government BZE$650 for Ambergris Caye (taking over every parcel of land except one set aside for the Catholic church) and began collecting rent from people who had been there for many years. After this, the history of the island was tied up with the fortunes of the Blakes and their in-laws, the Parhams and Alamillas. Their story reads like a script from a novel—including love affairs, illegitimate children, unlikely marriages, and (some say) power trips. The Blakes controlled everybody and everything on the island, including the coconut and fishing industries, though in the end (after almost 100 years) the good guys won out—or so it seems today. After many years, the rule of the Blake family came to a close when the Belizean government stepped in and made a "forced purchase" of San Pedro. It redistributed the land, selling lots and parcels to the same islanders who had been living on the land for generations.

The Fishing Industry

The caye saw industry change according to the political climate: from logwood to chicle to coconuts, and then to lobsters. Before 1920, the spiny lobster was thrown away and considered a nuisance, constantly getting caught in fishing nets. That all changed in 1921 when the lobster became a valuable export item. Though the fishermen were getting only a penny a pound, the business became lucrative when freezer vessels and freezer-equipped seaplanes began flying between the cayes and Florida. After struggling long and hard, the islanders established fishing cooperatives. Once they shook off the human "sharks," the fishing industry on the cayes became successful, with the benefits finally going to the fishermen.

Today's Ambergris

The island is rich in lore, some of which still reaches out and taps the modern islander on the shoulder. The establishment of the fishermen's co-op enabled the population of Ambergris to develop a good middle-class economy over the years. The financial upswing has allowed the town to improve the infrastructure of the island, which in turn has created a good atmosphere for tourists. Lots of stores, cafés, and hotels are waiting to be enjoyed, and the streets are becoming crowded with golf carts as the island develops.

The earliest tourists came to Ambergris Caye aboard the boat *Pamelayne* in the 1920s. By 1965 the first real hotel was established, and the industry has been growing ever since. The caye is considered the most developed and successful tourism area of Belize. It boasts 24-hour-a-day electricity, modern telephone communication to anywhere in the world, and medical services. You can buy the beautiful Belizean stamps and mail letters from the caye. On the downside, who knows how this influx of outsiders will affect the culture, values, and traditions of the tiny island? The ecology is threatened, but scientists in the country are on the alert and taking precautions to preserve the flora and fauna. Ambergris Caye is a laid-back combination of tropical paradise (with accommodations from simple to upscale, but not glitzy) and old-flavor fishing village: the best of both worlds, which must be seen and experienced.

THE OCEAN

A circus of underwater color and shapes is the main reason people first started traveling to Belize in large numbers, because they wanted to explore its pristine dive areas. Today if you get

SAN PEDRO

MATA CHICA ●

CASA CARIBE ●

GREEN PARROT RESORT ●

MEXICO ★
ROCKS

JOURNEY'S END CARIBBEAN CLUB ▼

CAPTAIN MORGAN'S RETREAT ●

CAPRICORN RESORT ●

EL PESCADOR ▼
▼ SWEET BASIL

San Pedro River

FERRY

★

Park/Playground

BUSH MASTER KOOL SPOT

■ HOTEL DEL RIO

SEVEN SEAS HOTEL

TIDES BEACH RESORT

■ PATOJO DIVE SHOP

HIGH
SCHOOL

LAGUNA ST.

SEA GULL ST.

BOCA DEL RIO DR.

ISLA EQUESTRIAN ■

SANDPIPER ST.

SAN PEDRO MARKET ■

Laguna de
San Pedro

PARADISE VILLAS ■

ROCK'S INN ●

HUSTLER TOURS

PARADISE
RESORT HOTEL

DOCKSIDE BAR
AND RESTAURANT

CARIBENA
FISHING
CO-OPERATIVE

CARIBENA ST.

PELICAN ST.

BARRIER REEF DR.

SCALE NOT AVAILABLE

ANGEL CORAL ST.

AMBERGRIS ST.

Caribbean Sea

BUCCANEER ST.

Plaza/
Park

BLACK CORAL ST.

PESCADOR DR. ST.

SEE "SAN PEDRO DOWNTOWN" MAP

TARPON ST.

HYPERBARIC
CHAMBER ■

ISLAND
AIR ■

AIRSTRIP

COCONUT ST.

■ SPORTS ARENA

BELIZE TRAVEL AND TOUR ●

TROPIC AIR ●

● SEADUCED

SUNBREEZE HOTEL ●

● PRIMARY
SCHOOL

THE PALMS CONDOMINIUMS ●

■ LIBRARY

CHANGES IN LATITUDE
BED & BREAKFAST ●

RAMON'S VILLAGE ●

● BELIZEAN REEF SUITES

HIDEAWAY SPORTS LODGE ●

● DEL MAR
Park

★ BELIZE YACHT CLUB

PLAYADOR HOTEL ●

COCONUTS HOTEL ●

● CORONA DEL MAR/
WOODY'S WHARF

CARIBBEAN VILLAS ●

● MATA ROCKS RESORT

ROYAL PALMS VILLA AND INN ●

● VICTORIA HOUSE

Barrier Reef

© AVALON TRAVEL PUBLISHING, INC.

together with a group of serious divers anywhere in the world, at least one will rave about an underwater adventure in Belizean waters. Since dive stories can be even more remarkable than fish stories, neophytes normally should take it all with a grain of sand—except in Belize. Divers tell of swimming with wild dolphins, swarms of horse-eye jacks, and more than two dozen eagle rays at one time. Some divers go strictly to photograph the eerie underwater beauty and color. Others enjoy the excitement of coming head to head with pelagic creatures that are carrying on with life as though the two-legged outsider were invisible, such as during the January full moon when hundreds of groupers gather at their primeval mating grounds on the reef. These stories tell of so many groupers (hundreds!) that the reef face is covered with these thick-lipped, ugly fish releasing sperm and eggs in such a fury and quantity that you cannot see two feet in front of you.

Beaches

Don't expect Cancún-type beaches on Ambergris. A few hotels have good sand; most don't. But the Caribbean is as beautiful as ever, and when you want to get into the water, small docks are provided where it might be difficult. In some areas you wade through sea grass, and it's worth it. The sea is clear, warm, and seductive.

Coral and Sponges

Belizean waters are universally clear except where, during heavy rains, the river outlets gush silt-clouded water into the sea. Particularly pristine areas are around the atolls, the reef, and certain cayes. In some cases visibility is extraordinary: more than 200 feet. Coral heads are magical with unique shapes reaching, floating, and quivering, interspersed with minute-to-immense fish all with personalities of their own. Garish-colored sponges decorate steep vertical walls that drop into black nothing. Bright red-and-yellow tube sponges grow tall, providing habitat for similarly colored fish.

Ships and Treasure

Some divers prefer searching for sunken ships. All have heard the stories of magnificent sunken treasure never found—but then who would tell if they did find it? For more than 300 years the

---

REEF FISH

Atlantic spadefish	schoolmaster
banded butterfly fish	sergeant major
bar jack	smallmouth grunt
blue tang	southern stingray
bluestriped grunt	Spanish grunt
dog snapper	spotfin butterfly fish
four-eyed butterfly fish	spotted drum
French grunt	trunkfish
green moray	white grunt
honey damselfish	yellow jack
nurse shark	yellowtail damselfish
queen triggerfish	yellowtail snapper

Belize Reef has served as a watery grave for ships thrown into the destructive limestone wall during forceful unexpected storms, including hurricanes. According to some divers, the bottom of the sea along the Belize Reef between Mexico's Isla Mujeres and Honduras Bay is littered with wrecks both ancient and modern.

SCUBA DIVING

The Cuts and Atolls

When flying over the reef and as you approach Ambergris Caye, study the seascape around the island. The Belize Reef is clearly visible about a half mile in front of the island. If the plane is low enough, you can see marine life suspended in the sea: coral heads, large fish, and, of course, the inviting multicolors of blue that lure even the nondiver to learn how to snorkel. You can also see the layout of the reef, how shallow the water is, and how close to the surface the corals rise, making it impossible for even the most shallow-draft craft to cross over.

The cuts (or channels) are also clearly visible; these seven channels are the areas where most day boats bring their divers to explore, both on the seaward side and at the cut itself. This part of the Caribbean attracts divers for many reasons, one of which is the location of three of the only four atolls in the entire Caribbean Sea: Turneffe Islands Atoll, Lighthouse Reef Atoll, and Glover's Reef Atoll.

Almost every hotel on Ambergris employs the services of local divers, and some have on-site

*divers off
Ambergris Caye*

PATTI LANGE

dive shops and dive masters. Local guides for the most part have lived on the island most of their lives and operate island-built skiffs 20–30 feet long that are generally powered by two outboards. Other options for the visiting diver are live-aboard dive boats that travel farther and stay out at sea longer, from overnight excursions to seven-day cruises that originate from a variety of ports in the United States, Belize City, or San Pedro. This is a world meant for divers.

Other Dive Locations around Ambergris

Probably no "secret" dive spot is left along the Belizean mainland or island coasts. But if you talk to divers who continue the search, some go away with curious smiles on their faces—do you suppose they know something they aren't sharing? **Hol Chan Marine Reserve** is probably the most popular dive destination of the cuts or channels. The words *hol chan* mean "little channel" in the Maya language. The reserve covers about five square miles and is located four miles southeast of San Pedro in the northern section of the Belize Reef. The channel is about 30 feet deep, and since no fishing is permitted in the reserve, it is rich with sea life of every description. Divers can expect to see abundant angelfish, blue-striped grunts, schoolmaster snapper, and hundreds of other varieties. It's also well known for the green moray eels living in tiny caves along the wall. The areas for recreation are marked with buoys. The usual rule: take only photos! It is clearly spelled out: do not collect coral or fish whether in with spear or handlines. Mooring buoys are in place to help protect against anchor damage.

Note: The current at Hol Chan is very strong. Snorkelers should take care. At least one person has drowned because of the current.

Palmetto Reef is another dramatic dive site for the experienced. Divers will see flamboyant blue vase and purple tube sponges along with other reaching and twisting corals. Coral shelves plunge 50–150 feet into dark chasms. **Mexico Rocks** offers a variety of coral heads and clouds of tiny fish. **Caverns** offers swim-through caves filled with colorful fish and sponge-covered walls. At **Sandy Point Reef** myriad caverns and deep canyons provide dramatic diving.

Dive Shops

There are *many* dive shops on the island. They all offer pretty much the same thing: resort courses, PADI and/or NAUI certification classes, day trips, and snorkel trips. Some offer things like night dives, and a few have NITROX capabilities. What really makes the difference is the instructor or dive master. This is by no means a conclusive list but notes some of the better facilities.

Amigos del Mar, located on the pier off of Cholo's Bar, tel. 26/2706, fax 26/2648, email amigosdive@btl.net, is a thriving place recommended by many locals.

INTRODUCTORY DIVING COURSES

You're in Belize on vacation and want to dive—but you don't want to spend four of seven precious days going through a certification class. What can you do? How about a resort course—an introduction to scuba and the underwater world with minimum instruction?

Diving is a very safe sport, and if you know the right questions to ask before you make the plunge, you can avoid many problems. Both PADI and NAUI (the biggest dive agencies in the Americas) have detailed requirements and guidelines for instructors and dive masters. The following is not complete, nor is it even a list, but is meant to enable the nondiver to ask the right questions.

Find out if you'll be with an instructor or a dive master. A dive master is qualified to lead certified divers; an instructor has been trained to teach the necessary diving skills. There is a *huge* difference between the two: Just because someone has been diving 30 years does not mean they know how to teach scuba diving or have the patience new divers sometimes require.

Ask how many divers you will be diving with. One instructor should not have more than four new divers to watch. Some might say otherwise, but think about it—how far can two hands go toward four bodies? If there are eight in the group, don't go.

Find out how deep you will be going. Forty feet is the limit for a resort course. The deeper you go the more quickly you use up your air, so a shallow dive means a longer dive. The marine life tends to be more numerous and varied in the shallow waters, and if there are problems, you are a lot closer to the surface to fix those problems.

Assess your health. Reputable dive shops will have you fill out a medical form and legal release. The legal stuff doesn't mean much south of the border, but your instructor needs to be aware of any health problems you might have. Hiding or lying about problems is not advised, as this could make the difference between life and death. If you have heart problems, asthma, diabetes, or epilepsy, stick to the wonders of snorkeling. Forgo binging on alcohol until after the dive, and finally, don't dive the day before you fly home. At the very least, wait 12 hours between diving and flying; it's recommended that you wait 24 hours.

Most important, have fun! Relax, breathe, look

The **Victoria House** (email victoria@btl.net) has the **Bradley brothers,** great dive masters who lead a very personal and educational tour—they enjoy their jobs and want you to enjoy their environment.

The **Coral Beach Dive Shop,** Barrier Reef Dr., tel. 26/2013, not only has been around for a long time, but also has the *Offshore Express,* the only live-aboard based on San Pedro. **The Holiday Hotel,** Barrier Reef Dr., has the **Bottom Time** dive shop, a full-service facility.

Patojo's, located on the pier off Boca del Rio Drive, tel. 26/2283, email patojos@btl.net, is not as new or fancy as some of the others but has a good reputation for professional service. There is also the **Blue Hole Dive Center,** next to the Spindrift Hotel on Barrier Reef Dr., tel. 26/2982 or 3776, email bluehole@btl.net, home to the *Blue Hole Express,* one of the few boats that will go to *the* Blue Hole. **Journey's End,** tel. 26/2173, email jorneyend@btl.net, offers Nitrox fills.

BOATING, SNORKELING, AND FISHING

Take a boat ride. Explore the Caribbean Sea in and around the many cayes of the area. Some vessels are **glass-bottom boats,** such as the **Reef Seekers,** tel. 26/2802, so the nonswimmer can enjoy the beauty of the sea too. Two trips daily; 9 A.M. and noon. Snorkeling is also part of the activity on many boats, and gear is readily available. Ask at your hotel about trips to Hol Chan Marine Reserve or Caye Caulker.

A day-boat with a long history of success is the **Rum Punch II,** run by brothers Tony and George. A snorkeling stop at the **Coral Garden,** lunch at Caye Caulker, and captivating stories make a pleasant day. True to the boat's name, rum punch is served throughout the trip. US$45. For a romantic evening, check out the sunset cruise.

The **Winnie Estelle,** tel. 26/2394, is a converted freight boat offering comfortable day trips to the reef and Caye Caulker for snorkeling. This classic wooden 66-foot island trader docks at the Paradise Resort Hotel.

Rocky Point Ultimate Snorkeling Trip, tel. 26/2422 or 26/2234, offers a day of snorkeling, with stops at three snorkel sites, and a beach barbecue lunch of freshly caught seafood, often times lobster, dessert, and drinks; US$50.

L'il Alfonse, tel. 26/2584, offers half-day, full-day, and nighttime snorkel trips. The best part is the guide—he gets in with you and gets just as excited, showing you critters you'd probably miss on your own. The all-day trip stops at three sites; US$35.

Many guides who lead snorkeling trips also do fishing trips. Among the many who offer both are **Fred Alamilla,** tel. 26/2006; **John Alamilla,** tel. 26/2009; **Alfonso Graniel,** tel. 26/2584; **Abel Guerrero, Jr.,** tel. 26/2517; **Daniel Nunez,** tel. 26/2314, also takes people to the ruins; and **Andy Nunez,** with his boat, *Flashdancer,* tel. 26/2442.

For those wanting to take a kayak tour, contact **Seaduced,** tel. 26/2254, email seabelize@btl.net. They're a bit pricey but at last visit the only ones offering the tour.

The area within the reef is a favorite for such fish as tarpon and bonefish. Outside the reef the choice of big game is endless. Most hotels and dive shops will make arrangements for fishing, including boat and guide. One resort, **El Pescador,** tel. 26/2975, specializes in fishing packages that include all types of angling.

Rubie's Hotel has a shack on the beach, and the guys working there are rumored to be the best local guides. Good local fishing guides include **Freddie Waight,** through the Belize Yacht Club, tel. 26/2777; **Jose Gonzales,** tel. 26/2344; **Nestor Gomez,** tel. 26/2063; **Luz Guerrero,** tel. 26/2705; and **Luis Perez** through Amigos del Mar, tel. 26/2706.

At the Marina
The **Belize Yacht Club,** tel. 26/2777, fax 26/2768, offers slips to visiting boaters. Gas and water are available.

Water Toys and Where to Find Them
Ambergris has joined the high-tech tourist community, and most of the upscale hotels have fun toys for rent. Along with the latest in diving equipment and dive boats, fun-seekers will find **sailboards, personal watercrafts, catamarans,** and **water skis.** If you've never done any of these things, schools and instructors are available.

Catamarans are available for guests at **Ramon's Village, Mata Chica,** and **Journey's End.**

The dock at **Fidos,** tel. 26/4804, rents Hobie cats—US$60 half-day; pedal boats—US$15/hour; banana boats with a 4HP motor—US$60 for a half-day; and WaveRunners—US$60/hour, US$35/half-hour. Credit card deposit required. Closed on Wednesday.

The wind often blows off the caye and **Sailsports Belize,** tel. 14/8070, offers sailboard instructions and rentals on modern equipment. Gear rents for US$20/hour; lessons are US$30/hour. Open year-round and located on the beach at the Holiday Hotel.

windsurfing along the caye

ACCOMMODATIONS

For such a tiny island, you'll find a wide variety of accommodations. Most rooms downtown are very simple, with more and more upscale hotels and condos popping up, spreading out from the center of town. Many of the downtown hotels are in a cluster separated by narrow walkways in between and along San Pedro's narrow beachfront. In the center of town, most of the "beach" is little more than a narrow strip of sand on which to pull up boats, and a pedestrian walkway. Many of the hotels on Barrier Reef Drive (formerly Front Street—on the eastern side of the island and running north and south) provide porches that look out over the sea and reef just offshore. The downtown hotels are right in the middle of things, close to the restaurants, bars, gift shops, dive shops, and all other commerce. For something a little more deluxe, check out the hotels on the edges of town, where you'll find more traditional beach resorts—and where you'll pay considerably more as well.

Special Rates and Extra Taxes

Most hotels offer special rates during the summer and early fall. Year-round, expect a 7 percent hotel tax, and a 10–15 percent service charge; in some cases an extra 4–5 percent is charged for the use of a credit card. Prices change frequently, and you'll pay even more during Christmas. Traveler's checks usually are accepted. Be sure to ask about any special rates and taxes when making reservations.

Under US$50

For one of the best budget hotels, take a look at **Rubie's (Ruby's) Hotel** (yes, they are one and the same), P.O. Box 56, San Pedro, Ambergris Caye, Belize, C.A., tel. 26/2063, fax 26/2434, email rubys@btl.net, on Barrier Reef Drive at the south end of town. The beds might be a bit lumpy, and your sink might sit at an angle, but you can't beat the location—right on the beach. New rooms have been added with great balconies and private baths. Other rooms come with shared or private baths. You can arrange a wide array of activities through the hotel, including snorkeling and dive trips. Fishing is a specialty; tailored trips feature light spin

casting or fly-fishing for bonefish and tarpon, or trolling for reef fish with live bait. Look for the coffee pot sign; Rubie's also has a café serving breakfast, lunch, and dinner; it's open 6 A.M.–6 P.M. Credit cards are OK. Rooms are US$48 with a/c, ocean view; US$30 with fans; US$15 for shared bath.

It isn't very pretty, but **Thomas Hotel,** Barrier Reef Dr., Ambergris Caye, Belize, C.A., tel. 26/2061, has seven rooms and is one of the cheapest places in town. One room has three beds. US$35 with a/c US$25 fan cooled.

No, **Martha's Hotel** is not on the beach, but this great little budget hotel, P.O. Box 27, San Pedro, Ambergris Caye, Belize, C.A., tel. 26/2053, fax 26/2589, email julian@btl.net, is two blocks from the waterfront, close to everything, and across the street from **Elvi's Kitchen.** Rooms are upstairs; downstairs is a general store where you can pick up almost anything from a cooler of ice to a pair of sandals. Originally someone's home, the rooms are clean and unpretentious with private baths, ceiling fans, linoleum floors. Ask for a corner room. US$35, credit cards OK. You can arrange a variety of tours for diving, fishing, caving, and other land tours.

The old classic **Hotel San Pedrano,** Barrier Reef Dr., Ambergris Caye, Belize, C.A., tel. 26/2054, fax 26/2093, email sanpedrano@btl.net, offers six rooms just a block from the ocean on the corner of Barrier Reef Drive. From the breezy upstairs veranda, it's easy to eat a bite, read a book, or watch the street life below. It's a favorite of both European and American travelers, who offer nothing but favorable comments. It offers good value for your dollar. Each room has h/c water, private bath, ceiling fan or a/c. Some have full kitchens. US$40 with a/c; US$30 without. Credit cards are OK. The hotel can also arrange a variety of excursions including diving, fishing, shelling, and beach picnics.

Allan and Helen Forman invite guests at the **Coral Beach Hotel and Dive Shop** to have a welcome piña colada and a choice of 19 clean rooms, each with private bathroom, h/c water, and a/c or fan. Rates are US$45 with a/c. Meal plans are available. The building is across the road from the sea, and they run a top-notch dive shop. Their *Offshore Express* is the only boat on the island with live-aboard facilities.

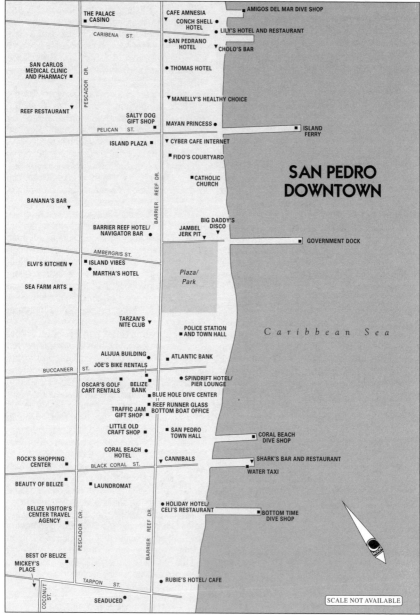

THE PALACE
■ CASINO

CAFE AMNESIA
▼
CONCH SHELL ●
HOTEL

■ AMIGOS DEL MAR DIVE SHOP

● LILY'S HOTEL AND RESTAURANT

CARIBENA ST.

● SAN PEDRANO
HOTEL
▼ CHOLO'S BAR

SAN CARLOS
MEDICAL CLINIC
AND PHARMACY ■

● THOMAS HOTEL

PESCADOR DR.

REEF RESTAURANT ▼

▼ MANELLY'S HEALTHY CHOICE

SALTY DOG
GIFT SHOP

MAYAN PRINCESS ●

■ ISLAND
FERRY

PELICAN ST.

ISLAND PLAZA ■

▼ CYBER CAFE INTERNET

■ FIDO'S COURTYARD

BARRIER REEF DR.

● CATHOLIC
CHURCH

SAN PEDRO
DOWNTOWN

BANANA'S BAR
▼

BARRIER REEF HOTEL/
NAVIGATOR BAR ●

BIG DADDY'S
DISCO
JAMBEL
JERK PIT ▼

■ GOVERNMENT DOCK

AMBERGRIS ST.

ELVI'S KITCHEN ▼
■ ISLAND VIBES
● MARTHA'S HOTEL

SEA FARM ARTS ■

*Plaza/
Park*

Caribbean Sea

TARZAN'S
NITE CLUB ▼

POLICE STATION
■ AND TOWN HALL

ALIJUA BUILDING ●
■ ATLANTIC BANK

BUCCANEER ST.

JOE'S BIKE RENTALS ●

● SPINDRIFT HOTEL/
PIER LOUNGE

OSCAR'S GOLF
CART RENTALS ■

BELIZE
BANK
■ BLUE HOLE DIVE CENTER
■ REEF RUNNER GLASS
TRAFFIC JAM ● BOTTOM BOAT OFFICE
GIFT SHOP ■

LITTLE OLD
CRAFT SHOP ■

■ SAN PEDRO
TOWN HALL

■ CORAL BEACH
DIVE SHOP

CORAL BEACH
HOTEL ●

ROCK'S SHOPPING
CENTER ■

▼ CANNIBALS

▼ SHARK'S BAR AND RESTAURANT

BLACK CORAL ST.

■ WATER TAXI

BEAUTY OF BELIZE ■

■ LAUNDROMAT

BELIZE VISITOR'S
CENTER TRAVEL
AGENCY ■

PESCADOR DR.

● HOLIDAY HOTEL/
CELI'S RESTAURANT

BARRIER REEF DR.

■ BOTTOM TIME
DIVE SHOP

BEST OF BELIZE
MICKEY'S
PLACE ■

TARPON ST.

● RUBIE'S HOTEL/ CAFE

COCONUT ST.

SEADUCED ●

SCALE NOT AVAILABLE

© AVALON TRAVEL PUBLISHING, INC.

The Coral Beach offers several package prices, dive packages include a boat, guide, equipment, room, meals, transportation to and from Belize International Airport, tackle, etc. All packages include tax. The hotel bar, **The Tackle Box,** is out at the end of the dock and has a daily happy hour 5–8 P.M. For information, contact Coral Beach Hotel, P.O. Box 16, San Pedro, Ambergris Caye, Belize, C.A., tel. 26/2013, email forman@btl.net.

US$50–100

Right on the beach and around the corner from Hotel San Pedrano, **The Conch Shell Hotel,** P.O. Box 43, San Pedro, Ambergris Caye, Belize, C.A., tel. 26/2062, email conchsehll@btl.net, is inexpensive and has simple rooms with private baths, ceiling fans, linoleum floors, wood-paneled walls, and simple furnishings. Some have kitchenettes; ask for Room 5. About US$55.Credit cards are OK. This is one of the prettiest beachfront areas in the downtown area. Lie in a chaise lounge long enough and you'll probably have lobster fishermen and little kids with coconut crisps tempting you with their goods.

The old standard of budget travelers, **Lily's Hotel,** San Pedro, Ambergris Caye, Belize, C.A., tel. 26/2059, email lilies@btl.net, has moved up a notch with air-conditioning. The simple hotel is run by the Felipe Paz family—friendly, long-time residents of San Pedro. Ask a local where to find them, or if you see a dock with the *Andrea* and/or *Triple J* tied up, then look on shore and you'll find the hotel. Lily's has been known for years for offering excellent local food in plentiful family-style servings, and they offer complimentary coffee every morning. In addition, Lily's offers 10 basic clean rooms with a/c, h/c water, and private bathrooms and small fridge. Ask for one of the six rooms with an ocean view. US$75 Lily's accepts Visa/MC.

The **Hideaway Sports Lodge,** P.O. Box 43, Ambergris Caye, Belize, C.A., tel. 26/2141, fax 26/2269, email hideaway@btl.net, is another spot that's a short distance from the beach. It's run by a couple from Texas and has 24 rooms at reasonable rates. The rooms are very modest, but some are spacious with ceiling fans and funky decor. The owners are in the process of giving the hotel a facelift. The restaurant/bar serves home cooked meals like chicken-fried steak (US$8), pizza, and has a children's menu. The pool will be a hit with the kids. Rooms vary in size and number of beds, accommodating from two to six people. Rooms come with h/c water, private baths, fans. US$55 no a/c, US$65 with a/c. Packages available. Credit cards accepted.

In the center of town and across from the park, the **Barrier Reef Hotel,** Barrier Reef Dr., Ambergris Caye, Belize, C.A., tel. 26/2075, fax 26/2719, email bremek@btl.net, has 11 rooms, a restaurant, sports bar with big-screen TV, beauty parlor, and second-floor pool. It is especially popular with the diving crowd. The pool is nice on a hot day and the restaurant is known for its seafood pizza. Rooms have h/c water, private baths, cable TV, and ceiling fans or a/c. US$75, Credit cards OK.

At first glance the **Spindrift Hotel,** Barrier Reef Dr., Ambergris Caye, Belize, C.A., tel. 26/2174, fax 26/2251, U.S. tel. 800/688-0161, email spinhotel@btl.net, reminds one of the old Florida hotels with soft, art-deco corners and the center courtyard. Within its complex are a lively bar that hosts the "chicken drop," a small second-floor sundeck, 22 rooms, and three suites. All rooms have h/c water, private baths, and ceiling fans. Suites have a/c and so do some of the more expensive rooms. For cheaper rates, ask for a patio room with the inner balcony. Up to two children under 12 are free with adults. Credit cards are OK. Price range is US$48 for basic rooms to US$110 for beachfront apartments.

On the north end of town near the San Pedro River, in a more remote location by the mangroves and the sea, is the **Hotel del Rio,** Ambergris Caye, Belize, C.A., tel./fax 26/2286, U.S. tel. 318/984-9655, email hodelrio@btl.net. Here, surrounded by sea grapes, palms, lilies, banana trees, and hibiscus you'll find a pleasant family atmosphere and whimsical little touches like a circular wood table on the beach and brightly colored rowing paddles. Accommodations range from basic economy rooms with shared baths and cold water to the Cabaña Grande, an apartment-style bungalow with full kithchen, to the Casa Blanca with a/c. Rates US$30–35. Anglers, take note: the owner's husband, Fido, is a well-known fishing guide with his own 28-foot-foot boat. Just around the corner is a little store/bar called **Bush Master Kool Spot** where you can stock your fridge and buy toiletries.

How about a little bed-and-breakfast near the beach and next to the yacht club? **Changes In Latitude B&B,** San Pedro, Ambergris Caye, Belize, C.A., tel./fax 26/2986, email latitudes@btl.net, has strong appeal for divers looking to spend their days in the water and then have comfortable rooms and beds for the evening. It's a quiet place run by Canadian transplant Lori Reed. The cleverly painted sign says it all with an igloo perched on a tropic isle. In fact, cleverness has everything to do with how she runs the bed-and-breakfast and the way she's furnished the six rooms. Lori lives on the grounds and, with the help of her wonderful staff, caters to the needs of guests. At one end of the lower level is a common room that serves as a kitchen/eating area and library. Inside the small but comfortable rooms, you'll find fans and a/c, h/c water, private baths, good mattresses, phones, lots of wood furnishings, and Guatamalan fabric bedspreads. Breakfasts are great—you might even get Lori's Famous French Canadian Crepes with coffee and fresh fruit. After a pickup at the airport, Lori provides her guests with a packet that contains tips on the best places for food, fun, and diving. US$90, includes tax and breakfast. Credit cards are OK.

Tides Beach Resort, tel. 26/2283, email patojos@btl.net, is on the beach away from the center of town and is reminiscent of a southern colonial home. The 12 rooms are named after animals and are light and airy with tile floors. Six of the rooms have a/c. Some have king-size beds, other have doubles, all have private bathrooms and refrigerators. The upstairs rooms get better breezes. Room with a/c and king bed is US$85. The on-site **Jumping Frijoles** bar is tiny but has all the right stuff. This is also the home base for **Patojos Scuba Center,** one of the more respected dive outfits on the caye.

At the north end of Barrier Reef Drive, you'll find the entrance to the compound of **Paradise Resort Hotel,** P.O. Box 25, San Pedro, Ambergris Caye, Belize, C.A., tel. 26/2083, fax 26/2232, email paradise@btl.net. This casual resort has a pleasing range of amenities and a good location on a sandy beach with its own dock and beachside bar, conveying a relaxed "barefoot" feeling. You'll find a deli, gift and dive shops, and you can make all fishing arrangements on the premises. You'll have your choice of a thatched cabaña, a villa, or a minisuite with a/c. US$85 fan, US$100 a/c. Room rates vary according to season, location, and type. Meal plans are available.

US$100–150

The **Hotel Playador,** should have new condos by the time you're there. All the amenities needed are here. A one-bedroom US$135, at least that was the projected price.

Banana Beach Resort, tel. 26/3890, email bananas@btl.net, has 35 one-bedroom suites with fully stocked kitchens. Some of them have private balconies. All have a/c, fans, cable TV. Rates start at US$125—rooms with a pool view. Ocean-view rates are more.

The **Seven Seas Hotel,** Ambergris Caye, Belize, C.A., tel. 26/2382, email reservations@sevenseasresort.com, is another comfortable hotel on the water. The one-bedroom suites have h/c water, private baths, kitchenettes, ceiling fans, a/c, ocean views, Belizean furniture, and tile floors that add a tropical ambience. The living room area also has a queen-size sofa with fold-out bed. Credit cards are OK. Children under 12 stay free. Maid service even takes care of dishes. Views from the upper floor are especially nice. The pool is handy for those too lazy to walk to the sea and the pier is great for kicking back with a Belikin. The hotel can arrange tours and trips of all kinds. US$125, except during the Christmas holiday season when rooms top out at US$185. They offer a substantial discount if you book directly through them.

BOB RACE

The pleasant **San Pedro Holiday Hotel,** P.O. Box 61, San Pedro, Ambergris Caye, Belize, C.A., tel. 26/2014, fax 26/2295, email holiday@btl.net, just keeps getting better. It offers a charming ambience—the pink-and-white wooden structure faces the sea with wide verandas open to the cooling tradewinds of the tropics. Other services include a full-service dive shop, **Bottom Time,** and the glass-bottom boat, *Reef Finder.* On the premises are a small but pleasant lobby bar known for its ceviche and bartender, an economical deli, and popular **Celi's Restaurant.** Celi's serves delicious food: try the fish dishes. They serve lunch and dinner. Wednesday the restaurant is closed; go instead to the beach barbecue with live music.

Rooms come with h/c water, private baths, fans, and a/c. Some have refrigerators. Apartments include a/c in the bedroom, tabletop stove, and some have a fridge. US$95 for standard room; US$120 for room with refrigerator. Credit cards OK. Write or call for more information and reservations.

The Emerald Reef Suites, tel. 26/2306, email travltour@btl.net, US$125, offers spacious suites on the beach. Each has a balcony, fully equipped kitchen, a/c, safety deposit box and king-size bed. TV is available.

A 20-minute walk from downtown is **Coconuts Caribbean Hotel,** P.O. Box 94, San Pedro, Ambergris Caye, Belize, C.A., tel. 26/3500, fax 26/3501, email coconuts@btl.net, This small, airy 12-room hotel is on the beach. The spacious rooms have firm futon-type beds covered with colorful throw pillows. Each room has a/c, fans, hot and cold water in private bathrooms; TV available The best part of the hotel is the people—friendly and smiling. Rates include continental breakfast and the use of bicycles. US$95–125.

The small, intimate **Green Parrot Resort,** P.O. Box 36, San Pedro, Ambergris Caye, Belize, C.A., tel./fax 26/4211, email gparrot@btl.net, is six miles north of San Pedro but just a quarter mile from famous Mexico Rocks. Expect spectacular snorkeling. The Green Parrot offers double and triple cabañas on the beach; the restaurant comes up with great food (guests only) and an intimate bar is open to anyone wandering down that way. Full American Plan (FAP, three meals) and Modified American Plan (MAP,

two meals) are available. All cabañas have ceiling fans and hot showers. Snorkeling and fishing are provided by the resort at a minimum fee (but bring your own gear.) Diving, deep-sea fishing, and numerous tours are also available. Write or call for more information. US$110, includes breakfast.

About a mile south of town is **Mata Rocks Resort,** P.O. Box 47, tel. 26/2336, fax 26/2349, U.S. tel. 888/628-2757, email matarocks@btl.net, is a small intimate resort on the beach that has 11 rooms and two suites. Rooms are comfortable wood-sided suites with stucco exteriors and tile roofs. Inside they have h/c water, private baths, ceiling fans, and maid service. The deluxe and junior suites come with a/c. The resort arranges a full range of island activities and offers dive packages. Credit cards OK. Ocean-view rooms start at US$95; continental breakfast included in the room rate.

Four miles north of San Pedro on a broad beachfront with seawall, **Journey's End Caribbean Club,** 5847 San Felipe, Suite 2195, Houston, TX, 77057, or P.O. Box 13, Ambergris Caye, Belize, C.A., U.S. tel. 800/460-5665, fax 713/780-1726, Belize tel. 26/2173, fax 26/2028, email info@journeyseendresort.com. The hotel offers a wide range of activities and accommodations, two bars, and a good restaurant. This is the resort to visit for isolation and an all-in-one kind of vacation. Here you will find a swimming pool and a screened room with Jacuzzi, volleyball, a fine dive shop, snorkeling trips, mountain bikes, tennis, sailboats, Hobie cats, sailboards, canoes, and paddleboats. While additional charges are associated with some of these activities, they are all conveniently available. Less-active types have ample opportunity for beachcombing, sun worshiping, or reading a book by the pool. The resort also has the Barefoot Conference Lounge, a large room with sand floor and thatched bar equipped with slide projector, TV, and pretty much anything else you might need for seminars, reunions, or whatever the occasion calls for up to 100 people.

Transportation back and forth between the resort and San Pedro is by water taxi. It takes about 10 minutes one way and the resort has a schedule of three trips daily. Otherwise, you can arrange to pay for trips on your own schedule.

Guests have a choice of rooms overlooking

the back lagoon (great sunsets), pool cabañas toward the center, or thatched cabañas off to one side. The rooms by the lagoons offer the most isolation and views of wildlife. The poolside cabañas are the most charming and convenient to the sundeck and poolside bar/grill. The thatch cabañas are nearer the restaurant and beachside activities. Lagoon-view rooms are the least expensive at US$122 and an oceanfront villa goes for US$220. The resort also has a three-bedroom villa available for larger families/groups. Dive packages and meal plans are available. Contact for the specifics.

Will and Susan Lala have one of the finest suite-type accommodations on the island in **Caribbean Villas,** Ambergris Caye, Belize, C.A., tel. 26/2715, fax 26/2885, email c-v-hotel @btl.net. In a lovely two-story building with white-washed walls and red-tile roof, it's close enough to town to bike in and out at your leisure (bikes are compliments of the hotel) or walk the 15 minutes along the beach. When Will picks you up at the airport in the golf cart, he gives you a tour of San Pedro, pointing out the best places to eat, daily specials you don't want to miss, and where the happening spots are. Once at the hotel relax in a hot tub, fish, dive, snorkel, or just take in the view. Bird enthusiasts should check out the "people perch"—a four-story tower on the edge of the bush—and watch the birds at treetop height. Over 200 species have been spotted. Nonguests are welcome to use it; please check in with the front desk beforehand.

Spacious, attractively furnished lodgings come in all sizes from a double room to a deluxe suite with a loft. Rooms have h/c water, private baths, and ceiling fans. More-luxurious suites include a/c, full kitchens, and more living and sleeping area (they can accommodate up to six people). Double couples will prefer Unit 4 with its wrap-around loft, large balcony, and dual bathrooms. Rates start at US$85 for a room with a queen bed to US$150 for a one-bedroom suite with a king bed to US$245 for the deluxe suite that can sleep six people. Call for details.

Three miles north of San Pedro the **Capricorn Resort,** P.O. Box 65, San Pedro, Ambergris Caye, Belize, C.A., tel. 26/2809, fax 21/2091, email capricorn@btl.net, offers intimate seclusion on its beachfront property. There are only three cabañas—so far—but it won't get much bigger than that. Owners Annabel and Clarence live on the grounds and pride themselves on making guests feel at home. The restaurant is one of the best on the island. Reservations are a must—once you have a table, it is yours for the night. Rates include a continental breakfast. The small beach bar serves lunch for those not wanting to hop a water taxi into town. Plenty of hammocks just hanging around and the people are so friendly and the setting so right, you just might not want to leave—ever. They offer cabañas or a suite, and both are spacious. The cabaña has a balcony and two double beds; the suite has a queen bed and sundeck. US$110–US$135.

A full-service resort, **Ramon's Village,** in the United States, P.O. Drawer 4407, Laurel, MS 39441, tel. 800/624-4215 or 601/649-1990, fax 601/425-2111, in Belize tel. 26/2071, email info@ramons.com, has the best beach (all 500 feet of it) on the island. Just south of San Pedro, its attractive surroundings, good restaurant and bar, a myriad of activities, and a long pier with a *palapa* at the end make it a favorite among divers and nondivers alike. The recreational pier features two dive shops with boats, guides, and all diving equipment available for reef trips. The pool is steps away from the cabañas and one end of it is a Jacuzzi. Airport pickup is just one of the courtesies provided guests.

If you stayed at Ramon's years back, you'll notice it has expanded and added many more cabañas so the space on the beach is much more crowded. Visitors fond of thatched-hut cabañas will fall in love with the castaways look of the place. Ramon's offers many types of rooms—beachfront, seaside, garden, luxury, multiroom suites and honeymoon cabañas, totaling 61 units. They have either two double beds or one king size, all are spacious, pleasantly decorated, and have a/c and ceiling fans. Credit cards OK. The restaurant is one of the best on the island. Dinner averages about US$20, and room service is available. Recreational rentals include sailboards, aqua cycles, speedboats, bicycles, and golf carts. Scuba instruction is available.

Another charming suite hotel, **Mayan Princess,** P.O. Box 79, San Pedro, Ambergris Caye, Belize, C.A., tel. 26/2778, fax 26/2784, email mayanprin@btl.net, sits near the center of town. All 23 condo units face the ocean and have a kitchenette and eating counter, a/c, cable TV, a hide-a-bed, and a tropical ambience. Spacious verandas overlook the sea and provide shady views of the beach and ocean. Nonsmoking and luxury honeymoon suites available. The hotel has a gift shop and dive center. US$125 per night; dive packages available. Credit cards OK.

Take a look at **Paradise Villas Condominiums,** Ambergris Caye, Belize, C.A., U.S. tel. 510/792-2639, fax 510/791-5602, Belize tel. 26/3077, fax 26/2831, email susangg @megapathdls.net. These deluxe resort suites next door to the Paradise Resort Hotel have all the amenities of a hotel, including a pool, plus a fully equipped kitchen and a spacious living room. The one-bedroom units feature h/c water, private baths, a/c, full kitchen, and daily maid service. One bedroom for two people, US$115.

Inside an elegant three-story building of tropical colonial design, on the corner of Sandpiper Street and the ocean, are the 14 suites of **Blue Tang Inn,** (formerly Rocks Inn), P.O. Box 47, San Pedro, Ambergris Caye, Belize, C.A., tel. 26/2326, fax 26/2358, U.S. tel. 800/288-8646. All suites have fully decorated bedrooms, living rooms, and kitchens with h/c water, private baths, ceiling fans, and a/c, and can accommodate up to six adults. Third-floor rooms have Jacuzzi tubs. Credit cards OK. Shady verandas provide a pleasant perch from which to take in the ocean and beach scene. Hammocks and easy chairs under the palms make for lazy afternoons. Rates US$90–US$115, depending on first-floor or second-floor rooms and include hotel transfer. Snorkeling or diving can be arranged.

On the beach amid pleasant palmy surroundings sits the **SunBreeze Hotel,** tel. 26/2191, fax 26/2346, U.S. tel. 800/688-0191, email sunbreeze@btl.net. Very convenient for arriving air passengers; it's across the street from San Pedro's small airstrip. Because of the U-shaped building, with the open end toward the ocean, and the small size of the planes, the proximity to revving aircraft engines is not the problem you might expect. Barrier Reef Drive starts next door, so it's an easy walk to almost any point in town. The hotel has a variety of rooms—standard rooms with private bath; a/c, cable TV, and phones; deluxe rooms have

whirlpool baths. All have h/c water, private baths, ceiling fans. The on-site restaurant serves good Italian food as well as lots of seafood. An inviting pool sits near the restaurant along with an on-site dive shop. Cheapest rooms are US$120. Credit cards OK.

You'll find good value in **Corona del Mar,** P.O. Box 37, Ambergris Caye, Belize, C.A., tel. 26/2055, fax 26/2461, email corona@btl.net, referred to by many locals as **Woody's** after Woody's Wharf. Longtime residents Woody and Helen Canaday have four one-bedroom suites, each with h/c water, private bath, a/c, full kitchen, cable TV, direct-dial phones, and veranda. There are also four penthouse rooms with queen bed, a/c, TV, phone, small refrigerator, and wonderful ocean views. Rates include a hearty breakfast and a free juice and rum punch bar that is open all day; you might be able to have a chat with Woody, a humorous, good-natured guy there. The wooden doors with the carved Maya motif are a nice touch. Suites are US$135; penthouses are US$110. Prices go up a bit during Christmas. The hotel accepts Visa/MC. Laundry service, diving, and fishing can be arranged.

US$150–200

The handsome **Victoria House,** with lush tropical gardens two miles south of town, offers delightful (though pricey) oceanfront casitas or deluxe rooms. The resort includes stucco and thatched casitas with tile floors; rooms have ocean views, private bathrooms, and ceiling fans or a/c. Excellent meals are served in the restaurant, and diving and fishing equipment is available; a bar and a gift shop are on the premises, an inviting pool cools you down on a hot day, and a masseuse is on call. The dive masters are some of the best in the country—of all the snorkel and dive trips we sampled, the Bradley brothers pointed out and described many little critters that untrained eyes would never see. Also available are two- and three-bedroom villas that are spacious, airy, with kitchenettes, TV, VCR, lots of deck space, and a sense of privacy. Packages are the best deals if you're content to sit tight on the premises for all meals. Five-night minimum during peak season. US$155–US$235. For more information and reservations: in the U.S., 579 S. Carrollton Ave., New Orleans, LA

70118, tel. 800/247-5159, fax 504/865-0718; in Belize, P.O. Box 22, Ambergris Caye, tel. 26/2067, email dc@victoria-house.com.

What would it be like to be a castaway on a luxurious tropical paradise, where the palms really sway, and the staff is to love? Guests at **Captain Morgan's Retreat** will find out. Accommodation choices are 14 clean, attractive beachfront casitas with a/c or a more modern villa with kitchen and a/c. There's an on-site pool complete with swim-up bar, and restaurant with excellent food. On arrival, the activities director explains and helps arrange all fishing, diving, snorkeling, and sailing trips.

Captain Morgan's is a few miles north of San Pedro and it's a long walk to town. The best way to go in and out of town is by boat—the resort has daily scheduled trips on their private boats. For reservations and more information, call 888/653-9090 US$185–US$200 d., email belizevacation@yahoo.com. As with many of the upscale places on the island, Captain Morgan's also offers time-shares.

Even from the air, it's easy to spot the **Belize Yacht Club,** U.S. tel. 800/396-1153, Belize tel. 26/2777, fax 26/2768, email frontdesk @belizeyachtclub.com. Its red-tile roofs and white walls surround a swatch of green and turquoise. About a 10-minute walk south of town, the complex boasts a friendly staff, pier/marina, gift shop, manicured lawns, pool, dive shop, 40 units, and on-site security.

These are among the plushest suites on the island and they are priced accordingly. There are one-, two-, and three-bedroom suites. All units come with h/c water, private baths, a/c, cable TV, telephones, full kitchens, huge closets, and large verandas. Call for more specifics. The new sports bar has a pool table, 60-inch TV, PingPong, darts, and poker machines. Rates start at US$125. Children under 12 stay free with parent. Marina services are available for the boating crowd. Time-shares available here; credit cards accepted.

True to its name, **El Pescador Lodge,** P.O. Box 17, San Pedro, Ambergris Caye, Belize, C.A., U.S. tel. 800/245-1950, Belize tel. 26/2398, email pescador@btl.net, three miles north of San Pedro, is focused on fishing, though some come just to get away from it all. Anglers will find one of the best selections of quality gear in the country: line, lures, rods, and reels. Boats and guides specialize in tarpon fishing and cast the lagoons for ladyfish or snook; much of the fishing is catch-and-release. Others take guests outside the reef for sailfish or wahoo. Or they troll the reef for kingfish and barracuda and jig the bottoms with bait for snapper and grouper—something for everyone. Fishing package rates include transfers from Belize City, all meals, boat, and guide; guide tips, bar tab, and gear are extra. Packages are structured for couples of avid anglers and for those where only one likes to wet a hook. The resort has 12 rooms and one

Captain Morgan's Retreat, Ambergris Cove

PATTI LANGE

suite, all with private baths in a large colonial building. A long veranda faces the sea within sight of the reef just 200 yards offshore. For snorkelers, beach bums, and less-active types, the lodge offers less-expensive packages. Rooms only, on a daily basis, are also available. A pool sits alongside the beach. The restaurant serves buffet-style meals, with fish and meat dishes. Hors d'oeuvres are served before dinner. They offer many multinight packages based on fishing or not fishing. Prices start at US$200/day. Call for details.

US$200–250

A little more than four miles north, **Mata Chica** beach resort, tel. 21-3010/21-3011, fax 21-3012, email matachica@btl.net, is an isolated pampering station for vacationers who love the sea and the tropical ambience. Fourteen spacious a/c casitas are decorated in a Caribbean-mod flare and individually named. Shower in a private jungle atmosphere. Continental breakfast is included, a l42-foot catamaran is available for private charter, the sand is good, service is good, and the Italian food at the **Mambo Restaurant** is outstanding. Kids 10 and over welcome to stay here. US$190 for a sea-view bungalow or US$275 for beachfront casita. You might even run into some leftover *Temptation Island* lovers from TV.

For those who truly want to be pampered, **Cayo Espanto** is the place. Located on its own island off of Ambergris, the resort has five casitas and a guest to staff ratio of 2:1—all of which you pay for.

The casitas are all different but have king-size beds, a/c, TV, terry robes (in the tropics?), private pool, and personal butler—seclusion and luxury in a posh, tropical environment.

Guests at the resort have daily dining experiences with the award-winning chefs. Tours can be arranged.

Rates in high season are US$695–US$1,320 per night and include all meals and drinks. Call 888/666-4282 for more information.

Condotels

More and more condotels—privately owned condominiums that are rented out by a single management group—are popping up on the island. The following are just some of the condotels that are available on Ambergris:

The **Caribe Island Resort,** tel. 26/3233, email ccaribe@btl.net, three miles south of town, offers a range of accommodations with oceanfront minisuite US$130. All suites have a/c, cable TV, fully equipped kitchens—including blenders and microwaves, queen beds, and ceiling fans. Golf cart and bicycle rentals available. Rooms are cheerfully decorated. Fishing, snorkeling, and diving offered. A freshwater pool sits in front of the three-story units.

Ah, the Suite Life! Kenneth Krohn has created a wonderful condotel getaway, **Belizean Reef Suites,** San Pedro, Ambergris Caye, Belize, C.A., tel./fax 26/2582, email vkrohn @psnw.com, where you can have gleaming white suites with a/c and many of the amenities you'd expect in fancier Caribbean locations. Everything is spotless: the large one- or two-bedroom suites, the big bathrooms, and the spacious kitchens and living rooms. The shady verandas, with beautiful views of the ocean, are especially pleasant on a hot sunny day. Guests can use the facilities at Ramon's with the understanding that a little patronage of bar, etc., would be appreciated. Fair enough; Ramon's has the nicest slice of sand on the island. Laundry service, bikes, water toys, tours on land or sea, and transportation can all be arranged. One-bedroom suites are US$115.

FOOD

Those who like to eat are in for trouble in San Pedro—but not for lack of good food. Instead there are almost too many tempting chances to sample the culinary arts. This is a change from years past. At one time, the only place to have a good meal was at your hotel. Most of the hotels still serve good food—in fact some are outstanding—but today the visitor also has a choice of other cafés springing up around town. The selection grows each year.

Rubie's has good pastries and coffee in the morning. Several good spots to try for sandwiches and quick fare are **Celi's Deli,** near Rubie's, and **Mickey's Place** on Tarpon Street, home of the huge Wednesday special burrito for US$4. At **Tarzan's Nite Club,** the conch fritters and ceviche are worth a try. For the cheapest and ultimate in satisfying meals, don't overlook the street vendors selling rice, beans, and "stew chicken" by the playground. There is usually a good selection of desserts as well. If you're hankering for a latte or cappuccino, try **Café Olé,** across from the airstrip.

For inexpensive Mexican food, try the **Reef Restaurant,** next to Elvi's on Pescador Drive, and **Tropical Takeout,** across the street from the airport and next to the SunBreeze, has great homemade salsa *(muy picante!),* the better to douse tasty tacos of chicken, pork, or beef. A good value, a plate of them will put you back about US$2.50. And they're good! So are the *boletos,* Tropical Takeout's version of a sandwich, but actually a taco by still-another name. And you can get eggs and trimmings any time of day. No wonder the cabbies hang out here.

Cannibals serves three meals a day and offers salads, marinated chicken (US$5), breakfast burritos(US$4), baked potatoes with various fillings, and nachos—a bit of everything.

The **Dockside Bar and Grill** is good and cheap—US$3.50 for rice and beans with ginger chicken. The house special is pork chops for US$6.50. True to their name, Dockside is located on a dock. Eat indoors or out—indoors has TVs with sports on.

Barbecues

Beach barbecues seem to be the wave of the now in San Pedro—*everyone* seems to be hosting a barbecue at least one night a week, and you can eat barbecue every night if you so desire. Rating them is difficult, as they are all good. The following are some of the better ones. The **Holiday Hotel** has live music to accompany its beach barbecue on Wednesday night; **BC's** on the beach has one of the very best on Sunday 11 A.M. to 3P.M. Your choice of chicken, US$5, ribs US$10, or fish US$5. All are good. The **Lions Club** donates the money it makes from its Friday and Saturday night barbecues to those who need medical help and can't afford it, and **Ramon's** has a Tuesday and Friday barbecue.

Moderate

The **El Patio Restaurant** on Coconut Drive offers good value, nice servers, tasty food, and a strolling mariachi. The lime-marinated grilled grouper with cilantro and garlic and wine sauce is heavenly, US$10; so was the key lime pie. Open daily. **Big Daddy's** has great barbecue, especially the lobster. **Duke's Place** has a nice selection of seafood dishes. **La Margarita,** Coconut Dr., serves up tasty Tex-Mex for lunch and dinner and is home to a 40-ounce margarita—ouch! **Sweet Basil,** tel. 26/3870, is a gourmet café on the north side of the split (a cut in the island). They have deli selections as well as healthy and vegetarian meals. The Greek salad is wonderful, likewise the lobster kabobs. **Caruso's** at the SunBreeze Hotel serves Italian made by Italians. Large portions for a moderate price, are all served on the outside patio tables covered with linens. Spaghetti Carbonara is US$9; the linguini pescatore—with shrimp, snapper, and conch—is US$14 and good. They also serve pizza and Italian wine.

Island Cuisine, serves up good Belizean fare at reasonable rates on a nice outdoor patio.

If you don't feel like going out to eat, **Powerhouse Pizza,** tel. 2661, will deliver.

Duane's Surf and Turf serves breakfast all day—the lobster omelette will set you back US$7.50. Lots of seafood items as well as filet mignon. The **Jambel Jerk Pit** is known for its spicy jerk chicken. Open 7 A.M. to 2 P.M.

More Upscale

Customers enjoy a thatched-roof, fan-cooled tropical café at **Elvi's Kitchen,** Pescador Drive and Ambergris Street. The seafood specials are especially good (quality and quantity) even though they may cost a bit more. Burgers are good too.

Would an icy piña colada and some of the best conch ceviche on the island put you in the proper mood? **Celi's Restaurant** at Holiday Hotel, Barrier Reef Drive between Black Coral and Tarpon Streets, delivers the goods.

The **Capricorn Restaurant,** tel. 26/2809, three miles north of San Pedro, accessible by water taxi (or for the romantic, check out the sunset cruise on the *Rum Punch*), is a small, intimate, beachfront dining experience that can be described as gourmet. Reservations are a must; your table is yours for the night. Fish, Italian, French, and daily specials tantalize the taste buds as you read the menu. The seafood crepes and seafood combo are excellent; the focaccia with roasted garlic and olive oil is heavenly. Save

Ambergris coast

room for desserts such as the creamy rum chocolate cake.

For a special occasion, try **Rendezvous Restaurant,** tel. 26/3426. It is one of the best on the island and offers a blend of Thai and French cuisine. Start with escargot with lemon-garlic butter sauce for an appetizer, US$10; for your main course the grilled shrimp (US$22) or the marinated chicken with a coconut red-curry sauce (US$15) is sure to hit the spot. They serve lunch and dinner; need to take a water taxi here.

We didn't make it to **Mambo's** at the Mata Chica Resort, but everyone else says it's well worth the splurge.

ENTERTAINMENT

Diving by day and drinking by night can best describe the activities of Ambergris. There are bars for all shapes, sizes, and age groups in San Pedro—here are some of the better ones.

Start your night on the town watching the sun go down. The best places are **Bananas** rooftop bar and the **Coral Sands Sports Bar** at the Belize Yacht Club. They have two-for-one rum drinks.

The Boatyard offers free rum drinks every Wednesday during ladies night (sorry guys, for the women.)

Something is always going on at **Big Daddy's Disco,** on the edge of the park and the ocean at Ambergris Street. Thursday and Friday nights dazzle the crowd with your karaoke voice; Saturday night the place rocks to live music until 3 A.M.

For some really funky entertainment, drop into the **Pier Lounge** (in the Spindrift Hotel at Buccaneer St. and Barrier Reef Dr.), a favorite haunt of dive masters and other locals. On Monday evenings the hotly contested crab races take place. And on Wednesday evenings take in the "World Famous" **Chicken Drop.**

Located in Fido's courtyard, **Purple Parrot Bar,** at Barrier Reef Drive between Ambergris and Pelican Streets, is one of the livelier spots in town. Several nights a week it offers live entertainment (boo away the guy with the harmonica when the band wants to take a break), and with a restaurant, an art gallery, and a jewelry shop in the courtyard, there are always lots of new faces around.

The **Tackle Box Bar,** end of Black Coral Street, is a favorite watering hole of locals and travelers who have some time and a thirst. You never know whom you'll run into—a boat captain, a government minister, or an eye surgeon from the States.

For those wanting to sample the discos of Belize, **Tarzan's Nite Club,** Barrier Reef Drive and Ambergris Street, across from the park, is another jumping joint on Thursday through Saturday nights, with karaoke every Thursday. And with tasty and inexpensive edibles next door at **Tarzan's Huts,** you have the option of eating before or between dance sessions. It's a good place to meet local 24-year-olds or a good place to leave because of the 24-year-olds—take your choice!

The **Barefoot Iguana Disco** is THE place to go for dancing, says the young, local crowd. This large cement, boxy disco is dark, smoky, and loud.

Ambergris has **The Palace,** a casino that lets you lose your money at slots and blackjack. They open every day at 2 P.M. Closed Wednesdays.

SHOPPING

Arts and Crafts

Gift shops abound in San Pedro, especially on Barrier Reef and Pescador Drives. If you want postcards, shells, colorful swim-and beach-apparel, towels, hats, T-shirts, or any of the other usual knickknacks, they're easy to come by, either in the hotels or independent stores. Browse them all. Some are more than just souvenir shops and have displays of fascinating crafts—Belize has several artists who create world-class art with excellent portrayals of life and nature in Belize on canvas, and at least one artist who works in clay.

In Fido's Courtyard is the ambitious little **Belizean Arts,** tel. 26/2638, fax 26/63347. It features primitive and native art by local and neighboring-country artists as well as a great variety of crafts. If you're looking for more than the run of the mill T-shirts, this store might be worth checking out.

Artist John Westerhold has made himself right at home near Rubie's in **Iguana Jack's,** Ambergris Caye, Belize, C.A., tel. 26/2767. Here he has a shop and kiln where he creates and sells his paintings (and those of others), along with his ceramic sculptures, masks, and signature pots with the whimsical iguanas. Pass by on the beach and through the back of his shop watch John at work while pots dry on the little veranda before glazing. An amiable type, John enjoys talking to visitors. Stop by for a look and a brief word at the south end of Barrier Reef Drive.

The spacious **Best of Belize,** on Pescador Drive at the south end of town, has a wonderful selection of Belizean wood furniture (tables, clam chairs, and calypso chairs), cutting boards, other wood items, and ceramics.

Island Vibes, near Elvi's, has nicer clothes and is the place to stock up on Belizean food specialties, cookbooks, and T-shirts. **Traffic Jam** has a good selection of T-shirts, books, bathing suits, spices—a bit of everything. The tiny **Beauty of Nature Gift Shop** on Pescador Drive has colorfully painted picture frames, wall

decor, and chairs with toucan backrests. A little different from all the others. **The Little Old Craft Shop** on Barrier Reef Drive sells jewelry carved from coral, wood, and shell. Bring in a design; they also do custom-made mementos.

For divers looking for the perfect T-shirt, check out the **Coral Reef Dive Shop.** Besides snorkel gear, they carry the best selection of dive T-shirts. And if you're going snorkeling and forgot an underwater camera, **Blue Hole Dive Shop** sells the disposable kind, as well as the usual assortment of T-shirts.

Groceries, Sundries, and Other Basics

You can buy groceries and basic supplies at a number of stores. **Rocks Shopping Center** on the south side of town, at the corner of Pescador Drive and Buccaneer Street., has cereal, bread, meat, vegetables, cleaning solutions, wines, and just about anything else you'd expect to find in a grocery store. Its little sister, **Rocks II,** is on Coconut Drive.

Island Supermarket, on Coconut Drive, is a big market American style. You'll find everything here; they accept traveler's checks. **San Pedro Super Market** is another supermarket on Sandpiper Drive.

Patty's Fresh Fruit & Vegetables, tel. 26/2388, has a wonderful array of whatever's in season: star fruit, papayas, pineapples, grapefruit, watermelon, grapes, limes, bananas, squash, chayote, okra, lettuce, ginger, bell peppers, and potatoes. Patty's, just south of Elvi's Kitchen, delivers free to condos and docks.

Those on the north end of town also will find **Bush Master Kool Spot,** near Hotel del Rio. It carries a limited but useful selection of canned goods, cereal, eggs, bread, meats, garlic, dried beans, paper products, and cleaning supplies. Remember: This is an island and everything must cross the sea, so the choice is limited and pricey. But you should find just about everything you need on the shelves, along with Belikin beer and Belizean rum.

SERVICES AND INFORMATION

The **Atlantic Bank** is next to the **Spindrift Hotel.** The **Belize Bank** is across the street and south of Buccaneer Street. The **post office** is in the **Al-**

ijua **Building** on the corner of Barrier Reef Drive and Buccaneer Street, open Mon.–Fri. 8 A.M.–5 P.M. It's always fun to look at Belize's beautiful, artistic, and often very large postage stamps; they make great gifts for the folks back home and are perfect for framing or for the traditional stamp collector.

Get tourist information at the **Belize Tourist Board** office at Island Plaza on Barrier Reef Drive

Visitors will find answers to all of their travel questions at several local **travel agencies** in San Pedro; a few hotels have their own agencies. Independent agencies include **Amigo Travel,** tel. 26/2180, and **Travel & Tour Belize,** the oldest in San Pedro, tel. 26/2137; they can handle all of your travel needs, whether airline tickets or a tour into the countryside of Belize.

Head to **Cyber Coffee Internet** for all your email needs. US$2.50 for 15 minutes. Open 9 A.M.–9 p.m. Mon.–Sat.; 12–9P.M. on Sun.

Have a **real estate** question? Many people fall in love with the easygoing, water-oriented lifestyle of Ambergris Caye. For all those who just can't tear themselves away, condos and property are for sale on Ambergris Caye and elsewhere in the country. The **Belize Yacht Club, Belizean Reef Suites, and Mayan Princess,** are just a few examples of the condominiums around San Pedro. More are on the way. For more information, contact John Edwards of **Southwind Properties,** P.O. Box 1, San Pedro, Ambergris Caye, Belize, C.A., tel. 26/2005 or 2060.

Dellie's laundry, tel. 26/2454, on Pescador Drive, can keep you smelling fresh if your hotel doesn't offer laundry services. Open every day, US$5 a load.

Belicolor one-hour photo, tel. 26/3304, is in the Island Plaza.

Prescriptions and other medicines can be found at **R&L Pharmacy,** tel. 26/2890 by the airstrip. Open daily. If you need medical attention, there's **Dr. L Rodriguez Medical Services,** tel. 26/3197.

GETTING THERE

By Air
A 2,600-foot-long runway accommodates both private and commercial small planes on Am-

bergris, and from the strip it's just a few minutes' walk to downtown San Pedro (although there's been talk for years of moving this strip to a 550-acre spot south of town). Two airlines (Maya Island Air and Tropic Air) run regular and frequent flights to San Pedro and Caye Caulker. From Belize City, it's 15 minutes to the caye; flights to Ambergris are available from other towns in Belize as well. For schedules and prices contact U.S. travel agents or **Maya Island Air,** U.S. tel. 800/521-1247, San Pedro tel. 26/2435 or 2485, email mayair@btl.net. **Tropic Air,** P.O. Box 20, San Pedro, Ambergris Caye, Belize, C.A., U.S. tel. 800/422-3435 or 713/440-1867, Belize tel. 26/2012, email tropicair@btl.net, offers the same service. Several charter planes make custom flights: **Cari-Bee Air Service,** Municipal Airstrip/San Pedro, Belize City, C.A., tel. 2/44253, for local and international charters; and **Su-Bec Air Service,** P.O. Box 182, Belize City/San Pedro, Belize City, C.A., tel. 2/30388.

The flight from Belize City to San Pedro takes about 15 minutes and fare is about US$66 roundtrip. Leaving from the Municipal Airport can be cheaper if traveling in a group of two or more.

By Boat
Between Belize City and Ambergris, the trip takes about 75 minutes. The water taxi station at one end of the swing bridge in Belize City offers daily trips to San Pedro via Caye Caulker. Cost is US$12.50 one way. Boats leave Belize City at 9 A.M., noon, and 3 P.M. Other boats making the crossing are the *Triple J* and *Andrea II.* The *Andrea II* leaves San Pedro for Belize City at 7 A.M. daily from the Texaco dock by the **Conch Shell Hotel.** On a windy or rainy day, you stay dry on this vessel because it's enclosed. In Belize City, the *Andrea II* departs for San Pedro from the Bellevue Hotel pier (south of the swing bridge) at 3 P.M.

The *Hustler* leaves San Pedro daily at 7 A.M. and returns from Belize City about 4 P.M. The *Thunderbolt* docks at the swing bridge in Belize City and has the same schedule as above. Rates for all these boats should be around US$12.50 one-way. No regularly scheduled trips are available between cayes other than Ambergris and Caye Caulker; ask around the docks at Caulker and San Pedro, and you'll probably find a private boat owner willing to take you for a fee.

downtown Ambergris

The sea is usually calm on trips to the cayes thanks to the offshore reef. However, there's always the exception. (If it's extraordinarily rough, the boats will not run to the cayes.) But, if you happen to be traveling by boat when there are lots of whitecaps, sitting toward the stern of these boats usually nets you a smoother ride. In the case of an enclosed boat, such as the *Andrea II,* you may also smell more fumes back there. So, you have to weigh which will affect you more. And some sailors say that keeping your eyes on the horizon in rough weather helps to avoid seasickness. If you're always prone to seasickness, whether calm or rough, there are always seasick pills or wristbands for seasickness. Both of these are best brought from home just in case you can't find them here in a pinch.

GETTING AROUND

Friday, Saturday, and Sunday evenings no vehicles are allowed on Barrier Reef Drive. How pleasant to stroll the street and not to have to dodge a motor vehicle!

Rent a bicycle at **Joe's Bicycle Rentals,** tel. 26/2982, across from the Spindrift and cruise the island. Rentals by the hour, day and week.

Even on an island this small the occasional need for a **taxi** arises. Some hotels offer a steady stream of them. Otherwise you can have one called or take matters into your own hands and call **Chi's Friendly Taxi Service,** tel. 26/2635 or 2850, or **Tun's Taxis,** tel. 26/2038.

The most frequently seen modes of transport are **golf carts.** Very few cars exist on the island, and it really is fun to explore San Pedro and the rest of the island with one of the ever-present, ever-increasing number of carts. **Island Auto Golf Cart,** tel. 26/2790 on the town side of the airstrip, is just one of many places you can rent carts. Yes, San Pedro *does* have a **gas station** a short distance south of town.

Water taxis to the northern end of the island are available from the **Island Ferry.** Buy tickets at the dock office in front of Fido's Courtyard. Price depends on how far you are going. Cost to the Capricorn Restaurant is US$5 per person, one way. Ask about return schedule.

CAYE CAULKER

This tiny island offers its own special brand of laid-back tourism. Though the major industry traditionally has been fishing, tourism is beginning to edge up as a close second, maybe even number one by now. Only a few cars mar the tropical scenery and disrupt the two main sandy roads running north to south, though cut by a number of crossroads. Even that is changing *a little,* with more cars than ever before. Caulker is a place to recover from "burnout"—no traffic, no smog, no high-tech anything (OK, email has found its place here—but that's about it), no business meetings (for anyone), no lawn mowers (no lawns), no Burger Kings, and no frozen orange juice. To rejuvenate the psyche, Caulker lures one with swimming, snorkeling, diving, and a chance to study the sea and sky and all of God's creatures above and below. There's little else to do besides "experiencing" a small "desert island." And the best part? It's good value for your dollar, though not quite as cheap as in the past.

THE LAND

Caulker lies 21 miles northeast of Belize City, 11 miles south of Ambergris Caye, and one mile west of the Belize Reef. The island is four miles long; however, the inhabited part is an area less than a mile long, measuring south from the Split at the northern end. The land north of the Split is uninhabitable, consisting mostly of mangrove swamps with a narrow strip of land along the east coast. The dry season is December–February. Because the island sits on a limestone escarpment, most houses have wells. The water, though drinkable, is used mostly for utility purposes because of its slight saline flavor. Drinking water is collected in rain gutters from the aluminum roofs and then channeled into tanks kept by the side of most houses. In the dry season, drinking water becomes scarce.

New Development

When new houses were built on the south end of Caulker, friction was rampant between development and no-development factions. Bringing in electricity was a source of contention, but all agree that there will be no signs in this neighborhood. This private war will be an ongoing action as long as there are two people on the island. Several years ago, issues of disagreement were the sewage treatment plant and the building of the airport. Seventeen acres of crocodile and bird-nesting lands were destroyed with the construction; 120 species of birds nest on the southern end of Caye Caulker. As it is, the island can ill afford much more development. The next discussion was over sand dredging. Sand was brought from the backside of the island and dumped and spread along the front side. So far it has been spread from the split working its way along the coast, even Hurricane Keith didn't take away all of the forty feet of sandy beach along the waterfront. It looks very nice.

FLORA AND FAUNA

Caulker is a sandy island that does not support general agricultural production, although coconut, papaya, lime, breadfruit, banana, plantain, and cacao flourish. Colorful flowering trees and plants such as hibiscus, ginger, *flamboyanes,* crotons, succulents, spider lilies, bougainvillea, and periwinkle add an exotic touch to the otherwise stark white (sandy) landscape. The ziricote tree does nicely, and locals candy the fruit, or use it in salads. Jungle weeds and vines thrive in the sandy soil, and no matter how often they are cut back (by hand with machetes), they soon reappear.

Pelicans and frigate birds decorate the sky as they soar along the coast hunting for fish. Bird-watchers can see ospreys dropping on fish in the shallows or perching occasionally on the post of a pier. One has even built a nest by the airstrip.

A few creatures are endemic to the island, such as a variety of lizards, a few snakes (including the boa constrictor), and two types of crabs. During the rainy season, May–September, sand flies and mosquitoes are on the attack and drive all human life indoors. On rare occasions, malaria and dengue fever have shown up on the island, but not in recent history.

HISTORY

Caye Caulker (sometimes called Corker or Hicaco) is another former playground of the pirates—at least they played in the general vicinity. Most historians agree that the island was not permanently inhabited in that era by anyone. However, an anchor dating from the 19th century was found in the channel on the southern end of the island; a wreck equally as old was discovered off the southern end of Caye Chapel. The island was known to be visited by Mexican fishermen during those centuries because for generations they handed down stories of putting ashore at Caye Caulker for fresh water from a "big hole" on the caye. The island was uninhabited as late as the 1830s. It wasn't until the outbreak of the Yucatán Caste War in 1848, when refugees (Spanish and mestizos) fled across the border into Belize by the thousands, that many permanently settled on Ambergris Caye, a few found their way onto Caye Caulker. Many of today's Jicauqueños (Caulker Islanders) can trace their family histories back as far as the Caste War and even know from which region in Mexico their ancestors originated.

Exact dates of settlement on Caye Caulker are uncertain, but one of the remaining families on the island, the Reyes family, tells of their great-grandfather, Luciano, who arrived in Mexico from Spain and worked as a logwood cutter along the coast of Yucatán and later fled south to avoid the bloodletting in Mexico. He first settled in San Pedro on Ambergris Caye and decided it was going to be his permanent home. Then, when land fever erupted, he competed in the intense bidding for Ambergris Caye, only to lose out to James Blake, who became the owner with a bid of BZE$650. Reyes decided to buy Caye Caulker instead and, with BZE$300, became the owner of the small caye. Over the years land was sold to various people; many descendants of the original landholders are still prominent on Caye Caulker.

Early Economy

Though the town developed into a fishing village, *cocales* (coconut plantations) were planted from one end of the caye to the other. Though no written records have been found, it is believed the original trees were planted in the 1880s and 1890s at about the same time as those planted on Ambergris Caye. It took a lot of capital to plant a *cocal*. The land had to be cleared of jungle growth, holes dug, seaweed gathered and placed in the holes for fertilizer, and then seedlings planted. After that it took many man-hours to keep the *cocales* clear of brush, pick the coconuts, husk them, and then deliver the harvest to Belize City. Reyes was one of the original planters. His workers would begin at the northern end and stack the coconuts all along the shore, where they were picked up by boats. It was time-consuming, laborious work. When the workers finished their sweep of the island, it was time to begin again—the trees produced continually. Slavery was never a part of the Caulker economy, which prevented the development of the stereotypical plantation hierarchy based on race and class that was so common in the Caribbean. Laborers earned a cash wage (albeit small) enabling them to use their income to buy the necessities to supplement their subsistence fishing. The people were very poor. Some of the older folks remember their grandparents and great-grandparents working long days and making only pennies.

Maybe because of the economic conditions, the families on the caye began helping each other out early on. When one man got a large catch of fish, his family and neighbors helped him with it and, in turn, always went home with some. When one man's fruit trees were bearing, he would share the fruit, knowing that he would benefit later. This created very strong ties, especially between families and extended families. Today's longtime fishing families on Caulker make an above-average living, and many of them add to it by providing some type of service to the tourists that are coming more regularly every year.

Lobstering

Lobsters are sought today to feed the tourists. Many lobsters are taken undersized and as a result the quantities are diminishing. The lobster

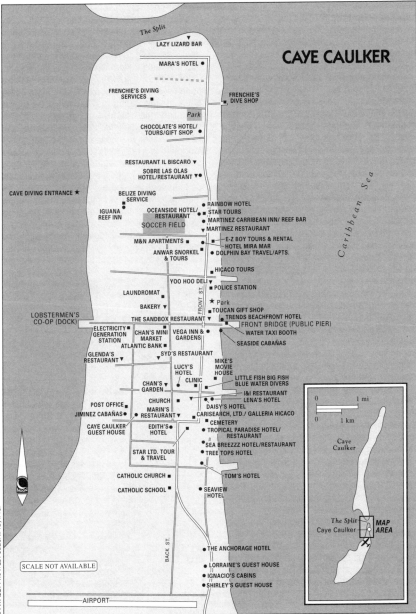

CAYE CAULKER

The Split

LAZY LIZARD BAR ▼

MARA'S HOTEL ●

FRENCHIE'S DIVING
SERVICES ■

FRENCHIE'S
DIVE SHOP ■

Park

CHOCOLATE'S HOTEL/
TOURS/GIFT SHOP ●

RESTAURANT IL BISCARO ▼
SOBRE LAS OLAS
HOTEL/RESTAURANT ▼●

CAVE DIVING ENTRANCE ★

BELIZE DIVING
SERVICE ■

IGUANA
REEF INN ■

OCEANSIDE HOTEL/
RESTAURANT ▼

SOCCER FIELD

● RAINBOW HOTEL
■ STAR TOURS
▼ MARTINEZ CARRIBEAN INN/ REEF BAR
▼ MARTINEZ RESTAURANT

M&N APARTMENTS ■

ANWAR SNORKEL
& TOURS ■

● E-Z BOY TOURS & RENTAL
■ HOTEL MIRA MAR
● DOLPHIN BAY TRAVEL/APTS.

■ HICACO TOURS

YOO HOO DELI ●

LAUNDROMAT ■

BAKERY ▼

■ POLICE STATION

★ Park
● TOUCAN GIFT SHOP
▼ TRENDS BEACHFRONT HOTEL

Caribbean Sea

LOBSTERMEN'S
CO-OP (DOCK) ■

THE SANDBOX RESTAURANT ▼

FRONT ST.

FRONT BRIDGE (PUBLIC PIER)
WATER TAXI BOOTH

ELECTRICITY
GENERATION
STATION ■

CHAN'S MINI
MARKET ■

ATLANTIC BANK ■

VEGA INN &
GARDENS ■

SEASIDE CABAÑAS

GLENDA'S
RESTAURANT ▼

SYD'S RESTAURANT ■

LUCY'S
HOTEL ■

CHAN'S
GARDEN ▼

CLINIC ■

MIKE'S
MOVIE
HOUSE ■

LITTLE FISH BIG FISH
BLUE WATER DIVERS ■

POST OFFICE ■

JIMINEZ CABAÑAS ●

CHURCH ■
MARIN'S
RESTAURANT ▼

■ I&I RESTAURANT
● LENA'S HOTEL

● DAISY'S HOTEL
CARISEARCH, LTD./ GALLERIA HICACO

CAYE CAULKER
GUEST HOUSE ■

EDITH'S
HOTEL ■

■ CEMETERY

● TROPICAL PARADISE HOTEL/
RESTAURANT

STAR LTD. TOUR
& TRAVEL ■

● SEA BREEZZZ HOTEL/RESTAURANT
● TREE TOPS HOTEL

CATHOLIC CHURCH ■

● TOM'S HOTEL

CATHOLIC SCHOOL ■

SEAVIEW
HOTEL ●

0   1 mi

0   1 km

Caye
Caulker

The Split
Caye Caulker

MAP
AREA

BACK ST.

● THE ANCHORAGE HOTEL

SCALE NOT AVAILABLE

● LORRAINE'S GUEST HOUSE
● IGNACIO'S CABINS
● SHIRLEY'S GUEST HOUSE

AIRPORT

© AVALON TRAVEL PUBLISHING, INC.

MOON

economy has suffered, and those in the know have suggested that the lobster season be shortened; the lobster season has been shifted to June 15–February 15.

THE PEOPLE

In the early days, fish brought in very little cash. However, fishing was still preferred to working on the *cocal*. It was less strenuous and less time-consuming, and the fishermen enjoyed greater independence. Eventually fishing began to pay off for the people and co-ops were established. Lobster was an important part of their success, as it was on Ambergris. Fishermen liked being their own bosses and, as a result, to this day Jicauqueños (in Spanish the island name is Cayo Jicaco, which has degenerated into Caye Caulker) are independent thinkers with a lot of self-assurance. They take pride in their early roots on the island, and while color-class social thinking is seen in other parts of Belize, the distinction between peoples in Caulker is not based on color, rather on whether they are islanders or nonislanders! Along with the title "Jicauqueños" you usually know an islander from such comments as, "I belong to Caye Caulker." Most of the original island families were mestizo (commonly referred to in Belize as Spanish). But today the mixture also includes Creoles and a few immigrant Anglos. The Caulker community has been fairly successful in keeping the ownership of land among the locals. Every once in a while someone talks of bigger and better tourist accommodations, but face it: The locals are happy with their small island, small guest houses, small home-style cafés and want to keep it just the way it is. It appears they don't really *want* more outsiders!

TOURISM

Early Tourism
Until the 1960s, few visitors reached the shores of Caye Caulker. But once the hippie backpackers discovered the small, relaxed island, more and more travelers began arriving. This was becoming the hushed secret among adventurers making their way south along the Central American trail. Although most people had never heard of Belize in the 1970s, they did recognize the name of British Honduras and had a rough idea of where it was located. The usual description was that Belize was the next country past Mexico. Such people as Jacques Cousteau and *National Geographic* writers began spreading the word that Caulker was the place for the young or the young at heart. It soon became apparent to islanders that incoming visitors *needed* food and lodging, and this was a new way for the women to earn extra money. The men's lives changed little with the influx as they continued fishing. Houses on Caulker were generally wooden structures built on stilts with a separate cooking shack. The first accommodations, such as **Edith's Hotel,** were simple cubicles created by enclosing the space under the house. Others followed, and soon islanders built simple hotels next to their homes. Most offered only the barest of necessities (shared toilet, no hot water) and were

jungle Christmas tree

often dormitory style, but they served the purpose and were satisfactory for the young adventurers who came. The first "cafés" were women selling food out of their windows on the sandy lanes. Some women would place chalkboards in front of their houses announcing that they were cooking "boil up," or fish, or *whatever,* that evening and the price. If you wanted to come for dinner, all you had to do was knock on the door early in the day and tell her. It was wonderfully casual, unbelievably cheap, and a marvelous opportunity to get to know the warm, friendly people of Caulker. Probably the only black mark during this era was the substance users who became obnoxious and insulting. The people didn't approve of having "stoned" or drunken folks wandering around the small community. In the Caulker of the new millenium, a close watch is kept on anyone who looks the part—that's not to say that the islanders themselves have never indulged in growing—and smoking—a little pot. It's a given that you will be approached at least once by someone trying to sell you pot or cocaine. It's annoying but not threatening. Little is done by the police due to the brother-nephew-son syndrome of such a small place. Police are frequently moved city to city to new locales and as a result, the locals find it amusing that their grandmothers know who is selling drugs, but the police can't seem to figure it out.

Tourism Today
Today's Caulker is changing—a little. The population has grown to 1,300 in the last decade. The islanders don't want to "lose" their island as they believe the San Pedranos have lost San Pedro on Ambergris Caye. The islanders have adamantly kept out foreign investors, and they keep the prime pieces of land for their homes. Newer hotel cabañas now provide cable TV and air conditioning, but they still maintain the low-key Caribbean ambience.

Visitors are not just backpackers anymore. Though the island still attracts many young adults, it also finds whole families who thrive on the unhurried, uncrowded atmosphere visiting. Visitors can expect nice people, productive fishing, exotic snorkeling and diving, a laid-back atmosphere—and reasonable prices! More hotels are springing up around the island

each year. In February and March you'll run into the largest number of tourists from the States. In August the island is filled with the European contingent. The slowest months are in the fall and in January.

The caye has sandy streets and very few are marked with street signs; just ask anyone for directions. You can walk from one end of the island to the other, and backside to frontside, on a lazy morning. If you want to take a little rest, flake out on one of many wooden docks that jut out over the clear turquoise sea along the waterfront—just ask for permission first. In case you didn't know, that's what Caye Caulker is all about—being lazy, lying on your back, and studying the sky and all the winged creatures that prefer flying just above Caulker. You might see the graceful and magnificent frigate (fish bandit extraordinaire that never gets its feathers wet), always on the lookout for a handout from any *real* fishing bird flapping away with its loaded beak— whammo! The frigate steals the fishing bird's catch and it doesn't know what hit it. In spring you might see the black male frigate's brilliant red gular pouch (under its beak) inflated like a bright red balloon—that means it's courting. When you get tired of that view, flip onto your stomach and look over the side of the dock—you can spend the rest of the day studying the constantly changing underwater scene through crystal-clear water, no dive-glass needed.

OFFICIALDOM

The pace here is very slow. Don't believe anyone who tells you it is OK to partake in illegal substances because the cops are easy on tourists. Not true. Foreigners are just as welcome in the Caulker jail as locals. The **Tourist Police** are on the island to check that tour guides are licensed, and, in theory, to keep the locals from pestering the tourists to buy drugs. The mayor says they love the low-budget travelers—as long as they don't sleep on the docks or wander around nude (both against the law). Fortunately, the crimes on Caye Caulker are small transgressions. Also, keep in mind the law does not allow camping on public or private property without permission. The only "official" camping is at Vega Inn and Gardens (see "Accommodations" below), and as at many places in Belize, the price is almost as much as a cheap room in a few hotels.

ORIENTATION

Caye Caulker is cut into two pieces. **The Split** or **the Cut** separates the southern inhabited part of the island from the northern mangrove swamps. This feature earned its name after a hurricane widened a channel, causing a "cut" or "split" in the island. Travelers and locals alike come to enjoy the water around the Cut.

Moving south past the Cut toward town on **Front Street,** the street that skirts the eastern shore (there are two more north-south streets, inland), the traveler soon encounters the first of seven sandy roads that cut across the island. Turn right on any of these roads and you'll get to Back Street.

On the western pier, there's a fuel pump. Sailors exploring the nearby cayes anchor in the shallow protected waters offshore.

Back on Front Street, the **cemetery** lies at the sixth road inland. This is also where Front Street dead-ends. By turning right and then cutting to the left one street over, you'll come upon the seventh and final street. Follow this street west one block, take a left, and you can follow this dusty track called **Back Street** (even though there's one farther west than this) all the way to the airstrip. Turn left at the airport until you reach the beach and stroll the sand path past **Shirley's** and **Tree Tops Hotel** until you reach Front Street. Going south past the airport are private homes and secluded beaches—not much for tourists.

WATER ACTIVITIES

Snorkeling and Diving Services
There are many reputable dive shops for such a small island. All offer snorkeling excursions, dive trips, and certification courses. Look for **Frenchie's Diving Services,** P.O. Box 1812, Caye Caulker, Belize, C.A., tel. 22/2234, email dolphinbay@btl.net, on the pier past Chocolate's.

At **Belize Diving Services,** P.O. Box 20, Caye Caulker, Belize, C.A., tel. 22/2143, fax 22/2217,

email bzdiveserve@btl.net, owners Dawn Williams and Kathy Dalton offer three boats, PADI certification, and an on-site classroom. To find it, turn west at the **Martinez Caribbean Inn** and proceed across the width of the island past the soccer field and look for the sign.

Caye Caulker School of Scuba, tel. 22/2292, owned by local guide Abel Novelo, offers certification as well as dive trips, boating, and snorkeling. Ask around for directions.

Little Fish Big Fish Blue Water Divers, located on northern Front St., tel. 22/2250, offers PADI instruction, trips to the Blue Hole, and a friendly staff to help you with your dive questions.

Note: It only makes sense that divers and passengers check out the boat they're boarding. Ask questions—does it have two motors? Extra gas? How far will you be going? What's the weather outlook both inside the reef and outside? In short, take steps to ensure your own safety. Ask a local about the diving reputation of your dive master.

Licensed Guides
The **Caye Caulker Tour Guide Association** has worked hard to standardize prices so the prices on the island are fairly uniform. All guides in town should be licensed; ask to see a badge. This ensures proper training. More importantly, it provides you with the peace of mind that you won't lose your guide if the Tourist Police make a random check and your guy doesn't have a license.

The guides and dive shops of Caulker work well together. Most shops require a minimum number of people to run a trip and if they don't have the minimum, they'll combine groups so you *will* go out.

Touring with Captain Chocolate
Probably the best known of all the guides is Captain Chocolate, owner of **Chocolate's Tours,** Caye Caulker, Belize, C.A., tel. 22/2151, email chocolate@btl.net. Chocolate and his fleet of boats are near-legends in the trade. Whenever you talk with groups of travelers who've been to Caulker, the name Chocolate is bound to come up. For years he ran a water-taxi service and is now a member of the **Caye Caulker Water Taxi Association.** During this time, Cap-

tain Chocolate became the first to take people on trips to a nearby caye to see manatees. It's still a top-rated trip. This all-day excursion first stops in an open area where it is possible to approach manatees in their element, while being careful not to disturb the gentle creatures. The effect is exhilarating as you near a creature weighing hundreds of pounds, yet which, with the flick of a tail, can instantly leave you far behind.

The second stop is an area that Chocolate describes as the manatees' feeding area. He approaches slowly and quietly with his engines off to ensure no harm comes to these curious beasts. Instead, he uses a stout stick to pole in close. A couple of minutes' wait and the curious manatees begin to surface around the boat to breathe and continue feeding.

Other guides are often not so careful; some manatees show recent scars from boat propellers. Captain Chocolate is very protective of local manatees, and when guides from other islands come to visit the area with engines running, he sees to it that they learn the ground rules in a hurry.

After viewing the manatees for an hour or two, Chocolate heads to the white sand island of Goff Caye for an afternoon of snorkeling.

Chocolate and his wife, Annie, were involved with the creation of a manatee reserve in the Swallow Caye area. Funding and government bureaucracy are always a problem, but the reserve is finally a reality. In July 1999, **Swallow Caye** became an official manatee reserve; those wanting to donate funds can contact Chocolate and Annie at email chocolate@btl.net.

A new tour is a snorkeling trip to the Turneffe Islands with guide Carlos, who works for Captain Chocolate. He lived there for years and knows all the great snorkeling spots. Lunch is on the island where Carlos's grandfather and dog, Ninja, live. Cost is about US$42 and well worth it.

More Good Guides
Anwar Tours, tel. 22/2327, is run by brothers Rico and Javier Novelo, along with Carlos Arce, who specialize in snorkel trips to the local reef, Shark Ray Alley, and Hol Chan Preserve. Snorkeling with Carlos is great—he enjoys snorkeling as much as his passengers do and goes out of his way to show and explain the mysterious critters you wouldn't have noticed on your own.

Carlos Tours specializes in snorkeling tours to the many sites around the reef. Safety is his priority and he carries a fire extinguisher and first aid kit. Book through the Seaview Hotel, tel. 22-2205, or ask around town. He should have his own shop by publication time.

Jim and Dorothy Beveridge of **Sea-ing Is Belizing,** P.O. Box 10, Caye Caulker, email tourism@cayecaulker.org.bz, tel. 21/2079, offer nature walks that explore and explain the mangrove forests as well as the trees and critters of the island. They give slide presentations on topics ranging from the local ecosystems to marine birds. They also specialize in organizing custom trips for academic groups and wildlife photography buffs. Signs are usually posted for the slide shows; a small fee is charged. If you've ever wanted to see crocodiles, they do an A.M. nature walk that includes a croc watch. Call for details.

Fishing
This is good fishing country; inquire at your hotel about making arrangements with a fisherman (tackle provided) to take you on a hunt for the sweetest seafood in the Caribbean. Or take a walk to the backside of the island, where you'll find fishermen cleaning their fish, working on lobster traps, or mending their nets in the morning. Many will be willing to take you fishing. Main trophies are groupers, barracuda, snapper, and amberjack—all good eating. Small boats are available for rent by the hour. If you want a more organized trip, contact **Porfilio Guzman,** tel. 22/2152, a well-known fishing guide for reef or flats fishing. Guide **Roque (Rocky) Badillo,** tel. 22/2214, of **Roque's Fishing and River Tours** is another good choice.

Rolando "Roly" Rosado offers fishing and diving charters. He'll take you to the reef to dive, or on daylong fishing expeditions. Talk to Roly or his brother, Ramon, at tel. 22/2190 2058 or 2073. **Raul Young,** tel. 22/2133, takes travelers snorkeling or fishing on the reefs and is known for flats fishing.

Swimming the Split
While meandering around the island, you'll notice the **Split,** a channel that was widened by Hurricane Hattie's big blow in 1961. The violent force of the wind and water rammed through the

land, blowing away a piece of the mangrove forests—and suddenly the island was cut in two by a wider swath of water. There is sand here, but most people sunbathe on the cement walkway that sits above the water. Swimming and snorkeling are possible, but be aware that swimming in the "new" channel can be dangerous; this is a shallow and heavily trafficked area. The pull of the swift current can be enough to overpower children or weak swimmers. Another, and even more dangerous, threat is the passage of fast skiffs through the Split. Fatal accidents have occurred. Around the bend only a few meters out of the channel, the water is calm and safe. Swimming off the "back bridge" on the western side of the caye is even safer.

ACCOMMODATIONS

It used to be that none of the hotels on the island were luxurious, and then there was a room at Chocolate's that was special. Slowly more and more nice hotels are going up on the island. Most of the budget hotels are very basic. The newer ones offer electricity, private baths, and ceiling fans. A few have air-conditioning and cable TV, but still there's a taste of tropical-island life with just a few frills. There are about 300 rooms and 31 hotels on the island. The following is *not* a complete list of hotels. Remember, prices are negotiable depending on the time of the year, the number of tourists on the island, and how persuasive you are. Don't forget to add in the 8 percent sales tax, 7 percent hotel tax, and whatever service charge hotels may tack on, including a few extra bucks if you're using a credit card. You're never too far from the sea on Caulker, but few places are right on the water's edge. During the high season, most rooms are taken as soon as the tourists from Belize City arrive. Make reservations if possible.

Hotels on the front side of the island are happy places, both owners and guests. In the summer of 2000, approximately 40 feet of beach was added to the waterfront there. Crews dredged the backside of the island to fill the front. It looks nice and offers a relaxed invitation to those in search of lazy beach days.

Under US$25

On the beach, **Ignacio's Cabins,** Caye Caulker, Belize, C.A., tel. 22/2212, offers 13 small, purple clapboard wooden huts on stilts that are surrounded by a scattering of palms, sea grapes, and cassarina trees. Each cabin comes with a private, cold-water bath, is very small, and may not be everyone's cup of tea—but they have lots of island character. The cabins in the back are cheaper. US$10–25.

Daisy's Hotel, Caye Caulker, Belize, C.A., tel. 22/2150, is another oldie. Run by a great, friendly family of many daughters, Daisy's is on the east side of the island, on the main street and south of the public pier, just inland from Lena's Hotel. Daisy's has 11 simple rooms with fans and hot water in shared baths. US$18.

Lena's Hotel, Caye Caulker, Belize, C.A., tel. 22/2106, has 18 rooms in an old building. Some have shared baths; others have private baths. Rooms come with fans. Under US$25.

Edith's Hotel, Caye Caulker, Belize, C.A., with smallish, tidy rooms is a hallmark on the center street of the island. Four rooms come with h/c water, private baths, and ceiling fans; another four have shared baths. Under US$25.

Lorraine's Guesthouse, next to Shirley's on the beach, tel. 22/2002, offers seven simple cabins, three of them on stilts. A nice dock is available for sunbathing, and chairs and hammocks are on the beach. US$17–25.

Lucy's Guesthouse Hotel, Caye Caulker, Belize, C.A., tel. 22/2110, is farther inland from Daisy's and across the street from the church. Rates considerably less for shared rooms. Under US$25.

The six **Jimenez Cabañas,** Caye Caulker, Belize, C.A., tel. 22/2175, are owned and operated by George Jimenez. The cabañas have h/c water, private baths, ceiling fans, and nightlights. Under US$25.

The six nice wood cabins at **Mara's Hotel,** Caye Caulker, Belize, C.A., tel. 22/2156, are a great value with private hot-water baths and cable TV. Each unit has a small porch with hammocks. The property has a private dock with lounge chairs for guests to use. US$25.

The **Martinez Caribbean Inn,** Caye Caulker, Belize, C.A., tel. 22/2196, with its friendly staff, has been around for a long time under various names. The 24 rooms are basic with h/c water, private baths, fans, and ocean views that afford a glimpse of breakers crashing against the Belize Reef. Five rooms have a/c. The inn has a restaurant/bar nearby that contributes to the already noisy area.

Hotel Mira Mar, Caye Caulker, Belize, C.A., tel. 22/2157, is a two-story hotel a couple of blocks north of the public pier on Front Street. Its 19 rooms face the ocean across the street, and each has fan, cold water in its shared bath, and hot water in its private bath. US$10 for shared bath, private bathroom is US$18. There is also a small store.

M & N Apartments, Caye Caulker, Belize, C.A., tel. 22/2111, 2229, is on the corner of the second cross street south of the Split. Rooms at US$30 come with h/c water and are simply furnished. These are the same folks who rent the golf carts; no doubt you've seen this newest form of transport for the lazy who don't want to use their feet.

Tom's Hotel, Caye Caulker, Belize, C.A., tel. 22/2102, is popular with the young crowd and backpackers: simple bungalows (36 rooms), clean, with h/c water, shared or private baths, fans, louvered windows, tile floors, and a sea view. Both rooms with shared bath US$16, and cabins with private baths US$26.

In a concrete building by the water, Ilna Auxillou runs **Dolphin Bay Apartments.** The two fully furnished apartments are rented to those wishing to stay for a week or longer. Both feature cold water (soon to be upgraded to h/c), private bath, full kitchen with stove and fridge, and fans. The upstairs apartment is larger, catches a bit more of the sea breeze, and rents for US$175 per week. The lower apartment rents for US$125 per week. Contact **Dolphin Bay Travel,** tel. 22/2214.

Sobre Las Olas Hotel, Caye Caulker, Belize, C.A., tel. 22/2243, has a restaurant on the water; the rooms are across the street. They range in size, price, and amenities. Rooms have h/c water, private baths, and fans or a/c, and some have TVs. Rooms with a/c US$25; no a/c US$19.

US$25–50

Ramon Reyes has one of the more popular spots on Caye Caulker and with good reason: **Tropical Paradise Hotel,** Caye Caulker, Belize, C.A., tel. 22/2124, represents good value and has an equally good restaurant. It is separated from the village cemetery by a worn white picket fence. If the cemetery next door doesn't give you pause, you'll enjoy this location—both look out to sea. The wooden cabañas have private ceiling fans, baths, h/c water. Rooms have a/c. Rooms (cheaper) and suites (more expensive) are also available. The staff at Tropical Paradise can help you make arrangements for snorkeling, fishing, or lobster trapping with guides as well as arrangements to visit neighboring cayes. US$20 for simple rooms; US$32 for a/c; US$50 for deluxe rooms that have cable TV

Two stories high, the brightly colored **Rainbow Hotel,** Caye Caulker, Belize, C.A., tel. 22/2123 or 2172, sits on the edge of the lane going north of the public pier toward the Split. Seventeen clean, motel-style stucco rooms offer h/c water, private baths, electricity, a/c and/or fans, TVs, tile floors, and two suites. US$35 without a/c, US$52 with a/c. The hotel accepts Visa/MC. The Rainbow Restaurant is across the street at the water's edge.

Don't overlook **Tree Tops Hotel,** P.O. Box 29, Caye Caulker, C.A., tel. 22/2008, fax 22/2115, email treetops@btl.net, a comfortable gem set off the beach. The owners are a husband-and-wife team; Terry is English and Doris is German. Influenced by their years in Africa, they have created beautifully decorated rooms with atmosphere. Each room is different and all have high ceilings. Combine that with genuine sincerity and pleasant people, and you will find a true Caulker experience. Two rooms share a bath; the others are private. All have hot water, cable TV, ceiling fans, and a refrigerator. Visa/MC OK, a small discount given for cash and traveler's checks. Shared-bath rooms with sea view, US$35; private bath with sea view, US$40; private bath, back room US$36.

The new, clean hotel to your right as you get off of the water taxi is **Trends,** tel. 22/2094, fax 22/2097, email trendsbze@btl.net. Rooms have comfortable queen-sized beds, refrigerator, fans, and private baths, and run about US$40, w/ac US$60. A restaurant is on the premises, and a fine beach offers great sunbathing.

The **Seaview Hotel,** P.O. Box 11, Caye Caulker, tel. 22/2205, email seaview@btl.net, offers four simple rooms in a building on the beach past Tree Tops. Simple touches like a table and chairs make it homey, and the Guatamalan rugs make it colorful. Rooms are about US$35.

The newish **Seaside Cabañas,** tel. 22/2498, email seasidecabanas@hotmail.com, is the first hotel on your left as you get off of the water taxi. They have five cabañas with varying amenities. The rooms are small but tidy, private or shared bath, hot water, small porch, thatch roofs; rates about US$35. The front cabaña is large and spacious with wood floors. It can sleep six US$100.The managers are friendly Canadians and can help you make snorkeling, diving and fishing arrangements at the on-site **Hummingbird Tours** shop. No restaurant here, but it's close to everything, including **Brutus Bar,** which is steps away for cold drinks and watching the arrival of the water taxis.

US$50–100

The **Anchorage Hotel,** P.O. Box 25, tel. 22/2391, email anchorage@btl.net, Caye Caulker, Belize, C.A., tel./fax 22/2304, email tourism@caye caulker.org.bz, has upgraded from simple beach cabañas to the increasingly popular modern cement building with 12 comfortable rooms, orthopedic beds, refrigerators and fans (no a/c—owners want to help "save the environment"). Located on the beach close to many Front Street eateries. US$50.

Vega Inn and Gardens, P.O. Box 701, Belize City, Belize, C.A., tel. 22/2142, fax 22/2269, email lifestyles@vega.com.bz. This is one of the originals, and it's still a favorite. The inn offers simple rooms in an old two-story building on the sand. Owned by the Vega family, longtime island residents, the hotel has a warm and friendly atmosphere. This is a family affair and they're a font of information about the island—past and present. The family will talk for hours about establishing the fishing cooperatives, struggling against the big money-and-power folks who controlled the cayes—and winning out. Lydia rents the rooms, US$65, with fan. With only 10 rooms, reservations are a must, especially during the holiday seasons (Christmas and Easter). Rates for shared bath are considerably cheaper. The inn accepts Visa/MC.

You can rent campsites on Vega Inn and Gardens property (beware of the sand flies), but the management doesn't put up with loud or drunken parties! Camping fees are US$7 per person per night.

Clean and comfortable, at **Shirley's Guest House,** P.O. Box 13, Caye Caulker, Belize, C.A., tel. 22/2145, fax 22/2264, email shirley@btl.net, rooms are all on the beach and built with beautiful tropical woods—great wooden floors and walls. Shirley's has a variety of rooms and cabins with different amenities. Rooms with private bath US$60, shared bath US$45. The cabin has a fridge. The outside is neatly painted white with a green trim. This is the lodging closest to the airstrip on the eastern side of the island. Adults only, please.

Chocolate's Guesthouse, P.O. Box 332, Belize City, Belize, C.A., tel. 22/2151. It started with one room, but what a beautifully furnished room it is—many say the best on the island! If you're lucky enough to snag this one, remember this is a nonsmoking house. You'll have h/c water, private bath, fan, cross-ventilation, a porch with a swing, a coffee maker, bedpost lights, tile floors—even terry cloth robes. US$60. A new addition is in progress, but probably won't be ready for awhile because of delays brought on by Hurricane Keith. Check with Annie. And staying here makes it a good bet you'll get a spot on one of Chocolate's trips to Goff's Caye and a look at the manatees along the way, an experience you'll not soon forget.

The Lazy Iguana B&B, P.O. Box 59, Caye Caulker, tel. 22/2350, fax 22/2320, is a four-story private home that has four spacious rooms, all with private baths, hot water, and a/c. The top floor has a deck for lounging and a 360 degree view of the island.Their motto says it all: "Where the elite sleep and eat in bare feet!" US$85.

The **Iguana Reef Inn,** P.O. Box 31, Caye Caulker, Belize, C.A., tel. 22/2213, email iguanareef@btl.net, touts itself as the first upscale hotel on Caulker. Located next to Belize Diving Services, its rooms are spacious and colorful. The upstairs rooms have high vaulted ceilings and comfortable touches: minifridge, pleasing tile in the bathrooms and porches, cable TV, and many other modern conveniences, US$95.

FOOD

For such a tiny island, Caye Caulker boasts a number of small cafés and other eateries; just don't expect lace and linen service. For the most part, meals are simple, with fresh seafood and chicken as the featured menu items.

At the **Sand Box**, open 7 A.M.–10 P.M., north end of Front Street, you'll find (what else?) a sand floor inside and a casual atmosphere with a lot of local color. This is an evening spot for seeing and being seen. Lots of seafood: fish with curry rice, conch ceviche is US$2.25, seafood salad is US$9, and stuffed eggplant and mushrooms is US$3.75. Beer, liquor, soft drinks, and fresh juices (watermelon, orange, and pineapple) round out the menu. Breakfasts are good. Try the banana waffles, US$2.75, or one of their many omelettes, US$3.25. Happy Hour is 3–6 P.M.; rum drinks are about a buck.

Tropical Paradise Restaurant, at the south end of Front Street, has a pleasant interior. Among other selections, it serves pancakes and bacon for US$3, French toast US$2.50, and fresh orange juice for US$1.75. For lunch or dinner, some of the specialties are lobster ceviche US$4, burgers US$3, shrimp pasta salad US$6, curried lobster US$9, and pork chops US$7.50. Nearby **Popeyes** has upgraded. It's bigger, the enclosed room has a sand floor, and the breeze can keep the skeeters at bay when there's an outbreak. Icicle lights give a soft glow to your dining experience. Dinner includes chicken curry at US$10, three different-sized pizzas from US$7–22, salads, fish, and conch soup, pricey compared to the other places in town. Young, cocky waiter is free!

Sobre Las Olas, a beachfront bar and grill, turns on the barbecue and chars burgers, lobster, shrimp, crab claws, pork chops, fish, and chicken, or whatever else is in season. **Il Biscaro** offers a delightful change of pace, *real* Italian food. Homemade lasagna and ravioli are the specialties, US$8. Closed Tuesday.

Marin's, down the street from the Tropical Paradise, has a good menu and always-fresh fish; **Glenda's,** on the west side of the island, serves inexpensive Mexican food and good, cheap lobster burritos. In the morning, try her homemade cinnamon rolls and fresh-squeezed orange juice—by the glass or in an at-home recycled bottle—the best two bucks you'll spend on the island. **Syd's,** east of Glenda's, makes good burritos and has a great Saturday night barbecue. And then there's **WishWilly's,** where you get not just food with an attitude, but friendly conversation and fun. The selections are good—fresh seafood, tropical drinks—and vegetarians say thumbs up. **Martinez Restaurant** offers three meals a day year-round with burgers, tacos, and lobster heading the menu. **Chan's Garden,** on Back Street across from

local girls selling powder buns, lemon crusts, and other homemade pastries

Lucy's Hotel, serves Chinese food and decent T-bone steaks.

The **Yoo Hoo Deli,** tel. 22/2232, is a great place to pick up a bag lunch for your daily excursions. Call ahead to order. A roast beef and cheese sub sandwich, US$3.25. They also have things like a baked potato with choice of topping for about US$2 and key lime pie and ice cream sandwiches for your after-dinner meander through town.

Groceries

If you're lucky, you may run into some cute kids strolling the sandy lanes balancing pans of homemade sweet crusts and wheat bread on their heads—for sale, of course! The banana bread is heavenly.

Look around and you'll find **Chan's Mini Mart** (across from the Atlantic Bank). They've got a decent selection of fruits, drinks, and snacks for cheap meals. And if you want fresh fish or lobster, ask at the Lobstermen's Co-op Dock on the backside of the island what time the fishermen come in with their catch. This is always a good place to buy fresh fish.

NIGHTLIFE AND ENTERTAINMENT

For such a small island, it's somewhat surprising that there *are* more options than just drinking. **Sea-ing Is Belizing** offers slide shows of island birds, reef ecology, and other eco-minded topics. Call 22/2189 or ask around.

Mike's Movie House and email services, located near Tropical Paradise, has a large selection of movies to choose from and watch on their TV. It's a private home so don't be shy. US$2.50 per person with a US$7.50 minimum. Email available here too—US$2.50 for 15 minutes.

There are many bars that hop for most of the night. For the liveliest, just walk down the street and see for yourself.

Be sure to stop in at the **Lazy Lizard Bar** at the Split. This *palapa* bar is a good place to meet locals and the *best* place to watch the sunset. No food here unless you believe *Guinness* is a meal in itself. This isn't a late-night bar, and they close on bad sand fly or mosquito days. The **Sand Box** always has a crowd; **Popeye's** has bands once in a while and **Oceanside** rocks.

ISLAND ART AND GIFT SHOPS

You'll find a sprinkling of small shops in and around Front Street. Several sell T-shirts, island art, photos, books, shells, suntan lotion, maps, and typical Belizean souvenirs.

For batik lovers, **Chocolate's Gift Shop,** P.O. Box 332, Belize City, Belize, C.A., tel. 22/2151, is a must stop. Operated by Captain Chocolate's wife, Annie Seashore, this gift shop (really more boutique) has women's dresses, skirts, shirts, and sarongs acquired during Annie's yearly trips to Indonesia. (There's even a small selection for men.) Colorful, high-quality Guatemalan bags, place mats, belts, and other goodies are also found here. Open daily. Sign up here for Chocolate's trips.

If you forget your camera, James Beveridge is an excellent photographer of underwater marine life, terrestrial wildlife, and people. He sells slides and prints of his work. James and his wife, Dorothy, offer evening slide presentations featuring the natural history of Belize. To reach the Beveridges, contact **Sea-ing Is Belizing,** P.O. Box 10, Belize City, Belize, C.A., tel. 22/2189, email tourism@cayecaulker.org.bz.

Galeria Hicaco, tel. 22/2178, is a small gift shop in the front of a house at the south end of Front Street near the Tropical Paradise.It has something for everyone: handmade Belizean crafts, kayak rentals, and reef snorkel tours.

Don't stop looking; there are more. Wander through **Salty Dog** and **Toucan Gift Shop,** both on Front Street.

SERVICES AND INFORMATION

Because of the size of the island and limited number of visitors to Caulker, most of the businesspeople who make a living from tourism do so through multiple services. For the most part, the local men carry on with their fishing, and until recently their wives were the backbone of the food businesses and hotels. You'll find that the shops are generally owned by multitalented people who are artists, photographers, guides, or divers. They all have one thing in common; they're dedicated to saving natural resources—especially the reef and its rich sea life. A few newcomers have opened businesses in recent years.

Among services that you will find helpful: **Atlantic Bank,** open 9 A.M.–1 P.M., is on Back Street, half a block south of Chan's Mini Mart and the cross street with the public piers at each end.

The **post office** is also on Back Street at the last crossroad as you go south, across from the primary school and church. It's open 9 A.M.–noon, 2–5 P.M. Mon.–Fri., 9 A.M.–noon only Saturday. The mail goes out three times a week—Monday, Wednesday, and Friday.

If you should have a medical problem, a small clinic on Front Street just north of Lena's Hotel offers limited services.

Travel Agencies

Need a local travel agent to arrange dive trips, plane reservations, inland trips, or accommodations? There are many, and they keep coming. **Dolphin Bay Travel,** tel. 22/2214, has been around for a long time.

Hicaco Tours and Travel, tel. 22/2073, can make arrangements for tours to the cayes or inland. **Star Tours,** tel. 22/2375, has an office at the Tropical Paradise Hotel and the boat dock. Wendy de la Fuente runs **Caye Caulker Travel and Tour,** tel. 22/2214, and can get you to most anyplace in the country.

Newspapers

The summer of 2000 saw the restarting of a local paper, this time called the *Conch Telegraph.* It touts itself as "the only newspaper on the island." It's lighthearted, but serious issues are also discussed. We're still waiting for a new edition, but after about edition three, Hurricane Keith hit and nothing's happened since.

Email

Many hotels offer email services to their guests but if yours doesn't, **Seaside Cabañas** has Internet service. Fifteen minutes will cost you US$2.50. The **Caye Caulker Cyber Coffee Café** offers not only Internet services but is a coffee shop, Belizean style. Rates are US$2.50 for 15 minutes.

TRANSPORTATION

Getting There

Maya Island Air and **Tropic Air** make regular flights to Caye Caulker, flying from Belize City's municipal and international airports. The airstrip on Caulker is pretty simple—you wait under a tree or on the veranda of the small building that serves all flights. Fares are about US$25 one-way to the municipal airport (about 10 minutes), about US$43 to fly to the international airport. Note: Fares can change, so check them out.

If you prefer getting there by boat, outboard skiffs/launches go to and from Caye Caulker every day. The **Caye Caulker Water Taxi Association** boats haul travelers, groceries, dive equipment, and other small freight to the island daily, leaving Belize City at 9 A.M., 10:30 A.M., 12 P.M., 1:30 P.M., 3 P.M., and 5 P.M. It takes about 45 minutes between Belize City and Caye Caulker and is usually an enjoyable ride, allowing passengers to get in the island mood a bit before they touch shore at Caye Caulker. Boats leave Caye Caulker for Belize City at 6:30 A.M., 7:30 A.M., 8:30 A.M., 10 A.M., 12 P.M., 3 P.M., and 5 P.M.

Boats to San Pedro leave Caulker at 7 A.M., 8:30 A.M., 10 A.M., 1 P.M., and 4 P.M. The schedule from San Pedro to Caulker is 8 A.M., 9:30 A.M., 11:30 A.M., 2:30 P.M., and 4:30 P.M. All the boats are open air, a light wrap is handy for windy trips. A poncho is a godsend on rainy voyages. The boats are oftentimes packed to the point of being overloaded. They are supposed to have a limit, but it isn't always observed. Cost to Caulker is US$7.50 one-way, US$12.50 round-trip.

Getting Around

Caye Caulker is so walkable and the pace so languid that most people hoof it wherever they go. However, taking a spin around town in a **golf cart** is a pleasant way to get one's bearings upon first arriving. At **Island Rentals,** tel. 22/2111, carts are rented by the hour or day. Credit cards are accepted.

Quietly paddling a brightly colored kayak is a great way to visit the mangrove forests that surround the island. The wind can really blow in the afternoons, so plan accordingly—go upwind while you're still fresh. **EZ Boy Tours** rent kayaks for US$10/hour or $60/day.

OTHER POPULAR CAYES

CAYE CHAPEL

Just one-by-three-miles long, Caye Chapel is about 15 miles and 25 minutes by boat from Belize City. The caye is owned by a wealthy Kentuckian who is trying to attract corporate America to his piece of paradise, starting with 8 US$2,000-a-night villas for up to four people. No meals, but use of golf course and all non-mechanized sports equipment. Meals can be pricey: US$30 breakfast, US$90 dinner. A resort will eventually be built, but meanwhile the public will be allowed to stay overnight only if there are no corporate groups on the island. To contact the hotel and golf course (see below), visit or write to P.O. Box 912, Belize City, C.A., tel. 2/28250; email bzgolf@yahoo.com

The island also has the **Caye Chapel Golf Course and Marina** (the name will probably change). Long in coming, the developers of the caye achieved their goal of making the first golf course in the country. Hard-core golfers may be happy, but it wasn't built without controversy.

Those against it say that the dredging done and the run-off from the fertilizer and pesticides used on the greens is wreaking havoc on the fragile coral and marine life. They cite that no long-term studies were done ahead of time and that big money is the only reason the golf course exists.

The 18-hole course is challenging, or so we've been told, and as far as cost, a round of golf will cost anywhere between US$75–200. Call for details. The water taxi will drop you off here.

Developers of the resort say that they are using a grass called Paspalum that requires less watering, fertilizer, and pesticides than other grass and that it isn't as harmful to the environment. Only time will tell. Meanwhile, if you can afford to stay here, you'll probably want to fly in—they do have an airstrip.

ST. GEORGE'S CAYE

This small caye, nine miles from Belize City, is shaped something like a boomerang with its open ends facing the mainland. The caye is steeped in history and was the first capital of the British settlement (1650–1784). It was also the scene of the great sea battle between Spaniards and British settlers. Today the small cemetery gives evidence of St. George's heroic past.

St. George's Caye is far from commercialized—on the contrary, it's very quiet with mostly

St. George's Caye

TURTLE PENS TURNED SWIMMING POOLS

In the days when pirates roamed the high seas for months at a time, they had regular stopping places: islands with abundant supplies of water were probably the most important. St. George's Caye was a favorite spot to pick up giant sea turtles. The seamen built large square pens (called kraals) at the end of wooden docks and would keep the captured turtles there until they left for the bounding main. Several turtles were taken on board and fed, kept mostly on their backs and out of the way (they would live that way for a month or two), until they were slaughtered for their meat. Often, turtle was the only sweetmeat the crews would eat for many months. No doubt animal-rights groups would have plenty to say about that today!

Over the years the pirates dwindled and St. George's Caye became the unofficial capital of Belize. Many more homes were built along the waterfront, and kraals became "crawls," swimming pens for people. Today many of the bright-white wooden houses still have the small "pools" at the ends of their docks.

residential homes and their docks. However, two small resorts, **Cottage Colony** and **St. George's Lodge,** attract divers and people searching for total peace and relaxation near the sea. Both have great diving and snorkeling facilities.

Accommodations

Cottage Colony is a marvelous little resort of small colonial-like white- and pastel-painted wooden cottages surrounding a large sandy courtyard with hammocks slung between shady palms (for a leisurely nap or a good read). The attractive second-floor dining room/bar overlooks the sea, and serves tasty food. The collection of individual cottages accommodates as many as 25 people. The suites have a sitting room, a kitchen, and a/c. The rooms are fan-cooled, simply but comfortably furnished, and have private bathrooms. The resort is 20 minutes from the Bellevue Hotel dock in Belize City. Cottage Colony has a good diving program with several boats capable of handling large dive groups. PADI certification classes are available. Room rates are about US$93, transportation from Bellevue dock to St. George Caye is US$25 pp round-trip. The dive package with all meals is about US$1,000. You can make reservations at either the Bellevue Hotel, 5 S. Foreshore, P.O. Box 428, Belize City, Belize, C.A., tel. 2/77051, fax 2/73253, email bellevue@btl.net, or at Cottage Colony, tel. 2/12020.

At the southern end of the caye and less than a mile from the reef, visitors are invited to stay at the delightful **St. George's Lodge,** P.O. Box 625, Belize City, Belize, C.A., U.S. tel. 800/678-6871 or 941/488-3953, Belize tel/fax 2/12121. Divers are regulars here, but it's a quiet and relaxing spot for anyone who takes pleasure in the beauty of the sea, sky, and lovely surroundings. Don't expect a nightlife other than the good fellowship of other travelers, either in the comfortable bar/lounge or outdoors under the palms watching the stars over the sea. The main building consists of a lovely dining room, secluded sundeck, and bar—all made of beautiful Belizean hardwoods—and 10 lodge rooms with h/c water, private baths, fans, and 24-hour electricity. Six thatch cottages with the same amenities sit on a dock over the water. Electricity is provided by the lodge's own windmills, and a solar-heated hot tub is always available for the guests. Good home cooking is provided—lots of fresh fish, fresh breads, and great lobster pizza. A bar offers you a choice of libations or you may bring your own.

The resort brags about their dive safety record; they also offer Nitrox Diving.

Rates come as packages with meals, airport transfers, tips, taxes, tanks, weights, and full diving privileges with boats and guides (two boat dives daily, weather permitting) included, varying by whether or not the guest is a diver. Weekly packages are US$1,496 to $1,999, for divers, US$1,124 to $1,495 for nondivers. A three-night package is available.

SOUTH WATER CAYE

South Water Caye is another scenic, postcard-pretty, privately owned island 35 miles south/southeast of Belize City and 14 miles

THE GRAY LADY

As in all good myths and legends, details are sketchy, but facts are usually delicious. It is said that Henry Morgan often roamed the waters of the Caribbean, frequently off the coast of Belize City. In his wanderings, Henry brought his fair lady with him, a very independent miss. It's easy to imagine that lovers occasionally got testy living in such close quarters aboard a caravel. And though Henry and his lady usually kissed and made up, one lightning-slashed night, just off the coast of St. George's Caye, they were unable to settle a nasty argument—something to do with the seaman standing watch the night before? He was the captain after all; his word was law! The lady ended up walking the plank into the stormy sea, gray gossamer gown whipping around her legs in the angry wind. Since that fateful night, the lady in gray has been roaming the small caye of St. George trying to find her blackguard lover. Don't scoff; some islanders will speak no ill of the Gray Lady, and on stormy nights they stay safely behind closed doors.

offshore from Dangriga. Carrie Bow Caye, where the Smithsonian Institution has a research station, is just a mile southeast.

Onshore are several lodging choices and a research operation. A British organization called **Coral Caye Conservation** has a group of volunteers with headquarters at South Water Caye studying how tourism affects the cayes and their environment. The volunteers (fewer than 30) are all divers and study the fish, sea grasses, algae, currents, and tides, and test seawater samples regularly looking for changes. Volunteers also investigate the culture of the people, lifestyle changes, and their boating activities.

Accommodations

Leslie Cottages (elevation three feet) is right on the beach. Inland is an octagon-shaped marine lodge that can house groups of up to 15 and has bath and dining facilities. Each of the three cottages (one on the east side, two on the west side of the island) has a kitchen and private

bathroom. There are two cabañas as well, which have no bathrooms; guests use the lodge. Kayaks, Sunfish sailboat, and sailboard are free for guests to use.

Accommodations are rented by the week and include meals and transfers from Dangriga Airstrip on the mainland to South Water Caye, and either snorkeling or a boat excursion each day. Weekly prices only. A bargain with meals and transfers. For more information, contact International Zoological Expeditions, 210 Washington St., Sherborn, MA 01770, 508/655-1461, fax 508/655-4445.

Blue Marlin Lodge, 15 Mahogany Street, P.O. Box 21, Dangriga, Belize, C.A., U.S. tel. 800/798-1558, Belize tel. 5/22243, fax 5/22296, email marlin@btl.net, offers 12 double rooms and six cabañas just steps away from the sea. The domed cabañas have a/c, beautiful furniture, and immense bathrooms, phone service at the office, and well-kept grounds. All rooms come with h/c water, private bath, and electric fans; the bar/dining room over the sea serves meals, snacks (included), and drinks. Diving equipment, dive master, fishing boats, and guides are available—and best of all, South Water Caye is only 120 feet from the reef. Day trips are available to Glover's Reef, the Blue Hole, and other wonderful nearby dive spots. Diving classes for certification are available.

Lodging prices are based on four-night or seven-night packages, all transfers and meals included. Call for prices.

In addition to their mainland **Pelican Beach Resort** in Dangriga, Stann Creek District, the Rath family owns Belizean-style vacation homes on stilts on South Water Caye. Called **Osprey's Nest** and **Frangipani House,** they have great views of the ocean, each sleep six, and all are fully furnished. You have no refrigeration here; cooling is by block ice in coolers. All lighting is solar. Call or write Pelican Beach Resort, P.O. Box 14, Dangriga, Stann Creek District, Belize, C.A., tel. 5/22044, fax 5/22570, email pelicanbeach@blt.net. Student groups can stay in a two-story, five-bedroom building (moderate). Includes three meals.

LESSER KNOWN CAYES

Scattered along the coast is a constellation of small (and not so small) cayes. You can make arrangements to visit well in advance or wing it, if you feel like taking a chance. Accommodations are limited.

BLUEFIELD RANGE

The Bluefield Range is a group of cayes a short distance south of Belize City. On one of the islands, 21 miles south of the city, is **Ricardo's Beach Huts and Lobster Camp,** the ultimate of funky. Originally two shacks on stilts built over a sand spit of shallow water leading out from a mangrove island, Ricardo's now is four very basic huts built on cleared land. A path has been built up and leads to the swimming and snorkeling beach on the west side of the island. Units face east, overlooking a lagoon surrounded by more mangrove islands. Some manatees live in the lagoon and you might see them at sunrise and sunset. Ricardo's father cooks fresh seafood and local dishes. Snorkel and fish the nearby reefs and cayes. That's dinner.

Ricardo and his father appreciate the conservation value of mangroves and have underbrushed just enough so guests can watch the bird life of the area. It's one of the best anchorages for any weather (even a recent tropical wave with 30- to 40-knot winds caused nary a problem).

Expect camp-out conditions: outhouse, bucket shower, bugs. Bring mosquito coils, repellent, and a mosquito-net bed/tent. On the upside, this is one of the few chances to experience outer-island living just as it has been for the people who spend their lives fishing these waters. Ricardo's is "bloody ethnic with some really genuine people running it," observed a recent visitor.

A trip here is a package deal; a fish and lobster camp. Because the island has no bar, feel free to bring your favorite bottle; soft drinks and ice are provided. Bring your own fishing and snorkeling gear. For five or more, the price drops. The price includes two nights and three days at Ricardo's, including accommodations, meals, and round-trip boat transfers to and from Belize City. A bargain. Visitors are picked up at the Mira Rio Hotel, 59 N. Front St., Belize City. For more information, contact Ricardo Castillo or Anna Lara, P.O. Box 55, Belize City, Belize, C.A., tel. 2/44970.

ENGLISH CAYE

Though this is just a small collection of palm trees, sand, and coral, an important lighthouse sits here at the entrance to the Belize City harbor from the Caribbean Sea. Large ships stop at English Caye to pick up one of the two pilots who navigate the 10 miles in and out of the busy harbor. Overnights are not allowed here, but it's a pleasant day-trip location.

GOFF'S CAYE

Near English Caye, Goff's Caye is a favorite little island stop for picnics and day trips out of Caye Caulker and Belize City, thanks to a beautiful sandy beach and promising snorkeling areas. Sailboats often stop overnight; camping can be arranged from Caye Caulker by talking with any reputable guide. Bring your own tent and supplies. Goff's is a protected caye, so note the rules posted by the pier.

LAUGHING BIRD CAYE

Another protected area, **Laughing Bird Caye National Park** is a popular day trip from Placencia. It's easy to see why. Swaying palms, small but beautiful beaches, an absence of biting bugs, shallow sandy swimming areas on the leeward side of the island, and interesting diving on the ocean side add up to a lot of pleasure in a relatively small package.

This particular kind of caye is referred to as a *faro* island, and the arms on each end make a kind of enclosure around a lagoon area on the leeward side. In this way the island acts much

kayakers at Long Caye

PATTI LANGE

like a mini-atoll. That's good news for those wishing to dive the eastern side of the island. You'll find a lot of elkhorn coral and fish life. Grunts, damselfish, parrot fish, houndfish, bonefish, and even rays and nurse sharks are to be found here.

MONTEGO CAYE

Not much is on this small caye 10 miles from Belize City. If you are interested in learning more, contact Luis Rosado, 2818 Belama II, Belize City, Belize, C.A., 2/30061, in the U.S. 415/ 452-0418, email wendy@montegocaye.com.

SPANISH LOOKOUT CAYE

Spanish Bay Resort
The reason to come to Spanish Lookout Caye, which lies 10 miles east-southeast of Belize City (about a 30-minute boat ride), is to stay at the **Spanish Bay Resort.** When you approach the resort from the sea on a sunny day, the simple white cabañas built over the blue-green water are quite spectacular. Five cabañas with 10 rooms, hot showers, and private baths are connected to the island by a dock. The rooms are furnished with two double beds, and a circular bar/dining room overlooks the sea. Power is solar, with backup generators. Diving is one of the favorite activities here. The

resort is only one mile west of the main barrier reef and about eight miles west of central Turneffe Island. The resort offers popular three-night packages that include all meals and transfer to the island. Prices start at US$337 pp. Nightlife is good conversation. Contact 71 North Front St., Belize City, Belize, C.A., Belize tel. 2/12024, email sbrturton@btl.net.

FRENCH LOUIS CAYE

You won't find much on this caye besides hammocks and sand, and a simple guest house with a surly looking caretaker who makes scrumptious meals. Spend your day kayaking or spend hours snorkeling the clear, shallow water near the mangroves; free dive the mini-wall that drops off to 60 feet, or read in a hammock strung between two palms. The island is tiny—you can easily swim around it or cover ground in about 50 paces. Rates are US$50 and include three home-cooked meals accentuating local fish. Accommodations are basic but provide the necessities, including an outhouse-style toilet. For more information, contact Kitty's Place, tel. 6/23227, email kittys@btl.net.

LONG CAYE

Thirty-five miles off of Dangriga at Glover's Reef is Long Caye, surrounded by shallow patch reefs on one side and a wall that drops to 3,000 feet on the other. Accommodations range from simple cabins on the beach to tents protected by lean-tos. Kayakers will be in heaven. The tour operation Slickrock Adventures, Inc., is based on this island; for more information, see "Tour Operators" in the On The Road chapter.

AND MANY MORE CAYES

A myriad of other little-known cayes have names such as: **Baker's Rendezvous, Deer, Drowned, Frenchman's, Hunting, Little Peter, Middle Long, Negro, Pajaros, Paunch, Ramsey's, Rider's, Romero, Rosario, Sapodilla, Simmonds, Spanish, Swallow,** and **Tostado.**

While some of the tinier cayes, which were around in days long gone, have been washed or blown away by hurricanes and other natural forces over the years, new mangrove-bits and sandy cayes are forming all the time. And there are still plenty of others that are hundreds of years old. If the cayes could speak, they'd probably have exciting stories to tell—tales of ancient Maya ceremonies, of battles won, treasure lost, and the shenanigans of rip-roaring pirates.

BOB RACE

KATHY ESCOVEDO SANDERS

THE ATOLLS
INTRODUCTION

The atolls are startlingly beautiful when approached by sea or air. Like necklaces of coral, the islands and reefs surrounding the lagoons create large areas of protected waters. Boating, diving, fishing, sailing, and windsurfing in these areas is exhilarating. The islands vary from palm-covered spits of sand to lush mangrove cayes. Most of the islands have mangroves; it is best to come prepared with plenty of bug repellent containing at least 30 percent DEET. Citronella seems to work well too. The mosquitoes are sometimes fierce. However, if you're planning to snorkel, please use a nonpolluting repellent.

Dolphin sightings are common in the atolls as well as around the cayes of Belize. Often dolphins in a playful mood will catch a ride on the bow wave of boats. The power and grace of the animals are remarkable. Other times, divers may see them underwater. Usually dolphins make a pass or two and go about their business. Sometimes they pay no attention at all; other times they approach closely. It all depends on the time

of day, their mood, and the presence of young. It's OK to touch them if the animals approach closely; dolphins enjoy the stroke of a hand. Do not, however, grab the dorsal fin or impede the animal in the water. These creatures are immensely strong and occasionally respond aggressively to rough treatment or what they perceive to be threats.

DIVING AROUND THE ATOLLS

Live-Aboard Dive Boats
Several excellent live-aboard vessels based in Belize City take their guests to Lighthouse Reef and Turneffe Islands atolls. These boats are designed for scuba divers but can also accommodate an avid diver's companion if he or she is a sea lover and/or a casual angler. Nondivers pay less. Your hotel and chef travel with you to some of the most scenic spots in the tropical world. Tariff includes all meals, diving, fishing, cruising, guides, and equipment. Alcohol and tips are

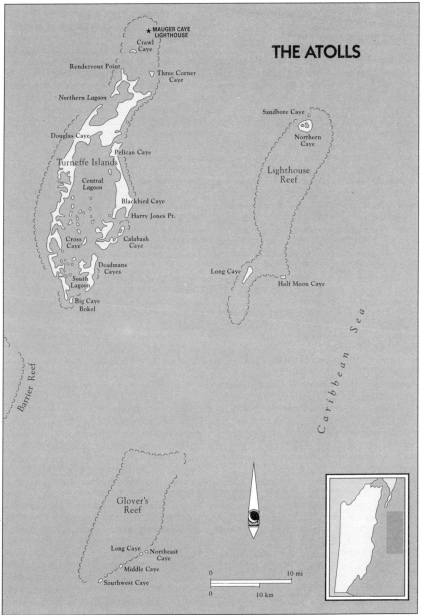

THE ATOLLS

★ MAUGER CAYE LIGHTHOUSE

Crawl Caye

Rendezvous Point

Three Corner Caye

Northern Lagoon

Douglas Caye

Pelican Caye

Turneffe Islands

Central Lagoon

Blackbird Caye

Harry Jones Pt.

Cross Caye

Calabash Caye

Deadmans Cayes

South Lagoon

Big Caye Bokel

Sandbore Caye

Northern Caye

Lighthouse Reef

Long Caye

Half Moon Caye

Caribbean Sea

Barrier Reef

Glover's Reef

Long Caye

Northeast Caye

Middle Caye

Southwest Caye

0   10 mi

0   10 km

© AVALON TRAVEL PUBLISHING, INC.

extra. (See the callout "Live-Aboard Dive Boats" in the On The Road Chapter.)

In the luxury category and accommodating 14–18 people, the **Aggressor III** offers carpeted, a/c staterooms with single and double berths, hot water, a desalination water maker, self-service bar, stereo, and VCR, as well as a spacious dining room for buffets and barbecues on the sundeck; plenty of good food.

Divers enjoy unlimited diving (twin compressors for an unlimited air supply, tank, backpack, weight belt, and weights are provided). A personal dive locker is available right on the dive deck with a wide dive platform plus two ladders. Camera buffs will find a complete video and photo center with daily E-6 processing (camera rentals available). You'll also find certification courses, photo and wildlife seminars, and lots of TLC, including airport transfers. Live the good life from Saturday to Saturday. For more information, contact Aggressor Fleet Limited, P.O. Drawer K, Morgan City, LA 70381, 800/348-2628, fax 504/384-0817. Rates for a one-week diving vacation are US$1,395 per person based on double occupancy.

Equally famous, **Peter Hughes Diving,** 800/932-6237 or 305/669-9391, email dancer @peterhughes.com, has a fleet of top-end dive boats. The *Belize Wave Dancer,* which goes to Turneffe Islands, Lighthouse, and Glover's Reef, is no exception. The boat accommodates 20 guests on a seven- or ten-day dive adventure they will not soon forget. Packages include dives, all meals, beverages, and airport transfers. US$1,895 pp. Guests have a choice of five dives per day on two separate sites; one of these is a night dive. Dive instruction is available including advanced certifications. The 120-foot *Wave Dancer* has E-6 processing and video center onboard. In addition, it has a sundeck, outside bar, and freshwater showers on the stern to rinse off in when boarding the boat. All cabins have a private head and shower.

Offshore Express can handle up to 18 people, but the trips are usually for shorter periods of time. It offers either one- or two-night excursions to dive around Half Moon Caye. Passengers can either sleep aboard or in tents on the beach, with showers and meals aboard. Prices are about US$250 pp for one night or US$350 pp for two nights. For more information, visit or contact the Coral Beach Dive Shop in San Pedro, tel. 26/2817 email: forman @btl.net.

TURNEFFE ISLANDS ATOLL

The islands are mostly small dots of sand, mangrove clusters, and swampy land, though **Blackbird Caye** and **Douglas Caye** are quite large. With the preponderance of mangroves and coconut palms, many cayes are home only to sea and wading birds, ospreys, manatees, and crocodiles; a few support small colonies of fishermen and divers.

This atoll is a great fishing destination, just 25 miles east of Belize City. If you're into bonefish and permit, miles of crystal flats are alive with the hard-fighting fish. Tarpon are abundant late March–June within the protected creeks and channels throughout the islands. Those who seek larger trophies will find a grand choice of marlin, sailfish, wahoo, groupers, blackfin tuna, and many more. Check with fishing guides in Belize City or Ambergris Caye, or the resorts listed below under "Accommodations."

DIVING

Divers will find different dive spots every day and any type of diving they want—wall dives, shallows for photography, fish life, creek dives, coral heads, or drift dives. At the northern end of the atoll, divers especially enjoy the walls and reefs around **Rendezvous Point.** Others investigate the colorful tube sponges and black coral at **Vincent's Lagoon.** Live-aboards frequently visit this northern end of Turneffe Islands and **Mauger Caye.**

Rendezvous Point

This is a popular first-dive of overnighters out of Ambergris Caye. It provides a great opportunity for divers who haven't been under in a while to get their feet wet again. The depth is about 40–50 feet and affords sufficient bottom time to

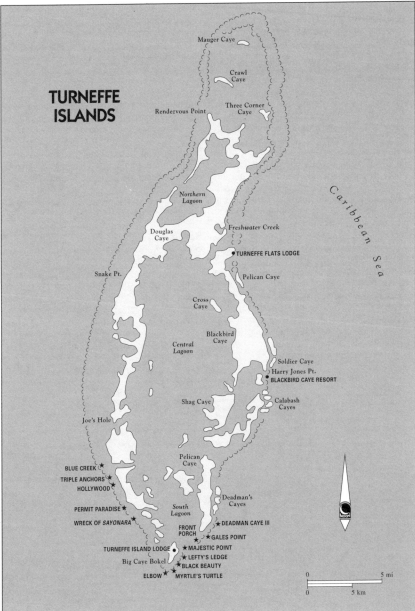

TURNEFFE ISLANDS

Mauger Caye

Crawl Caye

Three Corner Caye

Rendezvous Point

Northern Lagoon

Caribbean Sea

Douglas Caye

Freshwater Creek

● TURNEFFE FLATS LODGE

Snake Pt.

Pelican Caye

Cross Caye

Blackbird Caye

Central Lagoon

Soldier Caye

Harry Jones Pt.
● BLACKBIRD CAYE RESORT

Shag Caye

Calabash Cayes

Joe's Hole

Pelican Caye

BLUE CREEK ★

Deadman's Cayes

TRIPLE ANCHORS ★
HOLLYWOOD ★

South Lagoon

PERMIT PARADISE ★

WRECK OF *SAYONARA* ★

★ DEADMAN CAYE III

FRONT PORCH ★
★ GALES POINT

TURNEFFE ISLAND LODGE ● ★ MAJESTIC POINT

Big Caye Bokel ★ LEFTY'S LEDGE
★ BLACK BEAUTY

ELBOW ★ ★ MYRTLE'S TURTLE

0   5 mi

0   5 km

get a good look at a wide variety of reef life. Angelfish, butterfly fish, parrot fish, yellowtails, and morays are represented well. This will only whet appetites for the outstanding diving to come.

The Elbow

Most divers have heard of the Elbow (just 10 minutes from Turneffe Island Lodge), a point of coral that juts out into the ocean. This now-famous dive site offers a steep sloping drop-off covered with tube sponges and deep-water gorgonians, along with shoals of snappers (sometimes numbering in the hundreds) and other pelagic creatures. Predators such as bar jacks, wahoo, and permits cruise the reef, and the drop-off is impressive. Currents sweep the face of the wall most of the time and they typically run from the north. However, occasionally they reverse or cease all together. When conditions are right, this is a dive you won't forget.

Lefty's Ledge

A short distance farther up the eastern side of the atoll is another dive to excite even those with a lot of bottom time under their weight belts. Lefty's Ledge features dramatic spur-and-groove formations that create a wealth of habitats. Correspondingly, divers will see a head-turning display of undersea life, both reef and pelagic species. Jacks, mackerels, permits, and groupers are present in impressive numbers. Wrasses, rays, parrot fish, and butterfly fish are evident around

the sandy canyons. Cleaning stations are also evident, and it's fascinating to watch large predators allow themselves to be groomed by small cleaner shrimp or fish. The dive begins at about 50 feet and the bottom slopes to about 100 feet before dropping off into the blue.

Gales Point

Another "don't-miss" dive, Gales Point is a short distance farther up the eastern side. Here the reef juts out into the current at a depth of about 45 feet, sloping to about 100 feet before the drop-off. Along the wall and the slope just above it are numerous ledges and cavelike formations. Rays and groupers are especially common here—some say this may be a grouper breeding area. Corals and sponges are everywhere in numerous varieties.

Sayonara

On the leeward or eastern side of the atoll the wreck of the *Sayonara,* a tender sunk by Dave Bennett of Turneffe Islands Lodge, lies in about 30 feet of water. Close by is a sloping ledge with interesting tunnels and spur-and-groove formations. Healthy numbers of reef fish play among the coral, and some barracudas tag along. Large schools of permits are often drawn down by divers' bubbles. They give a marvelous three-dimensional quality to the dive as you see them spiraling down from the surface like a squadron of fighter planes.

ready for lounging

PHIL LANIER

SEARCHING FOR SUNKEN TREASURE

Allied in the early 1950s, a group of Mexican divers (CEDAM—Conservation, Exploration, Diving, Archaeology, and Museums) from nearby Quintana Roo has salvaged several old vessels along the reef. The booty from these old ships wasn't gold treasure but other practical items such as equipment, kitchen implements, tools, arms, beads, and an occasional coin, all contributing to our understanding of another era.

The first ship discovered and explored was *Mantanceros.* It was named for Punta Mantanceros, the point off the Quintana Roo beach close to where it's believed the ship went down. On February 22, 1742, the Spanish ship ended up in a skirmish with a British ship. The British ship was part of the Admiral's fleet that ducked into the protection of Be-

lize and engaged in blockading any ships along the coast. The Spanish galleon was loaded with 270 tons of mixed cargo bound for New World ports. Many years after CEDAM salvaged the ship, the information about it was discovered in the Archives of the Indies in Seville, Spain. The real name of the ill-fated ship was *Nuestra Señora de los Milagros* ("Our Lady of the Miracles"). Again, no gold, but many fascinating artifacts from 18th-century Spain.

Another doomed ship was *La Nicolasa,* believed to be the Montejo fleet flagship. Montejo was one of the conquerors of the Maya. And at Chinchorro Banks, a 40-cannon mystery wreck has defied efforts to make a definitive identification for years. Chinchorro Banks, just off the southern Mexican shore, is a favorite dive spot.

Hollywood

A bit farther up the atoll, Hollywood offers divers a relatively shallow dive (30–40 feet) with moderate visibility unless the currents have reversed. Here you'll find lots of basket and tube sponges and lush coral growth. Many angelfish, parrot fish, grunts, and snappers swim here. So, although not as dramatic as an eastern side dive, Hollywood has plenty to see.

ACCOMMODATIONS

While limited in number, accommodations fall neatly into three categories: one that appeals primarily to divers but can easily accommodate anglers or beach bums, another for those who would like to participate in an ongoing research project, and a third for avid fishers.

The motto of guests at the friendly **Turneffe Island Lodge** could well be captured in the words written on the first sign a new arrival sees, "We're not here for a long time, just a good time!" How true. And that's what's in store for up to 16 guests on Little Caye Bokel, 12 acres of beautiful palm-lined beachfront and mangroves. It's a popular location for divers, anglers, and those who just want to swing in a hammock under the palms.

At the southern tip of the atoll, the resort is a short distance north of its larger relative, Big

Caye Bokel. This strategic location offers enthusiasts a wide range of underwater experiences within minutes of nearly 200 dive sites. Shallow areas are perfect for photography or snorkeling; you can see nurse sharks, rays, reef fish, and dolphins in the flats a few hundred yards from the dock. All the dives mentioned earlier and many more lie within 15 minutes by boat. The dive operation run by Kevin is first rate, and advanced instruction and equipment rentals are available. This would be an excellent place to get that underwater photography certification.

One diver we met had been on a 14-day visit, had dived three different sites each day (never repeating one of them), and had half an hour of underwater video of dolphins. He yawned at every diving tale he heard. Rather ostentatious, actually!

Anglers have a choice of fishing for snappers, permit, jacks, mackerel, and billfish off the dropoffs. They can stalk the near-record numbers of snook, bonefish, and tarpon in the flats and mangroves. George, the fishing guide, has an uncanny way of knowing where the fish will be.

The lodge is fish-camp comfortable. The friendly ease about the place makes even shy guests feel at home. Rooms are next to the sea, have h/c water, private baths, and 24-hour electricity. The main lodge boasts a small bar with wood deck overlooking the grounds, a spacious pine-paneled dining room that serves tasty meals in ample quantities, and a comfy lounge with TV, VCR, and ample reading material. The lodge also has a gift shop and evening activities so the guests won't get bored on their desert island. A one-week package includes meals, sports facilities, and transfers from Belize International Airport, with emphasis on either diving or fishing, US$1,285–2,520, pp. For more prices, information, and reservations, call 800/874-0118, email info@turnefflodge.com.

On the eastern side of Turneffe Islands lies **Blackbird Caye Resort,** 4,000 acres of a planned, environmentally responsible resort. At present, it offers 10 individual thatch cabañas, with hot-water showers, private baths, and double and queen beds, as well as a duplex and triplex featuring private rooms and a/c. A variety of seven-day fishing or diving packages are offered, includes 3 dives a day, all meals, lodging and airport transfers, US$1,450, pp.

Oceanic Society Expeditions, 800/326-7491, fax 415/474-3395, email office@oceanic -society.org, provides up-close encounters with dolphins. A favorite of the Oceanic Society, the Blackbird-Oceanic Society Field Station is a modern research center created to study dolphins. A resident researcher takes groups to assist in counting and observing dolphin behavior in their natural habitat and sometimes to swim with them. Plan on a 90-minute boat ride from Belize City. The reef is a stone's throw from the resort beach; prepare to snorkel in an untouched area. Ask for prices. Packages (land only) begin with your pickup at the Belize International Airport and include all meals; no alcoholic drinks are available on the island—feel free to bring your own.

For vacationing folks who want to concentrate on just a few things—fishing, fishing, and fishing—**Turneffe Flats,** P.O. Box 36, Deadwood, SD 57732, 800/815-1304 or 605/578-1304, fax 605/578-7540, email vacation @tflats.com, is the place to go. Flats fishing for bonefish, tarpon, snook, and permit have put the resort on the map with fly fishers. A fleet of boats and guides is available, or anglers can wade. Larger boats venture out for reef fish, including snappers, wahoo, and groupers. Bluewater fishing for tuna and billfish is also available.

Guests who want to dive or mix diving with fishing will have ample opportunity to indulge. Seven-day dive packages include lodging, all meals, three dives per day, and a trip to Lighthouse Reef. Or you can mix fishing and diving. US$1,285-2,700.

The resort features tidy raised wooden structures along the beach with h/c water and private bath. Meals are served on a pleasant breezy deck just off the lodge building.

LIGHTHOUSE REEF ATOLL

ORIENTATION

The most easterly of Belize's three atolls, Lighthouse Reef lies 50 miles southeast of Belize City. The 30-mile-long, eight-mile-wide lagoon is the location of the Blue Hole, a dive spot that was made famous by Jacques Cousteau and that is a favorite destination of dive boats from Belize City, Ambergris Caye, and Caye Caulker. The best dive spots, however, are along the walls of Half Moon Caye and Long Caye, where the diving rivals that of any in the world.

Think of the atoll as a large spatula with a short handle and a long blade. At the northern tip of the spatula blade, **Sandbore Caye** is home to a rusty lighthouse and a few fishing shacks. It is also the favorite anchorage of several of the dive boats doing overnight stops, including *Reef Roamer II.*

Big Northern Caye, across a narrow strait, is the location of **Lighthouse Reef Resort.** A landing strip just behind the resort is a convenient means of entry for resort guests and divers who wish to make only a day trip without the long water crossing going and coming, which eats up most of the day. Here are long stretches of beach to walk, beautiful vistas, and large areas of mangroves and lagoons, home to snowy egrets and crocodiles.

Halfway down the spatula-shaped atoll, about where the blade meets the handle, lies the magnificent **Blue Hole,** a formation best

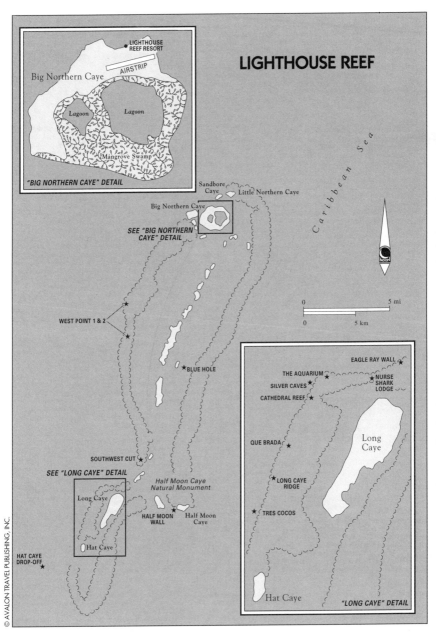

Caribbean Sea

LIGHTHOUSE REEF

Big Northern Caye

LIGHTHOUSE
REEF RESORT

AIRSTRIP

Lagoon

Lagoon

Mangrove Swamp

"BIG NORTHERN CAYE" DETAIL

Sandbore
Caye

Little Northern Caye

Big Northern Caye

SEE "BIG NORTHERN
CAYE" DETAIL

MoN

0   5 mi

0   5 km

WEST POINT 1 & 2

★ BLUE HOLE

EAGLE RAY WALL ★

THE AQUARIUM ★

SILVER CAVES ★

NURSE
SHARK
LODGE

CATHEDRAL REEF ★

Long
Caye

QUE BRADA ★

SOUTHWEST CUT ★

SEE "LONG CAYE" DETAIL

★ LONG CAYE
RIDGE

Half Moon Caye
Natural Monument

★ TRES COCOS

Long Caye

HALF MOON
WALL ★

Half Moon
Caye

Hat Caye

HAT CAYE
DROP-OFF ★

Hat Caye

"LONG CAYE" DETAIL

appreciated from the air, but impressive from the bridge of a boat.

At the elbow of the handle, and looking like some kind of Gilligan's Island, is **Half Moon Caye** with its lighthouse, bird sanctuary, shipwrecks, and incredible diving offshore.

Finally, on the imaginary handle we come upon **Long Caye,** a lonely outpost with a small dock, large palms, and glassy water.

Some anglers and beach bums do come to Lighthouse, but the lure of diving attracts most visitors. And at Lighthouse Reef, they are not disappointed.

DIVING

If you're looking for spectacular diving, Belize is the place. In Belize, this area rivals any in the country, or for that matter, around the world. You could easily spend a week or two diving this atoll and never tire of the coral and sponge growths, the amazing variety of invertebrates, and reef and pelagic fish. Expect visibility of more than 100 feet in most places except the Blue Hole (it can be silty) and the upper reaches of the leeward side of the atoll.

Blue Hole

If flying over the offshore coast, you'll easily recognize this large circular formation with its magnificent blue-to-black hues surrounded by neon blue. Though there are other, smaller, blue holes around Ambergris Caye, Caye Caulker, and elsewhere, this is the Blue Hole to beat them all. The submerged shaft is a karst-eroded sinkhole with depths that exceed 400 feet. In the early 1970s Jacques Cousteau and his crew explored the tunnels, caverns, and the listing stalactites that were angled by past earthquakes. This twilight world has suspended sediment and little fish life. Most dive groups descend in the caves to a depth of about 135 feet. Technically, this is not a dive for novices or even in-

termediate divers, though thousands have done it. It requires a rapid descent, a very short period at depth, and a careful ascent. For a group of 10 or more, at least three dive masters should be present.

From the standpoint of undersea life, the lip of the crater, down to about 60–80 feet, is a much more interesting dive. Be prepared for some of the largest midnight parrot fish you will see anywhere. Stingrays are also to be found in sandy areas, as are feather duster worms. Angelfish, butterfly fish, and small reef fish cluster around coral heads and outcroppings. Occasional barracudas and small groupers guard their territories.

Half Moon Caye Wall

They just don't come much better than this. Here on the eastern side of the atoll, the reef has a shallow shelf in about 15 feet of water where garden eels are plentiful. Their heads and a part of their bodies protrude from the burrows that protect them. They look to the untrained eye like blades of grass, but when you get closer to get a better look, the shy eels quickly disappear back into their tiny holes. Interesting to watch from a distance, they are but a precursor to what is in store as you go deeper into the water.

The sandy area broken with corals extends downward till you run into the reef wall, which rises some 20 feet toward the surface. Most boats anchor in the sandy area above the reef wall. Numerous fissures in the reef crest form canyons or tunnels leading out to the vertical face. In this area sandy shelves and valleys frequently harbor nurse sharks and gigantic stingrays. Feather duster worms of various types, sea anemones, shrimps, crabs, and starfish live here. All the reef fish you like to photograph are here: angelfish, damselfish, surgeonfish, triggerfish, butterfly fish, and parrot fish abound. You'll also see several cleaning stations, where tiny wrasses or shrimp rid fish of parasites. Divers who are lucky enough to be staying at Lighthouse Reef Resort or diving off live-aboards with photo processing aboard are sure to return with a wealth of wonderful slides.

lighthouse

BOB RACE

Cruise through one of the canyons and experience the sight of the reef falling vertically out of sight on a drop of a thousand feet and more. The wall here is simply spectacular with overhangs, caves, a riot of sponges, and coral growths of every kind. Gorgonians and sea fans grow everywhere. The eye hardly knows where to settle. Schools of the tiniest fish hover like gnats in protected crevices. Sea turtles, barracuda, lobsters, and morays are evident, along with the larger pelagics—jacks, wahoos, and groupers of various species. Occasionally you'll see eagle rays and mantas. This is a site you could dive many times without boredom, if there weren't so many other good areas to see.

Tres Cocos

On the western wall, "Three Coconuts" refers to trees on nearby Long Caye. But you'll hardly notice land. Your eyes will be focused on the neon shades of blue beneath your boat—lighter shades signifying shallower water with sand bottom, darker indicating coral growth, indigo signifying the deep. The sandy bottom slopes from about 30 feet to about 40 feet deep before it plunges downward. Overhangs here are common features, and sponges and soft corals adorn the walls. Another fish lover's paradise, Tres Cocos does not have the outstanding coral formations you'll see at several other dives in the area, but who cares; there's a rainbow of marine life all about. Turtles, morays, jacks, coral, shrimp, cowfish, rays, and angelfish are among the actors on this colorful stage.

Silver Caves

The shoals of silversides (small gleaming minnows) that gave this western atoll site its name are gone. But Silver Caves is still impressive and enjoyable. The coral formations are riddled with large crevices and caves that cut clear through the reef.

As you enter the water above the sandy slope where most boats anchor, you'll be in about 30 feet of water and surrounded by friendly yellowtail snappers. Once again you'll see the downwardly sloping bottom, the rising reef crest, and the stomach-flipping drop into the blue.

The crevices and sandy canyons provide ample habitat for a panoply of undersea life. Expect to see nurse sharks, gigantic stingrays, file fish, angelfish, morays, parrot fish, wrasses, and a multitude of small reef fish hovering around the reef crest, above, and slightly below. Cleaning stations are evident here too. You'll find feather dusters, sea fans, sea cucumbers, and starfish (including occasional basket stars).

Off the face of the reef, you'll see mackerel, jacks, barracuda, sea turtles, eagle rays, and large groupers. Barrel, tube, and vase sponges abound.

West Point

Farther north and about even with the Blue Hole, West Point is well worth a dive. Visibility may be a bit more limited (60–80 feet) than down south, but it's still very acceptable. The reef face here is stepped. The first drop plunges from about 30 feet to well over 100 feet deep. Another coral and sand slope at that depth extends a short distance before dropping vertically into very deep water. The first and shallow wall has pronounced overhangs and lush coral and sponge growth. Divers are likely to encounter triggerfish, morays, parrot fish, file fish, wrasses, and angelfish in abundance. Garden eels and rays inhabit the shallow sandy slope.

HALF MOON CAYE

Dedicated as a monument in 1982, this crescent-shaped island was the first reserve created within the new climate of protecting Belize's natural beauty. Half Moon Caye, at the southeast corner of Lighthouse Reef, measures 45 square acres.

As you approach Half Moon Caye you'll believe you have arrived at some South Sea paradise. Offshore, boaters use the rusted hull of a wreck, once known as the *Elksund,* as a landmark in these waters. Its dark hulk looms over the surreal blue and black of the reef world. The caye, eight feet above sea level, was formed by the accretion of coral bits, shells, and calcareous algae. It's divided into two ecosystems. The section on the western side has dense vegetation with rich fertile soil. The eastern section primarily supports coconut palms and little other vegetation.

Besides boasting offshore waters that are among the clearest in Belize, the caye's beaches are also Robinson-Crusoe wonderful. You must climb the eight-foot-high central ridge that divides the island and gaze south before you see the striking half-moon beach with its unrelenting surf erupting against limestone rocks.

Half Moon Caye's first lighthouse, built in 1820, sits on the eastern side of the caye. Another was built in 1848 and modernized and enlarged in 1931; today the lighthouse has entered the age of high technology with solar power.

Flora and Fauna

The variety of vegetation is not large, but you will see the **ziricote** forest, the **red-barked gumbo-limbo, ficus fig, coconut palms,** and the **spider-lily plant.**

The endangered **red-footed boobies** are the principal inhabitant of Half Moon Caye and the main reason for its status as a monument. Ninety-eight percent of the 4,000 adult breeding birds on the caye are a very rare white. Naturalists must travel to an island near Tobago in the West Indies to find a similar booby colony; most adult red-footed boobies are dull brown. Along with the boobies, 98 other species of birds have been recorded on the caye and include the **magnificent frigate, white-crowned pigeons, mangrove warblers,** and **ospreys.** A couple of varieties of iguana skitter through the underbrush, and in the summer **hawksbill** and **loggerhead turtles** return by instinct to lay their eggs on the beaches.

The Tower

Everyone should go to the observation tower provided by the Audubon Society in the ziricote forest and climb above the forest canopy for an unbelievable view. Every tree is covered with perched booby birds in some stage of growth. In the right season you'll have a close-up view of nests while feathered parents tend their hatchlings. The air is filled with boobies coming and going, attempting to make their usually clumsy landings (those webbed feet weren't designed for landing in trees). Visitors have a wonderful

opportunity to see the myriad inhabitants of the caye. Thieving magnificent frigates swoop by while iguanas crawl around in the branches, both always mindful of an opportunity to swipe a few eggs left unguarded.

Camping

Guests must register at the park warden's office near the lighthouse. You'll be directed to maps, camping and sanitation facilities, and given other general information about the caye. The biggest concern is the preservation of Half Moon Caye and its plants and animals. Please observe the rules of the house: bring your own water (island water is very scarce); no pets allowed; when camping use only designated sites and firepits; stay on trails to avoid damage to fragile plant life and to avoid disturbing nesting birds; no hunting or fishing; carry everything out with you; don't litter; and, finally, do not collect *anything*—eggs, coral, shells, fish, plants—even sand!

Getting There

If you go by boat, expect to spend a couple of hours or more getting to Half Moon Caye from Belize City, depending on the sea conditions. On occasion, the sea can be rough, and not all small-boat captains will leave the protected waters inside the barrier reef. Besides, on rough days divers will find poor underwater visibility at the atoll anyway. These conditions, especially the ones fed by strong northerlies in winter, seldom last more than a few days at a time.

Only chartered or privately owned boats and seaplanes travel to Half Moon Caye Monument; so far no regular public transportation is available. An option would be to take an inexpensive water taxi from Belize City to Ambergris or Caye Caulker and take one of the *Reef Seekers* out to Half Moon Caye (US$40 one-way, US$80 round-trip) the next day. You could catch a ride back with the same outfit the following week. All of this would have to be worked out in advance. Or you could check

BOB RACE

with **Belize Audubon Society,** tel. 2/34987, in Belize City for other suggestions.

Bringing in Your Own Vessel or Plane

Note: People traveling to Belize on their own vessels must clear with the authorities before entering Belizean waters. Check with the Belize Embassy in Washington, DC, tel. 202/332-9636, fax 202/332-6741.

On the leeward side of Half Moon Caye, sailors will find a dock with a pierhead depth of about six feet. Large ships must anchor in designated areas *only*. This will help to protect the reef from further (irreversible) damage such as that caused by large anchors in the past. Amphibious planes are welcome to land here.

NORTHERN TWO CAYE

When people talk about the fantastic sunrises and sunsets out here, believe them. Long walks on the shore, swims in the shallow waters offshore, and fantastic diving/snorkeling are hallmarks of Northern Two Caye and the **Lighthouse Reef Resort,** 800/423-3114, email donna@scuba-dive-belize.com. The island covers 1,200 acres, though almost half is mangrove lagoon with resident bonefish, crocodiles, and bird life. Sandbore Caye lies a short distance away.

On shore, the resort offers 16 acres of tropical beauty, and nature has provided wonderful, long alluring beaches, swaying palms, and a variety of bird and reptilian life. Accommoda-tions are in villas or duplex cabaña-like rooms. The three villas (one two-bedroom with kitchen, and two with one bedroom for two people) are colonial-style architecture with solid wooden roofs, facing the sea and the northeasterly trade winds. They have wallpapered walls, Persian rugs, "antique-type" furnishings, baths and showers, h/c water, a/c, space for diving equipment, an immeasurable supply of fresh water from four wells, and a dining room/bar where family-style meals can be served. The cabaña rooms have mahogany interior accents, Mexican-tile floors, h/c water, private baths, a/c, and modern interior decoration.

Diving, snorkeling, and fishing (bonefishing and deep-sea game fishing) are unsurpassed. Divers must have certification cards with them and should bring their own gear as rental equipment is limited. Slide processing is available. You're likely to spot dolphins nearby. It's possible to come into close contact with them. Remember: Treat them with respect—if in doubt, ask the dive guide what to keep in mind. Anglers usually bring their own gear too. Consult with the resort for further information including prices.

Getting There

You can arrange air transportation from Belize City's international airport to Northern Two Caye by way of **Tropic Air** or charter. For more information and reservations, write or call P.O. Box 1435, Dundee, FL 33838, 877/305-7503, Belize tel. 2/31205.

GLOVER'S REEF ATOLL

Seventy miles (a five-hour boat trip) southeast of Belize City brings you to **Glover's Reef,** a dream-come-true of island fantasy—white sand, blue sea, and coconut palms with a fringe of white water breaking over the nearby reef. It was named for pirate John Glover, who, in his own swashbuckling manner, also loved this offshore reef. The atoll is a circular necklace of almost continuous coral reef around an 80-square-mile lagoon with depths to 50 feet; the various colors of blue in the water are so in-tense they seem phony. Within the lagoon divers will find 700 shallow coral patches. And for the adventurer looking for sunken ships, the sea on the north and northeastern sides of the reef embraces the bones of at least four ships. This is a favorite destination for boaters large and small, including live-aboard dive boats that come from the United States and Belize City.

Anglers will have a chance at bonefish and permit, as well as the big trophies, including sailfish, marlin, wahoo, snapper, and grouper.

Diving

Glover's Reef is rightly known for the abundance of its marine life, especially turtles, manta rays, and whale sharks. Corals and sponges of many types crowd the walls and reef tops. The names of dive sites such as **Shark Point, Grouper Flats, Emerald Forest Reef, Octopus Alley, Manta Reef, Dolphin Dance,** and **Turtle Tavern** conjure visions of what lies in store. Because of

the Caribbean swells, most of the frequently dived locations lie in the southern parts of the atoll.

Long Caye Base Camp

Ever dream of living like a castaway on a deserted tropical island—palms swaying in the moonlit sky, and you feasting off of the sea and dodging coconut bombs? Well. Add a few people to that illusion, throw in a solar panel for

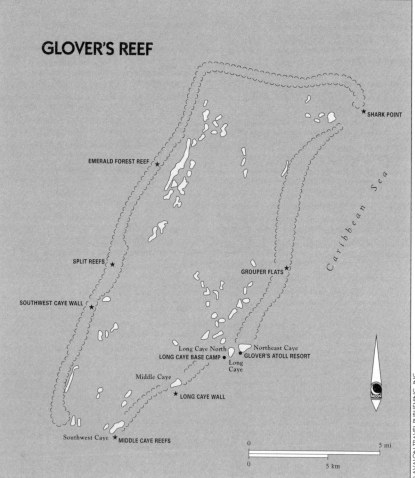

GLOVER'S REEF

SHARK POINT

EMERALD FOREST REEF

Caribbean Sea

SPLIT REEFS

GROUPER FLATS

SOUTHWEST CAYE WALL

Long Caye North

Northeast Caye

LONG CAYE BASE CAMP ● ○ GLOVER'S ATOLL RESORT

Long Caye

Middle Caye

★ LONG CAYE WALL

Southwest Caye ★ MIDDLE CAYE REEFS

0   5 mi

0   5 km

© AVALON TRAVEL PUBLISHING, INC.

limited electricity, allow yourself to be pampered by a fabulous cook, play on a variety of water toys, and make it a reality at Long Caye with the people from **Slickrock Adventures** (see "Tour Operators" in the On The Road chapter). Slickrock leads kayaking tours to Glover's Reef for both beginner and advanced kayakers. A shallow lagoon on one side of the island is the perfect saltwater pool for the beginner to master paddling technique and the intermediate paddler to learn rescues and rolls. For the advanced, kayak surfing is also a possibility if the conditions are right. When you get tired of paddling, a scuba shack on the island takes you under water, and snorkeling and windsurfing can be done right off the beach. Tag along with one of the resident staff in the hunt for dinner (fish, fish, or fish), or join the before-dinner lively volleyball game, just enough of a workout to justify another dip into camp manager Lord Jim's nightly happy hour rum-punch barrel (OK, plastic pitcher).

Accommodations are rustic cabins on the beach with kerosene lamps, foam pad mattresses, and great views. Chairs and/or hammocks grace the porch. When the cabins are full, some get tents to sleep in with palm lean-tos for privacy. Outhouse toilets are of the *plein air* variety, surrounded by palm leaf "walls"; similar shower "rooms" hold the sun-warmed well water in sturdy polyurethane bags that double as your shower. Neither has a roof but both undoubtedly provide the best views from a WC in the entire country.

Dinners consist of fresh fish. Grouper in horseradish sauce? I don't think Gilligan had it so good. Conch ceviche? To die for. The wonderful aroma drifting through the air? Probably another batch of homemade cookies. The food is always good and there is plenty of it. (They got rid of the cook who told guests they didn't need a second helping.) The kitchen cabin serves as dining and social area—it has the only light once darkness sets in—as well as a refrigerator with cold Belikin. A library holds several titles on Belizean natural history and there are plenty of games available. The staff is a mix of friendly Belizeans and experienced American kayak guides. They all must take a mellow-test and she or he with the lowest score gets the job—there are no attitudes out here, only smiling people who are happy to be where they are.

For information and a video, contact Slickrock Adventures, P.O. Box 1400, Moab, UT 84532, email slickrock@slickrock.com, 800/390-5715.

KATHY ESCOVEDO SANDERS

COROZAL DISTRICT

Corozal is the northernmost district in Belize. The ambience is "Spanish," but with a Belizean flavor. If arriving by way of Mexico the first time, you'll immediately notice the difference between the two countries. The people of Corozal are a happy bunch, and dozens of American expats enjoy the slow pace of Belizean living.

Nature lovers will not be disappointed by the Corozal District. Crocodiles, tapirs, jaguars, manatees, peccaries, tree frogs, and more live in the forests and creeks. Bird-watching is especially good around the bays, lagoons, marshes, and mangroves of coastal areas. Wading birds and waterfowl of all types frequent these areas. In drier places, parrots, toucans, hawks, and songbirds are plentiful. Shipstern Wildlife Reserve and Butterfly Breeding Center offers excellent opportunities to see all of the above and a treasure trove of wild butterflies as well. More than 200 species may be observed fluttering about on sunny days.

COROZAL TOWN

Just nine miles (15 minutes) from the Rio Hondo (the border separating Belize and Mexico) and 96 miles north of Belize City is the small town of Corozal. The population is about 10,000. While English is the official language, Spanish is just as common since many are descendants of early-day Maya and mestizo refugees from neighboring Quintana Roo. Historically, Corozal was the scene of many attacks by the Maya Indians during the Caste War. What remains of the old fort can be found in the center of town (west of Central Park). Today it's a quiet little village that lies near the tranquil shores of the Caribbean and close to the Bay of Chetumal.

The town was almost entirely wiped out during Hurricane Janet in 1955 and has since been rebuilt. As you stroll through the quiet streets, you'll find a library, a museum, town hall, government administrative offices, a Catholic church, two secondary schools, five elementary schools, three gas stations, a

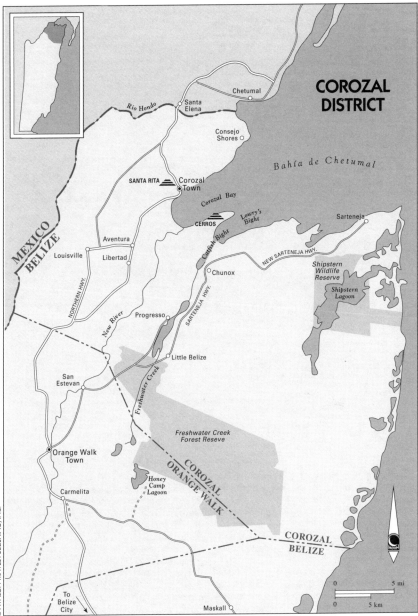

© AVALON TRAVEL PUBLISHING, INC.

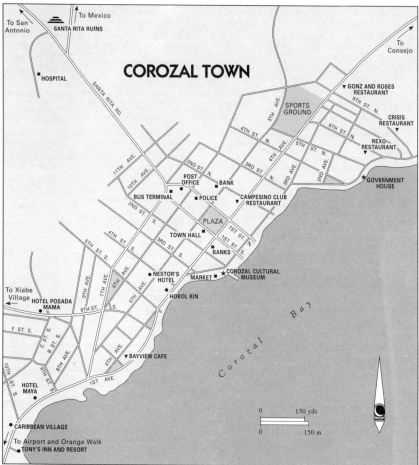

To San Antonio

To Mexico

SANTA RITA RUINS

To Consejo

HOSPITAL

COROZAL TOWN

SANTA RITA RD.

GONZ AND ROSES RESTAURANT

9TH ST. N.

5TH AVE.

SPORTS GROUND

CRISIS RESTAURANT

4TH ST.

6TH ST. N.

5TH ST. N.

REXO RESTAURANT

4TH AVE.

3RD AVE.

2ND AVE.

2ND ST. N.

3RD ST.

11TH AVE.

10TH AVE.

POST OFFICE

BANK

GOVERNMENT HOUSE

BUS TERMINAL

POLICE

2ND ST. S.

CAMPESINO CLUB RESTAURANT

PLAZA

1ST ST. N.

4TH ST. S.

3RD ST. S.

TOWN HALL

1ST ST. S.

5TH ST. S.

BANKS

8TH AVE.

7TH AVE.

6TH AVE.

5TH AVE.

NESTOR'S HOTEL

MARKET

COROZAL CULTURAL MUSEUM

To Xiabe Village

HOTEL POSADA MAMA

6TH ST. S.

HOKOL KIN

Corozal Bay

F ST. S.

C ST. S.

B ST. S.

9TH ST. S.

8TH AVE.

4TH AVE.

BAYVIEW CAFE

10TH ST. S.

HOTEL MAYA

1ST AVE.

CARIBBEAN VILLAGE

To Airport and Orange Walk

TONY'S INN AND RESORT

0   150 yds

0   150 m

© AVALON TRAVEL PUBLISHING, INC.

government hospital, a clinic, a cinema, a few small hotels, a couple of funky bars and discos, and several restaurants. Not a whole lot of activity goes on here, unless you happen to be in town during special holidays. The biggest excitement is during the Mexican-style "Spanish" fiestas of Christmas, *Carnaval,* and Columbus Day.

Many houses are clapboard, raised on wooden stilts to avoid possible floods and to catch the wind, creating a cool spot for the family to gather. More of the newer houses

are built out of cement blocks. Be sure to go into the town hall and take a look at the dramatic historical mural painted by **Manuel Villamour.** The flamboyantly colored mural depicts the history of Corozal, including the drama of the downtrodden Maya, their explosive revolt called the Caste War, and the inequities of colonial rule.

The Corozal District economy has for years depended on the sugar industry with its local processing factory. One of the oldest (no longer in operation), the **Aventura Sugar Mill,** began operating in the 1800s. Little is left today, but you can still see the antiquated chimney when driving past the village of Aventura on the New Northern Highway, seven miles from Corozal Town.

ORIENTATION

Enter Corozal either from the north (many drivers cross the Mexican border here) or from the south on the Northern Highway. Getting oriented to Corozal is easy since it's laid out on a grid system with **avenues** running north and south and **streets** running east and west. Corozal's two primary avenues, 4th and 5th, run completely through town. The majority of restaurants or stores of interest to travelers lie on, or adjacent to, these streets. The town square is in the center of town, with streets numbered outward from there in each direction (1st St. N, 1st St. S).

SIGHTS AND RECREATION

Corozal Town is a great base camp for fishing, nature watching, and water sports. Lots of folks just hang out for a couple of days, wander over to the town square, have a drink or two somewhere, and strike up a conversation with the locals and a few of the expats who've come to love the laid-back lifestyle.

Maya Archaeological Sites

Though not of the scope or interest to the casual traveler as Lamanai in Orange Walk District or Caracol and Xunantunich in the Cayo District, the nearby ruins of **Cerros** and **Santa Rita** are easy to visit. Both are mostly unexcavated. Cerros is especially intriguing as it looms over the jungle across the bay from Corozal Town. Located on a peninsula in Corozal Bay, Cerros was an important coastal trading center during the late pre-Classic period (350 B.C.–A.D. 250).

You can reach Cerros by boat; hire it in downtown Corozal. Check with your hotel or ask at Tony's Inn about transport. The trip is pleasant if a bit pricey. If there's no one else to split the cost of the trip and it's dry season (Jan.–April), you can get to Cerros by car.

Today's Corozal Town is built on the site of what was once the ancient Maya province of Chetumal. The bay was an important trading port. The remaining ruins are called Santa Rita. To explore this site either strike out on your own or go with a guided group from your hotel. The site is on the edge of town. Women traveling alone should team up with others or hire a guide.

River Trips

A favorite excursion from Corozal is a boat ride up the New River to Lamanai in Orange Walk District. Travel 30 miles past mestizo, Maya, and Mennonite settlements on a sun-dappled, jungle-lined river until you come to a broad

Corozal Town Hall historical mural

lagoon and then to the temples of Lamanai. The trip is through tropical flora and fauna, and you might see such exotics as black orchids and jabiru storks, the largest flying birds in the New World with a wing span of 10–12 feet. This is an all-day trip. The price for one to four people to Lamanai runs about US$250 (check with Manuel Hoare, tel. 4/22744). During the dry season (Jan.–April), you can reach Lamanai by road from San Felipe, preferably in a 4WD.

Consejo Shores
This suburb of Corozal Town is seven miles northeast of the town center. Look for the turnoff downtown; it brings you to Consejo Shores, which the locals call the "Miami Beach" of Belize (a wild stretch of the imagination unless you've seen the rest of the country). The name is rather odd, too, since Corozal has no "real" beach. Mostly this is an upscale neighborhood with some lovely homes (many owned by expats). Walking along the coast it's easy to find a place to enter the lovely blue sea; you'll find good swimming, for example, at Four Mile Lagoon.

Across the Border
Tours to Chetumal for shopping or to Bacalar with its Spanish fort and blue hole are popular activities. Henry Menzies, tel. 4/22725, specializes in such tours. In fact, Henry takes visitors back and forth to Tulum, Akumal, and Cancún in quality air-conditioned vehicles.

Other Activities
Fishing is good in Corozal. With its numerous creeks, bays, inlets, and the ocean, Corozal offers the angler a choice of fishing for saltwater or freshwater species. Tarpon fishing is especially popular.

ACCOMMODATIONS

Under US$25
Nestor's Hotel, 123 5th Ave., tel./fax 4/22354, rates about US$22, has been a budget favorite for a long time, but it sometimes has been a little loosely managed. However, the new owners are running a tighter establishment. Rooms are small, simple, and have fans, a/c, and private baths. Laundry service available. Downstairs a pleasant restaurant and bar with karaoke, audio, and video systems attracts locals and travelers. Try the barbecue dip steak sandwich for under US$5 or a T-bone in one of three sizes. It serves good vegetarian fare too. A locked parking lot is available.

    Caribbean Village, South End, Corozal Town, Belize, C.A., tel. 4/22725, fax 4/23414, was formerly known as the Caribbean Motel and Trailer Park. Once an old standard for simple cabins and campers, this pleasant shady resort offers five thatched cabins, renovated by owners Henry and Joan Menzies. This is for travelers who want simple but clean ac-

Tony's Inn and Resort

commodations with private baths, h/c water, and reasonable prices. The Menzies are reps for Tropic Air, and there's an added plus: Henry runs a good tour operation; he is a knowledgeable guide who specializes in tours of northern Belize and Mexico. Across the street from the bay, under palms that catch the breeze, an on-site restaurant is a pleasant family-style place to grab a bite to eat or to hang out. Cabins US$20. Campsites about US$5. Full hookups for RVs, US$17, for two people. They also have two houses for rent on a monthly basis; one furnished, one not. The Menzies accept Visa/MC.

Across from the bus stop at the south end of 7th Avenue is a small hotel, **Hotel Maya,** P.O. Box 112, Corozal Town, Belize, C.A., tel. 4/22082 or 4/22874, email hotelmaya@btl.net. It offers rooms with fans US$24, upgraded rooms with a/c and TV US$50, and a restaurant. Two buildings house the office, restaurant, and rooms. The hotel is fairly well maintained and the help is friendly. Mexican and regional dishes are served in the comfy little café. Enjoy a cold beer and ceviche at the bar; swim at the shore across the street. Although far from fancy, all rooms have private baths, h/c water, and fans. The furnishings are simple but comfortable. Check the corner rooms on the second and third floors facing the ocean. The hotel accepts Visa/MC. This is also the agency for Maya Island Air.

US$25–50

Off the beaten track in a residential neighborhood, **Hotel Posada Mama,** 77 G St. S, Corozal, Belize, C.A., tel. 4/22107 or 4/23245, is hard to find, but the small blue hostel is worth it. Very clean, tiny rooms have a toilet and shower tightly placed in separate corners. The eight colorful cement rooms have a/c, color TV, h/c water, and telephones, US$22. There isn't a restaurant here, but the owners will direct guests to their favorite eateries.

Just two blocks south of town center, look for **Hok'ol K'in Guesthouse,** P.O Box 145, Corozal Town, Belize, C.A., tel. 4/23329, fax 4/23569, email maya@btl.net. With nine guest rooms, private baths, veranda, no a/c (c/a instead—Caribbean air), and a book exchange shelf, the bright white guest house is located

right on the lovely sea. US$40. For those staying for three days, they offer a package that includes all meals, transfers to and from the international airport, and tours to Cerros, Altun Ha, Lamanai, and Cuello, and hotel tax. US$400 pp, double occupancy. There are no sand beaches in Corozal, but there's grass to the shore. They offer many tours, including a nighttime river safari where it is common to spot elusive wildlife. You can rent a car here (Budget) and bikes rent for US$10 a day. If you want a true cultural immersion, stay awhile at Hok'ol K'in. (In Yucateca Mayan, Hok'ol K'in means the "Coming of the Rising Sun.") At Hok'ol K'in, the staff can suggest both Maya and Garifuna families that will take you in, show you the ways of their lives, and perhaps tell old stories from their elders. Great experience. There's plenty to see; just ask and the staff will help you. This is one of the few lodgings in Belize that's equipped to handle a wheelchair—one room only so be sure to specify if needed. The restaurant is open 7 A.M.–10 P.M. and guests can get a meal 24 hours a day here. Food is tasty and reasonably priced: pork chops US$4.50; fish fillet US$5; great breakfast burrito US$4.50. If you want a *really* good cheeseburger, eat here; breakfast is served 24 hours.

US$50–100

Casablanca by the Sea, Box 212, Consejo Village, Corozal District, C.A. Tel. 4/38018, fax 4/38003, U.S. fax 781/235-1024, email: info @casablanca-bythesea.com, is where you can get a fine standard room for US$65. Depending on views and size, prices go up. Another intimate hotel with lovely grounds and views of the Bay of Consejo. Eight rooms with queen-size beds, two doubles, private bathrooms, indoor/outdoor dining, and a lot of secluded privacy yet with access to all the sights of the Corozal District. Rates in the summer are US$40, children under 12 free.

Corozal Bay Inn, P.O. Box 184, Corozal Town, tel. 4/22691, email doug@corozalbayinn.com, is next door to Tony's. This inn is actually apartments. The Podzuns are the friendly owner/operators.They live across the street and deliver fresh fruit to your room every morning. There are four suites, two on ground level, and they are clean, comfortably furnished with cable TV, couch, bookshelves with books, and a fully stocked kitchen. Phone and laundry services available. This is a nonsmoking hotel. US$50–65.

On the sea, facing the Maya site of Cerros across the bay, is one of Corozal's older hotels, **Tony's Inn and Resort,** P.O. Box 12, Corozal Town, Corozal District, Belize, C.A., tel. 4/22055, fax 4/22829; from the U.S., call **International Expeditions,** 800/633-4734, email tonys @btl.net. This two-story white stucco building is a modern hotel with large rooms that have a/c, private baths, electricity, and h/c water. Prices range from US$50–65, less in the summer. It has a good restaurant, though a bit pricey, and a manmade sandy beach, and beach bar (a good evening hangout) where you can enjoy the trade winds off the Caribbean, a marina, swimming, other water sports, and pleasant companionship with fellow travelers. Tony's has 20 double rooms. Rooms are less in the summer; credit cards OK.

On-site the Vista del Sol restaurant serves three meals a day. Tony's is 80 miles from the Philip Goldson International Airport in Belize City, 18 miles from Chetumal, Mexico, and 150 miles from Cancún, Mexico. Owners/managers Dahlia and Tony Castillo are friendly and always ready to assist their guests. They are agents for Budget Rent a Car. Write or call for more information and reservations.

FOOD

Corozal has a number of places to eat a decent meal. Most serve a variety of Creole and Mexican-style food.

Crisis (pronounced CREE-sees) is a neat little place with a lot of atmosphere, good local food, and reasonable prices. On 9th Street N, Crisis features a lounge, dancing, and live music on weekends. The rice and beans with stew beef is good for US$2.25. Check out the conch ceviche or steak for under US$4. The typical Mayan dishes *Chimole* (similar to a pot roast of beef made with the black version of a tasty spice called recado and served in a bowl) and *escabeche* (made with chicken that is boiled and then brushed with a sauce made from chicken broth, lots of onions, and the red version of the spice recado; then the chicken is broiled) cost about US$2.25 each. Find oil-cloth-covered tables and fans. It's open Sun.–Fri. 10 A.M.–10 P.M. On Saturday, it is closed in the morning, but open until midnight.

At the north end of town on the right, you'll find **Gonz and Roses,** 5 4th Ave. N, tel. 4/23137, really more of a bar than restaurant, but it's quaint with a cool interior, tables and private booths, all brightened by tiny blinking Christmas lights. Here from 11 A.M. till midnight, Ms. Gonzalez serves a variety of local and Mexican snacks. Tostadas are a tasty bargain, fried chicken is served with potatoes and veggies, and conch ceviche is a specialty.

Near the Corozal Cultural Center find **Café Kela** serving a mix of French and Caribbean cuisine at very reasonable prices, and good reports.

Black Orchid, tel. 4/20157 on 10th Street, is more bar than restaurant, but if you are driving by, they serve tasty stew chicken and rice and beans for under US$5. Music can be loud.

fishing from the docks in Corozal

Hok'ol K'in Guesthouse has good food open 7 A.M.–10 P.M. **Tony's Inn** is good if a bit pricey. **Casablanca by the Sea** in Consejo is known for its good eats.

SHOPPING AND SERVICES

Corozal has lots of little shops, grocery stores, bookstores, and a few gift shops. You'll find locally made jewelry, pottery, wood carvings, clothing, textiles, and a host of other mementos here and there. Not overrun with gift shops yet. A **U Sav Supermarket** is near the **Hok'ol K'in Guesthouse.**

Money

If you need to change money, go to **Belize Bank, Nova Scotia Bank,** or **Atlantic Bank** Mon.–Thurs. 8 A.M.–1 P.M., Friday 8:30 A.M.–4:30 P.M.

Local Guides and Tour Companies

Two good local guides know the country well, especially the Corozal District, and have well-kept vans: **Henry Menzies Travel & Tours,** P.O. Box 210, Corozal Town, Belize, C.A., tel. 4/22725, and Manuel Hoare of **Ma-lan's Tours,** 13 6th St., South Corozal Town, Belize, C.A., tel. 4/22744, fax 4/23375.

Garage Service

If you're driving your own car and have a mechanical problem, don't fret—**Johnnie's Auto Repair,** 23 8th Ave. S, offers 24-hour service.

GETTING THERE

In this chapter we tell you how to get back and forth to Corozal. However, for travelers already in Quintana Roo, Mexico, this is one way to get to and from Belize. From Cancún, it's a simple matter to take a bus to Chetumal, and then either a Batty or Venus bus across the border. Even simpler, arrange to be picked up in Chetumal by one of the Corozal guides and they will take you from Chetumal across the border and to the airport to fly either to San Pedro in Ambergris Caye or to Belize City. Tropic Air flies to both. Or rent a car in Corozal and make the drive; it takes a good part of the day to drive to Belize City.

By Air

Call **Tropic Air,** tel. 4/22725 or **Maya Island Air,** tel. 4/22874 for charter information to or from Corozal.

By Bus

Both **Venus,** tel. 4/22132 and **Batty,** tel. 4/23034, buses travel between Chetumal and Belize City and stop in Corozal about every two hours until 6 P.M.; Sunday service is less frequent.

By Car

In this area, driving is easy along the Northern Highway. Signs are plentiful, but watch for speed bumps outside Orange Walk and other small towns.

EAST OF COROZAL TOWN

SHIPSTERN WILDLIFE NATURE RESERVE

In the Corozal District, Shipstern is in the northeastern corner of the Belize coast. Thirty-two square miles of moist forest, savanna, and wetlands have been set aside to preserve as-yet-unspoiled habitats of well-known insect, bird, and mammal species associated with the tropics. The reserve encompasses the shallow **Shipstern Lagoon,** which, although hardly naviga-

ble, creates a wonderful habitat for a huge selection of wading and fish-eating birds. The reserve is home to about 200 species of birds, 60 species of reptiles and amphibians, and nearly 200 species of butterflies.

The **Audubon Society** and **International Tropical Conservation Foundation** have been extremely generous in their support. As at most reserves, the object is to manage and protect habitats and wildlife, as well as to develop an education program. This entails educating the local community and introducing children to the concept of wildlife conservation in their area. Shipstern, however, goes a step further by conducting an investigation of how tropical countries such as Belize can develop self-supporting conservation areas through the controlled, intensive production of natural commodities found within such wildlife settlements. Developing facilities for the scientific study of the reserve area and its wildlife is part of this important program. For information about a few cabins at the reserve, US$10, contact the Belize Audubon Society at email base@btl.net.

Shipstern began the production of live butterfly pupae through intensive breeding. Around the world, tourist attractions such as Disney World are providing butterfly habitats, where visitors can wander through an enclosure designed to resemble the deep jungle, with flitting tropical birds and colorful butterflies—all flying free. These butterfly habitats are gaining popularity. Great Britain has 60. Many of the large animal parks in the United States, such as San Diego Wild Animal Park, the San Francisco Zoological Society, and many others have either opened a habitat or are designing one. They are so much more pleasant than dead collections!

Pineapple is a lucrative crop for Sartaneja.

The Butterfly Life Cycle

A butterfly goes through four stages in its life cycle: egg, caterpillar, pupa, and adult. Shipstern gathers breeding populations of typical Belizean species in the pupal stage. Depending on the species, butterflies live anywhere from seven days to six weeks. If you plan to visit, go on a sunny day; you'll see lots more butterfly activity than on an overcast day—if it's raining, forget it!

In many areas of Belize, butterfly populations have been almost totally depleted for many reasons, including habitat destruction (from logging, for instance) and changing farming practices, particularly the use of pesticides. Shipstern's untouched steamy marshes, swamps, and rainforest have been a natural breeding ground for beautiful butterflies for thousands of years and maybe will continue to be so.

For a while, the pupae were gathered at Shipstern, carefully packaged in moist cotton inside a cardboard box, and then shipped. Once the pupae were unpacked they were carefully "hung" in what is called an emerging cage with a simulated "jungle" atmosphere—hot and humid. A short time later they shed their pupal skin, and a tiny bit of Belize flutters away to the amazement and joy of watching children and adults. However, costs exceed benefits, so the export business was stopped. But the butterfly breeding program continues for education and science.

Botanical Trail

Before starting your trek along the Botanical Trail, pick up a book with detailed descriptions of the trail and the trees at the center's headquarters. The lovely trail starts at the parking lot by the office and meanders through the forest. You will have the opportunity to see three types of hardwood forests and 100 species of hardwood. Many of the trees are labeled with their Latin and Yucatec Maya names.

It's essential that visitors go first to the visitors'

center; someone is there 24 hours a day. A guided tour of the visitors' center, Butterfly Breeding Center, and the Botanical Trail costs US$5 per person. The guides' discerning eyes spot things that most city folk often miss even though they are right in front of them. The forest is alive with nature's critters and fascinating flora. Hours for touring are daily 9 A.M.–noon and 1–3 P.M., except for Christmas, New Year's Day, and Easter.

Getting There

From Orange Walk, figure a little more than an hour to drive to Shipstern Wildlife Reserve. The road takes you through **San Estevan** and then to **Progreso**. Turn right just before entering Progreso, to **Little Belize** (a Mennonite community). Continue on to **Chunox; Sarteneja** is three miles beyond Shipstern. Don't forget a long-sleeved shirt, pants, mosquito repellent, binoculars, and a camera for exploring the reserve.

SARTENEJA

When you arrive, you'd almost think you were in Mexico; but why not? The small fishing village in northern Belize was established by Yucatán settlers from Mexico in the 19th century. The fishermen continue to use the skills handed down over the years along with the knowledge of boatbuilding. Obviously the immigrants were not the only people who felt that Sarteneja's location on the Corozal District coast was ideal for the seafaring life; it is apparent that the ancient Maya spent many years here also. To date, only one Maya structure has been partially restored, and archaeologists note that the remains of more than 350 structures have been discovered—but not excavated.

For generations, the people of nearby villages have robbed the Maya sites of building materials such as stone blocks and limestone to make plaster and cement. As the scavengers picked and dug around the structures over the years, artifacts made of gold, copper, and shells continued to turn up. Scientists believe Sarteneja was occupied by the Maya from the early Classic period into the 1700s.

Agriculture

Today Sarteneja is home not only to fishermen, but also to farmers. Pineapples grow well and for years were transported to Belize City by boat twice a week and sold at the Belize City wharf. But since the all-weather road from Sarteneja opened, the fruit can be delivered more frequently by truck. Farmers are planting other crops, and with the freedom of coming and going to Belize City more easily, this may develop into a major agricultural community—if tourism doesn't beat it out first! Already there are sport fishermen who prefer Sarteneja's mild climate (with rich catches of fish) to the southern, more humid part of the country.

Accommodations

Fernando's Seaside Guesthouse, tel. 4/32085, offers inexpensive, simple accommodations, about US$15–20.

KATHY ESCOVEDO SANDERS

ORANGE WALK DISTRICT
INTRODUCTION

Orange Walk is the second largest district of Belize, and its history is inexorably linked to Orange Walk Town, near the northern tip of the district. This busy town is one of the largest commercial and farming centers in the country. It was settled in the 19th century by refugees from southern Mexico during the Caste War; you'll still hear more Spanish than English. What's left of two forts, Mundy and Cairns, reminds one that this was the scene of violent battles between Belizean settlers and war-minded Maya trying to rid the area of outsiders. The last battle took place in 1872. Today the most striking people you'll notice on the streets aren't the Maya but the Mennonites, who still maintain their simple cotton clothes, horse-drawn buggies, and stoic countenances.

THE LAND

Orange Walk District is blessed with a wide array of habitats and wildlife. Like its neighbor, Corozal,

it has a riverine lagoon, marshes, and deep tropical forest. You'll find it has good trekking, around Lamanai ruins on the New River Lagoon, the Rio Bravo Conservation Area, and the country around Chan Chich Lodge. The vast New River Lagoon is Belize's largest body of fresh water (28 miles long). Its dark waters are smooth and reflective, changing with every cloud that passes over the sun. Morelet's crocodiles and hicatee turtles inhabit these waters along with numerous species of fish and waterfowl.

Logging

For centuries, before settlement by farming-inclined mestizo refugees from Yucatán in 1849, this was timber country. In years past, all the timber logged from the north and middle districts was floated down the New River to Corozal Bay, and then to Belize City; from there it was shipped all over the world. If you travel about two miles north past Orange Walk Town, you'll find a toll bridge over the New River. Today you'll encounter large logging trucks crossing the toll bridge.

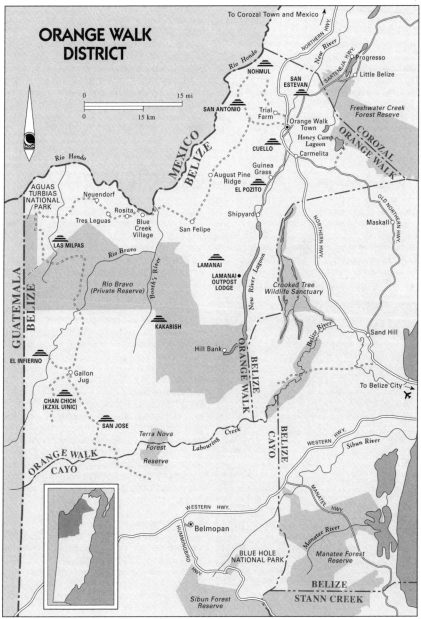

ORANGE WALK DISTRICT

To Corozal Town and Mexico

NORTHERN HWY.

Rio Hondo

NOHMUL

SARTENEJA HWY.

New River

Progresso

Little Belize

SAN ESTEVAN

Freshwater Creek Forest Reserve

SAN ANTONIO

Trial Farm

Orange Walk Town

Honey Camp Lagoon

CUELLO

Carmelita

COROZAL

ORANGE WALK

15 mi

15 km

MEXICO

BELIZE

Guinea Grass

August Pine Ridge

EL POZITO

Rio Hondo

AGUAS TURBIAS NATIONAL PARK

Neuendorf

Rosita

Tres Leguas

Blue Creek Village

Shipyard

Maskall

OLD NORTHERN HWY.

San Felipe

LAS MILPAS

Rio Bravo

Booth's River

LAMANAI

LAMANAI OUTPOST LODGE

New River Lagoon

Crooked Tree Wildlife Sanctuary

GUATEMALA

BELIZE

Rio Bravo (Private Reserve)

NORTHERN HWY.

Sand Hill

KAKABISH

ORANGE WALK

BELIZE

Belize River

To Belize City

EL INFIERNO

Hill Bank

Gallon Jug

CHAN CHICH (KZXIL UINIC)

SAN JOSE

Terra Nova Forest Reserve

Labouring Creek

BELIZE

CAYO

WESTERN HWY.

Sibun River

ORANGE WALK

CAYO

WESTERN HWY.

HUMMINGBIRD HWY.

★ Belmopan

BLUE HOLE NATIONAL PARK

MANATEE HWY.

Manatee River

Manatee Forest Reserve

Sibun Forest Reserve

BELIZE

STANN CREEK

© AVALON TRAVEL PUBLISHING, INC.

MOON

Sugarcane

At one time sugarcane was the most important Belizean crop. Now farmers grow more and more citrus, and beef producers supply not only the local market but also the export market. **Caribbean rum** (a product of sugarcane) is still big business in this area. During the cane harvest, the one-lane highway is a parade of trucks stacked high with sugarcane and waiting in long lines at the side of the road to get into the sugar mill. Night drivers beware: The trucks aren't new and often have no lights.

Mennonite Country

The picturesque Mennonite farming areas of Orange Walk seem strangely out of place as you ride through the countryside. At times you could believe you were in North Dakota or even Pennsylvania as you near Blue Creek and the mountains that straddle the Mexican border behind it. Today's Mennonite farmers have created lovely green pastures and rich gardens; they specialize in the dairy and egg industries. Agriculture is blossoming in many directions in Orange Walk.

LAMANAI ARCHAEOLOGICAL ZONE

Lamanai is an exciting site and one of Belize's largest Maya ceremonial centers. It was an imperial port city encompassing ball courts, pyramids, and the more exotic Maya features. Lamanai is believed to have been occupied from 1500 B.C. to the 19th century. (Historical Spanish occupation is also apparent with the remains of

Lamanai Archaeological Site

two Christian churches, and the sugar mill was built by U.S. Confederate refugees.) Lamanai huddles to one side of New River Lagoon. It's reachable by boat from Shipyard or by road during the dry season from San Felipe. A visit to this unreconstructed ceremonial center, which dates from 3500 B.C., is an Indiana Jones adventure into the deep shadowed home of the mysterious Maya. Besides Lamanai, the nearby ruins of **Cuello** beckon the visitor, as does the distant site of **La Milpa** in the **Rio Bravo Conservation Area** to the far west. (See the Mundo Maya chapter.)

Archaeological Research and Nature Study

Programme for Belize operates a Rio Bravo exploration tour offering a couple of days' involvement on the La Milpa ruins archaeological survey. Participants are allowed the time to study the flora and fauna of the area. Lamanai Outpost Lodge's ongoing archaeological program allows guests of the lodge to get involved. For more information, contact Programme for Belize, 2 S. Park St., Belize City, C.A., tel. 2/75616.

Accommodations

Right next door to Lamanai Reserve along the shore of the New River Lagoon is the comfortable **Lamanai Outpost Lodge,** tel./fax 2/33578, U.S. tel. 888/733-7864, email lamanai@btl.net. Guests of the lodge, just a half mile from the reserve's dock, can either walk or take a quick water taxi ride over. The lodge boasts 16 comfortable thatched-roof cabañas made of natural wood and other mostly Belizean materials. Below the resort's lodge and dining room, the cabañas lead down to the lagoon's shore, where you'll find a dock, swimming area, canoes, boats of various types, and a sailboard. This is a low-key, escape-to-nature kind of setting, perfect for the bird-watcher, Mayaphile, naturalist, or traveler who wants to get away from the tourist trail for a while. Ask about packages including meals and activities, which bring the daily cost way down. The area is rich in animal life, including more than 300 species of birds as well as crocodiles, margays, jaguarundis, anteaters, arboreal porcupines, and the fishing bulldog bat.

The owners are involved in several scientific research projects that also allow nature study opportunities for guests. One study concentrates on howler monkeys, another on recording bird-calls, and another on spiders. Guests through programs such as **ElderHostel** and **Oceanic Expeditions** can participate in the work. Quarters for the researchers will soon be completed. Ask about daily herbal and bird walks as well as night safaris.

ORANGE WALK TOWN

Orange Walk Town (population about 10,000), just off the Northern Highway, is easy to get to. Roads from Orange Walk Town enable you to explore, in four directions, as many as 20 villages. Daily buses from Orange Walk link Belize City and Corozal. Lying 66 miles north of Belize City and 30 miles south of Corozal Town, Orange Walk town is one of the larger communities in Belize. Though it does not qualify as a tourist destination, it's another facet of Belize with its own history and style. If passing through, stop and look around. The town has two banks, a cinema, a few hotels, and a choice of many small, casual cafés. Close by you'll find several interesting historic sites: **Indian Church,** a 16th-century Spanish mission; the ruins of Belize's original sugar mill, built by U.S. Confederate Civil War refugees; and if you head west and then southwest you'll find **Blue Creek,** a Mennonite development where Belize's first hydroelectric plant is located.

SIGHTS AND RECREATION

Cycling
Motivated cyclists with mountain bikes should have no trouble in most of Orange Walk District. Wet conditions in the rainy season can make riding impossible in some isolated areas, but the roads to Rio Bravo Conservation Area and Chan Chich are all-weather roads. Allow plenty of time and avoid night travel. In the hilly country around Blue Creek, the road rises over a short distance and curves around a *lot.* A gas station/general store at the top, **Linda Vista Credit Union,** offers food and drinks. Other than this section of road, the less than 40 miles to Chan Chich should be a good ride for

a looter's trench into the side of a Maya archaeological site

the *experienced* cyclist. From the point you bear off to the left, a little before Tres Leguas, till the point you reach Chan Chich, enjoy the great ride. Note: Expect fast-moving jeeps rounding the sharp turns in a hurry; there're no shoulders much of the way. It's a jungle out there!

Orchid Tours

The **Audubon Society** is very involved with the preservation of Belize's wildlife. One of Belize's most important features is 150 species of orchids growing wild throughout the country. **Godoy and Sons,** 4 Trial Farm, Orange Walk Town, Belize, C.A., tel. 3/22969, offers a tourist guide service that, along with the usual attractions, leads orchid tours. Luis Godoy, the eldest son, has developed an exciting tour during which visitors will see a variety of tropical blossoms, including the black orchid (the Belizean national flower). Ask about orchid sales. When not involved with touring, the Godoys export orchid plants for the Audubon societies from various parts of the country. Many resorts around the country buy the plants from the Godoys to use for landscaping.

Orchid fanciers who wish to buy Belizean orchids must go through special procedures to bring the blooms into the United States. Luis Godoy is one of just a handful of people in the country who know all the legal procedures involved, and he can handle all of it for you. Call or write the Godoys for information, or look them up when visiting Orange Walk Town.

River Trips

Trips up and down the **New River** and around the **New River Lagoon** are fun adventures for the entire family, with a chance to see Morelet's crocodiles and iguanas sunning on a bank. Night safaris are equally, if not more, exciting. It's a chance to see the habits of animals who come out to play only after the sun sets; you'll need the help of a good guide and spotlight of course.

By day you'll see the sights of verdant jungle and wildlife along the river. Many people combine a river trip with a visit to the ruins of Lamanai. It is the most impressive way to approach the site, and a time-saver as well compared to going by land. Contact **Jungle River Tours,** tel. 3/22293, fax 3/22201, at Lovers Lane road and talk to Antonio or Herminio Novelo, who run river tours to Lamanai and the surrounding area.

ACCOMMODATIONS

Few people choose to stay in Orange Walk Town due to all the stories of drugs and crime. It's hard to know just how badly this has impacted the town. Suffice it to say that this is not a resort community. If you *must* stay, there are a few choices. Check them carefully. Most of the hotels in Orange Walk Town are simple and not designed for upscale tourist comforts. However, the rooms are basic, clean, and, for the most part, inexpensive at under US$50.

D Star Victoria, 40 Belize Road, Orange Walk Town, Belize, C.A., tel. 3/22518, fax 3/22847, was formerly known as the Baron Hotel. This refurbished version is easily the best of the downtown hotels and is on the main road between Belize City and Corozal Town. With 31 rooms, it is also the largest. As you come into town it is hard to miss with its coral and white exterior. Even the pool appears to have had a facelift. Its disco comes to life in the wee hours. All rooms have h/c water, private baths, and ceiling fans or a/c.

Mi Amor Hotel, 19 Belize/Corozal Road, tel. 3/22031, is a roadside hotel on the town's main thoroughfare. It offers private bathrooms and a choice of a/c or fan; TV is extra. It also has a restaurant and a bar.

Chula Vista Hotel, tel. 3/23414, is a few miles beyond Orange Walk Town at **Trial Farm Village.** Take a look at this attractive motor court hotel. The Reyes family offers a restaurant, bar, and seven clean simple rooms with private baths.

FOOD

There's really only one good reason to linger in Orange Walk Town—on the far side of town in a nice neighborhood near the hospital is the best restaurant around, **The Diner,** 37 Clark St., tel. 3/23753. Here you'll find a surprising menu: peppermint steak (US$5), smoked pork chops

(US$8), filet mignon (US$12.50), lobster thermidor or grouper in bechamel sauce (US$15). Try the coconut pie or the homemade soursop ice cream!

It's easy to find Chinese food in Orange Walk Town, maybe because at one time it was home to so many Chinese laborers who worked the sugarcane fields. Now you can find Belizean, Mexican, and Jamaican specialties, even hamburgers, mixed in with so-so oriental offerings. Most of these eateries have little in the way of decor, many are inexpensive, and some for whatever reason ask too much for what you get in return. **Lee's Chinese Restaurant,** 11 San Antonio Road near the fire station, serves passable versions of chicken chow mein (US$3.25), sweet and sour fish (US$7.50), black soybean lobster or shrimp (US$12), and cocktails from a colorful bar on Yo Street.

Entering town on the Belize/Corozal Road you will see a **service station/convenience store** on the left. This store has light snacks, cold drinks, a few staples, medications, and cosmetics. If you are headed by car to Rio Bravo or Chan Chich, this is a good place to top off the gas tank.

GETTING THERE

By Bus

Novelo's and **Venus** travel between Chetumal and Belize City with stops in Orange Walk and Corozal about every two hours until 6 P.M.; Sunday service is less frequent.

By Car

Traveling to Orange Walk on the New Highway is easy; just point the car and go. Watch out for speed bumps as you near the toll bridge south of Orange Walk. The rugged Old Northern Highway is more comfortable with a 4WD vehicle because of the high clearance needed during the rainy muddy season.

By Boat

Going by boat is a pleasant way to get anywhere, especially to Lamanai. Enjoy nature's best along the shore of the river. You never know what you will see next—long-legged birds, orchids growing in tall trees, flitting hummingbirds? It's like a treasure hunt. Bring your binocs. Ask at your hotel for directions to the boat dock.

WEST OF ORANGE WALK TOWN

Four miles west of Orange Walk Town are the minor ruins of **Cuello.** As the road meanders west from there, numerous small villages dot the border region. Occasionally you'll see a soft drink sign attached to a building, but there's not much between Orange Walk and Blue Creek but wide open fields of crops, low forest, and dirt road.

Near **Blue Creek** the road rounds a bend to reveal a pleasant valley. The small village to the right is **La Union,** on the other side of the Mexico border. Then the road angles up sharply. At the top is **La Vista Credit Union,** the gas station/general store mentioned earlier. Fill the tank if you're driving to Rio Bravo or Chan Chich Lodge; it's your last gas station until you come back this way.

RIO BRAVO RESEARCH STATION

Here, on 250,000 acres of prime tropical jungle in the Rio Bravo Conservation Area, is a cluster of small thatched-roof buildings. The station, run by the Belizean conservation group **Programme for Belize,** 2 S. Park St., Belize City, Belize, C.A., tel. 2/71248, fax 2/75616, is dedicated to scientific research, agricultural experimentation, and the protection of indigenous wildlife and the area's Maya archaeological locations—all this while creating self-sufficiency through development of ecotourism and sustainable rainforest agriculture such as chicle production. A scientific study continues to determine the best management plan for the reserve and its forests.

Another focus is on environmental education. Every year the organization, which receives support from the Belize Audubon Society, the Nature Conservancy, and the World Wildlife Fund, expends a goodly effort in educating Belizeans and eco-specialists from abroad. In one program, young Belizean students are recruited to become field biology trainees. This one-year program allows young people the opportunity to work alongside international researchers in gathering knowledge of the jungle and its inhabitants. Another program, sponsored through Save The Rain Forest, Inc., brings in groups of high school teachers and students to experience and learn about the forest and its ecosystems.

For visitors here, Rio Bravo provides the chance to experience the outdoors while supporting a worthy environmental effort. You'll have opportunities to experience the wilderness and see archaeological work underway at La Milpa, the ancient Maya ruins on the property. Activities include nature walks (both day and night), more in-depth study of local birds, mammals, and reptiles, and swims in the Rio Bravo. Visitors may or may not see crocodiles, deer, peccaries, fer-de-lances, coatis, boa constrictors, margays, and jaguars in the surrounding jungle. Bird life is plentiful with waterfowl and jungle birds represented. Scientists, research volunteers, donors, and interested travelers are encouraged to contact Programme for Belize.

CHAN CHICH

Built in an ancient Maya plaza and surrounded by miles of steaming jungle, **Chan Chich Lodge,** P.O. Box 37, Belize City, Belize, C.A., U.S. tel. 800/343-8009, fax 508/693-6311, Belize tel. 2/34419, fax 2/34419, email info@chanchich .com, has an ambience all its own. When you're flying in, it's apparent that civilization is scarce. Driving in on the miles of oft-times bumpy road confirms it. For bird-watchers, naturalists, horseback riders, canoers, or those who love being out in the middle of nowhere (250,000 acres of it here), the experience can be exhilarating. Cleared trails wind through the rainforest, with a green canopy high above. Almost daily, guests run into a flock of beautiful ocellated turkeys out for their morning feed or hear the nightly roar of the howler monkey. Deer, peccary, puma, spider monkey, tapir, and the jaguar live in this country. Parrots and toucans, great curassows, crested guans, and several hundred other species inhabit the branches overhead.

Chan Chich means "little bird." Actually the word has many translations, depending on which Maya dialect you use. The Maya site itself is a fairly recent discovery in the northwestern corner of Belize. Because of its isolation, it was a favorite spot to raise marijuana, and looters attempted to steal the treasures buried within the tombs. But no more! Now, under the watchful

Chan Chich Lodge

PATTI LANGE

eye of Chan Chich managers/builders Tom and Josie Harding and the ardent guests wandering the jungle trails, it is no longer an easy task for robbers to dig their trenches and tunnel unseen, or to raise the weed.

The lodge offers an adventurer's ambience with a jungle location and rustic architecture that blends surreptitiously into the surroundings of Maya and nature. When you drive your own car into Chan Chich, you are especially amazed at what you find. After miles and miles of backcountry, rugged roads that might even be washed out at places, and sights of rainforest and streams that have seen little human touch, suddenly the trees part and you find yourself in a beautiful green world. Green grass everywhere! Green grass covering obvious Maya pyramids surrounded by lovely, well cared for cabañas.

Each of the 12 cabañas has a thick thatched roof (good natural insulation against the jungle heat), beautiful hardwood interior, private bathroom with hot-water shower, electricity, ceiling fan, two queen-size beds, veranda, and walkways (paved with rounds of cabbage bark logs)

that lead to the river. A charming community dining room/salon offers excellent food, a handsome outdoor bar, and a swimming pool and spa. Guides are available for bird-watching. Canoeing the New River or the adjoining lagoon is a pleasant way to spend a few hours and have a chance to see some wildlife along the way. Guests at Chan Chich Lodge can arrange to ride quarter horses from nearby Gallon Jug stables and explore numerous jungle trails, fields, and sparsely traveled dirt roads. Additional Maya ruins are hidden in the recesses of the jungle. Nearby lakes are pretty sites for picnics. It helps to have a guide.

Chan Chich is 130 miles from Belize City (the Hardings say, plan an all-day drive to get here) on all-weather roads from the international airport, or (much easier) a 30-minute charter flight to nearby Gallon Jug. Rates are US$140, full meal packages run US$40 adults, US$30 children under 12; all-inclusive prices available. Tours and guides to the surrounding areas are easily arranged through Josie. Call or write for more information.

BOB RACE

KATHY ESCOVEDO SANDERS

CAYO DISTRICT
INTRODUCTION

Cayo, in western Belize is the largest of the six districts of Belize, and one of the most visited. Belmopan, the nation's capital, is located here close to some of the most beautiful countryside in the land. From savanna-covered plains and rich groves of citrus, the land gradually rises into the mountains. The magical beauty of the mountains offers outdoor lovers such enticing activities as climbing up steep ridges, hiking along the banks of myriad rivers, swimming through a waterfall in the rainforest, and discovering caves, colorful birds, and shy jungle animals.

The Cayo District is a rich mixture of people, places, and marvelous creatures—mythical and real. Maya, Mennonites, mestizos, Anglos, Creoles, and Chinese all commingle in government, commerce, agriculture, and tourism. The Maya Mountains, Vaca Plateau, and Mountain Pine Ridge are important geological features. Several major rivers drain the highlands, including the Branch, Macal, Mopan, and Sibun Rivers. Savanna, broadleaf jungle, and pinelands form a patchwork of habitats for a great diversity of animals. A few of the protected lands and private reserves are Blue Hole National Park, Chiquibul National Park, Guanacaste National Park, Slate Creek Reserve, and Tapir Mountain Reserve. Two of the countries major Maya sites, Xunantunich and Caracol, are part of Cayo's past along with Cahal Pech.

The geological wonders of this area contribute to the growing popularity of caving. Visitors can explore myriad caves that were once used by the Maya. Among them are Chechem Ha, Actun Tunichil Muknal, Rio Frio Cave, and Blue Hole.

Driving a car is the best way to get around the Cayo District. You never know when you'll come upon a beautiful valley or a Maya ruin, and the land is criss-crossed with small dirt roads that take you to surprise destinations. (Car rentals are available in Belize City and the airport.) While traveling in this part of the country you'll pass through many villages with quaint-sounding names such as Roaring Creek, Black

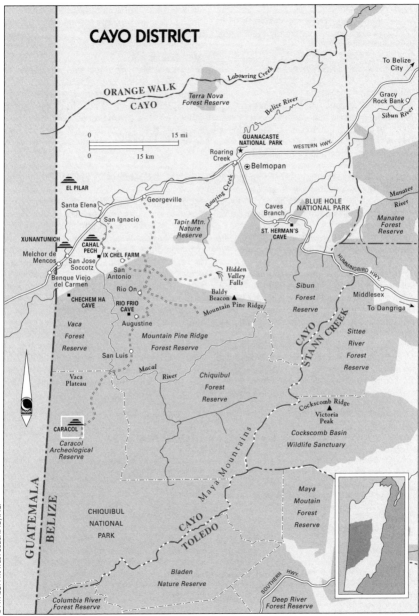

CAYO DISTRICT

ORANGE WALK
CAYO

Terra Nova
Forest Reserve

Labouring Creek

Belize River

To Belize
City

Gracy
Rock Bank

Sibun River

0   15 mi
0   15 km

EL PILAR

Santa Elena

Georgeville

GUANACASTE
NATIONAL PARK

Roaring
Creek

WESTERN HWY.

Belmopan

Manatee
River

San Ignacio

Roaring Creek

Caves
Branch

BLUE HOLE
NATIONAL PARK

Manatee
Forest
Reserve

XUNANTUNICH

Tapir Mtn.
Nature
Reserve

ST. HERMAN'S
CAVE

CAHAL
PECH

IX CHEL FARM

Melchor de
Mencos

San Jose
Soccotz

San
Antonio

HUMMINGBIRD HWY.

Benque Viejo
del Carmen

Rio On

Hidden
Valley
Falls

Sibun
Forest
Reserve

Middlesex

CHECHEM HA
CAVE

RIO FRIO
CAVE

Baldy
Beacon

Mountain Pine Ridge

To Dangriga

Vaca
Forest
Reserve

Augustine

Mountain Pine Ridge
Forest Reserve

CAYO
STANN CREEK

Sittee
River
Forest
Reserve

San Luis

Macal

River

Chiquibul
Forest
Reserve

Vaca
Plateau

MOON

Cockscomb Ridge

Victoria
Peak

CARACOL

Caracol
Archeological
Reserve

Maya Mountains

Cockscomb Basin
Wildlife Sanctuary

GUATEMALA

BELIZE

CHIQUIBUL
NATIONAL
PARK

CAYO

TOLEDO

Maya
Mountain
Forest
Reserve

Bladen
Nature Reserve

SOUTHERN HWY.

Deep River
Forest Reserve

Columbia River
Forest Reserve

© AVALON TRAVEL PUBLISHING, INC.

Man Eddy, Holdfast, Double Head Cabbage, Washing Tree, and Teakettle. All add a bit of their own exotic charm to an already exotic place.

HISTORY

The Mestizo Past
The Spanish influence is much stronger in the Cayo District than in either Belize City or Stann Creek. At one time the majority of the people in Cayo were mestizo, and their families had lived in the area for generations. In those days this bustling area depended mostly on the forests to survive, especially at the port of San Ignacio from which logs and chicle were sent down the river to the sea, loaded onto ships, and sent across the world's oceans. Access to the area around San Ignacio, bordered on two sides by rivers, was limited to river traffic. Thus arose the name, Cayo, or "island" in Spanish.

Refugees, Tourism, and Agriculture
But times change. Today, while many residents are descendants of the original settlers, a great many are refugees from unsettled areas in Guatemala and El Salvador as well as newcomers from all over. And while the Cayo District still produces lumber, it has developed into an agricultural area (citrus, peanut, and cattle) as well as a booming tourist center. On the one hand, you'll see Mennonite farms dotting the area between Belmopan and San Ignacio.

On the other, you'll find that the number of small hotels and cottage resorts is increasing rapidly.

Area Development
One recent advance in the area, which affects both agriculture and tourism, is the development of the hydroelectric dam on the Macal River below Benque Viejo. Power from the dam is lighting up the Cayo in unprecedented fashion, making it the envy of Belize's neighbor just across the border.

INLAND ADVENTURE

From Rough Camps to Comfy Resorts
The traveler to Cayo has a choice of camping or staying at numerous cottages, small hotels, lodges, or ranches. These more intimate accommodations—each with its own ambience and specialties, whether very basic or very upscale—are scattered across the Cayo countryside and attract the visitor interested in bird-watching, canoeing, caving, cycling, fishing, hiking, horseback riding, swimming, tubing, and general adventuring. Long treks through tropical foliage, canoe rides on a choice of rivers, horseback trips to hidden waterfalls, and quiet safaris to search out the shy animals and flamboyant bird life of the Belizean forest are all popular. Many visitors return year after year to their favorite spots.

A DAMMING PROJECT

The Belize government and a Canadian corporation want to put in a hydroelectric dam in the Chiquibul Forest Reserve. If this goes forward, 22 miles of the Macal River valley would be flooded, destroying many wildlife habitats and archaeological ruins.

The area to be flooded is well known for a huge diversity of plant and animal life, and it has the only known nesting site in the entire country for a species of the scarlet macaw. Currently the birds number less than 250. The proposed area is also home to some of the best jaguar habitat in the country as well as home to animals like the Morelet

crocodile, the ocelot, tapir, and spider monkey (all are becoming rare).

Animals won't be the only thing losing out: Four Maya ruins were recently found in the area and studies have yet to be done on them. If the dam becomes a reality, information about the ancient Maya in this area will be lost forever.

Proponents want to build the dam to increase water storage capacity and year-round water flow to make a downstream dam more profitable. As with many things, opponents are afraid that the clout of big money will win out over environmental concerns.

Canoeing and River-running Trips

One of the most popular activities in Belize is canoeing in its many rivers. These rivers were the highways of Belize during the days of the Baymen, and now offer a different kind of river journey. This is a very special kind of sight-seeing. You'll float past ever-changing flora: plants, trees, vines, and blossoms thrive along the river-banks. You'll watch for the timid animals that live within their own private worlds, including small underground burrows, sandy riverbeds, and leafy branches of tall hardwood trees. Sometimes it's so quiet you can hear a fish jump for a hovering mosquito. Other days you'll hear the dramatic roar of the howler monkey announcing its territory. By all means, keep your eyes and ears open; most will agree this really is the way to see the country.

For an exciting account of a river trip taken by local Jim Bevis and companions, go online and type in *sibun gorge belize.*

Check out the rafting trips offered by Slick-rock Adventures (see "Tour Operators" in the On The Road chapter). Every Friday full-day trips are offered to nonpackage visitors. You'll gather in San Ignacio, drive through lush jungle, and then raft a 20-mile stretch of the Macal River. Small, steep, and technical, you'll pass through drop pools, mazelike channels, and big waterfalls in class IV whitewater. Led by guides who have rafted all over the world, you know it's got to be good when even they get excited about it. Groups are small (six people), and the wildlife abundant—tapirs, iguanas, and river otters are only some of the animals to be seen. Slickrock is just one of the outfitters in the country running such trips. And remember: These trips are not run year-round as the water level drops during certain months.

For a smoother ride, check out the **Caves Branch** trip—five miles of floating through underground caves. Call for more information: Belize tel./fax 8/22800.

High Adventure Caving

Caving is fast becoming the compelling adventure trip of Belize. Why? Certainly more caves are being discovered and explored as more visitors show their interest. The real reason, however, lies most simply in the mysterious beauty of caves—stalagmites and sta-

lactites are often studded with crystal and sparkle in even the dim light of a match. Often cathedral-like caverns have rivers running through them. But by far the two most fascinating features of caving in Belize are the discovery of Maya artifacts and the reflection on the role caves played in Maya life. Skeletons, skulls, and clay pots found in many sizes are believed to have been used in ceremonial rituals as well as grain storage. There is even some evidence pointing to more frequent use of the caves due to the fact that some of the largest have more than one entrance.

It's really best to explore most of these caves—wet or dry—with a guide. And, of course, come prepared. Bring proper equipment—headlamps or flashlights and batteries—and proper clothing—sturdy shoes and quick-drying pants or shorts. Many Cayo resorts offer excellent guided trips of varying levels of difficulty, from the beginning spelunker on up to the speleologist, who does this professionally. There are day trips, overnights, and weeklong trips available.

CAYO ARTS AND CRAFTS

One of the premiere artists of Belize, **Carolyn Carr,** creates haunting images of local Belizean life in acrylic at her studio near Belmopan. Animals, too, are cherished subjects of hers, but our personal favorite is the painting that reminds us of what the old marketplace was like back in the early days of Belize. One of her murals graces the lobby of the Princess Hotel and Casino in Belize City. Prints of her canvases are sold in many Belizean shops; an original will cost you thousands. You'll find her studio at **Banana Bank Lodge,** P.O. Box 48, Cayo District, Belize, C.A., tel. 8/12020 or 8/23180.

In Benque Viejo, **Octavio Sixto** creates detailed miniature replicas of Belizean shacks and landmark buildings. His work is sold around the country but, not surprisingly, more of it is available in Cayo.

Slate Carvings

Maya and Belizean motifs set out in slate have become very popular and in some cases costly. Among the leading artists are **The Garcia Sisters, Lesley Glaspie,** and the **Magana**

family. Their work can be found in several Cayo shops as well as elsewhere in the country. The Garcia sisters started the slate craze, and their quality has always been high. Slate carvings require a lot of time to create. Now more artists produce them and wise shopping will net a treasured piece without draining your personal treasury. Though many artists use the same subject matter, if you find a piece that excites you, it's a good idea to buy it right away rather than later since you'll seldom find the identical piece.

Wood Furniture

Mennonite furniture is becoming increasingly popular as a take-home item. Cleverly executed chairs and small tables in mahogany and other tropical woods are the mainstays. In San Ignacio you can have them conveniently boxed and ready for baggage check at the airport.

Arts and Crafts Shops

Of the art houses that you are apt to hear about in Belize, many are in Cayo; a couple are really outstanding. Most of the gift shops at various resorts around the countryside offer the same things. Check out the jewelry. We found charming little necklaces, bracelets, and earrings made from the vertebrae of a shark. The clever artist buys the carcass after the fishermen are finished butchering the fish. She then buries the bones in the ground and lets nature's tiny subterranean creatures do the rest, and shortly the bones are clean of all lingering flesh. From there

the artist's methods are secret, but in the end she has created pure white, lightweight, attractive jewelry of symmetrical "fish beads."

In Belmopan look into **El Caracol Gallery & Gifts,** 32 Macaw Ave., Belmopan, tel. 8/22394. East of San Ignacio, **Caesar's Place,** a friendly hotel/bar/restaurant/gift shop at Mile 60, Western Highway, tel. 9/22341, fax 9/23449, has encouraged local artisans to create jewelry, slate carvings, and other works for sale. As a result, Caesar's has a huge selection, probably the largest in the area. Ask about its locally made furniture. It has a sister shop, **Black Rock Gift Shop,** in San Ignacio on Burns Avenue, with similar products.

In downtown San Ignacio, **Eva's Restaurant,** 22 Burns Ave., tel./fax 9/22267, has a small but first-class selection of Belizean arts and crafts in the gift shop area. **Arts and Crafts of Central America,** 1 Wyatt St., tel. 9/22253, specializes in "just what you're looking for."

The Magana family has two shops, **Magana Zactunich Art Gallery** south of Cristo Rey Village and **Magana's Art Center** at the east edge of San José Succotz. Both sell Belizean and Guatemalan arts and crafts of good quality at reasonable prices.

On the north edge of San Antonio, the Garcia sisters have their **Tanah Mayan Art Museum** and store, San Antonio Village, tel. 9/23310. Prices and quality are high. In Benque Viejo, **Galeria del Arte de Gucumaz** has a choice of Belizean and Guatemalan crafts at reasonable prices.

ALONG THE WESTERN HIGHWAY

As you pass the Belize Zoo and head west along the Western Highway, savanna and scraggly pines border the road and the traffic is rarely heavy. The milepost markers that run between Belize City and San Ignacio will help you find your way around the countryside. If you're driving, just set your odometer to match the markers as you turn onto Cemetery Road at the western edge of Belize City. You'll pass two service stations between the Western Highway and the turnoff for Belmopan. Another lies down Constitution Drive on the way into Belmopan.

Manatee Junction

Driving west, note the junction with **Manatee Road** on your left at about Mile 29. (Look for the **Midway Resting Place,** a service station and motel of sorts on the southeast corner; its tall Texaco sign makes an especially good landmark at night when the sign glows with bright colors.) This improved dirt road is the shortcut to Gales Point, Dangriga, and the Southern Highway. It's always a good idea to top off your tank, stock up on cold drinks, and ask for current road conditions here. Heavy rains can cause washouts on a lot of these "highways." This is a

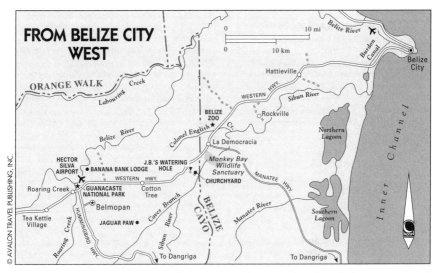

drive best done in daylight because of the picturesque views of jungle, Maya villages, and the Maya Mountains in the distance.

Monkey Bay Wildlife Sanctuary

A couple of miles farther down the Western Highway (Mile 31) and on the left, you will come to a sign for Monkey Bay Wildlife Sanctuary. Take the short road up to the main building and have a look around. Matt Miller, an American transplant to Belize, runs this 1,070-acre private reserve with a board of directors and the financial assistance of Monkey Bay Wildlife Fund Tokyo. The main house has a gathering place upstairs with library, bulletin boards, and panoramic views of the pines, palmettos, and savanna. There's a casual feeling here, something like a college student union. That's little wonder, since the main focus is on educating the student groups Miller and his staff bring in from the States.

You'll find two miles of trails, a 20-acre arboretum, and good swimming at nearby Sibun River. With the declaration by the Belize government in 1992 of the 2,250-acre **Monkey Bay Nature Reserve** across the river, there now exists a wildlands corridor between the **Manatee Forest Reserve** to the south and the sanctuary.

No, there are no monkeys and no bay, but the river does flow through the sanctuary and this is a good meeting place for backpackers. There are many tours offered here, and due to the remote location, it's common to spot more elusive animals like crocodiles and jaguars. These animals are often seen while canoeing the Sibun River on day and dusk trips. Cave and fishing excursions are also available.

If you stay here, be prepared for rustic conditions: cold water, outhouse-style toilets, and no showers. But it's cheap and wild and well worth giving up smelling clean for a day or two. You can camp here for US$5, sling your hammock under a palapa for US$5, stay in a bunkhouse for US$8, or splurge for a very simple room for US$20. Meals, mostly vegetarian and rated "excellent" by the students we talked to, cost US$4–6. For more information, contact Monkey Bay Wildlife Sanctuary, P.O. Box 187, Belmopan, Belize, C.A., tel. 8/23180, fax 8/23235, email mbay@pobox.com.

PRACTICALITIES

J.B.'s Watering Hole

At around Mile 32, legendary J.B.'s Watering Hole, P.O. Box 290, Belmopan, email neesemgm @btl.net, presents the traveler with an opportunity

PASS UP THE PLASTIC, PLEASE

Until 2000, beer and soda came in recycled glass bottles in Belize. But in early 2000 that changed with the introduction of soda in plastic bottles. The maker of those tasty Belikin beers and stouts are also the only distributors of Coca-Cola products. The distributor promised a recycling center to do something about the hundreds of thousands of bottles that are bound to end up in landfills and the side of the road; but as we go to press many months later, no arrangements have been established. Many businesses, especially in the Cayo District, refuse to sell plastic bottles until they can be properly disposed of. We encourage the same. Let's not contribute trash to mar the landscape of beautiful Belize.

to slake a thirst and chew the fat with locals and other travelers. This "watering hole" in the middle of nowhere has been around for years. A former favorite of British forces (now gone), it's one of the few such places worth stopping at between Belize City and San Ignacio. Locals say Harrison Ford was a regular during the filming of *Mosquito Coast*. Originally run by J.B., it's long since been under new management. It's a good stop for a burger, or stewed chicken and a Belikin. Lift one to J.B.'s memory and the fair ladies who run it still; you'll be in good company.

For those who've had too many or for those who want an inexpensive base for further exploration of the area, J.B.'s now offers one- or two-bedroom accommodations, hot water, and private baths. In one, known as the "jungle hut," furniture is made from local wood. Rates are US$30.

Jaguar Paw Jungle Resort

When first turning onto the Hummingbird Highway and then to the dirt road to Jaguar Paw, you don't perceive anything different. But after a couple of slow miles on the bumpy road, your mind-set transforms along with the terrain. Low-lying savanna turns into lush jungle as the road narrows and the trees loom taller. When the car rounds the final curve and goes down a steep hill, you arrive at the lodge. You have the feeling you've gone back in time and must tread carefully to protect the aura—until you get out of the

car and hear the din of the powerful generator. Welcome to Jaguar Paw where the motto is "adventure by day, comfort at night."

Jaguar Paw is located on 215 acres of a nature reserve. This is cave country, and recently more dry caves were found just 15 minutes from the main building of the resort. Jaguar Paw is literally steps away from the **Caves Branch River** and its innumerable shoreline caves. Perch yourself on an inner tube and let the river pull you in and out of water-filled black caverns; go on an all-day jungle walk with friendly guides and learn about medicinal plants, blossoms, and jungle creatures; walk through dry caves with bats by the hundreds zooming all around you. Or, put on your boots and go rock climbing. For the lazies, kick back at the pool and enjoy the refreshing scenery, or catch the latest game on satellite TV at the bar.

Cy and Donna Young have spent years creating a bit of high-tech beauty in their isolated piece of Eden. Sixteen rooms have electricity, hot showers, and air-conditioning. Ever the creative one, Donna gave each cabin a theme, from African décor to bordello. Art from around the globe is displayed on tables and decorates the walls, and handmade quilts and sheets by the Mennonites keep you warm on coolish nights; these personal touches add to guests' contentment.

The lobby, dining room, and bar are in a cement building styled as a Maya ruin. On one inside wall is a reproduction of the Bonompak murals, famous Maya murals in Mexico. The dining room is comfortable and an elegant menu is offered by friendly staff. Try the seafood pasta with fresh fettuccini in a delicious Alfredo sauce. For breakfast, the French toast with zesty spices is a favorite. Meals are tasty, although there's not enough food for some big appetites. Dinner runs about US$15–20.

Check out the building by the river with small kitchen/bar, gift shop, changing rooms, and six toilets. This structure will hold 125 people, enough for a nice-sized party.

For more information, contact Jaguar Paw Jungle Resort, P.O. Box 1832, Belize City, Belize, C.A., tel. 8/13023, U.S. tel. 888/77-JUNGLE, email cyoung@btl.net. Winter rates are US$170, much less in the summer months.

To get there from the Western Highway, turn

left at Mile 37 and follow the road seven miles; the signs are pretty good—otherwise, every time you come to a junction, keep to the right.

Banana Bank Lodge

One of the older working cattle ranches in the country, Banana Bank Ranch was originally run by artist Carolyn Carr and her Montana cowboy-husband, John. Today most of its pastures have been converted to growing corn and beans, and part of the ranch now contains the Banana Bank Lodge. Although the place has electricity and a phone, it retains the ambience of the tropical ranch it was. Rooms and cabañas are fanciful and no two are alike. The food is great, served family style. Five cabañas each sleep up to six people, and five more rooms in the main house accommodate guests, three with shared bathroom; one room is furnished with a water bed and has a private bath. Breakfast included in the room rate. Lunch is US$10, dinner US$15.

Half of the 4,000-acre ranch is covered in jungle, and within its borders guests will discover not only a wide variety of wildlife but a respectably sized Maya ruin. Scattered around the property are many more small archaeological "house mounds." The ranch's lagoon, hand-dug centuries ago, today harbors several Morelet's crocodiles and a bevy of frogs, happily croaking away.

With more than 20 saddle horses, Banana Bank Ranch features horseback riding. However, visitors can also bird-watch, fish, hike, or take a boating trip down the Belize River with plenty of time left for a cooling swim. A lazy ride via horse-drawn buggy into the surrounding countryside is another treat, as is nighttime stargazing with an eight-inch telescope.

An unusual sidelight is a small menagerie that includes a resident jaguar as well as spider and howler monkeys; most of the animals were given to the Carrs to care for. (Some were orphaned and others were pets who had outworn their welcome and could not live on their own in the wild.)

You'll find Banana Bank Ranch at Mile 47 on the right. Follow the signs; from the highway it's 1.25 miles on an all-weather road through fields and low jungle to the river. Park your vehicle to the right under the trees and amble down to the dock. Someone will pull a boat along the rope stretched from bank to bank to fetch you shortly. If you miss the first turnoff road, there's another past Roaring Creek Village at Mile 56, on the right. The sign says to take the road to the ferry, cross the river, and proceed to the ranch—a total of four miles.

For information and reservations, contact P.O. Box 48, Belmopan, Cayo District, Belize, C.A., tel. 8/12020, website www.bananabank.com. From the United States, book rooms through Great Trips, tel. 800/552-3419, fax 507/364-7713. Transfers are available from the hotel to the air-

PATTI LANGE

caves near Jaguar's Paw

port. There are many choices of rooms for different prices, averaging US$89, including breakfast.

Hector Silva Airport
Back on the Western Highway, you'll pass Hector Silva Airport on the left with its grassy field. So far there are no scheduled flights, but charter trips are available on **Maya Island Air** or any of the other airlines flying commuters around the countryside.

At Mile 48 on the left you'll find the **Hummingbird Highway,** which leads toward Belmopan, Dangriga, and the sea. To the right is Guanacaste National Park.

GUANACASTE NATIONAL PARK

A mere 56 acres, Guanacaste National Park packs a lot within its small area. This gem of a park is sponsored by the **Belize Audubon Society, MacArthur Foundation, World Wildlife Fund,** and the government. It gets its name from the huge specimen of guanacaste or tubroos tree near the southwestern edge of the property. Ceiba, cohune palms, mammee apple, mahogany, quamwood, and other trees also populate the forest. Agouti, armadillo, coati, deer, iguana, jaguarundi, and kinkajou have all been observed

in the park, along with more than 100 species of birds. Among the rarer finds are resident blue-crowned motmots. Picnic tables, benches, restrooms, and trash cans have been added slowly to the site, mostly by Peace Corps volunteers.

If you're going to Guanacaste, pack a lunch, bring a swimsuit, and take some time out at this quiet spot where the Belize River and Roaring Creek meet—you'll need very little coaxing to cool off with a swim.

The park was originally the home of the former British city planner who was commissioned to relocate the capital to Belmopan after Hurricane Hattie heavily damaged Belize City in 1961. It's said that he chose the spot because of the proximity to the spectacular old guanacaste tree. The official decided almost immediately that the meadow should be set aside as a government reserve for future generations to enjoy. The huge tree, well over 100 years old, is more than 25 feet in diameter and host to more than 35 species of exotic flora, including orchids, bromeliads, ferns, philodendrons, and cacti, along with a large termite nest and myriad birds twittering and fluttering in the branches—a tree of life! When rivers were the main method of transport, travelers stopped here to spend the night under the protection of its wide-spreading branches. The only thing that saved the tree from loggers was its crooked trunk.

As you enter the park, walk across the grassy field; go left to get to the trail that brings you to the guanacaste. Beyond the tree, there's a looter's trench—someone long ago thought there was treasure buried here. The trench graphically demonstrates how a looter excavates and works a would-be treasure site (including Maya structures). Farther on, the path meets the shore of **Roaring Creek,** the westernmost boundary of the park. This is a wonderful and easy trail; you may or may not see another hiker, but you'll certainly see birds, delicate ferns, flowers, and long parades of wiwi ants—"cutters"—on the trail carrying their green mini-umbrellas (really pieces of leaves that they're carrying back to their nest).

Another option from the entrance to the park is to cross the meadow and veer to the right. Here you'll find the steps that lead down to the **Belize River.** Along the shore nature quietly continues its pattern of creation and subsistence. The *amate* fig grows profusely on the water's edge and provides an important part of the howler monkey's diet. In the center of this scheme is the tuba fish, which eats the figs that fall into the water, dispersing the seeds up and down the river—starting more *amate* fig trees. And so it goes—on and on. At dusk on a quiet evening, howler monkeys roar the news that they're having dinner—keep your distance, world! Park hours are 8 A.M.–4 P.M.

BELMOPAN

About 50 miles from Belize City, Belmopan has been the capital of the country since 1961. The small, unpretentiously planned city was built far away from the coast to be safe from floods after two hurricanes in 30 years rammed their way through the coastal region with amazing destruction. After Hurricane Hattie in 1961, when the relocation was ordained, the government expected large numbers of the population of Belize City to move along with the government center. It didn't happen, and today the population of Belmopan is only about 5,400. Industry stayed behind and so did the jobs—the masses are still in Belize City, which remains the cultural and industrial hub of the country. Some capital employees continue to

commute the 50 miles back and forth each day. However, Belmopan was designed for growth and continues to expand. You can see the tiny city very quickly, or bypass the town and know you've not missed much.

Located in the geographical center of the country, Belmopan seems more like a quiet suburb than the capital of the country. It's worth a visit just to amble around the market, listen to the several languages being spoken, and buy a *punta* rock cassette tape or some fresh produce. As for the government buildings, they aren't particularly attractive with their all-over gray look and vaguely Maya design. Built of concrete, they should be sturdy enough to withstand the next hurricane. Government employees are friendly, though, and senior members are remarkably accessible.

Until a museum is built, the archaeological treasures of the country are stored in rooms in the government buildings. The town does have a large complex of sporting fields that includes basketball, volleyball, and tennis courts, as well as lots of space for spur-of-the-moment gatherings.

ORIENTATION

From the Western Highway, it's just a couple of miles down the highway's smooth pavement to the turnoff to Belmopan. Two roads allow the traveler to see what's useful and interesting. **Constitution Drive** curves gently to the left as it enters town, passing a handy gas station on the right and crossing **Bliss Parade** a couple of streets farther. Constitution Drive and Bliss Parade is one of the two most significant intersections in Belmopan. If you turn right onto Bliss Parade, the **Belmopan Hotel** will be immediately on your right, the **bus station** and **market square** on your left. If you follow Bliss Parade to the right, it joins **Ring Road.** As the name implies, this multilane extension circumscribes a loop around the central town district, meeting Constitution Drive, creating the other important intersection—Constitution and Ring—north of town. As you continue on Ring Road, **Bull Frog Inn** sits on the east end of town along Ring Road. After you turn the corner and head back west toward Constitution Drive, an unnamed road to your right leads to

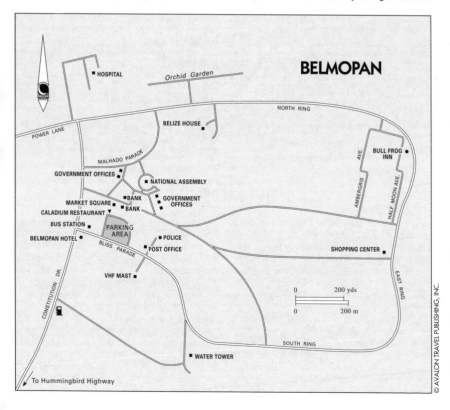

Moho Street and the budget **El Rey Inn.** Keep following the Ring Road and you will pass various government buildings and embassies on the left before you meet up with Constitution Drive again.

Once you're on the access road that runs west through the market and toward Constitution Drive, to your left will be the bus station. Past the station on the left is Bliss Parade. Ahead and to the right across the access road is the **Caladium Restaurant.** Closer and across a parking lot to the right are the two **banks.**

Market Square

This is where the action is for the locals, its lines of stalls alive with the commerce and gossip of the area. Hang out here for a little while and you are sure to see a parade of local farmers, government workers, and colorful characters going about business. Try a tasty tamale for next to nothing. Bananas, oranges, mangos, tomatoes, chiles, and carrots are cheap, too, and there's even some produce you won't recognize, such as wild cilantro, which is just as tangy as the cultured herb back home.

Department of Archaeology

At one time it was possible to visit the vaults of the Department of Archaeology in the capital. Here the government is preserving finds from Belize's Maya sites. However, the department has changed the rules and it no longer allows tourist visits. According to one archaeology commissioner, "Tourists on occasion became irate when they were denied access to the vault." There are plans for a new museum, and the Museum Building Fund is growing. According to the directors, the new museum is on the horizon. Right now, visitors and Mayaphiles must be satisfied with visiting the great structures scattered about the country and some of the caves where the Maya carried on ceremonies; many still have remnants of Maya occupation. Keep asking about the museum. It is truly needed, with valuable traces of the last 1,000 years all crammed into a small vault.

Anyone interested in helping out financially should contact the **Association for Belizean Archaeology,** Belmopan, Belize, C.A. For more information, call 8/22106.

ACCOMMODATIONS

Long a favorite of Belmopan visitors, the **Bull Frog Inn,** 25 Half Moon Ave., Belize, C.A., tel. 8/22111, fax 8/23155, email bullfrog@btl.net, sits in a quiet residential neighborhood with convenient access from Ring Road. With the clean modern lines of a prosperous motel chain, the inn has a/c and fans, private baths, cable TV, and lush tropical gardens. About US$50–65. The on-site restaurant serves good food.

Convenient to market square, government buildings, and the bus station, the contemporary **Belmopan Hotel,** P.O. Box 237, Belmopan, Cayo District, Belize, C.A., tel. 8/22130, email gsosa@btl.net, encourages groups to hold meetings and conventions here. It offers meeting rooms, swimming pool and poolside bar, restaurant, group facilities, and a communications center. However, it's still an intimate place for the independent traveler. The 20 comfortable but worn rooms have a/c, fans, and cable TV. Some of the carpeting is a bit long in the tooth and the interior decorating is a little confused at times, but the people are friendly and eager to please. Ask for one of the rooms with a refrigerator. Grilled lobster, seafood, surf and turf, and T-bone steak head the menu here. The restaurant, tel. 8/22130, serves three meals daily. The hotel accepts traveler's checks, MasterCard, and Visa. US$50.

FOOD

The **Bull Frog's** indoor/outdoor restaurant and bar have a solid reputation among even the elite of Belmopan, and this is one of the most popular spots in town to dine. The fish fillet, chicken, and burgers are all good here, and moderately priced. The inn serves fresh orange, lime, and grapefruit juice. The restaurant offers a breezy open-air design.

With economical daily specials listed on the chalkboard, the air-conditioned, family-run **Caladium Restaurant** is a convenient place to sip a milkshake or a beer, or to linger over a lunch of local Belizean fare as you plan your next excursion. As a rule Belizean beef can't stand up to the quality of its pork. Here, however, the sirloin steak smothered in onions, bell peppers, and a rich gravy is excellent. The prices are right, the waitresses couldn't be friendlier, and the service was quick when we were there. Look for the Caladium, tel. 8/22754, across the access road from the bus terminal, on market square.

GETTING THERE

If driving, Belmopan is located off Hummingbird Highway, just south of the Western Highway and Guanacaste National Park.

There's really little reason to fly into Belmopan, but if that's your choice, only charter flights are available into **Hector Silva Airport.** Most hotels in Cayo can arrange for pickup. Buses are much cheaper; take your choice of **Novelo, Z-Line,** and **Batty** buses. All buses from Belize City to San Ignacio and Dangriga stop in Belmopan at the Novelo bus station in market square.

SOUTH OF BELMOPAN

ALONG HUMMINGBIRD HIGHWAY

Anyone who has not driven the Hummingbird Highway for a few years will be surprised! It is paved and boasts some of the best road in Belize. The highway passes through towering hills and lush jungle as you cross the Caves Branch Bridge and enter the Valley of Caves. As the names suggest, nearby you'll find the many caverns of Caves Branch Estate, Blue Hole National Park, and St. Herman's Cave. After another 20 miles under your wheels, you climb into the Maya Mountains, pass the access road to Five Blues Lake National Park, experience the high pass known as **Over the Top,** and then descend toward the sea. The junction with the Southern Highway is 20 miles farther—Dangriga is 25. (For more information on Dangriga, see the Stann Creek District chapter.)

Maya Mountains

The high forested hills and green valleys of the northern end of the Maya Mountains provide beautiful scenery along much of the Hummingbird Highway. Sibun Valley is the most impressive of these. You'll see citrus orchards heavy with fruit, sleepy villages perched on the banks of rocky streams, craggy cliffs and gorges crusted with deep green beards of heavy jungle, and tracts of thick cohune forest. All will beckon you to stop, to explore, to linger a bit longer.

Blue Hole National Park and St. Herman's Cave

At about Mile 12.5 past Belmopan is a sign for St.

Herman's Cave; ignore it and continue to the main entrance about a mile down the road. You'll find a parking area and a cabaña for those wishing to change for a dip in the deep blue waters of the Blue Hole. Covering 575 acres, Blue Hole National Park encompasses this water-filled sink, St. Herman's Cave, and the surrounding jungle. (Belize's other Blue Hole lies in the ocean at Lighthouse Reef.) Rich in wildlife, Blue Hole National Park harbors the jaguar, ocelot, tapir, peccary, tamandua, boa constrictor, fer-de-lance, toucan, crested guan, blue-crowned motmot, and red-legged honeycreeper.

The pool of the **Blue Hole** is an oblong collapsed karst sinkhole 300 feet across in some places and about 100 feet deep. Water destined for the nearby Sibun River surfaces briefly here only to disappear once more beneath the ground. Steps lead down to the swimming area, a pool only 25 feet deep or so.

St. Herman's Cave is not as convenient to find. As you face the Blue Hole, the trail to St Herman's Cave lies to the right and requires a hike of a little more than a mile and a half over rugged ground that rises and falls. The trail begins by the changing cabaña. A flashlight and rugged shoes are necessities, and a light windbreaker or sweater is a wise choice for extended stays if you visit in the winter season. The nearest of the three entrances to the cave is a huge sinkhole measuring nearly 200 feet across, funneling down to about 65 feet at the cave's lip. Concrete steps laid over the Maya originals aid explorers who wish to descend. The cave doesn't offer the advanced spelunker a real challenge, but neophytes will safely explore it to a distance of about a mile. Pottery, spears, and the remains of torches have been found in many caves in the area. The pottery was used to collect the clear water of cave drippings, called *Zuh uy Ha* by the Maya.

The entire area is a labyrinth of caves where the ancient Maya once lived and roamed; some of the chambers still show signs of rituals long past. A variety of caves lie in the hilly limestone nearby and include **Mountain Cow** and **Petroglyph Caves.** The caves include cathedral-like ceilings hundreds of feet high as well as narrow cramped passageways. Some have crystal-coated stalactites and stalagmites; others have underground streams that seem to speak at times in murmured voices. And while you won't likely find any Maya living in the caves, you will find a number of harmless bats. Expect plenty of human company at these sites on weekends too; during the week you'll usually have the place to yourself. Remember: Bring a flashlight, extra batteries, and sturdy walking shoes. The surrounding lush jungle is thick with tropical plants, delicate ferns, bromeliads, and orchids.

It's best to visit most caves with a guide, and at the least, don't visit the park unless the wardens are there. Make sure you lock your car and don't leave valuables in view.

entering a wet cave

ADVENTURE TRIPS AND JUNGLE ACCOMMODATIONS

Ian Anderson's Caves Branch
Adventure Company and Jungle Lodge
Continue on Hummingbird Highway to Mile 41.5. About the time you see the sign for St. Herman's Cave (Mile 12.5), you should see another sign to Ian Anderson's place. Turn left and follow the dirt track about a mile into the jungle before you see signs of habitation to the left. Rounding a bend you'll drive directly to the lodge and up to the main building. Behind and to the left is the open-sided dining area. The main building has electricity, but accommodation lighting is by the glow of kerosene lamps—and yes, flush toilets and hot and cold water are available throughout. The lodge is surrounded by the jungle with all of its exotic critters and flying creatures, including 165 bird species, and hundreds of brightly-colored butterflies.

Visitors have a choice of camp sites, bunkhouse, jungle cabañas, and cabaña suites. All visitors come together in the open-sided dining room for meals, which are served family-style. Breakfast US$12 pp, lunch US$12 pp, dinner US$17 pp.

Camp sites (US$5 pp) are on the upper bank of the Caves Branch River, which is perfect for swimming, bathing, viewing sunsets, and listening to hundreds of birds. Bring your own tent to sites with outdoor flush toilets and leaf-shrouded showers. No fires allowed—whether for cooking or anything else.

The **bunkhouse** (US$15 pp) is a fine-screened thatched coed dormitory with eight bunk beds, linen provided. The washroom is located outside the Bunkhouse with modern toilet facilities and warm water and leaf-shrouded showers. This is a great gathering place for budget travelers.

Jungle cabañas (US$58), consist of six units on the rustic side, but comfortable. Washroom facilities located outside the cabañas with the same modern facilities as above. Double and twin beds are available.

Cabaña suites are four units (US$97) that offer comfort with a king bed, living room with pullout bed, and complete indoor bathroom with hot and cold showers. Units are fully screened and snug from flying critters, but open to the wonderful sounds of the outdoors. Though these are open-sided affairs, you feel a sense of coziness in the lantern's light before drifting off to sleep. Taxes are included in all prices given.

For more information, contact Ian Anderson's Caves Branch Adventure Co. and Jungle Lodge., P.O. Box 356, Belmopan, Belize, C.A., tel./fax 8/22800, email cavesbranch@pobox.com.

Below a steep embankment, the Caves Branch River swirls over sand and gravel. It is handy for swimming and bathing, depending on your modesty level. Several spots are perfect for Tarzanlike dives into the refreshing waters below—if only there were a sturdy vine! The lodge is all under a 100-foot jungle canopy. If you have a chance to talk to owner Ian Anderson, he makes it clear that this is not a resort or a sight-seeing camp. This is a hub for adventure seekers. He has very specific requirements for hiking clothes, shoes, and fitness levels. As he said a few years ago, "We're certainly not for everyone—thank God!!"

Adventure is the draw here and Ian delivers with an array of choices for adventurous spirits; jungle treks both day and night offer glimpses at elusive creatures. Don't be surprised to see coati, kinkajou, boa constrictors, fer-de-lance, paca, and more. You'll even find a Maya ruin nearby to explore.

This area is not called Caves Branch for nothing. On the 58,000 acres of the estate are 68 known caves, and Ian has discovered and explored them all as well as developed a variety of trips around many of these. The longest and deepest of these Maya ceremonial caves extends seven miles. Ian offers tubing trips through river caves where at times the murmur of the water takes on the sound of human voices. Pristine dry caves glisten with crystal formations. Some caves still have pottery shards, skeletal remains, and footprints coated with an icing of rock crystals. Ian offers one- to seven-day expeditions. Ask about his "BAD ASS" expedition in search of the Maya mystic domain, known as Xibalba.

All expedition guides have received intensive training in "cave and wilderness rescue/evacuation and first aid."

WEST OF BELMOPAN

On the highway, anticipate lots of big trucks, slow-moving traffic, and pedestrians.

Tapir Mountain Nature Reserve
Covering 6,741 acres, Tapir Mountain is one of the newest jewels in the country's crown of natural treasures. The deep, steamy jungle is ripe with an abundance of plant life. Every wild thing native to the region roams its forests, from toucans to tapirs, coatis to kinkajous. To the southwest lie the towering cliffs of the Mountain Pine Ridge, the lush valley called the **Vega** in **Slate Creek Preserve,** and the vast forest lands of the **Chiquibul Forest Reserve.** For access to these areas, contact the Belize Audubon Society, P.O. Box 1001, Belize City, Belize, C.A., tel. 2/35004 or 34987, fax 2/34985 or 78562.

ACCOMMODATIONS AND FOOD

US$50–100
For yet another taste of the Cayo, stay at **Warrie Head Creek Lodge,** P.O. Box 244, Belize City, Belize, C.A., tel. 2/77257, fax 2/75213; in the United States, call International Expeditions, 800/633-4734. Walking into this ranch house is reminscent of visiting grandmother's house— comfortable, touchable, and user-friendly. Upstairs in the ranch house a TV room is full of videos on the natural history of the area; another room has a big wooden table, perfect for a Yahtzee game with new friends. Rooms are decorated with antique Belizean colonial furniture, comfortable patterned bedspreads, and extra touches of pretty lamps and pictures that feel

PATTI LANGE

Pook's Hill Resort

more like home bedrooms than hotel rooms. Rates are US$70.

The lodge is close to the main highway (and the treasures of San Ignacio and the surrounding areas), yet far enough away that you forget about the outside world. A stroll down a grassy hillside brings you to bubbling cascades and waterfalls where the Belize River and Warrie Head Creek meet, a walking trail, and a spring-fed pool that's perfect for swimming. This is a bit of paradise with orchid trails, 189 species of birds, and 40 varieties of fruit trees.

Ten comfortable rooms are fan-cooled, and have h/c water, showers, and an honor system self-service bar. Miss Lydia runs the dining room and serves delicious food with a smile. Owners Bia and Johnny Searle offer river trips, excursions to the popular sights in the country, and horseback riding. If you have the chance, take the time to talk to Bia. She was born and raised in Belize and can tell you about Belize past and Belize today. She has wonderful stories about growing up with a Creole nanny who became her surrogate mother and grandmother to her children for many years before her death.

Caesar's Place, P.O. Box 48, Belmopan, Belize, C.A., tel. 9/22341, fax 9/23449, is a hotel/gift shop/restaurant/bar of some renown at Mile 60, about 10 miles from San Ignacio. Caesar Sherrard rents a number of clean garden rooms. Each has a private bath, h/c water, tile

floors, and ceiling fans for US$50. Camping is available for US$5 per person; full RV hookups can be negotiated too. For simple cabañas in beautiful jungle river surroundings, ask about **Black Rock.**

This is also a lovely spot to sit in the shade under the vines and trees and have a glass of wine or a meal. The food is a mix of Belizean and Mexican. Breakfast and lunch cost about US$7, dinner about US$14. On weekends there's live entertainment, and travelers who are *talented* musicians can get free room and board for jamming with the house band.

Have a look around the grounds planted with a variety of tropical greenery. Or wander through the gift shop noted for its massive selection of handmade Belizean crafts and other Central American wares. You'll spot some fine woodwork, especially an unusual folding hardwood chair that many visitors have shipped home, plus carved slate and wood, jewelry, clothing, and a variety of other crafts.

US$100–150

For an alluring, rustic lodge located in a 300-acre jungle reserve adjacent to Tapir Mountain Reserve, stay at **Pook's Hill Lodge,** P.O. Box 14, Belmopan, Belize, C.A., tel. 8/12017, email pookshill@btl.net. By day, explore the trails on horseback or look for the many species of birds that call this area home while walking in the footprints of cats—big cats. Feel the warmth

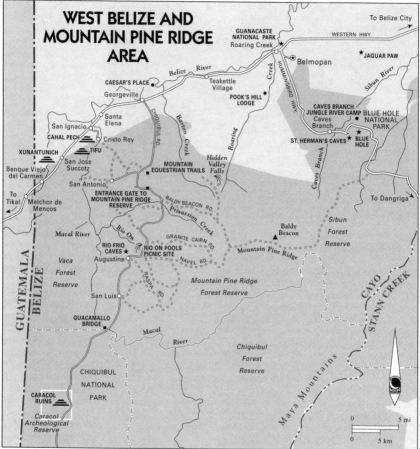

WEST BELIZE AND
MOUNTAIN PINE RIDGE
AREA

To Belize City

GUANACASTE
NATIONAL PARK
Roaring Creek

WESTERN HWY.

★ JAGUAR PAW

Belize River
Teakettle
Village

Belmopan

Creek

CAESAR'S PLACE
Georgeville

POOK'S HILL
LODGE

HUMMINGBIRD HWY.

Sibun River

Santa
Elena

San Ignacio

CHIQUIBUL RD.

CAVES BRANCH
JUNGLE RIVER CAMP
Caves
Branch

BLUE HOLE
NATIONAL
PARK

CAHAL PECH

Cristo Rey

Barton Creek

Roaring

ST. HERMAN'S CAVES ★ BLUE
HOLE

XUNANTUNICH
TIFU

Benque Viejo
del Carmen

San Jose
Succotz

MOUNTAIN
EQUESTRIAN TRAILS

Hidden
Valley
Falls

San Antonio

Caves Branch

To Dangriga

To
Tikal

Melchor de
Mencos

ENTRANCE GATE TO
MOUNTAIN PINE RIDGE
RESERVE

BALDY BEACON RD.

Privassion Creek

Baldy
Beacon

Sibun
Forest
Reserve

GUATEMALA
BELIZE

Macal River

Rio On

GRANITE CAIRN RD.

Mountain Pine Ridge

RIO FRIO
CAVES ★
Augustine

RIO ON POOLS
PICNIC SITE

NAVEL RD.

Vaca
Forest
Reserve

RASTA RD.

Mountain Pine Ridge
Forest Reserve

San Luis

GUACAMALLO
BRIDGE

Macal

River

Chiquibul
Forest
Reserve

CAYO

STANN CREEK

CHIQUIBUL
NATIONAL
PARK

CARACOL
RUINS

Caracol
Archeological
Reserve

Maya Mountains

0   5 mi

0   5 km

© AVALON TRAVEL PUBLISHING, INC.

of the sun at the swim hole or look for wildlife while floating downriver on an inner tube. At night, experience the stillness of this nirvana; watch fireflies illuminate the darkness. If there is a full moon, you'll never want to leave. US$118, 30 percent less from May–October, children under 12 sharing a room with parent, free. Meals are breakfast US$6, lunch US$9, dinner US$16.

The lounge/bar area overlooks a grassy knoll that gently slopes toward the creek. This is the social center of the lodge. The lodge is owned by Ray and Vicki Snaddon—hospitable, attentive

people who are more than happy to make your stay pleasant and memorable. Gather in the lounge/bar after the day's activities and tell tales with these kind folk. If they can, and you are receptive, they will sit and visit at mealtime, recanting their efforts and experiences building the lodge and the lifestyle they now live. Be sure to take advantage of one of the many natural history books in the bookcase.

All eight cottages have private baths with h/c water and palm-thatched roofs (and the occasional scorpion). Some have electricity (all will eventually have it) and others are lit by kerosene lamps. Guatamalan fabrics decorate the comfortable, simple, circular walls and double beds. For families, two rooms are side by side and share a bath. The dining room is downstairs from the lounge, and good, filling meals are served family style. They accommodate vegetarian or other preferences when given advance notice.

To get there, look for the sign to the lodge at Teakettle Village (around Mile 52.5), turn left onto the road, and follow the signs that lead the way. After four miles turn right and the property begins less than a mile down the road. Another three-quarters of a mile will take you to the lodge. Transfers are available from the international airport to Teakettle Village.

GEORGEVILLE TO MOUNTAIN PINE RIDGE

Georgeville is not much more than a bump in the road at Mile 63. For the traveler it has no real attraction, other than that it is across the road from an abundance of small lodging signs where one turns left onto the Pine Ridge Road (also known as Chiquibul Forest Road). Down this long, curving, bumpy road lie the treasures of the Mountain Pine Ridge. For some travelers to Belize, this area is the highlight of the trip. The road winds through the tropical foothills past orange and cattle farms before the terrain begins to gradually change to sand, rocky soil, then red clay, and tall pine trees. Soon the road rises and you are surrounded by tall pines, rushing streams, small and large waterfalls, and patches of thick forest with the echoing calls of the *chachalaca* and *tinamou*. Creases of land within narrow river valleys are rich with stands of tall hardwood trees, many covered with orchids and bromeliads. At certain times of the year bright-colored clouds of flamboyant butterflies float from tree to bush. Here and there small clearings have been carved out of the jungle by *milperos* (slash-and-burn farmers), and picturesque clusters of thatch huts surrounded by banana and cohune trees with delicate blossoms show Belizean life in the slow lane.

This is another "wily" road; some of it is fine, but the rest is rocky, uneven, and bumpy, and will shake even the sturdiest vehicle. Certain sections are impassable during the rainy season; check out conditions before you head up.

SIGHTS

While there is plenty of opportunity to relax in the piney woods, broadleaf jungle, or by rushing streams, Mountain Pine Ridge tends to draw energetic people. This is as true of those who

Rio On River cascades through the mountains.

manage its resorts as the guests themselves. For active people of all ages, the Mountain Pine Ridge offers bird-watching, caving, Maya ruins, horseback riding, jungle treks, mountain biking, opportunities for nature study, and swimming.

Slate Creek Preserve
Mountain Equestrian Trails and several other private landowners have set aside 3,000 acres as a private preserve. The purpose of the preserve is to protect the watershed, plants, and animals of a valley called the Vega. This limestone karst area teems with life. Mahogany, santa maria, ceiba, cedar, and cohune palms tower above. Orchids, ferns, and bromeliads are common. Birds such as the aracari, emerald toucanet, keel-billed toucan, keel-billed motmot, king vulture, and various parrots and hummingbirds are to be found here. Puma, ocelot, coati, paca, and anteater roam the forests.

Green Hills Butterfly Farm
Located at Mile 8 on Mountain Pine Ridge Road in Cayo District, this outstanding butterfly breeding, education, and interpretive center is run by Jan Meerman and Tineke Boomsma. Displays include all stages of the life cycle of a butterfly (egg-caterpillar-pupa-butterfly), and visitors can watch them all. Between 25 and 30 different species are raised at the center, including the tiny glasswing, the banana owl—the largest butterfly in Belize—and of course the magnificent blue morpho.

Arrive early enough in the morning and watch a butterfly emerge from a pupa right before your eyes—a grand experience. Jan's newest guidebook on butterflies in Belize, *Lepidoptera of Belize,* should be available soon. Tineke, also involved in research, spends many hours each day feeding and caring for these wondrous miracles of life. Both Tineke and Meerman have spent years studying butterflies, nourishing the plants they eat, and watching the interaction of different species of butterflies. Tours of the center take about an hour and give you a chance to see and learn about these beautiful fluttering creatures. The tour through the flight rooms (2,700 sq. feet), brings you up close to hundreds of flitting butterflies of all colors. Open daily 8 A.M.–5 P.M. Last tour begins at 4:00 P.M. Entrance fee for guided tour, US$4 pp, mini-

mum of two people. Group rates available. For more information call or fax 91/2017 or email meerman@btl.net.

Hidden Valley Falls
Mountain Pine Ridge Forest Reserve covers almost 300 square miles, and only controlled logging is allowed. Follow the reserve's main road for about two miles beyond the entrance and you'll come to the turnoff for Hidden Valley Falls. From the turnoff, the road keeps going down for about four miles and brings you to the falls and a picnic area. These spectacular falls plunge about 1,000 feet over the granite edge down to the jungle. It's a moderately difficult hike to climb the rocks to the falls.

Rio On Pools
Continuing south toward Augustine village you will cross the Rio On. It's well worth the climb over an assortment of worn boulders and rocks to a delightful site with waterfalls and several warm-water pools; don't forget your camera. There's a parking area just off the road.

Rio Frio Cave
Back on the highway, turn right at **Douglas De Silva** (the western division of the Forestry Department) and continue for about five miles. Follow the signs to the parking lot. From here visitors have a choice of exploring nature trails (note the purple ground orchids growing along the paths) and two small caves on the road or continuing to the largest and most well-known river cave in Belize, the Rio Frio, with an enormous arched entryway into the half-mile-long cave. Filtered light highlights ferns, mosses, stalactites, and geometric patterns of striations on rocks. Each step stirs up the musty smells of the damp rocky cave. Watch where you walk; sinkholes are scattered here and there, and a narrow stream flows along the gravel riverbed.

Caracol Archaeological Site
This is the Maya city state that toppled Tikal. Located in a nationally declared archaeological preserve, within the **Chiquibul Forest Reserve,** this site offers a wealth of natural wonders as well as the fabled Maya ruins. (For more details, see the Mundo Maya chapter.)

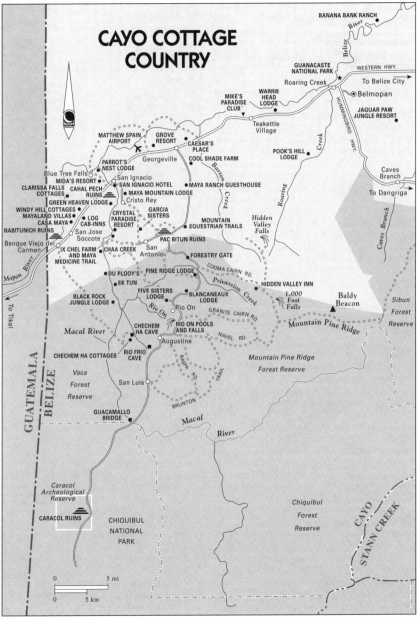

CAYO COTTAGE COUNTRY

BANANA BANK RANCH

Belize River

GUANACASTE NATIONAL PARK

WESTERN HWY.

Roaring Creek

To Belize City

Belmopan

MIKE'S PARADISE CLUB

WARRIE HEAD LODGE

JAGUAR PAW JUNGLE RESORT

Teakettle Village

MATTHEW SPAIN AIRPORT

GROVE RESORT

CAESAR'S PLACE

COOL SHADE FARM

Georgeville

POOK'S HILL LODGE

Caves Branch

To Dangriga

PARROT'S NEST LODGE

Blue Tree Falls

MIDA'S RESORT

San Ignacio

SAN IGNACIO HOTEL

MAYA RANCH GUESTHOUSE

CLARISSA FALLS COTTAGES

CAHAL PECH RUINS

MAYA MOUNTAIN LODGE

GREEN HEAVEN LODGE

Cristo Rey

WINDY HILL COTTAGES

GARCIA SISTERS

Caves Branch

MAYALAND VILLAS

CRYSTAL PARADISE RESORT

CASA MAYA

LOG CAB-INNS

MOUNTAIN EQUESTRIAN TRAILS

Hidden Valley Falls

NABITUNICH RUINS

San Jose Soccote

Benque Viejo del Carmen

PAC BITUN RUINS

IX CHEL FARM AND MAYA MEDICINE TRAIL

CHAA CREEK

San Antonio

FORESTRY GATE

Mopan River

DU PLOOY'S

PINE RIDGE LODGE

COOMA CAIRN RD.

To Tikal

EK TUN

FIVE SISTERS LODGE

BLANCANEAUX LODGE

Privassion Creek

HIDDEN VALLEY INN

1,000 Foot Falls

Baldy Beacon

Sibun Forest Reserve

BLACK ROCK JUNGLE LODGE

Rio On

Rio On

GRANITE CAIRN RD.

Mountain Pine Ridge

Macal River

CHECHEM HA CAVE

RIO ON POOLS AND FALLS

NAVEL RD.

CHECHEM HA COTTAGES

RIO FRIO CAVE

Augustine

Mountain Pine Ridge Forest Reserve

RASPA RD.

Vaca Forest Reserve

San Luis

BRUNTON RD.

GUACAMALLO BRIDGE

Macal River

GUATEMALA

BELIZE

Caracol Archeological Reserve

Chiquibul Forest Reserve

CAYO

STANN CREEK

CARACOL RUINS

CHIQUIBUL NATIONAL PARK

0   5 mi

0   5 km

ACCOMMODATIONS

Travelers will find only a handful of places to stay near Mountain Pine Ridge. But, within that limited number is great variety. Visitors have a choice of a working citrus farm, a couple of ranch/equestrian resorts, or resorts with miles of hiking trails and panoramic vistas of the river gorges and their roaring waterfalls. Cabañas on piney hillsides offer caving hikes nearby. Two resorts sit on the banks of Privassion Creek, one a luxurious resort owned by Hollywood director Francis Ford Coppola and the other a more modest lodge owned by local Belizeans.

Those interested in camping must get permission from the forest guard at the entrance of Douglas De Silva Reserve (formerly called Augustine); camping is permitted both at the entrance to the reserve and at Augustine village, about 10 miles south. Neither spot is particularly scenic. But traveling the circular route will take you past beautiful scenery and to the falls and the caves.

Five Sisters Lodge

The **Five Sisters Lodge** tel. 91/2005, email fivesislo@btl.net, U.S. tel. 800/447-2931, is owned by local Carlos Popper and is poised above Privassion Creek. Prices vary depending on time of year, type of room, shared bath or not; a standard room is US$105, includes continental breakfast, bathroom, and warm water. Restaurant prices are US$6 breakfast and lunch, US$17.50 dinner, and packages for longer stays are offered. All perched on the top of the steep canyon, accommodations range from simple boxy rooms to beautifully thatched cabañas overlooking the river; 14 units in all. The honeymoon suite has brightly colored bedspreads, mosquito netting, and complete privacy—even when sitting on the screened balcony, nothing mars the view of the beauty of the mountains and river.

The dining room serves Belizean and Mexican dishes. Hardwood furniture and colorful paintings decorate the inside; a small deck with wooden chairs and tables beckons you to come outside. A piano in the bar area invites fingers (anyone's) to dance on its keys.

Even if you don't stay here, come by, have a beer on the outdoor deck, and enjoy the com-

PATTI LANGE

Five Sisters Lodge

manding view above the river. The hearty can walk the 300 steps down to the river and quench their thirst at the small island bar. If you have a few too many down there, not to worry—the funicular allows even the laziest an opportunity to enjoy the natural wonders of Five Sisters, the five small waterfalls and namesake for this lodge—at least between 8 A.M. and 4 P.M.

Blancaneaux Lodge

This is the place for people who *do* want to be pampered! Choices of rooms include riverfront cabañas, garden view cabañas, villas, and a honeymoon suite. Prices are just as spread out. However, you can get a riverfront cabaña for US$150, including continental breakfast, plus taxes. Blancaneaux is a director's fantasy on a bluff overlooking the rocks and falls of Privassion Creek. Here Francis Ford Coppola has created an exotic little hideaway for those who want a softer, more exclusive, experience in Belize. He built his own hydroelectric dam to provide 24-

hour electricity, planted gardens to grow fresh vegetables, put in an espresso machine, and a coffee roaster, and, he says his is the only wood-burning pizza oven in the country. Possible? Could be.

Accommodations range from lodge rooms with shared bath to cabañas made of native hardwoods to villas to the spacious Coppola family villa. The cabañas and two-bedroom suites overlook the Privassion Creek and are decorated with colorful Guatamalan fabrics and locally made furniture. They also have panoramic screened decks in back. In fact, the deck with its flamboyant view is the focus of each cabaña; it can be screened off from the rest of the room at night. A few luxurious villas include kitchens, but who wants to cook here when the lodge has a gourmet chef? The dining room offers delicious pastas (a *lot* of pastas) and other Italian foods with a selection of wines from Coppola's Napa Valley vineyards Niebaum-Coppala—smooth, but costly. If you like exotic drinks, try the one they call Jaguar Juice. The staff is friendly and hardworking and comes from a variety of ethnic backgrounds. The staff even includes a licensed massage therapist; the word from guests is that he really gets the kinks out. Got that screenplay to finish? Computer hookups, fax, and other modern communications are available.

Look for the sign for Blancaneaux Lodge, Box B, Central Farm, Cayo District, Belize, C.A., tel. 9/23878, fax 9/23919, at about Mile 14.5 and turn right. The **Blancaneaux Airstrip** will appear on the right. Turn left at the splashy gate and head down to the end of the drive; don't be put off by the stockade fence to the right. You'll notice a grassy courtyard (perfect they say for croquet) and fountain to one side, the lodge and planted gardens to the other, and the cabañas and villas below. The lodge of rustic wood and stone features a restaurant, bar, deck, fireplace, and two double rooms upstairs.

Mountain Equestrian Trails (MET)

Before the Bevis family took over and built the lovely cabañas, only the "horse people" thought of coming here. No more. This small resort now offers a relaxing alternative to a seaside vacation. To take advantage of the location—close to the Mountain Pine Ridge area, the mountains, Caracol, and the entire Cayo District—it helps to

have a car to get around. No matter that the small cantina is a 20-minute drive from San Ignacio, it still attracts visitors and locals from all around for drinks, dinner, and good conversation. **Chiclero Trails Campsite** offer safari-style tents located under the rainforest canopy, with beds, mattresses, linens, private covered deck, and close access to restrooms and showers, US$15 pp per night. Meals are served in an insulated tent in the camp.

Guests will find lovely, comfortable cabañas of thatch, stucco, and exotic wood interiors with private bathrooms and h/c water (no electricity—yet). Room rates are US$120–140. Meals are served in the cozy cantina/restaurant, which serves a variety of excellent food. Breakfast US$9, lunch US$10, dinner US18.

Horse people have a choice of gentle or spirited horses. Trips are designed to suit every taste, from mountain trails that wander past magnificent waterfalls and pools where everyone is lured for a swim, to pine forests that take in creeks, Maya caves, Caracol, exotic butterflies, and more than 150 species of orchids. The equestrian trails are only a few miles from **Rio Frio Caves** and **Hidden Valley Falls,** where the water drops into the jungle below. Programs are designed for both beginners and experienced riders—children at least age 10 with previous riding experience are welcome. Riding fees are extra. Riders are required to carry personal liability insurance to cover themselves while touring.

Set on a hill beside the Little Vaqueros Creek is **Pine Ridge Lodge,** P.O. Box 2079, Belize City, Belize, C.A., tel. 8/23180, U.S. tel. 800/316-0706, fax 216/781-1273 email PRLodge @mindspring.com. Rates are US$75, US$15 per extra person. The lodge is five miles inside the Mountain Pine Ridge Reserve (be prepared to stop at the gate) and a bit past Mile 14. Turn right at the sign.

Owners Vicki and Gary Seewald have extensively planted the grounds, and various epiphytes and orchids live on the pines. The lodge consists of six renovated cottages, each with a colorful Maya-inspired wall painting on the exterior. All six cottages have screen porches, lanterns, private bathrooms with cold-water showers (they are being upgraded to hot water), original Maya-style art, pottery, and Guatemalan textiles.

The open-air café serves good home cooking, fresh juices, and fruits, eggplant parmigiana, great vegetarian choices, and, as Gary (the owner) says, the best French toast in Belize. A large outdoor grill awaits barbecues, and two screened *palapas* nearby allow parties to eat together in semiprivacy, and of course there's a grand hammock-palapa. The Seewalds advertise the **Pine Ridge Tavern** as being the "last stop for a cold beer before heading off to Caracol." Ask for a river-view cottage; the calming sound of the stream is wonderful. Room rates include continental breakfast; lunch US$7, dinner US$17.50 per person. The lodge is only seven miles north of Rio On pools; ask about tours and transfers, especially a trip through.

Those looking for the solitude of long hikes through pines and jungle to waterfalls and pristine pools should take a look at the lovely **Hidden Valley Inn**, P.O. Box 170, Belmopan, Belize, C.A., tel. 8/23320, fax 8/23334, U.S. tel. 800/334-7942, email info@hiddenvalleyinn.com. It's always a surprise to find this upscale resort in the midst of tall sparse pine trees in the middle of nowhere. To get there, turn left at Mile 14 onto Cooma Cairn Road. Then just follow the signs. Ask about transfers from Belize City. On the left, set on 18,000 acres of private reserve, this is really a "get-away" vacation.

The main house is the gathering place for guests in several spacious public rooms: a comfortable lounge, card room, TV room, library filled with good reading material, and the dining room, where dinner is served in candlelit splendor. The 12 cottages have *saltillo* tile floors, vaulted ceilings, cypress-paneled walls, fireplaces, ceiling fans, screened louvered windows, comfy beds, and private baths with h/c water. When the main electricity goes out at night, 12-volt bedside lamps and night-lights are available. The room rate, US$103.50 pp, includes breakfast, dinner, hotel tax, and gratuities. Packages available. For those who enjoy hiking, well-tended trails on the property lead past **Tiger Creek Pools and Falls, King Vulture Falls** (where the king vulture nests), **Dragonfly Pool, Butterfly Falls** and **Crystal Pools, Lake Lollyfolly,** and the famous **Hidden Valley Falls** (also known as 1,000 Foot Falls). For birders, bird blinds are set up where you can glimpse such beauties as orange-breasted falcons, rose-breasted grosbeak, indigo bunting, and the ocellated turkey. Picnic lunches are provided.

At Mile 8 turn left at the MET sign and follow the road back to the left. Jim and Marguerite Bevis offer a wonderful change of pace and an opportunity to see areas of Belize that are without roads—this is especially interesting if you're an equestrian. For a brochure and more information, write to Mountain Equestrian Trails, Central Farm Post Office, Cayo District, Belize, C.A., or P.O. Box 180, Belmopan, Belize, C.A., tel. 8/23180 or 22149, fax 8/23361, email met@pobox.com.

GEORGEVILLE TO SAN IGNACIO

Mennonite Country

Follow the sign to **Spanish Lookout Village.** It's always a surprise in the tropics—the landscape suddenly changes from ragged forest covered with vines, creepers, and delicate ferns to neat barns and rolling green countryside. This is one of the Mennonite communities whose founders brought a small bit of Europe with them and, over the years, developed a fine agricultural industry that supplies a large part of the milk, cheese, and chicken for the country.

Santa Elena

The **Aguada Hotel,** P.O. Box 133, San Ignacio, Cayo District, Belize, C.A., tel. 9/23609, email aguada@btl.net, is a short distance from the stir of San Ignacio and offers a quiet night of sleep. The hotel has simple colorful rooms with hot water private baths, a pool, email, and laundry services. A restaurant serves breakfast, lunch, and dinner to their guests; no breakfast to nonguests. Good value here. US$25 for the rooms, add US$5 for a/c.

At the moment there's not much more for the average visitor in Santa Elena other than its proximity to its sister city across the Macal River. But give it time; things are changing all over.

SAN IGNACIO

San Ignacio is the largest city in western Belize and the district capital. This agricultural community is a peaceful, though busy, hub nestled in rolling hills with clusters of houses scattered on hillsides and valleys along with the remains of once-elegant Maya ceremonial centers. The Maya, the country's first farmers, also appreciated these rich valleys.

At one time a busy port, now the river is a placid part of both San Ignacio and Santa Elena. Here you'll see women doing their wash, kids splashing around to keep cool (and accomplishing a bath at the same time), and at least a few canoes cruising the quiet waters.

ORIENTATION

Hawksworth Bridge
The impressive Hawksworth Bridge links the highway between Santa Elena and San Ignacio. As the only suspension bridge in Belize, it's a high-tech dot on the landscape of the low-key Belize countryside. It even has one of the few traffic lights in the entire country. In the past, whoever reached the center of the one-lane bridge first had the right of way, and the other vehicle had to back off the bridge; occasionally the local gendarme had to come along and measure car distances to settle the drivers' arguments. But that's a thing of the past now with a neat line of traffic waiting patiently at the red light. Old-timers say the water rose as high as this bridge during Hurricane Hattie!

The police station is immediately to your left as you leave the Hawksworth Bridge. But the main action in town is to your right down Burns Avenue. This short strip about two blocks long is where the heart of the town pulses. Here you'll find Eva's Restaurant, several hotels in a row, banks, and stores to provide you most anything you need. It's as convenient a street as you will find in all Belize. But there's more to explore within a block or two east or west.

San Ignacio Information
The **Belize Tourist Board** has an office at the Cahal Pech ruins entrance, and the staff can give you general maps and information, but don't expect any nitty-gritty details. To get the real facts go to **Eva's Restaurant and Bar,** 22 Burns Ave., San Ignacio, Cayo District, C.A., tel. 9/22267, email evas@btl.net. The government should take a lesson; this is probably the best information center in the entire country. Some say the Cayo is its own little universe. If so, then

Hawksworth Bridge

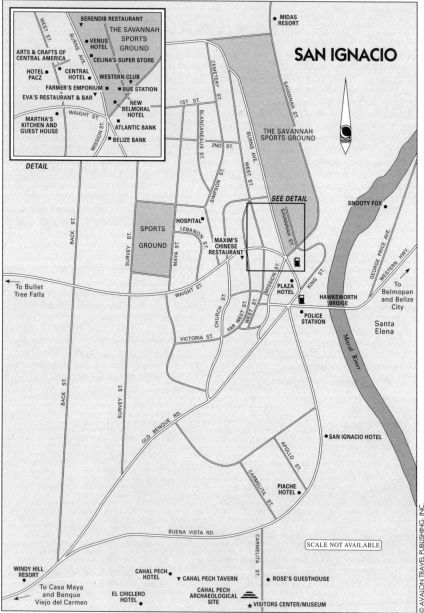

DETAIL (inset)

SERENDIB RESTAURANT

WEST ST.

BURNS AVE.

THE SAVANNAH SPORTS GROUND

VENUS HOTEL

ARTS & CRAFTS OF CENTRAL AMERICA

CELINA'S SUPER STORE

HOTEL PACZ

CENTRAL HOTEL

WESTERN CLUB

FARMER'S EMPORIUM

BUS STATION

EVA'S RESTAURANT & BAR

NEW BELMORAL HOTEL

WAIGHT ST.

MISSION ST.

MARTHA'S KITCHEN AND GUEST HOUSE

ATLANTIC BANK

BELIZE BANK

SAN IGNACIO (main map)

MIDAS RESORT

WEST ST.

CEMETERY ST.

SAVANNAH ST.

THE SAVANNAH SPORTS GROUND

MooN

SNOOTY FOX

1ST ST.

BLANCANEAUX ST.

2ND ST.

SIMPSON ST.

WEST ST.

BURNS AVE.

SAVANNAH ST.

SEE DETAIL

GEORGE PRICE AVE.

WESTERN HWY.

To Belmopan and Belize City

BACK ST.

SURVEY ST.

SPORTS GROUND

MAYA ST.

HOSPITAL

LEBANON ST.

MAXIM'S CHINESE RESTAURANT

MISSION ST.

KING ST.

To Bullet Tree Falls

WAIGHT ST.

PLAZA HOTEL

HAWKSWORTH BRIDGE

Mopal River

Santa Elena

CHURCH ST.

FAR WEST ST.

WEST ST.

POLICE STATION

VICTORIA ST.

BACK ST.

SURVEY ST.

OLD BENQUE RD.

San Ignacio Hotel

APOLLO ST.

CARMELITA ST.

PIACHE HOTEL

BUENA VISTA RD.

CARMELITA ST.

SCALE NOT AVAILABLE

WINDY HILL RESORT

To Casa Maya and Benque Viejo del Carmen

CAHAL PECH HOTEL

CAHAL PECH TAVERN

ROSE'S GUESTHOUSE

EL CHICLERO HOTEL

CAHAL PECH ARCHAEOLOGICAL SITE

VISITORS CENTER/MUSEUM

Eva's Restaurant must be the center of that cosmos. Many travelers make Eva's their first stop in town, a gathering spot not only for knowledgeable wanderers but also for many people who run the cottages and activities in the area. Sit down long enough and all the information will come to you. But if you're anxious to taste Cayo's treasures, bulletin boards on the walls keep visitors up to date on all the activities offered in the area. The biggest asset is owner Bob Jones, a walking database of information for just about anything that's happening in San Ignacio and along the river.

So, if you need help finding a budget room (Eva's has pictures and rates of most of the budget resorts along the river), or a guide, or a tour operator, or information on almost anything in the area from nightlife to natural history, look for the information on the wall; if you can't find what you're looking for, ask for Bob. He's never impatient though he undoubtedly answers the same questions thousands of times each month.

Send or receive email here for US$2.50 for 15 minutes.

PATTI LANGE

Tineke Boomsma of Green Hills Butterfly Farm

SIGHTS

Cahal Pech Archaeological Site
Though they have been partially excavated and restored, the ruins of Cahal Pech ("Place of the Ticks") still have a covering of jungle around them. The site was discovered in the early 1950s, but scientific research did not begin until 1988, when a team from San Diego State University's Department of Anthropology began excavation. (For more information, see the Mundo Maya chapter.) Info and a pamphlet are available at the site. Admission is US$2.50. Nearby **Tipu** was an important Maya-Christian town during the early years of colonization. Tipu was as far as the Spanish were able to penetrate in the 16th century.

Chechem Ha Cave
Loaded with Mayan pottery, this ceremonial cave is near the farm of the same name owned by the Morales family. The government allows only guided tours and (of course) nothing can be removed from the cave. The pottery inside is estimated to be as old as 2,000 years. You can climb and explore various ledges and passageways, but the highlight is a deep ceremonial chamber in the heart of the hill. In some places, you need a rope to help you get around. While those of average physical abilities can enjoy Chechem Ha Cave, you should take care when moving amid the pottery; a clumsy patron some years ago seriously damaged one of the pots.

Though rewarding, the cave is not easy to reach. Take your choice—it's either a very long drive via Benque Viejo and the hydro dam road followed by a short walk, or a short drive to a parking spot down Chaa Creek Road and a long hike down the river and up the face of the Vaca Plateau. For more information, contact Eva's, tel. 9/22267.

Ix Chel Farm and the Maya Medicine Trail
About Mile 4.5 out of San Ignacio, a sign indicates the turnoff to the left for duPlooy's and Chaa Creek. Down this road you bear left at

the fork to go to Chaa Creek. Past the parking area and to the left is Ix Chel Guesthouse and Wellness Center. Here visitors are welcome to take part in a walking tour through the forest, where they will see examples of plants and trees that can cause damage (scratches, rashes, poison) and then, close by, the antidote. Rosita Arvigo and husband, Greg Shropshire, are both graduates of Chicago National College of Naprapathy. Those interested in holistic medicine will be fascinated with the Maya Medicine Trail, named for the late Maya bush doctor, Don Eligio Panti, former teacher and mentor of Rosita's. It's an especially fun trip if you combine it with a canoe ride up the placid Macal River to the docks at Ix Chel. Check in at the gift shop and enjoy the stroll along the shady, tree-lined trail. Expect to pay a small usage fee. Around the house, small garden plots produce fresh vegetables and a pineapple or two, and fruit trees are scattered about.

There are a few simple guest rooms avail-able here. Rooms have electricity, ceiling fans, and all share a hot water bathroom. Guests have free use of the medicine trail. A restaurant serves organic, healthy meals. US$60.

The small gift shop/entrance office has books on Rosita's experiences with Panti as well as her book, *Rainforest Remedies,* and natural medicines for various ailments. I will personally vouch for the effectiveness of Flu Away—ingredients include jackass bitters and cayenne pepper—needless to say, it tastes horrible but it works! And for those bug bites you have all over your legs? To quote a dear friend, the green pasty Jungle Salve "rules." Rub some of that on the bites and you will get instant relief. For more information about the herbs and roots, and details about the Maya Medicine Trail and Don Eligio Panti, who continued treating and teaching until he died at 103, contact Ix Chel Farm, San Ignacio, Cayo District, Belize, C.A., tel. 9/23870, email info@ixchelbelize.com.

Due mainly to the influence of Rosita Arvigo, the Belizean government established **Terra Nova Medicinal Plant Reserve,** referred to in 1993 as the world's first medicinal plant reserve. The 6,000 acres are administrated by the **Belizean Association of Traditional Healers,** dedicated to the preservation of what might be important scientific help in future treatments of illnesses, and inspired by a long history of successes by Maya medicine man Don Eligio Panti. Seedlings are brought here from threatened areas of the rainforest to live on.

ACTIVITIES

San Ignacio is a great base camp for almost any activity the Cayo and nearby Guatemala have to offer. Most hotels and resorts can arrange for any of them. However, when in doubt, drop in at Eva's Restaurant and check the bulletin boards.

Animal Observation and Bird-Watching
Looking for the furred and feathered inhabitants is especially productive in the Mountain Pine Ridge, the national parks and forest reserves, along the Macal and Mopan Rivers, and in the remote reaches of the Vaca Plateau. Lodges at Black Rock, Chaa Creek, Chechem Ha, Crystal

on the Medicine Trail

Paradise, duPlooy's, Ek Tun, Hidden Valley, Mountain Equestrian Trails (MET), and Pook's Hill all have large tracts of land where you'll likely find abundant wildlife and knowledgeable staff members. Most lodges can arrange for trips to productive areas with qualified guides who know the area well.

Nature Study

Many study groups come to Belize to learn about the rainforest, its wildlife, and ancient cultures. Workshops are held all over the countryside. If this kind of a vacation interests you, check with **Chaa Creek Cottages,** tel. 9/22037, fax 9/22501, where there's a local natural history museum and learning center. **Maya Mountain Lodge,** tel. 9/22164, fax 9/22029, gives regular classes in ecology and multiculturalism. **MET,** tel. 8/23180, fax 8/23361, a participant in Slate Creek Reserve, has a resident biologist and organized study in the reserve through its **Chiclero Trails Organization. International Expeditions,** a stellar U.S. tour operator (see "Tours Organized in the U.S." in the On the Road chapter), organizes archaeology and rainforest workshops in the area.

Exploring Archaeological Sites

With **Cahal Pech, Caracol, El Pilar,** and **Xunantunich** within easy driving distance of the town, exploration is a very popular activity among those visiting San Ignacio. Countless other mounds and ruins are scattered throughout the surrounding jungle. Ask at your lodging. Two independent guides who specialize in such trips are **Ramon Silva** (ask at Eva's) and **Herman Velasquez,** tel. 9/22467.

Hiking

The areas listed above also lend themselves well to extended hikes. Even the smaller resorts can accommodate the desires of the average tourist and can arrange for more-serious hikes.

Cycling

Biking the Cayo District is fun, beautiful, and a great way to burn off those Belikins. Routes abound—stick to the main highway (boring) or set off on small dirt roads around San Ignacio and Bullet Tree, or head up into the Mountain Pine Ridge area. Start early and bring lots of water. If you aren't used to the heat, plan short rides to see how your body adapts—if you are out in the middle of nowhere and need help, there's a good chance you'll be on your own. Bikes can be found at **Tropicool** in San Ignacio. Bikes with front suspension are for rent at **Chaa Creek;** bike tours are also available. Call for more info: tel. 9/22037, email chaacreek @btl.net.

Horseback Riding

The equestrian resorts offer good riding adventures. Those who like to saddle up should also check with **Guacamallo Treks,** part of Maya Ranch, tel. 1/49117, fax 9/23075. Another, **Easy Rider,** tel. 9/23310, is an independent operator who charges reasonable rates and gives good service. Or check with Paul, tel. 9/23907. He is highly recommended and has reasonable rates.

Caving

Numerous caves lie in the surrounding hills along Mountain Pine Ridge and Vaca Plateau. Check with **Mayawalk Adventures,** 19 Burns Ave., tel. 9/23070, email mayawalk@btl.net, **David's Tours** 9/23674, **MET,** tel. 8/23361; **William Morales** (ask at Eva's); **Jerone Tut,** tel. 9/22823; or **Gary Seewald,** tel. 9/23310.

Canoeing and Tubing

Canoeing and tubing are exhilarating ways to enjoy the Macal and Mopan Rivers. Most hotels and cottage resorts in Cayo District have canoes and tubes; **Tony's Guided Tours,** tel. 9/23292, is probably the most economical, independent trip on the river at US$12.50 per person. For the more adventurous, he also offers a five-day canoe/camp trip to Belize City. He provides everything except your personal effects.

Swimming

It's pretty easy to find a "swimming hole" in the San Ignacio area. Rivers, ponds, and creeks are abundant. Many hotels built along or above the river have small beaches along the water, and of course several hotels offer pools as well.

ACCOMMODATIONS AND FOOD DOWNTOWN

Choices abound for such a small town, many of them pretty cheap, although quality isn't always the highest. This isn't an area where you want to hang out in your room all day anyhow—there's too much to do!

Under US$25

You can't be more centrally located than this budget favorite, the **Central Hotel,** 24 Burns Ave., San Ignacio, Belize, C.A., tel. 9/22253. It's next door to Eva's and within walking distance from the bus station. The bath is shared and the rooms are small, but they're usually clean. There are almost always interesting folks in their 20s to 40s from Europe and the States here. About US$10. Cash or traveler's checks only.

Just a few doors up the street is the **Tropicool Hotel,** 30A Burns Ave., tel. 9/23052. It's simple and the shared bath only has cold water, but it is clean. Under US$25.

The **Hi-Et,** tel. 9/22828, is a basic hotel in the owner's large home, right across from Martha's (see below). With simple, shared baths and cold water, this is will fit into anyone's budget, about US$10. The people are nice too.

Another low-cost lodging is the **Venus Hotel,** 29 Burns Ave., San Ignacio, Belize, C.A., tel. 9/23203, fax 9/22225, email daniels@btl.net. Only if you really need a cheap stay, and first check out a few things: the deadly slippery waxed floors, the linens, (hopefully you won't have stains on the sheets from the night before), and especially note any exposed wiring in the shower. Rates: US$22, no a/c, and US$30 with a/c.

In the center of town on Far West Street, **Hotel Pacz,** tel. 9/22477, email pacz@btl.net, a small hostelry owned by Diana Zugrzycki, has five clean, simple rooms with h/c bath. Free tea or coffee is available in the morning. Rates: US$17.50. They also offer lots of exciting tours.

Just a couple of streets behind Burns and on the corner, you'll find **Martha's Kitchen and Guesthouse,** 10 West St., San Ignacio, Belize, C.A., tel. 9/23637. John and Martha have eight rooms that offer an atmosphere of privacy and conviviality in a homey setting. The rooms come with fans, hot water, and cable TV. Some share a bath US$21; rooms with private bath cost about US$28. Laundry services are available. Food is also available downstairs; breakfast is US$3.50 and a lunch or dinner—T-bone steak with rice, salad, and fried plantain is US$8. They can make tour arrangements here.

US$25–50

The **New Belmoral Hotel,** 17 Burns Ave., San Ignacio, Belize, C.A., tel. 9/22024, fax 9/23502, has jumped a level in class from its previous life. The hotel has a lobby on the second floor and comfortable wicker furniture for guests. Centrally located, and run by a warm, friendly family, the only drawback is its proximity to the bus station—some rooms are very noisy early in the morning. Ask for a front room. The large common balcony allows guests to check out the local scene from above and some of the back rooms have nice views of the surrounding hills. There are eleven rooms in all; management accepts traveler's checks and Visa/MC. US$28.

Food

Eva's Restaurant and Bar, 22 Burns Ave., tel. 9/22267, is not only the tourist and activity center, it's also the place for a good meal and a cold Beliken. Check out the beer garden outside. If you're going touring for the day, pick-up a boxed lunch here—a sandwich, chips, fruit, and a bottle of water—for US$4. Burgers, pork chops, and stewed chicken cost about US$4.50, French toast and coffee US$3, fruit salad US$4, and tasty fresh squeezed OJ is only US$1. Open for breakfast, lunch, and dinner.

Near the Venus Hotel you'll find the **Serendib Restaurant,** 27 Burns Ave., tel. 9/22302, a café owned by Sri Lankan Hantley Pieris. Along with good hamburgers and chow mein, he serves excellent curries. Reasonably priced, a broiled lobster dinner or San Ignacio Giant Steak will set you back only about US$12. A coffee shop serves continental breakfast for about US$3 and a full breakfast for about US$5. The Serendib accepts traveler's checks and Visa/MC.

Maxim's Chinese Restaurant, 23 Far West St., has a good reputation among the locals. It has numerous ceiling fans and a freezer in the main dining area. A family-run café, it serves mainly lunch and dinner. Prices are moderate; you won't pay much over US$10 for the best meal in the house and a beer.

Martha's Kitchen and Guesthouse also serves a variety of dishes including pizza, stir-fried vegetables (about US$6), T-bone steak served with gravy and fries, US$7.50, and a club sandwich, US$3.50. Ask about local dishes, including gibnut. **Hanna's Bar and Restaurant,** on Burns Avenue near Atlantic Bank, serves a mix of Indian and Belizean food in the US$4–10 range.

ACCOMMODATIONS JUST OUTSIDE OF TOWN

Camping

Cosmos, 15 Branch Mouth Road, San Ignacio, tel. 9/22116, is a 20-minute walk from town, just past Midas Resort, and has pretty grounds and mowed lawns for tents for US$3 per person. A few simple cabañas rent for US$3.75 per person. Hammock hanging also available. Follow the signs. Campers are also welcome at **Midas Resort,** tel. 9/23845, for US$7.

US$25–50

About a quarter-mile out of town at Branch Mouth Road, check out **Midas Resort,** a small family-run lodging. You'll find seven cottages with thatched roofs, situated on five acres along the banks of the Macal River (down a 300-yard path from the cottages). All cabins offer private bathrooms. No electricity is available yet, but oil lamps and hot water are provided. Campers are welcome. For more information and reservations, call 9/23845. A restaurant serves breakfast and lunch, and a small gift shop in the reception area has a few knickknacks. Credit cards OK.

EL Chiclero Camp Resort, near the Cahal Pech archaeological site, tel. 9/24119, offers five thatch-hut cabañas on shaded grounds interspersed with many plants and tall trees. The lodge has simple cabañas with handmade furniture. "Everything is from the bush" and offers the visitor insight into the chiclero camps of the old days. Chicle comes from the sapodilla tree and was the base for gum in the early Wrigley days. In the large screened dining room, a human-sized model wears the outfit typical of the loggers, and a few artifacts used in the cooking process of the chicle hang on the walls. Outside behind the restaurant is the "cooking" area where chicle was made. Breakfast, lunch, and dinner served for around US$5–8. Room rates are US$25.

Near the crest of Cahal Pech Hill are **Cahal Pech Cabins,** tel. 9/23380, a sprinkling of about a dozen cabañas. The views are panoramic and the breeze refreshing. The cabañas are built with an updated Maya theme using a blend of traditional and modern materials, all with colorful trim. Some cabañas have walls made of small palm trunks or bush stick. Each has a thatched roof with two double beds, h/c water, private bath, louvered windows, and veranda. Rates: US$35. One of the rooms has eight double beds for US$70. There is no restaurant here, only the Cahal Pech Tavern, one of the biggest bars in the country and one of THE places to party in the area, so count on some noise during the weekend.

US$50–75

The **Cahal Pech Village,** tel. 9/23740, fax 9/22225, offers a variety of rooms and cabins spread out on spacious grounds overlooking San Ignacio. All rooms are named after Belizean ruins, have private bath, and cable TV, and should have a/c by now. Junior suites and family rooms are available. A restaurant, bar, and gift shop round out the resort. Rates are about US$50.

The **Log Cab-Inns,** tel. 8/23367, fax 8/22289, is run by super-friendly people. They have nine mahogany cabins that indeed look like log cabins spread out on the property. The comfortable cabins have cement floors, two double beds, windows with curtains, and small private bathrooms with hot water. A large group can be accommodated in the three rooms that share a common veranda. The restaurant is a mix of wood—cedar, cabbage bark, ziricote, and mahogany. Breakfast is a filling meal of eggs, fry jacks, sausage, fruit, and all-you-can-drink fresh-squeezed OJ for US$6. Lunch and dinner will cost about US$6–10. Cabins are US$55; the three rooms that share a veranda are US$35 each when split up.

US$75–100

You could say the **San Ignacio Hotel,** P.O. Box 33, San Ignacio, Cayo District, Belize, C.A., tel. 9/22034 or 9/22125, fax 9/22134, email sanighot@btl.net, is a hotel fit for a queen; Queen Elizabeth *did* stay here on a visit to Belize in 1994. To try it for yourself, you'll have to take the first left (Buena Vista Road) after crossing the Hawksworth Bridge into town. Because of the one-way street just past the end of the bridge, you will have to circuit the little center triangle until you can cross over and take Buena Vista Road up the hill. The hotel is a hundred yards up on the left. The San Ignacio Hotel overlooks the Macal River and the hills of Cayo. Its 25 rooms are pleasant and roomy with private bathrooms and h/c water; the hotel also has a restaurant and bar, patio deck, swimming pool, ball court, disco, gift shop, sightseeing tours, and convention facilities. As an added touch, it has 10 acres of forest along the river with marked trails and a swimming beach. Bird-watching tours are available with a guide or a birding list. Rates US$90–110. Most major credit cards OK.

Iguana lovers, the hotel has the **Green Iguana Conservation Project** going on the grounds. When the iguana population was on a noticeable downward cycle, the manager took the lead and created the conservation project. Groups go on hunts, capture the females, and highjack the eggs. (Ask someone for details about that story!) The hatchlings are then kept until they are older and stronger and more likely to live a longer life. It is working; there are more iguanas thriving in the bush. Tours are available.

Once about a mile out of town on the Western Highway, today **Windy Hill Resort,** tel. 9/22017, fax 9/23080, email windyhill@btl.net, sits next to the highway at the edge of San Ignacio—the town has grown out to meet it. Here on **Graceland Ranch,** you'll find rustic charm with thatched-roof cottages, green grass, private baths, h/c water, ceiling fans, 24-hour electricity, a swimming pool, and recreation hut complete with TV, hammocks, bar, table tennis, and billiards. Credit cards accepted. US$80. Packages with meals and tours available. Guests enjoy the friendly efficiency with which the place is run and the variety of activities: canoeing, caving, horseback riding, nature tours, and hiking trails. Ask about escorted tours to Guatemala and archaeological sites in the area. Meals served in a casual thatched-roof dining room.

ENTERTAINMENT AND SERVICES

Cayo Nightlife

If you have the energy after a day on the river or hiking the jungles, you have several good choices for a quiet drink or more boisterous nightlife. You'll find a placid atmosphere and a nice view at the patio of the **San Ignacio Hotel** or the bar at **Windy Hill Resort. Eva's Restaurant** on Burns Avenue and the **Western Club** behind the New Belmoral Hotel are centrally located and have lots of conviviality. At the Western Club you can also try out your footwork on the dance floor.

For high-visibility nightlife try the **Cahal Pech Tavern,** tel. 9/23380, the giant longhouse on top of the hill just south of town. It probably has the largest *palapa* roof in the entire Cayo, if not the country. This lively tavern also has great views of the area at night and plenty of sociable goings-on, with lots of dancing space and enough seating space to accommodate a thousand. This is a fine place to meet fellow travelers and mix with the locals. Close by is **Piache's** bar, which can get lively, especially on the weekends.

If you want to go a little farther than San Ignacio, you'll find nighttime activity at **Caesar's Place** (Mile 60). Weekends can be especially good depending on who drops in for the jam session. If you know how to pluck, strum, or fiddle, drop by and join in.

Shopping

For gifts, **Eva's Restaurant, Farmer's Emporium** (24 Burns Ave.), **Arts and Crafts of Central America** (1 Hyatt St.), and **Black Rock Gift Shop** (Burns Ave.) sell Belizean arts and crafts. Farmer's Emporium also offers fresh bread and orange juice. **Celina's Super Store,** 43 Burns Ave., tel. 9/22247, sells groceries.

Services

Fill your tank at the **Shell Station** on the San Ignacio side of the bridge. **Atlantic Bank, Scotia Bank,** and **Belize Bank** are all on Burns, just past the Hawksworth Bridge as you come into town. The station for all buses, **Novelo** and **Z-Line**, is behind the New Belmoral Hotel. The **Taxi Co-op** is here too. **The Pharmacy,** 24 West St., tel. 9/22510 has all the (legal) drug paraphernalia you might need. **Martha's Kitchen and Guesthouse** offers daily laundry service 7 A.M.–8 P.M.

GETTING THERE

By Air

Chartered flights into **Spanish Lookout** and **Blancaneaux** Airports are the most expensive way to arrive. They are also the quickest. Blancaneaux is a less dependable point for a return flight because of frequent foggy conditions in the rainy season and weight limitations due to altitude and runway length. However, if conditions aren't right, a 30-minute ride to Spanish Lookout is a good fallback plan.

All the resorts can arrange for a pickup at the **international airport** in Belize City. The cost for such a transfer is about US$120–130 but can be split. **DuPlooy's,** tel. 9/23101, email duplooys@btl.net, has a daily bus running to

and from the airport. Cost is US$25, reservations recommended. Pickup at specified places like Eva's.

By Bus

Novelo runs through here from Belize City to the Guatemala border. The first bus reaches San Ignacio from Belize City about 9 A.M. and continues to the Guatemala border; the last one leaves in the opposite direction at about 6 P.M. The buses stop at the town circle near the police station, at the bridge, or at the parking area off Burns Avenue. Expect only limited service on Sunday. For current schedules between Belize City, San Ignacio, and Benque Viejo (Guatemala border), call the **Novelo Bus,** tel. 2/77372.

By Car

Armed with the map the rental car agent will supply, the drive is simple; enjoy the scenery and follow the signs. You'll be happy to note that many of the speed bumps that peppered the roadways in years past are gone. Keep your eyes peeled for the few that remain and drive more slowly than the locals; they know what's ahead.

VICINITY OF SAN IGNACIO

NORTH OF TOWN

Sights

A few dusty miles north of town is the little village of **Bullet Tree Falls.** Not much here, just a playing field and an intersection. But continue to the far side of town to where the road splits just before the bridge. This is an important landmark. Go forward and you're going toward El Pilar Ruins; take a right and you are headed to the Parrot's Nest.

The fascinating **El Pilar Ruins** lie on about 50 hilly acres northwest of Bullet Tree. Here two groupings of temple mounds, courtyards, and ball courts overlook a forested valley. Aqueducts and a causeway lead toward Guatemala, within sight 500 meters (450 yards) away. Unexcavated except for the handiwork of looters here and there, the ruins hold onto their air of mystery. Many trees shade the site: allspice, gumbo-

limbo, ramon, cohune palm, and locust. It's a beautiful hiking area with ridge after ridge of beckoning jungle.

Accommodations

Pass the bus stop and keep going, sticking to the biggest dirt road. It eventually narrows, passing the cemetery on the left, and you come to a fence that surrounds the Parrot's Nest.

The whimsical **Parrot's Nest,** P.O. Box 108, San Ignacio, Cayo, Belize, C.A., 93/7008, email parrot@btl.net, has four simple yet comfortable cabins and two tree houses on stilts, some under the spreading limbs of a gigantic guanacaste tree. Each cabin has 24-hour electricity, linoleum floor, and a simple single or double bed, with the breeze providing "natural" air-conditioning along with the help of fans. Cabin 6 has a private toilet US$37.50; the others share facilities. The new owners are upgrading to include more private bathrooms. Call for prices, since almost each of them is a different price. Breakfast and dinner are available, and they will cater to vegetarians. Breakfasts cost about US$3, dinners about US$7.

Getting There

If you don't have your own wheels, the owners offer a free shuttle into town in the mornings and back to the resort in the afternoon. Just make arrangements ahead of time. There is also a bus from San Ignacio or hop in a taxi. If you're mountain biking, it's an easy, scenic 20-minute ride.

SOUTH OF TOWN

Sights

Probably the most famous Maya art gallery and museum is **Tanah Mayan Art Museum,** featuring the well-known Garcia sisters. The Garcia sisters took their Maya heritage and began re-creating slate carvings reminiscent of those of their ancestors. Today they have made a nationwide name for themselves. The Tanah Museum is built in the old Maya way with limestone and clay walls; the floor is a parquet of logs and limestone, and the roof is typical thatch of bay and palm leaves, picked and placed on the nights of the full moon to give them a longer life. These sisters are charming ambassadors of the San Antonio neighborhood, as well as clever artists who make hand-drawn art cards depicting the wildlife of Belize, Belizean dolls, native jewelry, and medicinal herbs (who more qualified than the nieces of Don Eligio Panti, Belize's most renowned bush doctor? See "Healing" under "Health and Safety" in the On the Road chapter). If you're traveling to **1,000 Foot Falls, Rio Frio Cave,** or the falls of the **Rio On,** stop by and visit the Garcias in San Antonio, P.O. Box 75, San Ignacio, Belize, C.A.

Accommodations

In Santa Elena a sign directs you to **Maya Mountain Lodge,** P.O. Box 46, San Ignacio, Cayo District, Belize, C.A., tel. 9/22164, fax 9/22029, U.S. tel. 800/344-MAYA, email maya_mt@btl.net. This jungle hideaway is operated by Suzi and Bart Mickler. The lodge is only a short distance off the Western Highway, yet miles from the rest of the world. A meandering trail with signs introduces the neophyte to a variety of plants and trees and birds. Take along the guidebook the Micklers have created and discover the secrets of the jungle on your own. Or better yet, take a tour with one of the guides, some of the nicest and most knowledgeable according to Bart. Accommodations range from simple to quaint cottages with batik and other colorful fabrics and wood furniture. Clean and comfortable, the baths are private with h/c water; fans keep you cool and the requisite hammock is found on the front porch. The Micklers take pride in their restaurant—the menu includes Belizean and international dishes, along with homemade breads and buckets of fresh-squeezed orange juice; no liquor is sold (you can, however, bring your own). Breakfast costs US$8, lunch US$8, dinner US$16. Ask about workshops on biodiversity and multiculturalism. Write or call for reservations and more information. Kids six and under free, 7–11 half price.

At about Mile 4 and only a quarter of a mile past Cristo Rey Village, you'll find the friendly, family-owned **Crystal Paradise Resort** off to the right. Contact Jerone Tut, tel. 9/22823. Ever wonder who does all those roofs you see in the area? The patriarch of the Tut family runs a successful thatching business. Mrs. Tut is in charge of the resort's kitchen and the rest of the clan run tours and entertain guests. In fact, son Jerone is a well-known birding, horseback riding, river and cave guide with an impressive and growing library of nature guides.

Accommodations come in several styles on the property. If you're lucky you may get one of the simple thatched cabañas near the dining *palapa* that overlooks the river. These have compelling views of the valley and feature cement walls, tiled floors, h/c showers, and shaded verandas for relaxing. Others are clean and comfortable but more of a clapboard style. All offer ceiling fans and electricity. The Tuts also own other property nearby that's great for birdwatching and nature walks, and they offer tours around the countryside. Rates include breakfast and dinner. Traveler's checks and Visa/MC are accepted.

WEST OF TOWN

Accommodations

About two miles west of town, on 68 spacious acres is **Casa Maya,** tel. 9/12020. You have your choice of a bed in a dorm-type room for US$12 or cabañas with private bath and views for US$80. Tours can be arranged here; a restaurant and bar are on the grounds.

Clarissa Falls Resort, at Mile 70.5 on the Western Highway, P.O. Box 44, San Ignacio, Cayo, Belize, C.A., tel. 9/23916, is a laid-back resort where guests camp or stay in simple cottages with 11 rooms, eight with private bath, all with electric lighting, with inner paneled walls, two twin beds, and a hammock space in each, with room to add a cot. Also find a hammock house called the "bunkhouse," (US$7.50) where good screens keep out flying critters, and the shared toilet and shower building has hot and cold water. Activities include horseback riding through the jungle, floating tube-style down the river, and walking along the Mopan River to the Maya archaeological site of Xunantunich. You can see the ruins from Clarissa Falls Cottages. Campers (US$3.75 pp) and motor homes (US$7.50) are welcome. The dining room serves good Mexican food, including a few specialties such as black mole soup and great Mexican-style tacos. It also serves vegetarian fare. Food can be as inexpensive as US$0.40 for an order of tacos to US$6 for a meal such as stuffed squash. Breakfast with fresh fruit juice is US$5. This is a food hangout for locals. Could it be? A pet parrot named Larry predicts when rain is coming by crying *agua, agua!*

To reach **Black Rock Belize Jungle River Lodge,** P.O. Box 48, San Ignacio, Belize, C.A., tel./fax 9/22341, email blackrock@btl.net (contact Caesar Sherrard), from the Western Highway, turn at the Chaa Creek Rd, Mile 4.5, and take the right fork toward duPlooy's. If it makes you feel better, on your way stop by Caesar's Place, at Mile 62 on the Western Highway, for details and exact directions. For those who thrill to the outdoors, the vistas include jungle foliage, wildlife, and the unspoiled river. Guests have a choice of deluxe cabañas, US$95; private bath cabañas, or shared bath cabañas, both US$70. Excellent food is served in an open-air dining pavilion. Though in a primitive setting of 250 jungle acres, Black Rock uses modern technology to provide solar electricity, solar hot water, and solar water pumps.

From here guests strike out on their own to hike, explore on horseback, or canoe, swim, and lounge around the riverside beach, watch birds, or take day trips to nearby caves and Maya archaeological sites. Caesar's Place will arrange for pickup and transfers. Meals are US$8 full breakfast, US$9 lunch, US$16 dinner.

If you aren't driving a vehicle, the easiest way to get to Black Rock is to hop the airport bus

Chaa Creek Lodge

going to Belize City, get on Novelo's bus on the way to San Ignacio, and ask to be dropped off in front of Caesar's Place.

On the edge of the Vaca Plateau, the farm of Antonio and Lea Morales looks out over the magnificent Upper Macal River Valley. Here **Chechem Ha Cottages** offer simple accommodations to travelers who want to visit **Chechem Ha Cave.** Though this farm is just upstream from Black Rock and Ek Tun, the easiest way to reach it is by taking the turnoff at Benque Viejo by the cemetery and heading toward the new hydroelectric dam, about 10 miles (ask at Eva's in San Ignacio for directions or to share a ride). This is truly living with the locals as you witness around you family life on a small jungle farm. Bunks are simple affairs in clapboard buildings, and are best appreciated by backpackers. Fireflies will light up the night and all manner of jungle birds will call from the trees. You'll eat under a thatch *palapa* and bathe in the nearby stream or under the waterfall below the lip of the plateau. The toilet is a latrine. Stop at Eva's to radio the Morales family and make arrangements to stay; cost includes all meals.

Chaa Creek Resort and Spa and Inland Expeditions takes you from simple to the sublime (well almost), P.O. Box 53, San Ignacio, Cayo District, Belize, C.A., tel. 9/22037, fax 9/22501, email reservations@chaacreek.com or chaacreek@btl.net. Rates have multiple choices, however, you can expect a fine cabaña for two for US$165, breakfast US$10, packed lunch, US$8, dinner US$26. On the Western Highway about Mile 4.5, look for the Chaa Creek sign and make a turn onto the dirt road to the left. Stay to the left at the fork and the road leads to a secluded hideaway on the edge of the Macal River. This is a favorite to which guests return year after year. Owners Mick and Lucy Fleming, an American wife/British husband team, are both world travelers who came to visit Belize in the late 1970s, fell in love with the land, and never left. Chaa Creek was one of the first cottage resorts in Cayo, and if you ask Mick he'll tell you its colorful history, from overgrown farm to private nature reserve of 330 acres where three small Maya plaza groups lie along the resort's Ruta Maya trail system. Ask for a map or take one of the daily walks with a Chaa Creek guide.

A bright, flower-lined path brings you to the white stucco cottages with tall, peaked *palapa* roofs and wooden shutters that close over bright-colored curtains. (You don't need glass—no mosquitoes here!) The 20 double cottages have private baths and h/c water, Mexican-tile floors, and decorations of rich Guatemalan fabrics. The cottages, reminiscent of Africa design from the Flemings' earlier years in Kenya and Uganda, are scattered across the brow of a grassy hillside that slopes down to the edge of the Macal River. Guests can swim along the shore, go sightseeing on the trails, or take a leisurely two-hour paddle in a canoe down the river to San Ignacio. The river drifts through thick trees and tangled growth. Local housewives pound sudsy clothes clean on river rocks under a leafy arbor, while iguanas blink at you in the lazy afternoon sun. It's a great outing, and you can relax knowing that someone will pick you up in the van or Land Rover in San Ignacio for the trip back if you wish.

Chaa Creek is an easy gateway to the Guatemala border and the fabulous **Tikal** ruins. Day trips to the ruins of **Xunantunich** (close by) as well as to Tikal can be arranged here. After dinner, look for nocturnal critters on a night walk with one of the conversant guides, enjoy the art of conversation, or gaze at the starry sky from the quiet wooden bar deck; in short, enjoy the magic that intertwines night and jungle. Ask about the many all-inclusive packages and bargains including trips to see the sights of Belize.

The spa part of the resort is getting rave reviews; its amenities include a Vichy shower, massage therapy, body wraps and scrubs, or aromatherapy.

For those who like to rough it (a little), the **Macal River Camp Site,** about a mile from the lodge, offers luxury camping in a remote setting. US$50 pp includes all meals. Located one mile downstream from the lodge, 10 raised platforms with casitas are interspersed throughout the lush forest high above the riverbank. Nicely furnished, twin beds, comfy bedding, and the rates include breakfast and dinner—you are well fed. Mick says the food at the campsite is even better than at the lodge, hard to believe! If that is the case, camping out will be worth it solely for the food. This is a wonderful place to hike and to have a unique rainforest experience. Nearby both the lodge and the campsite is the new bird-viewing house. Surrounded by dense vegetation, the house was built as inconspicuously as possible so as not to infringe on the nesting and natural habits of the bird population. Many small creatures call this area home, and the new structure makes them easier to observe.

Ever innovative, the Flemings created the **Blue Morpho Butterfly Breeding Center.** A small flight room houses the blue beauties; naturalists on the grounds gladly explain the various stages of life that the butterfly goes through; if you arrive early in the morning there is a good chance you will witness the birth of a butterfly from the pupa, truly an amazing transformation. On the same grounds is the **Chaa Creek Natural History Museum.** The museum includes exhibit areas that examine ecosystems, geology, and Maya culture in the Cayo area, a research room and archives, a lecture area, and a reading porch.

If you received a "challenge" in the mail offering a free weekend in an isolated jungle guest house in Central America's Belize to the first couple who brought a gallon of still-frozen Häagen-Dazs ice cream to said resort, what would you do? Well, several adventurers packed up their Häagen-Dazs and hit the airport on the run. The first couple (from Davis, California) arrived undaunted by jungle heat with a cooler filled with dry ice and not one, but two gallons of their favorite flavors. **duPlooy's Cottage Resort** had one heck of a party all weekend. And not only did the resort guests enjoy the treat, but also special friends from all over Belize came with a multitude of exotic fruit toppings and lots of chocolate sauce.

This is typical of the feeling you get at du-Plooy's—a really fun place to stay that's a kind of nature-inspired Disneyland. This is a family-run resort (all daughters) with fun-timers Judy and Ken duPlooy at the helm. The small resort is set on what was originally 20, now 90, acres of rolling countryside wrapped on the east and north by the Macal River. The duPlooys have planted the additional acres with thousands of trees, part fruit orchard and part botanical garden, and built a pond that is already attracting lots of birds and fish (where do they come from?).

Guests have several choices. The Jungle Lodge, with its stucco cabañitas with red-tile roofs, screened porches, private bathrooms, hot showers, and ceiling fans, has large rooms with many windows to bring in the pleasant views. DuPlooy's Bungalows house large rooms in three individual buildings, each with its own deck looking down on the bird-laden bush and beautiful Macal River. Each room has a king bed and queen-size sofa bed, refrigerator, coffeepot, bathtub, and hammocks on the deck. Jungle Lodge Connecting Rooms, with two rooms connected by a bath, is perfect for a family and can sleep as many as seven. The Pink House guest house has six rooms with two shared bathrooms, living room, and screened-in porch around the building with comfy hammocks and seating areas, and a dining area where simple meals are served.

Meals can be included for US$35 pp, per day. Lunch can be a voucher in a local restaurant, a packed picnic, or a meal served in the river-view dining room. Dinner consists of four courses served in the dining room. Vegetarian meals are available, and do try some of the great exotic fruit dishes (many fruits and veggies come straight from the garden). A room in the Pink House is US$50, at the Jungle Lodge US$115, La Casita US$250, and a bungalow US$250. Package rates, including sight-seeing trips, are available. For more information, call duPlooy's, tel. 9/23101, fax 9/23301, email duplooys@btl.net.

duPlooy's is a very special place; they treat the earth and its creatures well. You have a choice: Use duPlooy's as a place to relax on a sandy beach by the river, or as a base from which to explore the caves, the nearby waterfalls, the Maya ruins, or even Guatemala and Tikal. Guests choose their mode of exploring: horseback, ferry, canoe, or on foot. But whatever you do, don't miss exploring duPlooy's grounds. Ken is a great gardener. Take a look at the orchids hanging on the trees, and as Ken says, if a cutting isn't *stolen,* it won't grow well. The newest venture of duPlooy's was to pack up a little piece of Belize's rainforest, put it in a climatized container, and ship it across the seas to London. There it was displayed at the *Chelsea Flower Show* where it took a silver medal in the education category. British arborists and researchers, as well as tourists, were quite impressed. Many things are in the hopper: an herbarium, seed depository, research lab, and nursery.

One of the well-trained guides holds fort on the "deck" every morning, and one of the bird guides guarantees 75 bird sightings by the time breakfast is served—and that's before the bird walk. Night-birding expeditions in the back of his pickup with a powerful beam reveal a new world of birds that play in the dark.

Equestrians enjoy night riding when the moon is full. Or, by day, a ride through the woods to Cahal Pech Maya ruins, followed by a ride into San Ignacio, where you can tie up in front of a restaurant, feels remarkably like an old Western adventure. Check out the Maya medicine garden, run by an old healer, Mr. Green, and the Maya hut where Maya-style lunches will soon be served. The trail along the river is a pleasant place to walk and observe nature at its finest.

Ek Tun is a scenic half-hour drive from San Ignacio; the last leg is an added adventure by boat along the Macal River. Contact Merlin Dart in the U.S., P.O. Box 18748, Boulder, CO 80308-8748, 303/442-6150; or Ken and Phyllis Dart in Belize, General Delivery, Benque Viejo, Cayo District, Belize, C.A., tel. 9/22881, fax 9/22446. Rates US$241.48 including breakfast and dinner; lunch and snacks available. The owners encourage you to bring your own snack food. When you make reservations, you will receive detailed directions. Once there, the adventure continues on 200 acres with jungle trails, a waterfall, and Maya mounds and ceremonial cave to explore. Tapir, deer, peccary and a variety of bird life use the property. Howler monkeys have been heard nearby, and from the dining room you can still see the critically endangered orange-breasted falcons. Other excursions include river trips that explore fascinating limestone caves once inhabited by the Maya in the nearby **Vaca Cave** system.

Ek Tun accommodations include two luxurious stick-and-thatch huts that can house up to four people each. The cabins are charming and about 500 square feet with two double beds in the loft and another downstairs. Antiques are among the furnishings, and each hut offers h/c water, flush toilets, stucco walls in the bathroom, and kerosene lamps—described by former guests as "rustic elegance." The dining and lounging areas are in a lush tropical setting. By the time you have this book, new solar panels at each cottage will provide reading lights, bathroom lights, and fans. Excellent meals include Mexican specialties, lots of fresh fruit, spicy local dishes, and each day an elegant dessert. Most of the fruits and vegetables served are grown in the Ek Tun gardens. Meals are served in the open dining room overlooking the surrounding mountains and the surging Macal River. The intimate atmosphere makes Ek Tun a favorite for honeymooners. Children under 12 stay for half price. Packages are available.

Green Heaven Lodge, tel. 9/12034, email ghlodge@btl.net, is just a short drive off the Western Highway on the road to Chaa Creek. The hacienda, which is yellow on the outside, opens to a large tiled lobby of many colors. Reminiscent of Mexico, I for one was pleasantly surprised at the decisive French flavor of this resort that is owned and operated by a French family. The four simple cabins are spread away from each other and have colorful bedspreads and matching drapes, NO thatch roof, a private bath with hot water, a step-down tile bath, and ceiling fans. Also on the grounds are a volleyball court, badminton, and an inviting pool. In the dry season the grounds look dismal but the atmosphere has a relaxed vivaciousness to it. The restaurant serves three meals a day, has no screens, and serves tasty French dishes, including daily specials like chicken Cordon Bleu US$10, and quiche Lorraine US$6. Other choices are stewed pork with curry with white and port wines and pinenuts for US$10, or shrimp spaghetti for US$9. Rates US$90.

Mayaland Villas, Mile 69, Western Highway, tel. 9/12035, email mayaland@btl.net, is one of the many new hotels popping up in the area. The owners have some experience in the tourist business as owners of Mayaland Tours and Travel, as evidenced by all the tour vans in the parking lot.

Even though the hotel is just off the highway, it sits on 16 acres and the cabins are away from the road. This hotel was once a private home and farm, and during the building of the cabañas and restaurant, they cut down as little as possible. Colorful bougainvillea and banana trees make up just some of the plant life that adds color to the grounds. A stream runs through the property, visible from the back porch of some of the cabañas.

Guests can stay in one of three rooms in the main house or in one of the cabañas spread out on the grounds. Rooms in the main house are clean and spacious, have ceiling fans and queen beds. The cabañas either have double beds or a king, private baths, fans, a cozy breakfast nook, and a porch with chairs and plants. Rooms run about US$80, cabañas about US$100.

A palapa restaurant and bar serve good, filling meals. Breakfast choices include pancakes US$4, or Belizean breakfast—scrambled eggs, refried beans, and johnnycakes for US$4.50. For lunch try the pasta salad for US$4 or everybody's favorite, stewed chicken and rice and beans US$4. The dinner menu has a lot of Mexican selections as well as burgers.

TO THE GUATEMALA BORDER

SAN JOSÉ SUCCOTZ

About Mile 6.5 you'll find the village of San Jose Succotz. Ancestors of the Mopan Maya migrated from San Jose (in Guatemala's Petén) and throughout the years have preserved the ancient Maya culture and folklore they brought with them to the isolated small village. In Succotz the first language is Mopan, and the people still wear the bright-hued fabrics that the women weave on their back-strap looms. The most colorful time to visit is during one of their fiestas. The two biggest celebrations are March 19 (feast day of St. Joseph) and May 3 (feast day of the Holy Cross).

Sights

If you're interested in local art, check out **Magana's Art Center** at the entrance to San José Succotz village, not too far from the Xunantunich ferry. David Magana has been working with the youth of the area, encouraging them to continue the arts and crafts of their ancestors. You'll find the results inside in the form of local wood carvings, baskets, jewelry, and stone (slate) carvings unique to Belize. It's open 9 A.M.–4 P.M.

The **Xunantunich Archaeological Site,** an impressive Maya ceremonial center, rests on a natural limestone ridge and provides a grand view of the entire Cayo District and Guatemala countryside. The tallest pyramid on the site, **El Castillo,** has been partially excavated and explored, and the eastern side of the structure displays a stucco frieze. The plaza of the ceremonial center houses three carved stelae. Eight miles past San Ignacio on the Western Highway going toward Benque Viejo and the Guatemala border, you'll reach the turnoff and the Succotz

Ferry (look for a small wooden sign on the side of the road). After another mile you'll reach Xunantunich. You can park here, hop on the hand-cranked ferry (free) that shuttles you across the river, and you have about a mile's hike up gentle hills to the site. If you wish, drive your car on the ferry, which operates daily 8 A.M.–5 P.M., and then motor on to Xunantunich.

You'll pay a small fee to enter the grounds, and a guide will explain the site: the history, what's been restored, and what's in the future. For more details about Xunantunich, see the Mundo Maya chapter.

As you make your way south on the Western Highway past the Xunantunich turnoff and before you arrive at Benque Viejo, the Mopan River runs alongside the road—more than likely you'll see women under shady trees scrubbing the family laundry on the rocks. Close by the kids have a good time playing and splashing around in the cool water. These are Mopan Maya from San José Succotz.

Accommodations

The Trek Stop, tel. 9/32265, email susa@btl.net, is a simple budget hotel. Close to the Xunatunich ruins, it offers simple cabins, camping facilities, a restaurant with inexpensive Belizean dishes, and outside composting toilets and solar showers. Rates are US$10. The **Tropical Wings** butterfly center is also here.

As time goes on, new and more convenient hotels are rising. Now you can stay very close to the most popular archaeological site, **Xunantunich.** This also puts you close to the Guatemala border and Tikal, as well as various mountains, waterfalls, and caves. The **Inn at Xunantunich** is at Mile 72 on the Western Highway in Succotz Village, tel. 9/23739, fax 9/32584, email xunhotel@btl.net. The hotel offers modern rooms, doubles, triples, and quads, private bath, cable TV, pool, and is very close to its archaeological namesake. Dining room/lounge/bar overlook the Mopan River, quite nice. US$58, with ac. Airport pickup available. Very convenient for those people who are driving a car, and a bus stops in front of the hotel.

Getting There

Novelo buses stop here on their way to neighboring Benque Viejo. If you're traveling by car, watch for the speed bump (sleeping policeman) at the east end of town. There are several more between here and the center of Benque.

BENQUE VIEJO DEL CARMEN

Eight miles beyond San Ignacio on the Western Highway going toward the Guatemala border lies **Benque Viejo,** the last town on the Belize side (the border is about one mile farther). Like the rest of the area, the houses sit on posts, and the town is scattered across hillsides with lush mountains standing guard.

This is a quiet little town with a peaceful atmosphere. Benque Viejo has been greatly influenced by the Spanish, both from its historical past when Spain ruled Guatemala and later when Spanish-speaking *chicleros* (chicle workers) and loggers worked the forest.

The Latin influence persists with today's influx of Guatemalans. A group of foreign doctors who donate free medical assistance visit **Good Shepherd Clinic** in Benque Viejo every year. People come from all over the district for this needed service; families even come from across the Guatemala border.

Many residents are Mopan Maya Indians, and even more of these descendants live in the nearby Maya village of San José Succotz. At one time Benque Viejo ("Old Bank"—riverside logging camps were referred to as banks) was a logging camp. This was the gathering place for chicle workers, and logs were floated down the river from here for shipment to England.

Accommodations and Food

The area has recently acquired another fine hotel. The **Mopan River Resort,** tel. 9/32047, fax 9/33272, email mopanriver@btl.net, set on 10 beautiful acres across the Mopan river, is the Club Med of Cayo but without the crowds and the nightlife. It's a place to relax in a beautiful environment and enjoy the solitude. Owned by expats Jay and Pamela Picon, you reach the lodge by taking a very short ferry ride across the Mopan River.

The lodge is all-inclusive—you pay one reasonable rate and get lodging, meals, alcohol, tours, transportation (to and from the airport)—everything. The spacious, hilly grounds have rock walkways through the trimmed grass and

river ferry boat on the way to Xunantunich

many fruit trees; at night lanterns on posts light your way. The cabins are scattered about for privacy and each has a large deck with chairs and tables to enjoy the scenic, peaceful view. The rooms have big bathrooms and double sinks, mahogany furniture, exotic hardwood flooring, minibars stocked with Belikins and sodas, a coffeepot, and either two twin beds or one queen. Suites are also available and have a full fridge, cable TV, and VCR.

Dinner is served between 7 and 8 P.M. preceded by the 6 to 7 P.M. cocktail hour. The cheery kitchen is the cleanest I've ever seen in Belize, or the United States for that matter, and it puts out good meals. Dinners are themed and breakfasts are cooked to your liking.

The resort arranges and leads all tours, and you can go on as many or as few as you want—they are paid for. If Tikal is on your list of to-do's, make sure you stay here on a Tuesday or Friday as those are the only days they go.

There purposely is little nighttime entertainment here. Evenings are for sharing stories with fellow travelers, listening to the night noise, and hearing the life story of the Picons (worthwhile).

The river looks inviting but swimming isn't advisable as it's reportedly polluted. Swim in the pool instead. Package rates break down to about US$120 per person a day. Sometimes their specials are even better, US$798 per person, double occupancy for seven nights, including tax.

The **Royal Mayan Resort and Spa,** U.S. tel. 888/271-3482, is another new resort. It sits on the top of a steep hill and the grounds, not necessarily the rooms, offer beautiful views of the valley below. Some of these smallish rooms have queen beds, most have doubles, and all have a/c, hot water, louvered windows, small fridge, and private baths. The resort opened in 1999 and they are still adding on. When we were there, the spa was marginal. The gym facilities are downright ugly, but the pool is inviting, and it's easy to enjoy the other aspects of this overpriced resort. The amiable staff, the upstairs bar, the beautifully set dining room and the hot tub that sits on a deck away from the rest of the resort are definite plusses. US$140, including breakfast. The restaurant serves three meals a day. Dinner choices US$12–17.

A couple of other places around Benque appeal primarily to backpackers and budget travelers. Hotel Maya and Restaurant is one such place. According to readers, **Maxim's Palace Hotel and Restaurant,** 41 Churchill St., Benque Viejo, Belize, C.A., tel. 9/32259, is the best of the bunch

Vista del Carmen Cafe perches at the east end of town up on a high hill overlooking Benque and the surrounding countryside. Like the Cahal Pech Tavern, you can see this from some distance away due to a large *palapa* with tables and a bar. Off to one side are two simple, whitewashed cabañas (under US$25).

Shopping
Galeria de Arte Gucumaz sells Belizean and Guatemalan handicrafts at some of the best prices around. The textiles are bright and well made. Otherwise there's not much shopping. A few small general stores sell a little of everything: canned goods, sweets, sundries, and cold drinks. You'll also find a gas station, police department, fire station, and telephone service. This is a good place to fill your gas tank before entering Guatemala.

By Bus to and from Guatemala
Novelo buses move through town fairly often, starting with a 6:30 A.M. departure from Belize City. Some bus drivers going to the border pick you up and waive the fee since it's so close. Traveling in the other direction (from Benque Viejo to Belize City), buses begin moving through at 4 A.M. Remember when traveling on Sundays in Belize that the schedule is much shorter, so check ahead of time.

At the Guatemala Border
You'll have to get off the bus at the border and go through customs (you'll have to pay about US$15 in exit fees). If you're trying to get to **Tikal,** take the early **Batty bus** from Belize City, which passes through Benque Viejo, crosses the border, and arrives at the first town, Melchor de Mencos, about 10 A.M. Here it meets with the bus to Flores, where you'll hope to connect with a bus to Tikal from the El Cruce junction. Occasionally you can hitch a ride, but if you're not a gambler, you may want to go directly to Flores, where buses run more frequently to Tikal. (For more

detailed information about crossing the border, traveling into Guatemala and Tikal, accommodations, and Maya archaeological sites, see the Across Belize's Borders chapter.) Those going straight to Tikal should change money at the bank in Melchor de Mencos (or even with the moneychangers who hang out at the border station). The bank at Flores closes daily at 2 P.M. Tikal has no banks, and though hotels and restaurants will accept U.S. dollars and traveler's checks for payment, they will *not* change traveler's checks into Guatemalan quetzals.

BOB RACE

KATHY ESCOVEDO SANDERS

STANN CREEK DISTRICT
INTRODUCTION

For those looking for the real rainforests of Belize, beautiful beaches, and fascinating local culture, a trip to the Stann Creek District in southern Belize is in order. This section of the country has not been high on the list of advertised destinations, but that is all beginning to change. Of course this means more and more resorts will come along, changing life here ever-so-slightly. However, as more people arrive in response to the Mundo Maya ("World of the Maya") movement, many new doors of financial opportunity are opening for the locals. This movement is an ecotourism plan that involves five countries in the Mundo Maya to collaborate and encourage special tours for visitors. This southern district of the country has a lot to offer, especially to those who are looking for this Maya world. As well as being one of the richer rainforests in the country (with more than 120 inches of rain per year), southern Belize offers white sand and blue sea, waterfalls, jungle pools, vine-edged trails, a vast cave system, and a plethora of hidden Maya

cities of the past. Another plus—more and more divers are discovering the southern cayes and their opulent undersea life and comparing them with the best of the more touristed regions.

THE LAND

Stann Creek District begins just after Over the Top ridge on the Hummingbird Highway where the surrounding lush rainforest is thick with tropical plants, delicate ferns, bromeliads, and orchids. As you get closer to Dangriga, the rainforest gives way to vast groves of citrus. Stann Creek is not the smallest district in Belize, but it's next in line.

Agriculture
Over the millennia, rivers and streams gushing from the Maya Mountains have deposited a rich layer of fertile soil, making the coastal and valley regions ideal farming areas. The banana

industry, once vital in the area, was wiped out by a disease called "Panama Rot" many years back. However, with new technology, a strain of bananas has been developed that appears to be surviving and promises to grow into a profitable operation.

Stann Creek's citrus industry produces Valencia oranges and grapefruit, which are then processed (on-site) into juice—one of Belize's most important exports. The business center of the citrus industry, Dangriga has rebounded with vigor since being wiped out by Hurricane Hattie in 1961. The town itself bears little resemblance to its big brother, Belize City. Dangriga has a bright potential in agriculture.

ON THE ROAD

Hummingbird Highway

For those who drive into Stann Creek, the Hummingbird Highway passes picturesque villages, bountiful orchards, and jungle landscapes, all on a comfortably paved road.

Manatee Road

Another route into Stann Creek District and onward to Dangriga or the Southern Highway is the Manatee Road (check conditions before you head out during wet weather). This dirt road can

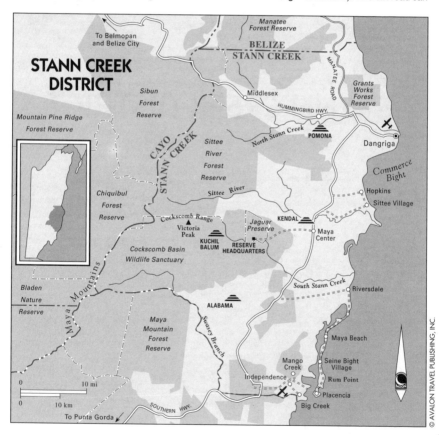

TODD CLARK

Dangriga coastline

charm you with beauty one moment and jar your fillings loose the next. Many short wooden bridges with no rails are large enough for a single vehicle only. Sections of the twisting road are lined with jungle or pine forests on each side, with not a sign of human intrusion. You'll drive through washouts, where rain-swollen streams empty over their banks and carve rim-bending channels and pits into the submerged roadway. But you'll be rewarded with the sight of eclectic Maya villages, towering forests, and distant looming mountains.

HISTORY AND THE PEOPLE

Stann Creek, as all of Belize, is a rich mix of cultures, including Garifuna, East Indian, European, and Maya. Historically, African heritage is especially strong here, and for that reason both Stann Creek and Toledo Districts are considered by some to be the most "Caribbean" sections of Belize. The indigenous people of southern Belize (dating back 3,600 years) are the Maya, and they, too, are still well represented.

MAYA

Small villages of Maya, still practicing some form of their ancient culture, dot the landscape. Little is known of their early history except what has been learned from the amazing structures that are continually uncovered in thick jungle. Records show that in more recent times (soon after Columbus visited the New World), many of the Maya moved away from the coast to escape hostile Spanish and British intruders who arrived by ship to search for slaves. The independent Maya refused to be subjugated, so traders brought boatloads of African slaves into the Caribbean. Both the Maya and the Africans had religious beliefs that were extraordinarily inconsistent with the lifestyles of Christians, who considered them subhuman. As a result, the Maya and the Garifuna for years kept to themselves.

Even now, the Mopan, Yucatec, and Kekchi continue to live much as their ancestors did. Most of them practice some form of Christian religion integrated with ancient beliefs—in southern Belize the Kekchi have their own Mennonite church. But ancient Maya ceremonies are still quietly practiced in secluded pockets of the country, many in southern Belize. Curiously today's Maya have little connection with the Maya structures that remain. Not too far from Dangriga, many of these ceremonial centers have been discovered, with indications that many more lie waiting under thick jungle growth.

GARIFUNA

The earliest Black Caribs were farmers, fishermen, trappers—and warriors—originating on St. Vincent Island in the West Indies. Here, escaped West African slaves mixed with the aboriginal people called Red Caribs.

Though the Black Caribs were dominated by the Europeans and confined to the islands of St. Vincent and St. Dominica, they never stopped their fight for freedom. They were persistent warriors, and under the leadership of a valiant fighter, Joseph Chatoyer, they continued the battle. But with European firepower against their bows and arrows, they were no match. The Caribs were put down in 1796, and to try to contain them the victors moved about 5,000 captives once again to the Bay Islands off the coast of Honduras.

From the time that ships flying the Spanish flag began using the ocean to export the riches of the New World to Spain, the Bay Islands (because of their location) were thrust into the middle of the fight over who would control these sea-lanes. At one time or another the fight included Dutch, English, French, and U.S. ships, either pirating or smuggling goods in and out of what Spain considered its personal territory. The Bay Islands off Honduras shifted ownership reg-

ularly as all of those countries vied for control of the sea-lanes.

After arriving in the Bay Islands, the Caribs, still seeking peace, began wandering in their dugout canoes and over the years began to settle in coastal areas of Honduras, Guatemala, Nicaragua, and southern Belize. In 1802 the beginnings of a settlement took hold in Stann Creek with 150 Caribs. The isolated band supported itself by subsistence fishing and farming. In 1823 a civil war in Honduras forced more Caribs to leave, and they headed for Belize. They landed in Belize under the leadership of Alejo Beni and began what has been a peaceful, poor community. Only recently, after more than 150 years, has Dangriga become a thriving agricultural center thanks to the efforts of the whole community, including the Maya and the Caribs.

The Black Caribs are known today by the language they speak, referred to as both Garifuna and Garinagu. According to Phylis Cayetano, who devotes much of her time and effort to preserving the Garifuna culture and language, the group is a mixture of Amerindian, African, Arawak, and Carib, but the mothers were mostly Arawakan. The Garifuna developed their own language, and, according to a dictionary that dates from the 1700s, very few words are African; most are Carib.

The Garifuna continued to practice what was

GARIFUNA HISTORY

Garifuna history really began more than 300 years ago when two ships filled with African slaves were wrecked on the Caribbean's Windward Islands. The next century is shadowy, and the only certainty is that with the passage of time they intermarried with the Carib people, creating the Garifuna. They were defeated and controlled over the years by the Spanish and British, the latter deporting them to the inhospitable island of Roatan off the coast of Honduras. Finally, after decades, the people got their freedom and sailed to the southern coast of Belize, where they began a new life.

Freedom and integration into Belize in the 1800s was not easy. And though the Garifuna were allowed to settle in the Stann Creek District when they

first arrived, the British isolated them from the rest of the country. They allowed the Garifuna into Belize City only with 48-hour passes to let them sell their harvests. City dwellers who did not farm and for years were forced to exist on limited imported British food welcomed this fresh produce.

The populace in general was frightened of the Garifuna, believing the lies told by slave owners that they ate babies and cast evil spells. These stories were spread by slave owners convinced their slaves would run away to live with the outsiders if they saw the relative freedom the Garifuna enjoyed in southern Belize. Finally, on November 19, 1832, the Garifuna were given a voice in government affairs at the public meeting in Belize City.

still familiar from their ancient African traditions—cooking, dances, and especially music, which consisted of complex rhythms with a call-and-response pattern that was an important part of their social and religious celebrations. An eminent person in the village is still the drum maker, who continues the old traditions, along with making other instruments used in these often night-long singing and dancing ceremonies.

Obeah

One of the most enduring customs, the practice of black magic known as *obeah,* was regarded with great suspicion and concern by the colonialists in Belize City, even after laws were enacted that made it illegal "for any man or woman to take money or other effects in return for fetishes or amulets, ritual formulas, or other magical mischief that could immunize slaves from the wrath of their masters." However, the practice continued—though in more secretive ways. (No doubt, if you have a need and have established a trust with the Garifuna, you can find an *obeah* man today.) The *obeah* works through dances, drumbeats, trances, and trancelike contact with the dead. Small, black *puchinga* (cloth dolls) stuffed with black feathers can strike dread into the hearts of the Garifuna; if buried under the doorstep of an intended victim, the doll can supposedly bring marital problems, failure in business, illness, or death. It's not unusual for sacrifices to involve the blood of live chickens and pigs. Small Garifuna children occasionally are seen with indigo blue crosses drawn on their foreheads to ward off evil spirits.

Exile

Shortly after the Garifuna established themselves in southern Belize, they brought their home-grown produce in dugouts to sell in Belize Town, where the people were delighted to have fresh vegetables. But because of the fear generated by the slave owners of Belize Town, these southern people were ostracized when they tried to become part of the Town Public Meeting. The fear pervaded the colonial town for many years.

Now each year on November 19, the whole country remembers the day the Garifuna arrived in Belize, and Settlement Day is celebrated with a reenactment of the landing in 1823—a happy celebration and an opportunity for the curious to witness the exotic tempos of Garifuna dancing and singing. Be adventurous and taste the typical, though unusual, Garifuna foods. If you drink too much "local dynamite" (rum and coconut milk), have a cup of the strong chicory coffee said by the Garifuna "to make we not have goma" (a Garifuna hangover).

Recognizing that schooling is essential, the Garifuna, along with the entire country of Belize, are staunch advocates of education—every desk in the classrooms of Dangriga is filled. In schools all across the country, Garifuna women excel as teachers.

The people are, generally, still farmers; their plots often are 5–10 miles outside of town. In the early days they walked the long distances; today they take a bus, tending their fields from early morning to late afternoon. The district's leading crop is citrus, and the people of Dangriga figure strongly in this production.

Traditions

Traditionally and continuing today, the Garifuna raise cassava to make *eriba,* a flat bread made from the meal of the cassava root. The large bulbous roots of the shrubby spurge plant are peeled and grated (today mostly by electric graters, but formerly by hand—a long, tedious job on a stone-studded board). The grated cassava is packed into a six-foot-long leaf-woven tube that is hung from a hefty tree limb, then weighted and pulled at the bottom, squeezing and forcing out the poisonous juices and starch from the pulp. The coarse meal that remains is dried and used to make the flat bread that has been an important part of the Garifuna culture for centuries.

Today's Garifuna are still aloof and seldom marry out of their group. However, a friend is treated warmly. The women are extremely hard working, the central influence of the family, and generally the caretakers of the family farm.

WHITE SETTLERS

The earliest white settlers were Puritans from the island of New Providence in the Bahamas. These simple-living people implemented their knowledge of raising tobacco on nearby offshore cayes (today called Tobacco Cayes), began a trading post (also known as a "stand," which

GARIFUNA SETTLEMENT DAY

The hour before dawn we made our way through the darkness along the edge of the sea heading toward the persistent beat of distant drums. Orange streaks began to widen across the horizon as we climbed over a half-fallen wooden bridge spanning a creek, cutting a muddy path to the Caribbean. We were on our way to Dangríga on Garifuna Settlement Day, one of Belize's lively national holidays, celebrated each year on November 19 to commemorate the arrival of the Garifuna people to Belize.

The ancestors smiled. Rains that had been pouring down for a week subsided, and by the time we reached the center of town and the river shoreline, crowds of revelers were beginning to gather in the breaking dawn. This was a day of reflection and good times in Belize, a severe contrast to Garifuna beginnings that for decades were filled with misery and tragedy.

Settlement Day is a happy celebration. Everyone dresses in colorful new clothes, and while waiting for the "landing," family, friends, and strangers from all over Belize catch up on local gossip, make new acquaintances, and enjoy the party. Sounds of beating drums emanate from small circles of people on both sides of the river, from the backs of pickup trucks, and from rooftops. In lieu of drums, young men push through the crowds shouldering giant boomboxes that broadcast the beat. Excitement (and umbrellas) hangs in the air as the assemblage waits for the canoes and the beginning of the pageant.

Now, in the early dawn, the crowd cheers. It spots two dugout canoes paddling from the open sea into the river. Years ago, the first refugees from Roatan crowded into just such boats along with a few meager necessities to start a new life in a new land. Today's reenactment is orchestrated according to verbal history handed down through generations. Leaves and vines are wrapped around the arrivals' heads and waists. Drums, baskets that carry simple cooking utensils, young banana trees, and cassava roots are all among the precious cargo the Garifuna originally brought to start their new lives in Dangriga.

The canoes paddle past cheering crowds. No matter that this pageant is repeated every year (like the Fourth of July in the United States); each November is a reminder of the past, and even this outsider is swept along in the excitement and thoughts of what this day represents to the Garifuna citizens of Belize.

The canoes travel up the river and under the bridge and back again so that everyone lining the bank and bridge can see them. When the "actors" come ashore, they're joined by hundreds of onlookers. The colorful procession then winds through the narrow streets with young and old dancing and singing to the drumbeats; they proudly lead the parade to the Catholic church, where a special service takes place. Dignitaries from all over Belize attend and tell of the past and, most important, of the hopes of the future.

The Catholic church plays a unique part in the life of the Garifuna. Some years back the church reached an unspoken, working agreement with the Garifuna: nothing formal, just a look-the-other-way attitude while their Garifuna parishioners mix Catholic dogma with ancient ritual. It wasn't always this way. For generations the people were forced to keep their religion alive in

a low-key, heavy-footed, repetitive shuffle with subtle hand movements accompanied by timeworn words that we don't understand but are told tell a tale of survival.

Every few minutes a reveler filled with too much rum pushes through the circle of people and joins the dancing women. He's quickly chased out of the ring by an umbrella-wielding elder who aims her prods at the more vulnerable spots of his body. If that doesn't work, she resorts to pulling the intoxicated dancer off the floor by his ear—a little comic relief that adds to the down-home entertainment.

The *paranda* continues, and little kids energetically join in the dances on the outside of the "circle" or watch wide-eyed from the rafters near the top of the *palapa* roof, entranced by the beat, dim light, and music—the magic of the holiday. The recurring rain adds an extra beat to the exotic cadence of the drums; dance after dance continues.

The *huguhugn* dance is open to everyone, but the sexy *punta* is the popular favorite, with one couple at a time in the ring. Handsome men and beautiful women slowly undulate their bodies with flamboyant grace and sexual suggestion. This is the courtship dance born in African roots. In case you miss Settlement Day parties, stop by a bar or nightclub anywhere in Belize and you'll see locals doing a modern version called *punta* rock.

The Garifuna are a matriarchal society, and the elder women are trying hard to keep the old traditions alive. While English is the language of the country and taught in the classrooms of Belize, one of the concerns of the elders is the preservation of the ethnic language of the Garifuna.

Most of the older Garifuna women wear bright-colored dirndl skirts and kerchiefs tied low over their foreheads, symbolic of days spent in the fields. Only a few wear the traditional costumes trimmed with shells; today's young women and girls prefer T-shirts and jeans or modern tight skirts—and no one wears a kerchief. The men wear jeans, and years ago they traded their straw hats for baseball caps.

During Settlement Day, a walk down the narrow streets takes you past small parties and family gatherings under stilted houses where dancing and singing is the rule; others enjoy holiday foods (including cassava bread) and drinks. If invited to share a cup of coffee dipped from an old blue porcelain kettle heavily laced with rum, join in—it could turn out to be the best part of the celebration!

clandestine meetings or suffer severe punishment and persecution.

Rain, much like time, has not stopped the Garifuna celebrations nor the dancing that is an integral part of the festivities. Street dances (traditionally held along village streets for many nights leading up to Settlement Day) continue and are moved indoors to escape the flooded streets. Small bars and open *palapa* (thatch) structures are crowded with fun-lovers and reverberate with the pounding of exotic triple drums (always three). Drums bring their magic, and parties continue with both modern punta rock and traditional dances into the early hours of the morning. The Garifuna are a people filled with music. The songs sung in the Garifuna language tell stories—some happy, some sad—and many melodies go hand-in-hand with daily tasks.

At an open *palapa* hut, three talented drummers begin the beat. The old Garifuna women, heavily influenced by their African beginnings, insist on marshaling the dances the old way. The first tempo is the *paranda*, a dance just for women. A circle is created in the dirt-floored room and the elderly women begin

over time deteriorated to "Stann"), and spread south into the Placencia area. The trading post ultimately faded away, and Dangriga continued its almost stagnant existence. During the American Civil War, arms dealers became familiar with the Belizean coast. In the 1860s British settlers encouraged Americans to come and begin new lives in Belize. Hundreds of Confederates did arrive after the Civil War and began clearing land to develop. However, it was not to last.

Most of the American settlers returned to the United States, though one group of Methodists from Mississippi stayed in Toledo District long enough to develop 12 sugar plantations. By 1910 most of the Mississippians were gone. During the U.S. Prohibition, boats decked out as fishing crafts ran rum from Belize to Florida.

Despite its slow start, today's Dangriga is a community, population about 9,000, with a bright future of growth.

DANGRIGA

The town of Dangriga, a Garifuna word meaning "standing waters," was perhaps the heart of what began as Stann Creek. The small community is on the coast, 36 miles south of Belize City as the crow (or Maya Island Air) flies. However, by bike, bus, or car the trip is much longer, roughly 75 miles along the twisting Manatee Road or about 100 miles on paved Hummingbird Highway from Belmopan. By Stann Creek standards, the city of Dangriga is a bustling, though easygoing, place. It's thriving because of the successful citrus industry that has finally begun a healthy growth (after more than 50 years). Tourism today attracts a moderate number of curious citizens-of-the-world, especially divers, owing to Dangriga's location near the sea and enticing underwater world.

Dangriga Culture
Dangriga is home to the well-known **Warribaggabagga Dancers,** the **Punta Rebels,** and the **Turtle Shell Band.** It is the heart of Garifuna folk culture. The music and dancing, including syncopated African rhythms, is an enchanting mixture of the various cultures of southern Belize. Some of Belize's most accomplished artists live in Dangriga. **Austin Rodriquez,** is known for his authentic Garifuna drums. **Benjamin Nicholas** paints the local scene, and **Mercy Sabal,** makes colorful dolls that are sold all over the country.

Arts and Crafts
Drums and other typical musical instruments are favorite souvenirs. Women make charming purses woven from reeds. Another memento is a mask, carved and painted by an artisan, used during various ceremonies in the south of Belize, both in Maya and Garifuna ceremonies. Note: There have been a couple of complaints from readers who have commissioned artwork with payment in advance. Some of these people did not receive *exactly* what was expected when it was due. Perhaps only a partial advance payment would be better?

Activities
Activities include cycling, exploring ruins, fishing, hiking, nature watching of all kinds, snorkeling, and scuba diving.

ACCOMMODATIONS

Under US$25
Rio Mar Hotel, 977 Waight St., P.O. Box 2, Dangriga, Stann Creek District, Belize, C.A., tel. 5/22201, is a guest house with three tiny, fan-cooled clean rooms and paper-thin walls. You may not be enthralled by the blaring music from the bar downstairs, but some say this is the place to be on Garifuna Settlement Day. US$12.50.

Other inexpensive basic hostelries are **Dangriga Central Hotel,** 119 Commerce St., and **Riverside Hotel,** 5 Commerce St., tel. 5/22168, fax 5/22296, simple and comfortable with shared baths and fans. US$20 private; US$10 shared.

On the second street south of Central Bridge, in a quiet residential area on the second floor of a clapboard building, is the charming little **Bluefield Lodge,** 6 Bluefield Road, Dangriga, Stann Creek District, Belize, C.A., tel. 5/22742. The owner, Miss Louise, has six clean, attractively

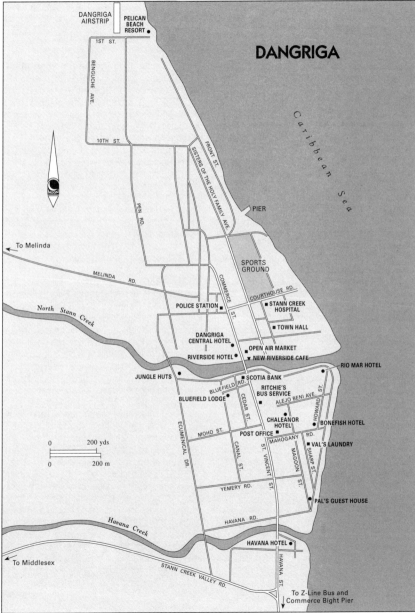

DANGRIGA AIRSTRIP

PELICAN BEACH RESORT

1ST ST.

BENGUCHE AVE.

10TH ST.

DANGRIGA

FRONT ST.

SISTERS OF THE HOLY FAMILY AVE.

PEN RD.

Caribbean Sea

PIER

To Melinda

MELINDA RD.

COMMERCE ST.

SPORTS GROUND

COURTHOUSE RD.

North Stann Creek

POLICE STATION

STANN CREEK HOSPITAL

TOWN HALL

DANGRIGA CENTRAL HOTEL

RIVERSIDE HOTEL

OPEN AIR MARKET

NEW RIVERSIDE CAFE

RIO MAR HOTEL

JUNGLE HUTS

SCOTIA BANK

BLUEFIELD RD.

RITCHIE'S BUS SERVICE

BLUEFIELD LODGE

CEDAR ST.

ALEJO BENI AVE.

HOWARD ST.

CHALEANOR HOTEL

BONEFISH HOTEL

ECUMENICAL DR.

MOHO ST.

POST OFFICE

MAHOGANY RD.

VAL'S LAUNDRY

0   200 yds

CANAL ST.

ST. VINCENT ST.

MAGOON ST.

SHARP ST.

0   200 m

YEMERY RD.

PAL'S GUEST HOUSE

Havana Creek

HAVANA RD.

To Middlesex

HAVANA HOTEL

HAVANA ST.

STANN CREEK VALLEY RD.

To Z-Line Bus and Commerce Bight Pier

furnished rooms with fans, h/c water, private baths, and special little touches in wallpaper, bedcovers, and curtains. US$25 private; US$16 shared. Everything about the place bespeaks the pride and care she takes in her lodge. Parking is on the street. No food service, but sodas are available for purchase at the front desk.

US$25–50

If you are looking for waterfront accommodations in the center of Dangriga, **Pal's Guest House,** 868 Magoon St., Dangriga, Stann Creek District, Belize, C.A., tel. 5/22095, is the place. You'll find 10 clean, modest rooms at the corner of North Havana Road and Magoon Street. Across the road and on the beach is another building. Rooms have linoleum floors, ceiling fans, h/c private showers, TV, and balconies with views of the ocean. Louvered windows on both ends of the rooms create good cross-ventilation. Boats are beached or tied nearby. Rates on seafront rooms are about US$30; rooms with shared bath in the back building are about US$20.

The **Chaleanor Hotel,** 35 Magoon St., tel. 5/22587, fax 5/23038, email dssusher@btl.net, is run by very accommodating owners Chad and Eleanor. Ten rooms have private baths, hot water, mismatched colorful bedspreads, some have TV and a/c and a homey atmosphere in a residential neighborhood. Eight rooms share a bathroom. Laundry service is available; a gift counter in the lobby carries a few things. Help yourself to the tray with coffee and bananas in the morning. There's even a rooftop restaurant with traditional Belizean fare if you don't feel like walking the short distance to other restaurants. US$32, private, US$13 shared.

Along the river on the west side of town, look for an unexpected surprise just by the bridge. **Jungle Huts Hotel,** Ecumenical Drive, P.O. Box 10, Dangriga, Stann Creek District, Belize, C.A., tel. 5/22142, fax 5/23166, is run by the local dentist, Arthur Usher, and his wife, Beverly. You'll find hot water, tiled private bathrooms, pleasant furniture, and two double beds in each of the four rooms in the main building. Some have a/c. In addition, there are four basic cabañas of a rustic Belizean design. All feature private h/c baths or showers. The hotel and its cabañas are very secure (behind the Usher home). The whole family is very friendly, and you have more

of a feeling of staying with relatives than with strangers. US$25 for basic rooms; US$37 for TV and private bath.

US$75–100

An old favorite of divers, the **Bonefish Hotel,** 15 Mahogany Road, P.O. Box 21, Dangriga, Stann Creek District, Belize, C.A., tel. 5/22165, fax 5/22296, is a pleasant little place with 10 rooms and a second-floor lobby and bar. It's in downtown Dangriga a couple of blocks east of Havana Street and across the street from a grassy park at the end of Mahogany Road. It caters to active travelers who want to tour the area, fish, or dive. Across the street to the east is the ocean a short distance away. The resort is allied with Blue Marlin Lodge on South Water Caye. Rooms are clean and simple, and carpeted. Upstairs rooms have private h/c baths, minibar, cable TV, and a/c. It accepts Visa/MC. Downstairs rooms don't have the minibar and are US$70; upstairs are US$84.

US$100–150

You'll find the casual **Pelican Beach Resort,** P.O. Box 14, Dangriga, Stann Creek District, Belize, C.A., tel. 5/22044, fax 5/22570, email pelicanbeach@btl.net, along the beachfront just north of town. It's run by Therese and Tony Rath. The most attractive lodging in Dangriga and the closest to the small local airstrip, Pelican Beach offers a fine waterfront location, friendly atmosphere, and good food prepared by local cooks in the restaurant/bar. An aquarium in the bar is a mini living coral reef. Iguanas, turtles, land crabs, and butterflies inhabit the surrounding greenery. A palm-studded beachfront adds to the charm. Rooms are clean, simply but comfortably furnished, and include fans, h/c private baths, and telephones; some have balconies. Rates are based on four- to seven-day packages and work out to be about US$120 a day, including excursions. The resort has its own travel agency, and sight-seeing trips to the cayes or to Cockscomb Basin Wildlife Sanctuary are easily arranged. Dangriga is a 15-minute walk along the shore. Ask about their cottages and group accommodations on South Water Caye (see "Other Popular Cayes" in The Cayes chapter). Discounts are available for longer stays, and children under 12 are free with adult. All major credit cards are OK. Follow Ecumenical Drive past the tall transmission tower, across the bridge, until the road dead-ends. Turn right and it's by the beach on your left. Contact the resort for reservations.

FOOD

In Dangriga Town don't forget what time it is; the small cafés are open only during meal times. The **New Riverside Café** opens early and serves a tasty breakfast, including fresh-squeezed orange juice. For a change of pace try the **King Burger**. It serves great burgers, fries, shakes, ice cream—oh yes, and conch soup. The **Rio Mar Hotel** also has a bar and restaurant. **Pelican Beach Resort** has delicious food prepared by Creole cooks.

GETTING THERE

By Air
The 20-minute flight from Belize City to Dangriga is by far the easiest and quickest way to arrive. **Maya Island Air** and **Tropic Air** have daily scheduled flights in and out of Dangriga from both Belize City airports. It's also possible to fly back and forth between Dangriga, Placencia, Big Creek, and Punta Gorda. The strip itself is similar to the Belize City Municipal Airport, about the length of a few football fields. Check with Maya Island Air, tel. 2/31140, and Tropic Air, tel. 5/22129, for fares and schedules.

By Boat
Dangriga is roughly 36 miles by boat from Belize City. Because there isn't a scheduled boat trip to Dangriga, ask around—at the Belize City docks by the Texaco station, your hotel, or the Belize Tourist Board in Belize City. They tried running a regularly scheduled shuttle, but it didn't make money. Expect to pay a decent sum for this trip.

By Bus
From Belize City's Magazine Road terminal, the **Z-Line Bus** offers several departure times daily. Call for schedule; in Belize City call 2/73937, in Dangriga call 5/22211 or 22160. It's about a five-hour ride.

    Ritchies Bus Service on St. Vincent Street serves the local area and continues to Punta Gorda.

By Car
It pays not to be in a big rush when meandering the highways and byways south of Belize City. Building roads through swamps and marshes takes lots of money, so up until now it's just been easier to go around the problem areas. Remember, "highway" doesn't necessarily denote a smooth, paved road. Most of the highways in southern Belize are graded, potholed, dirt roads that can be impassable during the rainy season (June–Oct.) although things are slowly improving, including the 100 percent paved Hummingbird Highway.

    Those inclined to drive, however, will do best with a 4WD vehicle (rentals available); the reward is a chance to see the lovely countryside up close. **Driver's Note:** Fill up your gas tank whenever you run across a gas station; a fill-up at Belize City should get you to the next gas at Dangriga.

SERVICES

Belize Bank and **Scotia Bank** are on St. Vincent Street near the bridge; get film developed at **Dangriga Photo Plus** on Bluefield Road. Mail your postcards at the **post office** on Mahogany Road. Medical problems can be addressed at the **Southern Regional Hospital** tel. 5/22078, Mile 1.5 on Stann Creek Valley Road; **Val's Laundry** is near the post office on Sharp Street; they also provide **Internet** services.

ALONG THE SOUTHERN HIGHWAY

HOPKINS

There are those who say that Hopkins is going to be *the* area to watch for new development. Right now it's still a low-key Garifuna fishing village, about eight miles south of Dangriga. Wooden boats are dragged onto the beach when fishermen are finished for the day, making picturesque photos. Craftsmen carve dugout canoes out of one large tree trunk and weave their own nets—life is simple here. Will it change? The small seaside village, four miles from the main road, has about 1,100 people with the main source of income from fishing. Until recently Hopkins was virtually untouched by tourism, getting only the occasional visitor. But listen to the hammers and watch while upscale lodges begin popping up just south of Hopkins.

PATTI LANGE

Maya musicians having a party

Accommodations and Food

Hopkins is one of the best places to join in the festivities for Garifuna Settlement Day. You can probably drop in and find a room most of the year, *except* around Garifuna Settlement Day (November 19). You have several choices.

At the southern end of the village, **Sandy Beach Lodge,** Hopkins Village, Stann Creek District, Belize, C.A., tel. 5/37006, email vals@btl.net, offers six cabins for rent. This is run by an all female co-op. Four cabins have private baths; others share a bathroom, outhouse-style. These accommodations are extremely basic, but generally clean and cost about US$20. Meals are served. Don't expect too much and you'll enjoy your stay in the village. Though the co-op is right on the beach, the shoreline looks trashed, although the women try to keep it clean.

Jungle Jeanies, tel 5/37047 offers simple accommodation by the beach. Cabins US$30, US$7 pp to camp. The sand flies here are really bad, and I don't think that bug repellent will stave them off!

Tipple Tree Beya Inn, P.O. Box 206, Dangriga, tel/fax. 5/12006, email tipple@btl.net, in Hopkins, offers a night's sleep for all budgets: campers pay US$5 a night (bring a tent; again, sand flies come in swarms), simple rooms with private baths are about US$30, and rooms with shared bath US$20. There is also an apartment, US$40.

Hopkins Inn, tel. 5/37013 (Oct.–May) or 907/683-2518 (June–Sept.), email hopkinsinn @btl.net, offers two cabañas on the beach with private baths, double beds, fans, refrigerators, and coffeepot; rates, with breakfast, are US$50.

Visitors have noticed a building project along the beach here for some time. Well, the rumor is that this will be completed by summer of 2001, so hopefully by the time you have this book in your hands, **Kanantik Jungle & Reef Resort** will be a reality. According to managing director, Roberto Fabbri, this will be quite special with privacy, luxury, excellent service, and primo cuisine. Sounds good! They *think* the introductory all-inclusive price will be US$300 per day, pp, all-inclusive, everything: lodging, meals, Belizean beer and rum, a daily excursion that will include scuba diving and everything else that people like to do in Belize. On 300 acres that includes beach and forest, there will be 25 cabañas, with thatch roofs, large and with a/c, luxury bathroom, and a private deck. For more info, P.O. Box 1482, Belize City, Belize, C.A., tel/fax 6/12048, email info @kanantik.com.

Still looking for lodging? You might just ask around; many homes in the village are happy to have a guest at the table for a small fee.

SITTEE

A couple of miles farther down the Southern Highway brings you to a turnoff to the left for Sittee. This qualifies as a village only in the loosest sense; it's just a cluster of fishing shacks, a few other houses, **Reynold's Store,** and amiable people scattered around the Sittee River. And that's the way it's been for a long, long time. But things change even here. In years past the accommodations were limited to a clapboard home offering the most basic of accommodations and owned by congenial locals. Today there are more, upscale options currently being built.

Accommodations and Food
Glover's Guest House, P.O. Box 563, Belize City, Belize, C.A., tel. 5/23048, is a very spartan lodging primarily for guests of Glover's Atoll Resort, a palm-studded caye on the barrier reef. Backpackers may want to try here; if it's full, there's always room for camping. Meals are available.

A short distance farther down the river, you'll find the **Toucan Sittee,** Sittee River, Stann Creek District, Belize, C.A., tel. 5/22888, a pleasant basic lodging with very good local food. On the right as you head for the ocean you'll see the sign, and a main house. The cabin nearest the river has two doubles, each with a kitchen, cold water, private bath, and a screened porch. The other cabin is a bunkhouse with bunk beds. About US$10 a day, with shared cold water bath; and the diehards can camp out for about US$5/day. Travelers can lodge here per

person or in private groups of four or more. One of the owners, Neville Collins, can arrange guided river and lagoon fishing. Snook, tarpon, peacock bass, sheepshead, and barracuda are his specialties. He also rents canoes. Delicious meals are based on local dishes, including *serre* (fish cooked in coconut milk), steak with onions and bell peppers, baked barracuda with yogurt, curries, and fresh fruit pies.

Lillpat Sittee River Resort, U.S. tel. 805/963-2501, email lillpat@btl.net, is 26 miles south of Dangriga and is dedicated to the fisherpeople of the world. Their guides are knowledgeable and snook, tarpon, and kingfish are the most abundant in nearby waters—contact the hotel for specific seasons. Note that they are catch-and-release friendly.

The lodge has four a/c rooms. They are simple but comfortably decorated. The pool is close to the bar. Rates are all-inclusive, starting about US$1,900 per person for six nights and include all meals, fishing guides, and boat.

The **Jaguar Reef Resort,** Box 297, Dangriga, Stann Creek District, Belize, C.A., tel. 2/12041, U.S. tel. 800/289-5756, email jaguarreef @btl.net, just keeps getting better. This full-service resort has seven cottages and 14 a/c rooms with fridge. All are spacious and comfortably furnished. The restaurant not only serves delicious meals, but for a night of romance, enjoy a candlelit dinner on the patio. A new pool can cool you off since the beach waters—although pretty—are often muddy and might not be inviting to everybody.

Rates for cabañas are US$185; for one-bedroom suites, US$275 (cheaper during the summer season). Rates drop considerably in low season (June 1–Oct. 31). Ask about their great packages, including tours, meals, transfers, and snorkeling on the cayes. Mountain bikes, kayaks, and a sand volleyball court are available.

The water just off the beach can be a bit muddy at times (like most Belizean mainland beaches) because of the close proximity of rivers and streams. Clear water is only a matter of minutes out to one of the near-shore cayes. But the reason to come here is the interesting mix of tours available, including dive trips to offshore cayes and Glover's Reef Atoll, or trips to the nearby Cockscomb Basin Wildlife Sanctuary.

Tours are available that combine both. Write or call for more information.

Just south of Sittee Village, **Hamanasi Resort** sits on 17 acres, including 400 feet of beachfront. It offers eight rooms and four suites, all with a view. Tiled bathrooms, a/c, fans, porches, colorful Guatemalan bedspreads, and all tile floors. Rates US$160, includes breakfast and taxes. Good pasta and, of course, fresh seafood. U.S. tel. 877/5-dive, in Belize tel. 5/12073, email info@hamanasi.com.

Driver's Note
Driving the causeway, which cuts through the marsh from the mainland to a kind of barrier island by the beach, is a one-way affair. A couple of places have been fashioned to allow one vehicle to pull over while another passes. Do not attempt to pass a vehicle on this causeway, especially in wet weather; the shoulders have a habit of crumbling beneath the weight of vehicles, causing them to slide or roll into the marsh.

COCKSCOMB BASIN

The land rises gradually from the coastal plains to the Maya Mountains; the highest point in the Cockscomb Basin range is Victoria Peak (3,675 feet). Geologists believe that Victoria Peak is four million years old, the oldest geologic formation in Central America. Mountain climbers find this peak a real adventure. The first climbers (a party that included Roger T. Goldsworth, governor of then-British Honduras) reached the peak in 1888; British soldiers recorded another climb in 1986. Heavy rain along the granite peaks of the Maya range (as much as 160 inches a year) runs off into lush rainforest thick with trees, orchids, palms, ferns, abundant birds, and exotic animals, including peccaries, anteaters, armadillos, tapirs, and jaguars. Until recently, the jaguar was a prize for game hunters. Today the beautiful cat has thousands of acres to roam protected from man in the Cockscomb Basin Wildlife Sanctuary.

The archaeology buff should check out the ruins in the vicinity of Cockscomb Basin: **Pomona** on North Stann Creek, **Kendal** on the Sittee River, and **Pierce** on South Stann Creek.

COCKSCOMB BASIN WILDLIFE SANCTUARY

Maya Center Village
A few miles south of the Sittee turnoff you'll come to the entrance to the sanctuary at Maya Center Village. This small town's claim to fame is the entry into the sanctuary. Check in here if you're interested in seeing the reserve (or the re-

mains of the Maya ceremonial site called Kuchil Balum). You'll find a selection of Belizean crafts for sale, including carved slate Maya images. Maya families within the sanctuary were relocated to this small village to protect the sanctuary environment. Since then the Maya have changed their lifestyles; the men work as guides and the women concentrate more on crafts. They have organized a crafts co-op, and their art is for sale at the **visitor's center** just past the gate into the sanctuary.

The Cockscomb Basin Wildlife Sanctuary is one of the best undisturbed nature centers in the country and easily one of the most beautiful. If you came to Belize to see luxuriant jungle, if you came to get close to the "skeeters" and all of God's creatures, and if you came to share sleeping space in a clapboard building with a bunch of strangers from all over the world who have the same interests as you, then you've come to the right place.

Most of the hotels in southern Belize provide transportation and guided tours of the wildlife sanctuary, or you can make arrangements with your hotel in other parts of the country for a side trip to southern Belize.

Sanctuary Beginnings
A large tract of approximately 155 square miles of forest was declared a forest reserve in 1984, and in 1986 the government of Belize set the region aside as a preserve for the largest cat in the Americas, the jaguar. The area is alive with wildlife, including the margay, ocelot, puma, jaguarundi, tapir, deer, paca, iguana, kinkajou, and armadillo (to name just a few),

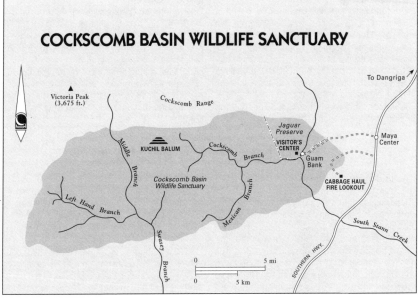

hundreds of bird species, and some unusual reptiles, including the red-eyed tree frog. And though you probably won't see the large cats roaming during the day (they hunt at night), it's exciting to see the large jaguar paw print; it's a real sign that the cat does indeed exercise ownership of this jungle. The peccary is said to be the jaguar's preferred diet, but, according to locals, the jaguar enjoys a love/hate relationship with the animal. Maya legend has it that the jaguar learned to climb trees to get away from the peccary because, as large and feared as the jaguar is, a group of the piglike peccaries can tear the great cat apart. The jaguar prefers to search from its tree branch for a single peccary.

Alan Rabinowitz and sponsors from the New York Zoological Society had a great deal to do with bringing the sanctuary to fruition. (See the special topic "Jaguars 1, Hunters 0" in the Introduction.) Rabinowitz did extensive research in this area, studying the jaguar, its habits, and its range. He lived in the jaguar's neighborhood for about 18 months and urged the government to create this protective hideaway for

the large cat. He has put it all down in a book titled *Jaguar: A Struggle and Triumph in the Jungles of Belize,* published in 1986 by Arbor House, New York.

Visitor's Center and Accommodations
Just past the entrance gate into the sanctuary is a small gift shop and office where you sign in. Seven miles into the sanctuary you'll find the visitor's center with its small museum, picnic area, and outhouse/restroom. You'll also find an "office" of the **World Wildlife Fund,** an important sponsor of the park, along with the **Belize Audubon Society** and the government. The overnight accommodations are in a couple of clapboard buildings with about a dozen bunks and metal roofs. A walled-off washing area has buckets, and a separate cooking area has a gas stove, a few pots and such; we're talking basic here. Or bring your own tent, US$2.50; US$3.50 if you want to use their cooking facilites. No campfires. And just in case, bring a poncho, mosquito netting, and insect repellent with enough DEET to pack some punch (30 percent or higher).

Hiking the Trails

From the visitor's center, many trails go off in different directions into the park. The trails are well cared for and comfortable even for hikers without lots of experience. Check out the front of the visitor's center building and you'll see a detailed map of the trails nearby. If you wish to take a guide for trekking farther afield, ask about availability at the center. Bring your swimsuit; you'll find cool natural pools for a refreshing plunge, especially along Stann Creek.

If You're Driving

Driving into the Cockscomb is best done with a 4WD vehicle. In the rainy season, even those can get stuck in the parking lot of the visitor's center—the best stretch of level ground in miles! And if you do get stuck, on a slow day it could take a long time and a few bucks before you are discovered and pulled free; however, there is a villager from Maya Center who can winch you out; it just might take a while to get him there.

PLACENCIA PENINSULA

Continuing on the Southern Highway, take the road to Riversdale, about 10 miles. In Riversdale a right turn will put you on the road down the strip of land called the Placencia Peninsula.

Belizeans and visitors alike agree that the finest beaches in the country are along this 11-mile slender strip. It feels like an island with the Caribbean on one side and the Placencia Lagoon on the other. It is predicted that eventually this will be the next big tourist development—so come quickly! Placencians will tell you that the best time to vacation here is anytime (although more rain falls May–Nov.). The informality and relaxed atmosphere are very special and highly contagious. Nature provides white sand fringed with waving green palms and the azure sea; the reef is visible in the distance. The water is clear enough to watch fish through the glasslike surface. Gentle breezes give way to strong winds on occasion but rarely long enough to mar any vacation. And from the Placencia coast you can hoist anchor and within a short time find a score of idyllic offshore cayes.

MAYA BEACH

Accommodations

As you proceed south on the peninsula you'll come to a small cluster of houses. Its particular attraction is a nice beach and almost complete isolation from tourists, minus the new resorts and cabins that keep popping up.

US$25–50

Xcape, P.O. Box 162, Dangriga, Belize, C.A., tel. 6/37002, email xcape@btl.net, is a simple four-room building on 10 acres of quiet beautiful beach. The rooms aren't fancy, but they are clean and have private bathrooms and still go for US$50 a night. An airy, large, screened-in room serves as dining room and general hangout area; a generator provides electricity (goes to battery at night). Meals are available. Camping is also allowed on the beach for US$5 per tent. Cold showers and access to the common room allowed.

Maya Playa, Seine Bight Village, Maya Beach, Belize, C.A., run by Stanley Torres, offers three cabañas on the beach. Each is two stories with a loft, private bath, and a mini-jungle in the bathroom. Restaurant and bar keep you fed and watered with local dishes and exotic drinks. Rates are inexpensive during the high season, about US$50 in high season.

Barnacle Bill's Beach Bungalows, tel.06/37010, email taylors@btl.net, offers two roomy cabañas on the beach. Many creature comforts like a comfy queen-size bed, full-size bath, beautiful wood counter tops, reading lights and coffee table makes this feel like your home away from home, including the American owner's two dogs. The kitchen has everything you need to cook your own meals. Outside there are picnic tables and tiki torches between the two cabins to enjoy this very quiet and secluded feeling neighborhood. Beach towels are available and kayaks are for rent. US$85 in the high season.

Orchid lovers will enjoy the grounds of **Singing Sands,** Maya Beach, Placencia Peninsula, Belize, C.A., tel./fax 6/22243, email

the Dockside Bar

PATTI LANGE

ssi@btl.net. It's a small resort geared for families with cabañas and a bar/restaurant along a beach sprinkled with palms. The pool will make the kids happy. Each of the cabañas has a fridge, some of them have bunk beds and a double bed, paneled wood walls, screened windows, ceiling fan, private bath, h/c water. US$90–120 a night. Meals are available in the restaurant for about US$30 a day. Canoes and bikes are complimentary to guests.

The Green Parrot Beach Houses and Resorts, 1 Maya Beach, Placencia, Belize, C.A., tel./fax 6/22488, email greenparot@btl.net, is a comfortable beachside resort with new owners and two-story A-frame cabañas. The upstairs loft has a queen and a single bed; downstairs is a double hide-a-bed. About US$125 a night. The dining area includes indoor and outdoor seating.

The **Maya Breeze Inn,** tel. 6/37012, is a blue-gray wood resort with five rooms of varying sizes, all close to the beach. The rooms sit on stilts and inside are shiny wood floors, colorful weavings on the wall, and a fridge and sink; all have a porch. One "room" has an upstairs with two bedrooms and a downstairs with a futon to sleep six. They say they are building a restaurant across the street. US$85–125.

SEINE BIGHT

For a taste of the Garifuna lifestyle, stay or at least visit Seine Bight, 2.5 miles south of Maya Beach, where you'll find a village of simple one-room wooden houses on stilts and about 550 people. In this tiny town most of the men are fishermen, and the women tend the family gardens, which they depend on for their basic food needs. It takes a while for the locals to strike up a friendship. In fact, unless you make the first move, about all that happens is that people will look you over, especially the kids. Some are realizing that they are sitting on a gold mine and are attempting to clean up the town, with hopes it will someday become a prime, low-key tourist destination. For now, the traditional lifestyle prevails.

The people here are different; they have a carefree intact culture that reflects ancient tribal customs. Men and women have a major split; the women have their own language that they say the men don't understand. The men will do absolutely nothing that might be construed as women's work. According to the women, the men lounge around in hammocks and drink most of the day. However, they have been known to help a stranger with car trouble. Ask before you take pictures, and accept "no" graciously.

If interested in diving (and who isn't?), the **Nauti One Dive Shop** is a full-service dive shop with two dive boats and a 24-foot boat for snorkeling and scuba trips to the Silk Cayes and elsewhere.

For a bus tour of Maya ruins, contact Ben and Janie Ruoti, Seine Bight, Placencia Peninsula, Belize, C.A., tel./fax 6/22310. You'll see the countryside on this 22-passenger bus.

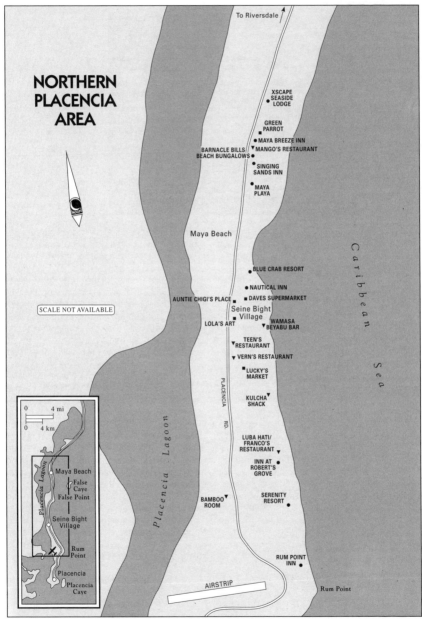

NORTHERN
PLACENCIA
AREA

To Riversdale

XSCAPE
SEASIDE
LODGE

GREEN
PARROT

MAYA BREEZE INN

MANGO'S RESTAURANT

BARNACLE BILLS
BEACH BUNGALOWS

SINGING
SANDS INN

MAYA
PLAYA

Maya Beach

Caribbean Sea

BLUE CRAB RESORT

NAUTICAL INN

AUNTIE CHIGI'S PLACE

DAVES SUPERMARKET

Seine Bight
Village

LOLA'S ART

WAMASA
BEYABU BAR

TEEN'S
RESTAURANT

VERN'S RESTAURANT

LUCKY'S
MARKET

PLACENCIA RD.

KULCHA
SHACK

LUBA HATI/
FRANCO'S
RESTAURANT

INN AT
ROBERT'S
GROVE

Placencia Lagoon

SERENITY
RESORT

BAMBOO
ROOM

RUM POINT
INN

AIRSTRIP

Rum Point

SCALE NOT AVAILABLE

0   4 mi
0   4 km

Placencia Lagoon

Maya Beach
False
Caye
False Point

Seine Bight
Village

Rum
Point

Placencia

Placencia
Caye

© AVALON TRAVEL PUBLISHING, INC.

SOUTHERN
PLACENCIA
AREA

AIRSTRIP

RUM POINT
INN

Rum Point

KITTY'S PLACE
PLACENCIA
DIVE SHOP

SUNSEA CABAÑA

TURTLE INN

MOTHER OCEAN'S
TROPIC HOTEL

CAMPING BEACH

Placencia Lagoon

PLACENCIA RD.

Mango
Creek

The "Sidewalk"

Caribbean Sea

CONRAD AND
LYDIA'S ROOMS

JENE'S FLAMBOYANT
RESTAURANT

SEA SPRAY HOTEL

D&L RESORT

RANGUANA
LODGE

PARKING

CREOLE GAL
GIFT SHOP

KINGFISHER
SPORTS LTD.

DAISY'S
ICE CREAM

JULIA'S
BUDGET
HOTEL

DEB AND DAVE'S
LAST RESORT

BTL

SEA MONKEY AND GRILL

CUNCHS

SUNRISE VILLAS

COZY CORNER

BLUE RUNNER GUIDING

POLICE

Placencia

OMAR'S DINER/
SUNRIDER GUEST HOUSE

ONE WORLD GIFT SHOP

WESTWIND HOTEL

COCONUTS CABAÑAS

JOHN THE
BAKERMAN

J. WESTBY FISHING GUIDE/
MISS LIZZY'S

The "Sidewalk"

BARRACUDA & JAGUAR INN/
PICKLED PARROT BAR & GRILL

TRADEWINDS HOTEL

HARALD
WALLEN'S
MARKET

ORANGE PEEL
GIFT SHOP

FISHERMAN'S
CO-OP

PLACENCIA
DIVE SHOP

DR. TED'S
ACUPUNCTURE

ICE

THE GALLEY
RESTAURANT
AND BAR

SOCCER
FIELD

PLACENCIA
TOURISM CENTER

PLACENCIA
BUS STOP

PURPLE SPACE MONKEY
INTERNET CAFE

PHONE

CHILI'S

SEA HORSE
DIVE SHOP

MIKE'S CARIBBEAN CLUB

BRENDA'S

TENTACLES
RESTAURANT

Big Creek

ICE

DOCKSIDE
BAR

SCALE NOT AVAILABLE

To Monkey River, Punta Gorda,
Nim Li Punit, and Lubaantun

0   4 mi
0   4 km

Maya Beach

False
Caye
False Point

Seine Bight
Village

Rum
Point

Placencia

Placencia
Caye

© AVALON TRAVEL PUBLISHING, INC.

Accommodations

As with Maya Beach, accommodations are growing in Seine Bight.

In the middle of town you'll find **Auntie Chigi's Place,** the colorful green building with the yellow trim. It's of simple wood-frame construction that will appeal to backpackers and those who really want local flavor. Auntie Chigi's offers four rooms with very simple but clean surroundings and shared bathrooms.

On a clean, shallow beach about a half-mile north of Seine Bight is **Blue Crab Resort,** Seine Bight, Placencia Peninsula, Belize, C.A., tel. 6/23544, fax 6/23543, U.S. tel. 800/359-1354 or 618/549-7347, email kerry@btl.net. American-owned, the resort offers a couple of rooms and a few cabañas. Each has a high thatched roof, louvered windows, h/c water, private bath, and three fans. Children under 16 stay free in adult's room. Two rooms take a/c, US$85. Meals are generally for guests only (nonguests with reservations only) and include a mix of Asian and American cuisine—try the Thai curry and garden shrimp. For those wanting regional dishes, Creole-style dishes are available on request. The resort arranges trips for night and day fishing, diving, snorkeling, Maya ruins, and the Cockscomb. Credit cards OK.

Just north of town is the **Nautical Inn,** tel. 6/23595, fax 6/23594, U.S. tel. 800/688-0377, email nautical@btl.net. The resort has an outside barbecue, an on-site travel agency, beauty salon, gift shop, and massage service and the **Oar House,** a restaurant and bar. The rooms feature Belizean-made furniture, ceiling fans, h/c water, private baths with deftly designed glass shower stalls, and "porthole" motif mirrors. Four rooms have a/c. Ask for an upper-level room, right at "coconut" height. Rainwater is used for drinking and in the showers and toilets. Children under 12 free in same room with adults. Rates range from US$105 to 125. Credit cards OK. Three meals can be provided. On the beach, a catamaran, canoes, and volleyball net await energetic guests. Beyond the beach stretches a 100-foot dock with a *palapa* at the end. Every Monday at 3:30, the inn offers the lagoon sunset booze cruise—all the rum punch you can drink while you watch the sunset over the Placencia lagoon.

KULCHA SHACK MENU— A FEW GARIFUNA DISHES

hudut: fish simmered in thick coconut milk with herbs and cooked over an open fire—served with *fu-fu* (beaten plantain)

tapow: green banana cut in wedges and simmered in coconut milk with fish, herbs, and seasonings—served with white rice or *ereba* (cassava bread)

seafood gumbo: a combination of conch, lobster, shrimp, fish, and vegetables, cooked in coconut milk, herbs, and grated green banana or plantain—served with rice or *ereba*

Irish Moss: a seaweed shake

Food and Culture

Take an evening to discover the one-of-a-kind **Kulcha Shack** (pronounced SHOCK), tel. 6/22015. By day it's just another small forlorn structure on the beach with some friendly people serving drinks and snacks. But at night it takes on magic. You'll hear the haunting drums of the Garifuna accompanied by melodies from the past. If you're lucky enough to have a translator with you, you'll learn a bit of Garifuna melodrama. The drummers know their craft well, and with reservations on the weekends, you'll see modern entertainment (*punta* rock) as well as traditional fare. The lamp-lit café serves authentic Garifuna food. For a great souvenir to take home, ask to see Darlene's (the owner's wife) handmade Garifuna dolls. For the special dinner and show, minimum of four people, the price is US$25 per person; make reservations and call before 6 P.M. Ask about the simple cabins on the beach.

Lola's Art Gallery and Cafe Lagundo is a definite must-stop (located behind the soccer field—follow the well-marked signs). Lola sells handmade dolls, as well as a selection of more whimsical artwork, including oil and acrylic paintings on canvas (US$14–150), notecards (US$0.50 cents), and holiday cards (200 varieties in all). She also sells shell craft of different kinds, carvings, and painted plaques and coconut shells. If you miss her sign, just ask around for Lola Delgado.

For a taste of local food and culture, make a reservation for dinner or lunch with Lola at her **Cafe Lagundo,** (same location). Garifuna and

Creole food and entertainment—be it storytelling or music—awaits you. Bring your own bottle if you want a little libation.

If you want to drink a beer with the locals, **Wamasa Bar** is it. Mostly men here, so beware you single woman travelers.

PLACENCIA TOWN

Sitting at the southern tip of the palm-dotted peninsula, Placencia Town is more than 100 miles south of Belize City. To get there you can travel by land, sea, or air. Placencia has been a fishing village from the time of the Maya, except for the intrusion of a pirate settlement now and then. Even with the arrival of tourists, it is still home to many fishermen. Modern conveniences (including electricity, telephones, and email) also have arrived!

The town itself is about a mile long. Delightful guest-house resorts continue to develop in the area along the coast, and the people who run these isolated resorts offer a warm pioneer spirit of cordiality. Fortunately (for now at least) they all fit into the environment—Placencia hasn't been spoiled by high-rise, jet-set, hundreds-at-a-time tour groups that have filtered into and transformed many other once-placid Caribbean locations.

In lieu of a newspaper, local cafés are the places to hear all the news and daily gossip of Placencia. If something is really important, it'll be posted on a tree or a fence around the gas pump and grocery store.

ORIENTATION

In Placencia, there really isn't a main road through the "downtown business section," but there *is* a mile-long "main sidewalk." The road into town (Placencia Road) comes down the peninsula, skirts the airport, runs alongside the lagoon, and parallels the sidewalk on the west. More and more businesses are springing up along Placencia Road. The road passes a large soccer field and at its far end you'll see a turquoise building (the Galley Restaurant); the road continues to the service station, ice house, bus stop, and main dock at the end of town.

"Downtown" Placencia

This stretched-out community doesn't really have a "downtown," but if I had to pick a "central

downtown" or "heart" of Placencia Town it would probably be along the shoreline near where the old post office once held fort. Placencia's post office is an open-air affair near the sea. A gas pump sits just a few feet away near the bank, and close by is a small harbor with cafés and bars—gathering places for locals and visitors alike.

Use the gas pump as a reference point; just east of it is the dock and marina, which accommodate good-sized vessels. You'll see a mixture of fishing boats and yachts in the harbor. This is a good mooring area for visitors, and for those looking for a boat to head out to the cayes, ask at the dock, the post office, or the grocery store—someone will direct you. Need a boat ride to Big Creek? This is the place to get that as well. Allow a good half-hour on the water to get to Big Creek bus station, and at the bus station transportation is available to the airport. You'll need to make arrangements ahead of time to have a taxi pick you up shoreside in Big Creek. The Placencia airstrip is just north of Rum Point Inn, and the bus stop is close to the gas pump.

South of the Gas Pump

South of the gas pump, you'll find a sandy path that leads southwest along the water past a few houses and businesses, including Chili's and Mike's Caribbean Club. Farther down, past a few mangroves and houses, and you'll pass Paradise Vacation Resort. Next to the resort is Tentacles Restaurant, and out on the dock, Dockside Bar. Both are relaxing places to spend the cocktail hour meeting other travelers and locals; sip a little, nibble a little, and enjoy the end of the day.

Back at the gas pump going in the opposite direction, across from the post office and the road, you'll see a warehouse-like building; that's **Olga's** local grocery store. This is not a modern supermarket, but you'll find most of your needs, fresh breads, cheese, produce, sundries, and this and that.

SIGHTS

When visiting Placencia allow yourself to be lulled into a lazy funk with the beautiful sea, sandy beaches, and a chance to meet the friendly people of Placencia. Once you've relaxed and you're ready to go again, this is a great hub from which to investigate the surrounding countryside. In Placencia you can be as busy as you desire with snorkeling, beachcombing, scuba diving, or land trekking to the Maya Mountains, Monkey River, the jaguar preserve, and Maya ruins, or bird-watching and photographing the rich wildlife of the region. This is not to be missed. Consider yourself fortunate; you made it here before the crowds!

Along the "Sidewalk"
A short distance from the grocery store down a dirt path is the beginning of the "sidewalk," or as the *Guinness Book of Records* puts it, "the world's most narrow street." It's about 24 inches wide and meanders through the sand for a mile. Houses and businesses line both sides. The townsfolk had better keep this sidewalk intact forever; it receives almost as much publicity as Beverly Hills' Rodeo Drive. Just off the sidewalk you'll pass the **fishermen's co-op, ice, guide services, and fishing;** if you're hungry check out and **Jene's Flamboyant Restaurant.** At the very end of the sidewalk you'll be at the beach designated for campers, tents and all. Along the sidewalk look for **Daisy's,** a tiny little ice-cream/pastry shop with a few tables. The tasty ice cream here is hand-cranked in a variety of flavors, including local papaya and rum raisin.

WATER SPORTS

Diving and Snorkeling
From the **Placencia Dive Shop** trips can be designed to take in the reef and inner cayes, with camping on the reef, lagoon fishing, and deep-sea fishing. Dive trips to the cayes usually include two tanks, dive equipment, lunch, and guide. Scuba divers must bring their "C" cards. For more information, call/fax 6/23313 or email pds@btl.net.

This 24-inch-wide sidewalk serves as Placencia's "main street."

Out on their own pier, **SeaHorse Dive Shop,** tel./fax 6/23166, email seahorse@btl.net, teaches both PADI and NAUI courses and offers day dives to the surrounding area. Laughing Bird Caye is a popular dive site with a small beach where you stop for lunch. In April and May these guys are the only ones to take people to dive with the whale sharks. If this interests you, plan your trip near the full moon as that's when the big guys tend to show up. Definitely email ahead to plan this trip.

Rum Point Divers is yet another good dive shop. Divers travel to the cayes and other dive destinations on the *Auriga II,* a comfortable PRO 42-foot dive boat. Dive packages are offered for extended or short periods. For more information, contact Rum Point Inn, tel. 6/23239, fax 6/23240; in the U.S. call the Belize specialists at **Toucan Travel,** tel. 800/747-1381, email rupel@btl.net.

Sea Kayaking

This is a great way to explore the near-shore cayes, mangroves, creeks, and rivers. Kayaks are available to guests at several resorts, including **Kitty's, The Inn at Robert's Grove,** and **Turtle Inn,** as well as **Lagoon Saloon** from Kevin Madeira, tel. 6/23178. **Toadal Adventure,** tel. 6/23207, email debanddave@btl.net, offers guided trips.

Exploring the Cayes

Find a boat and captain through your hotel or at one of the many tour stands along the sidewalk. Take a morning to cruise around the southern sea and discover tiny little islands scattered about, including **Laughing Bird Caye.** This mini-atoll is a narrow S-shaped caye with three small harbors and easy access for snorkelers to discover, just offshore, a crystalline underwater world of fascinating corals and beautiful tropical fish. Clumps of palm trees offer a tiny bit of shade, and the sea around the caye is brilliant turquoise—no lie!

Fishing

Anglers consider Placencia the "permit capital of the world." **Kingfisher Sports, Ltd.,** is noted for a good fishing operation. Fishing guide Charlie Leslie has a reputation for being *the* best fly fisherman anywhere. He has many years of experience in these waters, and some visitors have been returning almost that long because of Charlie.

Kingfisher Sports takes you to a wide variety of fishing spots, from inshore places that include nearby flats to **Tarpon Caye,** and to the remote area of **Ycacos.** Bonefish, tarpon, snook, snapper, and permit that weigh in at up to 30 pounds are some of the rewards.

Offshore fishing will take you outside the reef, where the depth increases dramatically. It's common to find wahoo, sailfish, marlin, kingfish, and dolphin fish. Sight-seeing trips inland, as well as diving and picnicking trips on the nearby cayes, are available. Ask about package prices, which include room, food, boat, guide, and fishing. For more information, contact Robert Hardy in the United States, 107 Lafayette Ave., San Antonio, TX 78209, 512/826-0469, fax 512/822-6415. In Placencia, contact Charles Leslie, tel. 6/23323.

Another great place to catch bonefish to your heart's desire is **Big Creek,** a short skiff-ride away from Placencia. "Good bones," as well as wily permit and torpedo-size tarpon, are to be expected. Ask about boat charters to Guatemala.

Hints: Gear is usually provided but come prepared if you have a feel for specific gear; there's little choice of equipment in Placencia. For bonefishing, experienced anglers suggest a sturdy reel, a good nine-foot fly rod, and a no. 8-weight, floating, saltwater, tapered fly-line. Recommendations for the newcomer to tropical fishing locations: Bring good polarized glasses with side shields and a heavy-duty sunscreen (don't forget the ears, nose, and lips). Wear a long-sleeved shirt to keep out the sun and lightweight ripstop nylon pants for wading as the sun's rays will go right through the water and burn your legs. For even more protection, wear a hat—those funky, double-billed, fore-and aft-style hats with bandannas are excellent sun shields. You will need shoes for wading knee-deep along the coral flats; sneakers or Patagonia Reef Walkers serve the purpose. Standing in the shallow water with the sun's reflection for three or four hours can burn your skin to a crisp unless you take precautions. Above all, have fun and remember, *catch and release!*

OTHER RECREATION

Cycling

Biking between outlying resorts and Seine Bight or Placencia Town is an airy way to see everything there is to see on the lower part of the peninsula while burning off some of those Seaweed Punches. Singing Sands, Rum Point Inn, the Inn at Robert's Grove and Kitty's Place are just some of the resorts that have bikes available for their guests. Bikes are available for rent at **Deb 'n' Dave's,** tel. 6/23207. Those with a car can easily take a boat over to Big Creek or Mango Creek and head out into the surrounding countryside for some exploring. Or, when you're ready, take off for Punta Gorda and points south. It's only about a 20-minute trip through the mangroves and channels into Big Creek.

Weekend Sports

If you feel like hanging with the locals, don't miss Saturday's **horseshoe tournament** at the Lagoon Saloon and Sunday's **ring toss** at the Dockside Cafe. Both are drinking games and draw the locals, some of whom even close their own businesses to partake in the weekly festivities.

More to Explore

An hour's drive off the peninsula takes you to the luxuriant rainforest of the Cockscomb Basin. And if possible go to **Golden Stream** on this side of Nim Li Punit. Go by boat across Mango Lagoon to more lush forest, small pools, and waterfalls—these can be coolish, although a higher waterfall is warmed as it flows across hot rocks into an eight-foot-deep pool, complete with tiny aquarium fish to keep you company. Nearby, stop at a small craft shop where you'll find carved slate, small baskets, embroidery, and other crafts of the area; there's an outhouse here.

If you have a chance while visiting in Placencia, take a trip out of town to the banana packing plant—very interesting. Ask one of the locals for directions.

MONKEY RIVER VILLAGE

Placencia is a good base for exploring some beautiful jungle areas. A one-hour boat ride brings you to the mouth of the Monkey River, a good picnic spot with noisy howler monkeys, tall trees, toucans, oropendulas (birds that nest in hanging bags that they weave), and wading birds. Monkey River Village lies at the mouth of the river on the Caribbean Sea—the best of two worlds. For a long time this has been a fine day trip from Placencia. But more and more people are traveling to Monkey River Village for a night or two of total isolation. A few fishermen in the know have made this a Belize *destination.* Anyone who really likes isolation, primitive surroundings, and nature might enjoy a visit here. Monkey River Village today is almost a ghost town compared to earlier years, back before the banana blight stifled that industry. Sound good? Then take a look.

At one time this entire area and the area up the river provided a home to profuse numbers of spider monkeys and howler monkeys. Today most of the spiders are gone. However, you'll first hear and then see the black howlers that live in the trees. If it's wildlife you want, come to Monkey River. Like to fish, discover exotic birds, meander through the jungle, or snorkel along offshore cayes? The accommodations are few, but the adventurer will find what he/she wants here.

Accommodations: These are barefoot-casual inns. Most offer a set menu (a different entrée served each day). Reservations are required for meals, though all of these small cafés will serve drop-ins something such as a burger or a beer. The village is accessible only by boat, but you may drive to the parking lot across the water from the village and a boat will come pick you up. Be sure to inspect your accommodations before you move in.

Enna's Hotel, tel. 6/12033 or 22014, is nestled in coconut trees and hibiscus, and is spartan-simple. It's two stories with four rooms on each floor with double bed and single bed, screened windows, floor fan, one shared bath on each floor with h/c water. Rates are US$25, US$5 each additional person. Friendly and relaxed, the people of the village are around to share stories and adventures. On the premises, **Ms. Alice's Restaurant** offers a set menu, served in a large dining room with a view of the sea.

Sunset Inn, tel. 6/12028, is tucked in at the end of the lagoon and surrounded by beautiful tropical plants. Off the beaten path, it offers an atmosphere that is quiet and relaxed. The two-story structure boasts nine rooms on the top floor, plus a spacious shared veranda with a lovely view of the river. Each room has a double bed, floor fan, private bath with h/c water, and screened windows. Rates are US$25. On the premises you'll find the **Sunset Inn Dining Room.** Reservations required.

A little more upscale, **Bob's Paradise,** tel. 6/12024, offers a contact in Florida—E.J. at 954/429-8763—email bobsparadise@webtv.net, website at www.bobsparadise.com. Surrounded by vibrant jungle with the blue Caribbean out front, Bob's Paradise is set about one mile north of Monkey River in a private, relaxed, and friendly atmosphere. It's accessible by boat only; if driving, park your vehicle in the parking lot at the end of Monkey River Road and catch a water taxi or call Bob for pickup. Three

Placencia Tour Guides

A number of guides are available in Placencia to take you to the surrounding areas. Dave Vernon of **Toadal Adventure,** tel. 6/23207, email debanddave@btl.net, is one of, if not the best, guides in Belize. He offers numerous unique trips and each year he seems to come up with something even better and more adventurous than the last. His day trips include biking to untouched ruins, mangrove ecology kayak paddles to see manatees and other wildlife, and guided hikes through the Cockscomb Basin rainforest, ending with a leisurely tube float down a river or a "rock slide"—making your way down a river by sliding down the smooth, natural grooves of rocks that have been worn from hundreds of years of water flowing. Dave is a walking encyclopedia and a must-speak for the eco-traveler. Call for info or stop by the office of **Deb 'n' Dave's Last Resort.**

Local Sam Burgess drives a taxi in town, but his main occupation is as a guide for his company, **Jaguar Tours,** which you can reach at his **Sea Shell Giftshop,** tel. 6/23139. He has a 12-passenger van and escorts guests to Garifuna villages, nearby caves, rivers, and to the jaguar reserve and Maya ruin sites.

private beach-side cabañas have screened windows, two full-size beds, ceiling fans, private bath with h/c water, small refrigerator, and a view of the sea. The **Tiki Bar** offers meals—no reservations required. In summer, rates are US$75, US$25 each additional person; in winter, US$100, US$40 each additional person; more during holidays. A small dory is available for guests. Credit cards accepted.

Monkey House Resort, tel. 6/12032, email monkeyhous@btl.net. In the United States, call Walter in Texas, 409/755-1659, fax 409/755-4126, email watheriot@juno.com, website www.monkeyhouseresort.com. Sitting between the lush jungle and the sparkling Caribbean, the resort is approximately 300 yards north of exotic Monkey River. Intimate and exclusive, it combines old world Belize and new world conveniences, with emphasis on relaxation interspersed with adventure. It's accessible by road or boat. Two private beach-side cabañas with two full beds, ceiling fan, floor fan, private bath with h/c water, screened windows on all sides, and a fully screened front porch with an open view of the sea. The tropical dining room/bar offers floor-to-ceiling views of the Caribbean. Reservations required. Rates in summer are US$75, US$35 extra person; in winter, US$100, US$50 extra person; more on holidays. Paddleboats are available. Credit cards are accepted. The owners, the Scotts, are ticket agents for Tropic and Maya Island Air. Little Monkey Caye bird rookery is just 500 yards out in front of the Monkey House Resort.

All hotels and resorts offer sea and land tours and trips. The Monkey River boat- and jungle-walk tour is the highest-rated tour in the south of Belize. Local guides and fishermen are experts. Sorry, . no dive shop yet, but bring your snorkeling gear. Overnight caye trips are available as are river camping trips. (You're dropped off at the Bladen bridge and canoe down the river, stopping at night to camp.)

local children getting a lesson, Monkey River

PATTI LANGE

Placencia Tours, tel./fax 6/23186 takes visitors to Cockscomb Basin Wildlife Sanctuary for day or overnight trips—if you really want to look for the jaguar take a nocturnal stroll. They also travel to the Maya sights of Lubaantun, Nim Li Punit, Uxbenka, and Blue Creek. Placencia Tours is in Placencia Town, across from the ball field; Ellis says, "Drop by the veranda for information." Other guide services are available through most of the hotels and guest houses.

Kurt and Earl Godfrey, who are experienced in manatee watching, camping, river tours, and fishing, operate reliable **Southern Guides,** tel. 6/23277.

Ocean Motion guide service, tel. 6/23162 or 23363, offers fishing, Monkey River trips, and snorkeling at Laughing Bird Caye.

ACCOMMODATIONS

Most of these budget lodgings lie within the central part of Placencia Town, and many are close to the "sidewalk." Options are also given should you choose to meander north of town; the area continues to grow, adding good-looking resorts and simple cabañas, all with the personalities of the people who have chosen to make Belize "home." During our last visit many of the hotels were for sale—be prepared for some changes, new owners, and possible new additions.

Note that the resorts on the peninsula take turns during the week offering fun stuff—be it beach barbecues, booze cruise, etc. Check the local paper as it's all posted.

Under US$25
Check out **Julia's Guesthouse,** tel. 6/23185. Some of the rooms share a bath and are cheaper. Rooms are US$15–40. **Lucille's Rooms,** tel. 6/23190, offers eight rooms; four share a bathroom.

Lydia's Guesthouse, tel. 6/23117, fax 6/23354, email lydias@btl.net, has simple rooms with shared bath that range in price from US$18–20. Miss Lydia will make you breakfast if you make arrangements the day before; she also bakes such delectables as Creole bread; there's always a line when it comes out of the oven. Anyone can get his or her laundry washed by Lydia. She also rents kayaks and is the lady to

talk to if you are looking to rent a house.

Deb 'n' Dave's Last Resort, tel. 6/23207, email debanddave@btl.net, is on the back road into town. The four small, clean rooms share a bath and are close to everything, US$20. Owner Dave has a wealth of information about Belize and is head guide for **Toadal Adventures,** one of the best tour outfits in the country.

A *palapa* restaurant and bar of the same name but different owners is adjacent to the hotel. Cold beers and big burritos available every day except Monday. A lot of local guides hang out here, making it easy to get a feel of what Placencia is all about. Deb and Dave also have mountain bike rentals available.

US$25–50
The **Barracuda and Jaguar Inn,** tel. 6/23330, fax 6/23250, email wende@btl.net, offers two hardwood cabañas with screened balcony, private baths, coffeepots, and refrigerators. It's one of the few places that has parking available. Rates are about US$40. It's not on the ocean side of the path and on the sand, as is the **Pickled Parrot Restaurant** with seafood and vegetarian pizza specialties. Includes local airport pickup and continental breakfast.

The **Serenade Guesthouse,** tel. 6/23163, email serenade@btl.net, is a two-story cement building right off of the path. Ten simple, clean rooms, upstairs and down and are all either triples or quads. The upstairs rooms catch great breezes. Air-conditioning is more. A tiny but breezy restaurant and bar is on the top floor and serves three meals a day. Room rates vary from US$23–55. Owners also operate **Frank Caye,** 28 miles away. The four and a half acre island has three cabañas that sleep four each. A caretaker on the island cooks meals, utilizing the abundant conch and lobster. US$50 per person a night; transportation to get there is extra.

Look for the **Tradewinds Hotel,** tel. 6/23122, fax 6/23201, email trdewndpla@btl.net, on five acres near the sea, offering six cabañas and three rooms. Cabañas have spacious rooms, fans, refrigerators, coffeepots, and private yards just feet away from the ocean. The rooms are smallish but have private bath with hot water, fans, and a small porch with a hammock. For the cabañas pay US$55; the rooms about US$25.

The family-run **Sea Spray Hotel,** tel./fax 6/23148, is 30 feet from the beach on the point and is one of the best places in town for homeyness. They've upgraded and added a second floor. The Sea Spray offers four different types of rooms, plus a cabaña for a total of 18 rooms, all with private bathrooms, refrigerators, h/c water, and coffeepots. Some rooms are basic. The people are warm and friendly. For land- or sea-based tours, owner Jodie will help with details. Rates US$25–55. **De Tatch** restaurant on the premises serves breakfast, lunch, and dinner and offers email and Internet services.

US$50–100
The bright yellow **Cunchs Villa,** tel. 6/23271, email lgodfrey@btl.net, is owned and run by local fishing guide Curt Godfrey and caters to the fishing crowd with four rooms on the beach with private baths, refrigerators, and coffeemakers. Rooms are US$55. Expect a day of fly-fishing here to cost about US$200.

Kitty's Place

Coconut Cottage, tel. 6/23155, fax. 6/23234, email harbaks@btl.net (subject: Coconut Cottage), is a two-room cottage on the beach, 50 feet from the water's edge, run by ex-pat Kay Westby. This is a spacious room with double and single beds, private bath, refrigerator, and coffeepot. US$55 in high season.

The **Ranguana Hotel,** tel./fax 6/23112, right off the strip, has five private cabañas, three of them on the beach. All are spacious with beautiful wood floors, walls, and ceilings. Amenities include double and single beds, coffeepots, refrigerators, private baths with hot water, and a large deck. No restaurant here, but you are close to everything "downtown." US$60. They also have simple accommodations on their caye. Cabins are about US$30 a night and camping is US$10/night. As with all of the offshore islands, getting there is the expensive part, but worth it if you want your own island for a night or two.

Westwind Hotel, tel. 6/23255, email westwind @btl.net, has eight rooms with great views, sunny decks, h/c water, private baths, and fans. This resort provides all the amenities of some of the resorts north of town, right in the heart of the village. Rooms US$45–55 a night. Credit cards OK.

Serenity Resort, tel. 6/23232, fax 6/23231, email serenity@btl.net, is an attractive family resort sitting on 21 acres of land with 12 cabañas and 10 rooms. Cabañas have tiled roofs and floors, high ceilings, h/c water, ceiling fans, private bathrooms, and patios US$85. The dining room, with blue tablecloths and blue-upholstered chairs, has a thatched veranda that faces the sea. The pricing structure reflects the "family" part of the resort: Children under five stay and eat free; those 5–11 stay free and pay half price for meals; those 12–18 pay US$10 per person per day for lodging and full price for meals.

On the other side of the street from the Serenity is the **Bamboo Room,** an open air palapa bar with tables that overlook the lagoon. This is a beautiful spot to watch the sunset over the lagoon, and, talented—and not so talented—locals are known to get up and sing here on occasion.

US$100–150
Another favorite, **Kitty's Place,** P.O. Box 528, Belize City, Belize, C.A., tel. 6/23227, fax

6/23226, email info@kittysplace.com, is owned and operated by Kitty Fox and Ran Villanueva. Just on the other side of the airstrip from Rum Point, it's a growing resort, with a nice beach and comfortable rooms, casitas, and apartments. The economy rooms share a bath and cost US$40; the casitas, US$140, on the beach are beautifully decorated, rich in Guatemalan fabric, and spacious with a fridge and a coffeemaker. The Garden Rooms, US$100, overlook a small pond and lush greenery, and feature queen beds.

Kitty's Restaurant and Bar has tasty food—check out the nightly specials. Sunday night try their chicken Pibil, served with conch fritters. If you're looking for a romantic dinner for two with candlelight, go to the veranda. The gift shop off the reception desk is the best in Placencia in variety and selection. Activities offered include day trips to Monkey River, snorkeling trips, and sea kayaks rentals. The daytrip snorkel to Laughing Bird Caye and French Louis Caye shouldn't be missed. The clear aqua waters are surrounded by beautiful deserted islands. Lunch is at French Louis, Kitty's private caye, served by the caretaker. Hammock and kayak time a must.

Laughing Bird Caye is a national park so there are no accommodations. But on French Louis Caye, Kitty offers a simple guest-house cabin for those who want to get away from it all. The caye is about six miles off the coast. It's never crowded—only a few beds. The snorkelers from Kitty's stop here for lunch, but other than that it's all yours. (You do have to share with the caretaker—a great cook, if a little scary looking.) Around the tiny caye, the sea is filled with those colorful swimming critters. A kayak is available. US$75 per night.

Just a half mile north of Placencia on what may be the widest single strip of beachfront on the island (1,000 feet) is **Mother Ocean's Tropic Hotel,** tel. 6/23233, fax 6/23224, U.S. tel. 800/662-3091, which has six waterfront cabins with a/c and kitchenettes on a cleared lot with palms swaying in the breeze. A tennis court on the beach is for guests to use; snorkeling and other activities can be arranged. Each renovated cabin has two queen-size beds, a private bath, and a large screened porch.

US$150–200

The **Luba Hati,** Placencia Peninsula, Belize, C.A., tel. 6/23402 or 6/23571, email lubahati@btl.net, is a great addition to Belize—a lovely, different design, great food, and friendly people all in one. Meaning "House of the Moon," it is a Mediterranean-inspired villa resort and offers simple elegance in a quiet, lush area. The eight spacious rooms have king or queen beds, full baths, freestanding sinks, and colorful tiles along with batik prints and African decor. Some rooms have balconies and swinging shutter doors. One room has a kitchenette, dining table, queen bed, and trundle bed.

Downstairs, tile floors and wood tables with colorful ceramic-tile tops sit in front of large doors that open to face the sea and its fresh breezes. Other amenities include an airy dining room, an outside lounge area with wooden chairs and hammocks, and a dock ideal for sunbathing. A third-story viewing platform is perfect for stargazing or for viewing the surrounding area. On the beach, a simple shack is home to a sauna downstairs and a massage room upstairs. Rates US$80–150.

Franco's Restaurant is open daily except Sunday. A garden on the grounds grows "whatever we can get to grow," and these fresh things are used in many dishes. An extensive wine list and Mediterranean dishes such as penne alla béchamel and eggplant with a tahini garlic sauce tempt the taste buds. Pizza and nightly specials round out the menu.

Rum Point Inn, tel. 6/23239, fax 6/23240, in the U.S. call Toucan Travel, 32 Traminer Dr., Kenner, LA 70065, 800/747-1381, fax 504/464-0325, is operated by George and Corol Bevier and is a favorite of guests and divers from around the world. The Rum Point offers some of the best accommodations on the peninsula and a bustling dive business. The 42-foot jet boat *Auriga II* is another good dive boat on the peninsula. Condo-style rooms and cabañas house guests. The cabañas: Do they look more like mushrooms or igloos? It's a toss-up. But once you're inside, they become magical (at least for many guests). Expect a cool, spacious, tropical atmosphere, each attractively furnished with two queen beds, brightly woven Guatemala fabrics, rich hardwood furniture, tropical plants, roomy bathrooms, tile floors, and fans. Each dome-shaped cabaña is pristine white inside and out, with artfully shaped peek-a-boo screen openings cut into the walls. It's probably the most modern and unusual hotel in Placencia. If these cabañas aren't for you, ask for the newer buildings; they offer equally spacious, conventionally shaped rooms, enormous but furnished in the same pleasant way, and they offer a/c. The pool pleases kids of all ages.

Dining is family-style, meaning all guests sit together and eat at the same time. Honeymooners who want to be alone should check with the Beviers. In a week the daily menu never repeats itself. Foods are fresh and innovative, and a lovely dining room and veranda overlook the water.

In the main house, Corol runs a nice little gift shop, but it's the lounge that's so terrific, with a library offering an amazing variety of books about Central America, mammals, invertebrates, the Maya, plants—you name it. The cozy bar is a great gathering place for cocktails and delicious toasted coconut chips before dinner. Town is about a 20-minute walk away. Tours to the cayes and reef are available as well as bikes to ride into town or to Seine Bight.

Down the road from Kitty just a bit is the **Turtle Inn,** tel. 6/23244, or Dr. Lois Kruschwitz, 2190 Blue Bell, Boulder, CO 80302, 303/444-2555, email turtleinn@btl.net, off to the left on a palmy beach. It doesn't come much more comfortably casual than this lodging run by American Skip White. Turtle Inn offers great atmosphere, diving, and adventure travel. The curious will find excursions to far-off cayes, the reef, and Maya Mountain jungles. Sea kayaks are available for rent by the day and half-day. The Turtle Inn is a series of quaint thatched-roof cabañas on the beach with ceiling fans, hot water, verandas, and hammocks. All meals included; an option with continental breakfast only is less. One beach house is also available. All electricity is solar-powered. But no mention of Turtle Beach is complete without mentioning the bar/restaurant area. The wood deck that spills out onto the beach at just above sand level invites one to step up, plop down, and strike up a conversation with the nearest fellow wayfarer. It's a great spot for late afternoon drinks about the time guests come in from their adventures. Sharing tales of a day in the ocean or jungle whets the appetite for food as well as conversation. The CD collection is vast, to say the least, and the restaurant here won't disappoint with a menu heavy on seafood and local dishes.

Sitting on the beach, the **Mariposa,** tel.6/24069, email foxbuddy@btl.net, has two studio rooms, complete with all kitchen utensils and fridge for those who want to do their own cooking. Rates are US$125 a night, high and low season.

Perched on eight acres of beachfront is the spacious **The Inn at Robert's Grove,** tel. 6/23565, from the United States call 800/565-9757, email info@robertsgrove.com. Owned and operated by easygoing, transplanted New Yorkers, Robert and Risa Frackman, the inn is one of the most luxurious in the country. The 20 rooms are spacious with high ceilings and king-sized beds. Two are luxury suites and if you can afford to stay here, it's a bit of heaven. The bathrooms are big and have a huge funky-shaped tile bathtub. Tasteful wood furniture surrounds you and the a/c refreshes when the heat kicks in. There's an in-room safe to keep your valuables protected. The staff is wonderful—pleasant yet casual, efficient but not overbearing.

The food is delicious. Try the prime beef wrapped with bacon and served with coconut shrimp or the daily homemade soups like cold chicken curry and cream of mushroom. Pasta specials include pasta rags—a homemade pasta in a tangy tomato sauce—and how about penne pasta, black olives, and artichoke hearts in olive oil? And yes, homemade desserts, like fresh coconut cream pie—a graham cracker crust, layered with custard and topped with grated coconut is as good as you can handle. Pricey, but oh so worth it. Around the pool and outside bar enjoy local dancers and musicians as they entertain. The pleasant evening breeze and candlelit atmosphere makes a romantic evening.

Three outdoor hot tubs on 3-story high rooftops offer great views of the ocean and nighttime stargazing. Look for the lap pool and a dock with chairs and hammocks.

The tennis court is one of very few in the area and the scuba shop is handy, with a knowledgeable dive master. Robert's has its own offshore caye to visit. Kayaks, bikes, and small sailboats are available to the guests. Rooms are US$150; suites about US$225.

FOOD

You'll find some of the finest Creole cooking in Belize in Placencia. Most of the cafés are low-key and the real "stuff" includes fresh seafood cooked in coconut milk and local herbs, with liberal amounts of plantain or banana. However, if something less daring sounds good, you'll find sandwiches, tamales, hamburgers, and great Italian food.

For a quick burrito or hot dog, try **Chili's. Omar's Diner** can fix you up with pork chops, T-bone steak, or conch steak for about US$6, lobster for US$10, or breakfast specials for about US$3. Omar's Diner is on the sidewalk and Chili's is close by.

The **Galley Restaurant and Bar,** tel. 6/23133, should not be missed by jazz lovers or those who enjoy good food. Owner Cleveland is a jazz and blues musician, handy with a guitar, flute, or keyboard. Some evenings he'll play his own music, other times he covers the greats. The Galley has the best jazz CD collection in the whole of Belize; count on great tunes to eat by. And where the music leaves off, the kitchen picks up. The stuffed baked fish is great, US$7; try Creole-style lobster, US$12.50; shrimp-fried rice, US$9; or vegetarian stir-fries. Prompt smiling service has been a hallmark of this establishment. Try the Galley's famous Seaweed Drink; it claims to have created this common Placencia concoc-

tion in its present frothy form. It's similar to egg nog with a pleasing flavor and a shot of brandy for good measure. Local men (especially husbands) chuckle sheepishly and say, "It's good for de back mon!"

The **Purple Space Monkey Internet Café** serves breakfast and lunch under a palapa with a modern twist: computers for Internet access and TV's that offer continuous movies—and noise. OK food, cold beers. They're threatening to offer dinner when they can find a cook.

You can't miss **Jene's Flamboyant Restaurant,** tel. 6/23174, or at least you can't miss the tree just across the sidewalk that it's named after, especially if it's in full bloom. Uncle Jay, the proprietor, prides himself on using the freshest ingredients and accommodating most any special request. Every day he offers Belizean specials for about US$6–8. Continental specials appear frequently in the evenings.

The **Sea Monkey Bar and Grill** on the beach offers simple but filling dishes.

The **Dockside Bar,** just off of the sometimes-open Tentacles Restaurant, hosts a popular afternoon happy hour on Saturday and Sunday, 4–6 P.M. This is a great gathering place for visitors and local boatmen, and better yet, the only good place to thank the sun god on its way down into the horizon. The **Lagoon Salon** has US$1 rum drinks during its happy hour, good sandwiches and the ever-popular Belizean-style horseshoe tournament every Saturday at 3 P.M., something a number of town folk look forward to.

mammee fruit

Other options include **B.J.'s Restaurant,** Placencia Road, tel. 6/23108, which offers fresh orange juice and good barbecue chicken in a screened dining room with wooden tables. Serving simple fare, it's open 7 A.M.–10 P.M. **Malu's Kitchen,** between the bank and Nitewind Snorkel Shop, doesn't look like a restaurant but serves some mean local food. A few stools and a picnic table under a *palapa* are usually occupied by locals. Homemade seafood specialties are her trademark—the conch fritters are hot and spicy! Saturday she offers barbecue, but she admittedly closes down for the horseshoe tournament and "comes back drunk." **Sonny's** also serves everything from seafood to burgers. Or, take a taxi or the shuttle from town and treat yourself to the fine dining at the resorts.

Franco's is a way out of town but offers Mediterranean cuisine in a beautiful dining room. Pizza, salads, pastas, and other delectables are available. Call for free shuttle service.

Next to Luba Hati, **The Inn at Robert's Grove,** is an upscale resort with an equally up-scale menu. Robert imports beef from the States, and daily seafood specialties are mouth-watering. Pricey but worth the splurge if you're not on a budget.

Further north on the peninsula, **Mangos** is back, in a larger location on the beach. Christine Duffy has relocated her former three-table restaurant to a large, funky, four-point palapa on the beach. Not only is this a cool place to hang out at night, but her food is just as good as ever. Food is served 11:30 A.M.–10 P.M. Chicken satay goes for US$8; there are tasty inexpensive daily specials and my all-time favorite—fresh basil, tomato, and mozzarella salad. Lots of vegetarian meals—try the veggie quesadilla US$8.

The hardy might want to give long-timer **Brenda's** a go. Some have complained that she is a hustler; others agree she can make the best spicy conch stew around. The "restaurant" is a camplike site on the beach with a table or two. If you eat here, know that hot water doesn't clean your dishes. Also, if she asks you for money ahead of time don't give it as you might not see anything when you return for your meal. With that said, she's a hoot and it's fun to be adventurous once in awhile.

Sweet Stuff

Got a sweet tooth? The Belizeans will fix that. Downtown, ask where to find **Miss Lily's;** she's a great baker and makes delicious powder buns to sell from her house (under the stilts). Like all of the ladies (following), she works on Belizean time—when she sells out, she closes up. They all bake village favorites: Creole bread (with shredded coconut), cinnamon rolls, johnney cakes (journey cakes), and other favorite snacks. Anyone will point you to these local bakers: **Miss Lydia's, Miss Cuncu,** and, to these lady bakers, let's add **John the Bakerman** (great breads!). **Daisy's,** on the sidewalk, makes its own ice cream and offers cakes, pies, and other goodies.

PRACTICALITIES

Cara's Laundry, next to Omar's Diner, is open daily 8 A.M.–5 P.M., except Saturday.

Atlantic Bank, near the gas pump, is open 9 A.M.–2 P.M.

At both **Olga's Market** and **Wallen's Market** you can find almost all of your needs, including groceries, dry goods, and sundries. If you run low on cash and can't use the credit card, Olga's will usually cash traveler's checks, especially if you buy something.

Email services are available at De Tatch restaurant; and the Purple Space Monkey Internet Café. Rates are about US$2.50 for 15 minutes.

GETTING THERE

By Air

Flying is easiest, quickest, and gentlest to the body. For current schedules and fares call, **Maya Island Air** in Belize City, tel. 2/44234. **Tropic Air** in Belize City, 2/45671 or Placencia, tel. 6/23410, makes about five flights daily between Belize City and Placencia.

By Bus

Richie's Bus leaves Dangriga for Seine Bight and Placencia every day at 12 P.M. and 5 P.M. From Placencia to Dangriga, it's an early 5:30 A.M. or 6 A.M. departure; ask around or check at the **SeaSpray** for the current schedule. Cost is less than US$5 each way.

Or take the **Z-Line** bus to Mango Creek for US$7.50; ask at the post office about the boat to Mango Creek or the mail boat for Big Creek. The buses also continue to Punta Gorda for US$8.50. A bus leaves from Dangriga at **The Hub** guest house for Punta Gorda at 3 P.M.; fare is about US$5. This particular bus ride gets three goose eggs for discomfort. From Mango Creek you can travel by dory across the lagoon to Placencia.

By Car

If driving, continue past the Dangriga turnoff (can it be possible that this strip of road to Placencia is worse than other southern roads? Yes!). If it's been raining, four-wheel-drive is a necessity, especially for the last five miles from the small village of Seine Bight to Placencia Town.

GETTING AROUND

Getting around on the peninsula has gotten easier with the **Penninsula Shuttle Service,** tel. 14/3928. The shuttle leaves Maya Beach on the even hour, starting at 6 A.M.; it leaves Seine Bight on the half hour; and it leaves Placencia on the odd hour. The shuttle takes a break between noon and 2 P.M. Cost is US$2.50 one way; an all-day pass costs US$6.

Taxis can also get you around. **Kingfisher Taxi,** tel. 6/23322, **Seine Bight Taxi,** 014-4438 and **How Now Taxi and Tour Service,** tel. 6/23424 can take you around for a moderate fee. Or, just ask your hotel and they can probably call a reliable taxi for you.

BOB RACE

KATHY ESCOVEDO SANDERS

TOLEDO DISTRICT
INTRODUCTION

Locals refer to southern Belize as the neglected stepchild of the country. Money earmarked for development and tourism rarely finds its way south, and on arrival in Punta Gorda (or P.G., as it is called by locals), the largest town of the district, this is quite evident. P.G. is not a tourist town, and at first seems to have little to offer: no regularly scheduled boats to the cayes, and no trips wrapped up in glitzy little "tour" packages to the archaeological sites, to the mountains, or the caves. Instead, it's the springboard for a discovery experience favored by the real adventurer. Supply and demand. Good Belizean guides are available, and a few are beginning to call themselves tour operators, but it's a long way from the Cancún variety. There are indications that all of this is going to change with various plans and activities on the drawing board. The Maya people and other eco-wise organizations in the country have voiced their objections to anything that smarts of destroying the forest. But the government often finds it hard to turn down big money from companies who covet the hardwood trees in this unspoiled wonderland. Only time will tell who will win out.

But for now, take advantage of the "purity" of the Toledo District, be prepared for the unexpected, and take it as it is. Truly this is the magic of the area. Obviously not for everyone, this is a poor section of a third world country, but it's definitely for those looking to find the true splendor of the rainforest and its inhabitants. Take the opportunity to visit with the Maya "up close and personal," while learning a bit about the Kekchi or Mopan culture right in their homes. Up till now, tourism has been coming to the district in small doses, small groups, lone independent travelers, or backpackers. Hurry! Toledo is waiting.

THE LAND

Toledo is the most southerly district in Belize and the third largest in the country. To the south and west it shares a border with Guatemala. The district has the highest population of Maya (Kekchi and Mopan) of any district in Belize.

Toledo District presents the traveler numerous opportunities to experience the Caribbean, rivers, jungle, and mountains. Nearby, travelers find offshore cayes, tranquil waterways, outlying villages, and Garifuna communities. Stretches of pine and savanna, lowland broadleaf jungle, and the peaks of the Maya Mountains are just short distances from Punta Gorda.

ACTIVITIES

Punta Gorda is a vital hub for a variety of activities. Kayaking is popular both in the sea or on the tranquil rivers, or you can dive and snorkel in glass-clear water and on rarely visited cayes. Lounging in a hammock never fails to relax, while adventurous souls can explore the nearby mountains and rainforest. Not that many divers find their way this far south, so divers find virgin reefs near small spits of sand or mangrove in the clear Caribbean. Nature lovers are thrilled at the glimpse of an elusive animal. Swift boats cross the sea to favored fishing spots or go to Guatemala for a day of shop-

---

GUEST VILLAGES OF THE TOLEDO DISTRICT

Santa Cruz
San José
San Pedro Columbia
San Miguel
Laguna
Blue Creek
San Antonio

Some of these villages are within an hour's walk from each other. Most of them are surrounded by thick forest. It's work to keep the paths between villages clear in this thick forest.

---

ping or exploring. Archaeological buffs have easy access to Maya ruins and see artifacts only recently unearthed from a sleep of a thousand years. For spelunkers, one of the largest cave systems of Belize is within easy reach. The daring climb up tall poles to narrow swinging walkways that lead to wooden platforms where a jungle watch really offers a "bird's-eye view" of the rainforest canopy. If you are very still you can watch the everyday life of exotic birds at 100 feet above Blue Creek. The opportunities are endless and for the most part unheard of. Talk to Chet Schmidt at Nature's Way Guest House (see Accommodations, below); as a great supporter of the area, he's a font of information.

HISTORY

Maya Mysteries

The first Maya built several ceremonial centers in the Toledo area. Little is known about this group of people. However, as archaeologists continue to make discoveries, they learn more and more—some fact, and some fiction. One favorite mystery that lingers suspended between truth or fiction is the one surrounding the crystal skull found by the 17-year-old daughter of explorer Benson Hedges on her birthday. Experts have vacillated about the authenticity of the crystal skull for years. Was it made by the Maya? Does it have inexplicable powers? Is it a phony? Where did it really come from? Did Hedges plant it for the pleasure of his daughter? The questions persist over the decades. The skull still belongs to the Hedges family; you can see it in the British Museum in London.

Later Settlers

Just as in the Stann Creek District, the Garifuna followed the Maya into this remote area in the 1800s. Ironically, in 1866 they were followed by Americans—Southerners who'd been buying guns from the British during the American Civil War. When their side lost, they asked for and received refuge and land grants from the British, and then tried their hand at raising sugarcane. Most eventually returned to the United States. Over the years laborers from distant parts of the world were brought into the country for logging and sugarcaning and made Toledo District their permanent home.

Today's Toledo

Today the district is a blend of many unrelated cultures—Caucasian, Kekchi and Mopan Maya, mestizo, Garifuna, Creole, Chinese, Palestinian, and East Indian. More than 10,000 Kekchi and Mopan Maya are subsistence farmers in the Toledo countryside.

ECOTOURISM

Tourism is on the rise even though the infrastructure of southern Belize lags far behind that of the rest of the country. More and more travelers are passing up generic high-rise hotels and luxury accommodations in exchange for a chance to peer into another time and culture, and in Toledo the culture is in its purest form. Obviously this is not a vacation for everyone. But for those with a curiosity about old traditions and the beauty of the rainforest creatures, a world of adventure awaits.

It used to be that Toledo District's only accommodations were in Punta Gorda, except for one tiny guest house in San Antonio 15–20 miles away. However, that's changed with a program of small Maya guest houses coming to life in the ethnic villages in Toledo. More than anything, this program is intended to help the villagers find a safer economy—another way to support their families besides total dependency on the meager subsistence farming that entails slashing and burning the rainforest. Concern includes the

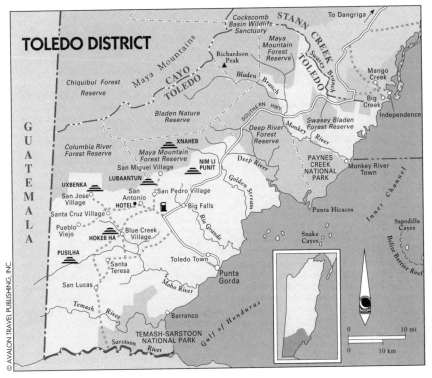

© AVALON TRAVEL PUBLISHING, INC.

preservation of jungle growth where so many of the pharmaceutical world's biggest discoveries have been made, with the promise of many more.

And though this is a much-discussed subject worldwide, it's becoming a vital problem in southern Belize because of the growth of the various Maya communities. Not only will the guest-house project protect natural resources, it is also designed to preserve an ancient culture that is in danger of becoming diluted by outside influences and lifestyles, especially with the increased interest from tourism.

Garifuna Village Project

Garifuna people make up one of the largest ethnic groups in Toledo. Life has never been easy for the Garifuna, and in recent years there's been a real danger of old traditions slipping away entirely. Fortunately a group of Garifuna volunteers have used 40 acres of a 1,000-acre plot (a legacy from their ancestors) to re-create an authentic Garifuna village at St. Vincent's Block, calling it Habiabara Ginagu Cerro. Farming is part of the project, and this re-created village is a small living museum. The workers in the field become docents, showing visitors around and serving them lunch Garifuna style. The project was originally an independent effort, but St. Vincent's Block volunteers have added themselves to the Toledo Eco-Tourism Association ranks.

The Maya Guest House

For a truly unique and unforgettable experience, consider an overnight stay in a Maya village in

COFFEE, TEA, OR IGUANA?

I sat at the front of the bus, not wanting to miss my stop. As the bus started to slow down in the middle of nowhere, the driver pointed at me and I stepped off onto the dirt road. Five Maya women also got off, going home to their village, the same village I was heading for. As we walked toward the lush Maya Mountains, I began talking to a woman my age. I learned about her family as we walked the three miles to Laguna Village. The closer we got to the mountains, the farther away we were from my reality, but by the time we arrived I had made a new friend.

The trees got taller, and green brush and jungle surrounded me. My guest-house destination was easy to find, very near one of the two roads in the village. Arriving at my wooden, thatched-roof "hotel," I waved good-bye to my new friend. The door was locked, so I sat on the steps and waited, wondering what was to happen next. Hot and tired, I was somewhat dismayed to notice that the electric line did not come anywhere near the guest house. With a sigh of resignation that I *would* enjoy myself, I leaned against the building and soaked up the warm sun.

Eventually Santos Pop arrived, a short, quiet-spoken man. He brought bedding and showed me the simple layout of the building—a wooden hut with a thatch roof, concrete floor, and four sets of bunk beds. It was serviced by an outhouse and a small room with a bucket of water for bathing facilities. At night kerosene lamps provided the light. Once I was

settled, he offered to show me around.

In the late afternoon sun, Santos and I set off for the village tour. The population of 250 people was spread out over a large area. The water pump was the pride of the town, and most of the villagers had running water in their yards. The first thing I noticed was the complete lack of noise. During the day the loudest sounds are toucans that live in the trees, even louder than the laughter of the children. Although electricity has been brought in to some houses, there are no TVs, CD players, or telephones, and especially no cars to break the silence. Everyone speaks quietly—not out of shyness but because there is no need to talk loud. The woman of the family runs the household, and when she speaks, everyone listens.

After our tour, Santos brought me to his home. When I walked into the thatched-roof house, it took my eyes a few minutes to adjust to the dim light. A fire pit in one corner was the stove, and the light in the rectangular room came from a couple of small windows. A few wooden shelves held dishes, plastic cups, and a few other utensils. The furniture was a small table against a wall with one chair pushed in and a well-worn hammock hung in the middle of the room. Just inside the doorway was a huge pile of dried corn. The family had raised the corn, dried it, and was now using it every day. The neatly stacked pile was almost ceiling high and extended into the room about 10 feet.

the surrounding areas of Punta Gorda, where life is carried on much the same as generations ago. The founder of this project, the Toledo Eco-Tourism Association (T.E.A.), created the program to help the indigenous people of the district—the Mopan and the Kekchi Maya—benefit from tourism in a controlled manner, while giving them an opportunity to voice their opinions regarding the development going on in their district—their farming and hunting grounds.

Simple guest houses are set up in the participating villages, giving you privacy and basic necessities. Meals are eaten in homes of the villagers and activities include tours of the village, surrounding caves, and canoe trips. For nighttime entertainment, traditional dancing, singing, and music can usually be arranged.

It was originally planned that all the villages would follow the same protocol, but this does not happen and there is something different about each one. It may not be exactly as the brochure describes. You can visit each of the 13 villages and have 13 completely different experiences. Most of the villages have 150–250 people, yet some will seem like virtual ghost towns.

For more information or to make sure someone in the village knows you will be coming, contact the **Toledo Eco-Tourism Association,** P.O. Box 157, Punta Gordo, tel. 7/22096, fax 7/22199, email tea@btl.net. You can visit the T.E.A. office at Vernon and Front Streets. Expect to pay about US$45 for one night accommodations, three meals, and two tours.

Thirteen-year-old Nigel, the eldest child of five, sat on a small stool on the hard-packed dirt floor, cleaning dinner—a headless iguana. They asked if I liked iguana. Laughing, I mumbled "I don't know." One of his sisters was grinding corn on the meat grinder—something that would go on for over an hour, at every meal, every day. Irminia, Santos's wife, prepared a *caldo,* a stewlike meal, with iguana as the chief ingredient. Tomatoes and a cilantro-type herb grown in their garden gave flavor to the firm white flesh. The iguana was female and had eggs, considered a delicacy by the Maya. They looked like large yellow garbanzo beans and had a similar texture. I alternated between disgust and fascination (of course I kept my feelings to myself). I had trouble knowing I was eating the critters I'd enjoyed watching from my canoe as they lounged on fat tree branches taking in the sun along the riverbank.

It is the custom in the villages for guests to eat by themselves while the family sits and, basically, watches you. At first this is awkward, but asking a steady stream of questions breaks the chewing noises that seem amplified in the already silent house. At this meal the father ate with me, because he had to go to a meeting. After he left I was free to speak with the wife, a quiet, calming woman who was very happy to talk about her life. She is one of the few village wives who works outside of her home; she works at a children's home three miles from her village.

Laguna was the first of three participating Toledo Eco-Tourism Association villages that I was to visit. The brochure touted the programs for each village, saying that each would be the same, but I encountered three completely different experiences. This probably is not for everyone, but for those who are intrigued with a different way of life, don't wait too long. As we learn from the Maya, so are they learning from us. It may all change in another generation.

the Santos Pop family

PATTI LANGE

CONSERVATION ORGANIZATIONS IN BELIZE

Manomet Bird Observatory: P.O. Box 936, Manomet, MA 02346, 508/224-6521

Tropical Conservation Foundation: P.O. Box 31, CH-2074, Marin-Ne, Switzerland, tel. 038/33-4344

Wildlife Conservation International: N.Y. Zoological Society, 185th St. & So. Blvd., Bronx, NY, 10460, 718/220-5100

U.S. World Wildlife Fund: 1250 24th St. NW, Washington, DC 20037, 202/293-4800

Or, if you happen to be in the bush near a village and want a place to crash for the night, just ask anyone to direct you to the guest house and more than likely there will be a bed available. Unless some college group is in the area, there is a good chance you'll be the only visitor in the village, especially those farther out.

Benefits

The benefits go both ways. Travelers are certainly enriched by the cross-cultural exchange and the exposure to nature. Observing and participating in making the day's tortillas, listening to the strains of Maya music by firelight in a thatched hut, swimming in the chilly waters of a clear forest stream, following a jaguar track down a jungle trail—these experiences can turn into cherished memories that last a lifetime. The same can be said for fishing from dugout canoes, hacking open coconuts to slake a thirst, cruising twisting mangrove channels, and dancing to the beat of Garifuna drums. On the communal level, everyone in the village benefits, even though each individual may not be directly employed as a guide, arts and crafts demonstrator, dancer, singer, or one of the other positions needed to provide service to the visitors. The money goes into a general village fund; salaries are paid first and the balance is used for education or health.

Is a Guest House for You?

Guest houses are designed after the local style: thatched roof, wooden walls, and cement platform base. So far each village has one guest house that will accommodate eight people. Guests are provided with beds with clean linens, mosquito netting, bucket showers, and outhouses.

Visitors, please note: It's best to be very flexible when visiting Toledo District. Although accommodations can be as described one day, they can change overnight—especially those in the outback. In many cases these are new, small guest houses, still ironing out the kinks in a whole new industry for most of these people. So to really enjoy the experience, be ready for *anything.*

Meals

Breakfast in Maya villages is generally eggs, homemade tortillas, and coffee or cacao drink. All meals are ethnic and lunch is the largest meal of the day; it is often chicken *caldo* (like a stew cooked with Maya herbs), although it isn't unusual to get local dishes like iguana or gibnut. Fresh tortillas round out the meal. Supper is the lightest meal of the day and generally includes "ground" food (a root food such as potatoes) that the guide and visitors might "harvest" along the jungle trail. The *comal* (tortilla grill) is always hot, and if you're invited to try your hand at making tortillas, go ahead—this is a wonderful way to break the ice with the usually shy Maya women. In a Garifuna village be prepared for simple but traditional cooking. It can be tasty, but guaranteed to be different. We especially like the *serre,* or fish in coconut milk.

What to Bring

Bring comfortable walking shoes, bug repellent (with 30 percent DEET or more), poncho, swimsuit, flashlight with extra batteries, and lightweight slacks and long-sleeved shirt. A picture of your own family or postcards of your hometown will give an immediate connection and will help break the ice.

PUNTA GORDA

At about Mile 100 on the Southern Highway, Punta Gorda (or P.G., as it is called by locals) is Toledo District's most important town as well as the last sizable town you'll come to before reaching the Guatemala border. To the northwest lies a cluster of Maya villages; to the east, the Gulf of Honduras; to the southwest, Guatemala. Most folks in town speak English, including the Maya in outlying villages. The majority of inhabitants in town are Garifuna and East Indian. Fishing was the main support of the local people for centuries; today many fishermen work for a high-tech shrimp farm. Farmers grow rice, mangoes, bananas, sugarcane, and beans—mainly for themselves and the local market.

ORIENTATION

This is a casual village—many people in town know only a few street names. Coming into Punta Gorda across Joe Taylor Creek from the north, the Sea Front Inn on the right is the first to greet you as you skirt the Caribbean on the left. Fifty or so yards down the way, the road splits at a Texaco station, forming North Park Street (a diagonal street a block long) on the right and Front Street on the left. Following Front will take you through town past the ferry pier, the Mira Mar Hotel, and several eating establishments, then all the way to Nature's Way Guest House at the bottom of Church Street. Behind Front, going away from the coast, only a few parallel avenues are of interest to most travelers.

SIGHTS

The Waterfront
You might expect a more colorful waterfront in P.G. In reality it's a simple port, not super clean, framed by many old, dilapidated wooden buildings. The waterfront is quiet and tranquil, with small waves lapping the shoreline, but when the ferries to Guatamala arrive and during market days, the port comes alive with activity.

Central Park
The town park, on a small triangle of soil roughly in the center of town, has an appropriately sleepy air to it. At the north end is a raised stage dedicated to the "Pioneers of Belizean Independence." In the center of the park is a dry fountain, and here and there some green cement benches. A clock tower on the south end has hands everlastingly stuck as if holding time

Punta Gorda coast

PATTI LANGE

PUNTA GORDA TOWN

To Dangriga

Joe Taylor Creek

SEA HUNT DIVE AND
FISH CHARTERS

GOMIER'S RESTAURANT ▼
T.E.A. OFFICE ■

● SEA FRONT HOTEL

NORTH ST.

MANGROVE'S
RESTAURANTS

LUCILLE'S
KITCHEN ▼

CHARLETON'S INN ●

■ TEXACO STATION

KING ST.

PALLOVIS HOTEL ●

ST. CHARLES INN ●

▼ GRACE'S RESTAURANT

QUEEN ST.

BTL TELEPHONE OFFICE ■
VERDE'S RESTAURANT/
GUEST HOUSE ●

■ JAMES BUS
LINE TERMINAL

POLICE ■

AIRSTRIP

MAYA ISLAND AIR ■

PRINCE ST.

■ POST OFFICE

MIRA MAR
HOTEL ■

● CUSTOMS

TROPIC AIR ■

INFORMATION CENTER
■ ● FERRY

FRONTIER
● GUEST HOUSE

Central Park

BELIZE
■ BANK

AUGUSTO
MAC'S STORE

AIRPORT HOTEL ●

AUNT J'S RESTAURANT ▼

MORNING
GLORY CAFE ▼

BTB TOURIST
INFORMATION

CLEMENTS ST.

ICE CREAM
PARLOR ▼

PACO'S BOAT
SERVICE ■

CHURCH ST.

FRONT ST.

MAIN ST.

JOSE MARIA NUNEZ ST.

BACK ST./

NATURE'S WAY
GUEST HOUSE ●

Caribbean Sea

GEORGE ST.

FAR WEST ST.

CIRCLE
C HOTEL ●

PUNTA CALIENTE
HOTEL ●

VICTORIA ST.

● TRAVELLERS INN
■ BUS STATION

WEST ST.

■ HOSPITAL

VOA RD.

CEMETERY

To Orange Point Marina and VOA

0   300 yds
0   300 m

© AVALON TRAVEL PUBLISHING, INC.

at bay. On Monday, Wednesday, Friday, and Saturday this is especially a pleasant spot to take a break, enjoy the blue sky, and watch the activities of the villagers who have come in to sell their produce.

Saturday Market

On the waterfront near the ferry pier is the colorful Saturday market. Many Maya vendors sell wild coriander, yellow or white corn, chiles of various hues, cassava, tamales wrapped in banana leaves, star fruit, mangoes, and much more. Laughing children help their parents. If you're inclined to snap a photo, it doesn't hurt to buy something, smile, and ask permission. If refused, smile and put your lens cap in place. Many of the women and children bring handmade crafts as well.

RECREATION

Boating Activities

Requena's Charter Service, 12 Front St., Punta Gorda, Belize, C.A., tel. 7/22070, makes daily trips to Puerto Barrios, Guatemala, at 9 A.M. for US$10. It can also arrange boat trips, both inland and ocean, especially to **Snake, Hunting,** and **Moho Cayes.** The company will also transport you to caves, ruins, and to **Deep, Moho, Monkey, Sarstoon,** and **Temash Rivers** and their associated villages.

Paco's Boat Service, 3 Clement St., tel. 7/22246, also has daily trips to Puerto Barrios. Be at the pier by 8 A.M. for the 8:30 A.M. departure. Trips to the cayes and Puerto Cortez, Honduras (12-person minimum), can also be arranged. Ask about diving and fishing trips.

Robert Hanggi operates **Sea Hunt Adventures,** tel. 7/22845, email seahunt@btl.net, a dive and fishing operation catering to small groups, offering fishing and diving packages, as well as tours to local caves, ruins, and waterfalls. Accommodations are available: a two-bedroom cottage facing the ocean with kitchen, a/c, and cable TV for US$20–25. Sailing available.

Tours

P.G. is now the base for many tours. Not so long ago there weren't many official tour companies. That is starting to change as many people are discovering the wealth of pristine rainforest, fishing, diving—and everything else that makes this a fascinating area to explore.

Trips worth looking into include a visit to the Lubantuun ruins, including sharing lunch with a Maya family and a swim in a river; US$38 pp, based on three people. Or, go in search of the howler monkey and do some bird-watching, about US$27.

Tour companies who make these trips are **Tide Tours,** tel. 7/22129, **Fish and Fun,** tel. 7/22670, and **Romero's Charters,** tel. 7/22924.

ACCOMMODATIONS

Accommodations are very simple but relatively plentiful in Punta Gorda. *Most* rooms are clean, some only have cold water, offer shared bathrooms (a few are not much more than outhouses), and don't take credit cards. The majority of accommodations in P.G. are family run, and that alone can be a great experience. However, do check out your room, sit on the bed, and take a peek into the bathroom before you sign your name.

Under US$25

As you step off the airport grounds you will see the **Frontier Guest House,** tel. 7/22450, a two-story white cement building with simple rooms, private bath, and hot water. Four rooms have a/c for US$27; two fan-cooled rooms are US$18.

Sixteen rooms with fans are available at the **Airport Hotel,** Ogaldes St., Punta Gorda, Belize, C.A., tel. 7/22495, a block away from the airport.

A block west of the bus station, the fine but basic **Circle C Hotel,** 117 West St., Punta Gorda, Belize, C.A., tel. 7/22726, is run by a local family. It's a quieter location, away from the action in town but convenient to the bus. Rooms are clean with ceiling fans and shared or private baths and cost US$20–25. You can arrange laundry services.

If you're really tight in the pocketbook, check out **Verde's Guest House,** 22 Main St., Punta Gorda, Belize, C.A., behind the restaurant with the same name. Verde's has simple rooms with louvered windows, screens, fans, cement floors, and shared outhouse-style toilets. About US$14.

Sea Front Inn, Punta Gorda

PATTI LANGE

Pallavi's Hotel, 19 Main St., tel. 7/22414, has 10 basic clean rooms with a small common balcony that overlooks Front Street. Check out Grace's Restaurant next door. Yes, you must walk through a messy yard to get to the stairs to reach the rooms. US$21.

The small **Mahung's Hotel,** P.O. Box 92, Punta Gorda, Belize, C.A., tel. 7/22044, is just across from the Texaco station at the corner of North and Main Streets. Rooms have shared or private baths, h/c water, fans, and TV, US$25

The **St. Charles Inn,** 21 King St., Punta Gorda, Belize, C.A., tel. 7/22149, is a two-story building with comfortable rooms and a shady veranda that allows you to observe village life below. Rates vary depending on shared or private bath; laundry service is available. About US$22.

You're apt to run into all sorts of interesting travelers from around the world who have somehow heard of **Nature's Way Guest House,** 65 Front St., P.O. Box 75, Punta Gorda, Belize, C.A., tel. 7/22119. Rooms and furnishings are simple but comfortable, clean with pleasant sur-roundings, and fan-cooled; good breakfast is served on a regular basis, and you'll have access to all activities in the area. The place is run by Chet Schmidt and his Belizean wife. He is an American expat who, after serving in the Vietnam War, decided to move south—way south. He often sits in the common area in the mornings and is very willing to answer questions on what to do, and to give his opinion on life in the area. Ask about kayak trips to nearby Joe Taylor Creek (US$20), jungle treks, camping, exploring unin-habited cayes, visits to archaeology sites, and Maya and Garifuna guest-house stays. Write or call for information. US$18.

For those traveling by bus, **Punta Caliente Hotel,** 108 Jose Maria Nunez St., Punta Gorda, Belize, C.A., tel. 7/22561, delivers great loca-tion, value, and food. Next door to the bus sta-tion, it's impossible to miss with its strings of tiny Christmas-tree lights lending a festive air. It offers eight rooms (under US$25), on-site laundry ser-vice (air dried, about US$5 per bag of laundry), a second-story common balcony, and a rooftop sundeck. The bright airy rooms have cold water, private baths, cross ventilation, and ceiling fans. The restaurant prepares delicious versions of local food, especially seafood; for a lesson on Garifuna culture, check out the implements on the walls that are used in cassava making. Note: It's one of very few places in town to serve meals on Sunday.

US$25–50

Those traveling by bus will find **Charleton's Inn,** 9 Main St., Punta Gorda, Belize, C.A., tel. 7/22197, at the north end of town convenient to everything. The Z-Line and James buses stop across the street. The 22 rooms are a bit worn but have h/c water, private baths, TV, and ei-ther a/c or fans (those with a/c have color TV instead of black and white). US$30 with a/c; US$25 or US$18 for rooms with fans.

Tate's Guest House, 34 Jose Maria Nunez St., Punta Gorda, Belize, C.A., tel. 7/22196, email teach@btl.net, is a comfortable lodging with five double rooms in a neighborhood setting. Rooms without a/c are considerably less. Ask for room 4 or 5; they are spacious with ceiling fans, remote-controlled color TV, sunrooms, louvered win-dows, and tile floors, and each has an additional entrance through the backyard. US$25.

The **Sea Front Inn,** P.O. Box 21, Punta Gorda, Belize, C.A., tel. 7/22682, email seafront@btl.net, IS on the sea front just as you enter the northern end of town and is the best place in P.G. Owner/operators Larry and Carol Smith have lived in Belize for more than 25 years, coming first as young missionaries. This comfortable friendly inn is family operated—daughter April is often found at the front desk or in the kitchen—and very comfortable. Before the Smiths' were hotel operators, they hosted many doctors, dentists, and other volunteers in their home. They felt that they knew what people wanted in a hotel and so—they built one.

Each room is named after a local animal, with that animal painted on the door. Guests find comfortable, spacious rooms, no two alike, with cable TV, fans, a/c, private bath, handmade furniture built with hardwoods. The third floor is the kitchen/dining room/common area that overlooks the ocean. Large tables and chairs made by Larry—including one made out of one piece of huge mahogany that required a block and tackle system and a lot of men to get it into the room—catch the cooling breezes off of the ocean. Books with local information, games and puzzles, a help-yourself snack bar and unique souvenirs are here.

The best part of the hotel are the wonderful sincere people. For some fascinating stories, ask Carol about her experiences teaching Maya women how to read—and Larry is a font of information for local diving. The restaurant caters to vegetarians but also has food for carnivores. Depending on the season, they might only serve breakfast but there are many restaurants close by. About US$55. They are in the process of building apartment-style lodging for longer term. Contact the Smiths for information.

"If you build it they will come"—that seems to be the mantra behind the luxurious (by P.G. standards) **Travellers Inn,** tel. 7/22568, Jose Maria Nunez St., Punta Gorda, Belize, C.A., which is the closest thing you'll find to a Holiday Inn here. Next to the bus terminal, its eight rooms have h/c water, private bathrooms, a/c, cable TV with remote and ceiling fans. One room is family size. The carpet is a bit faded and worn but it's clean, and the staff is efficient. US$65 to US$72 for the family room. Breakfast only is served at the restaurant. No credit cards. For information, call 7/22568, U.S. tel. 800/552-3419 or 218/847-4441, fax 218/847-4442.

TC's by the Sea Hotel, tel/fax 7/22963, is about a mile and half north of town and has six rooms, some with water beds. All have cable TV and rates include breakfast. The cement building appears worn on the outside but once inside you'll find spacious and comfortable rooms, some with mahogony doors with Maya-motif carvings. One room is family-sized, designed for parents to have a bit of privacy. Rates start at US$25 for singles and go up to US$70. Meat lovers, enjoy! The restaurant offers some of the biggest steaks in Belize. A 22-ounce porterhouse costs about US$15. Other menu choices are chicken-fried steak, hush puppies, and smoked ham. TC's can also arrange all tours.

FOOD

Don't expect gourmet in P.G.; most of the restaurants serve simple good food. Take the opportunity to taste local specialties, and there are many. The town has several good bakeries, and fruit and veggies are cheap and abundant on market day (Saturday).

Note: If you arrive on Saturday night, ask which cafés are open on the morrow. Many close on Sunday.

Mangrove's Restaurant is recommended by most locals and serves Belizean and Chinese dishes, all moderately priced.

When you enter **Punta Caliente,** 108 Jose Maria Nunez St., tel. 7/22561, and see the locals really tucking into plates of seafood, stewed pork (US$4), and fried chicken (US$7), with sautéed vegetables and cole slaw, you know you've come to the right place. The conch soup (US$5) is particularly good. The restaurant is open seven days a week. You can arrange early breakfasts (6–7 A.M.) for groups.

Aunt J's, tel. 7/22756, near the town square, is open 7 A.M.–3 P.M. and 6–10 P.M. seven days a week. This cheery, clean place is family operated and serves tasty, simple filling meals. Lots of egg choices on the breakfast menu; fried shrimp is US$7, burritos US$2.

Patti Lange crossing Blue Creek Canopy Walk high above the rainforest.

Gomier's Restaurant, near Nature's Way Guest House, is owned and operated by Gomier who offers homemade food made from organic ingredients he's grown himself. The restaurant is small but has tasty and creative daily specials. The day we were there he had barbecued tofu served with baked beans, grain bread, and coleslaw, and a veggie grain casserole, served with a salad. Both were filling and good. He also has many fresh fruit juices and soy ice cream. Gomier opens around 8 A.M., closes around 5 P.M. and is not there at all on the weekends.

Among other options, **Nature's Way Guest House** serves a good breakfast; the **Sea Front Inn** serves a filling breakfast. **Grace's Restaurant** is our favorite with typical Belizean fare. Good stew chicken (US$4), tasty conch soup (US$5) and great fry jacks with breakfast.

The tortilla factory, located just south of the bank, makes fresh tortillas every day.

ENTERTAINMENT

There are many small bars scattered around town, some with pool tables, all with lots of booze. Women—notice that there aren't any Belizean women in most of the bars. It's been said that only women looking for trouble go into these small, dark dives.

P.G. Sports Bar sits on the southern end of Central Park, and whether you are inside or out you can hear the loud cheers of the crowds

watching whatever game is on—or the crooning of the karaoke singers. I'm not sure which one is the better of the two.

SHOPPING

Gift Shops

Don't expect to find a lot of souvenirs in P.G.—this is a working town. Probably the best local crafts are found at **Fajina Craft Center of Belize,** at Front Street near the ferry pier. It's a small co-op for quality Maya crafts run by the Kekchi and Mopan women. Baskets, slate carvings, handwoven textiles, and embroidered clothes are available. It is not open daily, only when the ferry and the occasional cruise ship docks. To see the goods, ask around.

Tienda La Indita Maya, 24 Main Middle St., tel. 7/22065, lies just north of Central Park (the end opposite the clock tower). This store has arts and crafts by Maya Indians from Belize, Guatemala, and El Salvador. It also carries footwear and clothing.

The **Sea Front Inn** has a nice selection of handmade wood frames and other crafts.

This and That

At **Johnson's Store,** three of them spread around town, you'll find film of all types, shirts, cassettes of local musicians, pots and pans, mosquito netting, and more. **Wallace Supaul Store,** at the north end of Main Street, has great yogurt, cheese, juice, fruit, and canned meat at reasonable prices. If you are going off into the jungle, check out the rubber boots, flashlights, and film at **Witz Wholesale/Retail** on Main Middle Street.

Calvert's Grocery, the big white clean store just south of the town plaza, has the best selection of groceries, snacks, and drinks in the area.

INFORMATION AND SERVICES

Toledo Visitors' Information Center

Look for this office at the Toledo Dock. Here you'll find the owners of Dem Dats Doin', who come into town every Monday, Wednesday, Friday, and Saturday and who are willing to answer questions about Punta Gorda and the entire Toledo District, especially the "host family network," the Maya homestays. Also, contact the Toledo branch of the **Belize Tourism Industry Association,** Punta Gorda, Toledo District, Belize, C.A., tel. 7/22119.

Internet

An expat woman operates **The Cyber Café,** next door to the Sea Front Inn. She's open 9 A.M.–10 P.M. US$2.50 for 30 minutes.

Post Office and Immigration

Near the ferry dock, you'll find the immigration office. Opposite that are a couple of government buildings, where you'll find the post office.

Money

A few businesses readily accept credit cards, but many don't, so it's best to have Belize currency along, especially lots of small bills. The **Belize Bank,** 43 Front St., is open Mon.–Thurs. 8 A.M.–1 P.M., Fri. 8 A.M.–1 P.M. and 3–6 P.M. It's across from the Civic Center on the town square.

If you're headed toward Guatemala, go to the dock and look around for someone arriving from Guatemala who might want to exchange Belize dollars for Guatemala quetzals; often a freelance moneychanger hangs around the dock at boat time.

Gas Station

Fill your gas tank at the **Texaco Station** at the north end of Front St. 6 A.M.–6 P.M., tel. 7/22126 or 22926. They accept traveler's checks.

GETTING THERE

By Air

Daily southbound flights from Belize City to Dangriga continue to Placencia and then to Punta Gorda. This is the quickest and most comfortable way to get to Punta Gorda, and you have a choice of scheduled flights on **Maya Island Air** or **Tropic Air.** In Punta Gorda you can buy your Maya Island tickets at the airstrip. For a current schedule and fares, call Maya Island at the airstrip, tel. 7/22856. Or in Belize City, call the airport office, tel. 2/31140 or 35371. Call Tropic Air in Punta Gorda at the airstrip, tel. 7/22008, or in Belize City 2/45671, fax 2/62338.

By Bus

Even though P.G. is only about 100 miles from Belize City, it's a long haul if you're driving. Count on seven to eight hours by bus; four to five hours by car. Buses go on both the coastal route and on the Hummingbird Highway—it's much shorter from Placencia and Dangriga. The **Z-Line,** runs daily trips. **James Bus Line** leaves P.G. at 6, 8, and 11 A.M. and noon and drop you off at the Pound Yard in Belize City, US$11 one way.

To the Maya Villages: Every day has a different schedule. Buses go to the Maya villages on Monday, Wednesday, Friday, and Saturday, generally around noon, departing from the Central Park. From here it's possible to get to the villages of **Golden Stream, Silver Creek, San Pedro, San Miguel, Aguacate, Blue Creek, San Antonio** and the others. Some buses drop you off at the entrance road, leaving a walk of a mile or two. Check at the T.E.A. office or the Toledo Visitors' Information Center for more bus information and most recent schedules.

By Car

No matter who does the driving from Belize City, this is one long trip! In wet weather certain of the small bridges can be slick; others are so narrow only one vehicle at a time can pass, so be ready to back off. On sunny days the going is long and hot. On rainy days the drive is interminable. Work is still in progress on the Southern Highway and much of it is still unpaved.

INTO GUATEMALA FROM PUNTA GORDA

Across the bay from Punta Gorda are **Livingston** and **Puerto Barrios, Guatemala,** mostly inhabited by Garifuna. For those interested in doing a little exploring across the border, you have the option of flying or taking a boat.

By Boat

Two companies make daily trips to Puerto Barrios and sometimes on to Livingston if numbers make it worth their while. Arrive early to do the paperwork at the customs office at the foot of the pier; you will be asked for your passport. From Puerto Barrios, it is possible to catch a bus to Livingston. Boats leave P.G. at 9 A.M. The return boat leaves Puerto Barrios at 2 P.M.

WEST OF PUNTA GORDA

San Pedro Columbia and San Antonio are just two of the Maya villages taking part in the **Toledo District Maya Village Guest House and Ecotrail Program,** and the two easiest to reach. But for those interested in wandering the countryside on their own, Punta Gorda is a good starting point from which to wander off in many different directions.

ARCHAEOLOGICAL SITES

Nim Li Punit

At about Mile 75 on the Southern Highway near the village of Indian Creek, 25 miles north of Punta Gorda, you'll find Nim Li Punit (expect a 15-minute walk from the highway). The site was briefly surveyed in 1970, and about the only thing known for sure is that it held a close relationship with nearby Lubaantun. One of the memorable finds was a 29.5-foot-tall carved stela, the tallest ever found in Belize—and in most of the rest of the Maya world. It's possible to make arrangements to see these ruins and the villages before your arrival in Punta Gorda if you don't have your own car and would like a guide. In any case, if you plan on visiting these ruins, check with the Department of Archaeology in Belmopan before you go, tel. 8/22106.

Lubaantun

North of the Columbia River and one mile beyond San Pedro is the Maya ruin of Lubaantun ("Place of the Fallen Stones"). It was built and occupied during the late Classic period (A.D. 730–890). Eleven major structures are grouped around five main plazas—in total the site has 18 plazas and three ball courts. The tallest structure rises 50 feet above the plaza, from which you can see the Caribbean Sea, 20 miles distant. Lubaantun's disparate architecture is completely foreign to Maya construction in other parts of Latin America. Maya buffs will want to examine this site. For more detailed information, see the Mundo Maya chapter. A small museum is at the entrance as are clean toilets. Guides are available.

MAYA VILLAGES

San Pedro Columbia

To get there, take the main road in Punta Gorda that goes inland about 10 miles toward San Antonio. Just before you get to San Antonio, a dirt track to the right breaks off to the village of San Pedro. If you're without a vehicle, take the bus, which makes this trip about three times a week. Or you can hire a cab by day—a bit pricey, but the most convenient way to come and go according to your personal schedule. The owner of the Shell station you pass once in the general area has also been known to take people into the villages for a fee.

San Pedro is small and friendly. On the outskirts of town the dwellings are rather primitive; they often have open doorways covered by a hanging cloth, and hammocks and dirt floors. Chickens and sometimes dogs wander through the houses in search of scraps. People use the most primitive of latrines or just take a walk into the jungle. They bathe in the nearest creek or river, a routine that becomes a source of fun as well as a cleaning procedure. Electricity is found in some of the villages.

BUTTERFLIES

Most people know about the butterflies in the jungles of Belize. The fluttering little beauties are everywhere. And anyone who has ever bought a postage stamp in the country knows that the variety, the color, and the beauty are magnificent. However, as more civilization moves in, the butterflies move out. Several groups of people have initiated "butterfly farms." If you have the opportunity, visit one or all of them. Each offers guided tours by request.

The folks at **Fallen Stones Butterfly Ranch and Jungle Lodge** have established a "breeding ranch," both for exporting butterflies into cities where there's nothing but concrete and asphalt (so they must open special places to exhibit the butterflies) and for the protection and encouragement of the beautiful little critters right here in Belize.

Fallen Stones is in real rainforest country. The average yearly rainfall of 160 inches encourages the rich flora that attracts butterflies. Wandering the trails, you'll see the intense **blue morpho** as well as the **white morpho**, which is white but shot with iridescent blue. Three species of the **owl butterfly** (genus *Caligo*) love to come and lunch on the overripe fruit the keepers of the ranch leave hanging on the trees—just for them. You'll also see tiny **heliconians** and large yellow and white **pierids,** among many, many more.

At Mile 8 on Mountain Pine Ridge Road is **Green Hills Butterfly Farm,** a butterfly breeding, educational, and interpretive center. All the butterfly farms pay as much attention to the plants that provide the larval food as to the pupae. And these fussy little creatures often have different tastes. Here again you see platters of ripe fruit placed about the farm for the fluttering little "fly-abouts" to feast on.

Chaa Creek Lodge has developed the **Blue Morpho Butterfly Breeding Center.** A small flight room houses the blue beauties; naturalists on the grounds gladly explain the various stages of life the butterfly goes through.

A butterfly goes through four stages in its life cycle: from tiny teardroplike egg, to colorful caterpillar, to pupae, and then graceful adult. Butterfly farms gather breeding populations of typical Belizean species in the pupal stage, and then the pupae are carefully "hung" in what is called an emerging cage with a simulated "jungle" atmosphere—hot and humid (not hard to do in Belize). A short time later they shed their pupal skin, and a tiny bit of Belize flutters away to the amazement and joy of all who behold.

Depending on the species, butterflies live anywhere from seven days to six weeks. If you plan to visit a farm, or to go into the rainforest on a butterfly safari to observe the beautiful creatures, go on a sunny day: you'll see lots more butterfly activity than on an overcast day; if it's raining, forget it!

In many areas of Belize, butterfly populations have been almost totally depleted for many reasons, including habitat destruction (from logging, for instance) and changing farming practices, particularly the use of pesticides. Belize's steamy marshes, swamps, and rainforest have been a natural breeding ground for beautiful butterflies for thousands of years and hopefully will continue to be so.

As you walk into town past the thatched homes on each side of the road, it becomes apparent that the effects of modern conveniences are only beginning to arrive. When a family can finally afford electricity, the first things that appear are a couple of lights and a refrigerator—the latter allows the family to earn a few dollars by selling chilled soft drinks and such. After that, it's a television set; you can see folks sitting in open doorways, their faces lit by the light inside.

A small Catholic church in town has an equally small cemetery. It sits on a hilltop surrounded by a few thatched dwellings. Not far away is a prefab-looking school that was erected, we were told, with the assistance of National Guardsmen from the United States who were getting jungle training.

Local guides take visitors out of their village past a towering ceiba tree and into what appears to be secondary forest. If there's been rain, the going is muddy. We slogged up and down hilly trails, over little streamlets, and through glens. It's worth it. Everywhere is a stunning parade of life. Hummingbirds, toucans, parrots, and other birds flit about the canopy. Our guide pointed out a jaguar's track, plainly imprinted in the mud of the trail. We were able to follow it for a spell before it led off into the bush. We were impressed by the coolness of the jungle interior and more impressed with the guide's knowledge. He could point out and name every variety of flora and fauna along the path. He plucked wild coriander for us to savor and led us to a farmer's *milpa,* where corn was drying under a *palapa.* What a difference between the oppressive heat in the open cornfields and the cooling relief in the dark shadows of the jungle.

Accommodations

Fallen Stones Butterfly Ranch and Jungle Lodge, P.O. Box 23, Punta Gorda, Belize, C.A., tel./fax 7/22167, is the other most notable option for accommodations in the San Pedro Columbia area. Actually the name is a bit misleading; the ranch is for the butterflies. For the people you'll find a very handsome lodge with a covered wooden outdoor deck/dining area and thatched-roof cabañas scattered about 42 acres of jungle hillside. Butterflies flutter about the grounds, but the real work with the winged creatures takes place in buildings down the hill, where they are fed and bred.

The Butterfly Ranch is only one and a half miles from San Pedro, yet it could be a hundred; as far as the eye can see are rolling jungle hills and valleys stretching off into the Maya Mountains. The various trails about the property lead through heliconia groves, forest trees, and many native plants that appeal to the appetites of butterflies.

The cabañas are built along the lines of traditional Kekchi Maya homes, using rustic wood with high-pitched ceilings and deep shady verandas. Screened, louvered windows provide bug protection. Rates are US$105; more with meals. Meals are special, especially dinner, which might include pork chops in orange sauce with roasted potatoes and carrots. And for dessert, the house specialty is chocolate cake filled with sweet oranges and ginger that has been soaked in rum, sprinkled with shaved chocolate, and served with cream. Expect to pay US$23 for a four-course dinner. You can arrange various tours with local guides at reasonable rates.

Another option for accommodation is the **San Pedro Village Guest House,** which you can reach by writing P.O. Box 75, Punta Gorda Town, Belize, C.A., tel. 7/22119.

SAN ANTONIO VILLAGE

After leaving San Pedro and returning to the main road, make a right turn and you'll soon be in San Antonio just down the road. Inhabitants of these thatch-hut villages of San Pedro Columbia and San Antonio, the Kekchi and Mopan Maya, are people who fled to Belize to escape from oppression and forced labor in their native Guatemala at the turn of the century. The older folks continue to maintain longtime traditional farming methods, culture, and dress. No modern machinery here—they use a simple hoe to till the soil, and water is hand-carried to the fields during dry spells. The village of San Antonio is famous for its exquisite traditional Kekchi embroidery. However, the younger generation is being whisked right along into 21st-century Belizean society, so who knows how much longer it will survive.

A local tourism representative lives in San Antonio. He is friendly and happy to give helpful advice about the area, and can direct you to local guides in town willing to take you to archaeological zones (including a trip to the caves) called **Hokeb Ha/Blue Caves** and **Blue Creek** (bring your swimsuit). This is great bird-watching country. From here the road is passable as far as Aguacate ("Avocado"), another Kekchi village. But if you intend to visit the ruins at **Pusilha,** near the Guatemala border, you must travel either on foot or horseback. Another ruin, **Uxbenka,** is west of San Antonio near the village of Santa Cruz, easy to get to by trucks that haul supplies a couple of times a week. Not known by anyone but locals until 1984, Uxbenka is where seven carved stelae were found, one dating from the early Classic period.

Check out a tiny guest house that's been around for a long time, **Bol's Hilltop Hotel.** No electricity, very simple.

BLUE CREEK RESERVE

A Skywalk Stroll through the Top of the Rainforest

Continuing toward the mountains brings you to Blue Creek. Rivers, caves, birds, and all of nature's wonders are here to greet you; best of all this is primary rainforest! For something different and heart-stirring, check out the skywalk above the river. Right now, this is the only rainforest canopy observation system in Belize, spanning a river and rising over 100 feet. It was installed by **International Zoological Expeditions,** IZE for short.

For the hardy, getting to the canopy is half the excitement. Six sturdy aluminum ladders are nailed to a tree, and after being hooked up to a mandatory harness you climb up and up and up. Suspended (rope) bridges link the wooden platforms (some have chairs!) that were built for educational purposes. It is quite extraordinary to be in the treetops, at eye level with the birds, looking down on the lazing iguanas and the river below—stay long enough and you might see one of the lizards fall into the river after losing a fight. This adventure is not for those scared of heights: though it's only 120 feet off the ground, it might as well be a thousand; nothing feels really solid under your feet until you are once again on the floor of the jungle.

IZE has been bringing educational groups to the Belize rainforest for many years. They are the founders of this outstanding tropical rainforest field station. On the grounds visitors find a central lodge, a field station, and individual cottages, plus the marvelous skywalk constructed in the rainforest canopy. The company has an ongoing relationship with Maya guides, and a permanent resident stays on the property at all times. Independent travelers to Belize are welcome to stay in the cabins (just call ahead)—as long as there are no groups at the lodge.

It isn't necessary to be a guest of IZE to climb into the canopy. It costs US$5 per person to use the canopy walk and a guide is required (US$12.50). There was a lot of talk about signing a waiver before we got there, yet we never signed anything. As in many tropical countries you take risks, but it was a thrill not soon to be forgotten.

Blue Creek Caves
The Blue Creek Cave system is farther upriver from the canopy walk and has a variety of caves worth exploring. You need a guide who's familiar with these caves; ask at Punta Gorda or at one of the Maya villages. Many of these folks know the nearby caves well. Go prepared with flashlights.

Accommodations
In Blue Creek, a T.E.A. guest house that is rarely used is available. An outhouse is your toilet and a bucket of water (or the river) is your shower. Bring your own food, or meals can be eaten in villagers' houses. The people are friendly, though very reserved, and they are happy to share with you Maya specialties, you can always expect handmade tortillas. No shops are here so bring whatever you need.

IZE's Blue Creek Rainforest Lodge has seven simple wood cabins with bunk beds; one has a double bed. Restrooms are in the common area, as are the showers. All meals are served in the common lounge room and are included in the cost, plus a trip into the canopy. This is a great experience. For more information, call 5/22119, U.S. tel. 800/548-5843, email ize2belize @aol.com.

kids in Blue Creek Village

PATTI LANGE

At the lodge you can make arrangements with experienced Belizean guides (half-day US$20, full-day US$40); choices of trips are many. However, the Blue Creek Cave system should not be missed. You can opt for a wet-cave trip or a dry-cave trip.

ADDITIONAL ACCOMMODATIONS IN MAYA COUNTRY

A few more villages have guest-houses available for overnighters. You can contact **San Miguel Village Guest House, San José Village Guest House,** and **Santa Cruz Village Guest House** by calling 7/22119 or writing to P.O. Box 157, Punta Gorda Town, Belize, C.A. Another contact for village homestay programs is through the Toledo Visitors' Information Center in Punta Gorda.

Note: After talking to a lot of people in Punta Gorda, it seems that the village homestay program is not always as successful as the guest-house program. Visitors often feel as though they are kicking someone out of their hammock, or just in general intruding on the lifestyle of the villager. Generally there is just one room for the entire family for cooking, sleeping, eating, etc. Others are not happy with the primitive conditions they may find, even though they are told in advance.

Having said that, to get more information about the homestay program, call 7/22470.

GETTING THERE

To get to Maya country from Punta Gorda, you have several choices. If you plan on an overnight with the homestay or guest-house programs, T.E.A. will assist you.

Another alternative is to go by bus from Punta Gorda. Take the **Chun Bus** that makes the run to San Antonio Monday, Wednesday, and Friday, returning to Punta Gorda Tuesday, Thursday, and Saturday. Fare is US$1.75 one-way, US$3.50 round-trip. The bus doesn't stop in San Pedro; instead you will have to leave the bus at the road and trek in several miles. You can also catch a bus as far as Pueblo Viejo, "the edge of the known world": ask any backpacker in Punta Gorda. Catch the Chun Bus at Central Park. For times and additional information, call Antonio Chun, tel. 7/22666. If traveling by bus, remember that there is no Sunday bus service. Be sure your scheduled trip does not include a one-night stay on Saturday and a return on Sunday. Either you'll be stranded until Monday, or will have no other choice but to walk to wherever you are going with only the hope of a kind soul picking you up as you hitchhike.

If traveling by car, you have the option of exploring every little road you see. Yes, of course it's more sensible to drive a 4WD. From the turnoff for Punta Gorda at Mile 86 on the Southern Highway, take the road north. At about Mile 1.5 there will be a turnoff on the right that heads for San Pedro and other villages.

KATHY ESCOVEDO SANDERS

ACROSS BELIZE'S BORDERS
GUATEMALA (TIKAL)

The Tikal ruins, in the Petén (jungle) district of Guatemala, are among the more outstanding in the Maya world. They have been excavated and restored extensively, mostly by archaeologists and students from the University of Pennsylvania. What you'll see is only a small part of what is still buried and unexplored in the rainforest. It's been a national park for more than 30 years, so the forest has been protected from loggers—and parts of it are considered virgin. This is a *don't-miss* site.

As is the case with most Maya ceremonial centers, archaeologists are learning more and more about life in Tikal and its 3,000 structures (with 10,000 more foundations). They have mapped 250 stelae that the Maya left behind. In recent years, they have learned to decipher the Maya hieroglyphs, and about 80 percent of the Maya's written record has been translated.

Tikal is not only a treasure trove for the ar-

chaeology buff but also for nature lovers. You'll hear and, with luck (if you're up very early in the morning), see the howler monkeys that live in the treetops on the site. You'll see and hear hundreds of parrots squawking at you as you wander through **Twin Complex Q and R**—this is their domain. And while wandering the **Great Plaza** and the **Lost City,** you'll see colorful toucans fly between ancient stone structures and tall vine-covered trees.

Throughout the site, you'll see several twin complexes with identical pyramids facing each other across a central plaza. No one knows why they were built this way. At Twin Complex Q and R, one pyramid has been excavated and restored while its opposite is just as it was when found—covered with vines and jungle growth. You'll see this sort of juxtaposition frequently throughout Tikal. And if you saw the film *Star Wars,* you may recognize the five great pyramids of Tikal as the rebel base.

ACROSS BELIZE'S BORDERS

Gulf Of Mexico

Cancun

Merida

Cobá

Tulum

Isla de Cozumel

Campeche

Bacalar

Caribbean Sea

Chetumal

MEXICO

Corozal Town

Villahermosa

Tuxtla Gutiérrez

Tikal

Belmopan

Belize City

Flores

Dangriga

BELIZE

Placencia

Punta Gorda

Gulf of Honduras

Puerto Cortes

Santo Tomas Morales

San Pedro Sula

GUATEMALA

Copán

HONDURAS

Guatemala City

Santa Rosa de Copan

Tegucigalpa

PACIFIC OCEAN

San Salvador

EL SALVADOR

Golfo de Fonseca

NICARAGUA

0   100 mi

0   100 km

HISTORY

The Maya

The first Tikal Maya were farmers who, as far back as 750 B.C., chose the high ground that rose above the vast, steamy swamps of Petén for their settlement. The earliest evidence of their presence is some of the trash they left behind. Living on a major route between the lowlands and the cooler highlands, the Tikal villagers began a healthy trade in flint. The stone was plentiful here, and was prized for tools and weapons.

By 600 B.C., the Maya had begun their construction of Tikal ("The Place of Voices). Over the next 1,500 years, they built their platformed city in layers, razing structures to gather material to build more.

By about 200 B.C., the Maya were building ceremonial structures. By 100 B.C., the great Acropolis was in place, and the Great Plaza was already as large as it would be hundreds of years later, when the population of Tikal reached its peak of about 55,000 people. From 50 B.C.–A.D. 250, the Maya created even more elaborate architecture on these early foundations. They also carved monuments, though they did not yet use hieroglyphics.

With the beginning of the early Classic period in about A.D. 250, the Maya's monuments grew larger and became more formal and less ornate, but the plans for their temples changed little. They built the causeways to connect the parts of their city and carried on a thriving trade. Carvings on monuments and burial practices show a close relationship with Teotihuacán in Mexico. The monuments also describe Great-Jaguar-Paw and Smoking-Frog's conquest of nearby Uaxactún in A.D. 378. In 562, Lord Water of Caracol defeated Tikal in a great "ax war," and Tikal produced no monuments for 135 years. But in 682, Ah-Cacau took the throne and began to restore Tikal to its former glory. The great king was buried in the Temple of the Giant Jaguar.

Most of the construction at Tikal was in the late Classic period, which began in A.D. 550 (shortly before Tikal's defeat by Caracol) and ended in A.D. 900 (when the entire society collapsed). In and around the ceremonial parts of the city lie 200 stone monuments in the form of stelae and altars. Archaeologists have pieced together Tikal's history from the carvings. The burials at Tikal also hold a clue to the structure of the society.

In the six square miles of Tikal that have been excavated, archaeologists have found hundreds of little buildings that they believe were domestic. Usually they're found in small clusters on elevated sites suitable for housing an extended family. Most people were buried beneath the floors of their houses. Their bones were smaller and weaker than the bones of the folks buried in the great tombs. The range of the housing construction, in size and quality, also suggests great variety in people's status and wealth.

But in A.D. 900, the entire society fell apart, not only at Tikal but throughout the Maya world. Post-Classic Maya continued to use the site for several centuries, and even moved several of the stelae around in an attempt to restore the city for their own purposes, but the jungle eventually reclaimed Tikal.

The Archaeologists

Hidden Tikal was mentioned in 18th-century Guatemala archives, but not until 1848 did the government mount an official expedition. The governor and commissioner of the Petén visited Tikal, and their report, along with an artist's drawings of the stelae and lintels, attracted attention in Europe, where the report was published. A Swiss doctor, Gustav Bernoulli, visited in 1877. He had some of the lintels removed (from Temples I and IV).

The first maps of Tikal were drawn by Alfred Percival Maudslay, who visited in 1881 and 1882 and whose workmen liberated the temples from the forest. He published his accounts, along with the first photographs of the site. Teobert Maler continued in this vein; he visited in 1895 and 1904, mapping and photographing as he worked for the Peabody Museum of Harvard University. He wouldn't relinquish his site map, though, and the museum hired Mayanist Alfred Marston Tozzer and R. E. Merwin to finish the job.

Sylvanus G. Morley, for whom the Tikal museum is named and who was head of the Carnegie Institution's archaeology department, used Maudslay and the Peabody Museum's reports as a base, and devoted himself to recording the writing of the Maya. In 1956 the University of Pennsylvania launched the project to excavate Tikal and appointed Carnegie archaeologist Edwin Shook to lead the project. Since then, part of the immense site has been excavated and restored.

Exploring Tikal

It's so large and complex that unless you have a week to really explore Tikal, it pays to hire a guide. Official guides are available at the site and the fee is fairly standard (about US$30), varying according to the size of your group and the length of your tour. Try negotiating if the price is not to your liking. Wear good walking shoes to cover the six square miles of excavated sites. Photographers, bring lots of film because you'll become maniacal with your camera trying to capture it all—the white-gray stone buildings with the vibrant green of the grass and surrounding jungle.

THE RUINS

Site Entrance

At the gate to Tikal expect a fee (about US$10). Hang on to your ticket; you may be asked to show it. If you want to have the really memorable experience of watching the sunset from the top of Tikal pyramid, have the ticket man stamp yours for an after-hours stay; it's good till 8:30 P.M. Otherwise you must be out of the park by 5 P.M.

When you enter Tikal, note the large visitor's center/museum. Take a look at the scale model of the site and you'll get an idea of where everything is. The visitor's center has photos of the reconstruction, as well as some fine artifacts. The good little museum displays some excellent pieces of Maya history. Don't miss the fascinating tomb exhibit, including a skeleton and funerary offerings, just as they were found. Clustered around the visitor's center you'll find a few cafés, and nearby is a bazaar of Guatemalan artisans selling mostly items made from their colorfully woven fabrics.

Tikal is huge, too vast to fully describe here. Listed below are a few highlights, but to get the most out of a visit, do some reading first. An in-dispensable book to read and then carry with you to read again at the site is prominent archaeologist William Coe's book, *Tikal: A Handbook of the Ancient Maya Ruins,* available through the University Museum at the University of Pennsylvania (be sure to carry the map from the book with you—it's easy to get lost in this large complex). If you don't get it before you leave home, it's available at the site.

Note: Only VIPs of the park are allowed to drive on most of the roads; expect to walk a lot.

The Great Plaza

It's one mile from the museum to the Great Plaza. This plaza, considered the heart of ancient Tikal, is highly complex in design. The Great Plaza covers three acres; its plastered floor, now covered with grass, is made of four layers, the earliest laid in 150 B.C. and the latest in A.D. 700. Two great temples, I and II, face each other across the plaza, around which are scattered palaces, altars, a ball court, and 70 stelae—the memorial stones carved of limestone that tell of Maya life and conquest. Terraces and stairways lead up and down into a plethora of architecturally intense buildings. Most of these palaces were ceremonial centers, but a few are believed to have been apartments. If you climbed and poked around into every structure at the Great Plaza alone, it would take you at least an entire day.

Temple I

Because of its grace, form, and balance, this is probably the most photographed temple at Tikal. Also known as the **Temple of the Giant Jaguar** (named for a carving on one of its lintels), it rises 172 feet above the East Plaza behind it. Nine sloping terraces mark its sides, and its roof comb sits 145 feet above the Great Plaza floor. Atop the building platform is a three-room temple. Its central stair was used by workmen to haul building materials to the top of the temple. It's believed to have been built in about A.D. 700 for King Ah-Cacau, who brought Tikal out of its dark ages after its defeat by Caracol. His tomb was found inside during the restoration, and some of the grave goods, including 180 jade ornaments, pearls, and bone carvings, are on display in the museum/visitor's center.

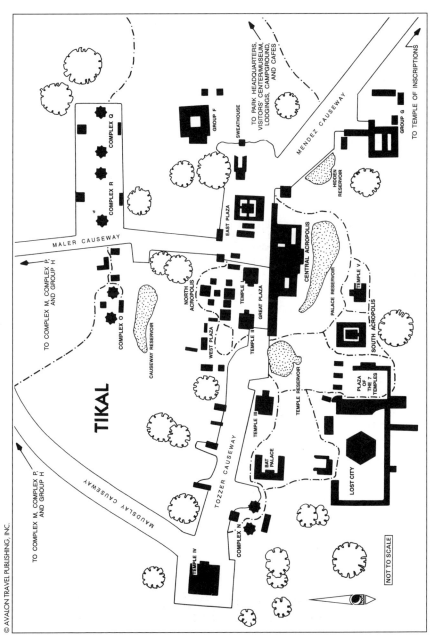

© AVALON TRAVEL PUBLISHING, INC.

Temple II

Called the **Temple of the Masks,** for the carvings on its lintel, this smaller structure faces Temple I across the Great Plaza. One of the few Maya temples ever dedicated to a woman, it was built for Ah-Cacau's queen, and is smaller and less steep than his. It stands about 125 feet above the Great Plaza, though if its roof comb were intact, the temple would have stood close to 140 feet. Like its counterpart across the way, it also has three rooms at the crest. In front of Temple II lies a large block that archaeologists speculate served as a reviewing stand—priests standing on it could see the crowds in the plaza below and in turn they could be seen by all.

East Plaza

The immense East Plaza, east of the Great Plaza and backing up to the Temple of the Giant Jaguar, was once a formal plastered area covering 5.5 acres. Two of the city's causeways, **Mendez** and **Maler,** lead from here. This plaza is the site of the only known sweathouse at Tikal, and it's also the site of a ball court and what appears to be the marketplace. Trash and other evidence shows that the Maya continued to use the ball court after the collapse of Tikal in A.D. 900.

Temple IV

It's another long walk, but follow your map and visit challenging Temple IV, the **Temple of the Double-Headed Serpent.** Facing east, it's a popular spot from which to watch the sunrise. The platform itself has not been excavated, and only those in good physical condition will want to climb the six ladders (sometimes all you can cling to are roots and branches) to the top. Yaxkin Caan Chac, the son and successor of Ah-Cacau, built Temple IV about 40 years after Temple I was built for his father. Today Temple IV is the tallest surviving Maya structure from pre-Columbian history—212 feet from the base of its platform to the top. Not until the turn of the century, when elevators came along, were taller buildings constructed in this hemisphere. Temple IV also houses a three-room temple, with walls up to 40 feet thick. From the summit of Temple IV, the sight of the entire area is breathtaking. The jungle canopy itself rises 100 feet into the air, and the tops of the other white temples of Tikal rise above the tops of the trees.

Temple V

Though the climb to the top of Temple IV is strenuous, it pales in comparison with the ascent to the north-facing Temple V. Like Temple I, it was built about A.D. 700; it rises about 190 feet. After clambering through underbrush to reach the top of the former stairway, hardy climbers have the option of hoisting themselves up through a hole in the roof comb that appears to have been dug sometime before archaeologists discovered Tikal. Some travelers have reported that the dark, for-

Tikal in all its glory

*Temple IV is a challenge
even for the hardy climber.*

bidding interior of the roof comb contains ropes and ladders to gain access to the very top of Temple V, from which there is a remarkably focused view of the other temples of Tikal.

Hieroglyphs and Stelae
The earliest stela at Tikal, number 29, was probably carved in A.D. 292. The latest is number 11, carved in 869. In between, the stelae record the births and deaths of kings, the cycle of festivals and seasons, and sagas of war. Even a long pause in the production of stelae, beginning in 557 and ending in 692, has a story to tell. Mayanists have deduced (now that they have discovered how to read as much as 80 percent of Maya writing here and at other Maya sites) that Tikal lost a great battle with Caracol, and the hiatus coincides with Caracol's dominance of the region. The inscriptions of Tikal also show that a single dynasty ruled the kingdom from the early Classic period until the society collapsed in

A.D. 900. Yax-Moch-Xoc founded the line and ruled from about 219 to 238. Though he was not the first leader to be memorialized at Tikal, he apparently was so magnificent that he was recognized as the founder of a dynasty—the inscriptions are the first in which the Maya recorded the concept of a founding ancestor. His descendants made up the royalty of Tikal. Among them were kings with names such as King Great-Jaguar-Paw, the ninth successor of Yax-Moch-Xoc, Moon-Zero Bird, who took the throne in A.D. 320, and Curl-Snout (A.D. 379).

Other Sights
There's so much to see and experience in this lovely jungle—a lazy walk through one of many dirt pathways will bring you up close to striking orchids of all colors, bromeliads, exquisite ferns, delicate blossoms, and myriad trees of every variety.

TIKAL ACCOMMODATIONS AND FOOD

At the Ruins
Within the Tikal grounds, you'll have the choice of staying overnight at three locales or camping. Accommodations are very simple; most do not have 24-hour electricity or hot water, and some have shared baths. Don't rely on credit cards; most don't accept them.

The small **Jaguar Inn,** tel. 502/926-0002, offers rooms in the main building, as well as several bungalows around the pool. All beds have mosquito netting and you *do* need it. Rooms have private bathrooms and cold-water showers. Electricity (private generator) is on until about 10 P.M., candles for later. If you're a reader, bring a mini book light, and do bring a flashlight to light your way to the bathroom at night; it's easy for wiggly little critters—some tiny and some a little larger—to get into these rooms This is the least expensive of the accommodations on site, at US$55, probably not really worth the price if they were anywhere else. Remember, you are in the middle of the jungle. The dining room is a low-key, screened-in porch with tile floors. The inn provides transportation to Flores at 2 P.M. daily, US$24. The **Jungle Lodge** offers rooms with shared bath, at budget rates; those with

An orphaned ocelot at Jaguar Inn in Tikal gets lots of TLC from Belizean archaeological guide Tessa Fairweather.

private baths are inexpensive. On one of our trips, we had a baby jaguar running through the dining room and out the screen door, an orphan that the owners were caring for.

If you want to stay some place a little more upscale try the **Tikal Inn,** tel. 502/926-0065. Rates (US$55) include breakfast and dinner. Camping costs about $6 per person.

Near the entrance to the Tikal ruins you'll find several cafés selling good food at reasonable prices. Vendors may also be selling breadnut tortillas near the temples. Try them; the taste is quite unusual. Usually a youngster at the foot of Temple IV will have an ice chest filled with beer and soda for sale, quite welcome after a hike up and down the tall pyramids.

Remate Petén

For those who want something a little nicer, go about 15 minutes south of Tikal to Remate

Petén, just across from Lake Petén-Itza. Here you'll find the small, charming hotel called **Mansione del Pajaro Serpiente,** a group of cottages stepped up the side of a hill, giving wonderful views of the lake and the *petén* (jungle). The 10 rooms are really diminutive suites with sitting rooms, tile bathrooms, double beds, h/c water, electricity, and an open-air dining room close by. The buildings are built of stone with *palapa* roofs and furnished with a flair. Across the road, shops sell wood carvings, jade jewelry, and more. Pickup at the Flores airport and transportation to and from the park is available along with guided tours. For a cheaper rate, ask about two tiny rooms on the property without all the amenities (no sitting room). Add 20 percent tax to all prices. For more information, write Mansione del Pajaro, Remate, 17702, Guatemala.

Here also you can arrange to participate in the yearly **Maya Man Triathlon.** Usually held in the first week of March, the triathlon begins at Remate. It consists of a one-kilometer swim, 34-kilometer bike ride (to Tikal Park), and a seven-km run (through the park). For more information, contact the Mansione del Pajaro.

An upscale hotel, the **Westin Camino Real Tikal,** is about 40 minutes away from the Tikal site, in the village of San José Petén. A little costy, US$110, the hotel is in a lovely site on 220 acres that overlook Lake Petén-Itza and the *petén.* The hotel offers a wide selection of sporting options, including hiking, swimming, fishing, scuba diving, canoeing, bicycling, sailboarding, and sailing. In keeping with the area's environmental standards, no motor vehicles are permitted on Lake Petén-Itza. In 12 trilevel, thatched-roof bungalows, 72 attractive rooms provide luxurious bathrooms, a/c, minibars, international telephone service, cable TV, and individual balconies overlooking the lake. In the main building guests will find a full-service restaurant, swimming pool, snack bar, lounge, and lake-view bar open till midnight. Transportation is provided for a fee between the Tikal archaeological site and the Camino Real Hotel. For more information and reservations, call 800/228-3000, tel. 502/926-0208, or write the hotel in San José Lote 77, 17702, Guatemala.

Flores

Flores, about an hour by road from Tikal, serves as a popular base for tourist excursions to the ruins. Many visitors opt to come by plane, and flights are available from Belize, Guatemala, and Mexico cities. Flights from Belize's Philip Goldson International Airport are scheduled on Tropic Air (US$186 round-trip, pp). The airport in Flores is newish and modern, much more so than the town it services. You'll find several hotels and numerous restaurants scattered around the area; most are very simple and very cheap.

GETTING THERE

On Belize's Western Highway from the Xunantunich turnoff, the road passes through Benque Viejo, an old town with aged wooden houses. It's a good place to stop and have a cold drink before the long ride into Guatemala, where the culture changes immediately. For Americans (with passports), crossing the border is usually no problem. First you must stop at the Belize side, show your passport, and fill out a departure form. At the Guatemala side, you stop again, show your passport, and fill out some more papers for your visa. You'll be asked how long you expect to stay in the country; allow an extra couple of days just in case you are delayed. Expect to pay US$5 (unless you obtained the visa previously in Mérida, Belize, or the United States). You should not have to pay to have your passport stamped here, but as border guards often do, they may ask for more money. You can try and play dumb, act as if you don't hear or don't understand—it *sometimes* works—but be prepared to pay a few dollars! If you're driving your own car, make sure you have all the necessary papers of ownership, which they *will* want to see. You are required to have your tires fumigated (by law), for which the cost is a few Belizean dollars.

Once across the border it's pretty easy sailing, but keep a couple of things in mind. When passing military camps (and you will pass several on the way to Tikal), do not take *any* photos (even of the large vicious sign of a soldier pointing his gun at you saying, "I dare you"). If you're aiming your lens at the lovely river and the water happens to flow in front of the guard station, you can get into difficulties no matter how innocent it seems to you. The Guatemala military is very touchy. Don't be surprised if you're stopped by

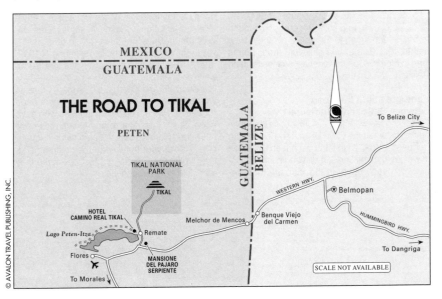

© AVALON TRAVEL PUBLISHING, INC.

the military and asked for your papers several times; keep your passport and visitor's permit handy, smile and answer all questions, and you'll soon be on your way.

The road in Guatemala is terrible, and it will take at least two hours to reach the entrance to Tikal National Park, after which the road is excellent for the final 30 miles to the site itself.

Note: If backpacking and taking public buses, be aware that no public transportation is available from the Belize border to Tikal. The only bus that runs from the border is a Guatemala public bus that goes to Flores. You can spend the night here and take the morning bus to Tikal (board in front of the San Juan Hotel). The border-to-Flores bus is usually very crowded with chickens and the works. If you wish to bypass Flores and take your chances of hitching a ride straight to Tikal, ask the bus driver to drop you off at the park crossroad (about US$3) that leads to Tikal. You won't find any stores or restaurants here, and you may wait quite a while for a car or taxi headed for Tikal. Many hotels from the Cayo District and Belize City run minibuses to Tikal. If you see one, flag it down; the driver will pick you up if there's room. From the Belize border, fare is about US$40–50.

Note: The airstrip at Tikal is no longer used since the coming and going of planes was found to be the damaging to the park's ecology. Now flights from Guatemala City and other points land in Flores. (See the sidebar "Airlines Serving Belize" in the On the Road chapter.)

**Footnote about the Road
between Belize and Guatemala**

Readers often write and ask why I don't mention driving between the Cayo District and Tikal more frequently. Well, it isn't that we haven't traveled it; we have, many times. It can be an interesting, though bumpy drive. In the rain, the road be-

TRAVEL IN GUATEMALA

As we go to press, things appear relatively peaceful for tourists in Guatemala; however, your best bet is to check before you go. For timely information as you depart for Guatemala, please call the **State Department Travel Advisory Office** in Washington, DC, 202/647-5225. Or for more detailed information, contact the **Guatemalan Embassy** in Washington, DC, 202/745-4952.

comes a quagmire of very deep mud; we have seen it when the road was so scattered with abandoned cars that we just could not make it the entire way. But more to the point, often around Christmas, people traveling by car (and sometimes bus) on their way to or from Belize have been stopped by bandits and robbed of money and watches. I know of *no* case when the bandits caused injuries, but some of them have been known to carry guns, making it a scary experience.

Many of the small cottage resorts offer escorted trips in vans, and they keep their ears open for any rumbles. At the first hint of a problem, they will cancel the trip. In some cases, drivers run their vans in tandem with other resort vans—safety in numbers! In the spring of 1992, after several robberies, we traveled in one van while another rode shotgun, both with Guatemala license plates and tinted glass. As many times as we have traveled that road, we have not been robbed, but we have spoken to those who have been. Since then, Belize and Guatemala have been friendlier and settled some of their squabbles. Ask at your hotel what they recommend; they'll give you the straight facts because they don't like to be robbed either.

MEXICO

CHETUMAL

Chetumal, capital of the state of Quintana Roo, is a good base from which to visit the many archaeological sights in the southern section of Quintana Roo and the eastern section of Campeche. It's also a gateway to Mexico's well-known Caribbean resorts: Cancún, Cozumel, Playa Del Carmen, and Akumal. Chetumal is without the bikini-clad, touristy crowds of the north and presents the businesslike atmosphere of a growing metropolis. A 10-minute walk takes you to the waterfront from the marketplace and most of the hotels. Modern sculpted monuments stand along a breezy promenade that skirts the broad crescent of the bay. Also explore the back streets, where worn, wooden buildings still have a Central American/Caribbean look. The largest building in town—white, three stories, close to the waterfront—houses most of the government offices.

Wide, tree-lined avenues and clean sidewalks front dozens of small variety shops. The city was a free port for many years (but no longer) and as a result has attracted a plethora of tiny shops selling a strange conglomeration of plastic toys, small appliances, exotic perfumes (maybe authentic?), famous-label(?) clothes, and imported foodstuffs. This is a popular place for Belizeans and Mexicans to shop. The population is an eclectic mixture of cultures, including Carib, Spanish, Maya, and British. Schools are prominently scattered around the town.

Sights

On Avenida Heroes five miles north of the city is **Calderitas Bay,** a breezy area for picnicking, camping, and RVing. The trailer park is one of the few in the state that provides complete hookups for RVs, including a dump station and clean showers, toilets, and washing facilities. Right on the water's edge, the spotless camp is in a parklike setting, fringed with cooling palm trees. Even amateur divers will find exotic shells, and the fishing is great. Nearby public beaches have *palapa* shelters that are normally tranquil,

but on holidays they're crowded with sun- and fun-seekers.

Tiny **Isla Tamalcas,** 1.5 miles off the shore of Calderitas, is the home of the primitive capybara. This largest of all rodents can reach a length of over a meter and weigh up to 50 kilograms; it's found in only a few other places in the world (South America and Panama). The shaggy animal is covered with reddish, yellowish-brown coarse hair, resembles a small pig or large guinea pig, has partially webbed toes, and loves to swim, even underwater. The locals call it a water hog, and it's a favorite food of the jaguar. Because it's been a favorite food, it's seldom seen anymore. Isla Tamalcas is easily accessible from Calderitas Beach.

Twenty-one miles north of Chetumal (on Highway 307) is **Cenote Azul,** a circular *cenote* 61.5 meters deep and 185 meters across filled with brilliant blue water. This is a spectacular place to stop for a swim, lunch at the outdoor restaurant, or just to have a cold drink.

Cenotes are created when the constant ebb and flow of underground rivers and lakes erodes the underside of limestone containers. In certain places, the surface crust eventually wears so thin that it caves in, exposing the water below, and the same time creating steep-walled caverns—natural wells. Around these water sources, Maya villages grew. Some of the wells are shallow, seven meters below the jungle floor; some are treacherously deep at 90 meters underground. In times of drought, the Maya fetched water by carving stairs into slick limestone walls or by hanging long ladders into abysmal hollows that led to the underground lakes.

Accommodations and Food

Chetumal has quite a few hotels in all price categories—and many fine cafés, many specializing in fresh seafood.

Getting There

Buses between Belize and Chetumal travel throughout the day to the modern Chetumal bus station on the highway 20 blocks south of town. **Taxis** are available from the station into town. With the expanding road system, bus travel is becoming more versatile and is the most inexpensive public transportation to the Quintana Roo coast. If you want to see more of Quintana Roo, buses from Chetumal make frequent trips to Playa del Carmen and Cancún. New express buses are appearing in many parts of Mexico. They are modern and clean, with bathrooms, a/c, and airline-type seats. Each bus has an attendant who will serve you coffee or cold drinks, and some buses have earphones for music—the 747s of the road. Chetumal is part of the loop between Campeche, Cancún, and Mérida. Check with a travel agent or **Belize Specialists,** 800/4-YUCATAN, for a pickup point in Chetumal or Cancún, usually at one of the hotels. Fares and schedules change regularly: to Cancún the fare is about US$30. Frequent bus service into Belize is provided by **Batty** or **Venus** bus companies. You will have to get off the bus when you go across the border into Belize. Have your passport handy; sometimes this takes a while.

If you're traveling **by car,** the drive is easy between Belize and Mexico on the Northern Highway. A good paved road connects Chetumal with Mérida, Campeche, Villahermosa, and Francisco Escarcega; Highway 307 links all of the Quintana Roo coastal cities. Expect little traffic, and gas stations are well spaced if you top off at each one. **Car rentals** are scarce in Chetumal; go to the Hotel Los Cocos for Avis. Chetumal is an economical place to rent your car (if one is available), since the tax is only 6 percent. If you're driving, watch out for "No Left Turn" signs in Chetumal.

BACALAR

Twenty-four miles north of Chetumal (on Highway 307) lies a beautiful multihued lagoon called **Las Lagunas de Siete Colores** ("Lagoon of Seven Colors"). Bacalar, complete with 17th-century Fort San Felipe, is a small town founded by the Spanish to protect themselves from the bands of pirates and Maya that regularly raided the area. Today part of the fort has a diminutive museum housing metal arms used in the 17th and 18th centuries. A token assortment of memorabilia recalls history of the area. The stone construction has been restored, and cannons are still posted along the balustrades overlooking the beautiful Bacalar lagoon. The museum is open daily except holidays and charges a small entry fee.

MAYA SITES OF MEXICO

If you have several days and would like to take in more Maya history, drive north to Tulúm and then inland to Cobá. Both are outstanding Maya sites. Head west on Highway 186 to Kohunlich, and into the state of Campeche to the ruins of Xpujil, Becán, Chicanná, and Calakmul Reserve.

TULÚM

In late 1994 many changes were made to Tulúm. A large new visitor's center with restaurant, restrooms, museum, and arts and crafts shops was built a couple of kilometers beyond the old turnoff road. Maybe just in time, considering the hundreds of buses that blew their foul contaminated fumes onto the already ancient structures. Services also include a shuttle for those who don't wish to take the 10-minute walk to the site from the parking lot (US$2 round-trip). Guides are available for hire at the entrance as well (not included in the entrance fee).

Tulúm's archaeological zone is open daily 8 A.M.–5 P.M. At 8 A.M., few tour buses have arrived yet, making the cooler early hours a desirable time to explore and photograph the aged structures. You pay a US$10 per person fee (plus about US$10 to bring in your camcorder) at the new entrance to the ruins. Parking is available there as well, US$2.

In the past it was permissible to climb the ruins. Now some have been chained off because of concern for the stability of the structures, so please do not climb. Areas are clearly marked.

Tulúm is made up of mostly small, ornate structures with stuccoed gargoyle faces carved onto the corners of buildings. In the **Temple of Frescoes,** looking through a metal grate you'll see a fresco that still bears a trace of color from the ancient artist. Archaeologically this is the most interesting building on the site. The original parts of the building were constructed around 1450 during the late post-Classic period, and as is the case with so many Maya structures, it was added to over the years.

Diving God

Across the compound, a small *palapa* roof protects a carved descending god. This winged creature is pictured upside down and is thought by some historians to be the God of the Setting Sun. Others interpret the carving as representing the bee; honey is a commodity almost as revered on the peninsula as maize. Visitors are no longer allowed to climb this ruin to view the carvings.

El Castillo

The most impressive site is the large pyramid that stands on the edge of a 40-foot limestone cliff overlooking the sea. The building, in the center of the wall on the east side, was built in three phases. A wide staircase leads to a two-chamber temple at the top; visitors are no longer allowed to climb this stairway, but the view from the hill on which the Castillo stands encompasses the sea, the surrounding jungle with an occasional stone ruin poking through the tight brush, and scattered clearings where small farms are beginning to grow. Two serpent columns divide the entrance, and above the middle entrance is another carved figure of the diving god. Until the 1920s, the followers of the "Talking Cross" kept three crosses in a shrine in this pyramid. It was only after curious visitors, as well as respectable archaeologists, showed an active interest in obtaining the crosses that the Maya priests moved the Tulúm crosses to Tixcacal Guardia, where they supposedly remain today, still under the watchful protection of the Maya priesthood.

Village of Tulúm

Tulúm pueblo is south on Highway 307 a short distance beyond the ruin's turnoff. It has always been the home of stalwart Maya people with the courage to preserve their ancient traditions; the descendants have vigorously chosen to enter the world of tourism (with tiny steps), and Tulúm pueblo is becoming a viable town.

COBÁ

This early Maya site covers an immense area (50 square km), and hundreds of mounds are yet to be uncovered. Archaeologists are convinced that in time Cobá will prove to be one of the largest Maya excavations on the Yucatán Peninsula. Only in recent years has the importance of Cobá come to light. Though Cobá was first explored in 1891 by Austrian archaeologist Teobert Maler, another 35 years passed before it was investigated by S. Morley, J. Eric Thompson, H. Pollock, and J. Charlot under the auspices of the Carnegie Institute. In 1972–75 the National Geographic Society in conjunction with the Mexican National Institute of Anthropology and History mapped and surveyed the entire area. A program funded by the Mexican government continues to explore and study Cobá, but the time-consuming, costly work will not be completed for many years.

Cobá was perhaps the favorite Maya ceremonial site of many independent travelers. The fact that the jungle hasn't been cleared away or all the mounds uncovered adds a feeling of discovery to the visit. For the visitor, it's important to know that the distances between groupings of structures are long (in some cases one to two km), and they're not located in a neatly kept park like Chichén Itzá. Each group of ruins is buried in the middle of thick jungle, so come prepared with comfortable shoes, bug repellent, sunscreen, and a hat. A canteen of water never hurts.

Flora and Fauna

Cobá in Maya means "Water Stirred by the Wind." Close to a group of shallow lakes (Cobá, Macanxoc, Xkanha, and Zacalpuc), some very marshy areas attract a large variety of birds and butterflies. The jungle around Cobá is good for viewing herons, egrets, and motmots. Once in a while, even a stray toucan is spotted. Colorful butterflies are everywhere, including the large, deep-blue *morphidae* butterfly as well as the bright yellow-orange barred sulphur. If you look on the ground, you'll almost certainly see long lines of cutting ants. One double column carries freshly cut leaves to the burrow, and next to that another double column marches in the opposite direction, empty jawed, returning for more.

The columns can be longer than a kilometer, and usually the work party will all carry the same species of leaf or blossom until the plant is completely stripped. It's amazing how far they travel for food! The vegetation decays in their nests, and the fungus that grows on the compost is an important staple of the ants' diet. The determined creatures grow to up to three centimeters long.

People

Thousands of people are believed to have lived in Cobá during the Classic period. Today the numbers are drastically reduced. They plant their corn with ceremony and conduct their family affairs in the same manner as their ancestors; many villages still appoint a calendar-keeper to keep track of the auspicious days that direct them in their daily lives. This is most common in the Cobá area because of its (up till now) isolation from outsiders and low profile. The locals live in communities on both sides of the lake. Those by the ruins operate small artisans' shops and restaurants and typically speak a smattering of Spanish. The community on the far side of the lake has a small clinic and a basketball court that serves as the town plaza. The communities have electricity, but no telephone service; the only phone in the area is the cellular one at the Villa Arqueológica.

THE COBÁ RUINS

White Roads

The most important reason to visit Cobá is to view the archaeological remains of a city begun in A.D. 600. These structures built near the lakes were scattered along a refined system of *sacbe* (roads). The remains of more than 50 *sacbe* have been found crisscrossing the entire peninsula, and there are more here than in any other location. They pass through what were once outlying villages and converge at Cobá, an indication that it was the largest city of its era. One such *sacbe* is 100 km long and travels in an almost straight line from the base of Nohoch Mul (the great pyramid) to the town of Yaxuna. Each *sacbe* was built to stringent specifications: a base of stones one to two meters high, about 4.5 meters wide, and covered with white mortar.

However, in Cobá some ancient roads as wide as 10 meters have been uncovered.

Archaeologists have even found a massive stone cylinder that was used to flatten the masonry. They have also discovered the mines where the inhabitants excavated the sand used to construct the roads. Sacbe 1, the longest, was an apparent attempt to extend Cobá's realm and challenge Chichén Itzá's rising aggression. It did not work, because Cobá was defeated in a mid-9th-century war. Cobá had a minor resurgence during the late post-Classic period when Tulúm-style temples were built on top of the site's pyramids and ceremonial platforms. In this last period, its main function was apparently as a pilgrimage destination. (Many caches of offerings, including jade, pearls, and shells, have been found in La Iglesia and other temples.)

Most of the stelae have been found in the Macanxoc area of the site, also known as Group A. Until recently, Stela 1 here was one of the great enigmas of Maya translation. It is covered with incredibly long date glyphs that resemble no other Maya inscription. Now researchers believe that Stela 1 commemorates two very ancient dates. One of these is August 13, 3114 B.C., the day on which the current era—as reckoned by the Maya—began (it ends A.D. December 23,2012). The other, more remarkable date is the longest one ever found in the Maya world; it marks the day that creation began: 41,943,040 followed by 21 zeros. Unfortunately, like most Cobá stelae, Stela 1 is badly weathered.

The Pyramids

While you wander through the grounds, it helps to use the map. When you enter, follow the dirt road a few meters until you come to the sign that reads Grupo Cobá directing you to the right. A short distance on the path brings you to the second-highest pyramid at the site (22.5 meters), called **La Iglesia**. After climbing many stone steps (the climb gets more dangerous each year as the steps disintegrate), you'll get a marvelous view of the surrounding jungle and Lake Macanxoc. Many offering caches, including jade, pearls, and shells, have been found in La Iglesia and other temples.

Back on the main path, a short trail leads to a stela with traces of carving, covered by a *palapa* to protect the stone from the elements.

From La Iglesia, farther on, the main path branches to the left, leading to **Nohoch Mul,** the tallest pyramid on the peninsula—42 meters, a 12-story climb! The view from atop Nohuch Mul is spectacular, and at the very top there's a small temple with a fairly well-preserved carving of the Descending God. After returning to the main path, turn left and continue to another fork. The path to the right leads to the **Grupo Macanxoc,** a collection of stelae covered with *palapas.*

From Grupo Macanxoc, the path to the left goes to **Conjunto Las Pinturas,** so named because of the stucco paintings that once lined the walls. Minute traces of the paintings, in layers of yellow, red, and blue, can still be seen on the uppermost cornice of the temple. This small building is well preserved, with groupings of pillars at the base and bright green moss growing up the sides of the gray limestone. It's nearly a half-hour walk from here back to the entrance to the ruins. Watch for signs and stay on the trails.

mask of Kohunlich

Scientists conjecture there may be a connection between the Petén Maya (hundreds of miles south in the Guatemala lowlands) and the Classic Maya who lived in Cobá. Both groups built lofty pyramids, much taller than those found in Chichén Itzá, Uxmal, or elsewhere in the northern part of the peninsula.

Undiscovered

All along the paths are mounds overgrown with vines, trees, and flowers—many of these are unexcavated ruins. More than 5,000 mounds wait for the money it takes to continue excavation. Thirty-two Classic-period stelae (including 23 that are sculptured) have been found scattered throughout the Cobá archaeological zone. Except for those at Macanxoc, most are displayed where they were discovered. One of the better preserved can be seen in front of the Nohoch Mul group. Still somewhat recognizable, it depicts a nobleman standing on the backs of two slaves and is dated 780 in Maya glyphs.

WEST OF CHETUMAL

Kohunlich

Forty-one miles west of Chetumal on Highway 186, turn right and drive five miles on a good side road to this Maya site. The construction continued from late pre-Classic (about A.D. 100–200) through Classic (A.D. 600–900). Though not totally restored nor nearly as grand as Chichén Itzá or Uxmal, Kohunlich is worth the trip if only to visit the exotic **Temple of the Masks,** dedicated to the Maya sun god. The stone pyramid is under an unlikely thatched roof (to prevent further deterioration from the weather), and gigantic stucco masks stand two-to-three meters tall. The temple, though not extremely tall as pyramids go, still presents a moderate climb. Wander through the jungle site and you can find 200 structures or uncovered mounds from the same era as the Palenque Maya archaeological site. Many carved stelae are scattered throughout the surrounding forest.

Walking through luxuriant foliage, you'll discover a green world. Note orchids in the tops of trees, plus small colorful wildflowers, lacy ferns, and lizards that share cracks and crevices in moldy stone walls covered with velvety moss. The relatively unknown site attracts few tourists.

Visitors feel that they are the first to stumble on the haunting masks with their star-incised eyes, mustaches (or are they serpents?), and nose plugs—features extremely different from carvings found at other Maya sites. Even the birds hoot and squawk at your intrusion as if you were the first. Like most archaeological zones, Kohunlich is fenced and opens 8 A.M.–5 P.M.; you'll pay an entrance fee. Camping is not allowed within the grounds, but you may see a tent or two outside the entrance.

STATE OF CAMPECHE

Several Maya sights in Campeche are close enough to the Belize border to be seen in a one-day (a long day) trip across the border, in conjunction with Kohunlich.

Xpujil, Becán, and Chicanná are the most accessible sites of south-central Yucatán's Río Bec culture. They share the distinctive Río Bec architectural style, whose hallmarks are "palaces" with flanking towers that appear on first glance to be Classic pyramids with temples on top. When you look closer, you realize that the "pyramid's" steps are actually reliefs and the temple is just a solid box with a phony door. It is as if they wanted the look of a Tikal-style temple without going through the trouble of building one. The towers are usually capped with roof combs, and sky serpent masks are frequent decorations on all ceremonial buildings.

The earliest occupation of the Río Bec area occurred between 1000 and 300 B.C. The great earthworks at Becán, which were probably defensive, were built around A.D. 150. Shortly afterward, the distant city of Teotihuacán's influence appears at the site in the form of ceramics and other evidence. Researchers believe that during the early Classic period Becán was ruled by trader/warriors from that great culture. Most of the existing structures in the Río Bec region were constructed between A.D. 550 and 830. Then the population gradually dwindled away; the area was completely abandoned by the time of the Spanish conquest. The Río Bec sites were rediscovered early in this century by chicle tappers.

The adventurous may also want to explore the sites of Río Bec itself and El Hormiguero,

which lie south of the road and are reachable only during the dry season along poor dirt roads.

The sites of Xpujil, Becán, and Chicanná are easy to get to from Belize. Cross the border and take the main highway (186) that cuts across the peninsula from Chetumal (and on to Escarcega) in southern Quintana Roo. You will reach the sites once you're across the Campeche border. In order to further develop the Mundo Maya project (also called La Ruta Maya), the Mexican government has agreed to spend big bucks in this area of Campeche, where some of the most interesting archaeological sites have been fairly well ignored until now. Water has always been a stumbling block for tourist development, but rumors circulating say there will soon be plenty of water and electricity with which to begin upgrading the area. INAH (the archaeological arm of the Mexican government) has begun work on some of the main structures, and many more structures and caves in the jungle continue to be "found." Because of the proximity to **Calakmul,** one of the largest Maya ceremonial centers found thus far, and the concentration of sites (though at present not fully developed), there will be many tourists coming through this part of Campeche.

Xpujil

About 110 km west of Chetumal, you'll pass the small village of Xpujil. Nearby stand three towers, a classic example of Río Bec architecture: the remains of three false towers overlook miles of jungle. On the backside of the central tower, check out what's left of two huge inlaid masks. Xpujil is one of the best-preserved Río Bec-style structures, unique for having a taller central tower in addition to the flanking twin towers.

If you're in a vehicle that can handle a primitive jeep road, you can reach Río Bec by taking the road south of the gas station near Xpujil.

Just past the small town of Xpujil, you'll see a large, circular *palapa* restaurant called **Maya Mirador.** This is a great lunch stop, serving good food and cold drinks—no wild game sold here! The café is run by a transplanted Frenchman, Serge Ríou, and his Mexican partner/engineer Moises, both also heavily into archaeology and nature. Behind the café, Serge offers four tiny sleeping *palapas*. This is spartan simplicity in pole houses. There's no electricity, just a roof to protect you from the rain and the bigger critters, but for those willing to carry a sleeping bag or a hammock, it's a convenient location to the ruins (a few more cabins are planned). Public restrooms are available. Serge speaks French, English, and Spanish and is a knowledgeable guide to the area. Recently he was involved in locating Maya caves that contained Indian drawings. At the newly discovered ruins, **Balam Ku,** robbers stripped the facing stones, but you can still see a portrait of kings. Sadly guards are necessary at Maya sites to keep out robbers who sell the artifacts to private collectors not only in Mexico but around the world.

This is also an ideal place for bird-watching in thick jungle with little or no tourist traffic. Don't forget your binoculars and bug repellent! If you're traveling by bus from Belize to Chetumal, check with the tourist office or a travel agency for bus trips to these sites. Not fully restored, the ruins will give you an indication of what the archaeologists find when they first stumble upon an isolated site. You will have renewed wonder at how they manage to clear away hundreds of years of jungle growth, figure out a puzzle of thousands of stones, and end up with such impressive structures.

Although you should be careful of those few strangers who are always looking to rob and steal, the majority of the people in the Yucatán Peninsula are friendly, kind folks. On a recent trip, our car gave up without warning. There we were, stranded—it was almost dark, no phones, or much of anything else. We walked to the nearby Maya Mirador Restaurant, where we eventually flagged down a pickup truck, and a kind-hearted farmer agreed to drive us to the Mexico/Belize border (as long as we didn't mind riding in the back with various and sundry animals). We were grateful, animals and all, for the friendly helping hand.

Becán

Six km west of Xpujil along Highway 186 is the turnoff to Becán. Becán offers archaeology buffs some of the largest ancient buildings in the state. Excavation is proceeding according to schedule. Becán dates back to 500 B.C. Structure VIII, just off the southeast plaza, offers a labyrinth of underground rooms, passageways, and artifacts, indicating this to be an important religious ceremonial center. You'll see an unusual waterless moat, 15 meters wide, four meters deep, and 2.3 km in diameter, surrounding the entire site. It's believed this protective-style construction indicates that warring factions occupied this part of the peninsula during the 2nd century. Historians claim that they were constantly at war with Mayapán, in what is now the state of Yucatán.

Chicanná

Another two km west is the turnoff to the Maya site of Chicanná, about a half km off Highway 186. The small city included five structures encircling a main center. An elaborate serpent mask frames the entry of the main palace, **House of the Serpent Mouth**—it's in comparatively good repair. Across the plaza lies Structure I, a typical Río Bec–style building complex with twin false-temple towers. Several hundred meters south are two more temple groups, though not as well preserved. Throughout the area are small and large ruins. If you're curious to compare the subtle differences of design and architecture of the ancient Maya throughout the peninsula, the group is worth a day's visit.

Calakmul Reserve

Located in the Petén region in the southern area of Campeche, 35 km from the border with Guatemala, Calakmul has given its name to one of the newest, largest biosphere reserves in Mexico. This site was once home to over 60,000 Maya. What may turn out to be the largest of all the structures built by the Maya, a massive pyramid, looms 175 feet over a base that covers five acres.

An archaeological team from the Universidad Autonoma del Sudeste in Campeche has mapped 6,750 structures; uncovered two tombs holding magnificent jade masks, beads, and two flowerlike earcaps; excavated parts of three ceremonial sites; and found more stelae than at any other Maya site. From the top of Pyramid 2, it's possible to see the Danta pyramid at Calakmul's sister site, El Mirador, and part of the Calakmul reserve on the Guatemala side of the border. Both of these sites predate Christ by 100 years.

Heading the archaeological team at Calakmul, William Folan has made startling discoveries, but even more important, he has been instrumental in pushing through the concept of the biosphere reserve. Today it has become a reality. Calakmul is not yet on the usual itinerary because of the difficulty reaching it; if you'd like more information, contact the tourist office in Campeche city. See the October 1989 issue of *National Geographic Magazine* for color photos of the Calakmul archaeological site.

HONDURAS

For Maya buffs, a trip to Honduras is essential. In the mountains, travelers will find Copán, one of the most prestigious ancient ceremonial cities of the Maya. For the scuba diver, a trip to the Bay Islands is in order.

SAN PEDRO SULA

The gateway to Honduras, San Pedro Sula, with its international airport is where many visitors land on their way to and from the **Bay Islands.** The ambience here is entirely different than in Belize; it has more the feeling of a Spanish colonial city, which of course it was hundreds of years ago. A day or two in the city, with its Spanish colonial buildings and lovely town square, will give you the flavor of another era. There's a good public market where arts and crafts from all over the country are sold—check out the great hardwood carvings. The **Gran Hotel Sula** across from the plaza is a pleasant place to overnight. Enjoy delicious (inexpensive) food at the hotel dining room. From San Pedro there are several other good side trips into the surrounding mountains.

Take a look at the cigar factory in **Santa Rosa de Copán** and then go on to the colonial town of **Gracias** at the base of **Celaque Mountain,** Honduras's highest peak, and the **Celaque National Park.** In the park, take some time to roam the trails of this dense pine-clad cloud forest. Be sure to check out the hot springs for a soak before you leave the park. You can camp in this great park, but bring *everything* you need with you.

Medical Concerns
In the Bay Islands, emergency **medical treatment** is available at a clinic in French Harbor; good hospitals are 35 miles away (about 20 minutes away by plane) on the Honduras mainland. Although malaria is rarely encoun-

tered in the islands, you may wish to ask your doctor or contact the Centers for Disease Control and Prevention in Atlanta, GA, 404/639-2888, before leaving the United States. A recompression chamber with trained staff is located on Roatan. Prescription drugs are unavailable in the tiny villages, so bring any necessary medicines in your carry-on luggage. Bring a bug repellent; though mosquitoes are a rarity, "no see-ums" and occasional sand flies can be a nuisance—Avon's Skin-So-Soft works great for *some* people—if you can stand the strong smell!

TEGUCIGALPA

Take a day or two to explore the city of Tegucigalpa, the capital of Honduras, with its colonial structures and left-over Spanish architecture. The graceful city offers a great **National Museum,** the **Presidential Palace,** and the beautiful **Basilica of Suyapa.** Don't miss the city market and wander through the streets to get acquainted. This is another good starting point into fascinating Honduran sites. The **Rio Platano Biosphere Reserve** is the forest habitat of the Pesch Indians. **La Tigra Cloud Forest** has myriad hiking trails and unique flora and fauna; birders would see more with a local guide. Mountain villages **Valle de Angeles** and **Santa Lucia** are typical with cobbled streets and red-tiled rooftops. Lush foliage makes everything green. Valle de Angeles is the home of the **National Artisans School** and a great place for shopping. The **Hotel la Ronda** and **Hotel Honduras Maya** in Tegucigalpa are good hotels. These are all places you can get to on your own with public transport. Or, for escorted tours and more information on prices and reservations and other destinations, contact Roatan Charters, Inc., tel. 800/282-8932.

COPÁN

With an interest perhaps stronger than we had ever felt in wandering among the ruins of Egypt, we followed our guide... to 14 monuments of the same character and appearance, some with more elegant designs, and some in work-manship equal to the finest monuments of the Egyptians.

Although these are the words of John Lloyd Stephens describing his first view of Honduras, they could easily be mine—and probably yours as well. Those who have visited archaeological monuments of ancient societies around the world will more than likely come to the same conclusion as they explore Copán as did the erstwhile explorers Stephens and his fellow-traveler, artist Frederick Catherwood.

The Maya

For a thousand years Copán lay covered by trees, embraced by roots of the tall strangler ficus amid layers of dust, dead-plant material, and loose particles that floated on the Honduran breeze and gradually covered most of this archaic wonderland. Since Stephens and Catherwood's visit, much has happened. Astounding carvings of immense heads, stairways lined with rearing stone jaguars, and many plazas have been uncovered and revealed to the sunlight once again. Stephens describes a colossal stone figure:

The front was a figure of a man curiously and richly dressed, and the face, evidently a portrait, solemn, stern, and well fitted to excite terror. The back was of a different design, unlike anything we had ever seen before, and the sides were covered with hieroglyphics.

Maya Sites

Copán is on the Copán River in a valley about 2,000 feet high. Stonework continues to be revealed throughout the valley. In Copán's 1,500

Maya stelae at Copán site

years of existence, the Maya moved its centers from one place to the other, building impressive structures at each site, perhaps improving each over the other until the middle of the 8th century, when it would seem that they reached the pinnacle of their accomplishments. Scientists believe Copán's beginnings were during the early Classic period, and these Maya continued in their advancements and structural designs until the late Classic period (A.D. 700).

While wandering through Copán with your guide (a guide is the way to go for good info), you will learn when the various structures were built and what archaeologists have learned about them over the years. The Acropolis, for example, is the largest complex at 130 feet high. This is where you'll find the well-known **Hieroglyphic Stairway,** covered with the longest "book" of hieroglyphics—2,500 glyphs on 63 steps. No, you cannot climb the steps; in fact, the public is not allowed to get too close. The Maya glyphs at Copán are considered the finest Maya art found to date. Look at the **Eastern** and **Western Courts.** At the Eastern Court you'll find **Temple 22,** the most breathtaking structure in Copán. Though much of the intricate carving has been destroyed, enough is left that visitors can see what complicated, tedious work was devoted to this temple—believed to have been the most sacred of Copán. The **Great Plaza** is at the northern end of the **Main Structure,** and those who have visited Tikal will notice the similarities between this one and the Great Plaza at Tikal.

On April 1, 1995, a group of U.S. and Honduran archaeologists discovered what they believe to be the tomb of Kinich Ah Pop, the second king of the Copán dynasty. They found the well-preserved skeleton surrounded by jade offerings in the Margarita Tomb. The bones were stained red, signifying blood in a mark of respect. Hieroglyphics at the tomb read, "May you be venerated, Kinich, lord of the sun, lord of the lake, lord of Copán." Carved on the facade of the tomb are figures of a macaw and a quetzal, preserved so well that the archaeologists said they were among the most beautiful and most important of Maya finds. The remains of Yax Kuk Mo, Kinich's father and founder of the dynasty who ruled from 426–437, were discovered in 1993. Eventually Kinich's bones and the artwork will be displayed in the Copán museum.

Don't miss the museum on the main plaza in the small town of Ruinas Copán; you'll see a booth to buy your ticket to both the archaeology zone and the museum (about US$3). At the museum you'll find the usual collection of stelae, a tomb, and other artifacts from the site. From the museum expect about a half-hour walk to the site. By the time you have this book, the new museum on the grounds of Copán should be open. The entrance to this beautiful museum is a reproduction of the entrance to the marvelous **Rosalila Structure** discovered in 1991. It's best to plan at least one full day to take in the site; two days are even better.

Accommodations and Food

A short distance from the site is the small village of Ruinas Copán where several very simple hostelries lie close by for an overnight stay. Simple eating places surround the small town square.

PRACTICALITIES

Getting to Honduras

TACA provides 727/737 service to the Honduras mainland and Bay Islands from U.S. gateways in Houston, Miami, or New Orleans. If you opt for an escorted two- or three-day tour from the Bay Islands, transportation, meals, and overnight hotel stay are arranged for you through several tour operators. Otherwise, to see Copán on your own, fly into either San Pedro Sula or Tegucigalpa and take a bus into the hilltop community of Ruinas Copán.

If you're traveling in Guatemala, it's a simple matter to cross the border into neighboring Honduras.

Miscellaneous Information

If you're looking for a school to learn Spanish, what nicer place than **Ixbalanque,** Copán's

A San Pedro Sula businessman. The oranges look green on the outside but are orange, sweet, and juicy on the inside.

Spanish language school? Room and board with families of the village are provided.

A valid passport is needed to enter Honduras; U.S. citizens do not need visas, but visas are required in advance for those traveling on Canadian passports. *Do* bring your passport. We read various reports of tourists saying that it's not necessary, especially if you're traveling into Copán for a day from Guatemala. However, we have also heard from travelers who found themselves stranded in Honduras for whatever reason, and without passports they had problems. So, be on the safe side, and bring your passport!

The official currency in Honduras is the lempira, referred to locally as the "lemp." Currently the exchange rate is US$1 to two lemps (but check, nothing is forever). Not all resorts accept **credit cards,** but **traveler's checks** are accepted almost every place (except the very smallest), and most resorts on the islands and the mainland are happy to take U.S. dollars. You must pay a **departure tax** of US$20 per person at the airport when leaving. Only a few hotels offer **car rentals;** as the roads improve, more are becoming available. **Hotel tax** is 7 percent.

Divers, remember to bring your certification card; PADI or SSI certification courses are available. Spearfishing is not permitted, and removing coral, shells, or fish is prohibited without express permission from the Honduran government. Bring whatever film you think you might use, as it is much more expensive on the islands and not all types are sold.

BOOK LIST

ARCHAEOLOGY

Carrasco, David. *Religions of Mesoamerica: Cosmovision and Ceremonial Centers.* San Francisco: Harper & Row, 1990.

Coe, Michael D. *The Maya.* New York: Thames and Hudson, 1984.

Coe, William R. *Tikal: A Handbook of the Ancient Maya Ruins, with a Guide Map.* Philadelphia: University Museum at the University of Pennsylvania, 1967.

Freidel, David. *Archaeology at Cerros, Belize, Central America.* Dallas: Southern Methodist University Press, 1986–89.

Garvin, Richard. *The Crystal Skull: The Story of the Mystery, Myth, and Magic of the Mitchell-Hedges Crystal Skull Discovered in a Lost Mayan City During a Search for Atlantis.* Garden City, NY: Doubleday, 1973.

Gifford, James. *Prehistoric Pottery Analysis and the Ceramics of Barton Ramie in the Belize Valley.* Cambridge, MA: Peabody Museum of Archaeology and Ethnology, Harvard University, 1976.

Kelly, Joyce. *The Complete Visitor's Guide to Mesoamerican Ruins.* Norman: University of Oklahoma Press, 1982.

Mercer, Henry Chapman. *The Hill-Caves of Yucatán: A Search for Evidence of Man's Antiquity in the Caverns of Central America.* Norman: University of Oklahoma Press, 1975.

Schele, Linda, and David Freidel. *A Forest of Kings: The Untold Story of the Ancient Maya.* New York: William Morrow and Company, Inc., 1990.

CULTURES OF BELIZE

Kerns, Virginia. *Women and the Ancestors: Black Carib Kinship and Ritual.* Urbana: University of Illinois Press, 1983.

CONTEMPORARY READING

Belize First. Lan Sluder, Publisher. Quarterly magazine dealing with living and visiting Belize. Equator Travel Publications, Inc. 280 Beaverdam Road, Candler, NC 28715, fax 704/667-1717.

DIVING AND THE SEA

Burgess, Robert. *Secret Languages of the Sea.* New York: Dodd, Mead, and Company, 1981.

Cousteau, Jacques-Yves. *Three Adventures: Galapagos, Titicaca, the Blue Holes.* Garden City, NY: Doubleday, 1973.

Kuhlmann, Dietrick. *Living Coral Reefs of the World.* New York: Arco Publishing, 1985.

Meyer, Franz. *Diving & Snorkeling Guide to Belize: Lighthouse Reef, Glover Reef, and Turneffe Island.* Houston, TX: Gulf Publishing, 1990.

FICTION

Edgell, Zee. *Beka Lamb.* London: Heinemann Educational Books, Ltd., 1982.

Highwater, Jamake. *Journey to the Sky: A Novel About the True Adventures of Two Men in Search of the Lost Maya Kingdom.* New York: Thomas Y. Crowell, 1978.

King, Emory. *Belize 1798, The Road To Glory.* Belize City: Tropical Books, 1991.

Westlake, Donald. *High Adventure.* New York: Mysterious Press, 1985.

HEALTH

Schroeder, Dirk. *Staying Healthy in Asia, Africa, and Latin America,* 4th ed. Chico, CA: Moon Publications, Inc., 1995.

Werner, David. *Where There is No Doctor.* Palo Alto, CA: Hesperian Foundation, 1992. Order from Hesperian Foundation, P.O. Box 1692, Palo Alto, CA 94302.

HISTORY AND POLITICS

Barry, Tom. *Belize: A Country Guide.* Albuquerque, NM: Inter-Hemispheric Education Resource Center, 1989.

Bernal, Ignacia. *The Olmec World.* Berkeley: University of California Press, 1969.

Bolland, O. Nigel. *Belize: A New Nation in Central America.* Boulder, CO: Westview, 1986.

Grant, C. H. *The Making of Modern Belize.* Cambridge, England: Cambridge University Press, 1976.

Sawatzky, Harry. *They Sought A Country: Mennonite Colonization in Mexico. With an Appendix on Mennonite Colonization in British Honduras.* Berkeley: University of California, 1971.

Setzekorn, William David. *Formerly British Honduras: A Profile of the New Nation of Belize.* Athens: Ohio University Press, 1981.

NATURE

Belize Audubon Society. *Snakes of Belize.* Belize City: The Society, 1990. Drawings by Ellen MacRae; available from 29 Regent St., P.O. Box 100, Belize City, Belize, C.A.

Lewis, Scott. *The Rainforest Book: How You Can Save the World's Rainforests.* Los Angeles: Living Planet Press, 1990.

MacKinnon, Barbara. *100 Common Birds of the Yucatán Peninsula.* Cancún, Quintana Roo, Mexico: Amigos de Sian Ka'an (Apto. Postal 770, Cancún, Quintana Roo, 77500, Mexico), 1989.

Rabinowitz, Alan. *Jaguar: A Struggle and Triumph in the Jungles of Belize.* New York: Arbor House, 1986.

Stevens, Katie. *Jungle Walk: Birds and Beasts of Belize, Central America.* Belize: Angelus Press, 1991. Order through International Expeditions, tel. 800/633-4734.

U.S. Department of the Navy, Bureau of Medicine and Surgery. *Poisonous Snakes of the World.* New York: Dover Publications, 1991. Originally published by and also available from the U.S. Government Printing Office, Washington, DC.

Wood, D. Scott, Robert C. Leberman, and Dora Weyer. *Checklist of the Birds of Belize.* Pittsburgh: Carnegie Museum of Natural History, 1986.

ACCOMMODATIONS INDEX

A
Airport Hotel: 299
Anchorage Hotel: 176
Auntie Chigi's Place: 278

B
Banana Bank Lodge: 225–226
Banana Beach Resort: 156
Barnacle Bill's Beach Bungalows: 274
Barracuda and Jaguar Inn: 284
Barrier Reef Hotel: 155
Belize Yacht Club: 160
Belizean Reef Suites: 161
Belmopan Hotel: 229
Black Rock: 233
Black Rock Belize Jungle River Lodge: 251–252
Blackbird Caye Resort: 192
Blancaneaux Lodge: 238–239
Blue Crab Resort: 278
Blue Creek Rainforest Lodge: 306–308
Blue Marlin Lodge: 182
Blue Tang Inn: 159
Bluefield Lodge: 266, 268
Bob's Paradise: 282–283
Bol's Hilltop Hotel: 306
Bonefish Hotel: 268
Bull Frog Inn: 229

C
Caesar's Place: 233
Cahal Pech Cabins: 247
Cahal Pech Village: 247
Capricorn Resort: 158
Captain Morgan's Retreat: 160
Caribbean Village: 204–205
Caribbean Villas: 158
Caribe Island Resort: 161
Casa Maya: 251
Casablanca by the Sea: 205
Cayo Espanto: 161
Central Hotel: 246
Chaa Creek Resort and Spa: 252
Chaleanor Hotel: 268
Chan Chich Lodge: 216–217
Changes in Latitude B&B: 156
Charleton's Inn: 300
Chechem Ha Cottages: 252
Chocolate's Guesthouse: 176

Chula Vista Hotel: 214
Circle C Hotel: 299
Clarissa Falls Resort: 251
Cockscomb Basin Wildlife Sanctuary: 273
Coconut Cottage: 285
Coconuts Caribbean Hotel: 157
Conch Shell Hotel: 155
Coral Beach Hotel and Dive Shop: 153, 155
Corona del Mar (Woody's): 159
Corozol Bay Inn: 205–206
Cosmos: 247
Cottage Colony: 181
Crystal Paradise Resort: 250
Cunchs Villa: 285

D
D Star Victoria: 214
Daisy's Hotel: 174
Dangriga Central Hotel: 266
Deb 'n' Dave's Last Resort: 284
Dolphin Bay Apartments: 175
duPlooy's Cottage Resort: 253–254

E
Edith's Hotel: 174
Ek Tun: 254
El Chiclero Camp Resort: 247
El Pescador Lodge: 160–161
Emerald Reef Suites: 157
Enna's Hotel: 282

F
Fallen Stones Butterfly Ranch and Jungle Lodge: 306
Fernando's Seaside Guesthouse: 209
Five Sisters Lodge: 238
Frangipani House: 182
Frank Caye: 284
French Louis Caye: 184
Frontier Guest House: 299

G
Glover's Guest House: 271
Graceland Ranch: 248
Gran Hotel Sula: 326
Green Heaven Lodge: 254
Green Parrot Beach Houses and Resorts: 275
Green Parrot Resort: 157

H

Hamanasi Resort: 272
Hi-et: 246
Hidden Valley Inn: 240
Hideaway Sports Lodge: 155
Hok'ol K'in Guesthouse: 205
Hopkins Inn: 270
Hotel del Rio: 155–156
Hotel Honduras Maya: 326
Hotel la Ronda: 326
Hotel Maya: 205
Hotel Mira Mar: 175
Hotel Pacz: 246
Hotel Playador: 156
Hotel Posada Mama: 205
Hotel San Pedrano: 153
Howler Monkey Lodge: 133

I

Ian Anderson's Caves Branch Adventure Company and Jungle Lodge: 231–232
Ignacio's Cabins: 174
Iguana Reef Inn: 176
Inn at Robert's Grove: 287
Inn at Xunantunich: 255–256
Ix Chel Guesthouse: 244

J

Jaguar Inn: 315
Jaguar Paw Jungle Resort: 224–225
Jaguar Reef Resort: 271–272
Jimenez Cabañas: 174
Journey's End Caribbean Club: 157–158
Julia's Guesthouse: 284
Jungle Huts Hotel: 268
Jungle Jeanies: 270
Jungle Lodge: 315–316

K

Kanantik Jungle & Reef Resort: 270–271
Kitty's Place: 285–286

L

Lamanai Outpost Lodge: 212
Lazy Iguana B&B: 176
Lena's Hotel: 174
Leslie Cottages: 182
Lilpat Sitee River Resort: 271
Lily's Hotel: 155
Log Cab-Inns: 247
Long Caye: 184–185

Lorraine's Guesthouse: 174
Luba Hati: 286
Lucille's Rooms: 284
Lucy's Guesthouse Hotel: 174
Lydia's Guesthouse: 284

M

M & N Apartments: 175
Macal River Camp Site: 252–253
Mahung's Hotel: 300
Manatee Lodge: 127
Mansione del Pajaro Serpiente: 316
Mara's Hotel: 174
Mariposa: 287
Martha's Hotel: 153
Martha's Kitchen and Guesthouse: 246
Martinez Caribbean Inn: 174–175
Maruba Lodge: 134
Mata Chica: 161
Mata Rocks Resort: 157
Maxim's Place Hotel and Resort: 257
Maya Breeze Inn: 275
Maya Guest House Project: 294–296
Maya Mountain Lodge: 250
Maya Playa: 274
Mayaland Villas: 254–255
Mayan Princess: 158–159
Mi Amor Hotel: 214
Midas Resort: 247
Monkey House Resort: 283
Mopan River Resort: 256–257
Mother Ocean's Tropic Hotel: 286
Mountain Equestrian Trails: 239

N

Nature's Way Guest House: 300
Nautical Inn: 278
Nestor's Hotel: 204
New Belmoral Hotel: 246

O

Oar House: 278
Osprey's Nest: 182

P

Pallavi's Hotel: 300
Pal's Guesthouse: 268
Paradise Resort Hotel: 156
Paradise Villas Condominiums: 159
Parrot's Nest: 249–250
Pelican Beach Resort: 182, 268–269

Pine Ridge Lodge: 239
Pook's Hill Lodge: 233–235
Punta Caliente Hotel: 300

R
Rainbow Hotel: 175
Ramon's Village: 158
Ranguana Hotel: 285
Ricardo's Beach Huts and Lobster Camp: 183
Rio Mar Hotel: 266
Riverside Hotel: 266
Royal Mayan Resort and Spa: 257
Rubie's (Ruby's) Hotel: 153
Rum Point Inn: 286–287

S
San Ignacio Hotel: 248
San José Village Guest House: 308
San Miguel Village Guest House: 308
San Pedro Holiday Hotel: 157
San Pedro Village Guest House: 306
Sandy Beach Lodge: 270
Santa Cruz Village Guest House: 308
Sea Front Inn: 301
Sea Spray Hotel: 285
Seaside Cabañas: 176
Seaview Hotel: 175–176
Serenade Guesthouse: 284
Serenity Resort: 285
Seven Seas Hotel: 156
Shirley's Guest House: 176
The Shores: 127
Singing Sands: 274–275
Sobre Las Olas Hotel: 175
Spanish Bay Resort: 184
Spindrift Hotel: 155
St. Charles Inn: 300
St. George's Lodge: 181
SunBreeze Hotel: 159
Sunset Inn: 282

T
Tate's Guest House: 300
TC's by the Sea Hotel: 301
Thomas Hotel: 153
Tides Beach Resort: 156
Tikal Inn: 316
Tipple Tree Beya Inn: 270
Tom's Hotel: 175
Tony's Inn and Resort: 206
Toucan Sittee: 271
Tradewinds Hotel: 284
Travellers Inn: 301
Tree Tops Hotel: 175
The Trek Stop: 255
Trends: 175
Tropical Paradise Hotel: 175
Tropicool Hotel: 246
Turneff Islands Lodge: 191–192
Turneffe Flats: 192
Turtle Inn: 287

V
Vega Inn and Gardens: 176
Venus Hotel: 246
Verde's Guest House: 299
Victoria House: 159–160

W
Warrie Head Creek Lodge: 232–233
Westin Camino Real Tikal: 316
Westwind Hotel: 285
Windy Hill Resort: 248
Woodys (Corona del Mar): 159

X
Xcape: 274

RESTAURANTS INDEX

A
Aunt J's: 301

B
barbecues: 162
BC's: 162
Big Daddy's: 162
B.J.'s Restaurant: 289
Black Orchid: 206
Brenda's: 289
Bull Frog Inn: 229

C
Café Kela: 206
Cafe Lagundo: 278–279
Cafe Olé: 162
Caladium Restaurant: 229–230
Cannibals: 162
Capricorn Restaurant: 162–163
Caruso's: 162
Casablanca by the Sea: 207
Celi's Deli: 161
Celi's Restaurant: 157, 162
Chan's Garden: 177–178
Chili's: 288
Crisis: 206

D
Daisy's: 289
De Tach: 285
Deb 'n' Dave's Last Resort: 284
The Diner: 214–215
Dockside Bar: 288
Dockside Bar and Grill: 162
Duane's Surf and Turf: 162
Duke's Place: 162

E
El Patio Restaurant: 162
Elvi's Kitchen: 162
Eva's Restaurant and Bar: 246

F
Franco's Restaurant: 286, 289

G
Galley Restaurant and Bar: 288
Glenda's: 177

Gomier's Restaurant: 302
Gonz and Roses: 206
Grace's Restaurant: 302

H
Hanna's Bar and Restaurant: 247
Hok'ol K'in Guesthouse: 207

I
Il Biscaro: 177
Inn at Robert's Grove: 289
Island Cuisine: 162

J
Jambel Jerk Pit: 162
J.B.'s Watering Hole: 223–224
Jene's Flamboyant Restaurant: 288

K
King Burger: 269
Kitty's Restaurant and Bar: 286
Kulcha Shack: 278

L
La Margarita: 162
Lagoon Saloon: 288
Lee's Chinese Restaurant: 215

M
Malu's Kitchen: 289
Mambo Restaurant: 161
Mambo's: 163
Mangos: 289
Mangrove's Restaurant: 301
Marin's: 177
Martha's Kitchen and Guesthouse: 246
Martinez Restaurant: 177
Maxim's Chinese Restaurant: 246–247
Maxim's Place Hotel and Resort: 257
Maya Mirador: 324–325
Mayan Wells Restaurant: 133
Mickey's Place: 161
Miss Lilly's: 289
Ms. Alice's Restaurant: 282

N
Nature's Way Guest House: 302
New Riverside Cafe: 269

O
Omar's Diner: 288

P
Pelican Beach Restaurant: 269
Pickled Parrot Restaurant: 284
Popeyes: 177
Powerhouse Pizza: 162
Punta Caliente: 301
Purple Space Monkey Internet Café: 288

R
Ramon's: 162
Reef Restaurant: 162
Rendezvous Restaurant: 163
Rio Mar HT: 269
Rubie's: 161

S
Sand Box: 177
Sea Front Inn: 302
Sea Monkey Bar and Grill: 288

Serendib Restaurant: 246
Sobre Las Olas: 177
Sonny's: 289
Sunset Inn Dining Room: 282
Sweet Basil: 162
Syd's: 177

T
Tarzan's Nite Club: 161
Tiki Bar: 283
Tony's Inn: 207
Tropical Paradise Restaurant: 177
Tropical Takeout: 162

V
Vista del Carmen Cafe: 257

W
WishWilly's: 177

Y
Yoo Hoo Deli: 178

GENERAL INDEX

A

abbreviations: xvi
accident evacuation: 54
accommodations: general discussion 63–64, 145; Ambergris Caye 153–161; atolls 80, 191–192, 196, 197–199; Belize City/vicinity 116–119, 126–127, 133–134; Belmopan 229, 231–235; Caye Caulker 170–171, 174–176; Cayo District 220, 224–226, 229, 231–235, 238–240, 249–257; Corozol District 204–206, 209, 214; Crooked Tree 138–139; Honduras 328; Orange Walk District 212–213, 214; San Ignacio 246–248; Stann Creek District 266, 268–269, 270–275, 278–279, 284–287; Tikal 315–216; Toledo District 293–296, 299–301, 306, 307–308; *see also* accommodations index; *specific place*
achiote: 65
acorn woodpecker: 16–17
Acropolis: 327
Actun Balam: 106
Actun Tunichil Muknal: 58
adventure tours: 231–232, *see also* tours
agouti (indian rabbit): 22
agriculture: 41, 64, 209, 220, 259–260, 263
airlines: 78–79
airports: Belize City Municipal Airport 78, 80, 109; Blancaneaux Lodge 80; Gallon Jug 80; Hector Silva Airport 226, 230; Philip Goldson International Airport 78, 80, 109z
air transportation: 77–70; atolls 197; Belize City 125; cayes 165, 179; Cayo District 226, 230, 239, 249; Corozol District 207; Honduras 328; Stann Creek District 269, 289; Tikal 318; Toledo District 303
alcohol: 86; and traveler's disease: 67
algae, ciguatera: 68
alligators: 26
Altun Ha: 101–102, 133–134
Amandala: 43
Ambergris Caye: 145–166; general discussion 145–149; accommodations 153–161; boating/fishing/snorkeling 151–152; entertainment 163–164; food 161–163; history 146–147; Maya 144; scuba diving 147, 149–151; services/information 68, 164–165; shopping 164; transportation 80, 165–166
Ambergris Caye Celebration: 60

American crocodile: 26
American tyrpanosomiasis: 69–70
ancient healing, Maya: 71–72
anemones: 54
angelfish: 31
animals: *see* fauna; wildlife
anole: 23, 144
anteater (tamandua): 22
antibiotics: 54, 69
antidiarrheals: 69
antivenin: 25–26; *see also* poisonous; snakes
ants: 9–10; leaf cutter ant: 27, 321–322
April the tapir: 23, 127, 130
aquaculture: 45
arachnids: 26–28, 75; *see also* insects
archaeologists: 98, 103, 104, 106, 311–312, 321
archaeological sites: Cahal Pech 243; Caracol 236; cayes 146–147; Corozol District 203–204; Lamanai 99–101, 204, 212–213; Mexico 321–326; Mundo Maya 94–106; Orange Walk District 212, 216; Punta Gorda 292; Tikal 309–318; Toledo District 304; Xunantunich ("Stone Lady") 102–104, 245, 255
archaeology: La Ruta Maya 37–38, 93; reading list 330; tours 84–85, 94–106
Archeological Research and Nature Study Programme for Belize: 212
area codes: 85
armadillo: 120
art galleries/artists: Ambergris Caye: 164; Belize City 119, 121–122; Caye Caulker 178; Cayo District 221–222, 248, 250, 257; San José Succotz 255; Stann Creek District 266, 278; Toledo District 302
Arvigo, Rosita: 71–72, 84, 244
Association for Belizean Archaeology: 94, 229
ATMs: 122; *see also* banking
atolls: 29, 30, 149–150, 186–199; accommodations 80, 191–192, 196, 197–199; Glover's Reef Atoll: 29, 84, 197–199; Lighthouse Reef Atoll 192–197; Turneffe Islands Atoll 29, 173, 188–192
Aventura Sugar Mill: 202–203
avocado: 12

B

babies, traveling with: 52, 89–91
Bacalar: 320

backpacking: 57–58, 87; *see also* camping
bacteria: 68
Balam Ku: 325
Ball Court, Lamanai: 99–100
bananas: 14, 45, 259–260
banking: Ambergris Caye 164–165; Belize City
    122–123; Corozol District 207; San Ignacio
    248–249; Stann Creek District 269, 289; Tole-
    do District 303
bare coral outcroppings: 29
Baron Bliss Day: 60
Baron Bliss Memorial: 114
Barracks Green: 78
barracuda: 31, 54–55, 67
barrier reef: 30, 56–57; *see also* Belize Reef
bars see entertainment; *specific place*
basilisk lizard, Central American (Jesus Christ
    lizard): 23–24, 144
Basil Jones area: 146–147
bats: 6, 23, 75
Bay Islands: 262, 326
Baymen: 39–40, 48–49; *see also* pirates
beaches: Ambergris Caye 149, *see also spe-
    cific place*
beauty, stylized Maya: 47
Becán: 324–325, 325
bed-and-breakfasts: *see* accommodations index;
    specific place
beer, local brews: 66
Belikin beer: 66
Belize Association of Louisiana (BAL): 50
Belize Audubon Society: 43, 58, 123, 133, 136,
    139, 207, 214, 273
Belize Bird Guide: 124
Belize City: 107–126; general discussion 107,
    109, 113, 123–124; accommodations
    116–119, 126–127, 133–134; churches 115;
    food 119–121, 133; Garifuna 48–49; hurri-
    cane damage 8; market 115; museums/art
    galleries 115–116; nightlife 121; recreation
    116; services 122–123; shopping 113–116,
    121–122; sights 113–116; St. George's Caye
    Day 60; taxis 77; transportation 124–126
Belize City Municipal Airport: 78, 80, 109
Belize Consulate: 56
Belize District: 107–140
Belize City: 107–126; Belize City vicinity:
    126–134; Crooked Tree 135–140; medical
    services 68
Belize Eco-Tourism Association: 43–44, 124
Belize Investment Code: 43

Belize Online, Tourist and Investment Guide: 85
Belize Reef: 29–21, 51, 141, 146, 149–151
Belize River: 109, 227
Belize Tourism Industry Associates: 66, 303
Belize Tourist Board: 77, 85, 123, 124, 144, 165,
    241
Belize Zoo: 23, 44, 127–131
Belizian Association of Traditional Healers: 244
Belmopan: 80, 227–235
Benque Viejo del Carmen: 255, 256–258, 317
Bermudian Landing Community Baboon Sanc-
    tuary: 21, 44, 123, 130, 131–133
bicycling: *see* cycling
Big Creek: 80, 281
Big Northern Caye: 192
biospheres: Calakmul Reserve 325–326; Rio
    Platano Biosphere Reserve 326
birds: 4, 16–19
bird-watching: 58; Caye Caulker: 167; cayes
    143–144; Corozol District 200; Crooked Tree
    Wildlife Sanctuary 135; Half Moon Caye 196;
    Lamanai Reserve 100; Manomet Bird Obser-
    vatory 296; San Ignacio 244–245; Santa Rita
    100; Shipstern Wildlife Nature Reserve 207;
    Tropical Education Center 131
Blackbird Caye: 59, 188
Blackbird-Oceanic Society Field Station: 192
Black Caribs: 262–263
black coral: 30
black howler monkey (baboon, *saraguate*):
    21–22, 130, 131–133
see also Bermudian Landing Community Ba-
    boon Sanctuary
black magic: 263
black mangrove: 28–29, 135
black-tailed indigo (snake): 144
Blake, James: 147, 168
Blancaneaux Lodge, airport: 80
Bliss, Baron Henry Edward Ernest Victor: 60,
    114
Bliss Institute: 114, 116
Blue Creek: 50, 213, 215, 306; Cave System 6,
    307; Reserve 306–308
Bluefield Range: 183
Blue Hole: 192, 194
Blue Hole (inland): 6, 230–231
Blue Hole National Park: 230–231
Blue Morpho Butterfly Breeding Center: 205,
    253
bluestriped grunt: 31
boa constrictor (wowla): 25, 144, 167

boating: Ambergris Caye 151–152; see also specific areas
boat transportation: 79; see also specific areas
"boil up" (seafood stew): 65
books: 87, 124, 330–331
border crossing: to/from Guatemala 317–318; to/from Honduras 328–329; to/from Mexico 78–79
Botanical Trail: 208–209
botfly: 26–27, 70
bottle-nosed dolphin: 32
bougainvillea: 13
Bowen, Barry: 101
breadnut: 72
British Honduras: 41–42
broadleaf jungle: 4–5
brukdown: 63
buccaneers: 39, 39–40, 48–49, 60, 144, 168, 182, 197
bug repellent: 66, 69, 90, 186, 326
bull horn acacia (cockspur): 9–10
Bullet Tree Falls: 249
burial chambers, caves: 6, 58, 221
burial sites: 94, 99–106
bus transportation: 80–81; see also specific areas
business hours: 86
busses: Belize City 125; Cayo District 231, 249, 256, 257–258; Corozol District 207; Mexico 319–320; Orange Walk District 215; Stann Creek District 269, 289–290; Tikal/Guatemala 318; Toledo District 303, 308
butterflies: 27, 305; Blue Morpho Butterfly Breeding Center: 205, 253; Fallen Stones Butterfly Ranch and Jungle Lodge 305; Green Hills Butterfly Farm 236, 305; monarch butterfly 27; Shipstern Wildlife Nature Reserve 208–209
buttonwood mangrove: 28–29, 143

C
cacao: 14
Cahal Pech ("Place of the Ticks"): 102, 243, 245
calabash: 12
Calakmul: 324
Calakmul Reserve: 325–326
Calcutta: 49
Calderitas Bay: 319
cameras: 52, 87–92
Campeche: 324–326
camping: 171–172, 183, 196, 231, 233, 239,
247, 252–253, 271
Cancún, flights from: 78
canoeing: 57, 221
canopy (rainforest): 307
Captain Chocolate: 172–173
car travel: 79, 249; see also specific areas
Caracol ("Snail"): 84, 104–105, 236, 245
Caribbean: 149–152
Caribbean rum: 212
Caribbean Tourism Association: 85
Caribs: 48, 262–263
Carnaval: 60
Carr, Carolyn: 221
Carrie Bow Caye: 182
cars: rental 81–82, 124–125; see also specific areas
casava: 263
cashew nut/seed: 15, 136–138
Caste War: 40, 47, 144, 147, 168, 200–201, 210
catamarans, rental: 152
"catch-and-release" fishing: 56, 281
Catholicism: 38–39, 261, 263–265
cats: 19–21
cattle industry: 46
Caverns: 150
caves: general discussion 5–7, 58, 221; Chechem Ha 243; Hokeb Ha/Blue Caves 306; Mauger Cave 188; Moho Cave 101; Mountain Cow 231; Petroglyph Caves 231; Rio Frio Cave 236; San Ignacio 245; Silver Caves 195; St. Herman's Cave 230–232; Toledo District 299, 306; Vaca Caves 254
Caves Branch River: 6, 221, 224, 232
Caya District, Cahal Pech ("Place of the Ticks"): 102
Caye Caulker: 167–179; accommodations 170–171, 174–176; flights to 80; flora/fauna 167–168; food 171, 177–178; history 168–170; land 167, 172; nightlife/entertainment 178; services/information 68, 171–172, 178–179; shopping 178; the people 170; tourism 170–171; transportation 179; water sports 172–174; Water Taxi Association fleet 113, 172, 179
Caye Caulker Tour Guide Association: 172
Caye Chapel: 80, 180
Caye Chapel Golf Course and Marina: 180
cayes: 141–185, 281, 299; general discussion 141; accommodations/food 145; Ambergris Caye 145–166; Caye Caulker 167–179; fauna 143–144; history 144, 145, 146–147;

other/smaller cayes 180–185; transportation 145; types 29

Cayo District: 218–258; general discussion 218–222; accommodations 220, 224–226, 229, 231–235, 238–240, 249–257; Belmopan 227–235; caves 6; food 223–225, 229–230, 232–235, 246–247, 256–257; medical services 68; shopping 221–222, 248, 257; sights 235–236, 243–244, 249; transportation 81, 226, 230, 239, 249, 256, 257–258; Western Highway 222–227

Cebada caves: 6

ceiba: 10, 58

Celaque National Park: 326

cell phones: 77

Cenote Azul: 319

Center for Environmental Studies: 94

Centers for Disease Control and Prevention: 66, 70, 72

Central American river turtle (hicatee): 26, 210

Central Farms, flights to: 80

Central Park, Punta Gorda: 297, 299

ceremonial centers: 47, 98–106

Kuchil Balum: 272; Tikal: 309–318

Cerros: 98, 203

ceviche: 65

Chaa Creek Cottages, Nature Study Center: 59

Chaa Creek Natural History Museum: 253

Chagas' disease: 69–70

Chan Chich (Kaxil Uinich): 100–101, 213–214, 216–217

Chan Santa Cruz Maya: 40–41

channels (cayes): 149–150, 173–174

charters: air 80, 125, 249; boat 56, 173, 196–197

Chase, Diane & Arlen: 94, 98, 104

Chau Hiix Ruins: 139–140

Chechem Ha Cave: 243

Checklist of the Birds of Belize: 16

Chetumal: 78–79, 204, 319–320

Chicanná: 325

children, traveling with: 52, 89–91

China root: 72

Chinchorro Banks: 191

Chiquibul cave system: 6

Chiquibul Forest Reserve: 104–105, 220, 232, 236

Christianity: 38–39, 261, 263–265

churches: 115, 213

ciguatera: 67–68

citizenship, sale of: 42

classic period: 36, 94, 99, 102

climate: 7–8

clinics (medical): 68, 70–71, 123, 165; *see also specific place*

clothing, what to pack: 87, 90, 296

coati: 22–23

Cobá: 321–323

Cockscomb Basin: 272–274

Cockscomb Basin Wildlife Sanctuary: 20–21, 84, 123, 130, 272–274

coconut plantations *(cocales):* 168

cohune forests: 4–5

collared peccary: 23

colonization: 40–42, 49

conch: 34, 65, 119–120

Conjunto Las Pinturas: 323

conquistadors: 38–39

Consejo Shores ("Miami Beach"): 204

Conservation, Exploration, Diving, Archeology, and Museums (CEDAM): 191

conservation/preservation: 2, 43; Archeological Research and Nature Study Programme for Belize 212; Belize Audubon Society 43, 58, 123, 133, 136, 139, 207, 214, 273; Belize Eco-Tourism Association 43–44, 124; Belize Zoo 23, 44, 127–131; Bermudian Landing Community Baboon Sanctuary 21, 44, 123, 130, 131–133; Blackbird-Oceanic Society Field Station 192; Blue Creek Reserve 306–308; Blue Morpho Butterfly Breeding Center 253, 305; Calakmul Reserve 325–326; Chiquibul Forest Reserve 104–105, 220, 232, 236; Cockscomb Basin Wildlife Sanctuary 20–21, 84, 123, 130, 272–274; Coral Caye Conservation 182; Crooked Tree Wildlife Sanctuary 123–124, 135–136; Fallen Stones Butterfly Ranch and Jungle Lodge 305; Green Hills Butterfly Farm 236, 305; Green Iguana Conservation Project 248; Guanacaste National Park 226–227; Half-Moon Caye bird sanctuary 58, 124; Hol Chan Marine Reserve 32, 150; International Tropical Conservation Foundation 207; jaguars 20–21; Lamanai Reserve 99–101; Laughing Bird Caye National Park 183–184; Manatee Forest Reserve 223; Manomet Bird Observatory 296; marine life/reefs 30–35, 44–45, 66; Monkey Bay Nature Reserve 223; Monkey Bay Wildlife Sanctuary 223; Mountain Pine Ridge Forest Reserve 3, 58, 84, 236; Mundo Maya 93–106; Nature Conservancy 216; Programme for Belize 44, 124, 212, 215–216; quetzal 17; Rio

Bravo Conservation and Management Area 44, 124, 212; Rio Platano Biosphere Reserve 326; Sea turtle Sanctuary 44; Shipstern Wildlife Nature Reserve 207–209; Slate Creek Preserve 44, 232, 236; Swallow Caye manatee reserve 173; Tapir Mountain Nature Reserve 232; Terra Nova Medicinal Plant Reserve 244; Tropical Conservation International 296; Tropical Education Center 131; Wildlife Conservation International 20, 296

Copán: 327–329

Coppola, Francis Ford: 238–239

coral: 29–31, 53–55, 92, 149

Coral Caye Conservation: 182

coral snake: 25

corn (maize): 64

Corozol District/Town: 200–209; accommodations 204–206, 209, 214; food 206–207; shopping/services 207; transportation 78–80, 207

Cortés, Hernán: 38

cortisone cream: 54

Costa Rica, quetzal sanctuary: 17

Cousteau, Jacques: 170, 192

crafts: 164, 266; see also art galleries/artists

crawfish, protection of: 30

credit cards: 86, 122–123, 153

Creoles: 48, 63

crime: 72, 76–77, 88, 91, 109

crocodiles: 26

Crooked Tree: 135–140; accommodations/food: 138–139; buses to/from 81; tours/guides 139

Crooked Tree Cashew Festival: 137–138

Crooked Tree Lagoons: 135

Crooked Tree Wildlife Sanctuary: 123–124, 135–136

cruise ships: 82

Cuello: 47, 98–99, 212, 215

cuisine, local: 64–66, 119–121, 278, 295, 296

culture: Dangriga 266; Olmec 36

currency: 85–86, 329

cuts (cayes): 149–150, 172

cutting ants: 27, 321–322

cycling: 59; Ambergris Caye 166; Orange Walk Town 213–214; San Ignacio 245; Stann Creek District 281

D

dance, Garifuna: 265

Dangriga: 266–269; Garifuna Settlement Day 62, 264–265; transportation 80–81

decompression chamber: 55

DEET: 66, 69, 90, 186, 326

de Landa, Bishop Diego: 38–39, 47

dengue fever: 69, 168

Department of Archeology: 7, 94, 99, 102, 105, 229

departure tax: 77, 86, 122, 329

development: 1–2, 42–46, 93–94, 143, 167, 180, 220, 270, 291

dialects: 47

diarrhea: 67–69

deities: 58

disinfectants: 68, 70

Divers Alert Network (DAN): 54

diving: dive shops/guides 53–54, 149–150, 172–173; live-aboard dive boats 52, 116, 150, 186, 188, see also scuba diving

Diving God: 321

docks: 56–57

doctors: 68, 70–71

documents, travel: 77

dolphins: 186, 192

domestic flights: 78, 79, 80, 125; see also air transportation

Douglas Caye: 188

Douglas DeSilva: 104–105

dreadlocks: 50

drugs, illegal: 76–77, 109, 171

dysentery bark: 71–72

E

early-classic period: 106, 311

East Indians: 49

East Plaza (Tikal): 314

Eastern Court (Copán): 328

ecological life zones: 9

economy: 42–46, 168–169

ecosystems, mangroves/turtle grass: 143

ecotourism: 1, 43–44, 293–296

education: 50, 263

eels: 194

Elbow, the: 190

El Castillo: 103, 255, 321

El Dia de San Pedro: 60, 145

El Pilar Ruins: 245, 249

Elderhostel: 52, 213

electricity: 86

Elksund: 195

Embassy of Belize: 85

emergencies: 54, 55, 123

endangered species: black howler monkey 21–22; crocodiles 26; hicatee 26; jaguar

19–21; manatee 32–34; quetzal 17; red-footed boobies 196; sea turtles 30, 34, 65
England, rule by: 40–42, 48–49
English Caye: 183
entertainment: 60–63; Ambergris Caye 163–164; Caye Caulker 178; Punta Gorda 302; San Ignacio 248–249
equipment, diving: 53–54
erosion: 143
estuaries: 28
evacuation, accident: 54
events: 60–63
excavation, cave: 7
explorers, early: 38–39

F
Fallen Stones Butterfly Ranch and Jungle Lodge: 305
false coral (snake): 25
fares, taxi: 125
farming: 41, 209, 220, 259–260, 263; pre-columbian agriculture 64
faro island: 183–184
fauna: 4–5, 16–18; Caye Caulker 167–168; cayes 143–144; Cobá 321–322; Crooked Tree Wildlife Sanctuary 123–124, 135–136; Half Moon Caye 196; Lamanai 100; Lighthouse Reef Atoll 196; San Ignacio 244–245
Feast of San Luis: 61–62
feather duster worm: 35
fees: 122
fer-de-lance (yellow-jawed tommygoff): 25–26
festivals: 60–63, 137–138, 264–265
film: 87–92, 122
fire coral: 54
firefly: 27
fire worms (bristle worms): 54
first aid: 54, 72–76
fish: 30–32, 54–55, 149; toxins (ciguatera) 67–68
Fisheries Administrator: 30
fishing; Ambergris Caye: 147, 151–152; Caye Caulker 173; Corozol District 204; Glover's Reef Atoll 197; industry 45, 170; recreational 55–56; regulations 30–31; Stann Creek District 281; Turneffe Islands Atoll 188, 191, 192
flamboyanes (royal poinciana): 12–13
flash floods, caves: 7
flora: 9–15: Caye Caulker 167–168; Cobá 321–322; Crooked Tree Wildlife Sanctuary 135; Half Moon Caye 196
Flores: 317

Florida, manatee breeding program: 33
flowers: 13–15
Folan, William: 325–326
food: 64–66, 90, 119–121; and traveler's disease 67, *see also* restaurants index; *specific place*
Forest Home: 49
Forestry Department, Western Division: 105
forests: 4–5, 9, 196
Fort Cairns: 210
Fort George Lighthouse: 113
Fort Mundy: 210
Fort San Felipe: 320
Freetown Road: 109
French Louis Caye: 184
fringing reef: 30
fruit: industry 46, 259–260; trees 12–15
furniture, Mennonite: 222

G
Gales Point: 126–127, 190
Gallon Jug, airport: 80
ganja (marijuana): 50
Gann, Thomas: 7, 94, 105
Garcia sisters: 221–222, 250
Garifuna: 48–49, 261–265, 275; food 65, 278
Garifuna Settlement Day: 49, 62, 84, 263–265
Garifuna Village Project: 294
Garinagu: *see* Garifuna
geckos: 23
geologic, history: 5
Georgeville: 235–240
germs: 68
Giant Cave: 6
giardia: 67
gibnut: 65, 66, 120
glass-bottom boats: 57, 151
Glover, John: 197
Glover's Reef Atoll: 29, 84, 197–199
gnats: 26
Goff's Caye: 183
Golden Stream: 282
golf: 60, 180; Ambergris Caye 146, 166; Caye Caulker 179
Good Shepherd Clinic: 256
government: 42, 331
Government House: 115
Government House Museum: 115
grapevine: 71
Gray Lady, the: 182
greased pole: 61–62

Great Plaza: 309, 311, 312, 328
Green Hills Butterfly Farm: 236, 305
Green Iguana Breeding Project: 131
Green Iguana Conservation Project, conservation/preservation: 248
green moray eel: 35
green turtle: 34
grocery stores: 279, 289, 303; Ambergris Caye 164; Belize City 122; Caye Caulker 178; Corozol District 207, 215
grouper (jewfish): 32, 67, 149
Grupo Macanxoc: 323
Guanacaste National Park: 226–227
guanacaste *(pich):* 10
Guatemala: 304, 309–318; border 39, 255–258, 317–318; border conflict 39; buses to/from 80–81
guaya: 12
guesthouses: Toledo District 293–296, 308; *see also* accommodations index; *specific place*
guides: *see* tours
gumbo-limbo: 10–11

H
Half Moon Caye: 192, 194, 195–197
Half-Moon Caye, bird-watching: 58
Half Moon Caye Wall: 194–195
Hammond, Dr. Neil: 98–99, 105
Hatchett Caye: 31
Haulover Creek: 107, 113
hawksbill turtle: 34
Hawksworth Bridge: 241
hazards, underwater: 54
healing/healers: 70–72, 244
health: 66–67, 331
Health Information for International Travelers: 72
Hector Silva Airport: 226, 230
Hedges, Benson: 292
Hieroglyphic Stairway: 327
hieroglyphs, Tikal: 315
hepatitis A: 68, 70
herbs, healing: 71–72
hermit crab: 144
hicatee (Central American river turtle): 26, 210
Hidden Valley Falls: 236
High Temple N10–43: 99
hiking: 57–58; Cockscomb Basin Wildlife Sanctuary 274; San Ignacio 245
history: 2; ancient: 36–38; Caye Caulker 168–170; cayes 144, 145, 146–147; Cayo

District 220; colonial 38–41; geologic 5; Maya 38–41, 144, 146–147, 311; reading list 331; Stann Creek District 261–266; Tikal 311–312; Toledo District 292–293
Hokeb Ha/Blue Caves: 306
Hol Chan Marine Reserve: 32, 150
holidays: 60–63, 264–265
Hollywood: 191
Holy Deer Dance: 61, 62
Honduras: 262, 326–329
Hopkins: 270–271
horseback riding: 59, 239–240, 245
Horwich, Robert: 132
hospitals: 68, 123, 269
hotels: *see* accommodations index; *specific place*
House of the Serpent Mouth: 325
howler monkey: 21–22, 130, 131–133, 135
Hummingbird Highway: 126, 226, 230–231, 260
hunting: jaguars: 20–21; sea turtles 30, 34; wild game 65
hurricanes: 7–8, 143, 173–174
hydroelectric dams: 220

I
Ice Age: 36
iguana: 24–25, 65, 120, 143–144; Green Iguana Breeding Project 131
illegal drugs: 76–77, 109, 171
Image Factory, The (museum): 115–116
immigration: 303
immunizations: 72
indentured workers: 48–49
independence, national: 41–42, 62
India, immigrants from: 49
Indian Church: 213
indigenous: peoples 47, *see also* Maya
industry: 44–45
information: general 85–86; tourist 85–86, 123; *see also* Belize Tourist Board; specific areas
inland Belize, habitats: 4
inns: *see* accommodations index; *specific place*
insect repellent: 66, 69, 90, 186, 326
insects: 26–28, 73, 74, 167–168, 321–322
instructors, diving: 53–54, 149–150, 172–173
insurance, car: 79, 82
International Expeditions: 138
international flights: 78, 79
International Traveler's Hotline: 72
International Tropical Conservation Foundation: 207
International Zoological Expeditions: 307–308

Internet: access 123, 165, 289, 303; online information 85
investment, foreign: 42–43
Isla Tamalcas: 319
Ixbalanque: 328–329
Ix Chel Farm: 243–244
Ix Chel Tropical Research Center: 71–72

J
jabiru stork: 17, 99, 135
jade: 99, 102
jaguar: 19–11, 130, 272–274
Jaguar: a Struggle and Triumph in the Jungles of Belize: 273
jaguarundi: 21
jellyfish: 55, 74
Jicaqueños (Caulker Islanders): 168, 170
jungle, broadleaf: 4–5
Jungle Walk, Birds and Beasts of Belize: 16

K
kayaking: 57, 84, 179, 184–185, 198–199, 281
keel-billed toucan: 16, 17
Kekchi Maya: 47, 63, 261, 306
ki bix: 72
King Ah-Cacau: 312
king vulture (King John crow): 17–18
Kinich Ahau: 102
Kinich Ah Pop: 328
"kissing bug": 69–70
Kohunlich: 323–324
Kuchil Balum: 272

L
Ladinos: 48
lagoons, Crooked Tree: 135–140
Laguna de San Pedro: 146
Laguna Village: 294–295
La Iglesia: 322–323
lakes: 4
Lamanai: 99–101, 204, 212–213
Lamanai Outpost Lodge, nature study: 59, 212–213
La Milpa: 212, 216
land: 3–4; rights 40
La Nicolasa: 191
La Ruta Maya: 36–38, 93
Las Lagunas de Siete Colores: 320
late-classic period: 103, 105, 311
La Tigra Cloud Forest: 326
La Union: 215

Laughing Bird Caye National Park: 183–184, 281
laundry: 165, 269, 289
leaf cutter ant: 27, 321–322
Lefty's Ledge: 190
legends: 6, 61, 146
Life Flight: 54
Lighthouse Reef Atoll: 29, 84, 192–197
Lighthouse Reef Resort: 80, 192, 197
limestone: 29–21
Lindburgh, Charles: 77–78
liquor: 86
literacy: 50
Little Quartz Ridge: 6
Little Rocky Point: 101
live-aboard dive boats: 52, 116, 150, 186, 188
lizards: 23–25, 144, 167
lobster farming: 45, 66, 120, 147, 168, 170
locust *(pac):* 11
loggerhead turtle: 34
logging: 9, 39, 41, 210
Long Caye: 184–185, 192, 194, 195
Long Caye Base Camp: 198–199
looting: 100–101, 106
Lost City: 309
Lubaantun ("Place of the Fallen Stones"): 105, 304
luggage: 86–87

M
Macal River: 220, 221
magnificent frigate bird (man-o'-war bird): 18, 171
mail: 86, 123, 165
maize: 64
malaria: 69, 168, 326
mammals
  land: 19–23; sea: 32–34
Manatee Forest Reserve: 223
manatee grass: 29
Manatee Highway: 126, 260–261
Manatee Junction: 222–223
manatees (sea cow): 32–34, 126, 143, 172–173
mangroves: 28–29, 141, 143, 186
Manomet Bird Observatory: 296
manta rays: 35
Mantanceros (Nuestra Señora de los Milagros): 191
maps: 124
Marco Gonzalez ruins: 147
margay (tiger cat): 21

mariculture: 45
marinas: 56–57, 116, 152, 180, 279
Marine Terminal: 113
Maritime Museum: 113, 115
market: Belize City 115; Punta Gorda 299
market square, Belmopan: 229
Maruba: 134
Mask Temple N9–56: 99
Matola, Sharon: 127–131
Mauger Cave: 188
"mauger" season: 7
Maya: ancient healing: 71–72; Chan Chich 213–214, 216–217; Chan Santa Cruz 40–41; Corozol District 202–203; dances 61–63; Feast of San Luis 61–62; Guest House program 294–296, 308; history 5–7, 36–38, 38–41, 144, 146–147, 311; Honduras 327–328; Kuchil Balum 272; La Milpa 212, 216; La Ruta Maya 37–38, 93; Lamanai 99–101, 204, 212–213; Maya Center Village 272; Mexico sites 320–326; modern culture 47; Mundo Maya 51, 93–106, 259; pre-columbian agriculture 64; ruins 51, 83–85, 93–106, 139–140, 147, 245, 249, 275, 306, 312–315, 328; San Ignacio 243–245; Sarteneja 209; Stann Creek District 261; Tanah Mayan Art Museum 250; Tikal 309–318; Toledo District 292–296, 304–306; tours 83–85; trading centers 101–102, 147; underworld/caves (Xibalba) 6, 58, 221, 230–232; Xunantunich ("Stone Lady") 102–104, 245, 255
Maya Beach: 274–275
Maya Man Triathlon: 316
Maya Medicine Trail: 84, 243–244
Maya Mountains: 6, 58, 230
Maya Mountains Lodge: 59
medical services: general discussion 68, 70–72, *see also* specific areas
medicines, prescription: 66, 87, 326
Melchor de Mencos: 257–258
Melinda's Hot Sauce: 44, 66
Memorial Park: 114
Mennonites: 48, 49–50, 210, 212, 222, 240
Mérida Maya: 38
Mesoamerica: 36, 39
mestizos: 41, 47, 48, 147, 168, 170, 200, 210, 220
"Mexican-Mestizo corridor": 48
Mexico: 319–326; accommodations/food: 319; transportation 80–81, 319–320; traveling from 78–79
Mexico/Jones Lagoon: 135
Mexico Rocks: 150
Miami Seaquarium: 33
milpas: 9, 10, 64, 132, 306
Moho Cave: 101
monarch butterfly: 27
money: 85–86, 122–123, 130, 207, 329
Monkey Bay Nature Reserve: 223
Monkey Bay Wildlife Sanctuary: 223
Monkey River Village: 282–283
monkeys: 21–22, 130, 131–133, 135, 223, 282–283
Montego Caye: 184
Montejo: 191
Mopan: 261, 306
Mopan Maya: 47
moray eels: 35, 54
Morgan, Henry: 182
Morolet's crocodile: 26, 210
mosquitoes: 26, 69, 74, 167–168, 186
moths: 27
Mountain Cow Cave: 231
Mountain Pine Ridge: 235–240
Mountain Pine Ridge Forest Reserve: 3, 58, 84, 236
Mundo Maya: 51, 93–106, 259; archaeological sites 94–106; general discussion 93–94
museums: Bermudian Landing Community Baboon Sanctuary 132–133; Chaa Creek Natural History Museum 253; Government House Museum 115; The Image Factory 115–116; Maritime Museum 115; Tanah Mayan Art Museum 250
music: 63, 264–266
mythology: 6, 61, 146

N
national anthem: 2
National Arts Council: 114
National Independence Day: 62
natural healers: 71–72, 84, 244
natural remedies, traveler's disease: 69
Nature Conservancy: 216
nature study: 59; reading list: 331; San Ignacio 245; tours 83–84
nature walks: 58–59; Bermudian Landing Community Baboon Sanctuary 21, 44, 123, 130, 131–133, 133; Caye Caulker 173; Cockscomb Basin Wildlife Sanctuary 274; Guanacaste National Park 227; Shipstern Wildlife Nature

Reserve 208–209; Tropical Education Center 131
NAUI: 150–151
New Highway: 215
New River: 203–204, 214
New River Lagoon: 210, 214
nightlife; Belize City: 121; Caye Caulker 178; San Ignacio 248
Nim Li Punit: 106, 304
Nohmul: 98
Nohoch Mul: 323
Northern Highway: 109, 125, 131–135, 203, 207, 213
Northern Two Caye: 197
"northers": 7
Nuestra Señora de los Milagros ("Our Lady of the Miracles"): 191
nuts: 14–15

O

obeah: 263
ocelot: 21
Olmec culture: 36
100 Common Birds of the Yucatán Peninsula: 16
Orange Walk District: 210–217; general discussion: 68, 210–212; accommodations 212–213, 214; Chan Chich (Kaxil Uinich) 100–101; food 214–215; Lamanai 99–101, 204, 212–213; Orange Walk Town 213–217; transportation 215
Orange Walk Town: 213–217
orchids: 13, 99, 214
oscellated turkey: 18–19
ospreys: 167

P

PABA: 70, 90
paca: 22
packing: 86–87, 89, 296
PADI: 150–151
palm trees: 11
Palmetto Reef: 150
Panti, Don Eligio: 71, 244, 250
Panti Trail: 71–72
papaya: 12
paranda: 265
parasites: 69–70
parks; Blue Hole National Park: 230–131; Celaque National Park: 326; Guanacaste National Park 226–127; Laughing Bird Caye National Park 183–184

parrot fish: 32
parrots: 16
passion fruit: 15
passports: 77, 317, 329
peccary (musk hog; javelina): 23, 127
Pendergast, David: 99, 101–102
peoples; ancient Maya: 36–38, 94–106; Caye Caulker 170; Cobá 322; modern Maya 47; polyglot 47–50; Stann Creek District 261–266; Toledo District 292–293
peppers: 44, 66
peregrine falcon: 4
personal watercraft: 57, 152
Petroglyph Caves: 6, 231
pharmacies: 123, 165; *see also* specific areas
Philip Goldson International Airport: 78, 80, 109
photography: 52, 87–92
pine: forests 5; trees 11–12
pineapple: 14
Pine Ridge: 136–139
pirates: 39–40, 48–49, 60, 144, 168, 182, 197
Placencia: 274–290; flights to 80; Town 279–290
plantlife: *see* flora; *specific place*
Pleistocene epoch: 36
poisonous: cashew nut/seed: 136–138; foods 73–75; sea life 35, 54–55; snakes 25–26, 71, 75; spiders 26, 28, 75
Poisonous Snakes of the World: 26
poisonwood *(chechem):* 12
polyglot: 47–50
polyps, coral: 30
Portuguese man-of-war: 55
post-classic period: 94, 99, 102, 146–147, 311
post offices: Ambergris Caye 165; Belize City 123; Punta Gorda 303; Stann Creek District 269
pre-classic period: 98, 102, 203
pre-columbian agriculture: 64
prescription medicines: 66, 87, 326
prices, accommodations: xvi, 63–64, 153
Programme for Belize: 44, 124, 212, 215–216
Protected Areas Conservation Trust: 122
publications, local: 124
puchinga: 263
puma: 21
Punta Gorda: 292, 297–308; general discussion 297–299; accommodations 299–301; entertainment 302; recreation 299; shopping/services 302–303; transportation 79, 80, 81
punta rock: 62, 63, 265
purification, water: 67

Puritans: 263, 266
Pusilha ruins: 106, 306
pyramids: 322–323, 324–325

Q
quamwood: 12
quetzal: 17
Quintana Roo: 40, 78, 319–320

R
rabies: 75
Rabinowitz, Alan: 20, 273
Radisson Fort George Dock: 114
rainfall: 3, 7–8
rainforests: 4, 306–308
Ras Tafari Makonnen: 50
Rastafarians: 50
rays: 35, 55
real estate agents: 119, 165
recreation: 51–60; Belize City 116; Corozol Town 203–204; Orange Walk Town 213–214; Punta Gorda 299
Recreational Equipment Incorporated: 67
recycling: 224
Red Caribs: 262–263
red coral: 54
red fire sponge: 54
red-footed boobies: 196
red mangrove: 28–29, 143
reefs: 29–31, 51, 141, 146, 149–151
refugees: 220
regulations, driving: 81
Relaciones de las Cosas de Yucatán: 38–39, 47
religious services: 86
Rendezvous Point: 188–189
rental cars: 81–82, 125
rental water sports/craft: 152, 173
reptiles: 25–26
Reservoir (Rockstone Pond): 101–102
resort course, scuba diving lessons: 151
restaurants: general discussion 66; *see also* restaurants index
Reyes, Luciano: 168
Rio Azul: 106
Río Bec: 324–325
Rio Bravo Conservation and Management Area: 44, 124, 212
Rio Bravo Research Station: 215–216
Rio Frio Cave: 6, 236
Rio Hondo: 78
Rio On Pools: 236

Rio Platano Biosphere Reserve: 326
river rafting: 203–204, 214, 221
rivers: 3–4
road conditions: 82; *see also* specific areas
Road Guide: 124
Roaring Creek: 227
Rockstone Pond (Reservoir): 101–102
Rocky Point: 146
rodents: 22
Rosalila Structure: 328
Ruinas Copán: 328
ruins: Maya 51, 93–106, 139–140, 147, 245, 249, 275, 306, 312–315, 328
tours: 83–85

S
sacbe: 322
safety: 66–67; cave 7; personal 72, 76–77, 94, 109, 318; personal items 72, 76–77, 86–87, 88, 91, 318; scorpions 28; snakebites 25–26; water 31, 35, 54–55, 174
sailboards: 152
San Antonio: 61
San Antonio Village: 61–62, 306
San Ignacio: 220, 240–255; accommodations/food: 246–248; activities 244–245; entertainment/services 248–249; general discussion 241–243, 249–250; sights 243–244, 250
San José Succotz: 255–256
San Pedro: 145, 147, 148, 165, 171
San Pedro Columbia: 304–306
San Pedro Sula: 326
Sandbore Caye: 192
Sandy Point Reef: 150
Santa Elena: 240
Santa Rita: 94, 98, 203
Santos Pop: 294–295
sapodilla fruit: 15
Sapodilla Lagoon: 140
sapote: 12, 15
Sarteneja: 209
savanna: 4–5
Save the Rain Forest, Inc.: 216
schools: 50
scorpion fish: 55
scorpions: 28
screwworms: 70
scuba diving: 52–57; Ambergris Caye 147, 149–151; atolls 186–199; Belize City 116;

Caye Caulker 172–173; Honduras 329; instruction 151, 172–173, 188; other cayes 180–185; reading list 52–57; Stann Creek District 275, 280; Toledo District 299
sea, general discussion: 28–31
seafood: 65, 120
sea-grass beds: 29, 143
sea life: 31–35, 53–55
seasons: 7–8
Sea Turtle Sanctuary: 44
sea turtles: 34, 54, 65, 143
sea urchins: 54
Secret Languages of the Sea: 31
Seeing is Belizing: 59
Seine Bight: 275, 278–279
Selassie I, Haile: 50
senior travelers: 52
service charges: 122, 153
services; Ambergris Caye: 68, 164–165; Belize City 122–123; Caye Caulker 68, 171–172, 178–179; Corozol District 207; Punta Gorda 302–303; San Ignacio 248–249; Stann Creek District 68, 269
settlers: Stann Creek District 263, 266; Toledo District 292–293
sharks: 35, 54–55
Sharp, Marie: 44, 66
shellfish: 34–35
Shipstern Lagoon: 207
Shipstern Wildlife Nature Reserve: 207–209
ship wrecks: 53, 149, 195, 197
Shipyard: 50
shopping; Ambergris Caye: 164; Belize City: 113–116, 121–122; Caye Caulker 178; Cayo District 221–222, 248, 257; Corozol District/Town 207; hours 86; Punta Gorda 302–303; San Ignacio 248
shrimp farming: 45
Shropshire, David: 71–72, 244
"Sidewalk" Placencia Town: 280; sights Belize City 113–116; Cayo District 235–236, 243–244, 249, 250; chetumal 319; Corozol Town 203–204; Georgeville to Mountain Pine Ridge 235–236; Guatemala border area 255; highlights 51; Orange Walk Town 213–214; Placencia Town 280; Punta Gorda 297–299; Stann Creek District 280, 282
sightseeing, highlights: 51
Silver Caves: 195
sinkholes: 6
Sittee: 271–272

Sixto, Octavio: 221
Skin Diver magazine: 53
skywalk, Blue Creek Reserve: 307
slash-and-burn farming: 41, 64
slate carvings: 221–222
Slate Creek Preserve: 44, 232, 236
slavery: 39–41, 48, 261–263
snail kite: 135
"snake doctors": 26, 71
snakes: 25–26, 71, 75, 144, 167
Snakes of Belize: 25
snapper: 67
snorkeling: 52–55; Ambergris Caye 151–152; Belize City 116; Caye Caulker 172–173; Stann Creek District 280–281
soka: 63
sooty tern: 19
South American tapir: 23
Southern Highway: 270–272
Southern Lagoon: 126
South Water Caye: 181–182
Spanish, occupation: 38–40, 47, 144, 146–147, 212, 256, 262
Spanish Lookout Caye: 184
Spanish Lookout Village: 50, 240
"Spanish tradition": 41
spicules, sponge: 54
spider monkey: 21, 22
spiders: 26–28, 75
spiny lobster: 34–35, 45, 66
spiny-tailed iguana: 24, 143–145
Split, the: 143, 167, 172, 173–174
sponges: 53, 54, 149
sports and recreation: water sports 52–57; *see also* specific areas
spur-and-groove formations: 190
Stain: 136–139
stalactites: 58
stalagmites: 58
Stann Creek District: 259–290; accommodations: 266, 268–269, 270–275, 278–279, 284–287; Cockscomb Basin 272–274; Dangriga 266–269; food 269, 270–272, 278–279, 288–289; Garifuna 48–49; general discussion 259–261; history and people 261–266; Placencia 274–290; services 289; Southern Highway 270–272; transportation 269, 289–290
Staying Healthy in Asia, Africa, and Latin America: 72
stelae: 106, 315, 322

Stephens, John Lloyd: 327
St. George's Caye: 40, 180–181
St. Herman's Cave: 6, 230–231
stingrays: 35, 55
St. John's Anglican Cathedral: 115
stoney coral polyps: 30
strangler fig: 12
St. Vincent's Block: 294
sugar industry: 41, 45, 202–203, 212
sunburn: 70, 75, 90, 281
Sun God Temple: 102
Supreme Court Building: 115
Swallow Caye manatee reserve: 173
swimming: 57, 173–174, 181, 245
swing bridge: 113–114

T
"talking cross": 40–41, 321
tamarind: 14
Tanah Mayan Art Museum: 250
tapir, South American: 23
Tapir Mountain Nature Reserve: 232
tarantula: 28
Tarpon Caye: 281
taxes: 122, 153: departure 77, 86, 122, 329
taxis: Ambergris Caye 166; Belize City 77, 125; Chetumal-Corozol 78–79; Stann Creek District 290
Tegucigalpa: 326
telephone service: 85
temples: Altun Ha: 102; Chan Chich (Kaxil Uinich) 100–101; Lamanai 99–101; Mexico 320–321, 323; Tikal 312, 314–315
tennis: 60
termites: 27–28
Terra Nova Medicinal Plant Reserve: 244
theft: 72, 76–77, 86–87, 88, 91, 318
ticks: 69, 76
Tiger Dance: 61
Tikal: A Handbook of the Ancient Maya Ruins: 312
Tikal ("Place of Voices"): 84, 104, 257–258, 309–318; accommodations and food: 315–316; the ruins 312–315; transportation 317–318
timber: 41
time: 86
tipping: 86
Tipu: 102, 243
Toledo District: 291–308; general discussion: 68, 291–293; accommodations 293–296,

299–201, 306, 307–308; caves 6; ecotourism 293–296; food 296, 301–302; Garifuna Settlement Day 62; music 63; Punta Gorda 297–308; transportation 303, 308
Toledo Ecotourism Association: 295
Toledo Maya Cultural Council: 62–63
Toledo Visitors Information Center: 303
toucans: 16, 17
tourism: 1–2, 43–44; Caye Caulker 170–171; Cayo District 220
tourist information: 85–86, 123; *see also* Belize Tourist Board
Tourist Police: 109, 171
tours: 83–85, 117, 123; adventure: 231–232; Ambergris Caye 151–152; Belize City 125–126; Bermudian Landing Community Baboon Sanctuary 21, 44, 123, 130, 131–133, 133; canoeing 221, 245; Caye Caulker 172–173; Corozol District 207; Crooked Tree 139; Maya archaeological sites 84–85, 94–106; Maya ruins 83–85, 275; nature study 245; orchids 214; river rafting 221; San Pedro Columbia 304–306; sportfishing 281; Stann Creek District 283–284; Toledo District 299
Tower, the: 196
Town Public Meeting: 49, 62, 84, 263–265
toxins, ciguatera: 67–68
trading centers, Maya: 101–102, 147
transportation: air 77–79; bus 80–81; car/boat 79; cruise ships 82, *see also* specific areas
travel agents: 123, 165
traveler's checks: 86, 153
traveler's disease: 67–69
treasure: buried 144; sunken 149, 191
Treaty of Paris: 39–40
trees: 9–13, 167
Tres Cocos (Three Coconuts): 195
Trial Farm Village: 214
Tropical Conservation International: 296
Tropical Education Center: 131
true coral (snake): 25
tubing: 57, 245
Tulúm: 320–321
Turneffe Islands Atoll: 29, 173, 188–192
turtle grass: 29, 143
turtle pens (kralls): 181
turtles: land: 26; protection of 30, 120; sea 34, 54, 65, 143
Twin Complex Q and R: 309
Tzimin Kax ("Mountain Cow"): 106

U

underwater: caves: 6; hazards 54; photography 91–92
underworld (Xibalba): 6, 58, 221, 230–232
U.S. Embassy: 114
Uxbenka ruins: 106, 306

V

Vaca Plateau, caves: 6, 254
Valle de Angeles: 326
venison: 120
Victoria Peak: 3, 20
Video Incorporated: 63
Vincent's Lagoon: 188
visas: 77, 86, 317, 329

W

Wallace, Peter: 42
Waribagabaga and Children of the Most High: 63
warries: 127
water: and traveler's disease 67; drinking 86, 121, 167
waterfowl see birds
waterfront, Punta Gorda: 297
water sports: 52–57, 280–281; Ambergris Caye 152; Caye Caulker 172–174
water taxis: Ambergris Caye 165–166; Belize City 125; Caye Caulker 179; Half Moon Caye 196–197
waterways: 3–5
weather: 7–8
Western Highway: 125, 222–227
West Point: 195
wet cayes: 29

wetlands: 4
Where There is No Doctor: 72
white grunt: 31
white-lipped peccary (warrie): 23
white mangrove: 28–29, 143
White Roads: 322
wild game: 65, 120; hunting: 65
wildlife: 4–5, 16–18; Caye Caulker: 167–168; cayes 143–144; Cobá 321–322; Crooked Tree Wildlife Sanctuary 123–124, 135–136; Lamanai 100; Lighthouse Reef Atoll 196; San Ignacio 244–245
Wildlife Conservation International: 20
windsurfers: 152
wishwilly iguana: 143–144
World Wildlife Fund: 273

X

Xibalba (underworld): 6, 58, 221, 230–232
Xpujil: 324–325
Xunantunich ("Stone Lady"): 102–104, 245, 255

Y

Yax Kuk Mo: 328
Yax-Moch-Xoc: 315
Ycacos: 281
yellow fever: 69, 70
yellowtail snapper: 32
Yo Creek: 47
Yucatán: 38–40, 147
Yucatec Maya: 47

Z

ziricote forest: 196

ABOUT THE AUTHORS

Chicki Mallan discovered the joy of traveling with her parents at an early age. The family would leave their Catalina Island, California, home yearly, hit the road, and explore the small towns and big cities of the United States. Traveling was still an important part of Chicki's life after having a bunch of her own kids to tote around. At various times Chicki and kids have lived in the Orient and Europe. When not traveling, lecturing, or giving slide presentations, Chicki and her photographer-husband, Oz, live in Paradise, California, a small community in the foothills of the Sierra Nevada. She does what she enjoys most, writing newspaper and magazine articles when between travel books. She has been associated with Moon Publications (now Avalon Travel Publishing) since 1983, and is the author of *Yucatán Peninsula Handbook, Mexico Handbook, Moon Handbooks: Cancún, Colonial Mexico,* and *Guide to Catalina Island.* In 1987, Chicki was presented the Pluma de Plata writing award from the Mexican Government Ministry of Tourism for an article she wrote about the Mexican Caribbean, published in the *Los Angeles Times.* Chicki is a member of the SATW, Society of American Travel Writers.

Chicki Mallan

Patti Lange

Patti Lange was part of the "bunch" that traveled with their mom, Chicki Mallan, to various parts of the world. Her mom urged everyone to keep a journal; Patti was the only one who was a faithful writer from age seven. She lived and went to school in Indonesia, France, and Paradise, California, and graduated from California State University, Chico. Once Patti was on her own, she began her trekking career through Europe, Mexico, and Belize. It was only natural to continue to write things down, and now she is a working/writing partner. When not traveling, Patti lives with husband Eric Addison and son Riley on Catalina Island. Besides being a mom, she works as a reporter and editor for the *Catalina Islander* newspaper, tests scuba gear for *Rodale's Scuba Diving* magazine, and leads kayakers around the wondrous coast of the island. She and Eric trekked the jungles of Belize with Riley, who got a free ride in a backpack, for the update of this book.

ABOUT THE PHOTOGRAPHER

Oz Mallan has been a professional photographer his entire adult career. Much of that time was spent as chief cameraman for the *Chico Enterprise Record.* Oz graduated from the Brooks Institute of Photography, Santa Barbara. His work has often appeared in newspapers and magazines across the country via UPI and AP. He travels the world with his wife, Chicki, handling the photo end of their literary efforts, which include travel books, newspaper and magazine articles, as well as lectures and slide presentations. The photos in *Moon Handbooks: Belize* were taken during many visits and years of travel in the small country. Other Moon books that feature Oz's photos are *Yucatán Peninsula Handbook, Mexico Handbook, Moon Handbooks: Cancún, Colonial Mexico,* along with *Guide to Catalina Island.*

ABOUT THE ILLUSTRATOR

The banner art at the start of each chapter was done by **Kathy Escovedo Sanders**. She is an expert both in watercolor and this stipple style that lends itself to excellent black-and-white reproduction. Kathy is a 1982 California State University—Long Beach graduate with a B.A. in art history. She exhibits drawings, etched intaglio prints, and woodcut prints, as well as outstanding watercolor paintings. Her stipple art can be seen in all of Chicki Mallan's books.

U.S.~METRIC CONVERSION

1 inch = 2.54 centimeters (cm)
1 foot = .304 meters (m)
1 yard = 0.914 meters
1 mile = 1.6093 kilometers (km)
1 km = .6214 miles
1 fathom = 1.8288 m
1 chain = 20.1168 m
1 furlong = 201.168 m
1 acre = .4047 hectares
1 sq km = 100 hectares
1 sq mile = 2.59 square km
1 ounce = 28.35 grams
1 pound = .4536 kilograms
1 short ton = .90718 metric ton
1 short ton = 2000 pounds
1 long ton = 1.016 metric tons
1 long ton = 2240 pounds
1 metric ton = 1000 kilograms
1 quart = .94635 liters
1 US gallon = 3.7854 liters
1 Imperial gallon = 4.5459 liters
1 nautical mile = 1.852 km

To compute celsius temperatures, subtract 32 from Fahrenheit and divide by 1.8. To go the other way, multiply celsius by 1.8 and add 32.

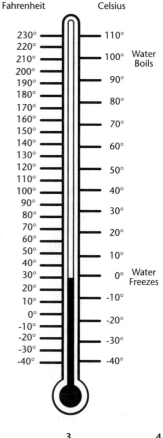

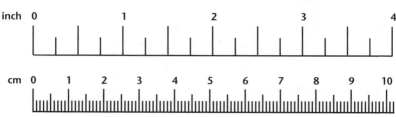